The International Handbook of Environmental Sociology, Second Edition

Edited by

Michael R. Redclift

Professor of International Environmental Policy, King's College, University of London, UK

Graham Woodgate

Senior Lecturer in Environmental Sociology, Institute for the Study of the Americas, School of Advanced Study, University of London, UK

Edward Elgar
Cheltenham, UK • Northampton, MA, USA

Published by
Edward Elgar Publishing Limited
The Lypiatts
15 Lansdown Road
Cheltenham
Glos GL50 2JA
UK

Edward Elgar Publishing, Inc.
William Pratt House
9 Dewey Court
Northampton
Massachusetts 01060
USA

A catalogue record for this book
is available from the British Library

Library of Congress Control Number: 2009938391

Mixed Sources
Product group from well-managed
forests and other controlled sources
www.fsc.org Cert no. SA-COC-1565
© 1996 Forest Stewardship Council
FSC

ISBN 978 1 84844 088 3 (cased)

Printed and bound by MPG Books Group, UK

Contents

Figures

Tables and boxes

Contributors

William M. Adams is Moran Professor of Conservation and Development in the Department of Geography at University of Cambridge, Cambridge, UK. wa12@cam.ac.uk.

Bianca Ambrose-Oji was Research Fellow at CAZS-Natural Resources, College of Natural Sciences, Bangor University, Bangor, Wales, UK. b.ambrose@bangor.ac.uk

Iñaki Barcena Hinojal is Professor of Political Science and Director of the Department of Political Science and Administration at the University of the Basque Country, Euskadi. inaki.barcena@ehu.es

Ted Benton is Professor in the Department of Sociology at the University of Essex, UK. tbenton@essex.ac.uk

Raymond L. Bryant is Professor of Political Ecology in the Department of Geography at King's College, University of London. raymond.bryant@kcl.ac.uk

Frederick H. Buttel (1948–2005) had a distinguished research and teaching career that took him to Michigan State University, Ohio State University, Cornell University and University of Wisconsin, Madison, USA. On his death, the International Sociological Association established in his honour the Frederick H. Buttel International Award for Distinguished Scholarship in Environmental Sociology.

Christine N. Buzinde, Department of Recreation, Park and Tourism Management, Penn State University, USA. cbuzinde@psu.edu

JoAnn Carmin is Associate Professor of Environmental Policy and Planning in the Department of Urban Studies and Planning at the Massachusetts Institute of Technology, USA. jcarmin@mit.edu

Thomas Dietz is Assistant Vice President for Environmental Research, Director of the Environmental Science and Policy Program, and Professor of Sociology and Crop and Soil Sciences at Michigan State University, East Lansing, MI, USA. tdietz@msu.edu

Riley E. Dunlap is Regents Professor of Sociology at Oklahoma State University, Stillwater, OK 74078, USA and Past-President of the International Sociological Association's Research Committee on Environment and Society (RC 24). rdunlap@okstate.edu

Arturo Escobar is Kenan Distinguished Teaching Professor of Anthropology in the Department of Anthropology at the University of North Carolina, Chapel Hill, USA. aescobar@email.unc.edu

John Bellamy Foster is Professor in the Sociology Department at the University of Oregon, Eugene, OR, USA and editor of *Monthly Review*. jfoster@uoregon.edu

Michael K. Goodman is Senior Lecturer in the Department of Geography at King's College, University of London, UK. michael.k.goodman@kcl.ac.uk

Nora Haenn is Associate Professor of Anthropology and International Studies at North Carolina State University, USA. nora_haenn@ncsu.edu

John Hannigan is Professor of Sociology, Department of Social Sciences, University of Toronto, Scarborough, Canada. john.hannigan@utoronto.ca

Emma D. Hinton is a PhD candidate in the Department of Geography at King's College, University of London, UK. edhinton@googlemail.com

Maria Kousis is Professor in Sociology of Development and Environment at the University of Crete, Gallos Campus, Rethymno, Greece. kousis@social.soc.uoc.gr

Rosa Lago Aurrekoetxea is a Lecturer in the Department of Electronics and Telecommunications of the University of the Basque Country, Euskadi. rosa.lago@ehu.es

Stewart Lockie is Professor of Sociology in the Research School of Social Sciences at the Australian National University. His recent research has addressed the incorporation of environmental and social values within agricultural commodity chains, the application of market-based instruments to environmental problems, the social impacts of mining and infrastructure development, and intimate partner violence in rural and regional communities. Professor Lockie is co-author of *Going Organic: Mobilising Networks for Environmentally Responsible Food Production* (CABI, 2006) and co-editor of *Agriculture, Biodiversity and Markets: Agroecology and Livelihoods in Comparative Perspective* (Earthscan, 2009).

David Manuel-Navarrete, Department of Geography, King's College, University of London, UK. david.manuel_navarrete@kcl.ac.uk.

Arthur P.J. Mol is Chair and Professor of Environmental Policy within the Department of Social Sciences at Wageningen University, the Netherlands and Professor of Environmental Policy within the School of Environment and Natural Resources at Renmin University, Beijing, China. Arthur.Mol@wur.nl

Raymond Murphy is Emeritus Professor of Sociology at the University of Ottawa, Canada, and author of *Leadership in Disaster: Learning for a Future with Global Climate Change* (McGill-Queen's University Press, 2009). Raymond.Murphy@uottawa.ca

Bradley C. Parks is a PhD candidate at the London School of Economics and Political Science and a Research Fellow at the College of William and Mary's Institute of the Theory and Practice of International Relations, Williamsburg, VA, USA. b.c.parks@lse.ac.uk

Michael R. Redclift is Professor of International Environmental Policy in the Department of Geography at King's College, University of London, UK. In 2006 he became the first recipient of the 'Frederick Buttel Award', from the International Sociological Association, for 'an outstanding contribution to international scholarship in environmental sociology'. michael.r.redclift@kcl.ac.uk.

J. Timmons Roberts is Professor of Sociology and Director of the Center for Environmental Studies at Brown University Providence, Rhode Island, USA. In 2008 Timmons Roberts was awarded the Fred Buttel Distinguished Contribution Award from the Environment and Technology Section of the American Sociological Association. timmons@brown.edu.

Eugene A. Rosa is the Edward R. Meyer Distinguished Professor of Natural Resource and Environmental Policy in the Thomas S. Foley Institute for Public Policy and Public Service and Professor of Sociology in the Department of Sociology, Washington State University, Pullman, WA, USA. rosa@wsu.edu.

Wolfgang Sachs is a Senior Fellow at the Wuppertal Institute for Climate, Environment and Energy, Berlin Office, and Honorary Professor at the University of Kassel, Germany. wolfgang.sachs@wupperinst.org

Jean-Guy Vaillancourt retired in May 2007 as *Professeur titulaire* in the Sociology Department at the University of Montreal, Canada. In October 2009 he was awarded the 2009 Michel-Jurdant Prize for Environmental Sciences by the ACFAS (Association Francophone pour le Savoir, previously known as the French-Canadian Association for the Advancement of Science). jean.guy.vaillancourt@umontreal.ca

Graham Woodgate is Senior Lecturer in Environmental Sociology at the Institute for the Study of the Americas in the University of London's School of Advanced Study. He is also an independent forestry consultant who specializes in the management of the UK's ancient semi-natural woodlands. Graham.Woodgate@sas.ac.uk

Steven Yearley is Professor of the Sociology of Scientific Knowledge at the University of Edinburgh, UK where he is also Director of the Genomics Policy and Research Forum (a centre funded by the UK's Economic and Social Research Council or ESRC). steve.yearley@ed.ac.uk

Richard York is Associate Professor in the Department of Sociology at the University of Oregon, Eugene, OR, USA. rfyork@uoregon.edu.

Introduction
Graham Woodgate

Volume aims and editorial reflections

This collection of original, commissioned essays provides an assessment of the scope and content of environmental sociology both in disciplinary terms and in terms of its wider interdisciplinary contribution, reflecting work by anthropologists, historians, geographers, ecological economists, philosophers and political scientists, as well as dedicated environmental sociologists. More than a decade has passed since the first edition of this handbook was published to considerable acclaim, and environmental sociology is now firmly established as a critical social science discipline, as well as a very broad and inclusive field of intellectual endeavour. Our goal in producing a completely new edition is to mark some of the changes, as well as the continuities, in the field of environmental sociology and to include chapters that draw attention to the substantive concerns and theoretical debates of today.

All the contributors have well-established academic backgrounds and many are also intimately involved in national, regional or global environmental policy processes from formulation through to implementation. Some of the authors provided chapters for the first edition (1997), but we have also commissioned pieces from other established scholars and younger colleagues who are challenging earlier approaches, highlighting alternative dimensions and bringing new perspectives to bear.

The volume is divided into three parts: I – concepts and theories; II – substantive issues; and III – international perspectives. While there is some overlap between these three parts, there is an overall progression from the general towards the particular. Each part begins with an editorial commentary that briefly outlines the contents of the constituent chapters and cross-references some of the more significant themes that link them. It may be useful to consult these commentaries before tackling the substantive chapters; however, each essay is entirely self-contained, so that the volume can be used as a reference source according to the particular interests of the reader.

The process of commissioning and editing the volume has been a fascinating, if at times challenging, project. The fascination and challenges are not just academic and intellectual, however. Together with the demands on comprehension and insight that editing a volume of this nature poses, personal and professional challenges are associated with accommodating such a project within a complex of other commitments and interests. This is mentioned not in preamble to any special pleading concerning the problems associated with bringing the project to fruition, but to highlight the fact that all the contributions to the volume have been produced by individuals who are deeply embedded and implicated in the very issues that they seek to illuminate (Bryant, Chapter 12).

Environmental sociology is usually defined as the study of societal–environmental relations or interactions (Dunlap, Chapter 1), yet this very definition contains within it one of the fundamental issues that many contributors to the field view as central to the emergence of our contemporary predicament: the ontological separation of people and societies from the rest of nature (see, *inter alia*, Dunlap, Chapter 1; Redclift, Chapter 8; Foster, Chapter 7; Manuel-Navarrete and Buzinde, Chapter 9; Benton, Chapter 13). This separation is a modern invention, a product of the scientific revolution and the underpinning of society's faith in its ability to transform the world in pursuit of 'progress'. Engrained in sociology and neatly summed up in Durkheim's claim that 'we can only understand society through recourse to social facts', this human exceptionalism prompted early environmental sociologists to call for a 'new ecological paradigm' (NEP) (see Dunlap, Chapter 1). Rather than view environmental problems as just another issue of societal concern, the NEP emphasized the ecological embeddedness of society and the idea that social structure and human behaviour are influenced by ecological as well as social facts. Developed from a basis in earlier works in various schools of eco-logical anthropology, as evidence of anthropogenic environmental change mounted and became recognized as a global as well as local phenomenon, environmental sociology has matured into what Vaillancourt (Chapter 3) terms 'global ecosociology'.

The chapters that comprise this volume emphasize different aspects of socio-environmental relations. What follow are our interpretations, reflections and attempts at synthesis, which, while we hope they are of some value, should be understood as products of our own academic backgrounds, intellectual endeavours and personal sentiments. We hope the contents of this book will provide sets and casts for your own productions.

Concepts and theories of nature, society, and environment

Human beings share many characteristics with other animals, particularly our fellow mammals. We are all organically embodied and ecologically embedded: we all need to breathe and eat, requiring the consumption of oxygen and nutrients for our bodily growth and maintenance. Our metabolic processes also result in the production and emission of 'wastes'. Every day people die and people are born at global average rates of approximately 110 and 250 per minute respectively. Thus the total global human popu-lation, which currently stands at around 6.75 billion, is increasing at a rate of about 70 million people per year.

The relationship between population growth, economic development and resource availability has been seen as problematic for at least 200 years, notably in early works such as Malthus's *Essay on the Principles of Population* and in the later work of Marx (see Foster, Chapter 7). In more recent times, the publication of Meadow's et al.'s report to the Club of Rome, *The Limits to Growth*, highlighted the finite character of resources such as fossil fuels and minerals, and in the same year, 1972, the UN Conference on the Human Environment (Stockholm) focused on the environmental impacts of industrial pollutants such as CFCs (chlorofluorocarbons) and noted early concerns over global warming.

These two events certainly stimulated the emergence of environmental sociology; however, population growth *per se* has not been the central focus of concern. Rather, relationships between population and resources are seen to be mediated by social structures (Buttel, Chapter 2; York, Rosa and Dietz, Chapter 5), which are themselves considered as both the context and outcome of human agency.

At the same time as human beings are organically embodied and ecologically embed-ded, we are also culturally embodied and socially embedded. Much of the corpus that comprises environmental sociology can be roughly divided into approaches that tend to favour one or other of these two 'realities' (Dunlap, Chapter 1). In contrast to the situation when the first edition of this volume was published, however, most people now acknowledge the relevance of both, while the more adventurous are seeking to combine them. Ideas such as 'coevolution', 'co-construction', 'conjoint constitution', and 'socio-ecological agency' refute the notion that human society can be separated from its ecological context and provide ways into theorizing the indivisibility of nature/society (Manuel-Navarrete and Buzinde, Chapter 9), while leaving room for their analytical separation.

There is also growing consensus surrounding the duality of structure: structure as both the context for and the result of social action, yet environmental sociologies generally tend to focus on either one or the other. Political ecology (Escobar, Chapter 6), while having structuralist roots, took a constructivist turn during the 1990s, and began to investigate the ways in which nature is socially constructed in discourses such as 'sustainable development' and 'biodiversity conservation', considering language to be constitutive of reality, rather than simply reflecting it. Manuel-Navarrete and Buzinde conceptualize the social and material possibilities of discourse in the figure of socio-ecological actors (Chapter 9), painting people as ecological actors, social actors and individuals all at the same time. They claim that reflexive socio-ecological agents will be indispensable mediators in the mutual co-creation of the social and material structures of successful 'post-carbon' societies.

On the other hand, Barcena Hinojal and Lago Aurrekoetxea (Chapter 10) focus on the structure of ecological debt to reflect the environmental injustices of capitalist development, or what Sachs (Chapter 17) calls the 'Euro-Atlantic development model'. Both of these contributions focus on the ecological character of South–North relations in order to counterbalance narrow, financial accounting that portrays a debt-ridden global South in hock to the global North. Any route out of our environmental predicament has to recognize and address these structural imbalances (Chapter 10; Chapter 17; Chapter 19). For Parks and Roberts (Chapter 19), unless imbalances in the economic, political and ecological structure of South–North relations are taken seriously, the prospects for achieving a meaningful post-2012 climate change agreement are severely limited.

Rather than seeking to apportion blame for escalating environmental problems, Mol's ecological modernizaton (Chapter 4; see also York, Rosa and Dietz, Chapter 5) is a structurally oriented social theory of environmental reform, focusing our attention on the social, economic and political structures of environmental governance. In John Hannigan's 'emergence model of environment and society' (Chapter 11) the aim is to understand how novel structures emerge in the context of accelerating environmental change. Drawing on the basic tenets of interactionist approaches, while there is no attempt to synthesize the biophysical and social elements of socio-environmental relations, the emergence model suggests that both individuals and collectivities are capable of acting, and that order and change can occur simultaneously.

Many of the concepts and theories that are discussed in the first part of the book are taken up in the subsequent sections, where they are employed in analyses of substantive issues and regional case studies.

Substantive issues and international perspectives

Globalization, global environmental change and global environmental governance are either referred to directly or are implicit in all the contributions to Parts II and III of the volume. When the first edition was published, there was still considerable debate over the accuracy and meaning of scientific data concerning changes in global mean temperatures and the possible link to climate change. Today, much more attention is focused on the character, efficacy and implications of the growing body of local, national and global policies and social movements that seek to promote climate change mitigation and adaptation.

The establishment of global scientific consensus around the phenomenon of planetary warming has created the impression, as Yearley (Chapter 14) puts it, that the world has 'grown eerily harmonious'. The issue of climate change stands out in this respect because of the way it gave rise to innovations in the production and certification of scientific knowledge – the establishment of the Intergovernmental Panel on Climate Change (IPCC) – and because of the novel positions into which it led environmental NGOs (non-governmental organizations); the IPCC consensus on global warming facilitated NGO campaigns urging governments to go much faster in responding to climate change. Yet prescriptions for action and policy to address global warming vary markedly between different national governments, industry coalitions and social movements.

In more general terms, the character and dynamics of environmental social movements have changed considerably in the wake of accelerated processes of globalization and in the context of the post-Washington Consensus aid environment. Information and communications technologies have been incorporated into the organizing and claims-making activities of social movements, while the recent emphasis on 'good governance' has created space for civil society representation within global environmental policy fora, leading to the professionalization of large-scale movements and their articulation with national and supra-state environmental agencies (Kousis, Chapter 15).

The shift towards more international and global configurations of the last ten to fifteen years has begun to slow, however. This may be linked to the inability of large-scale movements to incorporate local and regional concerns within frames of reference that gain purchase at the global scale, but it also reflects the growth of democratic spaces and processes within previously undemocratic nations and regions. The dynamics of civic engagement in environmental governance in Central and Eastern Europe following the end of the Soviet era and preparations for accession to the European Union (Carmin, Chapter 25), reflect some of the general trends noted by Kousis, but also reveal the enduring legacy of command-and-control economies and the curtailment of opportunities for engagement brought about by the demands of 'making a living' in the extended period of transition to free market economies. In Mol's assessment of the challenges of ecological modernization in China (Chapter 24), he also identifies the opening of space for civic engagement, although these are obviously spaces provided by the state rather than created by the people, and much more room is clearly needed for criticism and environmental activism.

Although the 2008 global financial crisis and consequent economic recession may have slowed the pace of globalization and unprecedented state intervention may suggest otherwise, the hegemonic position of the market as the most effective and efficient conduit for pursuing environmental reform appears to remain intact (Redclift, Chapter 8). Neoliberal regimes of environmental governance are examined in the context of Australian agri-environmental policy by Stewart Lockie (Chapter 23), in order to assess their potential in promoting climate change mitigation and adaption. Twenty years of experience using market-based policy instruments in pursuit of agri-environmental objectives suggest that they are not necessarily effective means for resolving the market failures that some environmental economists believe to be the root cause of agriculture's negative environmental externalities. The evidence from Australia suggests that in the absence of a more heterodox approach and greater grassroots support, policy is unlikely to gain much influence over the complex of social, ecological and economic relationships that shape rural land use and, by extension, global climate change.

Another issue that has gained significantly in prominence since the first edition of this book was published is 'sustainable consumption' (Hinton and Goodman, Chapter 16). Fitting comfortably with neoclassical economic orthodoxy and with the precepts of ecological modernization theory, the promotion of sustainable consumption through provision of 'information' in the form of media campaigns and green labelling, shifts responsibility for environmental reform from producers to consumers, whose purchasing choices will ostensibly send signals through the market mechanism, prompting more environmentally benign production processes and products. At the same time as sustainable consumption is promoted by public policy, alternative forms of green living are promoted by emerging discourses such as 'voluntary simplicity'.

The ethics of consumption are implicit in both mainstream and alternative sustainable consumption discourses, not only in terms of the environmental and social impacts of production and consumption, but also with respect to the moral consideration afforded to animals (Benton, Chapter 13). 'Animal liberation' activists have always been viewed as contentious contenders for membership of the 'club' of mainstream environmental movements, yet promotion of 'animal rights' has never been far from the centre of attention. But how does the discourse of rights hold up in a world where anthropogenic environmental change not only affects the conditions in which animals have to live but, by many accounts, has brought us into a new phase of rapid biodiversity extinction? Benton believes that while rights theory may offer a useful starting point, it needs to be more socially and ecologically sensitive and context-specific if it is to provide clear signposts towards a more benign relationship with the non-human world. Even then, he adds, a range of other moral concepts and codes of behaviour will be necessary.

Sachs (Chapter 17) is more concerned with the implications of ecological limits for global economic justice. Notwithstanding the growing importance attached to rights-based development by international institutions such as the United Nations, Sachs views rights discourse as entirely inadequate in terms of protecting ecological integrity, or for dealing with the continually widening gap between living standards and economic prospects in the global South and global North. In this context, Sachs suggests that Kantian ethics, concerning our duties, may be more helpful than promoting universal human rights. From the Kantian perspective economic and ecological justice demand sustainable consumption (Chapter 16), the eradication of ecological debt and a fair sharing of environmental space (Chapter 10), which together suggest a basic duty not to allow our own development to infringe on the development possibilities of others (Chapter 17). Nevertheless, in a world that is already running short of resources for conventional industrial development, the very concept of 'development' is moot.

At the very least we need to reassess the hegemonic status of the orthodox neoliberal discourse of sustainable development. This is not to deny the legitimate aspirations of those in the global South for secure and fulfilling livelihoods, but if greater justice is to be achieved along the road to a more sustainable future, it will be necessary to construct and act on a discourse of the 'overdeveloped North', rather than continuing to promote private property rights and free-market competition as keys to efficient resource distribution and global utility maximization. Were we to go further and revisit the biological roots of the development metaphor, we would find that it is inextricably linked to senescence. In nature, 'everything that goes up must come down' and everything that is born and develops must eventually grow old and die. As there is no obvious reason why these basic laws of physics and biology should not also apply to our fossil carbon society, perhaps we should focus on 'managed senescence' rather than continue to trumpet the goal of sustainable development?

The senescence of the 'eco-illogical ancient regime' must be accompanied by the florescence of a new 'ecosociety' that recovers some of the fossil carbon released by industrialization and adapts its own metabolism in line with the planet's biological carbon cycles. In Chapter 8, Michael Redclift turns a sociological eye to processes of transition away from carbon dependence. Recent influential reports such as the Stern Review in the UK (Chapter 8) and the Garnaut Review in Australia (Lockie, Chapter 23) have painted climate change as 'the worst market failure the world has ever seen' and stressed the economic opportunities associated with 'decarbonization'. Yet, despite what some have heralded as 'post-political' policy consensus, continuing international negotiations towards a post-Kyoto agreement reveal the deeply political nature of climate policy and science (Parks and Roberts, Chapter 19; Yearley, Chapter 14). In this context there is a need for environmental sociology to develop a better understanding of the ideological and political dimensions of climate policy (Redclift, Chapter 8), while at the same time taking care not to reduce the analysis of climate change risks to the study of discourses abstracted from their dynamic biophysical contexts (Murphy, Chapter 18; see also Hannigan, Chapter 11).

All discourses of nature presumably have at least some historical basis in experience, even if once adopted and marshalled in support of particular political interests they prove inadequate in terms of the purposes for which they are employed. This is well illustrated in Bill Adams's discussion of society, environment and development in Africa (Chapter 22). Through an analysis of relevant case study examples, Adams demonstrates some of the unintended consequences of poorly substantiated and overgeneralized environmental policy narratives and reveals that none of the narratives he analyses has provided an adequate explanation of the realities of rural life in Africa.

A similar situation is exposed in Nora Haenn's study of 'participatory' conservation–development policy in southern Mexico (Chapter 26). The establishment of the Calakmul tropical forest biosphere reserve was supposed to provide opportunities for development through conservation for the local communities of small-scale farmers. However, failure to take account of local histories, multiculturalism and longstanding social contracts led to increasing tensions among the various groups involved (the state, donors, NGOs and beneficiaries), and ultimately resulted in a very different form of conservation than that which was originally envisaged.

Adams and Haenn draw similar conclusions from their studies. For Adams (Chapter 22), 'what works for rural Africa is what rural Africans can make work', for Haenn (Chapter 26), conservation is only sustainable when it 'supports both the physical environment and the social relations that make conservation possible'. Both studies firmly refute the notion of post-political consensus and demonstrate the fallacy of believing that 'ecological debt repayments' can be made on the ecological debtors' terms alone. The overdeveloped countries of the North have achieved their status by occupying more than their fair share of environmental space and by accumulating an ecological debt. Twentieth-century efforts to promote market-driven development in the South have exacerbated, rather than ameliorated, socioeconomic inequality and ecological degradation. Market-based instruments such as carbon trading are unlikely to be able to address these issues successfully; alternative strategies will need to be devised to repair the social and ecological damage. Thus, establishing a successful global ecosociety will be a highly contentious and intensely political process.

Adams's and Haenn's contributions are also illustrative of the multiple roles that the world's trees and forests are expected to play in the North's transition out of carbon dependence and the South's search for 'carbon-lite' solutions for eradicating poverty and achieving human dignity. A much stronger focus on forests and what is termed the 'new forestry' is provided by Ambrose-Oji's essay on the influence of environmental sociological concepts and theories in international forestry discourse and practice (Chapter 20). Both environmental sociology and international forestry have rapidly had to come to terms with globalization and climate change. For international forestry the challenge has become how to integrate forest conservation and exploitation as crucial elements of the global carbon system, while moving forward on forest-based strategies for building resilient livelihoods and communities able to cope in the face of a range of future weather and climate scenarios.

Globalization studies and work on climate change have also begun to add credence to the view that ecological time is being compressed. For most of human history, nature's time has been understood as rhythmic and cyclical, reflecting the phases of the moon and the progression of the seasons. Other processes such as the advance and retreat of ice caps occurred so slowly as to be almost imperceptible before the development of geology in the nineteenth century. The pace of industrial developments in the twentieth century created the illusion of a timeless natural world, the most aesthetically pleasing aspects of which could be preserved for all time. Yet in the early twenty-first century it appears that nature's time is accelerating. Ecologists and natural-resource managers are revising their views of environmental change. The acceptance of non-equilibrium ecologies has moved on to the formulation of ideas about change that occurs not in incremental steps, but through major regime shifts (Ambrose-Oji, Chapter 20). Our ecological past is catching up with our social present and threatening our future survival. As Bryant (Chapter 12) so chillingly puts it, under 'fast capitalism', on 'peering into the abyss' we find ourselves on the road to a 'slow collective suicide'!

Whether we view the future with despondency or optimism, it is clear that mitigation of negative anthropogenic environmental impacts and adaptation to novel environmental conditions will depend on more than 'good science' and 'good governance'. Both may be necessary, but they are neither severally nor jointly sufficient. Part of what is needed is imagination, which is reflected in social mobilizations around climate and other environmental issues at the international level (see Kousis, Chapter 15). The Camp for Climate Action, for example, has been established by and for people who are 'fed up with empty government rhetoric and corporate spin, . . . worried about our future and want to do something about it' (http://climatecamp.org.uk/about, accessed 22 June

2009). Yet, much in the same way that Marx identified the 'noisy sphere of exchange' as a hindrance to our recognition of the ultimate source of all value and the 'secret of profit', post-carbon futures are difficult to imagine in the glare of ecological imperatives, social inertia and political inadequacy. As nature's time catches up with us we need to be able to match its pace of change with the speed of our imaginations. Perhaps the message here is, as Bryant (Chapter 12) suggests, to accept the absurdity of the situation and in the peace of hopelessness, develop our awareness and understanding of socio-ecological agency (Manuel-Navarrete and Buzinde, Chapter 9) and begin to imagine alternative socio-ecological structures and how they might emerge (Hannigan, Chapter 11). Environmental sociologists (*sensu lato*) are, as Bryant's reflections (Chapter 12) reveal, clearly aware of the absurdity of their situations – at least fleetingly – and thus well placed to undertake such abstract reflections.

In designing effective policies to facilitate the emergence of 'carbon-lite' socio-ecological agency/structure and the florescence of ecosociety, our imaginations must be matched by humility (Adams, Chapter 22), however, and a willingness to learn from place-based people. While climate change might be global, our experiences of its impacts will be local, and local conceptions, knowledges and cultures of place-attached people will be vital in responding to the challenges of change and the opportunities for pursuing greater social justice and repairing ecological integrity (Manuel-Navarrete and Redclift, Chapter 21).

To conclude, each of the contributions to this collection has been chosen because it reflects one or both of the following characteristics. First, the authors have pushed at the boundaries of 'environmental sociology', sometimes from dissatisfaction with what their own disciplines provide but more often because of the clear merits of drawing on several disciplinary and interdisciplinary traditions. Second, they have upheld environmental sociology's tradition in sociology by marrying an 'objective', critical stance towards subject matter with a strong moral commitment to address urgent human problems and concerns. They have not remained on the sidelines of policy discourse, for example, yet they remain highly critical of environmental 'policies' and 'policy processes'.

As the first edition of this handbook demonstrated, there is a global readership for most of these concerns, often made up of individuals for whom the main purpose of academic debate and theory is to arm themselves in the midst of positivist 'science' and political rhetoric. They are people who live their lives partly through adherence to the principles of robust scholarly dialogue and enquiry. It is to you, our readers, that we dedicate this new and challenging set of essays.

PART I

CONCEPTS AND THEORIES IN ENVIRONMENTAL SOCIOLOGY

Editorial commentary
Graham Woodgate

Environmental sociology has been at work since the first edition of this volume was published in 1997 and in ways that were not always apparent – for example, interpreting phenomena like climate change, biodiversity and food poverty, examining their politicization, and illuminating actual and possible social responses. In Part I of this edition, we have included chapters that elucidate some of the concepts and theories that are employed in framing analyses of socio-environmental relations. The complex and dynamic character of societies' interactions with the rest of nature, the discursive practices of environmental sociologists, and their experiences and reflections in both their professional and personal lives, all influence the ways in which socio-environmental relations are understood and the particular aspects of them that are the focus of attention. Thus it is more accurate to talk of environmental sociologies, envisaged as a dynamic set of cultural lenses through which to view and to make (non)sense of the world around us, and the ways in which our actions and institutions influence and are influenced by it.

Our aim, then, is to provide a snapshot that reflects something of the diversity of concepts and theories that constitute contemporary environmental sociological thought and practice. In Chapter 1, Riley Dunlap considers the way in which environmental sociology has matured and become more diverse over the three decades that have passed since he and his colleague William Catton Jr first proposed their 'new ecological paradigm' in the late 1970s. Dunlap notes that while the long-running debate over constructivist and realist approaches has subsided significantly in recent years, echoes still remain in what he terms 'environmental agnosticism' and 'environmental pragmatism' and that these two broad orientations reflect, to some extent, differences between the respective environmental sociologies of Europe and North America.

In the first edition of this volume, Dunlap's chapter was followed by a piece from Fred Buttel that focused on the links between social institutions and environmental change. Fred died in early 2005, but his work continues to influence the field of environmental sociology in numerous and significant ways, a fact noted in several of the contributions to this volume. His chapter from the first edition is the only piece that has been reproduced in this new edition and it has been included because of its prescience and continuing relevance. In Chapter 2 Buttel identifies three major issues that continue to dominate research in environmental sociology: the environmental implications of our political and economic institutions; whether growth is primarily an antecedent of, or solution to, environmental problems; and the origins and significance of environmentalism.

Dunlap and Buttel were both early pioneers in the field of environmental sociology in the USA, and their respective works follow parallel trajectories. In Chapter 3 Jean-Guy Vaillancourt documents the evolution of their ideas as reflected in their publications and the lively debates to which they both contributed over the best part of 30 years. It is hard to dismiss Vaillancourt's claim that Dunlap and Buttel were key players in the transition from human ecology to environmental sociology and, more recently, to the emergence of what he terms 'global ecosociology'.

Chapters 4 and 5 reflect on ecological modernization (EM), which Arthur Mol defines as 'the social scientific interpretation of environmental reform processes and practices at multiple scales' (Chapter 4). Ecological modernization has developed a very significant body of empirical and theoretical work that has received widespread attention from academics and also from policy-makers and politicians in terms of framing programmes of environmental reform. Mol's elaboration of EM theory is embedded within a historical analysis of social science contributions to understanding processes of environmental policy reform. Beginning in the 1970s, studies of environmental policies, protests and attitudes led to the initial introduction of the concept of ecological modernization. EM as a social theory of environmental reform was established during the 1990s, while the last ten years have witnessed moves to consider the role of consumers (see Hinton and Goodman, Chapter 16) in reform processes, the application of EM theory in the analysis of nations beyond the highly industrialized North, and also a trend towards more comparative, regional and global studies. During the last decade the impressive, if uneven, growth of China and India, in particular, has caused EM theorists to widen their analysis to reflect a more global perspective (see Mol on ecological modernization in China in Part III, Chapter 24).

Mol's contribution in Chapter 4 also includes a brief review of some of the criticism that has been levelled at EM theory, but a more thorough account is provided by Richard York, Eugene Rosa and Thomas Dietz in Chapter 5. Dunlap characterizes EM as falling into what he sees as the largely European tradition of environmental agnosticism, while York et al. fit his North American dominated model of environmental pragmatism. Indeed, the two fundamental criticisms that York and colleagues level at EM theory are: first that 'its purchase is not directly ecological . . . there is too little attention given to actual environmental change'; and second, while it has documented important cases of environmental reform, the general argument that ecological modernization is 'leading to increased sustainability in the aggregate is not consistent with a large body of empirical evidence'.

From EM theory we move to political ecology, another rapidly growing field that has attracted controversy in the last decade or so. In Chapter 6, Arturo Escobar traces the construction of political ecology and distinguishes three broad phases of development. Having initially emerged from the intertwining of political economy and human and cultural ecology in the 1970s and early 1980s, by the end of the 1980s this first phase of development, which sought to address the absence of nature in political economy and ecological anthropologies' lack of attention to power, was beginning to give way to the poststructuralist or constructivist turn. This 'second-generation' political ecology provided a 'vibrant inter- and transdisciplinary space of inquiry' throughout the 1990s and into the present decade, engaging with the epistemological debates fostered by constructivism and anti-essentialism. Over the last five years these epistemological concerns have been accompanied by ontological issues, prompting Escobar tentatively to identify a third-generation, postconstructivist orientation.

The relatively recent development of political ecology contrasts with the subject addressed by John Bellamy Foster in Chapter 7. As his title suggests, in 'Marx's ecology and its historical significance' Foster takes us back to the nineteenth century to explore in some detail the numerous and important linkages between Marx's historical material-ism and other major intellectual developments such as Liebig's agricultural chemistry and Darwin's theory of evolution by means of natural selection. Having established the significant ecological content of Marx's own work, Foster moves to the twentieth century to reveal its legacy in terms of the development of ecological science. For Foster, uncovering the contributions of Marx and subsequent socialist thinkers to the develop-ment of the modern ecological critique of capitalism plays a vital role in the construc-tion of an ecological materialist analysis that is 'capable of addressing the devastating environmental conditions that face us today'.

Michael Redclift's contribution to the volume follows Foster's chapter, providing an overview of environmental sociology's attempts to come to terms with what is, by general consensus, the most pressing environmental issue of our time: anthropogenic global warming. He begins by reviewing the major differences and divisions that have come to characterize the discussion of the environment and nature in the social sciences, distinguishing between critical realism and social constructivism. This is followed by a review of the main intellectual challenges to both positions. In the subsequent sections of Chapter 8, Redclift argues for a sociological perspective on transitions out of carbon dependence that includes better understanding of the ideological and political dimen-sions of 'decarbonization' (on which see Parks and Roberts in Part II, Chapter 19 of this volume), taking us beyond the current impasse and suggesting important areas for further theoretical development.

Some of the challenges identified in Michael Redclift's piece are taken up in the final four chapters of Part I. Within sociology there has always been a vibrant debate between exponents of 'agency' and 'structural' approaches. This central sociological concern has also surfaced within thinking about society and nature. In a very stimulating contribu-tion, David Manuel-Navarrete and Christine Buzinde (Chapter 9) argue for a recon-ceptualization of human agency as 'socio-ecological agency'. Building from concepts of society/nature 'conjoint constitution' and 'coevolution', Manuel-Navarrete and Buzinde argue that to maximize humanity's chances of overcoming the global environmental crisis, the mutual co-creation of social and material structures must be mediated by a transcendental form of agency enacted by individuals in their interactions not only with their societies and environments, but also with themselves. The requisite socio-ecological agency thus characterizes people as 'ecological actors, social actors and individuals all at the same time'.

Following a chapter that seeks to expand and redefine the concept of human agency, the next contribution (Barcena Hinojal and Lago Aurrekoetxea, Chapter 10) works to critique structures of economic development – in particular the financial indebtedness of less industrialized countries, which continues to exert economic pressure towards further exploitation and degradation of environments in the South and the social depri-vation of the 'bottom billion'. As a counterbalance to the structure of external debt, the authors draw our attention to the notion of 'ecological debt', a concept that has recently entered into academic circles, having emerged from social movement discourse and first-generation political ecology in the 1980s.

Established on the principle of environmental justice, ecological debt is the debt accu-mulated by the countries of the North towards the countries of the South through the export of natural resources at prices that take no account of the environmental damage caused by their extraction and processing and the free occupation of environmental space – atmospheric, terrestrial and hydrospheric – through the dumping of production wastes. For the purposes of their chapter, Barcena Hinojal and Lago Aurrekoetxea focus on revealing the content and dimensions of ecological debt in terms of a number of salient concepts: carbon debt, biopiracy, waste export and environmental liabilities. Their aim is to contribute to the search for solutions to both the problem of the South's foreign debt and climate change, and to the ecological restructuring of our societies in the search for sustainability.

Rather than seeking to explain the origins of the current environmental crisis (see Foster, and Barcena Hinojal and Lago Aurrekoetxea) or effective mechanisms for environmental reform (Mol), John Hannigan's chapter, 'The emergence model of environment and society' (Chapter 11), seeks to elaborate a sociological approach to the society–environment relationship that emphasizes 'elements of novelty, uncertainty, emergence, improvisation and social learning'. Building on the interactonist tradition in sociological inquiry, Hannigan makes no attempt to synthesize the material and symbolic elements of socio-environmental relations; instead, his aim is to shed light on the emergence of novel structures and associations and framings of risk in the context of accelerating environmental change. The emergence model of environment and society reflects a situation in which 'both individuals and collectivities are capable of acting, and order and change can occur simultaneously'.

The final contribution to Part I of this volume comes from Raymond Bryant (Chapter 12). In a piece that is at once alarming yet comical, Bryant draws on the absurdist tradition in his characterization of our current predicament as 'slow collective suicide under fast capitalism'. A theory of absurdity, suggests Bryant, casts our predicament as a manifestation of a fundamental 'lack of coherence and reasonableness in human thought . . . Absurdity emerges in the dawning consciousness of humanity that successive crises and predicaments can never be resolved via "knowledge fixes" let alone baseless mantras of hope.' Yet Bryant's message to us is not thoroughly pessimistic; as with early Dadaist and Surrealist artists, absurdity can bring liberation. With an acceptance of absurdity comes the opportunity to 'begin to unravel some . . . of the damage that the human species has done to the planet as part of a life that firmly rejects suicide, including the path of slow collective suicide that our species has embarked on'.

Many of the concepts and theories elaborated in Part I of this volume are taken up and employed in Parts II and III, which focus upon the use to which the conceptual apparatus has been put. As noted at the beginning of this commentary, environmental sociology is a broad and dynamic body of work, characteristics that are amply demonstrated in the coming chapters.

1 The maturation and diversification of environmental sociology: from constructivism and realism to agnosticism and pragmatism[1]

Riley E. Dunlap

Introduction

Environmental sociology has changed enormously since the first edition of this handbook was published. Both its theoretical perspectives and methodological approaches reflect increased sophistication and diversity, in part stemming from changes in its subject matter. Environmental problems are now regarded as more complex, intractable, globalized and threatening, partly due to increased knowledge and awareness, and partly as a result of objective changes in biophysical conditions. The increased salience of environmental problems combined with advances in the field have enabled environmental sociology to gain in legitimacy, exemplified by more publications in top-tier journals and growing job opportunities, and to continue its international diffusion. A result of all this is that even as environmental sociology is becoming a mature and well-institutionalized field, it is in a period of intellectual ferment, the home to major debates over foci, theory and methods that reflect in part international variation in intellectual approaches.

Nonetheless, in this period of flux, environmental sociology is still dealing with the same fundamental issues it faced when established as the study of societal–environmental relations or interactions (Catton and Dunlap, 1978; Dunlap and Catton, 1979a). From the outset, environmental sociology has grappled not only with how to approach such interactions, but with the nature of 'society' and 'environment' as well. Indeed, major developments in the field over the past three decades are linked to changing approaches to all three phenomena. I contend that societal–environmental interactions remain the most challenging issue, and divergent approaches to them the source of our most fundamental cleavages.

First, let me quickly note that trying to capture the social changes of the past three decades is well beyond the scope of this chapter. One need only consider that environmental sociology emerged during the transition from modernity to – depending on one's favored theorist – postmodernity, reflexive modernity, liquid modernity, risk society and/or network society (see, e.g., Lash et al., 1996; Spaargaren et al., 2000, 2006). While contemporary social change will be the subject of continuing theoretical debate, perhaps least disputed is that we are experiencing rapidly increasing globalization. The nature of globalization will continue to generate debate among environmental and other sociologists, but processes of globalization seem unlikely to abate and will have a profound effect on our field (Haluza-DeLay and Davidson, 2008; Jorgenson and Kick, 2006; Spaargaren et al., 2006; Yearley, 2007). I discuss the globalization of environmental phenomena in the next section, but otherwise confine my focus to the 'environmental' and 'interaction' components of societal–environmental interactions.

The rest of this chapter focuses first on key changes in 'the environment' over the past three decades and the resulting need to employ more sophisticated indicators of environmental conditions, and next on the continued struggles and debates over how to deal with societal–environmental interactions. I argue that while the realist–constructivist 'war' has subsided, one can discern a broader cleavage between constructivist-oriented scholars committed to 'environmental agnosticism' (a skeptical attitude toward evidence about environmental conditions) and realist-oriented scholars practicing 'environmental pragmatism' (an emphasis on measuring and investigating rather than problematizing such conditions), in part reflecting contrasting European–North American emphases. A result is that many environmental sociologists (particularly in Europe) limit their attention to the symbolic/ideational/cultural realm rather than examining the materialist nature of societal–environmental relations as increasingly common in North America. Then I continue to explore European–North American contrasts as part of a more general discussion of how historical/geographical contexts have influenced and continue to affect the evolution of our field, followed by a short conclusion.

The environment: changing conceptualizations and expanding foci of the field

The one issue that binds together environmental sociologists, regardless of theoretical or methodological orientation, is an interest in the biophysical environment (Dunlap and Catton, 1983). Indeed, this subject matter is what makes our field distinct. Of course, 'the environment' is an enormously complex phenomenon, open to highly diverse conceptualizations and operationalizations, and this is a key factor in generating diversity among environmental sociologists. When environmental sociology was being established in the USA, distinguishing among built, modified and natural environments was relevant because of the strong representation of scholars interested in housing and urban design (Dunlap and Catton, 1979a, 1979b; also see Dunlap and Michelson, 2002), while the simple distinction between 'additions' and 'withdrawals' (Schnaiberg, 1980) seemed adequate for conceptualizing societal interactions with non-built environments. However, on the one hand most built-environment analysts have moved into other areas, leaving us with an overwhelming focus on non-built environments (although renewed interest in energy consumption and heightened concern with sustainable cities may reverse this), and on the other it is increasingly recognized that withdrawals and additions are inadequate for capturing the complex processes by which societies interact with the biophysical environment (Mol and Spaargaren, 2006: 62). Thus the time is ripe for environmental sociology to embrace more sophisticated conceptualizations of the biophysical environment.

Ironically, but illustrative of the 'environmental agnosticism' to be discussed below, even those who recognize the need to move beyond withdrawals and additions (Spaargaren et al., 2006) appear hesitant to draw upon recent efforts of ecologists that provide far more comprehensive conceptualizations of the biophysical environment than were available when environmental sociology was launched. Current efforts to clarify ecosystem properties and services are largely ignored by those seeking more sophisticated conceptualizations of environmental phenomena. This is perplexing, as rich analyses distinguishing among, for example, the regulation, habitat, production and information functions of ecosystems take us well beyond the simplistic additions/withdrawals distinction and encompass virtually all of the biophysical phenomena of interest to environmental sociologists (deGroot et al., 2002).

Focusing on ecosystem services would also position environmental sociologists to engage more fruitfully in interdisciplinary endeavors such as the emerging field of 'sustainability science' (Kates cum al., 2001) and research on 'coupled human and natural systems' (Liu cum al., 2007) – the subject of a new program in the US National Science Foundation – as well as engage more effectively with major programs such as the United Nations Millennium Ecosystem Assessment project (Millennium Ecosystem Assessment, 2005). While some environmental sociologists may see such efforts, as well as use of the ecosystem services concept, as a case of allowing natural scientists and/or policy-makers to set our agenda (e.g. Szersznyski et al., 1996), I see it differently. Not only would greater use of ecological concepts provide us with more adequate conceptualizations of the phenomena most of us study, and help us interact more effectively with other disciplines and policy-makers, but there is no reason why we cannot bring a critical sociological eye to both the conceptualization and use of the notion of 'ecological services'. Indeed, an interdisciplinary team with two sociologists has recently done just that by demonstrating both the utility and limitations of current applications of the concept (Hodgson et al., 2007).

While I am hopeful that our field will make greater use of the rapidly developing literature on ecosystem services, for now I want to reintroduce a far simpler model of environmental phenomena that highlights only three ecosystem 'services' or 'functions' critical for human beings (Dunlap and Catton, 2002). To begin with, the environment provides us with the resources necessary for meeting our material needs and wants, and thus serves as our 'supply depot'. Second, in the process of using resources human beings produce waste products and the environment therefore functions as our 'waste repository'. Obviously use of the supply depot and waste repository functions involve environmental withdrawals and additions, but what has always been missing from investigations of the latter two is that they are not simply abstract processes but occur in specific places.

A concern with place points to the third function of the environment, which is to provide our 'living space' or where we live, work and consume. Political ecologists have long highlighted the geographical or spatial dimension of environmental problems, and in the contemporary globalizing world environmental sociologists have begun to do so as well (Spaargaren et al., 2006). In a global economy control over withdrawals and additions has become disembedded from sites of resource extraction and subsequent sites of processing, use and disposal of resulting products (Jorgenson and Kick, 2006). It is thus essential to combine the spatial along with the supply and repository functions if we are to have even a rudimentary model for conceptualizing the phenomena of interest to contemporary environmental sociologists, such as 'ecologically unequal exchange' (Rice, 2007), which will be discussed shortly.[2]

This deliberately simple model helps clarify the nature if not the sources of environmental problems. When human beings overuse a given environment (from local to global) for one of these three functions, 'problems' in the form of pollution, resource shortages and overcrowding and/or overpopulation result. Yet not only must a given environment (from local to global) serve all three functions, but fulfilling one may impair its ability to fulfill the other two and result in more complex environmental problems (see examples and diagrams in Dunlap and Catton, 2002). While problems reflecting functional incompatibilities at the local level (e.g. toxic contamination of living space and loss of agricultural land to urban sprawl) were common research foci in past decades, nowadays larger-scale conflicts resulting in regional deforestation and loss of biodiversity to global ozone depletion and anthropogenic climate change are receiving attention from sociologists (see Dunlap and Marshall, 2007: 331). Thus the foci of our field have become more complex and varied in scale, sometimes reaching the global level, as well as often posing greater risks that are difficult to detect (Beck, 1992).

Of course, it is not 'the environment' but 'ecosystems' that provide these three functions for human beings – and for all other living species – as the growing body of work on ecosystem services emphasizes (deGroot et al., 2002; Hodgson et al., 2007). Furthermore, it is increasingly recognized that the health of entire ecosystems, including the earth's global ecosystem, is being jeopardized as a result of rising human demands on them. Whereas historically the notion that human societies face 'limits to growth' was based on the assumption that we would run out of natural resources such as oil, contemporary 'ecological limits' refer to the finite ability of the global ecosystem to provide its vital services in the face of an increasing human load. Whether measured by human appropriation of net primary production or ecological footprints (Haberl et al., 2004), the evidence suggests that the growing demands of the human population for living space, resources and waste absorption are beginning to exceed long-term global carrying capacity (Kitzes et al., 2008) – with the result that the current human population is drawing down natural capital and disrupting the functioning of ecosystems from the local to the global level (Millennium Ecosystem Assessment, 2005).

Environmental sociologists have responded to these changes in environmental problems and ecological conditions in a variety of ways, but perhaps the two most noticeable are the increasing focus on global-level problems and use of a range of measures of environmental phenomena including deforestation, CO_2 and other greenhouse gas (GHG) emissions and energy consumption, as well as overall indicators of ecological load such as ecological footprints (a measure that encompasses all three functions of ecosystems – Kitzes et al., 2008). In a little over a decade there has been a quantum leap in the number of cross-national studies investigating societal characteristics associated with the ecological impacts of nations and their populations. Many of these studies have been guided by world systems theory (WST) (Ciccantell et al., 2005; Jorgenson and Kick, 2006), and these in particular have illustrated the importance of distinguishing among the supply depot, waste repository and living space functions, as well as disaggregating the human load on the global environment.

Although early WST analyses tended to use position in the world system (core, semi-peripheral and peripheral nations) to predict phenomena such as GHG emissions, over time studies have built on Stephen Bunker's pioneering efforts to trace the nature and consequences of the flow of ecological goods across borders (Ciccantell et al., 2005), and in the process have developed sophisticated models of ecologically unequal exchange that involve – at least implicitly – distinguishing among the three basic functions of the environment (Jorgenson, 2006; Rice, 2007). These studies demonstrate that wealthy (or core) nations are able to use poorer (both peripheral and semi-peripheral) ones as supply depots, obtaining from these nations a growing portion of the natural resources they consume. Likewise, wealthy nations increasingly use poorer nations as waste repositories by shipping wastes to them for disposal, locating polluting industries in them, and over-using the global commons (oceans and atmosphere) on which all nations depend. In the process, wealthy nations – including those implementing 'ecological modernization' – manage to protect their own living spaces by shifting their resource extraction and waste problems to poorer nations, despoiling the latter's living space and ecosystem viability in the process (Jorgenson and Kick, 2006; Ciccantell et al., 2005).

By adding the crucial spatial component to withdrawals and additions, and particularly by highlighting the fact that control over both of the latter is often located in distant centers of economic and political power, world systems analyses – as well as alternative analyses from a human ecology perspective (Dietz et al., 2007; York et al., 2003) – are offering keen insights into the relationships between social and ecological processes both intra- and internationally. Such cross-national studies promise to help move environmental sociology forward with progressively more sophisticated analyses of the societal causes and consequences of ecological disruptions.

Despite the progress being made in understanding global patterns of ecological disruption, many environmental sociologists remain more interested in problematizing rather than utilizing data on ecological phenomena, resulting in two divergent perspectives within the field that loosely reflect North American and European versions of environmental sociology.

Societal–environmental interactions

In the 1970s, when empirical studies of interactions were most likely to be micro-level studies of human behavior *vis-à-vis* built environments, and scholars interested in the 'natural' environment were more likely to examine the processes and actors involved in turning environmental quality into a social problem, a distinction was made between the 'sociology of environmental issues' and *core* 'environmental sociology'. The former referred to studies of public opinion, environmental activism, environmental politics and the social construction of environmental problems, while the latter was reserved for nascent efforts to investigate societal–environmental interactions (Dunlap and Cattton, 1979a, 1979b). As US environmental sociologists began to analyze empirically the relationships between social and environmental phenomena, such as the correlations between racial/ethnic and socioeconomic status and exposure to environmental hazards (Brulle and Pellow, 2006), and the field attracted scholars with a diverse set of interests and became more institutionalized, a more inclusive definition of environmental sociology as the sociological study of environmental issues/problems was, at least implicitly, adopted (Buttel, 1987).

By the early 1990s the cultural turn and postmodern sensibilities of the larger discipline, partially reflecting a growing European influence, generated a social-constructivist surge that threatened to replace the strong materialist grounding of environmental sociology with a more idealist orientation (Taylor and Buttel, 1992; Greider and Garkovich, 1994) and in the process return the field to (a new version of) the sociology of environmental issues (Dunlap and Catton, 1994).

Early on, Catton and I highlighted the importance of distinguishing between 'symbolic' and 'non-symbolic' interactions in a preliminary effort to emphasize that human societies obviously relate to the environment on both the ideational and materialist levels (Dunlap and Catton, 1979b: 75–6). We saw environmental sociologists increasingly focusing on both, and particularly the complex ways in which the symbolic and material realms intermingle, and subsequent analysts have continued to grapple with the problems posed in integrating the symbolic and materialist dimensions of societal rela-tionships with the environment (e.g. Freudenburg et al., 1995; Goldman and Schurman, 2000; Kroll-Smith et al., 2000; Murdoch, 2001; Woodgate and Redclift, 1998). What we did not foresee was that by the 1990s there would be a major push within environ-mental sociology to confine sociological analyses of environmental issues largely to the symbolic/ideational/cultural levels.

The realist versus constructivist debate
Rather than recreate the realist–constructivist battles in detail, let me note that the core of the debate was over what those of us in the realist camp saw as the excesses of postmod-ern relativism that, as Oreskes (2004: 1241) put it in her review of Latour's *The Politics of Nature*, 'led to silly and sterile arguments about whether there is or is not a real world and whether scientific knowledge bears any relation to it (if it exists)'. The debate seems to have subsided after scholars in the realist camp defended themselves against charges of 'naïve realism' by drawing upon critical realism to acknowledge that our understand-ing of environmental problems is socially constructed, while emphasizing that despite its imperfections science provides vital 'evidence' of real-world conditions (Dickens, 1996; Murphy, 1997). In turn, constructivists responded by disavowing 'extreme' constructiv-ism and dismissing its alleged ontological relativism as mere rhetorical excesses, while defending epistemological relativism and pointing to insightful examples of mild or contextual constructivist analyses that realists had never criticized and frequently cited. Most notable in this regard was Burningham and Cooper's (1999) rebuttal to critics of constructivism, a response that was subsequently critiqued by Benton (2001) and Murphy (2002), who showed the inherent limitations and contradictions of constructiv-ist analyses that adopt an agnostic stance toward the reality of environmental problems. The lack of response by constructivists to these trenchant critiques seems to have ended the formal debate between realists and constructivists, but not the continuing relevance of the underlying issues.

As both Benton (2001) and Murphy (2002) emphasize, eschewing an interest in the 'validity' of claims, particularly from those eager to weaken the credibility of scientific evidence, as recommended by Burningham and Cooper (1999) and other constructivists, can have important consequences in the 'real world' where the (often invisible) con-structions of the powerful already enjoy a privileged status (Freudenburg, 2000; 2005). Whether it is local citizens engaged in 'lay epidemiology' to challenge officials' dismissal of their claims of toxic exposure (Brown, 2007) or scientists, environmentalists and policy-makers attempting to develop policies to lessen deforestation, ozone depletion or greenhouse gas emissions, being able to argue that 'the evidence' supports their case is crucial. As Benton (2001: 18) puts it,

> Constructionist demonstrations of the intrinsic uncertainty and politically/normatively 'con-structed' character of environmental science sabotages environmental politics, and plays into the hands of powerful interests . . . who are only too pleased to discover that the environmental case against their activities is inadequate. (See also Murphy, 2002: 320)

Such stinging criticism was in response to Burningham and Cooper's (1999: 310–11) claim that being unwilling and/or unable to compare competing claims to objective conditions was non-problematic even in political debates.

Earlier criticism along these lines was stimulated by sociology's initial reaction to global environmental change, particularly anthropogenic global warming (AGW), being heavily skewed toward constructivist analyses (Dunlap and Catton, 1994: 20–23; see also Rosa and Dietz, 1998; Lever-Tracy, 2008). While such analyses provided valuable insight into the emergence of global warming as a 'problem' (Ungar, 1992) and the special challenges faced by climate scientists (Shackley and Wynne, 1996), realists were troubled by two interrelated problems: (1) the one-sided focus on deconstructing the IPCC and climate science while largely ignoring the counter-claims being issued by the fossil fuel industry and its political supporters, and (2) the extreme relativism involved in highlighting the 'contested nature' of AGW by uncritically citing skeptic sources such as the Marshall Institute (Taylor and Buttel, 1992: 413; Shackley and Wynne, 1996: 276). Granting a conservative think tank led by three physicists with no expertise in climate science *per se* (Lahsen, 2007), and best known for its support of Reagan's Strategic Defense Initiative (or 'Star Wars'), standing with the IPCC seemed unwise analytically,[3] and terribly naïve politically.

Realists believed that the constructions of critics of 'mainstream' climate science should be subjected to the same (if not more) scrutiny as those of the IPCC (McCright and Dunlap, 2000), and over time endeavored to demonstrate that conservative think tanks like the Marshall Institute function as key agents in a conservative-led movement to undermine climate science and thereby the need for climate policies (McCright and Dunlap, 2003). More generally, realists have called for greater attention to the (often subtle) ways in which economic privilege and political power are employed to suppress and deny scientific evidence of climate change and environmental degradation in general (Freudenburg, 2000, 2005; McCright and Dunlap, 2010).

Reflecting an acute awareness of the Right's success in deconstructing climate science, if not debates within environmental sociology, Latour (2004: 227) – a founding father of strong constructivism – has issued a stunning *mea culpa* in which he worries that 'dangerous extremists are using the very same argument of social construction to destroy hard-won evidence that could save our lives', and then adds, 'Why does it burn my tongue to say that global warming is a fact whether you like it or not?' More generally, he acknowledges a fundamental premise of the realist camp, which is that when dealing with issues like climate change we have no choice but to rely on scientific evidence, despite its imperfections (Benton, 2001; Dunlap and Catton, 1994; Murphy, 2002). While Latour's *mea culpa* could be seen as marking the official end of realist–constructivist battles, I believe a broader but related cleavage – between environmental sociologists who confine their analyses to the symbolic/ideational/cultural level and those who examine material conditions – continues to exist.

From constructivism versus realism to agnosticism versus pragmatism
Carolan's (2005) superb distillation of the relevant aspects of Roy Bhaskar's critical realism for approaching environmental issues is particularly helpful in shedding light on this broader divide in contemporary environmental sociology. Carolan (2005: 399–407) distinguishes among three strata of '"nature", nature and Nature'. First, 'nature' in quotes is clearly a sociodiscursive concept, one used to distinguish 'that which is not social', to refer to the natural world or human nature or human biology. Second, nature uncapitalized is 'the nature of fields and forests, wind and sun, organisms and

watersheds, and landfills and DDT' (p. 403). This stratum involves 'ubiquitous (and obvious) overlap between the sociocultural and biophysical realms'. Finally, there is 'deep' (capitalized) Nature, or 'the Nature of gravity, thermodynamics, and ecosystem processes. . .' (p. 406). It is this level of 'permanence-with-flux' that sociologists treat as a constant and thus bracket out of consideration.

This tripartite classification of a far-more complex 'real world' helps shed light on the current cleavage within environmental sociology that transcends the narrower realist–constructivist debate. To begin with, those who focus on the sociocultural construction of 'nature' frequently limit their attention to the first level, demonstrating that different cultures and social sectors (e.g. environmentalists) create and are motivated by differing images/views of the 'natural world' and thus that controversies over nature conservation/ development and environmental protection/degradation reflect divergent values and worldviews largely unrelated to 'objective conditions' (e.g. Eder, 1996; Greider and Garkovich, 1994; Macnaghten and Urry, 1998). Environmental realists appreciate the insights offered by these analyses, but take issue with the manner in which deconstructions of 'nature' are frequently and facilely overgeneralized to the world of ecological problems, or Carolan's second stratum.

This second stratum is the world of ecosystem services and disruptions that form the basis for environmental science and attract considerable attention from environmental sociologists. Yet there are clearly two distinct approaches to these phenomena. Drawing heavily on the sociology of science, constructivists typically confine their efforts to contextualizing, problematizing and deconstructing the claims about ecological conditions issued by scientists, activists and policy-makers (e.g. Lash et al., 1996; Wynne, 1996; Taylor and Buttel, 1992; Yearley, 2005, 2008) while realists employ various indicators of these conditions in studies of societal–environmental interactions (described below).

The third stratum of 'deep Nature' is of limited concern to sociologists, although Carolan's mention of 'ecosystem processes' along with the 'deepest' phenomena of gravity and thermodynamics opens up the possibility of the global climate system fitting here better than in the second stratum. Still, the general permanence of this level, at least in terms of human time spans, allows sociology to essentially ignore it, and only in exceptionally outlandish postmodern challenges to natural science as reflected in the 'Sokal Hoax' does it attract attention (Guillory, 2002).

We can draw several conclusions about contemporary environmental sociology from these distinctions. First, as noted above, realists have little problem with deconstructions of phenomena in the first stratum, which are primarily sociocultural products, but are troubled by constructivists' tendencies to generalize their deconstructions of cultural understandings of 'nature' to the ecosystem services and disruptions that comprise the second stratum and to conflate the two strata (Greider and Garkovich, 1994). Second, realists are critical of the (over)emphasis on problematizing and relativizing evidence, whether scientific or lay knowledge, of ecological problems as noted earlier. Third, and most pertinent here, realists see the emphasis on deconstructing both 'nature' and knowledge claims of ecological problems as reflecting a very restricted version of environmental sociology, essentially avoiding 'interactions' between sociocultural and biophysical phenomena (Dunlap and Catton, 1994).

Inglis and Bone (2006: 285) expand this cleavage beyond the confines of environmental sociology by analyzing the efforts of theorists such as Beck, Giddens, Latour and

Luhmann to deal with the 'nature/culture divide' in their various analyses of the growing significance of ecological problems. In the process Inglis and Bone complement and extend earlier efforts to show how disciplinary traditions and practices make sociologists reluctant to deal with the biophysical environment (e.g. Catton and Dunlap, 1980; Dickens, 1992; Benton, 1994) when they conclude that social scientists

> . . . have often conjured away the complexities of nature–culture interpenetrations at the ontological level in favour of epistemological assertions to the effect that such entities are purely cultural, claims which are implicitly aimed at vaunting the authority of the social sciences over that of the natural sciences. If we do indeed live in an age of reflexive modernity where all boundaries are made complicated and ambiguous, social scientists seem intent on clinging to their own favoured modes of boundary maintenance between 'culture' and 'nature', aggrandizing the former over the latter. (2006: 285)

In sum, we presently have two loosely defined but distinguishable 'camps' of sociologists focusing on environmental issues: the first, with somewhat disproportionate European representation, treats 'environmental matters' largely as symbolic/ideational/cultural phenomena best examined via a hermeneutic/interpretative approach, typically adopts a relativistic stance toward knowledge claims – including those issued by scientists – concerning environmental conditions, and is hesitant to deal with the materialistic dimension of ecological problems. Its efforts to incorporate the material world into sociological analyses are often limited to the discursive realm via talk about 'hybrids', 'cyborgs' and the like. The resulting perspective of 'environmental agnosticism' thus avoids societal–environmental interactions and represents a modern and theoretically sophisticated 'sociology of environmental issues' (York, 2006).

The second 'camp', predominantly but far from exclusively North American, is strongly interested in the material aspects of the environment, treats accounts of environmental conditions – whether lay or scientific – as potential indicators of ecological problems[4] and examines the complex ways in which these conditions/problems are interrelated with social phenomena via empirical investigations. Although recognizing that indicators of ecological conditions – as well as environmental values, issues and policies – are socially constructed, this camp's emphasis tends to be on analyzing linkages between the symbolic, social-structural and material realms. While reflecting a realist perspective, the diversity of empirical approaches might more aptly be termed 'environmental pragmatism' to capture their shared willingness to employ available indicators of ecological conditions in sociological analyses.[5] Broadly speaking, whereas the challenge for environmental agnostics is to understand differing stances on environmental issues, the challenge for environmental pragmatists is to shed light on the causes and consequences of ecological problems.

Examples of environmental pragmatism
Pragmatists tend to focus primary attention on Carolan's second stratum, the nature of ecosystem services and disruptions, in the form of resource extraction/use, pollution and land degradation. While enormously diverse in theoretical framework, methodology and research foci, their approach is characterized by a pragmatic employment of environmental indicators in empirical research investigating linkages between social and biophysical phenomena.

The 'data' employed by those in the pragmatist camp take diverse forms, ranging from quantitative national-level indicators like GHGs, deforestation, energy consumption and overall 'ecological footprints' (as employed in the WST studies reviewed earlier) to sub-national indicators of air and water quality to community-level indicators of environmental hazards. Often such data come from government agencies based on scientific measurements, or – as in the case of the USA's widely used Toxic Release Inventory (or TRI) – in the form of government-mandated industry reports collated and released by government agencies. Evidence reported, and in some cases carefully collected, by lay people also becomes data for analyses (Brown, 2007).

At the international level the WST-driven studies are most numerous and, as noted earlier, they demonstrate how historical paths of development, geographical distribution of natural resources and contemporary structures of international economic and political power drive global patterns of resource use and ecological degradation. Conversely, a growing number of studies anchored in a human–ecological perspective consistently document the pervasive role of demographic factors in ecological degradation, challenging both those who emphasize economic growth as the primary driver of degradation as well as those who see it as necessary for environmental protection (Dietz et al., 2007). Still a third set, drawing on world polity theory (WPT), focuses more on the diffusion of global environmental governance and its presumed ameliorative effect on environmental degradation (Shofer and Hironaka, 2005). The dramatic growth of such studies is stimulating robust debates among the various perspectives, and increasing efforts to compare their explanatory power relative to one another and frequently to ecological modernization theory (York et al., 2003).

Another 'growth area' in terms of empirical research, particularly in the USA, is sociological work on environmental inequality. The environmental justice movement, including its global diffusion, continues to attract sociological attention (Pellow and Brulle, 2005; Pellow, 2007). Of particular relevance here is the explosion of work on environmental inequality, or the 'inequitable' relationship between social (especially racial/ethnic and socioeconomic) hierarchies and exposure to undesirable environmental conditions. Early path-breaking work was understandably limited in establishing and especially explaining observed inequalities, often termed 'environmental racism', but in the past decade enormous strides have been made both theoretically and methodologically. Longitudinal studies have demonstrated that in some instances and eras the disproportionate exposure of racial/ethnic minorities and lower socioeconomic strata to environmental hazards may stem from complex processes in job and housing markets and general processes of segregation rather than direct targeting via siting decisions (Szasz and Meuser, 2000). The methodological rigor of these studies, including use of improved measures of proximity to environmental hazards (Mohai and Shaha, 2006), sometimes created with geographic information system (GIS) techniques (Downey, 2005), is improving rapidly. While debates over the impact of intentional siting and the relative roles of race and socioenomic status will continue, and eventually be arbitrated empirically, the existing body of evidence makes a compelling case that differential exposure to environmental conditions is a central component of overall inequality.

The combination of WST research on ecologically unequal exchange and research on environmental inequality demonstrates that in order to understand patterns of national and international inequality it is increasingly necessary to recognize that 'exploitation of the environment and exploitation of human populations are linked' (Brulle and Pellow, 2006: 36). Although such insights were offered in the early days of environmental sociology (Schnaiberg, 1980), few sociologists would deny them nowadays – a powerful illustration of how environmental sociology has helped the larger discipline overcome its historical blindness to environmental factors (Catton and Dunlap, 1978).

This quick sampling of realist-based studies that make pragmatic use of a range of indicators of environmental conditions, and whose results are often complemented by a wide range of in-depth qualitative case studies (Goldman, 2005; Pellow, 2007), reflects a more encompassing approach to environmental sociology than that of the agnostics. Both camps provide strong and often exemplary scholarly analyses, and any realist can value the insights offered by agnostics into the complexities of environmental science and the paradoxes created by environmentalists' reliance on it (Shackley and Wynne, 1996; Lash et al., 1996; Yearley, 2005, 2008). However, by delving deeply into the stratum of ecosystem services and disruptions and employing indicators (ranging from sophisticated measurements to lay perceptions) of these phenomena, I believe environmental pragmatists practice a more comprehensive version of environmental sociology. They should of course view 'environmental indicators' (along with measures of social, economic and political phenomena also used in their analyses) with a critical eye, interrogating concepts such as ecosystem services (Hodgson et al., 2007) and exposing flawed measures of 'environmental sustainability' rather than using them (York, 2009). But at its best, the pragmatists' approach seems to offer much promise for interdisciplinary collaboration and sometimes yields results of considerable policy relevance (Roberts and Parks, 2007).

Contextual factors in the evolution of environmental sociology
Fields of study are affected by the historical contexts in which they emerge, and this is certainly true for environmental sociology. For example, Catton's and my portrayal of the 'new ecological paradigm' we hoped would replace sociology's human exemptionalist worldview was heavily influenced by the energy shortages the USA experienced in the 1970s, which seemed to confirm the 'limits to growth' thesis (Catton and Dunlap 1980), but the limited capacity of the global ecosystem to serve as waste repository illustrated by ozone thinning and global warming currently overshadows its supply depot limits (at least until the full impact of 'peak oil' hits). Likewise, the role of geographical context is reflected in the fact that the agnostic and pragmatic camps described above are disproportionately (if far from exclusively) based in Europe and the USA, respectively.

The combination of historical and geographical contexts blend together and incorporate differing academic traditions and trends to create developmental paths (Mol, 2006) that yield various distinguishable approaches to environmental sociology beyond those noted already. For example, while the dramatic growth of environmental sociology in Japan has created a diverse body of work (Hasegawa, 2004), the impact of Nobuko Iijima's pioneering research on 'environmental victims' continues to be apparent. Similarly, because environmentalists played a vital role in highlighting ecological problems (and promoting openness) in the USSR, analyses of environmentalism continue to be a major focus of Russian scholars (Yanitsky, 1999). Likewise, the combination of Brazil's rich resources and its hosting of the 1992 UN Conference on Environment and Development probably contributes to Brazilian environmental sociologists' emphasis on sustainability, environmentalism and environmental politics (Ferreira et al., 2008).

Additional contextual factors emerge when returning to the European–North American contrast, and I explore them by building on selected aspects of Mol's (2006) detailed and informative comparison of these two versions of environmental sociology. There is probably no better illustration of the combination of the contextual factors Mol examines than the rise of ecological modernization theory (EMT) in Western Europe and the largely critical reaction it has received in the USA, touched on briefly by Mol (2006: 15). EMT emerged in response to observed progress in environmental protection programs in some European nations (enabled by their unacknowledged use of less-developed nations as supply depots and waste repositories). It was heavily promoted as an alternative to the political-economy perspective prominent in North American environmental sociology (Mol and Buttel, 2002), but provoked a reaction verging on incredulity from some Americans (Schnaiberg et al., 2002; York and Rosa, 2003), in part because of contextual factors.

In the USA, environmental sociology developed in response to mounting evidence of environmental degradation and it retains an emphasis on understanding the driving forces of degradation. Further, from the Regan Administration in the 1980s (and its institutionalization of a staunch neoliberal agenda) through the second Bush Administration not only did degradation worsen, but US efforts – with only slight abatement during the Clinton years – to dismantle national environmental protection policies and obstruct international policy-making reflected an 'anti-Environmental State' engaged in ecological *demodernization* (Dunlap and Marshall, 2007). The acceleration of these trends during the recent Bush Administration, complemented by its gross misuse of science (Brown, 2007: ch. 7), has been characterized as the institutionalization of 'anti-reflexivity' (McCright and Dunlap, 2010) and led Buttel (2006: 167) to describe the USA as 'a powerful engine of environmental destruction'. In this context it is not surprising that ecological modernization has been greeted with intense skepticism by many US environmental sociologists, particularly those hesitant to endorse the neoliberal worldview on which EMT is premised.

The Obama Administration's attempt to reverse these trends, and adopt a green agenda compatible with ecological modernization, will force US scholars to reconsider their views of EMT – particularly if the new administration achieves some success in putting the USA on a more sustainable path. Nonetheless, I predict that many North Americans will remain skeptical of the viability of solving ecological problems by greening capitalism until such efforts produce discernible *ecological* rather than just policy/institutional impacts (York and Rosa, 2003), and this leads to a revisiting of the contrasting stances toward the use of scientific evidence on the two continents. Clearly Mol and Spaargaren, the leading proponents of EMT, engage in empirical research not limited to the symbolic/ideational/cultural realm. Yet their reactions to critics employing various forms of data to argue that ecological modernization does not yield reductions in measurable human impacts on the environment sometimes borders on the agnostic stance of many fellow Europeans (Mol and Spaargaren, 2004: 262), further evidence of a transcontinental divide over reliance on natural science.

One of Mol's insightful observations is his contrast between US and European stances on 'theory and empirical research' resulting from an interplay of historical factors in both the broader discipline and within environmental sociology *per se* on the two continents. He suggests that European scholars are more likely to engage with current trends in general sociological theory, allowing them to be more innovative 'with respect to theoretical and conceptual contributions', but notes this may result in being 'more fashionable and trendy' and producing 'concepts and theories that have a much shorter life cycle than in the United States' (Mol, 2006: 5, 13).

Ironically, Mol provides the perfect prologue to a discussion of EMT's proposed successor, a theory of 'environmental flows' (Spaargaren et al., 2006). Drawing heavily from the work of Castells and Urry, Mol and Spaargaren (2006) view environmental flows as a theoretically sophisticated way of conceptualizing and examining dynamic interchanges between the sociocultural and biophysical realms, particularly at the global level. Yet their critical view of 'material flows analysis' and related approaches (Fischer-Kowalski and Haberl, 2007) creates the impression that they may be privileging analyses of non-material over material flows, once again bridging the social/environment divide more at the conceptual/discursive than material/empirical level. Only time will tell whether a theory of environmental flows delivers on its promise of shedding new light on global environmental processes, or turns out to be another trendy concept with a short lifespan. Although I would not label it 'grand' theory, which might seem pejorative, Mol's and Spaargaren's continuing commitment to infuse environmental sociology with cutting-edge theoretical developments from the larger discipline contrasts with what Mol (2006: 13) correctly describes as an emphasis on 'middle-range' theory-testing in the USA.

The last decade has seen a dramatic increase in efforts to apply WST, WPT and various forms of social movements, social-psychological and race theories along with more rigorous versions of human ecological theory in environmental research (as partially highlighted above). At its best, such work embodies the positive attributes of US environmental sociology nicely described by Mol (2006), and illustrated by the following example: after Dietz and Kalof (1992) introduced a measure of international environmental treaty ratification as an indicator of 'state environmentalism', Roberts (1996) used WST to predict ratification while Frank (1999) followed with an alternative predictive model based on WPT. Most recently, Roberts et al. (2004) employed an integrative model drawing on WST, WPT and other relevant theories to offer a parsimonious and empirically strong explanation of treaty ratification among 192 nations. Such work is unlikely to impact theoretical perspectives in the larger discipline, but it is superb scholarship that has interdisciplinary appeal and considerable policy relevance.

I highlight the work on environmental treaty ratification because it leads to two points on which I disagree with Mol. The first and least significant is that this strand of work along with the explosion of cross-national studies noted earlier indicates that US environmental sociology is no longer as locally/nationally focused as Mol (2006: 14) suggests, a pattern admittedly clearer now than when he wrote. Second, and more significantly, we may be seeing a reversal of the broad contrast Mol (ibid.: 11) offered of earlier tendencies in our field: 'whereas US environmental sociologists were more worried about getting environment into sociology, European environmental sociologists were preoccupied with getting sociology into studies of the environment'. It appears that as environmental sociology has become securely established in the USA, there is a tendency among US scholars to adopt interdisciplinary perspectives and engage in multidisciplinary projects aimed at producing policy-relevant results. Conversely, it appears that at least some European scholars – perhaps in reaction to disappointments over past engagement with natural scientists and the declining payoff from deconstructing environmental science

– are turning inward, emphasizing the use of 'mainstream' theory to raise the profile of environmental sociology within the larger discipline.

Should these potential trends bear out, they will reinforce Mol's (2006: 20) conclusion that even in the face of increased international exchanges in fora such as the International Sociological Association and large regional networks that enhance the diffusion of perspectives within our field, 'national geographies will remain important in environmental sociology, preventing . . . a universal, homogenized discipline'. As Mol further notes, tendencies toward homogenization will be dampened not only by lingering if evolving European–North American contrasts, but by the contributions of scholars from other regions. Thus the accelerating global flow of perspectives combined with a changing world will insure that environmental sociology remains in a state of flux, and its maturation will likely involve increased diversity.

Conclusion
In quickly tracing major developments in the evolution of environmental sociology I have admittedly emphasized those of North American scholars, but not out of ethnocentrism. Instead, my 'bias' stems partly from greater familiarity with work in the USA, but especially from feeling that US environmental sociology has gradually fulfilled the hope Catton and I had over three decades ago when calling for greater sociological attention to environmental problems (Dunlap, 2008). In particular, our plea to overcome the disciplinary tradition of ignoring environmental and other non-social phenomena, so that an environmental sociology focused on societal–environmental interactions – and not just societal attention to environmental issues – could take root, has been answered as reflected in the empirical research (a tiny sample of available work) reviewed above.

My strong commitment to our original goal also helps explain my critical reaction to the surge of strong constructivism in the 1990s, for despite the undeniable insights it offered, I felt it involved a retreat to a more limited (if sophisticated) sociology of environmental issues and even risked a return to an exemptionalist stance (Dunlap and Catton, 1994; see also see Murphy, 2002). While this also helps account for my preference for environmental pragmatism versus agnosticism, I hope to see greater efforts to merge the strengths of the two approaches, with agnostics using their rich analytical tools to delve more deeply into the material world and pragmatists paying greater attention to the impact of constructions, values, culture and the like.

The current situation – a mix of constructivist and realist, qualitative and quantitative, micro and macro, theoretical and empirical work – strikes me as a very healthy situation, creating opportunities for scholars of all persuasions to carve out niches and offer their goods in an increasingly global marketplace of ideas, one that despite imperfections functions more fairly than many economic markets. The operation of this marketplace and the entrance of new cohorts of scholars drawn from more geographical regions, combined with inevitable surprises from the biophysical world, guarantees that our field will continue to evolve – and in ways that cannot be foreseen. A third edition of this handbook will likely include chapters on topics not yet on the horizon.

Acknowledgments
Thanks to Robert Brulle, William Freudenburg, Andrew Jorgenson and the editors for helpful comments on an earlier draft.

Notes

1. This chapter is dedicated to the memory of Brent K. Marshall, a bright young environmental sociologist whose promising career was cut short by a tragic accident.
2. To avoid confusion, note that when Rice (2007) and others use the concept of 'ecospace' they are referring to the totality of an ecosystem's ability to maintain itself and provide 'services', and not the narrower notion of 'living space' I am using.
3. Compare Jastrow et al. (1990) with the accumulating evidence reported in IPCC reports.
4. Comparing the treatment of the lay–expert relationship in Brown (2007) and Wynne (1996) provides insight into the differing orientations toward science embedded in the pragmatic and agnostic approaches.
5. I am using 'pragmatist' in the lay sense of adopting a practical approach to problems, in this case making use of available indicators of ecological conditions in order to analyze their causes and consequences, rather than 'pragmatism' as philosophical tradition. However, my usage has parallels to the more practical stands of 'Environmental Pragmatism' in environmental philososphy (Light and Katz, 1996: 5).

References

Beck, U. (1992), *Risk Society: Toward a New Modernity*, London: Sage.

Benton, T. (1994), 'Biology and social theory in the environmental debate', in M. Redclift and T. Benton (eds), *Social Theory and the Global Environment*, London and New York: Routledge, pp. 28–50.

Benton, T. (2001), 'Environmental sociology: controversy and continuity', *Sosiologisk Tidsskrift*, 9: 5–48.

Brown, P. (2007), *Toxic Exposures: Contested Illnesses and the Environmental Health Movement*, New York: Columbia University Press.

Brulle, R.J. and D.N. Pellow (2006), 'Environmental justice: human health and environmental inequalities', *Annual Review of Public Health*, 27: 103–24.

Burningham, K. and G. Cooper (1998), 'Being constructive: social constructionism and the environment', *Sociology*, 33: 297–316.

Buttel, F.H. (1987), 'New directions in environmental sociology', *Annual Review of Sociology*, 13: 465–88.

Buttel, F.H. (2006), 'Globalization, environmental reform, and U.S. hegemony', in G. Spaargaren, A.P.J. Mol and F.H. Buttel (eds), *Governing Environmental Flows: Global Challenges to Social Theory*, Cambridge, MA: MIT Press, pp. 157–84.

Carolan, M.S. (2005), 'Society, biology, and ecology: bringing nature back into sociology's disciplinary narrative through critical realism', *Organization & Environment*, 18: 393–421.

Catton, W.R. Jr and R.E. Dunlap (1978), 'Environmental sociology: a new paradigm', *The American Sociologist*, 13: 41–49.

Catton, W.R. Jr and R.E. Dunlap (1980), 'A new ecological paradigm for post-exuberant sociology', *American Behavioral Scientist*, 25: 15–47.

Ciccantell, P.S., D.A. Smith and G. Seidman (eds) (2005), *Nature, Raw Materials, and Political Economy*, Greenwich, CT: JAI Press.

deGroot, R.S., M.A. Wilson and R.M.J. Boumans (2002), 'A typology for the classification, description and valuation of ecosystem functions, goods and services', *Ecological Economics*, 41: 393–408.

Dickens, P. (1992), *Society and Nature: Towards a Green Social Theory*, Philadelphia, PA: Temple University Press.

Dickens, P. (1996), *Reconstructing Nature: Alienation, Emancipation and the Division of Labour*, London: Routledge.

Dietz, T. and L. Kalof (1992), 'Environmentalism among nation-states', *Social Indicators Research*, 26: 353–66.

Dietz, T., E.A. Rosa and R. York (2007), 'Driving the human ecological footprint', *Frontiers in Ecology and the Environment*, 5 (1): 13–18.

Downey, L. (2005), 'The unintended significance of race: environmental racial inequality in Detroit, *Social Forces*, 83: 971–1008.

Dunlap, R.E. (2008), 'Promoting a paradigm change: reflections on early contributions to environmental sociology', *Organization & Environment*, 21: 478–87.

Dunlap, R.E. and W.R. Catton Jr (1979a), 'Environmental sociology', *Annual Review of Sociology*, 5: 243–73.

Dunlap, R.E. and W.R. Catton Jr (1979b), 'Environmental sociology: a framework for analysis', in T. O'Riordan and R.C. d'Arge (eds), *Progress in Resource Management and Environmental Planning*, Vol. 1, Chichester, England: John Wiley & Sons, pp. 57–85.

Dunlap, R.E. and W.R. Catton Jr (1983), 'What environmental sociologists have in common (whether concerned with "built" or "natural" environments)', *Sociological Inquiry*, 53: 113–35.

Dunlap, R.E. and W.R. Catton Jr (1994), 'Struggling with human exemptionalism: the rise, decline and revitalization of environmental sociology', *The American Sociologist*, 25: 5–30.

Dunlap, R.E. and W.R. Catton Jr (2002), 'Which functions of the environment do we study? A comparison of environmental and natural resource sociology', *Society and Natural Resources*, **14**: 239–49.

Dunlap, R.E. and B.K. Marshall (2007), 'Environmental sociology', in C.D. Bryant and D.L. Peck (eds), *21st Century Sociology: A Reference Handbook*, Vol. 2, Thousand Oaks, CA: Sage, pp. 329–340.

Dunlap, R.E. and W. Michelson (eds) (2002), *Handbook of Environmental Sociology*, Westport, CT: Greenwood Press.

Eder, K. (1996), *The Social Construction of Nature*, London and Thousand Oaks, CA: Sage.

Ferreira, L., C. Potiara, M. Giesbrecht and R. Martins (2008), 'Environmental issues, interdisciplinarity, social theory and intellectual production in Latin America', paper presented at the International Sociological Association's World Forum, Barcelona, Spain.

Fischer-Kowalski, M. and H. Haberl (eds) (2007), *Socioecological Transitions and Global Change*, Cheltenham, UK and Northampton, MA: Edward Elgar.

Frank, D.J. (1999), 'The social basis of environmental treaty ratification, 1900–1990', *Sociological Inquiry*, **69**: 523–50.

Freudenburg, W.R. (2000), 'Social constructions and social constrictions', in G. Spaargaren, A.P.J. Mol and F.H. Buttel (eds), *Environment and Global Modernity*, London: Sage, pp. 103–19.

Freudenburg, W.R. (2005), 'Privileged access, privileged accounts: toward a structured theory of resources and discourses', *Social Forces*, **84**: 88–114.

Freudenburg, W.R., S. Frickel and R. Gramling (1995), 'Beyond the society–nature divide', *Sociological Forum*, **10**: 361–92.

Goldman, M. (2005), *Imperial Nature: The World Bank and Struggles for Justice in the Age of Globalization*, New Haven, CT: Yale University Press.

Goldman, M. and R.A. Schurman (2000), 'Closing the "great divide": new social theory on society and nature', *Annual Review of Sociology*, **26**: 563–84.

Greider, T. and L. Garkovich (1994), 'Landscapes: the social construction of nature and the environment', *Rural Sociology*, **59**: 5–21.

Guillory, J. (2002), 'The Sokal Hoax and the history of criticism', *Critical Inquiry*, **28**: 470–508.

Haberl, H., M. Wackernagel, F. Krausmann, K.-H. Erb and C. Monfreda (2004), 'Ecological footprints and human appropriation of net primary production: a comparison', *Land Use Policy*, **21**: 279–88.

Haluza-DeLay, R. and D.J. Davidson (2008), 'The environment and a globalizing sociology', *Canadian Journal of Sociology*, **33**: 631–56.

Hasegawa, K. (2004), *Constructing Civil Society in Japan: Voices of Environmental Movements*, Melbourne, Australia: Trans Pacific Press.

Hodgson, S.M., L. Maltby, A. Paetzold and D. Phillips (2007), 'Getting a measure of nature: cultures and values in an ecosystem services approach', *Interdisciplinary Science Reviews*, **32**: 249–62.

Inglis, D. and J. Bone (2006), 'Boundary maintenance, border crossing and the nature/culture divide', *European Journal of Social Theory*, **9**: 272–87.

Jastrow, R., W. Nierenberg and F. Seitz (1990), *Scientific Perspectives on the Greenhouse Problem*, Ottawa, IL: The Marshall Press/Jameson Books.

Jorgenson, A.K. (2006), 'Unequal ecological exchange and environmental degradation', *Rural Sociology*, **71**: 685–712.

Jorgenson, A. and E. Kick (eds) (2006), *Globalization and the Environment*, Leiden and Boston, MA: Brill.

Kates, R.W. cum al. (2001), 'Sustainability science', *Science*, **292** (27 April): 641–2.

Kitzes, J., M. Wackernagel, J. Loh, A. Peller, S. Goldfinger, D. Cheng and K. Tea (2008), 'Shrink and share: humanity's present and future footprint', *Philosophical Transactions of the Royal Society*, **363**: 467–75.

Kroll-Smith, S., V. Gunter and S. Laska (2000), 'Theoretical stances and environmental debates: reconciling the physical and the symbolic', *The American Sociologist*, **31**: 44–61.

Lahsen, M. (2007), 'Experiences of modernity in the greenhouse: a cultural analysis of a physicist "trio" supporting the backlash against global warming', *Global Environmental Change*, **18**: 204–19.

Lash, S., B. Szerszynski and B. Wynne (eds) (1996), *Risk, Environment & Modernity: Towards a New Ecology*, London and Thousand Oaks, CA: Sage.

Latour, B. (2004), 'Why has critique run out of steam? From matters of fact to matters of concern', *Critical Inquiry*, **30** (Winter): 225–48.

Lever-Tracy, C. (2008), 'Global warming and sociology', *Current Sociology*, **56**: 455–66.

Light, A. and E. Katz (eds) (1996), *Environmental Pragmatism*, London and New York: Routledge.

Liu, J. cum al. (2007), 'Complexity of coupled human and natural systems', *Science*, **317** (14 September): 1513–16.

Macnaghten, P. and J. Urry (1998), *Contested Natures*, London and Thousand Oaks, CA, Sage.

McCright, A.M. and R.E. Dunlap (2000), 'Challenging global warming as a social problem: an analysis of the conservative movement's counter-claims', *Social Problems*, **47**: 499–522.

McCright, A.M. and R.E. Dunlap (2003), 'Defeating Kyoto: the conservative movement's impact on U.S. climate change policy', *Social Problems*, **50**: 348–73.

McCright, A.M. and R.E. Dunlap (2010), 'Anti-reflexivity: the American conservative movement's success in undermining climate change science and policy', *Theory, Culture and Society*, **27**, forthcoming.

Millennium Ecosystem Assessment (2005), *Ecosystems and Human Well-Being: Synthesis*, Washington, DC: Island Press.

Mohai, P. and R. Shaha (2006), 'Reassessing racial and socioeconomic disparities in environmental justice research', *Demography*, **43**: 383–99.

Mol, A.P.J. (2006), 'From environmental sociologies to environmental sociology', *Organization & Environment*, **19**: 5–27.

Mol, A.P.J. and F.H. Buttel (eds) (2002), *The Environmental State Under Pressure*, Amsterdam: Elsevier.

Mol, A.P.J. and G. Spaargaren (2004), 'Ecological modernization and consumption: a reply', *Organization & Environment*, **17**, 261–165.

Mol, A.P.J. and G. Spaargaren (2006), 'Toward a sociology of environmental flows', in G. Spaargaren, A.P.J. Mol and F.H. Buttel (eds), *Governing Environmental Flows: Global Challenges to Social Theory*, Cambridge, MA: MIT Press, pp. 39–82.

Murdoch, J. (2001), 'Ecologising sociology: actor-network theory, co-construction and the problem of human exemptionalism', *Sociology*, **35**: 111–33.

Murphy, R. (1997), *Sociology and Nature: Social Action in Context*, Boulder, CO: Westview Press.

Murphy, R. (2002), 'The internalization of autonomous nature into society', *Sociological Review*, **50**: 313–33.

Oreskes, N. (2004), 'A call for a collective', *Science*, **305** (27 August): 1241–2.

Pellow, D.N. (2007), *Resisting Global Toxics: Transnational Movements for Environmental Justice*, Cambridge, MA: MIT Press.

Pellow, D.N. and R.J. Brulle (eds) (2005), *Power, Justice, and the Environment*, Cambridge, MA: MIT Press.

Rice, J. (2007), 'Ecological unequal exchange: consumption, equity, and unsustainable structural relationships within the global economy', *International Journal of Comparative Sociology*, **48**: 43–72.

Roberts, J.T. (1996), 'Predicting participation in environmental treaties: a world system analysis', *Sociological Inquiry*, **66**: 38–57.

Roberts, J.T. and B.C. Parks (2007), *A Climate of Injustice: Global Inequality, North–South Politics, and Climate Policy*, Cambridge, MA: MIT Press.

Roberts, J.T., B.C. Parks and A.A. Vasquez (2004), 'Who ratifies environmental treaties and why?', *Global Environmental Politics*, **4**: 22–64.

Rosa, E.A. and T. Dietz (1998), 'Climate change and society: speculation, construction and scientific investigation', *International Sociology*, **13**: 421–55.

Schnaiberg, A. (1980), *The Environment: From Surplus to Scarcity*, New York: Oxford University Press.

Schnaiberg, A., D.N. Pellow and A. Weinberg (2002), 'The treadmill of production and the environmental state', in A.P.J. Mol and F.H. Buttel (eds), *The Environmental State Under Pressure*, Amsterdam: Elsevier, pp. 15–32.

Shackley, S. and B. Wynne (1996), 'Representing uncertainty in global climate change and policy', *Science, Technology & Human Values*, **21**, 275–302.

Shofer, E. and A. Hironka (2005), 'The effects of world society on environmental protection outcomes', *Social Forces*, **84**, 25–45.

Spaargaren, G., A.P.J. Mol and F.H. Buttel (eds) (2000), *Environment and Global Modernity*, London: Sage.

Spaargaren, G., A.P.J. Mol and F.H. Buttel (2006) (eds), *Governing Environmental Flows: Global Challenges to Social Theory*, Cambridge, MA: MIT Press.

Szasz, A. and M. Meuser (2000), 'Unintended, inexorable: the production of environmental inequalities in Santa Clara County, California', *American Behavioral Scientist*, **43**: 602–32.

Szerszynski, B., S. Lash and B. Wynne (1996), 'Introduction: ecology, realism and the social sciences', in S. Lash, B. Szerszynski and B. Wynne (eds) (1996), *Risk, Environment & Modernity: Towards a New Ecology*, London and Thousand Oaks, CA: Sage, pp. 1–26.

Taylor, P.J. and F.H. Buttel (1992), 'How do we know we have global environmental problems?', *Geoforum*, **23**: 405–16.

Ungar, S. (1992), 'The rise and (relative) decline of global warming as a social problem', *Sociological Quarterly*, **33**: 483–501.

Woodgate, G. and M. Redclift (1998), 'From a "sociology of nature" to environmental sociology: beyond social construction', *Environmental Values*, **7**, 3–24.

Wynne, B. (1996), 'May the sheep safely graze? A reflexive view of the expert–lay knowledge divide', in S. Lash, B. Szerszynski and B. Wynne (eds) (1996), *Risk, Environment & Modernity: Towards a New Ecology*, London and Thousand Oaks, CA: Sage, pp. 44–83.

Yanitsky, O. (1999), 'The environmental movement in a hostile context', *International Sociology*, **14**: 157–72.

Yearley, S. (2005), *Cultures of Environmentalism: Empirical Studies in Environmental Sociology*, Basingstoke, UK: Palgrave Macmillan.

Yearley, S. (2007), 'Globalization and the environment' in G. Ritzer (ed), *The Blackwell Companion to Globalization*, London: Blackwell, pp. 239–53.

Yearley, S. (2008), 'Nature and the environment in science and technology studies' in E. Hackett, O. Amsterdamska, M. Lynch and J. Wajcman (eds), *The Handbook of Science and Technology Studies*, 3rd edn, Cambridge, MA: MIT Press, pp. 921–47.

York, R. (2006), 'Review of Steven Yearley, *Cultures of Environmentalism*', *Organization & Environment*, **19**: 142–4.

York, R. (2009), 'The challenges of measuring environmental sustainability', *Political Research Quarterly*, **62**: 205–8.

York, R. and E.A. Rosa (2003), 'Key challenges to ecological modernization theory', *Organization & Environment*, **16**: 273–88.

York, R., E.A. Rosa and T. Dietz (2003), 'Footprints on the earth: the environmental consequences of modernity', *American Sociological Review*, **68**: 279–300.

2 Social institutions and environmental change[1]
Frederick H. Buttel

Introduction

Many environmental sociologists think of their scholarly speciality as being the study of social institutions and environmental change. But while the analysis of social institutions and environmental change could in some sense be said to encompass the whole of environmental sociology, the purpose of this chapter will be to examine institutional aspects of environmental change in a more specific and focused way. Our emphasis here will be on some of the major issues, particularly within North American environmental sociology, concerning the role of political–economic and sociocultural institutions in shaping environmental degradation and change.

The notion of 'institution' is one of the most common sociological concepts. But the notion is so commonplace in sociology, and so much a part of ordinary language, that it is often used in a vague or imprecise way. In this chapter we understand institution to refer to specific or special clusters of norms and relationships that channel behaviour so as to meet some human physical, psychological or social need such as consumption, governance and protection, primordial bonding and human meaning, human faith, and socialization and learning. Thus we may speak of economic, political, family, religious and educational institutions – the five institutional complexes of societies that are generally regarded by sociologists as being most important.

While institutions and institutional processes are analytically distinct with respect to one another, and tend to exhibit some autonomy or specialization, institutions of a society are also interrelated (or, to be more precise, people through their role[s] within one institution relate to social actors in other institutions). Among the most important kinds of institutional interrelations studied by sociologists are those of influence or dominance – the matter of which institutions are the predominant ones that affect or shape other institutions, and the processes, conditions or factors that determine the pattern of influence or dominance. Much of the classical tradition of social theory involved elaborating notions of which of society's institutions tend to be predominant (e.g. Marx's emphasis on the determinate role of the economy or mode of production, in contrast with Durkheim's on culture, collective conscience and the normative sphere). Likewise, many of the most important debates and research programmes in environmental sociology are those that relate to establishing which social institutions are most crucial in terms of relationships to biophysical environments and environmental changes. In the nearly 40 years since environmental sociology was first established, debates and research in the field have tended to focus on the relations of three master institutions – economic, political and cultural systems – to environmental change. In this chapter I shall give primary attention to these three important institutional complexes. In so doing I shall discuss three master institutional issues relating to environmental change: what are the environmental implications of economic institutions and economic expansion? Are there limits to growth, or do growth and development provide the capacity to solve environmental problems? What is the fundamental nature of ecological movements and environmental activism? But before proceeding to these tasks, it is necessary to explore the issue of how sociologists conceptualize the environment and environmental change.

Environmental sociology and environmental change

Environmental sociology as a subdiscipline of sociology was essentially founded in the immediate aftermath of the mobilization of the modern environmental movement. Most of the early generation of environmental sociologists, and a large share of subsequent cohorts, have been persons with strong pro-environmental commitments. Thus it is not surprising that members of this subdiscipline are pretty much united by the notion that the environment matters to *Homo sapiens* and to social life. Many environmental sociologists feel so strongly about the importance of the biophysical environment that they see the ultimate role of environmental sociology as not only the overhaul of sociology and of social theory as a whole, in the direction of greater recognition of the primacy of biophysical factors in social life, but also as playing a contributing role in aiding the cause of environmentalism (Catton and Dunlap, 1978; Dunlap and Catton, 1994; Murphy, 1994).

Given the strength of these convictions about the important status of the environment in social life, environmental change might seem to be a straightforward or unproblematic matter (e.g. that of environmental degradation or 'environmental problems'). However, many of the most important issues in the study of institutions and environment involve definite assumptions – often quite divergent and contested ones – as to how the environment and environmental change should be conceptualized. Five of the most important issues concerning the conceptualization of environments and environmental change will be briefly noted here.[2]

The first issue relates to the observation made above that many environmental sociologists feel very strongly that environmental sociology can and must strive for nothing less than revolutionizing the way that sociologists conceptualize the social world and the processes that shape societies. These sociologists grant that their mainstream sociological colleagues can (and sometimes do; e.g. Giddens, 1994) recognize the existence and the importance of environmentally related phenomena (such as ecology movements), or even do serious research on how social factors shape environmental problems. This mainstream sociological posture, however, remains consistent with the classical tradition, for example, the injunction by Durkheim to stress 'social facts' as explanatory variables and to de-emphasize psychological and biological factors. But from the earliest days of the subdiscipline many environmental sociologists have argued that rejection of the radical sociologism of the 'social facts paradigm' must be the hallmark of environmental sociology (for example, Catton and Dunlap, 1978; Dunlap and Catton, 1979). In this view, what concretely distinguishes environmental sociology from mainstream sociology is that the former recognizes that biophysical, as well as purely social, variables affect social structure and social change, while the latter does not.

While this agnostic or antagonistic posture toward the classical tradition retains many adherents to this day, it could be fairly said that the bulk of environmental sociological research draws substantially from, and very seldom argues for a rejection of, sociological schemas that give primacy to social variables (Buttel, 1987, 1996). Further, as suggested by Dickens (1992), while the injunction to incorporate biophysical variables as causal factors makes intuitive sense at a metatheoretical level, it has proven to be more difficult to bring this proposition to bear at a more straightforward theoretical and propositional level. Probably the majority of environmental sociologists today find value in examining biophysical explanatory factors, while not necessarily seeing inquiry that privileges biophysical explanatory variables as representing a more genuine or superior form of environmental sociology.

A second issue in the conceptualization of environments and environmental change concerns the matter of whether and how it is appropriate to conceptualize the biophysical environment in social–psychological, symbolic, social–constructionist or perceptual terms, as opposed to an objectivist or highly material sense of the environment as a source of resources, a set of systems that provide ecosystem services, and sites of human habitation (cf. Hannigan, 1995 and Yearley, 1996 with Dunlap and Catton, 1994). As will be stressed shortly in this section, this issue has come to the fore primarily (and perhaps unfortunately) as a result of debates relating to global climate change.

A third key issue relating to environmental change concerns the most appropriate or useful scale or unit of analysis of environmental change for theory and research. The conventional unit of social analysis is the society or nation, and much of environmental sociology (e.g. Schnaiberg and Gould, 1994) explicitly or implicitly employs society and the societal environment as the units of analysis. At the same time, it is widely recognized that ecosystems and environmental features do not coincide with political boundaries, and that the reciprocal impacts of social processes and environment occur at a variety of levels, from the local–regional to the global. These observations about units of analysis, and especially about the notion that social analysis will need to take a range of spatial units of analysis into account, are mostly uncontroversial. What has made the issue of the spatial scope of environmental change so contentious, however, have been rival views on the matter of global climate and environmental change.

Virtually all observers of the most recent stage of environmental mobilization across the world recognize that it has been anchored in research data on and scientific claims about 'global change' (the master dimension or component of which is global warming, though the notion also subsumes phenomena such as stratospheric ozone depletion, tropical deforestation, desertification, land degradation and loss of biodiversity). Many sociologists (and other environmental scientists and environmentally inclined groups and individuals) see global change, particularly global warming, as a profound and distinctive phenomenon that over the long term will have singular implications for societies across the world (e.g. Murphy 1994). Further, there are strong associated convictions that the importance of global warming requires the harnessing of environmental sociology to help build scientific, public and political/policy support for addressing the climate change issue (Dunlap and Catton, 1994).

Other environmental sociologists, however, are less willing to accord such unique importance to global warming, or to see the notion of the global environment as being a 'scientific' rather than a socially shaped construct. Some environmental sociologists, for example, contend that the significance of global warming lies as much or more in its contemporary role as an environmental movement ideology and symbol (Mol and Spaargaren, 1993) as in its long-term implications for social change. Still other sociologists suggest that seeing the essence of our most pressing environmental problems as being their global (versus regional or local) nature or incidence is somewhat arbitrary;

it is argued that privileging the 'globalness' of environmental problems could have the impact of obscuring the (largely local or regional) processes by which human beings and societies are affected by environmental changes (Taylor and Buttel, 1992; Yearley, 1996; see Redclift and Benton, 1994 for rival views on this issue).

The fourth key issue in the conceptualization of environmental change concerns the fact that the most influential theoretical perspectives in North American environmental sociology have tended to reflect a relatively singular conception of the environment. That is, 'the environment' – even if it is acknowledged to be multidimensional and a highly complex system – is nonetheless seen in some ultimate sense as having some upper bound of (long-term, sustainable) human carrying capacity, as being essentially or ultimately finite, and as having an underlying 'unity' (a particularly explicit expression of which is in Ophuls, 1977). While a particular region can exceed its carrying capacity by appropriating raw materials and ecosystem services from elsewhere (including 'deficit ghost acreage' over time; Catton, 1994), at a higher level of analysis the human community and global society cannot escape the carrying-capacity limits of the biosphere. Thus this singular conception of the environment ultimately presupposes a macro (particularly a global) level of analysis. And the notion of the singularity of the environment has been reinforced in recent years as a result of the widespread attention given to global environmental change and global warming; these phenomena carry the ultimate expression of the biophysical environment as an underlying global biospheric and atmospheric system, the degradation of which will have consequences for all peoples on the earth.

Such singular conceptions of the environment may, however, be problematic in their application to concrete empirical research. This is particularly the case when that research is sub-national in scope or focuses on ecological systems that are spatially diverse or unevenly affected by human activities.[3] To take an agricultural example, we may agree that there is validity to the notion that there are some definite global constraints or limits on the size of the human population that can be supplied with food, or on the extent to which the world's people can be supplied with diets based on animal sources of protein. Even so, empirical inquiry into the ecological constraints on, and consequences of, agriculture at a sub-national level will not find this notion of global carrying capacity to be a very comprehensive source of hypotheses about the ecology of agriculture and food. Agro-ecosystems are highly variable across space, and the global agro-food system is fundamentally a mosaic of multifold ecosystems and diverse modes of production and distribution. These singular–unitary versus plural or regionally variegated conceptions of the environment obviously both contain an element of truth. Neither warrants being exclusively privileged in theory, as is illustrated by the fact that an exclusive emphasis on one or another is often difficult to sustain in empirical research.

A final issue regarding the conceptualization of environmental change is one that has just begun to emerge. Since the founding of environmental sociology in the early 1970s, there has been an implicit consensus that its core mission was to account for processes of environmental degradation. Thus, while mainstream sociology was seen to be 'fiddling' – seeing the environment as irrelevant to understanding society while all around us serious environmental destruction was proceeding apace – environmental sociologists tended in the opposite direction. Environmental sociology's most influential theories were those that demonstrated how modern social institutions contained intrinsic dynamics toward environmental degradation. 'Environmental change' thus came to be seen as being virtually coterminous with environmental destruction. It must be recognized, however, that it is logically the case that social processes could involve (as either cause or effect) changes in the environment that are positive or neutral with respect to the 'quality' of the environment. Further, there is growing recognition, even among ecologists and environmental scientists (Botkin, 1990; Cronon, 1995), that environmental quality is highly multidimensional, and that environmental change should not be seen as a uni-linear construct of 'quality' in a straightforward biophysical sense. Thus there is now some appreciation, albeit at a relatively elementary level (e.g. Buttel, 1996), of the fact that environmental sociology must diversify its conception of the environment beyond the processes of scarcity and degradation. The ecological modernization perspective (Spaargaren and Mol, 1992; Mol and Spaargaren, 1993; Mol, 1995) has shown particular promise in being able to conceptualize processes of environmental improvement at the macrosocial, political and organizational levels.

Sociological models of environmental degradation: the materialist traditions of North American environmental sociology
Environmental sociology is in some sense a materialist critique of mainstream sociol-ogy. Environmental sociology's agenda is, in part, to demonstrate that the biophysi-cal environment matters in social life, and that ostensibly social processes such as power relations and cultural systems have an underlying material basis or substratum. Environmental sociology has thus long been anchored in a conception of the material embeddedness of social life. Not surprisingly, the earliest pioneers of the subdiscipline (e.g. scholars such as Fred Cottrell and Walter Firey, who trailblazed in the area decades before environmental sociology became a recognized subdiscipline) worked on topics such as the role of energy sources and converters in shaping social structure, and the interaction of culture and social structure in shaping conservation policies and practices. From the early 1970s to the present, the most influential components of the environmen-tal sociology literature have remained those originally contributed by Riley Dunlap and William Catton and by Allan Schnaiberg, both of which are materialist accounts of the institutional tendencies to environmental degradation and destruction in modern indus-trial capitalist societies. But despite the common commitments to materialist explana-tions of environmental degradation, their conceptions of the institutional processes that generate environmental destruction are quite distinct. Dunlap and Catton stress cultural institutions,[4] while Schnaiberg stresses the role of capitalist relations and the nature of modern state institutions.

Dunlap and Catton's environmental sociology (Catton, 1976, 1980, 1994; Catton and Dunlap, 1978; Dunlap and Catton 1994) is built around several interrelated notions: (1) environmental problems and the inability of conventional sociology to address these problems stem from worldviews (the dominant Western worldview in society at large, and the related human exemptionalist paradigm in sociology) that fail to acknowledge the biophysical bases of social structure and social life, or that see social structures and actors as being exempt from the laws of nature; (2) the dominant Western worldview has permeated the entire ensemble of societal institutions, and has led to widespread institutional norms of growth, expansion and confidence in indefinite material progress; (3) modern societies are unsustainable because they are living off what are essentially finite supplies of fossil fuels (what Catton, 1976, 1994, has called 'ghost acreage') and are using up 'ecosystem services' much faster than ecosystems can produce or replenish them; at a global level these processes are being exacerbated by rapid population growth; (4) societies are to a greater or lesser degree faced with the prospect of ecological vulnerability, if not 'crash', particularly on account of the exacerbation of global environmental problems; (5) modern environmental science has amply documented the severity of these environmental problems and is making it clear that major adjustments and adaptations will need to be undertaken if environmental crisis is to be averted; (6) recognition of the dimensions of looming environmental crisis is contributing to 'paradigm shifts' in society at large as well as in sociology (toward rejection of the dominant Western worldview and acceptance of a new ecological or environmental paradigm); and (7) environmental improvement and reform will be engendered through the spread of the new ecological paradigm among mass publics, and will be catalysed by comparable paradigm shifts among social (and natural) scientists.

Schnaiberg's (Schnaiberg, 1980; Schnaiberg and Gould, 1994; Gould et al., 1996) environmental sociology, by contrast, is centred around two key notions: that of the 'treadmill of production'; and that this treadmill tends to result in environmental degradation (through 'withdrawals' [that is, scarcity of energy and materials] and 'additions' [that is, pollution]). The treadmill of production concept has strong commonalities with the notions of fiscal crisis and the accumulation and legitimization functions of the state developed by O'Connor (1973). The treadmill of production notion holds that modern capitalism and the modern state exhibit a fundamental logic of promoting economic growth and private capital accumulation (along with a parallel imperative of devoting resources to 'legitimation'), and that the self-reproducing nature of these processes causes them to assume the character of a 'treadmill'.

According to Schnaiberg, the tendency to growth is due in part to the competitive character of capitalism, such that corporations and entrepreneurs must continually expand their operations and their profits lest they be swamped by other competitors. But there is also an analytically distinct, but complementary, growth logic within the sphere of the state. State agencies and officials prefer growth over stagnation in order to ensure tax revenues (the essential fiscal basis of the state) and to enhance the likelihood of re-election, or the continuity or span of power. In order to enhance private accumulation, the state undertakes spending aimed at subsidizing or socializing the costs of private production and accumulation (e.g. through public subsidy of R&D, transportation infrastructure, military procurement and tax incentives). The accumulation that is fostered tends to be capital-intensive, and thus leads to automation, unemployment and potentially to demands for job creation or welfare-state-type programmes on the part of those displaced or marginalized by capital-intensive accumulation. This tendency to legitimation crisis in turn dictates that progressively more subsidy to private capital accumulation be undertaken in order to provide employment and state revenues sufficient for paying the 'social expenses' associated with the dislocations of private accumulation. The fact that capital-intensive growth creates the dislocations and political demands that undergird even more state expenditure on and encouragement of capital-intensive growth is the essence of the treadmill character of modern industrial capitalism. Further, and of most importance to environmental sociology, Schnaiberg argues that the treadmill of production is directly linked to ecological crisis, since this accumulation process requires resource extraction ('withdrawals') and contributes to pollution ('additions').[5]

Growth machines and treadmills: the limits of generalization

Schnaiberg's notion of the treadmill of production stands today as a significant synthesis of what had previously been unrelated literature: (1) the work of O'Connor (1973), which integrated the concepts of the accumulation and legitimation functions of the state, the monopoly/competitive sectoral structure of the economy, and endemic state fiscal crisis as an expression of the contradictions of late capitalism; and (2) the 'limits to growth' and related neo-Malthusian literature. Schnaiberg's concept of the treadmill of production incorporated the growth–environmental degradation relationship specified by neo-Malthusianism – that there is some intrinsic growth–degradation relationship that over the long term cannot readily be obviated by technological or social-structural changes – while at the same time jettisoning neo-Malthusianism as the explanatory framework. While not relying on a formal Marxist logic, Schnaiberg's conceptualization of environmental degradation has some similarities to what neo-Marxists such as James O'Connor (1994) now refer to as the second contradiction of capital.[6]

Schnaiberg's treadmill notion has been very influential. His treadmill perspective, for example, has stimulated related work on the social antecedents and consequences of growth, with perhaps the most important instance being (urban) 'growth machine' theory (originally elaborated by Molotch, 1975; see also Logan and Molotch, 1987). Many observers now see the notions of the treadmill of production and the growth machine (or 'growth coalitions') as being essentially synonymous (e.g. Cable and Cable, 1995), and employ them interchangeably to depict powerful institutional pressures towards expansion and environmental degradation from the local to the global levels. Schnaiberg and associates and others have extended the notion of the treadmill of production up to the global level and down to the local level (for example, Schnaiberg and Gould, 1994; Gould et al., 1996; Cable and Cable, 1995). The general and flexible use of this and related concepts makes them an attractive framework.

This is not to suggest that Schnaiberg's concept of the treadmill of production is universally embraced. For example, Hannigan (1995: 22) has argued that Schnaiberg's (1980) notion of treadmill of production is based 'exclusively on the logic of the capitalist system', a contention that in these days of retreat from neo-Marxism and political economy is tantamount to being a devastating criticism. This critique, however, is somewhat off target. As implied earlier, Schnaiberg's political–economic explanatory framework is a nuanced one in that while it is anchored in propositions about the tendency to self-expansion of capital, it privileges neither the economy and class nor the state and politics. In fact, Schnaiberg's theory of the treadmill is more a theory of the role of the state than it is a theory of economic institutions *per se*. Schnaiberg draws heavily from the work of neo-Weberian political sociologists (for example, Robert Alford) and political scientists (for example, Charles Lindblom), and on related institutional economics arguments (for example, of Galbraith and Scitovsky), in developing his analysis of the role of states and state policies within the notion of the treadmill of production.

If anything, the most recent elaboration of the theory of the treadmill – in which Schnaiberg and colleagues seek to address simultaneously the processes of globalization and local environmental 'resistance' – demonstrates the political, rather than economic, underpinning of the theory. Schnaiberg in his joint work with Gould and Weinberg (Gould et al., 1996) has begun to reconsider the treadmill of production notion within the context of globalization and the transition to post-Fordism. Their argument is essentially that as the mobility of financial and industrial capital has increased and there has been increased international competition, there has emerged a 'transnational treadmill'. In this transnational treadmill, 'transnational treadmill market actors' predominate over 'national institutions of the nation-state, and its society' (Gould et al., 1996: 8). There has been an increase in the 'tilt' (that is, the pace or 'acceleration') of the treadmill. In the process, this transnational treadmill has involved an 'increase in the influence of market actors over political actors' (ibid.). But, in their view, the essence of the treadmill remains political and ideological in nature; nation-states and national labour forces have not only maintained, but have demonstrably increased, their commitment to the treadmill in order to address capital mobility and international competition and restructuring. Thus, while the self-expansion of capital is a powerful force, it is ultimately dependent on state support and social consent.

At the same time that Gould et al. (1996) have elaborated this concept of transnational treadmill, they have followed the lead of Cable and Cable (1995) in pointing out homologies between the notions of the treadmill of production and the local 'growth machine'. This equation of the treadmill of production with growth machines and coalitions, however, may well prove to be more problematic. By growth coalition, Logan and Molotch (1987) mean a coincidence of interest among spatially proximate (generally metropolitan) land-, real-estate-, commercial- and tourist-related development capitals and local state officials. This coincidence of interest is focused around the expectation that each will directly or indirectly benefit from growth in public subsidies to and private investments in infrastructure, civic capital, construction and related activities that help to attract people, employers and jobs to a local area.

There are some definite commonalities between the notion of the treadmill of production and the growth machine, especially in terms of the role that governments and worker–citizens play in providing ideological support for private sector expansion. But it should be noted that the theory of the treadmill, even in its most recent versions, has remained focused on theorizing the antecedents and socio-environmental consequences of capital-intensive manufacturing growth. The energy and materials 'withdrawals' and 'additions' attributed to capital-intensive industrial activity remain the major dimension of environmental destruction that is emphasized in treadmill theory. However, growth-machine-type growth as theorized by Logan and Molotch refers to quite different economic activities. Convention centres, professional sports franchises, housing subdivisions, freeway construction and shopping malls are the stuff of the growth machine, while activities such as these generally lie outside the purview of the treadmill.

Schnaiberg and associates have made a persuasive case that globalization reinforces national treadmills of production. They have also pointed out some provocative parallels between treadmill and growth machine theories. These concepts are likely to remain central to environmental sociology in North America. At the same time, theory and research that can identify the degree to which the notion of the growth machine is a comprehensive concept that can be employed at a variety of levels of analysis, or whether its usage is best confined to the nation-state level, is an important frontier of work in the field.

Limits to growth and dematerialization
Several intellectual traditions that have converged on the notion that there is an enduring contradiction between economic growth and the environment. While this notion did

not arise directly from the thought of Malthus, it has been one of the core premises of much twentieth-century neo-Malthusian scholarship. Before Earth Day 1970 there had been published a number of neo-Malthusian and related versions of the notion that there are ecological limits to growth (e.g. the works of Paul Ehrlich and Garrett Hardin). The Meadows et al. (1972) book, *The Limits to Growth*, which in a sense formalized the arguments of Ehrlich, Hardin and others through a global modelling exercise, had a particularly fundamental impact on the content of environmental sociology. The arguments and conclusions of *The Limits to Growth* – that exponential growth would lead to ecological collapse, even if technological solutions to resource scarcity and pollution control were assumed to be forthcoming at unprecedented rates – arguably became a widely shared domain assumption within environmental sociology. The course subsequently taken by environmental sociology was in many respects forged in dialogue or reaction to the notion of limits to growth. The work of Catton and Dunlap, for example, can be thought of as a sociologically sophisticated elaboration of *Limits'* basic thesis. Schnaiberg's work can be seen as putting some of the core ideas of *Limits* on a sounder sociological footing, primarily by excising *Limits'* neo-Malthusian underpinning. In the 1990s, major new statements in the field of environmental sociology (e.g. Murphy, 1994) continue to be rooted in this logic.

The continuing importance of issues relating to growth and environment has been due, in part, to the emergence of fresh theoretical and empirical debates on the implications of economic institutions for environmental quality. The most significant of these debates revolve around whether there is an ongoing trend towards, or clear potential for, developing meaningful solutions to environmental problems within the context of advanced capitalist development, or whether economic growth is actually good for the environment. There has been a vigorous programme of research on 'industrial ecology' (Socolow et al. 1994), 'industrial metabolism' (Ayres, 1989) and 'dematerialization' (Tibbs 1992) in which the case is made that ongoing technological changes and business practices are making it possible for manufactured goods to be produced with substantially fewer raw material, mineral and energy inputs than was the case decades earlier. Some observers have begun to generalize these results by arguing that there exists a tendency towards inverted-U-shaped (or 'Kuznets') curves for the relationships between per capita income and environmental attributes among world nations (see Arrow et al., 1995, for a discussion and critique). More sociologically, it has been found that the world system position bears an inverted-U relationship with CO_2 inefficiency (amount of CO_2 released per unit of economic output) among world nations, with semi-peripheral countries having the highest inefficiency scores (Grimes et al., 1993).

Related studies suggest that while there is no intrinsic tendency for technological change and economic growth to lead to environmental conservation, technological change under stringent environmental regulatory constraints will tend to lead to environmental improvement. As Mol (1995) has stressed, the stringent environmental regulations that tend to predominate in the countries registering progress in industrial ecology are ultimately due to the socioeconomic conditions (state regulatory capacity, social surpluses that can be captured by states to invest in regulation and private sector capacity for rapid technological innovation) that prevail in the richest industrial democracies (Mol, 1995). The concept of 'sustainable development', which rose to prominence during the late 1980s, is based on the notion that increased material well-being can have environmental benefits in the low-income as well as high-income countries. A related literature in the advanced countries has demonstrated that environmental regulation tends to have positive effects on growth and employment (see the summary in Repetto, 1995). Thus the 1980s and 1990s have increasingly witnessed the proliferation of theory and research about how and why contemporary economic growth can be environmentally friendly, and about how and why environmental regulation can be 'growth-friendly'.[7]

Does this emerging intellectual tradition serve to undermine the more standard environmental sociological view that there is some intrinsic contradiction between growth and environment? It is important in this regard to note that the evidence in support of environmental Kuznets curves is partial, and that there is some strong contrary evidence to sustain the more traditional notion of a growth–environment contradiction. It has been found, for example, that the evidence for environmental Kuznets curves exists mainly with respect to emissions of pollutants (e.g. particularly ones of predominantly local relevance such as sulphur and particulates, and also CO_2), but not for resource stocks (for example, soil, forests) or global ecosystem resilience (Arrow et al., 1995). Bunker's (1996) research on global trends in raw materials consumption has shown that aggregate materials consumption has tended to be a function of the growth of world income, and that in terms of aggregate consumption levels the dematerialization thesis is misleading. Thus the relationships between growth, income and environmental parameters should be regarded as quite complex and not well captured by notions such as limits to growth or environmental Kuznets curves.

Social institutions and environmentalism
Environmentalism has become one of the most widely researched modern social movements. Until recently, however, this was the case not because sociologists specializing in social movements and collective behaviour found the environmental movement a particularly important or interesting movement to explore. The bulk of research on the environment movement during the 1970s and through to the mid-1980s was done by environmental sociologists, rather than by social movements specialists. These early years of research on the 'modern' (post-1968) environmental movement were dominated by survey research on public environmental attitudes, mostly conducted with little guidance from social theory. Also, this literature tended to have a partisan flavour, with much of the research being done by academics and non-academics who had strong commitments in favour of – and occasionally against – it.

Over the past 10 to 15 years, however, environmental movement researchers have been drawn more from outside environmental sociology, and their research has aimed at a higher level of generality. In particular, most general theories in environmental sociology (e.g. Catton and Dunlap, 1978; Dunlap and Catton, 1979; Schnaiberg and Gould, 1994; Gould et al., 1996; Murphy, 1994) now place considerable emphasis on theorizing environmentalism. As noted earlier, the major general theories of environment and society have tended to take the form of theorizing how it is that there are pervasive, if not inexorable, tendencies for capitalist industrial development and modernization to lead to environmental degradation. Environmentalism and the environmental movement tend to be incorporated into these theories as the predominant social response to degradation, and as one of the principal mechanisms by which societies can escape the contradictions of growth and environmental destruction.

More recently, the analysis of environmentalism and ecological movements has been very strongly influenced by two interrelated trends in the sociological discipline. First, there has been a general tendency over the past decade or so for neo-Marxism and related materialist perspectives to decline in persuasiveness, and for various cultural, subjectivist or hermeneutic sociologies to be in ascendance. Second, many influential figures in the new cultural sociological ascendance (e.g. Beck, 1992; Giddens, 1994; see the reviews in Goldblatt, 1996, Hannigan, 1995; Martell, 1994) have come to see that environmentalism is, at least in an incipient way, one of the defining social forces in late twentieth-century societies. In particular, 'ecology' is now commonly regarded as the prototypical 'new social movement' (see the summary of this tradition in Scott, 1990). New social movements (NSM) theories have posited that ecology and related movements (feminism, peace) involve, embody or reflect new structural patterns in modern (or 'postmodern' or 'post-Fordist') societies. New social movements have become new vehicles of expression and self-identification on one hand, and/or are filling the political vacuum caused by the decline of traditional foci of political activism and interest aggregation (especially political parties and corporatist arrangements) on the other. Thus, while there are differences between materialist–environmental sociological and cultural sociological views of the environmental movement, they converge on the notion that the movement is becoming one of the principal axes of the cultural politics and institutions of advanced societies (e.g. Lash et al., 1996).[8]

Given the general agreement that environmentalism is an ascendant social force, the bulk of work in the field has been directly or indirectly aimed at understanding what are the factors in society and its environment that have contributed to this outcome. Three basic perspectives from the environmental sociology and related literature have been advanced. One influential tradition is that pioneered by Riley Dunlap and colleagues (e.g. Dunlap and Van Liere, 1984). They argue that as industrial society developed over the past several centuries, this was historically propelled and accompanied by a set of beliefs and institutional patterns that can be referred to as a 'dominant Western worldview' or 'dominant social paradigm' (DSP). The DSP denotes the belief that human progress should be seen primarily in material (production and consumption) terms, which in turn legitimates human domination of nature. The DSP has accompanied the long-term development of industrial society across a variety of societal types (ranging from capitalism to twentieth-century state socialism) and across a wide range of institutions within societies (e.g. the polity and popular culture as well as the economy). But while the social institutions of growth have led to material abundance, they have also created environmental destruction. Environmental problems and the growth of environmental knowledge are seen to be engendering a growing questioning or rejection of the DSP among many social groups. The DSP is now seen by many citizens of the advanced societies, and increasingly in the developing nations as well, to be environmentally insensitive, if not environmentally irresponsible. The result is that there is being nurtured a 'new ecological paradigm' – an ethic that involves more and more social groups rejecting DSP assumptions and seeing themselves more as a part of nature. Thus environmentalism is ultimately a social response to the biophysical realities of and scientific knowledge about environmental destruction.

Ronald Inglehart (1977) has pioneered a somewhat related view. Using neo-Maslowian reasoning, Inglehart has argued that as industrial societies have developed, and as absolute scarcity has been conquered and most basic material needs have been met, public concerns tend to rise up a definite hierarchy of 'needs' to a point where there is an articulation of 'post-material' values. Respect for nature and interest in the quality of life rather than in the quantity of material goods are seen as the prototypical post-material values. These values, in turn, predispose citizens to support movements such as ecology.

A third general orientation towards environmental mobilization locates the growing force of ecology within the transition from the institutions of mid-century Fordism to the post-Fordist or postmodernist institutions of the late twentieth century (see the overviews in Scott, 1990; Martell, 1994). The institutional disarray associated with the disintegration of Fordism has undermined traditional reservoirs of social meaning, and weakened associational and political party vehicles of interest aggregation. These social vacuums have increasingly been filled by movements such as ecology. For many citizens these movements are more satisfactory vehicles for allowing people to articulate post-industrial concerns (particularly concern about risks to health and about environmental integrity) than traditional political institutions.

Each of these master theories of environmentalism has strengths and weaknesses. Their strengths derive from the fact that they have identified important overarching features of institutional and environmental change that are related to organized environmentalism. Their weaknesses are generally due to the fact that in the quest for overarching explanations, they focus on particular forms or processes of environmentalism and downplay others. A comprehensive theory of environmentalism must be able to deal with a number of pivotal characteristics of ecology movements. First, the discontinuous surges and declines of the movement since the late 1960s suggest that biophysical (or scientific knowledge) factors do not play a predominant role in shaping movement mobilization. Second, the relatively widespread expressions of Third World environmentalism in recent years cast doubt on the notion that environmentalism is primarily a phenomenon among rich countries and affluent social classes (Martínez-Alier, 1995). Third, a comprehensive theory of environmentalism must also be able to explain anti-environmentalism, and account for the fact that in this neoliberal era anti-environmentalism at times rivals environmentalism as a political force. Fourth, there is a need to theorize the enormous internal diversity of the movement; expressions of organized environmentalism exhibit tremendous diversity in their class alignments, claims, goals and political ideologies, and the coexistence of these groups is often far more precarious than is recognized in academic treatments of them (Gottlieb, 1994). Acknowledging the internal diversity of the movement will cause environmental sociologists to recognize that there is no underlying coherence to the movement (or that it is more appropriate to see it as a series of movements rather than as a single movement).

Fifth, there is a need to recognize that environmentalism is in large part a social product. For example, many contemporary expressions of environmentalism (e.g. indigenous resistance to rainforest destruction in the developing world, environmental justice mobilization) would not have been seen as environmental activism three decades ago. Sixth, there is a need to distinguish between public support for the movement (which tends to be broad, but shallow and somewhat transitory), and movement participation (which is much less prevalent but more stable, and which tends to be drawn from well-educated and/or politically efficacious strata of civil society).

Concluding remarks

Almost from the start of environmental sociology the major axes of theoretical debate have revolved around its 'double specification' – that environmental sociology draws from material–ecological postures about human beings as a biological species in an eco-system on one hand, and from the classical–theoretical emphasis on the distinctly social and symbolic capacities of human beings and the social character of their institutions on the other. The major issues in the field have continued to revolve around the relative emphases that scholars place on the biological/ecological versus distinctly social nature of human societies. I have attempted to suggest, however, that rather than these two views being irreconcilably contradictory, there are some important opportunities for cross-fertilization. The issues identified in this chapter – the environmental implications of political and economic institutions, whether growth is primarily an antecedent or solution to environmental problems, and the origins and significance of environmental-ism – are not only important in their own right, but are among the major areas in which environmental sociology is working towards syntheses of the biophysical and social dimensions of environmental change (Freudenburg et al., 1995).

Notes

1. This chapter is reprinted from the first edition of this handbook: Michael Redclift and Graham Woodgate (eds), *The Handbook of Environmental Sociology*, Cheltenham, UK and Northampton, MA: Edward Elgar.
2. Some of these issues (e.g., whether environmental sociology should focus only on resource and habitat factors, or consider the urban or 'built' environment to be a proper focus of study) will not be examined in this chapter. See Mehta and Quellet (1995) and Cronon (1995).
3. Singular versus plural/variegated conceptions of the environment are, of course, not necessarily mutually exclusive. Note that singular and plural/variegated conceptions of the environment may both be represented in a single piece of research. A good example is that of integrated assessment models that have become the dominant focus of 'human dimensions' of global change research. At one level, the structure of these models is driven by regional contributions to greenhouse gas emissions, yielding both a global mean temperature response as well as disparate regional impacts and implications such as land-use and land-cover changes. Even so, we can say that the basic conception of the environment underlying integrated assessment modelling is a singular one – of the atmosphere and biosphere being a global system, perturbations of which will have a variety of implications for human communities and societies.
4. The fact that Dunlap and Catton stress cultural institutions while their analysis can be regarded as materialist may seem contradictory. Rather, this indicates the fact that my usage of the notion of materialism – actually, I prefer the term 'materiality' (Buttel, 1996) – is a broad one, transcending some of the more specific materialisms such as historical materialism and cultural materialism. The Dunlap and Catton style of reasoning is materialist, or involves materiality, in that the essence of their argument is that flows of energy and materials are the among the most critical parameters underlying social structure and social life.
5. Note, however, that Schnaiberg does recognize that environmental degradation will tend to engender environmental resistance and social movements. His notion of 'societal–environmental dialectic', though it has seemingly been discarded in his more recent work, acknowledges that political resistance to environmental degradation may shift the nature of the treadmill to a 'managed scarcity' synthesis in which the most pernicious aspects of degradation are socially regulated and accumulation is restricted but not eliminated (Schnaiberg, 1975).
6. The first contradiction of capital is that of capital–labour antagonism and class struggle.
7. Even so, it important to note that the notion of limits to growth has had virtually no political or policy currency (except the local politics of 'growth control'; Logan and Molotch, 1987). In the post-1973 milieu of economic stagnation, rising unemployment and declining real wages, the idea of actively constraining growth to achieve environmental goals has not been taken seriously within any nation-state, nor has this notion been actively advocated by any mainstream environmental group.
8. It is noteworthy in this regard that resource mobilization theory has tended not to be one of the most influential theories of the nature of the environmental movement. In part, this is because resource mobilization theory tends to place little emphasis on the content of movements, and instead is interested in matters such

as social-movement entrepreneurship, resource acquisition, the structure of movement organizations, and the relationships between movements and political opportunity structures. By contrast, most observers of environmentalism tend to be interested more in the content of the movement than in its structure. While resource mobilization theory is often overly preoccupied with how mobilization is made possible through 'resource' acquisition, observers of environmentalism often regard mobilization as unproblematic, that is, as being an understandable or logical result of environmental degradation or societal value shifts. While resource mobilization theory has limitations as a comprehensive explanation, a case could be made that theories of environmentalism often exaggerate the rationality of movement mobilization, a useful corrective to which would be cautious use of the resource mobilization perspective.

References

Arrow, K., B. Bolin, R. Costanza, P. Dasgupta, C. Folke, C.W. Holling, B.O. Jansson, S. Levin, K.G. Maler, C. Perrings and D. Pimentel (1995), 'Economic growth, carrying capacity, and the environment', *Science*, **268**: 520–21.

Ayres, R.U. (1989), 'Industrial metabolism', in J. Ausubel (ed.), *Technology and Environment*, Washington, DC: National Academy Press, pp. 23–49.

Beck, U. (1992), *Risk Society*, Beverly Hills, CA: Sage.

Botkin, D. (1990), *Discordant Harmonies*, New York: Oxford University Press.

Bunker, S.G. (1996), 'Raw material and the global economy: oversights and distortions in industrial ecology', *Society and Natural Resources*, **9**: 419–29.

Buttel, F.H. (1987), 'New directions in environmental sociology', *Annual Review of Sociology*, **13**: 465–88.

Buttel, F.H. (1996), 'Environmental and natural resource sociology: theoretical issues and opportunities for synthesis', *Rural Sociology*, **61**: 56–76.

Cable, S. and C. Cable (1995), *Environmental Problems, Grassroots Solutions*, New York: St Martin's Press.

Catton, W.R. Jr (1976), 'Why the future isn't what it used to be (and how it could be made worse than it has to be)', *Social Science Quarterly*, **57**: 276–91.

Catton, W. R. Jr (1980), *Overshoot: The Ecological Basis of Revolutionary Change*. Urbana, IL: University of Illinois Press.

Catton, W.R. Jr (1994), 'Foundations of human ecology', *Sociological Perspectives*, **37**: 74–95.

Catton, W.R. Jr, and R.E. Dunlap (1978), 'Environmental sociology: a new paradigm', *The American Sociologist*, **13**: 41–9.

Cronon, W. (ed). (1995), *Uncommon Ground*, New York: Norton.

Dickens, P. (1992), *Society and Nature*, Philadelphia, PA: Temple University Press.

Dunlap, R.E. and W.R. Catton Jr (1979), 'Environmental sociology', *Annual Review of Sociology*, **5**: 243–73.

Dunlap, R.E. and W.R. Catton Jr (1994), 'Struggling with human exemptionalism: the rise, decline, and revitalization of environmental sociology', *The American Sociologist*, **25**: 5–30.

Dunlap, R.E. and K.D. Van Liere (1984), 'Commitment to the dominant social paradigm and concern for environmental quality', *Social Science Quarterly*, **65**, 1013–28.

Freudenburg, W.R., S. Frickel and R. Gramling (1995), 'Beyond the nature/society divide: learning to think about a mountain', *Sociological Forum*, **10**: 361–92.

Giddens, A. (1994), *Beyond Left and Right*, Stanford, CA: Stanford University Press.

Goldblatt, D. (1996), *Social Theory and the Environment*, Oxford: Polity Press.

Gottlieb, R. (1994), *Forcing the Spring*, Washington, DC: Island Press.

Gould, K.A., A. Schnaiberg and A.S. Weinberg (1996), *Local Environmental Struggles*, New York: Cambridge University Press.

Grimes, P., J.T. Roberts, and J.L. Manale (1993), 'Social roots of environmental damage: a world-systems analysis of global warming and deforestation', paper presented at the annual meeting of the American Sociological Association, Miami Beach, August.

Hannigan, J.A. (1995), *Environmental Sociology: A Social Constructionist Perspective*, London: Routledge.

Inglehart, R. (1977), *The Silent Revolution*, Princeton, NJ: Princeton University Press.

Lash, S., B. Szerszynski and B. Wynne (eds) (1996), *Risk, Environment, and Modernity*, London: Sage.

Logan, J.R. and H.L. Molotch (1987), *Urban Fortunes*, Berkeley, CA: University of California Press.

Martell, L. (1994), *Ecology and Society*, Amherst, MA: University of Massachusetts Press.

Martínez-Alier, J. (1995), 'Commentary: the environment as a luxury good or "too poor to be green"', *Ecological Economics*, **13**: 1–10.

Meadows, D.H., D.L. Meadows, J. Randers and W.W. Behrens III (1972), *The Limits to Growth*, New York: Universe Books.

Mehta, M.D. and E. Ouellet (eds) (1995), *Environmental Sociology*, North York, Ontario: Captus Press.

Mol, A.P.J. (1995), *The Refinement of Production: Ecological Modernization Theory and the Chemical Industry*, Utrecht: Van Arkel.

Mol, A.P.J. and G. Spaargaren (1993), 'Environment, modernity, and the risk society: the apocalyptic horizon of environmental reform', *International Sociology*, **8**: 431–59.

Molotch, H. (1975), 'The city as a growth machine', *American Journal of Sociology*, **82**: 309–30.

Murphy, R. (1994), *Rationality and Nature*, Boulder, CO: Westview Press.

O'Connor, J. (1973), *The Fiscal Crisis of the State*, New York: St. Martin's Press.

O'Connor, J. (1994), 'Is sustainable capitalism possible?', in M. O'Connor (ed.), *Is Capitalism Sustainable?* New York: Guilford, pp. 152–75.

Ophuls, W. (1977), *Ecology and the Politics of Scarcity*, San Francisco, CA: W.H. Freeman.

Redclift, M. and T. Benton (eds) (1994), *Social Theory and the Global Environment*, London: Routledge.

Repetto, R. (1995), *Jobs, Competitiveness, and Environmental Regulation*, Washington, DC: World Resources Institute.

Schnaiberg, A. (1975), 'Social syntheses of the societal–environmental dialectic: the role of distributional impacts', *Social Science Quarterly*, **56**: 5–20.

Schnaiberg, A. (1980), *The Environment*, New York: Oxford University Press.

Schnaiberg, A. and K.A. Gould (1994), *Environment and Society*, New York: St Martin's Press.

Scott, A. (1990), *Ideology and the New Social Movements*, London: Unwin Hyman.

Socolow, R., C. Andrews, F. Berkhout and V. Thomas (eds) (1994), *Industrial Ecology and Global Change*, New York: Cambridge University Press.

Spaargaren, G. and P.J. Mol (1992), 'Sociology, environment, and modernity: ecological modernization as a theory of social change', *Society and Natural Resources*, **5**: 323–44.

Taylor, P.J., and F.H. Buttel (1992), 'How do we know we have global environmental problems?', *GeoForum*, **23**: 405–16.

Tibbs, H.B.C. (1992), 'Industrial ecology: an environmental agenda for industry', *Whole Earth Review*, **4**: 4–19.

Yearley, S. (1996), *Sociology, Environmentalism, Globalization*, London: Sage.

3 From environmental sociology to global ecosociology: the Dunlap–Buttel debates
Jean-Guy Vaillancourt

Introduction

Today, many European and North American environmental sociologists recognize the central role played by Fred Buttel, who died in January 2005, and by Riley Dunlap in the emergence of environmental sociology (Redclift and Woodgate, 1997; Yearly, 1991; Murphy, 1994; Hannigan, 1995). The ideas of those two major pioneers of US environmental sociology follow parallel and eventually converging trajectories. In fact, they both contributed to the transition from human ecology to environmental sociology, and then to an emerging global ecosociology. Their ideas evolved in seminal publications and through lively debates over many years. This chapter is based on the extended time span covered by their respective works.

Human ecology and social ecology: the HEP–NEP debate revisited

At first, like the Chicago human ecologists who inspired him, Dunlap (with William Catton) tried to show that modern societies depend on their natural environments. They were among the first sociologists to write that sociology overestimates the independence of human beings from their material environment. For them, mainstream sociology did not put enough emphasis on environmental factors, even though the earlier neo-Malthusian debate concerning the scarcity of resources showed that the natural environment influences social life.

Dunlap explained why sociologists had lacked interest in the impact of biophysical factors on society. Sociology emerged when the dominant sociological paradigms upheld unrealistic ideas concerning the power of human beings over nature (Dunlap and Van Liere, 1978: 1–2; 1984). According to Dunlap, this anthropocentric perspective is assumed by most social researchers, as when anthropologists and sociologists say that culture is gradually replacing nature. In opposition to biologists, geographers and some psychologists, who do not neglect the importance of the biophysical milieu for human beings, sociologists focus on the influence of social factors in order to legitimate the existence of their discipline (Dunlap and Catton, 1979a, 1979b).

With Catton, Dunlap presented the four postulates that undergird the old paradigm they first called the 'human exceptionalism paradigm' and then the 'human exemptionalism paradigm' (HEP) (Catton and Dunlap, 1978a; 1980): (1) human beings are unique among earthly creatures because they generate culture; (2) culture varies almost infinitely in time and space, and evolves more rapidly than biological traits; (3) thus many human differences are socially induced rather than genetically inherited; they are socially altered, and inconvenient differences can thus be eliminated; (4) consequently, cultural accumulation means that progress can continue without limit, making all social problems ultimately resolvable.

In opposition to this paradigm, which overestimates the power of human beings, they proposed a 'new environmental paradigm', subsequently called the 'new ecological paradigm' (NEP). It is more realistic, because it puts forward different postulates that take natural limits into account (Catton and Dunlap, 1978a, 1980): (1) human beings are only one species among the many that are interdependently involved in the biotic communities that shape social life; (2) intricate linkages of cause, effect and feedback in the web of nature produce many unintended consequences that are different from purposive human action; (3) the world is finite, so there are potent physical and biological limits constraining economic growth, social progress and other societal phenomena.

Their analysis highlights the impact of ecological constraints on human societies. From the outset, they were interested in analyzing the causes of environmental problems via Duncan's POET[1] or 'ecological complex' model (Duncan, 1959). In his empirical research, Dunlap examined the impact of dominant American values on environmental perceptions and behaviors (Dunlap and Van Liere, 1978, 1984). The HEP–NEP cleavage emphasized the sociological relevance of 'limits' and 'scarcity' and early US environmental sociology's tendency to focus on the societal impacts of energy and other scarce resources reflected this emphasis. Dunlap and Catton argued that cleavages between HEP and NEP adherents were more fundamental for the analysis of environmental problems than cleavages between the HEP-based sociological theories (Catton and Dunlap, 1978b), whereas Buttel believed the opposite to be true.

Buttel was more influenced by the German sociological tradition and by radical political economy, rather than by the Chicago School of human ecology. Although he shared Dunlap's interest in survey research for analyzing the social sources of support for environmental protection (Buttel and Flinn, 1974, 1976), Buttel also tried to understand the social causes of environmental problems (Buttel, 1976; Buttel and Flinn, 1977). He was opposed to environmental determinism, as were promoters of the new social ecology who, since the 1930s, had reacted against the Chicago ecologists, whereas Dunlap was more attuned to the positions of the Chicago School and of the neo-orthodox human ecologists such as Hawley and Duncan. Like Dunlap and Catton, Buttel admitted that for sociology to be recognized as a distinct science, the founding fathers had to struggle against biological and geographical determinism. This resulted in a tendency to dismiss ecological variables as explanatory factors for social behavior. However, Buttel did not endorse Dunlap's idea that environmental sociology should downplay mainstream theory and that the NEP represented an entirely new paradigm (Buttel, 1986a: 363–6). For him, environmental sociology had to move beyond middle-range theory, to grapple with the larger problems of the discipline: the reciprocal relationship between nature and society, highlighting the role of the state, social class issues and the laws of social change (Humphrey and Buttel, 1982: 10). Resource dependence, especially in the areas of energy and agriculture, was of particular interest to him (Buttel, 1978b, 1987; Buttel and Humphrey, 2002; McMichael and Buttel, 1980).

In regard to the HEP–NEP debate, Buttel (1978a) did not question the validity of the principles of the NEP, but denied that sociology needed a paradigm shift to analyze environmental problems since the classical theoretical approaches do not impede us from practicing environmental sociology (1986a: 369). Besides, Buttel (1976) had shown earlier that it was possible to find environmental perspectives in both the order and conflict traditions of sociology. Buttel implied that Dunlap's NEP put too much emphasis on the environment as a causal factor, or on the 'ecosystem dependence' of modern societies, at least in the area of natural resource scarcity, even if he himself accepted the notion of ecological constraints (Buttel, 1978a: 253).

Buttel gave a real but limited importance to the environment as a causal factor, although the growing scarcity of fossil energy resources did not play a unilateral role in social change (Humphrey and Buttel, 1982: 221). According to him, biophysical constraints contribute to the intensification of economic problems, but do not determine them. In fact, he thought that biophysical limits were created in interaction with structural societal dynamics (ibid.: 233–4). Buttel's main objective was to promote a theory of social structure where the study of the social causes and consequences of resource scarcity would be enmeshed in the ongoing dynamics of social change (Buttel, 1976: 309). Buttel was not totally opposed to Dunlap's NEP, since he also analyzed the impacts of the scarcity of resources on human societies, but after concluding that this problem was exaggerated, he ceased to give it much importance. His environmental sociology evolved towards the study of the impact that human activities have on environmental change, and the way solutions to environmental problems can be conceptualized through the notion of social justice.

Buttel chastised Dunlap for trying to replace traditional sociological perspectives with the NEP. Dunlap explained recently that his objective was only to justify the incorporation of environmental variables into sociological analysis, in order not to limit disciplinary analysis to social factors as sociologists were doing in the 1970s (Dunlap, 2002a, 1997). He did not want to replace social with environmental explanatory variables, but rather to give the latter a place alongside the former (Dunlap and Martin, 1983). He did not want to replace traditional theoretical perspectives with the NEP, but rather to encourage sociologists to pay attention to the biophysical bases of human societies and to incorporate environmental variables into their analyses, either as dependent or independent variables, in order to develop 'green' versions of traditional perspectives (Dunlap, 1997, 2002a).

Dunlap is convinced that his debate with Buttel was a matter of misunderstanding rather than a real opposition with contradictory positions. Dunlap was never a hard-core environmental determinist. Also, he has mellowed over the years on the issue of ecosystem dependence. Buttel saw Dunlap as an ontological realist who put too much emphasis on the material–ecological substructure of society in relation to social structure. Buttel saw opportunities for convergence and synthesis between society and the environment, and he insisted on seeing physical and social factors as 'conjointly constituted', in the sense that environmental sociology should take into account both material–structural and psychological–intentional phenomena (Buttel, 1996: 63–6). These diverse phenomena can be causes or consequences in a causal chain. Dunlap and Buttel thus agree basically that social change is not determined completely by environmental factors. Dunlap's advocacy of the NEP is really a highlighting of the ecosystem dependence of modern societies, not a plea for ecological determinism.

Environmental sociology from the late 1970s to the mid-1980s
Dunlap was interested in studying the environmental movement (Dunlap and Mertig, 1992) and public support for environmental protection (Dunlap and Scarce, 1991). He has stressed the importance of studies of psychosocial attitudes and values (Dunlap

and Jones, 2002), as well as of biophysical factors or variables (Dunlap and Michelson, 2002). With Catton, he defined environmental sociology as the study of 'societal–environmental interactions' (Catton and Dunlap, 1978a, 1978b; Dunlap and Catton, 1979a, 1979b), and he emphasized that a 'true' environmental sociology requires the study of 'environmental variables' as opposed to a sociology of environmental issues that simply applies traditional sociological perspectives to the study of environmentalism and environmental consciousness. In fact, Dunlap (2002a, 2002b) has noted that it was the desire to legitimate the sociological study of environmental variables that led him and Catton to criticize Durkheim's anti-reductionism taboo and the exemptionalist orientation of contemporary sociology.

Over time, Dunlap became more of a functionalist and empiricist. Much of his empirical research focused on the sociopolitical correlates of environmental concern and the measurement of an ecological worldview reflecting a societal version of the NEP (Dunlap and Van Liere, 1978, 1984; Dunlap et al., 2000). With Catton he emphasized that the physical environment fulfills three functions for human beings – a dwelling place, a source of supplies for human activities, and a repository for waste products – and that analyzing competing uses provides insight into the nature of environmental problems (Dunlap and Catton, 1983; 2002). However, Dunlap is not a structural–functionalist but a proponent of an ecological perspective on societies. Early on, he and Catton suggested that a useful way of showing how modern societies relate to their environments was to use Duncan's (1959) POET model of the human ecosystem as an analytical framework for environmental sociology (Dunlap and Catton, 1979a, 1983).

Beyond the ecosystemic interdependence of human societies, there is also the important impact of human beings on natural and built environments. Dunlap (1993) eventually related the POET model to the well-known formula $I = PAT$, where the impact (I) on the environment is a function of population (P), affluence (A, meaning economic consumption) and technology (T). In developing his environmental sociology with Catton, Dunlap has consistently drawn upon human ecology to develop a framework for analyzing societal–environmental interactions. Their efforts to build an analytical framework that clarifies the relations between society and the biophysical environment represent an attempt to provide an 'ecological perspective' for environmental sociology (Dunlap and Catton, 1983) that complements their proposal that the HEP be replaced by the NEP. This perspective has been extended by their colleagues into a sophisticated quantitative model (STIRPAT[2]) used to predict human impacts on the environment (York et al., 2003).

The fact that resource scarcity has proved to be less of a problem than anticipated in the early 1970s, and his realization that the problem had been exaggerated by oil producers, led Buttel to become more critical of the influence of capitalist producers on scientists, public opinion and environmentalists, since such producers are those who profit the most from the rise in the price of oil and other natural resources. Thus he became skeptical about how some environmentalists accepted the notion of 'limits to growth' and critical of their failure to challenge capitalism (Buttel et al., 1990). What interests are these Greens defending? Are they really protecting the environment or are they defending particular economic interests? Some members of green groups are members of socioeconomic, political and cultural elites, and the intervention of the state does not strongly affect their purchasing power and standard of living. On the contrary, their interventionism can lead to an increase of the state apparatus, and give more power to elites working for the state.

Buttel affirms that the major cause of environmental problems is the expansion of production, which leads to an intensive use of resources in order to stimulate economic growth (Humphrey and Buttel, 1982: 221). He blames the institutions of capitalist (and socialist) production rather than consumers, because it is supply that stimulates demand for goods and not the other way around. Furthermore, Buttel stresses the fact that it is not only the growth process that brings about the accumulation of capital and the development of monopolies and oligopolies. The state, unfortunately, also favors high levels of growth and profits, and does everything in its power to stimulate them. This concentration of capital in the hands of powerful economic elites, which puts pressure on the state, brings about an increase of social inequalities and further endangers the environment.

Concerning the impacts of environmental problems, Buttel is particularly interested in the socioeconomic ones. He stresses structural consequences and provides a radical political–economic analysis of the change process that unfurls in a series of stages: increase in the cost of production, lowering of profits, fall in the employment rate, diminishing purchasing power of individuals, and self-protective repression and violence by the bourgeoisie. This process leads to the following final consequence: the impossibility of re-establishing an economic equilibrium (Buttel, 1976: 319).

This process will continue to its inevitable conclusion if the resource base diminishes more rapidly than its rate of renewal. Here, the notion of the 'treadmill of production' put forward by Schnaiberg (1980) seems to Buttel to be quite appropriate, especially since it takes into account the role played by the state (Humphrey and Buttel, 1982). Because of increasing environmental problems and decreasing levels of employment, the state is forced to take charge of the social problems linked to these phenomena, leading to a financial crisis of the state and finally to a taxpayers' revolt. As long as the lack of resources is not critical, and the summit of the spiral of the treadmill of production is not reached, the state will give priority to the accumulation of capital while temporarily taking care of urgent social problems in order to maintain a minimum of social peace. This corresponds to what Schnaiberg (1980) calls 'the synthesis of planned scarcity'. Once again this shows that Buttel was a neo-Marxist Weberian who stressed a structural conflict position rather than functionalism. For him, this approach best explains the constraints on social and environmental change, a theme central to his environmental sociology.

Concerning strategies for coping with environmental changes, Buttel (2003) suggests that the green movement make alliances with disadvantaged social categories to provoke needed social changes, instead of thinking only of its own interests. In combination with other social movements, it could demand more social justice, and the state would then be forced to promote another kind of growth, which would be something like a steady state economy. Buttel also agrees with the radical biologist Barry Commoner (1971) that we should use softer appropriate technologies to protect the environment and to facilitate the closing of ecological cycles.

Ecological sociology or ecosociology for global environmental problems?

Since the publication of the Brundtland Report in 1987, a new global approach has been popularized that emphasizes that environmental degradation has reached planetary proportions and that it is necessary to promote sustainable development. Dunlap stresses that environmental problems have become global, and that the emergence of societal awareness towards those problems offers an opportunity to discard the HEP, which impedes sociologists from taking them seriously (Dunlap and Catton, 1994a, 1994b).

Dunlap believes that human beings have become so dominant on the planet that they have started to disturb fundamental natural processes. Being in a better position to analyze the interactions between society and environment, sociologists should examine the ways in which human beings affect the global ecosystem, indicate what behavior patterns should be modified, and what adaptations could be made in order to attain an ecological equilibrium. But sociologists have been slow in recognizing the significance of global environmental change (GEC), because they insist too much on the idea that these changes are a social construct rather than an objective phenomenon (Dunlap and Catton, 1994b: 16–18). Dunlap is afraid that the new focus among many sociologists on deconstructing the concept of global environmental change, rather than on analyzing its reality, will reinforce the HEP and the idea that climate change is not an important danger, and that this will limit sociological contributions to the understanding of the human dimensions of GEC.

In spite of their misgivings concerning constructionism, Dunlap and Catton refuse to accentuate the cleavage between constructionists and realists, since many scholars fruitfully employ both approaches in their work. Their view is that those perspectives are not irremediably opposed and exclusive of each other, but that the relativism of early deconstructions of the Intergovernmental Panel on Climate Change (IPCC) was problematic. Dunlap has subsequently endeavored to deconstruct climate change skepticism (McCright and Dunlap, 2000, 2003) to provide a more balanced sociological approach to the climate change debate. More generally, Dunlap and Catton argue that sociologists should develop an ecological sociology that focuses on the complex interdependencies between human beings and the ecosystem. As they put it: 'The recognition of GEC, including its human origins and especially its potential impact on society, clearly challenges the human exemptionalist orientation of mainstream sociology, and suggests the need for a full blown ecological sociology' (Dunlap and Catton, 1994b: 25). They believe that this ecological sociology must recognize that human beings ultimately depend on the ecosystems they inhabit, and that it must reject the HEP, which suggests that human beings are free from natural constraints.

In the French version of his article on the evolution of the sociology of environment, Buttel (1986a; see also 1986b) uses the word 'écosociologie' to describe the current phase of this subdiscipline. Since the publication of the Brundtland Report, much has been written on sustainable development as a solution to the problems caused by GEC. Nearly everyone who touches the subject proposes scenarios for the planet's future. In subsequent writings Buttel invited sociologists to be wary of hasty conclusions, recalling the sad consequences of the false alarm concerning the energy crisis during the 1970s. Thus Buttel wrote that ecosociology must take into account the social construction of environmental problems as well as the influence exercised by the material forces of production on ecological discourse (Buttel and Taylor, 1992: 16).

Buttel's position points in the direction of an ecosociology that is more critical towards the construction of environmental problems on the part of scientists and of environmental groups (Buttel et al., 1990; Buttel and Taylor, 1992: 2). Natural and social sciences are not naïve, and they open up certain possibilities of action while closing others. This is due to the intricate meshing of their activities with politics. Consequently, Buttel is inclined to examine quite critically the building of complex models to represent environmental problems. Global modeling, anchored in the conception of a collective 'us', places people in a position of spectators rather than of full-fledged participants involved in the formulation of different futures (Taylor and Buttel, 1992: 406).

Concerning green groups, Buttel mentions that they often depend on the conclusions put forward by natural scientists to elaborate their discourses, while these scientists depend on green groups for persuading governments to invest public funds in research. Scientific uncertainty in numerous areas forces environmentalists to construct their information according to their interests, in order to raise public consciousness, and this sometimes leads them to exaggerate the seriousness of a situation. This ideological dramatization also facilitates the internationalization of environmental activism (Hawkins and Buttel, 1992: 831). Consequently, green activists, like scientists, tend to socially construct reality and often give an impression that global environmental changes are real, even if this cannot be proven conclusively.

Just as he perceives that there are uncertainties concerning global environmental changes, Buttel discusses another concept charged with contradictions, namely sustainable development. He sees this concept as a symbol, an ideology, or even a 'buzzword' that occupies an area of conflict between various development groups. The groups critical of capitalist development want sustainability to become an ecological, social and ethical imperative of development, unlike the dominant capitalist-oriented institutions involved in this type of development that try to appropriate for themselves the concept of sustainability to legitimate their market policies or their pseudo-green marketing (Hawkins and Buttel, 1992: 833). However, the conflict concerning sustainable development cannot be resolved without one group ending up victorious over the others. Paradoxically, the discourse on global environmental change proposes certain modes of resolution of these problems that legitimize both of these positions, and this again indicates the fragility of ecological arguments (Buttel and Taylor, 1992: 16).

With his constructionism, then, Buttel comes close to questioning the reality of environmental problems. He is reluctant to admit that all global problems are really global, inasmuch as their purported causes, consequences and solutions can often be identified as social constructions. However, he admits that this is much less the case for global warming (Buttel and Taylor, 1992: 8). Thus, for Buttel, raising environmental problems to the global level is more a process of social construction of reality and of the production of political knowledge than a reflection on biophysical reality. This does not mean that the problems are not real, but only that their reality is often situated at local and national levels rather than at the global level (Buttel et al., 1990). Buttel is worried that economic elites will use a globalizing discourse to facilitate acceptance of the globalization of markets, an outcome that risks accentuating the gap between rich and poor countries (Hawkins and Buttel, 1992: 839). Buttel thus agrees partly with Agarwal and Narain (1991), for whom the globalization of environmental issues constitutes a disguised form of neocolonialism on the part of rich countries. Later, Buttel (2000a) seems to have moved from a weak form of constructionism to a position more akin to reflexive modernization theory and to the neo-Marxism he previously defended, as reflected in his interest in ecological modernization (Buttel, 2000b) and environmental reform (Buttel,

2003). His growing engagement with theory-oriented European environmental sociology evolved into an effort to develop an 'environmental flows' perspective in collaboration with Dutch scholars (Spaargaren et al., 2006), the final project of his career.

Environmental sociology in the twenty-first century
In 2002, two US journals specializing in environmental sociology each published a special issue on the history of this subdiscipline. *Organization & Environment* published the results of a symposium held by the American Sociological Association (ASA) in Anaheim, California. Dunlap and Buttel were among the major speakers, and their contributions are included in this issue. In his article, Dunlap offers a personal perspective on the first 25 years of environmental sociology, which he defines as the study of interactions between society and the environment. He also returns to his debate with Buttel, which 'stimulated' him and Catton to clarify their original 1978 argument in a subsequent publication (Catton and Dunlap, 1980; Dunlap, 2002b: 19). Dunlap adds:

> Our portrayal of the HEP seems to have been pretty well received by environmental sociologists (as Buttel, for example, 1996 and 2000, has acknowledged). It is frequently cited, often endorsed, and seldom criticized . . . leading me to think that many if not most environmental sociologists recognize our discipline's legacy of exemptionalism and the necessity of overcoming it. (Ibid.)

He ends his discussion about the HEP by affirming: 'In sum, it strikes me that the exemptionalist legacy of our discipline is more widely recognized now than in the 70s and that it has become less acceptable to endorse it – at least as an excuse for ignoring ecological problems' (ibid.: 20).

Dunlap goes on to defend his NEP, which seeks to affirm the ecological dependence of modern societies (2002b: 21, 2002a). He admits that Buttel's criticism of the NEP helped him realize that their argument was ambiguous and that Buttel was right in offering some constructive criticism to defend the value of classical perspectives in environmental sociology. Dunlap ends by putting forward a moderate interpretation of his argument in favor of the NEP, and suggests that growing efforts to 'green' various theoretical perspectives (ranging from symbolic interactionism to Marxism) reflects acceptance of the NEP as does the increasing incorporation of environmental variables into empirical sociological analyses. In sum, Dunlap revisits the history of US environmental sociology, evaluating and defending the role he played in its development, and highlighting the emergence of the field at the international level (see also Dunlap, 1997). He endorses Buttel's position that the subdiscipline is still far from having a strong influence on sociology as a whole, but concludes that climate change and resource scarcities validate his emphasis on the ecosystem constraints faced by modern societies and suggest the future vitality of environmental sociology.

Buttel's article (2002a: 42) starts off by asking if environmental sociology has finally 'arrived'. He notes that it is growing not only in America, but also in Europe and Asia. He sees it in the USA as divided between more theoretically oriented scholars who are active in the ASA, and applied experts whose professional lives gravitate around rural sociology, federal resource agencies and natural resource disciplines like forestry, and who are less preoccupied with the academic standing of the subdiscipline. He concludes with the following remark: 'Environmental or ecological questions are now gaining increased attention in a number of other specialty areas [besides political economy and world systems], for example, sociology of science, community and urban studies, economic sociology, cultural sociology, social movements, and political sociology' (ibid.: 50).

Buttel adds that environmental sociology has a smaller disciplinary impact in the USA than in Europe, where the field is less specialized but where environmental issues are taken more seriously in mainstream sociology, probably because green movements and parties are more prominent. To the question: 'Has US environmental sociology finally arrived?' Buttel answers by talking of mixed successes, but his verdict is basically positive:

> Environmental sociology is a fairly well-established subdiscipline, as evidenced by the fact that encyclopedias and compendia of sociology and social science now routinely include papers on environmental sociology. There is now a steady trickle of environmental sociological and environmentally focused papers in major, as well as minor, sociological journals. Environmental sociology, however, has been much less successful in its quest to reorient mainstream sociology toward embracing a more ecological point of view. (Buttel, 2002a: 51)

The special issue of *Society and Natural Resources*, also published in 2002, looks at the distinction between environmental sociology and natural resources sociology, from which the former partially emerged and with which it harmoniously coexists. It includes an introduction by Buttel and Field (2002), and Buttel's article (2002c), which traces the origins of both subdisciplines (see also Buttel, 1996). Buttel shows that these two subdisciplines are distinct, concerning subject matters, theories, literatures, institutional locators, scale of analysis and policy relevance. Environmental sociology is more theoretical and better rooted in general sociology rather than in applied work, as is much of natural resources sociology. Similarly, environmental sociology is centered on industrial and metropolitan production and consumption, and on pollution and resource scarcity at an aggregate level. He also notes: 'Environmental sociology has largely tended to have a national–societal unit of analysis, but increasingly environmental sociology has taken on a global or international level of analysis' (Buttel, 2002c: 209). Towards the end of his article Buttel stresses the emerging importance of the sociology of agriculture and of fisheries, before concluding that there is a need for greater cooperation between the environmental and natural resources sociology subdisciplines.

Dunlap and Catton's (2002) article focuses on the three basic and often conflicting functions that ecosystems fulfill for human societies, namely supply depot, waste repository and living space, mentioned in an earlier publication (Dunlap and Catton, 1983). Natural resources sociology focuses on the first of these functions while environmental sociology considers all three, ranging from the local to the global level. They describe how the latter emerged in the USA and how it focused primarily on energy issues, environmentalism, housing, the built environment, natural hazards and ecological theory. They also stress the importance of theory and the growing internationalization of the field.

The book *Sociological Theory and the Environment*, edited by Dunlap, Buttel, Dickens and Gijswijt (2002), constitutes the best illustration of what I have been saying for years, namely that Dunlap's and Buttel's contributions to environmental sociology are seminal and important, as well as conflicting, but also converging. The preface starts off by opposing Dunlap's new ecological paradigm and Buttel's 'sympathetic critique' (Dunlap et al., 2002: vii). The authors go on to say: 'the resulting debate ended up being only the first installment in an ongoing discussion' (ibid.: viii). Thus they show that environmental sociological theory has gone far beyond the original Dunlap–Buttel debate, and that it now engages the larger theoretical discussions that permeate the field of contemporary sociology while returning to the basic issues raised earlier.

In his contribution, Buttel shows that even if a materialist North American environmental sociology emerged in the late 1970s in opposition to mainstream sociology, the case can be made that Marx, Durkheim and Weber were aware of natural constraints and societal–environmental relations. They did not neglect the biophysical world, and for that reason, environmental sociology should not isolate itself from that classical tradition. He concludes by repeating that the recent straying away from materialism by constructionists, critical theorists and proponents of ecological modernization has largely been a positive development, arguing that this theoretical pluralism and diversification of environmental sociology 'is opening up avenues of theoretical innovation and synthesis that were not present a decade ago' (Buttel, 2002b: 47), adding that this increases opportunities for a closer integration with empirical research.

Dunlap's chapter (2002a) further refines his position on sociology's neglect of the biophysical environment. He admits that his first formulations contained some ambiguities that partly explain the ensuing misunderstanding of his intent. He recalls Buttel's critical response, and the illuminating exchanges and clarifications that followed, going on to say: 'In retrospect, I see that our debate with Buttel not only stemmed from differing notions of a paradigm, but also from the additional ambiguity of what constitutes a paradigm "shift" or "change" from HEP to NEP' (2002a: 339). Buttel unintentionally distorted Dunlap and Catton's argument by assuming that they were addressing the classical sociological tradition *in toto* and not just Durkheim's anti-reductionism, whereas their primary focus had been on mid-twentieth-century theorists like Talcott Parsons and Daniel Bell. Just as Buttel ended up recognizing 'these early works by Catton and Dunlap as having provided the template for modern environmental sociology' (ibid.: 342), likewise Dunlap retreated to a moderate interpretation of his argument on the HEP–NEP distinction in environmental sociology. In sum, the debate between Dunlap and Buttel abated to the point that both admitted that there was a gradual convergence of views between them rather than an irreconcilable divergence.

Conclusion: a lesson in agonistic friendship

This chapter has attempted to summarize and evaluate some of the debates that two leading US environmental sociologists have engaged in since the mid-1970s. Using Chicago School human ecology as his point of departure, Dunlap first put forward the argument that the dominant sociological traditions neglect the importance of environmental factors in relation to culture and society. He added that we should replace the anthropocentric human exemptionalism paradigm underlying these traditions with a new ecological one that takes into account natural limits and constraints. On the other hand, Buttel did not think it was necessary to adopt an entirely new paradigm and to discard previous approaches in order to give environmental variables their rightful place.

A second debate between Dunlap and Buttel referred to the causes and consequences of environmental problems, and to solutions to these problems. Both wanted to contribute to the development of a fully fledged environmental sociology. Dunlap stressed the importance of recognizing the interrelations between the multiple causes of environmental problems and the complexities that this creates for solving them. Buttel preferred to adopt a critical political-economy approach that centers attention on social movements, the state and capital, emphasizing the primacy of social, political and economic factors. He thought that the state is impelled to adopt pro-growth policies that favor the concentration of capital, and that green groups should align themselves with the oppressed poor in order to provoke social change and ecologically viable transformations. In his latter years, Buttel seems to have toned down this somewhat radical stance by his espousal of a moderate form of constructionism, use of reflexive modernization theory and interest in environmental flows.

Finally, the most recent debate between Dunlap and Buttel pertained not only to constructionism but also to the issue of the globalization of environmental problems. Buttel wanted to develop a new environmental sociology or ecosociology inspired by the sociology of science and knowledge, to challenge the way global environmental problems are being socially and politically constructed. He thought that decisions in this area should be taken at local, regional and national levels rather than globally. Furthermore, he considered it important to consider the way everyday lives of families are linked to the process of sociopolitical construction of environmental problems. Dunlap, on the other hand, believed strongly in the reality of global environmental problems, and he hoped that adopting an ecological approach would enable sociologists to contribute more effectively to interdisciplinary analyses of them.

Concerning their debate on constructionism versus realism, Buttel backed off from the strong constructionist approach he put forward in 1992 (Taylor and Buttel, 1992) after it was challenged by Dunlap and Catton (1994a). Reacting to an earlier version of their paper, Buttel wrote: 'Neither a "strong program" dissection of environmental knowledge nor a gratuitous postmodernist cultural sociology of environmental beliefs will or should change the reality of global environmental problems' (Buttel, 1992: 10). In sum, Buttel became a 'soft' constructionist when he recognized that GECs are real and not simply socially constructed, yet he continued to highlight the political-economic forces that influence differing views of GEC.

In a parallel fashion, Dunlap recognized the usefulness of a moderate form of constructionism, praising John Hannigan's development of a moderate perspective and his disavowal of extreme constructionism (Hannigan, 1995). While Dunlap's 'realist' orientation stems from his strong ecological orientation, he acknowledges the usefulness of developing a more moderate constructionist perspective and he admits that he was overzealous in intimating that the NEP should supplant classical sociology. He also notes that he does not expect the NEP to replace Marxist, Weberian, functionalist or other theoretical perspectives, but only to stimulate the development of green versions of them (Dunlap, 2002a, 2002b). He admits that since he apparently created unrealistic expectations concerning the NEP's usefulness for guiding empirical research, he is not surprised that it continued to be criticized by people like Buttel (1996). In sum, what Dunlap was trying to do, according to his more recent writings, was to legitimize integrations of environmental and sociological variables, both as causes and consequences of one another.

Somewhat more general strands can be woven together at this point. Dunlap's definition of environmental sociology as the study of societal–environmental interactions clearly requires a willingness to incorporate environmental variables into sociological analyses (Dunlap and Martin, 1983). Furthermore, Dunlap's ecological perspective leads to: (1) a concern about the 'exemptionalist' underpinnings of traditional sociological theories and a renewed call for an NEP; (2) a concern about trying to understand (via POET and IPAT) the complex origins of environmental problems; and (3) the use of a 'realist' perspective for analyzing GEC and other environmental problems (Dunlap and Martin, 1983).

In contrast, Buttel's tendency to draw from classical sociological theory leads to: (1) an emphasis on the continued relevance of classical theoretical perspectives for analyzing environmental problems and a certain skepticism regarding the need for a NEP; (2) the adoption of a political-economy perspective on environmental problems; and (3) the adoption of a weak to moderate constructionist orientation that challenges the formulation of GEC and highlights the roles played by various interest groups in debates over GEC.

The Dunlap–Buttel debate evolved in a series of friendly nuances and moderate concessions, rather than in rude confrontations. From the outset, Dunlap was concerned with legitimizing the incorporation of environmental variables in sociological analyses in order to establish a distinct field of environmental sociology, and he emphasized the utility of an ecological perspective for guiding analyses of societal–environmental relations. While not disagreeing with these aims, Buttel was more concerned with ensuring that environmental sociology should maintain strong links to the larger discipline by making use of both classical and contemporary sociological perspectives when analyzing environmental issues. While appreciating each other's views and occasionally modifying their own position somewhat, in reaction to friendly criticism, Dunlap and Buttel retained their respective emphases throughout their debates. In spite of their distinctive positions, their major contribution may have been to lessen the tension between competing perspectives and to foster fruitful collegial debates within the field.

In concluding, I would like to comment briefly on the short enlightening eulogy that Dunlap read at a memorial for Buttel at the August 2005 ASA meetings in Philadelphia. For him, Fred was not an enemy but 'one of [his] best friends and most highly valued colleagues' (Dunlap, 2005: 2). Early on in their careers, he says, they chose to be friendly colleagues rather than intense competitors. Buttel's sympathetic criticism of Dunlap and Catton's HEP–NEP helped them strengthen their argument and also contributed to making it more widely known. They had 'something of a running debate' during a quarter of a century, pushing Dunlap 'to keep a strong ecological orientation and a focus on environmental phenomena central to environmental sociology, and Fred pushing to ensure that our field was fully engaged with key theoretical currents in the larger discipline' (ibid.). Dunlap praises Buttel's far-ranging scholarship, his masterful theoretical work and empirical analyses, and his bridge-building between scholars internationally and locally. He considers Fred to have been 'one of the very finest, most decent human beings' with a 'wonderful sense of humor and positive outlook on life . . ., a role model' (ibid.). Dunlap ends his eulogy with the following paragraph:

> In short, I cannot find words adequate for expressing my affection and admiration for Fred Buttel. He was a rare gem among academics, a superb scholar and a wonderful and generous human being, and my life (along with many others) is richer because of him. Everyone should be so fortunate as to have an 'enemy' like Fred. (ibid.: 3)

I agree with Riley concerning Fred's eminent qualities. But I also know Riley quite well, and I must say that most of what Riley says about Fred also applies to Riley himself. Environmental sociologists and global ecosociologists everywhere are lucky to have these two outstanding scholars and gentlemen among the major co-founders of their subdiscipline.

Notes
1.   POET = Population, Organization, Environment, and Technology.
2.   STIRPAT = STochastic Impacts by Regression on Population, Affluence, and Technology.

References

Agarwal, A. and S. Narain (1991), *Global Warming in an Unequal World: A Case of Environmental Colonialism*, Delhi, India: Center for Science and Environment.

Buttel, F.H. (1976), 'Social science and the environment: competing theories', *Social Science Quarterly*, **57** (2): 307–23.

Buttel, F.H. (1978a), 'Environmental sociology: a new paradigm?', *The American Sociologist*, **13** (4): 252–6.

Buttel, F.H. (1978b), 'Social structure and energy efficiency: a preliminary cross-national analysis', *Human Ecology*, **6** (2), 145–64.

Buttel, F.H. (1986a), 'Sociologie et environnement: la lente maturation de l'écologie humaine', *Revue Internationale des Sciences Sociales*, **109**: 359–79.

Buttel, F.H. (1986b), 'Sociology and the environment: the winding road toward human ecology', *International Social Science Journal*, **109**: 337–56.

Buttel, F.H. (1987), 'New directions in environmental sociology', *Annual Review of Sociology*, **13**: 465–88.

Buttel, F.H. (1992), 'Environmentalization: origins, processes, and implications for rural social change', *Rural Sociology*, **57** (1): 1–27.

Buttel, F.H. (1996), 'Environmental and resource sociology: theoretical issues and opportunities for synthesis', *Rural Sociology*, **61** (1): 56–76.

Buttel, F.H. (2000a), 'Classical theory and contemporary environmental sociology: some reflections on the antecedents and prospects for reflexive modernization theories in the study of environment and society', in G. Spaargaren, A.P.J. Mol and F.H. Buttel (eds), *Environment and Global Modernity*, London: Sage, pp. 17–39.

Buttel, F.H. (2000b), 'Ecological modernization as social theory', *Geoforum*, **31**: 57–65.

Buttel, F.H (2002a), 'Has environmental sociology arrived?', *Organization & Environment*, **15** (1): 42–55.

Buttel, F.H. (2002b), 'Environmental sociology and the classical sociological tradition: some observations on current controversies', in R.E. Dunlap, F.H. Buttel, P. Dickens and A. Gijswit (eds), *Sociological Theory and the Environment: Classical Foundations, Contemporary Insights*, Boulder: Rowan and Littlefield, pp. 35–50.

Buttel, F.H. (2002c), 'Environmental sociology and the sociology of natural resources: institutional histories and intellectual legacies', *Society and Natural Resources*, **15** (3): 205–12.

Buttel, F.H. (2003), 'Environmental sociology and the explanation of environmental reform', *Organization & Environment*, **16** (3): 306–44.

Buttel, F.H. and D.R. Field (2002), 'Environmental and resource sociology: introducing a debate and dialogue', *Society and Natural Resources*, **15** (3): 201–04.

Buttel, F.H. and W.L. Flinn (1974), 'The structure of support for the environmental movement, 1968–1970', *Rural Sociology*, **39** (1): 56–69.

Buttel, F.H. and W.L. Flinn (1976), 'Environmental politics: the structuring of partisan and ideological cleavages in mass environmental attitudes', *The Sociological Quarterly*, **17**: 477–90.

Buttel, F.H. and W.L. Flinn (1977), 'The interdependence of rural and environmental problems in advanced capitalist societies: models of linkages', *Sociologia Ruralis*, **17**: 255–79.

Buttel, F.H. and C.R. Humphrey (2002), 'Sociological theory and the natural environment', in R.E. Dunlap and W. Michelson (eds), *Handbook of Environmental Sociology*, Westport, CT: Greenwood Publishers, pp. 33–69.

Buttel, F.H. and P.J. Taylor (1992), 'Environmental sociology and global environmental change: a critical assessment', *Society and Natural Resources*, **5** (3), 211–30.

Buttel, F.H., A.P. Hawkins and A.G. Power (1990), 'From limits to growth to global change: constraints and contradictions in the evolution of environmental science and ideology', *Global Environmental Change*, **1** (1): 57–66.

Catton, W.R. Jr and R.E. Dunlap (1978a), 'Environmental sociology: a new paradigm', *The American Sociologist*, **13** (4): 41–9.

Catton, W.R. Jr and R.E. Dunlap (1978b), 'Paradigms, theories, and the primacy of the HEP–NEP distinction', *The American Sociologist*, **13** (4): 256–9.

Catton, W.R. Jr. and R.E. Dunlap (1980), 'A new ecological paradigm for post-exuberant sociology', *American Behavioral Scientist*, **24** (1): 15–47.

Commoner, B. (1971), *The Closing Circle: Nature, Man and Technology*, New York: Alfred A. Knopf.

Duncan, O.D. (1959), 'Human ecology and population studies', in P. Hauser and O.D. Duncan (eds), *The Study of Population*, Chicago, IL: University of Chicago Press, pp. 678–716.

Dunlap, R.E. (1993), 'From environmental to ecological problems', in C. Calhoun and G. Ritzer (eds), *Social Problems*, New York: McGraw-Hill, pp. 707–38.

Dunlap, R.E. (1997), 'The evolution of environmental sociology: a brief history and assessment of the American experience', in M. Redclift and G. Woodgate (eds), *The International Handbook of Environmental Sociology*, Cheltenham, UK and Lyme, USA: Edward Elgar, pp. 21–39.

Dunlap, R.E. (2002a), 'Paradigms, theories and environmental sociology', in R.E. Dunlap, F.H. Buttel, P. Dickens and A. Gijswijt (eds), *Sociological Theory and the Environment: Classical Foundations, Contemporary Insights*, Boulder, CO: Rowman & Littlefield, pp. 329–50.

Dunlap, R.E. (2002b), 'Environmental sociology: a personal perspective on its first quarter century', *Organization and Environment*, **15** (1): 10–29.

Dunlap, R.E. (2005), 'Everyone should have an "enemy" like Fred: a tribute to Frederick H. Buttel', *Environment, Technology and Society*, **27**: 2–3.

Dunlap, R.E. and W.R. Catton Jr (1979a), 'Environmental sociology: a framework for analysis', in T. O'Riordan and R.C. D'Arge (eds), *Progress in Resource Management and Environmental Planning*, Vol. 1, Chichester, UK: John Wiley & Sons, pp. 57–85.

Dunlap, R.E. and W.R. Catton Jr (1979b), 'Environmental sociology', *Annual Review of Sociology*, **5**: 243–73.

Dunlap, R.E. and W.R. Catton Jr (1983), 'What environmental sociologists have in common whether concerned with built or natural environments', *Sociology Inquiry*, **53** (2–3): 113–35.

Dunlap, R.E. and W.R. Catton Jr (1994a), 'Struggling with human exemptionalism: the rise, decline and revitalization of environmental sociology', *The American Sociologist*, **25** (1): 5–30.

Dunlap, R.E. and W.R. Catton Jr (1994b), 'Toward an ecological sociology: the development, current status, and probable future of environmental sociology', in V. D'Antonio, M. Sasaki and K. Yonebayaski (eds), *Ecology, Society and the Quality of Life*, New Brunswick, NJ: Transaction Publishers, pp. 15–31.

Dunlap, R.E. and W.R. Catton Jr (2002), 'Which function(s) of the environment do we study? A comparison of environmental and natural resource sociology', *Society and Natural Resources*, **15** (3): 239–50.

Dunlap, R.E. and R.E. Jones (2002), 'Environmental concern: conceptual and measurement issues', in R.E. Dunlap and W. Michelson (eds), *Handbook of Environmental Sociology*, Westport, CT: Greenwood Press, pp. 482–524.

Dunlap, R.E. and K.E. Martin (1983), 'Bringing environment into the study of agriculture: observations and suggestions regarding the sociology of agriculture', *Rural Sociology*, **48** (2): 201–18.

Dunlap, R.E. and A.G. Mertig (eds) (1992), *American Environmentalism: The US Environmental Movement (1970–1990)*, Philadelphia, PA: Taylor & Francis.

Dunlap, R.E. and W. Michelson (eds) (2002), *Handbook of Environmental Sociology*, Westport, CT: Greenwood Publishers.

Dunlap, R.E. and R. Scarce (1991), 'The polls–poll trends: environmental problems and protection', *Public Opinion Quarterly*, **55** (1): 651–72.

Dunlap, R.E. and K.D. Van Liere (1978), 'The "new environmental paradigm": a proposed measuring instrument. Preliminary results', *Journal of Environmental Education*, **9** (4): 10–49.

Dunlap, R.E. and K.D. Van Liere (1984), 'Commitment to the dominant social paradigm and concern for environment quality', *Social Science Quarterly*, **65** (4): 1013–28.

Dunlap, R.E., K.D. Van Liere, A.G. Mertig and R.E. Jones (2000), 'Measuring endorsement of the new ecological paradigm: a revised NEP scale', *Journal of Social Issues*, **56** (3): 425–42.

Dunlap, R.E., F.H. Buttel, P. Dickens and A. Gijswijt (eds) (2002), *Sociological Theory and the Environment: Classical Foundations, Contemporary Insights*, Boulder, CO: Rowman & Littlefield.

Hannigan, J.A. (1995), *Environmental Sociology: A Social Constructionist Perspective*, London: Routledge.

Hawkins, A.P. and F.H. Buttel (1992), 'Sustainable development', in G. Szell (ed.), *Concise Encyclopedia of Participation and Co-Management*, Berlin/New York: Walter de Gruyter, pp. 831–41.

Humphrey, C.R. and F.H. Buttel (1982), *Environment, Energy, and Society*, Belmont, CA: Wadsworth.

McCright, A.M. and R.E. Dunlap (2000), 'Challenging global warming as a social problem: an analysis of the conservative movement's counter-claims', *Social Problems*, **47** (3): 499–522.

McCright, A.M. and R.E. Dunlap (2003), 'Defeating Kyoto: the conservative movement's impact on U.S. climate change policy', **50** (4): 348–73.

McMichael, P. and F.H. Buttel (1980), 'New directions in the political economy of agriculture', *Sociological Perspectives*, **33** (1): 89–109.

Murphy, R. (1994), *Rationality and Nature*, Boulder, CO: Westview.
Redclift, M.R. and G. Woodgate (eds) (1997), *The International Handbook of Environmental Sociology*, Cheltenham, UK Lyme and USA: Edward Elgar.
Schnaiberg, A. (1980), *The Environment: From Surplus to Scarcity*, New York: Oxford University Press.
Spaargaren, G., A.P.J. Mol and F. H. Buttel (eds) (2006), *Governing Environmental Flows: Global Challenges to Social Theory,* Cambridge, MA: MIT Press.
Taylor, P.J. and F.H. Buttel (1992), 'How do we know we have global environmental problems? Science and globalization of environmental discourse', *Geoforum*, **23** (3), 405–16.
Yearly, S. (1991), *The Green Case: A Sociology of Environmental Issues, Arguments, and Politics*, London: HarperCollins.
York, R., E.A. Rosa and T. Dietz (2003), 'Footprints on the earth: the environmental consequences of modernity', *American Sociological Review*, **68** (2): 279–300.

4 Ecological modernization as a social theory of environmental reform

Arthur P.J. Mol

Understanding environmental reform

During the late 1960s and especially the 1970s several social sciences witnessed the emergence of relatively small environmental subdisciplines: within sociology, political sciences, economics, and later also within anthropology and law. Strongly triggered by social developments in Western industrialized societies, social scientists started to reflect on a new category of phenomena: the changing relations between nature and society and the reflection of modern society on these.

In retrospect, the framing of environmental questions within sociology and political sciences during the 1970s was of a particular nature. The emphasis was primarily on the fundamental causes of environmental crises in Western industrialized society and the failure of modern institutions to deal adequately with these. Environmental protests and movements, state failures, the capitalist roots of the environmental crisis, and environmental attitudes and (mis)behaviour were the typical subjects of environmental sociology and political science studies in the 1970s. Many of these studies were strongly related to neo-Marxist interpretation schemes, and even today neo-Marxism is a powerful and far from marginal explanatory theory in environmental social science research.[1]

Strongly driven by empirical and ideological developments in the European environmental movement, by the practices and institutional developments in some 'environmental frontrunner states', and by developments in private companies, some European social scientists began reorienting their focus from explaining ongoing environmental devastation towards understanding processes of environmental reform. Later, and sometimes less strongly, this new environmental social science agenda was followed by US and other non-European scholars and policy analysts. By the turn of the millennium, this focus on understanding and explaining environmental reform had become mainstream, not so much instead of, but rather as a complement to, studies explaining environmental deterioration.

In what we might call – following the late Fred Buttel (2003) – the social sciences of environmental reform, ecological modernization stands out as one of the strongest, best-known, most used and widely cited, and constantly debated concepts in this body of literature. The notion of ecological modernization can be seen as the social scientific interpretation of environmental reform processes and practices at multiple scales. From the launching of the term by Martin Jänicke and Joseph Huber around 1980 and its insertion into social theory by Arthur Mol and Gert Spaargaren around 1990, ecological modernization has been applied around the world in empirical studies, has been at the forefront in theoretical debates, and has even been used by politicians to frame environmental reform programmes in countries including Germany, the Netherlands, the UK and China. There is now broad interest and much research in ecological modernization throughout the world, including Asia (especially China, Japan, Korea, Vietnam and elsewhere), North America, Latin America (especially Brazil, Argentina, Peru, Chile), as well as the wider European continent (including Russia).

In this chapter, I shall elaborate especially on ecological modernization theory. But I shall embed ecological modernization in a historical analysis of three generations of social science contributions to understanding environmental reform. Although these three generations have a historical dimension in that each has been developed in a specific period (and geographical space), they are not mutually excluding or full alternatives. First-generation theories on policy, protests and attitudes are still applied and relevant today, be it in a somewhat different mode as initially developed in the 1970s. In addition, insights from the first-generation theories have often been included in reform theories of later generations.

Policies, protests and attitudes

Although emerging as a more central theme in environmental sociology and political sciences only in the late 1980s, the subject of environmental reform was also present in the early days of the environmental social sciences. Initially in the 1970s (see Mol, 2006; Buttel, 2002), American and European environmental sociology and political sciences dealt with environmental reforms predominantly via three lines: analysing national environmental policies and environmental state formation, studying environmental non-governmental organizations (NGOs) and protests, and investigating individual environmental attitudes and related behaviour.

As environmental problems and crises were mainly conceptualized as (capitalist) market failures in the provision of collective goods, the emerging environmental state institutions were widely conceived as among the most important developments to deal with these failures. The establishment of national and local environmental ministries and authorities, new national frameworks of legal measures and regulations, new assessment procedures for major economic projects, and other state-related institutional innovations drove sociological and political science interests, analyses and investigations towards understanding environmental reform processes. To a significant extent, these analyses were sceptical of the nation-state's ability to 'tame the treadmill' (Schnaiberg, 1980) of ongoing capitalist accumulation processes and related environmental deterioration. Building strongly on neo-Marxist analytical schemes, the state was often perceived to be structurally unable to regulate, control and compensate for the inherent environmental side effects of an ongoing capitalist accumulation process. The environmental crisis was seen as being closely and fundamentally related to the structure of the capitalist organization of the economy, and the 'capitalist state' was considered to be unable to change the structure of the capitalist economy. Jänicke's (1986) study on state failure collected together many of the insights and themes of this line of investigation. Notwithstanding this dominant position during the early years of environmental sociology and political science, some did see and analyse the environmental state as of critical importance for environmental reform. This was the case, for instance, with tragedy of the commons/free-rider perspectives, more applied policy science analyses, or Weberian rationalization views. Much research was normative and design-oriented, focusing on the contribution to and development of new state-oriented institutional layouts for environmental policy and reform. Environmental impact assessment schemes, environmental integration models, policy instruments, control and enforcement arrangements, and the like were typical subjects for agenda-setting and implementation research.

Environmental NGOs and civil-society protests formed a second object of early environmental social science research on environmental reform. Investigations into local community protests against environmental pollution and studies of local and national environmental NGOs constituted the core of this second branch of environmental reform analyses in the 1970s and early 1980s. The resource mobilization studies in the USA (e.g. Zald and McCarthy, 1979; McCarthy and Zald, 1977) and the new social movement approach in Europe (e.g. Offe, 1985; Klandermans, 1986) were two dominant perspectives among a wide range of studies that tried to understand the importance of civil society in bringing about social transformations in the core institutions of modern society. In addition to a clear emphasis on the protests against what were seen as the fundamental roots of the environmental crises, many studies also focused on the contribution of the emerging environmental movement to the actual and necessary reforms of the modern institutional order, be it via escapism in small communities detached from the dominant economic (and often also political) institutions (cf. the 'small is beautiful' post-industrial utopians; Frankel, 1987); via public campaigning against polluters; via lobbying and influencing political processes; or via awareness-raising and attitudinal changes of citizens and consumers. Among environmental sociologists there was often a significant degree of sympathy with, and even involvement in, these new social movements. Many of the more radical and structuralist analyses of the 'roots of the environmental crises' saw – and still see – the environmental movement as the last resort for bringing about change and reform.

A third category of environmental reform studies emerged in the 1970s, although this category was more psychology – instead of sociology or political science – based: research on environmental values, attitudes and behaviour. Strongly rooted in psychological models and theories, a new line of investigation developed in the 1970s, relating changes in environmental values and attitudes of individuals to behavioural changes. Ajzen and Fishbein's (1975) model of reasoned action formed the basis for much fundamental and applied research, trying to relate polling and surveys on environmental values with concrete environmentally (un)sound behavioural actions and changes in social practices. In sociology, Catton and Dunlap's (1978a, 1978b) dichotomy of the human exemptionalism paradigm (HEP) and the new ecological paradigm (NEP) formed a strong model for survey research, although it was initially developed to criticize the parent discipline for failing to take environmental dimensions into account in explaining social behaviour (see Dunlap, Chapter 1 in this volume).

Reviewing these contributions to social science research on environmental reform, one can draw several conclusions. First, with Fred Buttel (2003) one can conclude that in the 1970s and 1980s the majority of the environmental social science studies were not focused on explaining environmental reform, but, rather, on understanding the continuity of environmental degradation. Second, among the relatively few environmental reform studies conventional political and civil-society institutions received most attention, whereas economic institutions and organizations, or mixes (hybrids) of institutions/organizations, were almost absent. This was, of course, related to the actual state of environmental transformations in OECD countries during the 1970s and 1980s.

Third, although neo-Marxist perspectives dominated the sociology/political sciences of environmental devastations during that period, no clear single dominant theoretical perspective emerged among the variety of environmental reform studies. Fourth, although these traditions in studying environmental protest, politics and attitudes originate in the 1970s, they still have strong positions in contemporary social sciences research on the environment. This is clearly illustrated in the environmental programmes of the annual, two-yearly or four-yearly conferences of, respectively, the American Sociological Association, the European Sociological Association, and the International Sociological Association.

Ecological modernization
From the mid-1980s, but especially since the early 1990s, a profusion of empirical studies has emerged focusing on environmental improvements, ecological restructuring or environmental reform. These studies have focused on distinct levels of analysis: individual producers, households or social practices; industrial sectors, zones, chains or networks; nation-states or countries; and even global regions. They all tried to assess whether a reduction in the use of natural resources and/or the discharge of emissions could be identified, either in absolute or in relative terms, compared to economic indicators such as GNP. This development is manifest in studies on cleaner production, industrial metabolism or industrial ecology; investigations on dematerialization and factor 4/10;[2] and perspectives on the greening of consumption, lifestyles and households. Although most of these empirical studies emerged in developed OECD countries, many of them have – be it often a little later – also found their way to less developed parts of the globe.

Although not all of the conclusions in these studies point in the same direction, the general picture can be summarized as follows. From the mid-1980s onward, a rupture in the long-established trend of parallel economic growth and increasing ecological disruption can be identified in most of the ecologically advanced nations, such as Germany, Japan, the Netherlands, the USA, Sweden and Denmark. This slowdown is often referred to as the decoupling or delinking of material flows from economic flows. In a number of cases (regarding countries and/or specific industrial sectors and/or specific social practices and/or specific environmental issues), environmental reform has even resulted in an absolute decline in the use of natural resources and/or in discharge of emissions, regardless of economic growth in financial or material terms (product output). These conclusions are sometimes also valid for rapidly industrializing and modernizing countries in, for instance, Asia (e.g. Sonnenfeld and Mol, 2006).

The social dynamics behind these changes, that is, the emergence of actual environment-induced transformations of institutions and social practices, became one of the key objects of social science research in the 1990s. I shall group the studies that try to understand, interpret and conceptualize the nature, extent and social dynamics of environmental reform processes in this era under the label of ecological modernization.

Fundamentals of ecological modernization
The basic idea of ecological modernization is that, at the end of the second millennium, modern societies witness a centripetal movement of ecological interests, ideas and considerations in their institutional design. This development crystallizes in a constant ecological restructuring of modernity. Ecological restructuring refers to the ecology-

inspired and environment-induced processes of transformation and reform in the central institutions of modern society.

Within the so-called ecological modernization theory, this ecological restructuring is conceptualized at an analytical level as the growing autonomy, independence or differentiation of an ecological rationality *vis-à-vis* other rationalities (cf. Mol, 1995; Spaargaren, 1997). In the domain of states, policies and politics an ecological rationality had already emerged in the 1970s and early 1980s, and 'materialized' or 'institutionalized' in different forms. The construction of governmental organizations and departments dealing with environmental issues dates from that era. Equally, environmental (framework) laws, environmental impact assessment systems and green political parties date back to the same period. The same is true in the domain of ideology and the lifeworld. A distinct 'green' ideology – as manifested by, for instance, environmental NGOs, environmental value systems and environmental periodicals – started to emerge in the 1970s. Only in the 1980s, however, did this 'green' ideology assume an independent status that could no longer be interpreted in terms of the old political ideologies of socialism, liberalism and conservatism, as argued by, among others, Giddens (1994).

However, the crucial transformation that makes the notion of the growing autonomy of an ecological rationality especially relevant is of more recent origin. After an ecological rationality had become relatively independent from political and socio-ideological rationalities (in the 1970s and 1980s), this process of growing independence began to extend to the economic domain in the 1990s. And because, according to most scholars, this growing independence of the ecological rationality from its economic counterpart is crucial to 'the ecological question', this last step is the decisive one. It means that economic processes of production and consumption are increasingly analysed and judged, as well as designed and organized from both an economic and an ecological point of view. Some profound institutional changes in the economic domain of production and consumption have become discernible in the 1990s. Among these changes are the widespread emergence of environmental management systems in companies; the introduction of economic valuation of environmental goods via the introduction of ecotaxes, among other things; the emergence of environment-inspired liability and insurance arrangements; the increasing importance attached to environmental goals such as natural resource saving and recycling among public and private utility enterprises; and the articulation of environmental considerations in economic supply and demand, for instance through the use of ecolabels. Within ecological modernization ideas, these transformations are analysed as *institutional* changes, indicating their semi-permanent character. Although the process of ecology-induced transformation should not be interpreted as linear, evolutionary and irreversible, as was common in the modernization theories in the 1950s and 1960s, these changes have some permanence and would be difficult to reverse.

Ecological modernization as environmental reform
Most ecological modernization studies focus on actual environmental reforms in specific social practices and institutions. An ecological modernization perspective on environmental reform can be categorized in five themes.

First, there are studies on three new interpretations of the role of science and technology in environmental reform. Science and technology are no longer analysed and judged only for their contribution to environmental problems (so dominant in the 1970s and early 1980s); they are also valued for their actual and potential role in bringing about environmental reforms and preventing environmental crises. In addition, environmental reforms via traditional curative and repair technologies are replaced by more preventive sociotechnological approaches and transitions that incorporate environmental considerations from the design stage of technological and organizational innovations. Finally, the growing uncertainties with regard to scientific and expert knowledge and complex technological systems do not lead to a denigration of science and technology in environmental reform, but, rather, in new environmental and institutional arrangements.

A second theme covers studies focused on the increasing importance and involvement of economic and market dynamics, institutions and agents in environmental reforms. Producers, customers, consumers, credit institutions, insurance companies, utility sectors and business associations, to name but a few, increasingly turn into social carriers of ecological restructuring, innovation and reform (in addition to, and not so much instead of, state agencies and new social movements). This goes together with a focus on changing state–market relations in environmental governance, and on a growing involvement of economic and market institutions in articulating environmental considerations via monetary values and prices, demand, products and services, and the like.

A third theme in ecological modernization relates to the changing role, position and performance of the 'environmental' state (often referred to as 'political modernization' in Europe (see Jänicke, 1993), or regulatory reinvention in the USA (see Eisner, 2004)). This theme evolved in the mid-1990s in environmental governance studies. The traditional central role of the nation-state in environmental reform is shifting, leading to new governance arrangements and new political spaces. First, there is a trend towards more decentralized, flexible and consensual styles of national governance, at the expense of top-down hierarchical command-and-control regulation. Second, there is a larger involvement of non-state actors and 'non-political' arrangements in environmental governance, taking over conventional tasks of the nation-state and conventional politics (e.g. privatization, public–private partnerships, conflict resolution by business–environmental NGO coalitions without state interference, and the emergence of subpolitics[3]). Finally, supranational and global environmental institutions and governance arrangements to some extent undermine the conventional role of the sovereign nation-state or national arrangements in environmental policy and politics. As I shall outline later in this chapter, this is more than just a matter of scale; it is, rather, a fundamental change in environmental reform dynamics, requiring a different environmental sociology and political science.

Fourth, the modification of the position, role, and ideology of social movements (*vis-à-vis* the 1970s and 1980s) in the process of ecological transformation emerges as a theme in ecological modernization. Instead of positioning themselves on the periphery or even outside the central decision-making institutions on the basis of demodernization ideologies and limited economic and political power, environmental movements seem increasingly involved in decision-making processes within the political and, to a lesser extent, economic arenas. Legitimacy, accountability, transparency and participation are the new principles and values that provide social movements and civil society with the resources for a more powerful position in environmental reform processes. Within the environmental movement, this transformation goes together with a bipolar or dualistic strategy of cooperation and conflict, and internal debates on the tensions that are a by-product of this duality (Mol, 2000).

And, finally, ecological modernization studies concentrate on changing discursive practices and the emergence of new ideologies in political and societal arenas. Neither the fundamental counterpositioning of economic and environmental interests nor a total disregard for the importance of environmental considerations is accepted any longer as legitimate positions. Intergenerational solidarity in the interest of preserving the sustenance base seems to have emerged as the undisputed core and widely shared principle, although differences remain on interpretations and translations into practices and strategies.

Hence, all in all, this gives a much wider agenda of environmental reform studies compared to the 1970s and early 1980s, partly reflecting the changing practices of environmental reform in and between OECD countries.

Ecological modernization studies: recent trends
While ecological modernization was coined in the 1980s and matured as a research tradition in the 1990s, recent years have witnessed a number of new trends in ecological modernization studies. These have resulted in a reformulation of the ecological modernization research agenda.

First, there is a growing research agenda on the ecological modernization of consumption practices (see Hinton and Goodman, Chapter 16 in this volume). This has developed in line with wider developments, such as the UNEP framework programme on Sustainable Consumption and Production and a more general idea, especially in the OECD countries, that consumption is increasingly seen as key to any environmental reform programme. Hence we see what has been labelled a consumerist turn in ecological modernization studies, with a growing number of ecological-modernization-inspired conceptual (see Spaargaren, 2003; Spaargaren and Mol, 2008) and empirical studies (see Cohen and Murphy, 2001; Jackson, 2006) on the greening of consumption. The consumerist turn has been accompanied by debates on the possibilities, priorities and modes of such ecological-modernization-inspired greening of consumption *vis-à-vis* alternative interpretations and consumption politics. Central in ecological modernization studies is a so-called contextual approach to consumer behaviour, where citizen–consumers are interpreted and analysed as change agents in their specific practices of consumption (e.g. tourism, shopping, cooking, travelling). Hence, such studies stand in contrast to ideas of greening consumption behind the backs of citizen consumers, and with the individualistic attitude–behaviour framings that dominated in the earlier generation of environmental reform studies.

The second main trend in ecological modernization studies relates to the growing interest in this interpretation framework outside the OECD geographies for which it was originally developed. Hence we see a growing interest in the ecological modernization paradigm in Southeast and East Asian studies of environmental reform (especially in South Korea, Japan, China (see Mol, Chapter 24 in Part III of this volume), including Hong Kong, Vietnam and Taiwan), with ecological modernization studies also emerging in Latin American countries such as Brazil, Peru, Argentina and Chile. This partly comes together with discussions on and reformulations of the key features of ecological modernization (see Zhang et al., 2007).

Third, while most ecological modernization research has been restricted to national studies, increasing numbers of comparative and more regional and global studies have been published. This has been true since the early 1990s for Europe and the EU, but increasingly also for wider geographies. The group around Martin Jänicke and Helmut Weidner has been especially instrumental in comparative studies with large numbers of countries. Others have focused on more in-depth comparative studies with a few countries. Yet others take a more global perspective and often abandon the state as the unit of analysis, to focus on environmental reforms related to global commodity networks, globalization processes, new global political arrangements, transnational infrastructures, or global material and non-material flows.

Finally, and related to the former point, the ecological modernization school of thought has started to rethink what a number of major social developments mean for environmental reform processes. Hence innovations emerge in theoretical and empirical environmental reform studies following processes of globalization and the information age, brought together under the banner of the environmental sociology of networks and flows. This will be further elaborated in the next major section.

Ecological modernization and its critics
From various (theoretical) perspectives and from the first publications onwards, the growing popularity of ecological modernization studies and ideas has met opposition and criticism. Coming from subdisciplines that had been preoccupied with explaining the continuity of environmental crises and deterioration, such a move to environmental reform perspectives cannot but meet (often fierce) debate. The debates and criticism surrounding ecological modernization have been summarized and reviewed in a number of publications[4] (see also Dunlap, Chapter 1, and York, Rosa and Dietz, Chapter 5 in this volume). Here I want to summarize these various critiques and debates in three categories.

First, several objections have been raised during the (relatively short) history of ecological modernization, which have been incorporated in more recent versions of the theory/idea. Although these objections to ecological modernization made sense in referring to the initial period of ecological modernization studies in the late 1980s, for more recent mature ecological modernization approaches they are no longer adequate. This is valid, for instance, regarding criticism of technological determinism in ecological modernization, of the productivist orientation and the neglect of the consumer/consumption, of the absence of 'power' from ecological modernization studies and of its Eurocentricity. Notwithstanding the increased incorporation of these critiques into ecological modernization studies at the turn of the millennium, they continue to be reiterated until recently (e.g. Carolan, 2004 on the productivist orientation; Gibbs, 2006 on missing power relations).

Second, there is a number of critiques of ecological modernization perspectives that find their origin in radically different paradigms and approaches. Neo-Marxist criticism by Schnaiberg and colleagues (2002) and others emphasizes consistently the fundamental continuity of a capitalist order that does not allow any environmental reform beyond window dressing. Deep-ecology-inspired scholars argue against the reformist agenda of ecological modernization, as it opts for a light green reform agenda, instead of a deep green fundamental and radical change of the modern order, sometimes even towards postmodernity. Human-ecologists, sometimes inspired by neo-Malthusianism, blame ecological modernization perspectives for their neglect of quantities, not least population growth and ever-growing levels of consumption. Consequently, ecological modernization perspectives are criticized as being inadequate, overly optimistic/naïve and incorrect. It is not so much that these objections are completely incorrect. From their starting points and the basic premises of these schools of thought, the points raised against ecological modernization are internally logical, consistent and coherent. However, their focus is often too narrow, limited and one-sided in claiming that there is nothing new under the sun. Although ecological modernization scholars would not deny that in various locations, practices, and institutions environmental deterioration is still forcefully present, they object to the common denominator among all this criticism: the conclusion that no institutional reforms can be identified and thus that it makes little sense to investigate it.

Third, and finally, there is a category of comments that is less easily either incorporated or put aside if we want to analyse and understand environmental reform in late modern society. These issues have to do with the nation-state or national society centredness of ecological modernization, the strong separation between the natural/physical and the social in ecological modernization, and the continuing conceptual differentiation among state, market and civil-society actors and institutions. Here it is especially the changing character of modern society – especially through processes of globalization – that makes new, early twenty-first-century environmental reform dynamics rest less comfortably with ecological modernization conceptualizations of the 1990s. This is not too dissimilar to the fact that the environmental reform dynamics of the 1990s did not fully fit the 'policy, protest and attitude' conceptualizations of the environmental reform studies of the 1970s and 1980s. It is especially these comments and discussions about ecological modernization that have induced the development of what can be called the environmental sociology of networks and flows.

Networks and flows: environmental reform for the twenty-first century

Via contributions from authors such as Manuel Castells, John Urry, Saskia Sassen and others, the second half of the 1990s witnessed the emergence of what we can now label the sociology of networks and flows. A new sociological perspective, a new social theory or even 'new rules of sociological methods' (Urry, 2003) never emerge with one publication. Crucial in the development of the sociology of networks and flows is the shift from states and societies as central units and concepts of analysis, to networks and flows of capital, people, money, information, images, goods/materials and the like. These networks and flows form the new architectures of a global modernity, according to its proponents. This new sociology is inspiring a change in the agenda of environmental reform studies and perspectives (see Spaargaren et al., 2006).

An environmental sociology of networks and flows

In applying the sociology of networks and flows for understanding twenty-first-century environmental reform, we cannot just rely on the work of Castells, Urry and other general – non-environmental – sociologists/social theorists. Their inclusion of environment in social theory is, at best, marginal (see Mol and Spaargaren, 2006). And, to some extent, this new social theory of networks and flows runs counter to the same frictions environmental sociologists had with earlier social theories (as was so strongly articulated in the HEP–NEP debate – see Dunlap, Chapter 1 in this volume). So, in applying insights from the sociology of networks and flows for a social theory of environmental reform, the sociology of networks and flows has to be combined with earlier environmental reform perspectives, most notably ecological modernization.

Whereas most of the flow literature in the social sciences emphasizes flows of capital, money, images, information and people (travel and migration), and analyses them from perspectives as diverse as economic development, governance and control, cultural diversity or democracy, an environmental sociology of flows focuses on an explicitly environmental interpretation of the flow concept. This environmental interpretation differs in two ways from the sociology of flows: (i) by analysing flows of information, capital, goods and persons from an ecological rationality point of view (by looking at environmental information, green products, green investment funds, sustainable management concepts, environmental certifications schemes, flows of environmental activists, and their ideas etc.); and (ii) by analysing environmental flows as such, that is: energy, water, waste, biodiversity, natural resources, contaminants and the like. Neither Castells nor Urry, nor any of the other social theorists in this tradition, has to date developed an in-depth account of environmental change in either of these two ways.

In relating environment to (global) networks and flows – both in terms of environmental flows as well as in terms of conventional flows – conceptual space for new forms and dynamics of environmental reform is constructed. Castells discusses inequalities and power in relation to the environment primarily in the context of a rather straightforward dichotomy: place-bound environmental movements attempt to resist the omnipotent actors of the space of (economic) flows. The environment or nature enters into Castells's (1996–97) analysis mainly as the traditional 'protest-approach' in environmental sociology (social movements organizing resistance against modernity, as we saw in the first generation of the social sciences of environmental reform). Saskia Sassen (2006) interprets global environmental NGO networks as constructive parts of what she calls the global assemblage. The global environmental movement constructs a new kind of authority, which is part and parcel of the global network society. This comes much closer to an ecological modernization interpretation of networks and flows. In the social theory of networks and flows, environment and environmental protection should be articulated and conceptualized in the space of place as well as in the space of flow. Place-bound environmental resistance and protection by local NGOs and communities are joined by articulation of the environment in international trade, in foreign direct investments, in global certification schemes such as ISO 14 000 or Forest Stewardship Council labels, in transnational company networks, in worldwide epistemic communities (such as those around water or climate change) and so on. By interpreting environment and nature as (also) attached to the 'space of flows' rather than seeing them only or primarily as part of the 'space of place', questions and analyses of environmental governance and reform move beyond a defensive position of only 'blaming' intrusions and infringements of global networks and flows on the environment of local places. The 'space of flows' then becomes a relevant analytical category for protecting and articulating nature and environment, opening up new sets of scapes, networks, nodes and strategies for environmental reform. Using such network and flow perspectives, Presas (2005), Bush and Oosterveer (2007), and Mol (2007) analyse environmental reform with respect to transnational buildings, food and biofuels, respectively.

New conceptualizations: power, inequality and beyond

The social theory of networks and flows changes the way environmental reform is conceptualized and investigated. As an example I shall elaborate on new ideas of power and inequality, as well as mentioning more briefly a few other points.

Within the social theory of networks and flows, power and inequality are no longer only related to ownership of capital, as has been the dominant view in neo-Marxist studies, nor to the state, as was the mainstream conviction in most other schools of thought. In addition to these 'conventional' categories of power and inequality, the sociology of flows defines new inequalities in terms of having access to, being included in or being decoupled from, the key networks and flows. Groups, persons, cities and regions with access to the core flows and located in or close to the central nodes and moorings of global networks, are the wealthy and powerful. Following Rifkin (2000), it is access to the information flows via the Internet, to the flows of monetary capital and to the skills of people moving around the world, that distinguishes the better-off people, groups, cities and regions from their marginalized counterparts. This 'access to' and 'inclusion in' concerns both direct access and inclusion as well as the ability and capability to structure the scapes and infrastructures to partially influence the mobile flows in terms of speed, direction, intensity and so on. Or, as Castells puts it: who has the power and capability to handle the switches between and the programmes of the networks that matter?

In following this analytical path, an environmental sociology of networks and flows perspective has two operationalizations of power and inequality. First, it pays attention to the conditions for access to environmental flows and to the scapes and networks that structure the current of strategic environmental flows. And it analyses in some detail the consequences for groups, actors and organizations to whom access is denied or who do not manage to establish links with the relevant global networks. Such an operationalization would reorient conventional environmental flow studies, which are currently dominated by natural science perspectives on flow (e.g. material flow analysis, industrial ecology), into different directions. It would also enrich present 'additions-and-withdrawals' studies, as power and inequality are being linked to flows in a more direct way. Power is thought to reside in the 'additions and withdrawals' themselves, and not only in the social practices of production and consumption. Second, power and inequality in an environmental sociology of flows perspective would also relate to the flows of capital, information, images and persons that structure, condition and enable environmental reforms. The power and inequalities related to non-environmental and non-material flows affect environmental reform trajectories. Those with access to and in (partial) control of the key economic and informational (Mol, 2008) flows can be said to dominate the new networked world order, at the expense of the place-bound local actors outside the core nodes of the global networks.

The sociology of networks and flows will also challenge our environmental reform ideas and research in other ways. Three deserve mentioning. The sociology of networks and flows blurs the sharp distinction between the social and the material world, between flows of information and money and flows of material substance, between the institutional infrastructure and the technological–material infrastructures. In trying to overcome (or do away with) the dichotomy of the social and the material, Urry goes way beyond the conventional schemes of environmental social scientists, who generally speaking remain comfortable with (1) asserting that social systems should be seen as systems having a material base, and (2) the recognition that material conditions do matter for social practices and institutional developments. Second, the strong separation between the conventional categories of state, market and civil society disappears, in favour of all kinds of new emerging hybrid arrangements in between. Networks and flows, scapes, and sociomaterial infrastructures, none can continue to be understood in terms of state and markets. Hence a new conceptualization invades the social sciences of environmental reform. Finally, ideas of (environmental) governance, management and control drastically change following the sociology of flows. Within Urry's (2003) work this is related to the emergence of complexity and the disappearance of agency, against the background of a strong systems-theoretical framework. How far will environmental reform perspectives for the twenty-first century travel in this direction?

Epilogue
Our theoretical elucidation of third-generation 'social theories' of environmental reform remains far from a systematic, coherent theory. We are only just starting to understand what environmental reform means in a global networked society and how and where such environmental reform processes differ from 'conventional', ecological modernization types of environmental reform. Several of the concepts, ideas and perspectives on environmental reform of the first and second generation will remain valid and useful under conditions of global modernity, where networks and flows seem to become increasingly important constituent parts. But the sociology of networks and flows, in its various forms and variants, suggests that environmental reform – among many other things – will not remain unchanged following globalization dynamics. The elaborations above give us some idea about the lines along which one might start thinking in developing new perspectives or social theories of environmental reform that fit the new social constellation. But much theoretical work and debate lies ahead before a more or less coherent theory of environmental reform in networked global modernity will emerge.

One of the debates in the emerging theoretical and empirical elaborations and discussions will without doubt be related to the necessity of a new theory and the continuing validity of 'conventional' ecological modernization theory. Ecological modernization theory remains to a major extent valid, and so do the – partly revised – policy, protest and attitude theories of the 1970s/1980s. In a considerable number of cases these models will be very helpful in explaining and understanding environmental reform in the twenty-first century. But in a number of cases and contexts – and most likely an increasing number – we are in need of new theories, along the lines of an environmental sociology of networks and flows.

Notes
1. Arguably, this is currently more the case in the USA than in European countries. For a comparison between the developments of US and European environmental sociology (including the position of neo-Marxism), see Mol (2006).
2. Factor 4/10 refers to the idea of being respectively 4 and 10 time as efficient with energy and material resources in producing the same economic output.
3. As Beck explains, 'sub-politics is distinguished from "politics," first in that agents outside the political or corporatist system are allowed to appear on the stage of social design . . ., and second, in that not only social and collective agents but individuals as well compete with the latter and each other for the emerging shaping power of the political' (Beck, 1994: 22).
4. For evaluations and critiques on the idea of ecological modernization as the common denominator of

environmental reform processes starting to emerge in the 1990s, see, for instance, Blowers (1997), Dryzek (1997), Gouldson and Murphy (1997), Blühdorn (2000), Buttel (2000), Mol and Spaargaren (2000), Schnaiberg et al. (2002), and Gibbs (2006).

References

Ajzen, Icek and M. Fishbein (1975), *Belief, Attitude, Intention and Behavior: An Introduction to Theory and Research*, Reading, MA: Addison-Wesley.

Beck, Ulrich (1994), 'The reinvention of politics: towards a theory of reflexive modernisation', in U. Beck, A. Giddens and S. Lash (eds), *Reflexive Modernisation. Politics, Tradition and Aesthetics in the Modern Social Order*, Cambridge, UK: Polity, pp. 1–55.

Blowers, Andy (1997), 'Environmental policy: ecological modernization or the risk society?', *Urban Studies*, **34** (5–6): 845–71.

Blühdorn, Ingolfur (2000), 'Ecological modernisation and post-ecologist politics', in G. Spaargaren, A.P.J. Mol and F. Buttel (eds), *Environment and Global Modernity*, London: Sage, pp. 209–28.

Bush, Simon R. and Peter Oosterveer (2007), 'The missing link: intersecting governance and trade in the space of place and the space of flows', *Sociologia Ruralis*, **47** (4): 384–99.

Buttel, Fredrick H. (2000), 'Ecological modernization as social theory', *Geoforum*, **31** (1): 57–65.

Buttel, Frederick H. (2002), 'Has environmental sociology arrived?', *Organization & Environment*, **15** (1): 42–55.

Buttel, Frederick H. (2003), 'Environmental sociology and the explanation of environmental reform', *Organization & Environment*, **16** (3): 306–44.

Carolan, Michael (2004), 'Ecological modernization: what about consumption?', *Society and Natural Resources*, **17** (3): 247–60.

Castells, Manuel (1996), *The Information Age: Economy, Society and Culture*, Volumes I, II and III, Malden, MA and Oxford: Blackwell.

Catton, William R. and Riley E. Dunlap (1978a), 'Environmental sociology: A new paradigm', *The American Sociologist*, **13**: 41–9.

Catton, William R. and Riley E. Dunlap (1978b), 'Paradigms, theories, and the primacy of the HEP–NEP distinction', *The American Sociologist*, **13**: 256–9.

Cohen, Maurie and Joseph Murphy (eds) (2001), *Exploring Sustainable Consumption. Environmental Policy and the Social Sciences*, New York: Elsevier.

Dryzek, John S. (1997), *The Politics of the Earth: Environmental Discourses*, Oxford: Oxford University Press.

Eisner, Marc A. (2004), 'Corporate environmentalism, regulatory reform, and industry self-regulation: toward genuine regulatory reinvention in the United States', *Governance: An International Journal of Policy, Administration, and Institutions*, **17** (2): 145–67.

Frankel, B. (1987), *The Post-Industrial Utopians*, Cambridge: Polity.

Gibbs, David (2006), 'Prospects for an environmental economic geography: linking ecological modernisation and regulationist approaches', *Economic Geography*, **82** (2): 193–215.

Giddens, Anthony (1994), *Beyond Left and Right: The Future of Radical Politics*, Cambridge, UK: Polity.

Gouldson, Andy and Joseph Murphy (1997), 'Ecological modernization: economic restructuring and the environment', *The Political Quarterly*, **68** (5): 74–86.

Jackson, Tim (ed.) (2006), *The Earthscan Reader in Sustainable Consumption*, London: Earthscan.

Jänicke, Martin (1986), *Staatsversagen: Die Ohnmacht der Politik in die Industriegesellschaft*, Munich: Piper (translated as *State Failure. The Impotence of Politics in Industrial Society*, Cambridge, UK: Polity, 1990).

Jänicke, Martin (1993), 'Über ökologische und politieke Modernisierungen', *Zeitschrift für Umweltpolitik und Umweltrecht*, **2**: 159–75.

Klandermans, Bert (1986), 'New social movements and resource mobilization: the European and the American approach', *International Journal of Mass Emergencies and Disaster*, **4** (2): 13–39.

McCarthy, John D. and Mayer N. Zald (1977), 'Resource mobilization and social movements: a partial theory', *American Journal of Sociology*, **82** (May): 1212–39.

Mol, Arthur P.J. (1995), *The Refinement of Production: Ecological Modernization Theory and the Chemical Industry*, Utrecht: International Books.

Mol, Arthur P.J. (2000), 'The environmental movement in an age of ecological modernisation', *Geoforum*, **31** (1): 45–56.

Mol, Arthur P.J. (2006), 'From environmental sociologies to environmental sociology? A comparison of U.S. and European environmental sociology', *Organization & Environment*, **19** (1): 5–27.

Mol, Arthur P.J. (2007), 'Boundless biofuels? Between vulnerability and environmental sustainability', *Sociologia Ruralis*, **47** (4): 297–315.

Mol, Arthur P.J. (2008*)*, *Environmental Reform in the Information Age. The Contours of Informational Governance*, Cambridge, UK: Cambridge University Press.

Mol, Arthur P.J. and Gert Spaargaren (2000), 'Ecological modernization theory in debate: a review', *Environmental Politics*, **9** (1), 17–49.

Mol, Arthur P.J. and Gert Spaargaren (2006), 'Towards a sociology of environmental flows: a new agenda for twenty-first-century environmental sociology', in G. Spaargaren, A.P.J. Mol and F.H. Buttel (eds), *Governing Environmental Flows: Global Challenges for Social Theory*, Cambridge, MA: MIT Press, pp. 39–83.

Offe, Claus (1985) 'New social movements: challenging the boundaries of institutional politics', *Social Research*, **52** (4): 817–68.

Presas, Luciana M. (2005), *Transnational Buildings in Local Environments*, Aldershot. UK: Ashgate.

Rifkin, Jeremy (2000), *The Age of Access. How the Shift from Ownership to Access is Transforming Modern Life*, London: Penguin.

Sassen, Saskia (2006), *Territory, Authority, Rights: From Medieval to Global Assemblages*, Princeton, NJ and Oxford: Princeton University Press.

Schnaiberg, Allan (1980), *The Environment: From Surplus to Scarcity*, Oxford and New York: Oxford University Press.

Schnaiberg, Allan, Adam S. Weinberg and David N. Pellow (2002), 'The treadmill of production and the environmental state', in A.P.J. Mol and F.H. Buttel (eds), *The Environmental State under Pressure*, London: JAI/Elsevier, pp. 15–32.

Sonnenfeld, David A. and Arthur P.J. Mol (2006), 'Environmental reform in Asia: comparisons, challenges, next steps', *Journal of Environment and Development*, **15** (2): 112–37.

Spaargaren, Gert (1997), *The Ecological Modernisation of Production and Consumption: Essays in Environmental Sociology*, Wageningen: Wageningen Agricultural University (PhD dissertation).

Spaargaren, Gert (2003), 'Sustainable consumption: a theoretical and environmental policy perspective', *Society and Natural Resources*, **16** (8), 687–702.

Spaargaren, Gert and Arthur P.J. Mol (2008), 'Greening global consumption: redefining politics and authority', *Global Environmental Change*, **18** (3): 350–59.

Spaargaren, Gert, Arthur P.J. Mol and Frederick H. Buttel (eds) (2006), *Governing Environmental Flows: Global Challenges for Social Theory*, Cambridge, MA: MIT Press.

Urry, John (2003), *Global Complexity*, Cambridge, UK: Polity.

Zald, Mayer N. and John D. McCarthy (1979), *The Dynamics of Social Movements: Resource Mobilization, Social Control and Tactics*, Cambridge, UK: Winthrop.

Zhang, Lei, Arthur P.J. Mol and David A. Sonnenfeld (2007), 'The interpretation of ecological modernization in China', *Environmental Politics*, **16** (4): 659–68.

5 Ecological modernization theory: theoretical and empirical challenges

Richard York, Eugene A. Rosa and Thomas Dietz

Introduction

There is little doubt that, over the past two centuries, 'modernization' – generally taken to mean the combined effects of industrialization (and more recently 'post-industrialization'), economic growth, the expansion of markets, urbanization, globalization, and the acceleration of scientific and technological development – has generated environmental problems that are unique in human history in their scale, type and diversity. Despite the consensus that modernization has historically led to detrimental environmental consequences, there is considerable disagreement about the contemporary and likely future environmental consequences of the modernization project. Although there is a striking diversity of views on this matter, this diversity of opinion can be usefully divided into two opposing perspectives. On one side, there are those who see the modernization project as anti-ecological to its core and, thus, incapable of being transformed along sustainable lines. Scholars of this theoretical opinion argue that the achievement of environmental sustainability requires fundamental changes to the social order and an abandonment of the modernization project as typically conceived or at least major aspects of it, such as the system of capitalism or the pursuit of economic growth. On the other side are those who see the modernization project as adaptable and capable of becoming ecologically sustainable. In fact, some go so far as to claim that not only is the modernization project not anti-ecological at its core; it is especially well equipped to deal with ecological crises and, therefore, its continuation is the best, and perhaps only, way to achieve sustainability. This summary of the contrast is perhaps more oppositional than the actual distinctions in the literature, but it does capture the flavor of most debates in a way that is useful for exposition.

The view that modernization can solve environmental problems is associated with 'ecological modernization theory' (EMT), which rose to prominence in the 1990s offering critiques of the neo-Marxian and human ecological traditions that were central to the field of environmental sociology (see Mol, Chapter 4 in Part I of this volume). Here we critically review the major theoretical features and research practices of EMT and examine empirical assessments of the effects of modernization on the environment. We argue that while some aspects of the EMT research program have been quite successful, one major claim of EMT – that modernization processes are leading to environmental sustainability – is flawed, and that a substantial redirection of research will be necessary to address this issue.

Ecological modernization theory in the context of environmental sociology

From its inception, environmental sociology was defined by its critique of the modernization project and its challenge to the techno-optimism and anthropocentrism that dominated Western societies and many other societies around the world (Catton and Dunlap, 1978; Dunlap, 1997 and Chapter 1 in this volume). Schnaiberg's (1980) influential 'treadmill of production' theory, as well as Anderson's (1976) and subsequent neo-Marxian analyses, argued that environmental degradation was an inherent feature of modernization. World systems theory (WST) broadened the neo-Marxist approach by delineating the historical emergence of capitalism to its current position of world dominance and driver of economic processes around the globe (Jorgenson, 2005, 2006; Wallerstein, 2004).

These theories offered a political–economic critique of elite-dominated, growth-dependent economic systems, particularly capitalism. They argued that ecological stability required a shift away from the dominant political, social and economic order. Otherwise, the dominant forms of economic structure, due to a self-reinforcing dynamic of growth, all but guaranteed continued ecological degradation. While this line of theorizing has been elaborated and has generated a substantial empirical literature, the principal focus has remained on critiquing the ecologically destructive institutions and practices associated with various aspects of modernity: capitalism, globalization, industrialism, economic growth, militarization, unequal trade relations and an inequitable distribution of impacts (Bunker, 1984; Clark and York, 2005; Dietz and Rosa, 1994, 1997; Dietz et al., 2007; Foster, 1992, 2002; Jorgenson, 2005, 2006; Jorgenson and Burns, 2007; Moore, 2003; O'Connor, 1994; Pellow, 2000; Rosa et al., 2004; Taylor, 2000; York, 2008; York et al., 2003a, 2003b, 2003c).

EMT has an alternative perspective to that of the foundational environmental sociology tradition and its critique of modernization (Mol and Spaargaren, 2000). EMT's early beginnings are traceable to German theorists Martin Jänicke and Josef Huber (for a discussion of EMT's origins, see Spaargaren and Mol, 1992; Mol and Spaargaren, 2000); however, it began its ascent to prominence in sociology (particularly American sociology) only in the 1990s with the work of Dutch scholars Gert Spaargaren and Arthur Mol (1992). Mol and leading American EM theorist David Sonnenfeld claim 'the aim of Ecological Modernization Theory has been to analyze how contemporary industrialized societies deal with environmental crises' (2000b: 5). However, EMT is defined not only by its domain of study, but also by its theoretical commitments. EM theorists reject human ecology and Marxian critiques of capitalism (Mol and Spaargaren, 2000). Mol (1995: 42) clearly articulates one of the key assumptions of EMT, when he asserts 'that the only possible way *out* of the ecological crisis is by going further *into* the process of modernization' (italics in original) (see also Mol, 1996: 305; Spaargaren and Mol, 1992: 336). Similarly, Spaargaren (1997: 25) declares 'the environmental crisis can and should be overcome by a further modernization of the existing institutions of modern society' (see also p. 169).

A key argument of EMT is that 'ecological rationality' will percolate through all aspects of society as modernity matures (Mol, 1995, 2001). For EM theorists, reflexivity is a key feature of late modernity – as it is for other European theorists such as Beck (1999), Giddens (1990) and Lash (1994). Modern societies are prone to critical and rational self-examination – driven in part by social movements, but also by non-movement NGOs and actors within government, business and the scientific establishment – with the capacity to rectify problems identified through this process. EM theorists argue that while the early stages of modernization were dominated by economic rationality, as the modernization project progressed new forms of rationality began to emerge, whereby ecological concerns increasingly received equal standing with economic ones. Through this process, ecological value is expected to be incorporated into economic choices, while economic valuation is simultaneously applied to ecological impacts. Central to EMT is the proposition that the institutions of modernity, including multinational corporations and governments, acting in their own self-interest for long-term survival, increasingly place ecological concerns center stage. EMT argues that these transformations lead to widespread ecological reforms, without requiring radical social or political–economic change (Mol and Spaargaren 2000, 2005). EM theorists further assert 'all major, fundamental alternatives to the present economic order have proved infeasible according to various (economic, environmental, and social) criteria' (Mol and Spaargaren, 2000: 23), and, therefore, efforts to achieve sustainability should focus on working toward further modernizing the institutions of modernity rather than seeking to replace them.

EMT has a number of engaging features worthy of serious consideration and elaboration. The geographical and case study reach of EMT studies has been expansive and the range of organizations and institutions covered in these studies is impressive (see, e.g., Mol and Sonnenfeld, 2000a; Spaargaren et al., 2006). Given the inherently pessimistic context of the alarms about environmental crisis in early environmental sociology, EMT provided a valuable counterpoint to assure the vitality of intellectual discourse that a dialectic brings. In our view, the importance of the role of dialectic in ensuring intellectual vitality cannot be overstated. Therefore, although we are critical of EMT, we think it is important to recognize the genuine contribution it has made to the field of environmental sociology. One purpose of our analysis is to differentiate what EMT has accomplished from where EMT has, in our view, fallen short as a theory of contemporary environmental change.

It may be helpful to think about three different aspects of the EMT approach. One is an emphasis on the *process* by which modern societies respond to environmental problems. In our view, this has been the most important contribution of EMT. Discussions of reflexive modernization have promoted thinking about how change in environmental policy and practices occurs. The rich body of case studies describing the history of specific firms, industries and governments is a strength of the EMT research programme. This empirical work also provides strong evidence in support of a second aspect of EMT. EMT provides a counterpoint to the more macro approach of neo-Marxian theories, particularly world systems theory (WST) and the treadmill, and the tendency of these theories to underemphasize the substantial variance in the behaviour of firms, industries and governments. Macro theories emphasize economy-wide processes, including feedback loops – the metaphorical forest. In doing so, they are sometimes not attentive to the many examples of successful environmental reform on a more micro scale and, therefore, miss the metaphorical trees. The EMT literature documents cases where environmental reforms have occurred. This encourages sociological work on environmental policy and practices to pay more attention to the variability in what firms, industries and governments do, and to explain that variability.

EMT's third aspect is the argument that modern, affluent, mostly capitalist societies can achieve sustainability and that there is indeed evidence of a broad trend in this direction around the world (Mol, 1995, 2001; Mol and Spaargaren, 2000). This aspect is the locus of our critique. We present some key challenges to EMT in an attempt to further our understanding of the forces driving environmental problems and to refine social scientific analyses of societal–environmental interactions. EMT claims that modern societies are prone to transformations that lead to environmental sustainability and that no radical change to the social, political and economic order is necessary to overcome the modern environmental crisis. Our focus here, then, is on assessing the validity of claims that modernization is a *general* process of environmental amelioration, even as we acknowledge the contribution of the EMT tradition in identifying examples of environmental reform and tracing the processes where it has occurred.

Epistemological and methodological challenges

As noted above, the bulk of EMT work comprises case studies focused on various institutions, organizations and governmental bodies. This is a wholly appropriate repertoire of methods for demonstrating that moves toward sustainability have occurred in specific firms, industries and governments, and for tracing the processes by which these changes have occurred. However, this methodology is insufficient to address another aspect of EMT: the argument that modernization processes tend to contribute to general societal changes that ultimately make modern societies more sustainable. As for this latter claim, what separates EM theorists from many of their critics is not simply disagreement about particular trends or specific theoretical positions, but a bedrock difference in epistemological approach.

As Dunlap and Marshall (2007: 339) have noted, EMT takes an epistemological stance that is at odds with some of the traditions of science. EM theorists, as is generally true of sociological theory in the European style, are skeptical of the application of the rigorous (particularly quantitative) empirical procedures of science to understanding the connection between modernization and environmental crisis, preferring qualitative interpretive approaches (see Dunlap, Chapter 1 in this Volume). Mol and Spaargaren (2005: 94–5), for example, criticize the use of quantitative methods and hypothesis-testing to assess the effect of modernization on the environment and declare 'the limitations of empirical studies in closing larger theoretical debates' (p. 94). Furthermore, they argue against relying on 'natural science "empirical facts"' and using mathematics in analyses of the environmental consequences of modernization processes (Mol and Spaargaren, 2004: 262). Although the interpretative approach preferred by EM scholars is appropriate for many sociological questions, particularly those addressing human meaning, debates about the environmental consequences of modernization are fundamentally about material issues. Questions about material conditions and processes can only reliably be answered with rigorous analyses of empirical evidence based on measurement of these conditions and processes. Hence we contend that it is necessary to take a scientific approach to assessing the effects of modernization on the environment.

The diversity of processes occurring in modern societies makes it difficult to characterize the net effects of modernization on the environment by focusing on a few successful examples, as is done in the case study approach (e.g. Mol, 1995; Sonnenfeld, 1998; Spaargaren et al., 2006). Since the social world is so diverse, typically there is a vast number of confirming (and disconfirming) examples to select from for any particular general claim. The key issue for nomothetic theories is the *relative dominance* of hypothesized processes or outcomes, not whether they occur at all. As we have pointed out elsewhere (York and Rosa, 2003), if one wanted to argue that smoking is not bad for human health, one could point to people who smoke heavily but live to a ripe old age. However, such an observation does not mean that smoking is not harmful to human health, since the overwhelming evidence indicates that smoking shortens the *average* lifespan of smokers – i.e. the effect of smoking on human health is clearly apparent when one compares the life expectancy of smokers to that of non-smokers. Likewise, pointing to specific instances of ecological reform in any particular modern institution is far from sufficient to demonstrate that modernization is a route to sustainability in general.

The *typical outcome and overall effects* of modernization are at the heart of debates between EM theorists and their critics, not whether an example of any particular claim can be found. While defending EMT from disconfirming empirical evidence about the tendency of modern societies to promote environmental degradation rather than reform, Mol and Spaargaren challenge the Popperian view of science, asserting: 'the black swan is never the falsification' (2005: 94) – a challenge to the oft-noted point in the hypothetico-deductive tradition that one black swan falsifies the claim that 'all swans are white'.[1] However, since the contested issue is not about whether there are metaphorical black swans at all but rather about the *relative frequency* of black and white swans, Mol and Spaargaren's comment misses the locus of disagreement between EMT and its critics. The most rigorous empirical critiques of EMT have not focused on single observations that contradict EMT (i.e. identifying individual black swans), but focused instead on the general pattern of environmental consequences stemming from modernization (i.e. the relative frequency of black swans) (York and Rosa, 2003). This is the proper framing in a world of stochastic processes. Thus, to assess nomothetic theories in a scientific manner there need to be systematic analyses of data that can detect general patterns, rather than seeking particular examples (or counter-examples) of any hypothesized process or outcome.

Conceptual challenges

Modernity and non-modernity

EM theorists have seldom systematically compared 'modern' societies to other types of societies. This is puzzling since EMT is inherently a process-based or evolutionary framework. Under such conditions historical comparison is a key analytic strategy, especially effective when there is substantial variability in the objects to be compared. It is unclear whether the features of modern societies that theoretically lead to the amelioration of environmental problems are indeed unique to modernity. For example, one assumption of EMT is that modern societies are especially capable of identifying and addressing environmental problems due to the sophistication of science and technology that comes with modernization (Cohen, 1997, 1998).

However, Diamond (2005) has presented several historical examples of past societies that effectively identified and addressed environmental problems even though they did not have 'modern' institutions or sophisticated technologies. Thus, in addition to the question of whether modern societies entrain a dynamic that generates environmental crises, it is important to add the question of whether modern societies are more or less prone than other societies to identify and address environmental problems. Demonstrating that modern societies recognize and address some environmental problems does not demonstrate that this is due to modernity itself. It is important to assess the extent to which environmental reforms are *driven by modernity* rather than simply *occurring in modernity*; being driven by processes that are not particular to modernity (or even that run counter to modernity). While EMT tends to assume that reforms that *occur in* modernity are *driven by* modernity, there is generally insufficient evidence to justify this assumption.

Real or symbolic reform

EMT generally argues that changes within existing institutions and the development of new institutions for purposes of protecting the environment are effective vehicles for achieving sustainability. It is important to keep in mind, however, that institutional change is merely a means to an end, not an end in itself. Hence it is crucial to examine critically the extent to which institutional changes aimed at addressing environmental problems are effective at doing so.[2] It is often the case that acts of government serve symbolic purposes, rather than the purported goals that promoted the acts. This could explain why the nations with the most developed environmental institutions are often the ones that have the greatest impacts on the environment. We have referred to the inappropriate assumption that institutions are effective at solving the problems they are intended to address as the 'death penalty fallacy' in reference to the fact that in the USA the death penalty is often justified on the belief that it deters crime, when in fact there is no compelling evidence that the death penalty does deter crime (York and Rosa, 2003). Further, it is important to distinguish between the reactions to or symptoms of a problem and genuine solutions to that problem. For example, as York (2004) points out, the growing availability of diet foods in the USA appears to be more a symptom of increases in obesity than an effective countermeasure. Similarly, the death penalty may be a symptom of the prevalence of crime, not a factor that serves to reduce crime. Likewise, many changes in institutional form that appear as a reaction to environmental problems may be symptoms of those problems rather than solutions to them. Thus it is imperative that we assess the effectiveness of political actions and institutional changes, rather than seeing them as confirming indicators of EMT in and of themselves.

Context

The focus of EMT on specific organizations or industries – such as the Dutch chemical industry (Mol, 1995) and the Thai pulp and paper industry (Sonnenfeld, 1998) – is both a strength and a weakness. It is a strength in showing that some reforms do take place and in providing a detailed understanding of those reforms. However, as we have noted, this approach cannot establish the larger claim that ecological modernization processes are moving societies toward sustainability in general. Since organizations and industries exist in larger contexts that they not only affect but also, in turn, are affected by, the full consequences of changes in organizations and industries must be assessed by examining these larger contexts. For example, one of the central arguments of critical political economists (Anderson, 1976; Foster, 1992; O'Connor, 1994; Schnaiberg, 1980) is that capitalism is the driving force behind environmental problems. Thus the emergence of so-called 'green' industries (e.g. ecotourism, recycled products) and businesses should not be taken uncritically as an indication of ecological reform, since the capital that these businesses generate can be invested anywhere in the economy. The effects of profits from a green business may be to expand resource consumption and waste production in other sectors of the economy as profits filter through the economy.[3] To capture these counter-vailing forces, as political economists have long recognized, the observed processes must be situated in the larger economic system.

The nation-state equivalent of this problem has been called the 'Netherlands fallacy', in recognition of the fact that small, affluent nations like the Netherlands can have high population densities and high levels of consumption without entirely spoiling their own environments because they import resources from elsewhere (Ehrlich and Holdren, 1971). They thus shift their environmental impacts beyond their own borders. Furthermore, just as industries and organizations are embedded in larger economic systems, nations, world systems theory reminds us, are embedded in a larger world system through which resources and wastes flow (Bunker, 1984; Frey, 1994, 1998; Jorgenson and Burns, 2007; York et al., 2003a). Wealthy, powerful nations, through unequal trade relations, can externalize their environmental impacts, making it necessary to track the flow of resources and wastes in the global economy. In the modern world system, poor nations are exploited by rich ones. Natural resources are often extracted from poor nations and exported to affluent nations, leaving behind environmental degradation (e.g. deforesta-tion) (Bunker, 1984). Likewise, hazardous industries and toxic waste are increasingly relocated from rich to poor nations (Frey, 1994, 1998). Therefore, if we want to know whether EMT has a valid purchase on the environmental consequences of modernity we need to look at larger economic and political contexts and the global structure of power, trade and environmental flows, rather than looking only at individual organizations, industries or even nation-states (Clark and York, 2005; York and Rosa, 2003).

Some work by EM theorists (e.g. Mol, 2001) examines the larger picture that world systems theorists have long emphasized, but without the critical lens of politi-cal economy. EM theorists have also recently addressed environmental flows (Mol and Spaargaren, 2005; Spaargaren et al., 2006) – a longstanding interest among world systems theorists (e.g. Bunker, 1984; Frey, 1994, 1998), ecologists (Ehrlich and Holdren, 1971; Wackernagel and Rees, 1996), and social metabolism[4] scholars (Fischer-Kowalski and Weisz, 1999; Weisz et al., 2006; Krausmann et al., 2007; Haberl et al., 2007). The flows perspective has led to a more specific focus on global processes and their dynamic interactions. However, the retention of the case study approach does not allow an overall assessment of the trajectory of modernization.

Efficiency
A key part of EMT logic rests on the assertion that economies and technologies can be transformed in a way that allows for growth in material affluence while improving envi-ronmental quality (Carolan, 2004; Mol and Spaargaren, 2004). Cohen (1997: 109) notes, 'a key element in executing this transformation is a switchover to the use of cleaner, more efficient, and less resource intensive technologies. . .'. Similarly, EM proponents Milanez and Bührs (2007: 572) and Fisher and Freudenberg (2001: 702) concur that technological innovation is the 'linchpin' of the EM argument. EMT, thus, is based on the important assumption that improvements in technology and eco-efficiency can lead to the demateri-alization of production (Carolan, 2004; Mol, 1995: 37–40, 2001: 47–8, 56; Spaargaren and Mol, 1992: 335), although some EM supporters, spurred by earlier critiques (York and Rosa, 2003), have come to acknowledge that eco-efficiency may be a misleading indicator of environmental improvements (Sonnenfeld and Mol, 2006). Nonetheless,

measures of eco-efficiency – i.e. economic production (typically measured as GDP) relative to resource consumption (e.g. energy), pollution emissions (e.g. carbon dioxide), or other indicators of environmental impact – have been used by EM adherents in support of EMT predictions. For example, Andersen (2002: 1404) writes, 'Because ecological modernization by definition is linked with cleaner technology and structural change . . . we can take changes in the CO_2 emissions relative to GDP as a rough indicator for the degree of ecological modernization that has taken place.'

The basic problem with a focus on economic eco-efficiency is that efficiency is a measure of what is gained economically per unit of environmental impact, not an account of the scale of environmental impact.[5] Efficiency often increases in tandem with total resource consumption and pollution emissions (Carolan, 2004; York and Rosa, 2003). This observation can be traced to the writings of William Stanley Jevons ([1865] 2001; see also Clark and Foster, 2001), who, in the nineteenth century, noted that as the efficiency of coal use in industry improved (i.e. more output per unit of coal consumed), the total amount of coal consumed *increased*. This has become known as the Jevons paradox, since one may expect consumption to decrease when efficiency increases because as a point of definition *all else being equal* (particularly scale remaining constant) greater efficiency in resource use leads to a lower rate of resource use. However, increases in efficiency of production make the use of coal (or another resource) more cost-effective for producers, who often respond to the increased efficiency by increasing the scale of production. Thus, if production increases faster than efficiency improves, total consumption increases and we observe the outcome characterized by the Jevons paradox. (In the next section, we shall discuss empirical work assessing the extent to which the Jevons paradox applies to large-scale economic processes.)

Similar to the Jevons paradox is what might be called the 'paperless office paradox' (York, 2006), a reference to the fact that the growth of electronic media has been associated with increasing, rather than declining, paper consumption. This observation suggests that the development of substitutes for a particular resource may not necessarily lead to conservation of that resource. This is particularly important in light of the fact that many technological substitutes – e.g. solar and wind power as substitutes for fossil fuels – are proposed to help overcome some environmental problems. However, the key question is whether these substitutes actually displace consumption of other resources, add to them, or increase them through dynamic processes, such as apparently happened with electronic media and paper consumption. Since EMT in some respects depends on the idea that technological changes can help overcome environmental problems without radical changes to the structure of the economy, the argument rests on the extent to which improvements in efficiency and the development of substitutes for various types of resources actually lead to reductions in resource consumption and pollution emissions.

Empirical challenges

Results of other research programmes
Our focus to this point has been on problems with the methodological approaches and conceptualizations used by EM theorists, especially in connection with EMT's claim that modernization is leading to more environmentally sustainable societies. Addressing this claim requires systematic analysis of the connections between key aspects of modernity,

such as economic growth and urbanization, and predicted environmental benefits. Thus, while EM theorists have provided an insightful summary about the social, cultural and institutional changes occurring in modern societies, the pivotal question is about the *ecological* consequences of those modernizing processes.

While this topic has not been much addressed by EM theorists, a growing body of quantitative cross-national empirical research in sociology and related fields has examined the extent to which macrostructural characteristics of modernization, particularly economic development and urbanization, are connected with environmental degradation. Questions about EM are related to a major debate in economics and elsewhere over the environmental Kuznets curve (EKC). The EKC predicts that environmental problems increase at early stages of development but eventually reach a turning point, after which further development corresponds with a decline in environmental problems (Dinda, 2004). Empirically the EKC appears as an inverted U-shaped curve when environmental impacts are plotted against affluence (typically measured as GDP per capita). The finding of an EKC is commonly taken to indicate that modernization, at least to the extent that it is connected with economic growth, facilitates environmental reform, or at the very least is not intrinsically incompatible with it.[6] So, a question of central importance is: what are the typical consequences of economic growth for the environment? Does economic growth consistently lead to an escalation in environmental impacts or does it in developed societies lead to declines in impacts?

Our own extensive STIRPAT[7] empirical research program addressed this question as one of its central tasks (see http://www.stirpat.org). We have examined the connection between economic growth (as indicated by GDP per capita) and a variety of environmental impacts using cross-national data. One indicator of environmental impact that we have found particularly important is the 'ecological footprint', which is a comprehensive hypothetical estimate of the land area required to support a society's consumption of resources and production of wastes (Wackernagel and Rees, 1996). Using the footprint helps to overcome some of the analytical challenges we noted above. Since the footprint is based upon a society's consumption of resources and production of waste without regard to where the resources are extracted or the wastes deposited, it avoids the Netherlands fallacy. So, for example, if forests are logged in Indonesia to extract wood that is consumed in Japan, this impact is included as part of Japan's footprint, not Indonesia's. The footprint is also helpful because it combines a variety of impacts – forest use, agriculture, urban growth etc. – into a single measure (all converted to land area), and therefore takes account of tradeoffs among different types of impact – e.g. a shift from extracting fiber from wild forests to producing it on agricultural land. This feature helps avoid being misled by shifts in the types of resources used.

Our research consistently has found a clear positive association between economic growth and the ecological footprint of nations, and no sign of a realistic EKC, indicating that economic growth is consistently associated with environmental degradation (Dietz et al., 2007; Rosa et al., 2004; York et al., 2003a). This clearly suggests that the diffusion of economic modernization around the world has led to increases, not decreases, in environmental problems. We have also assessed a variety of other measures of environmental impact, including carbon dioxide (CO_2) emissions and methane (CH_4) emissions, the primary greenhouse gases, and found that they consistently increase with economic growth (Rosa et al., 2004; York, 2008; York et al., 2003b, 2003c). Other scholars have had similar findings, indicating that economic development is not an ameliorative as predicted by EMT, but a key driving force behind global environmental impacts (Cole and Neumayer, 2004; Jorgenson, 2005, 2006; Jorgenson and Burns, 2007; Shi, 2003).[8]

It has also been suggested that urbanization may be, for some purposes, a better indicator of modernization than economic growth, since urbanization is linked with many of the institutions that EMT identifies as important and since the locus of economic activity is in urban centers (Ehrhardt-Martinez, 1998; Ehrhardt-Martinez et al., 2002). Our STIRPAT assessments have found that urbanization is consistently linked with larger ecological footprints, CO_2 emissions and CH_4 emissions (York, 2008; York et al., 2003a, 2003b, 2003c). Therefore two major features of modernization at the nation-state level, economic development (as measured by GDP per capita) and urbanization, do not conform to the predictions of EMT or its economic representation, the EKC. Instead, these processes are clearly linked with environmental degradation, and there is little support for the argument that there is an EKC for global impact measures.[9]

We have also empirically analyzed the connection between eco-efficiency and environmental degradation to assess whether the Jevons paradox applies as a general phenomenon at the nation-state level (York et al., 2004). We found that while the ecological intensity of production (ecological footprint per unit of GDP) is typically lowest in the most affluent nations, indicating that efficiency does improve with modernization, the decline in intensity is insufficient to counteract the increases in overall production. Therefore the richest nations have the most eco-efficient economies while simultaneously consuming the greatest amount of resources and producing the most waste. This finding challenges the belief that efficiency leads to resource conservation in the aggregate.

Conclusions

It is clear that EMT offers a range of attractive metatheoretical, theoretical and policy features, from abstract macrosocietal and global issues to connections to other approaches to sustainability otherwise uninformed by sociological knowledge. It has also launched a variety of creative ideas that has stimulated a large and growing body of research – as well as attracting a generous volume of critical response. However, the evidence reviewed cautions against accepting the promises of ecological modernization uncritically.

Efficacy

The main purpose of our critique of EMT is to refine social scientific analysis of environmental problems so that effective solutions to the modern environmental crisis can be found. By outlining problems with EMT we do not mean to suggest that other theories are problem-free, since, in fact, other theoretical approaches may share many of the same problems as EMT or have their own particular limitations. However, a critical approach to EMT is important because of EMT's growing sociological popularity and its potential motivation toward complacency: like the environmental Kuznets curve, EMT can be interpreted as indicating that the trends present in modern societies are leading to sustainability. Whatever EMT's architects intended, it is easy to see the theory as suggesting that the continued expansion of the global economy and its concomitant structural changes are sufficient for solving environmental problems. The unintended consequence could be to put serious efforts aimed at environmental protection on the 'back burner' in favor of policies aimed at enhancing globalization and economic growth. We believe the weight of empirical evidence suggests that modernization and economic growth lead to environmental degradation. It appears unlikely that we can overcome the modern ecological crisis without acknowledging the basic conflict between trajectories of population and economic growth and environmental sustainability. Although we are optimistic that sustainability can be achieved, the key question is whether it can be accomplished without a reorganization of the current political–economic structure, including a redefinition of well-being away from narrow economic measures (Dietz et al., 2009). Therefore we argue for the development of an alternative perspective that recognizes that fundamental environmental reform requires political–economic changes, not simply institutional, cultural, technological and behavioral ones.

We find two fundamental problems with EMT. First, its purchase is not directly ecological. With its focus on institutional change, there is too little attention given to actual environmental change. Second, while it has documented interesting and important cases of environmental reform, the argument that contemporary processes of reflexive modernization are leading to increased sustainability in the aggregate is not consistent with a large body of empirical evidence.

Our suggestion that sustainability is unlikely to occur as EM theorists predict does not necessitate the abandonment of EMT's embedded concern with human well-being and with processes of environmental reform. Indeed, it is quite likely that improving human well-being is contingent on progress toward sustainability. Our own research has shown that while economic measures of modernization are connected to environmental degradation, there is no direct link between human well-being, as indicated by measures such as life expectancy and education, and environmental degradation (Dietz et al., 2007, 2009). Furthermore, the link between economic growth and both 'objective' (Mazur and Rosa, 1974) and subjective well-being is weak, except in the poorest nations (Leiserowitz et al., 2005). While the modernization project as typically practiced may need to be fundamentally reformed or even abandoned in order to achieve sustainability, there is no necessary conflict between achieving human well-being and environmental sustainability. What is needed is a move toward a deliberative process of integrating human and ecological well-being – a change called for by Dewey (1923) and Habermas (1970) that is well suited to addressing the challenges of modern risks and sustainability (Rosa et al., 2008). However, moves toward more effective deliberative decision making are not a natural outcome of modernization but the result of structural change. The crucial question that remains for EMT and its competing theories is this: how can the world economic and political structure be changed to be fully responsive to the challenges of sustainability?

Acknowledgment

We thank Rachel Shwom for her insightful discussion of the topics we address.

Notes

1. It is of course logically correct that the definitive existence of one black swan falsifies the claim that 'all swans are white'. However, we take Mol and Spaargaren's point to be the fully valid one that few theories, at least in the social sciences, are of an absolutist and deterministic nature, and, therefore, single disconfirming observations do not undermine most theories.
2. This is a point that some EM supporters (Milanez and Bührs, 2007: 569) have recently acknowledged, although much of EMT work continues to focus on institutional change and to neglect environmental consequences.

3. It is also important to note that 'green' businesses, industries or programs are not necessarily environmentally sound. See Pellow et al. (2000) for an example of this with recycling efforts.
4. Although EM theorists are now examining flows, they have not yet engaged this research program with its long and distinguished track record.
5. Eco-efficiency has also been entrained in policy debates. In the USA the second Bush Administration promulgated climate change policy with goals based on 'greenhouse gas intensity' (the reciprocal of efficiency), thus avoiding focusing on total greenhouse gas emissions (which are what matters for the global climate) in favor of focusing on how much GDP is generated per unit of emissions (President George W. Bush, speech on 16 April 2008, accessed 22 September 2008 at http://www.cfr.org/publication/16043/).
6. Although EM theorists are aware of the EKC literature (see Mol, 2001), they apparently do not recognize it as a functional representation of some of the core propositions of EMT.
7. STochastic estimation of Impacts by Regression on Population, Affluence and Technology.
8. Contrary to this finding, Fisher and Freudenberg (2004) conclude that economic growth is not consistently linked with carbon dioxide emissions, but their analysis has serious methodological flaws (York and Rosa, 2005).
9. There is some evidence that urbanization ameliorates deforestation within nations (Ehrhardt-Martinez, 1998; Ehrhardt-Martinez et al., 2002). However, since a substantial portion of forest products are traded internationally, reductions in deforestation in one nation may be the result of increased deforestation in another. Rudel (2005) offers a nuanced analysis showing how the drivers of forest change interact with each other and differ across world regions.

References

Andersen, M.S. (2002), 'Ecological modernization or subversion? The effects of Europeanization on Eastern Europe', *American Behavioral Scientist*, **45** (9): 1394–416.
Anderson, C.H. (1976), *The Sociology of Survival: Social Problems of Growth*, Homewood, IL: Dorsey Press.
Beck, U. (1999), *World Risk Society*, Cambridge UK: Polity Press.
Bunker, S.G. (1984), 'Modes of extraction, unequal exchange and the progressive underdevelopment of an extreme periphery: the Brazilian Amazon, 1600–1980', *American Journal of Sociology*, **89**: 1017–64.
Carolan, M.S. (2004), 'Ecological modernization theory: what about consumption?', *Society and Natural Resources*, **17**: 247–60.
Catton, W.R. Jr and R.E. Dunlap (1978), 'Environmental sociology: a new paradigm', *The American Sociologist*, **13**: 41–9.
Clark, B. and J.B. Foster (2001), 'William Stanley Jevons and *The Coal Question*: an introduction to Jevons's "Of the Economy of Fuel"', *Organization & Environment*, **14** (1): 93–8.
Clark, B. and R. York (2005), 'Carbon metabolism: global capitalism, climate change, and the biospheric rift', *Theory and Society*, **34** (4): 391–428.
Cohen, M.J. (1997), 'Risk society and ecological modernisation: alternative visions for post-industrial nations', *Futures*, **29** (2): 105–19.
Cohen, M.J. (1998), 'Science and the environment: assessing cultural capacity for ecological modernization', *Public Understanding of Science*, **7** (2): 149–67.
Cole, M.A. and E. Neumayer (2004), 'Examining the Impact of Demographic Factors on Air Pollution', *Population and Environment*, **26** (1): 5–21.
Dewey, John (1923), *The Public and Its Problems*, New York: Henry Holt.
Diamond, J. (2005), *Collapse: How Societies Choose to Fail or Succeed*, New York: Viking.
Dietz, T. and E.A. Rosa (1994), 'Rethinking the environmental impacts of population, affluence and technology', *Human Ecology Review*, **1**, 277–300.
Dietz, T. and E.A. Rosa (1997), 'Effects of population and affluence on CO_2 emissions', *Proceedings of the National Academy of Sciences*, **94**: 175–179.
Dietz, T., E.A. Rosa and R. York (2007), 'Driving the human ecological footprint', *Frontiers in Ecology and the Environment*, **5** (1): 13–18.
Dietz, T., E.A. Rosa, and R. York (2009), 'Environmentally efficient well-being: rethinking sustainability as the relationship between human well-being and environmental impacts', *Human Ecology Review*, **16** (1): 113–22.
Dinda, S. (2004), 'Environmental Kuznets curve hypothesis: a survey', *Ecological Economics*, **49**: 431–55.
Dunlap, R.E. (1997), 'The evolution of environmental sociology: a brief history and assessment of the American experience', in M.R. Redclift and G.R. Woodgate (eds) *The International Handbook of Environmental Sociology*, Cheltenham, UK and Lyme, USA: Edward Elgar, pp.21–39.
Dunlap, R.E. and B.K. Marshall (2007), 'Environmental sociology', in C.D. Bryant and D.L. Peck (eds), *21st Century Sociology: A Reference Handbook*, Vol. 2. Thousand Oaks, CA: Sage, pp. 329–40.

Ehrhardt-Martinez, K. (1998), 'Social determinants of deforestation in developing countries: a cross-national study', *Social Forces*, **77** (2), 567–86.

Ehrhardt-Martinez, K., E.M. Crenshaw and J.C. Jenkins (2002), 'Deforestation and the environmental Kuznets curve: a cross-national investigation of intervening mechanisms', *Social Science Quarterly*, **83** (1): 226–43.

Ehrlich, P.R. and J. Holdren (1971), 'Impact of population growth', *Science*, **171**: 1212–17.

Fisher, D.R. and W.R. Freudenburg (2004), 'Postindustrialization and environmental quality: an empirical analysis of the environmental state', *Social Forces*, **83** (1): 157–88.

Fisher, D.R. and W.R. Freudenburg (2001), 'Ecological modernization and its critics: assessing the past and looking toward the future', *Society and Natural Resources*, **14** (8): 701–9.

Fischer-Kowalski, M. and H. Weisz (1999), 'Society as hybrid between material and symbolic realms: toward a theoretical framework of society-nature interaction', *Advances in Human Ecology*, **8**, 215–51.

Foster, J.B. (1992), 'The absolute general law of environmental degradation under capitalism', *Capitalism, Nature, Socialism*, **2** (3), 77–82.

Foster, J.B. (2002), *Ecology Against Capitalism*, New York: Monthly Review Press.

Frey, R.S. (1994), 'The international traffic in hazardous wastes', *Journal of Environmental Systems*, **23**: 165–77.

Frey, R.S. (1998), 'The export of hazardous industries to the peripheral zones of the world-system', *Journal of Developing Societies*, **14**: 66–81.

Giddens, A. (1990), *The Consequences of Modernity*, Stanford, CA: Stanford University Press.

Haberl, H., K.-H. Erb, F. Krausmann, V. Gaube, A. Bondeau, C. Plutzar, S. Gingrich, W. Lucht and M. Fischer-Kowalski (2007), 'Quantifying and mapping the human appropriation of net primary production of Earth's terrestrial ecosystems', *Proceedings of the National Academy of Sciences*, **104**: 12942–47.

Habermas, Jürgen (1970), *Towards a Rational Society*, Boston, MA: Beacon Press.

Jevons, W.S. (2001) [1865], 'Of the Economy of Fuel', *Organization & Environment*, **14** (1): 99–104.

Jorgenson, A.K. (2005), 'Unpacking international power and the ecological footprints of nations: a quantitative cross-national study', *Sociological Perspectives*, **48** (3): 383–402.

Jorgenson, A.K. (2006), 'Global warming and the neglected greenhouse gas: a cross-national study of the social causes of methane emissions intensity, 1995', *Social Forces*, **84** (3): 1779–99.

Jorgenson, A.K. and T. Burns (2007), 'The political–economic causes of change in the ecological footprints of nations, 1991-2001', *Social Science Research*, **36**: 834–53.

Krausmann, F., K-H. Erb, S. Gingrich, C. Lauk and H. Haberl (2007), 'Global patterns of socioeconomic biomass flows in the year 2000: a comprehensive assessment of supply, consumption, and constraints', *Ecological Economics*, **65**: 471–87.

Lash, S. (1994), 'Reflexivity and its doubles: structures, aesthetics, community', in U. Beck, A. Giddens and S. Lash (eds), *Reflexive Modernization: Politics, Tradition, Aesthetics in the Modern Order*, Stanford, CA: Stanford University Press, pp. 110–73.

Leiserowitz, A.A., R.W. Kates and T.M. Parris (2005), 'Do global attitudes and behaviors support sustainable development?', *Environment*, **47** (9): 23–38.

Mazur, A. and E. Rosa (1974) 'Energy and lifestyle: cross-national comparison of energy consumption and quality of life indicators', *Science*, **186**, 607–10.

Milanez, B. and T. Bührs (2007), 'Marrying strands of ecological modernisation: a proposed framework', *Environmental Politics*, **16** (3), 565–83.

Mol, A.P.J. (1995), *The Refinement of Production: Ecological Modernization Theory and the Chemical Industry*, Utrecht: Van Arkel.

Mol, A.P.J. (1996), 'Ecological modernisation and institutional reflexivity: environmental reform in the late modern age', *Environmental Politics*, **5** (2): 302–23.

Mol, A.P.J. (2001), *Globalization and Environmental Reform*, Cambridge, MA: MIT Press.

Mol, A.P.J. and D.A. Sonnenfeld (2000a), *Ecological Modernization Around the World: Perspectives and Critical Debates*, London: Frank Cass.

Mol, A.P.J. and D.A. Sonnenfeld (2000b), 'Ecological modernization around the world: an introduction', in A.P.J. Mol and D.A. Sonnenfeld (eds), *Ecological Modernization Around the World: Perspectives and Critical Debates*, London: Frank Cass, pp. 3–14.

Mol, A.P.J. and G. Spaargaren (2000), 'Ecological modernization theory in debate: a review', in A.P.J. Mol and D.A. Sonnenfeld (eds), *Ecological Modernization Around the World: Perspectives and Critical Debates*, London: Frank Cass, pp. 17–49.

Mol, A.P.J. and G. Spaargaren (2004), 'Ecological modernization and consumption: a reply', *Society and Natural Resources*, **17**: 261–5.

Mol, A.P.J. and G. Spaargaren (2005), 'From additions and withdrawals to environmental flows: reframing debates in the environmental social sciences', *Organization and Environment*, **18** (1): 91–107.

Moore, J.W. (2003), 'The modern world-system as environmental history? Ecology and the rise of capitalism', *Theory & Society*, **32**: 307–77.

O'Connor, J. (1994), 'Is Sustainable Capitalism Possible?', in Martin O'Connor (ed.), *Is Capitalism Sustainable? Political Economy and the Politics of Ecology*, New York: The Guilford Press, pp. 152–75.

Pellow, D.N. (2000), 'Environmental inequality formation: toward a theory of environmental injustice', *American Behavioral Scientist*, **43** (4): 581–601.

Pellow, D.N., A.S. Weinberg and A. Schnaiberg (2000), 'Putting ecological modernization to the test: Accounting for recycling's promises and performance', *Environmental Politics*, **9** (1): 109–37.

Rosa, E., A. McCright and O. Renn (2008), 'The risk society: theoretical frames and state management challenges', Working Paper, Pullman, Washington: Department of Sociology, Washington State University.

Rosa, E.A., R. York and T. Dietz (2004), 'Tracking the anthropogenic drivers of ecological impacts', *Ambio*, **33** (8): 509–12.

Rudel, T.K. (2005), *Tropical Forests: Regional Path of Destruction and Regeneration in the Late Twentieth Century*, New York: Columbia University Press.

Schnaiberg, A. (1980), *The Environment: From Surplus to Scarcity*, New York and Oxford: Oxford University Press.

Shi, A. (2003), 'The impact of population pressure on global carbon dioxide emissions, 1975–1996: evidence from pooled cross-country data', *Ecological Economics*, **44**: 29–42.

Sonnenfeld, D.A. (1998), 'From brown to green? Late industrialization, social conflict, and adoption of environmental technologies in Thailand's pulp industry', *Organization & Environment*, **11** (1): 59–87.

Sonnenfeld, D.A. and A.P.J. Mol (2006), 'Environmental reform in Asia: comparisons, challenges, next steps', *Journal of Environment and Development*, **15** (2), 112–37.

Spaargaren, G. (1997), *The Ecological Modernization of Production and Consumption: Essays in Environmental Sociology*, Wageningen, NL: Department of Environmental Sociology Wageningen Agricultural University (dissertation).

Spaargaren, G. and A.P.J. Mol (1992), 'Sociology, environment and modernity: ecological modernization as a theory of social change', *Society and Natural Resources*, **5**: 323–44.

Spaargaren, G., A.P.J. Mol and F. H. Buttel (2006), *Governing Environmental Flows: Global Challenges to Social Theory*, Cambridge, MA: MIT Press.

Taylor, D. (2000), 'The rise of the environmental justice paradigm: injustice framing and the social construction of environmental discourses', *American Behavioral Scientist*, **43** (4): 508–80.

Wackernagel, M. and W. Rees (1996), *Our Ecological Footprint: Reducing Human Impact on the Earth*, Gabriola Island, BC: New Society Publishers.

Wallerstein, I. (2004), *World-Systems Analysis: An Introduction*, Durham, NC: Duke University Press.

Weisz, H., F. Kraussman, C. Amann, N. Eisenmenger, K.-H. Erb, K. Hubacek and M. Fischer-Kowalski (2006), 'The physical economy of the European Union: cross-country comparison and determinants of material consumption', *Ecological Economics*, **58**: 676–98.

York, R. (2004), 'The treadmill of (diversifying) production', *Organization & Environment*, **17** (3): 355–62.

York, R. (2006) 'Ecological paradoxes: William Stanley Jevons and the paperless office', *Human Ecology Review*, **13** (2): 143–7.

York, R. (2008), 'De-carbonization in former soviet republics, 1992–2000: the ecological consequences of de-modernization', *Social Problems*, **55** (3): 370–90.

York, R. and E.A. Rosa (2003), 'Key challenges to ecological modernization theory: institutional efficacy, case study evidence, units of analysis, and the pace of eco-efficiency', *Organization & Environment*, **16** (3): 273–88.

York, R. and E.A. Rosa (2005), 'Societal processes and carbon dioxide (CO_2) emissions: comment on "post industrialization and environmental quality: an empirical analysis of the environmental state"', *Social Forces*, online rejoinder (http://socialforces.unc.edu/), August.

York, R., E.A. Rosa and T. Dietz (2003a), 'Footprints on the earth: the environmental consequences of modernity', *American Sociological Review*, **68** (2): 279–300.

York, R., E.A. Rosa and T. Dietz (2003b), 'A rift in modernity? Assessing the Anthropogenic sources of global climate change with the STIRPAT model', *International Journal of Sociology and Social Policy*, **23** (10): 31–51.

York, R., E.A. Rosa and T. Dietz (2003c), 'STIRPAT, IPAT, and ImPACT: analytic tools for unpacking the driving forces of environmental impacts', *Ecological Economics*, **46** (3): 351–65.

York, R., E.A. Rosa and T. Dietz (2004), 'The ecological footprint intensity of national economies', *Journal of Industrial Ecology*, **8** (4): 139–54.

6 Postconstructivist political ecologies
Arturo Escobar

Three generations of political ecology

Political ecology (PE) is an interdisciplinary field that has been under development for several decades; the process of constructing it has been marked by rich epistemological, paradigmatic and political debates since its inception. It is broadly recognized that it emerged in the 1970s out of the interweaving of several ecologically oriented frameworks and political economy. By bringing these two fields together, PE aimed to work through their respective deficiencies, namely, human and cultural ecology's lack of attention to power and political economy's undeveloped conceptualization of nature. Too mired still in structural and dualist ways of thinking, this 'first generation political ecology' (Biersack, 2006) has given way over the past decade to what could be termed a 'second-generation' political ecology; variously informed by those theoretical trends marked as 'post-' since the 1980s (poststructuralism, postmarxism, postcolonialism), the political ecology of the last 15 years has been a vibrant inter- and transdisciplinary space of inquiry drawing on many disciplines (geography, anthropology, ecology, ecological economics, environmental history, historical ecology, development studies, science and technology studies) and bodies of theory (liberal theory, Marxism, poststructuralism, feminist theory, phenomenology, postcolonial theory, complexity and natural science approaches such as landscape ecology and conservation biology). What distinguishes this second-generation PE from its predecessor is its engagement with the epistemological debates fostered by the theoretical positions known as constructivism and anti-essentialism.

Although very provisionally, given the newness of the trends in question, it could be said that a third-generation PE has been in ascension over the past five years. With roots in the second-generation PE and in the critical social theories of the 1980s, this emerging PE finds its direct conditions of possibility in the most recent debates on post-representational epistemologies in geography and science and technology studies (STS), on the one hand, and flat and relational ontologies in anthropology, geography, cultural studies and STS, on the other. At the social level, this tendency is influenced by persistent environmental problems for which PE did not have fully satisfactory answers and in social movement trends that resonate with similar problematics. The key difference between second- and third-generation PE is the attention that the latter gives to issues of ontology besides epistemology. Today, the three PEs can be seen at play in various works, although orientations from the second phase are still dominant. If PE1 could be said to be preconstructivist and PE2 constructivist, PE3 can be referred to as postconstructivist in the sense that, while informed by transformative debates on constructivism, anti-essentialism and anti-foundationalism that swept the critical scholarly worlds in the humanities and social sciences in many parts of the world, it builds on the efforts at working through the impasses and predicaments created by constructivism, radicalizing them, while at the same time returning to questions about 'the real'. As I shall suggest,

PE3 arises out of broader transformations in social theory – what could be called an 'ontological turn' in social theory, more concretely what a number of authors refer to as 'flat ontologies'.

The range of questions with which these various PEs deal, in both historical and contemporary terms, has remained relatively stable, although the list of problem areas keeps on growing: the relation between environment, development and social movements; between capital, nature and culture; production, power and the environment; gender, race and nature; space, place and landscape; knowledge and conservation; economic valuation and externalities; population, land and resource use; environmental governmentality; technology, biology and politics; and so forth. This range of questions, conversely, refers to problems whose very salience lends relevance to the field; these include, among others, destruction of biodiversity, deforestation, resource depletion, unsustainability, development, environmental racism, control of genetic resources and intellectual property rights, bio- and nanotechnologies, and global problems such as climate change, transboundary pollution, loss of carbon sinks, the transformation of agricultural and food systems, and the like.[1] Some recent trends discuss the multiplicity of socionatural worlds or cultures–natures, relational versus dualist ontologies, networked versus structural forms of analysis, and even a renewal of the question of what constitutes life. While these questions are more intractable theoretically, they seem to stem from the social more clearly than ever before, due in great part to the practice of some social movements.

The next section of this chapter deals with epistemologies of nature and their implications for PE. In the third section, I present a provisional outline of third-generation PE.

Varieties of nature epistemologies
The knowledge of nature is not a simple question of science, empirical observation or cultural interpretation. To the extent that this question is a central aspect of how we think about the present environmental crisis – and hence PE's constitution – it is important to have a view of the range of positions on the issue. To provide such a view is not a simple endeavor, for what lies in the background of this question – besides political and economic stakes – are contrasting epistemologies and, in the last instance, foundational myths and ontological assumptions about the world. The brief panorama of positions presented below is restricted to the modern social and natural sciences.

Nature epistemologies tend to be organized around the essentialist/constructivist divide. Essentialism and constructivism are contrasting positions on the relation between knowledge and reality, thought and the real. Succinctly, essentialism is the belief that things possess an unchanging core, independent of context and interaction with other things, that knowledge can progressively know.[2] Concrete beings develop out of this core, which will eventually find an accurate reflection in thought (e.g. through the study of the thing's attributes to uncover its essence). The world, in other words, is always predetermined from the real. Constructivism, on the contrary, accepts the ineluctable connectedness between subject and object of knowledge and, consequently, the problematic relation between thought and the real. The character of this relation yields varieties of constructivism.

As is well known, poststructuralism transformed the discussion on epistemology in many fields, including those concerned with nature. From a certain poststructuralist perspective (Foucaultian and Deleuzian in particular) there cannot be a materialist analysis that is not, at the same time, a discursive analysis. The poststructuralist analysis of discourse is a social theory, that is, a theory of the production of social reality that includes the analysis of representations as social facts inseparable from what is thought of as 'material reality'. Poststructuralism treats language not as a reflection of 'reality' but as constitutive of it. That was the whole point, for instance, of Said's (1979) *Orientalism*. For some, there is no materiality unmediated by discourse, as there is no discourse unrelated to materialities (Laclau and Mouffe, 1985). Discourse, as used in these approaches, is the articulation of knowledge and power, of statements and visibilities, of the visible and the sayable. Discourse is the process through which social reality comes into being.

There is an array of epistemological positions along the essentialist/constructivist divide, from positivism to the most recent forms of constructivism, each with their respective philosophical commitments and political attachments (see Escobar, 2008 for a more substantial discussion). The constructivist positions are difficult to classify. The following are said to be the most salient ones in the nature–culture field; these are not distinct schools but partially overlapping positions. They do not necessarily constitute highly visible trends (some are marginal or dissident within their fields, including biology). It is debatable whether all of them can be described in terms of a constructivist research program, although in these cases their effect *vis-à-vis* epistemological realism is similar to that of the constructivist proposals.

Dialectical constructivism

Besides the transformation of historical materialism through ecology – the account of capital's restructuring of production conditions (O'Connor, 1998) – the Marxist framework has produced the influential view of the dialectic of organism and environment, especially in the work of biologists Levins and Lewontin (1985). By complicating the binarism between nature and culture, these biologists contributed to rethinking theories based on this cleavage, including evolution and the ontogeny–phylogeny relation, although the implications of their work for ecology have been less explored. A similar contribution, although from different sources, including theories of heterarchy, comes from the field of historical ecology. This field studies long-term processes in terms of changing landscapes, defined as the material – often dialectical – manifestation of the relation between human beings and the environment (e.g. Crumley, 1994).

An altogether different conception of the dialectical method has been developed by Murray Bookchin and the school of social ecology, building on socialist and anarchist critiques of capitalism, the state and hierarchy. By weaving together the principles of social anarchism (e.g. decentralized society, direct democracy, humanistic technology, a cooperative ethic etc.) with what he sees as the natural dynamic that characterizes evolution itself, Bookchin developed a systemic analysis of the relation between natural and social practice (1986, 1990; Leff, 1998 for a critique). The cornerstone of his framework is the notion of dialectical naturalism, that is, the idea that nature presupposes a dialectical process of unfolding towards ever-greater levels of differentiation and consciousness. This same dialectic is found in the social order; indeed, social ecology poses a continuum between natural and social evolution (between first and second natures) and a general tendency towards development, complexification and self-organization. Extending Bookchin's insights, Heller (2000) identifies mutualism, differentiation and development as key principles affecting the continuities between natural and social life, natural and social evolution. For social ecologists, there is, then, an organic origin to all social orders; natural history is a key to understanding social transformation.

Constructive interactionism
This approach, proposed by Susan Oyama, deepens the insights of dialectical biology by infusing it with debates on constructivism, including feminist critiques of science. Oyama's focus is on rethinking biological development and evolution, taking as a point of departure a critique of gene-centric explanations in evolution (Oyama 2000, 2006). Oyama's call is for a dynamic and holistic approach to biological processes, which she advances, in her own field, through the concept of 'developmental system', defined as 'a heterogeneous and causally complex mix of interacting entities and influences' that produces the developmental cycle of an organism (2000: 1). She also proposes a non-dualist epistemology called constructive interactionism; rather than relying on a distinction between the constructed and the pre-programmed ('reality'), it upholds the idea that 'our presence in our knowledge, however, is not *contamination*, as some fear, but the very *condition* for the generation of that knowledge' (p. 150). Oyama's biology thus 'recognizes our own part in our construction of internal and external natures, and appreciates particular perspectives for empathy, investigation and change' (p. 149).

Phenomenological perspectives
Tim Ingold (1992) has long argued against the Cartesian assumption of the divides between humanity and nature and living and non-living things characteristic of most neo-Darwinist approaches. Besides the ethnography of non-Western groups, his main source of inspiration for overcoming this dualism is phenomenology, according to which life happens in the engagement with the world in which we dwell; prior to any objectification, we perceive the world because we act in it, and we similarly discover meaningful objects in the environment by moving about in it. In this way, things are neither 'naturally given' nor 'culturally constructed' but the result of a process of co-construction. In other words, we do not approach the environment primarily as a set of neutral objects waiting to be ordered in terms of a cultural project, although this certainly happens as well (what Heidegger, 1977 called 'enframing'); rather than this 'designer operation', in much of everyday life 'direct perception of the environment is a mode of engagement with the world, not a mode of [detached] construction of it' (Ingold, 1992: 44). Knowledge of the world is obtained not so much through abstraction, but through a process of 'enskillment' that happens through the active encounter with things (for related approaches in biology see Maturana and Varela, 1987; in computer science, Winograd and Flores, 1986).

Poststructuralist anti-essentialism
Donna Haraway's effort at mapping 'the traffic across nature and culture' is the most sustained anti-essentialist approach to nature. The notion of 'traffic' speaks to some of the main features of anti-essentialism, such as the complication of naturalized boundaries and the absence of neatly bounded identities, nature included. For Haraway, contrary to the positivist view in which the world/real informs knowledge, it is the other way around: knowledge contributes to making the world in profound ways. The disembodied epistemology of positivist science ('the god trick' of seeing everything from nowhere, as she descriptively put it (1988: 188)) is at the root of the modern culture of white capitalist

patriarchy, with its subordination of nature, women and people of color. Haraway offers a profoundly historicized reading of the making of socionatural worlds, particularly by contemporary techno-science. Building upon other proposals for a feminist science, she articulates an alternative epistemology of knowledge that is situated and partial but that nevertheless can yield consistent, valid accounts of the world (Haraway, 1988, 1989, 1991, 1997, 2003).

A great deal of work being done today at the interface of nature and culture in anthropology, geography and ecological feminism follows the strictures of anti-essentialism, and it would be impossible to summarize it here.[3] Among the basic tenets of these works are, first, the idea that nature has to be studied in terms of the constitutive processes and relations – biological, social, cultural, political, discursive – that go into its making; second, and consequently, a resistance to reduce the natural world to a single overarching principle of determination (whether genes, capital, evolution, the laws of the ecosystem, discourse, or what have you). Researchers following these principles study the manifold, culturally mediated articulations of biology and history – how biophysical entities are brought into social history, and vice versa; one suggestion is that it is possible to speak of different cultural regimes for the appropriation of nature (e.g. capitalist regime, as in the plantations; organic regime, as in the local models of nature of non-Western peoples; and techno-natures, as in the recent biotechnologies; see Escobar, 1999). Whether speaking about forests, biodiversity, or recent biotechnologies, in these analyses there is always a great deal of history, culture, politics, and some (not yet enough) biology. Third, there is a concern with biological and cultural differences as historically produced. In this respect, there is an effort at seeing both from the center – looking at dominant processes of production of particular socionatural configurations – and from the margins of social/natural hierarchies, where stable categories might be put into question and where new views might arise (e.g. Cuomo, 1998; Rocheleau, 1995a, 1995b; Rocheleau and Ross, 1995). As Rocheleau (2000, 2007; see also Whatmore, 2005) puts it, we need to understand how living and non-living beings create ways of being-in-place and being-in-networks, with all the tensions, power and affinities that this unprecedented hybridity entails. Finally, there is a reconstructive strain in many of these works that implies paying attention to particular situations and concrete biologies/ecosystems, and to the social movements that emerge out of a politics of difference and a concern for nature. The hope is that this concern could lead to envisioning novel ecological communities – what Rocheleau aptly calls instances of ecological viability. From this perspective, all PEs could be said to be reconstructive, in the sense given to the term by Hess (2001) in STS to indicate a shift towards actively envisioning and contributing to alternative world constructions.

While constructivism restored a radical openness to the world, for its critics the price was its incapacity to make strong truth claims about reality. There is a growing set of epistemologies that could be called neo-realist, including the following two positions:

Deleuzian neo-realism A non-essentialist, yet realist, account of the world exists in the work of philosophers Deleuze and Guattari (see especially 1987, 1994). Deleuze's starting point is that the world is always a becoming, not a static collection of beings that knowledge faithfully represents; the world is made up of differences, and it is the intensity of differences themselves – flows of matter and energy – that generate the variety of geological, biological and cultural forms we encounter. Matter is seen by Deleuze and

Guattari as possessing its own immanent resources for the generation of form. This difference-driven morphogenesis is linked to processes of self-organization that are at the heart of the production of the real. Differentiation is ongoing, always subverting identity, while giving rise to concrete biophysical and social forms, the result of processes of individuation that are relational and always changing. Instead of making the world depend on human interpretation, Deleuze achieves openness by turning it into a creative and complexifying space of becoming.

One of the problems with most epistemologies and ontologies of nature is that they are based entirely on the human experience; they distinguish between the real and the non-real according to what human beings are able to observe (de Landa, 2002). We need to drop the 'non-realist baggage' if we want to arrive at a new ontological commitment to realism that allows us to make strong claims about, say, emergent wholes. 'Deleuze is such a daring philosopher' – de Landa concludes – 'because he creates a non-essentialist realism' (2002: 11). In the end, de Landa advocates for a new form of empiricism that allows us to follow the emergence of heterogeneous and multiple forms out of the larger field of the virtual. We shall return to this discussion in the next section, when we situate the Deleuzian proposal within a broader trend towards 'flat ontologies', theories of assemblages, complexity and self-organization.

Holistic realism   This view has been articulated most explicitly by complexity theorist Brian Goodwin (2007). His reading of research on emergence, networks and self-organization leads him to conclude that meaning, language, feelings and experience are not the prerogative of human beings but are found in all living beings; creativity is an inherent aspect of all forms of life, and it is on this basis that coherence and wholeness is produced. His proposal is for a hermeneutic biology and a holistic realism that accept that nature expresses itself in embodied reality and that opens up towards the epistemological role of feelings and emotions. The implication is that scientists can become

> co-creators of [the] world with beings that are much more like us cognitively and culturally that we have hitherto recognized . . . We are within the history of that unfolding . . . The task before us now is to rethink our place in the stream of creative emergence on this planet in terms of the deeper understanding of the living process that is now taking form. The life of form, of which we are a part, unfolds toward patterns of beauty and efficiency that satisfy both qualitative and quantitative needs in such a way as to maintain diversity of species, cultures, languages and styles of living. (2007, pp.100, 101, 110)

What then is left of the question, 'What is nature?' Within a positivist epistemology nature exists, pre-given and pre-discursive, and the natural sciences claim to produce reliable knowledge of its workings. For the constructivist interactionist, on the contrary, we need to 'question the idea that Nature has a unitary, eternal nature that is independent of our lives. . . Nature is multiple but not arbitrary' (Oyama, 2000: 143). The positivist might respond that if this is the case, there must be an invariant that remains, a central core of sorts that we can know, thus missing the point since, for Oyama, there cannot be one true account of nature's nature. For Leff (1986, 1993, 2002), while nature is a distinct ontological domain, it has become inextricably hybridized with culture and technology and increasingly produced by our knowledge. For Ingold (1992: 44), nature exists only as a construction by an observer; what matters for him is the environment, that is, the world as constituted in relation to the activities of all those organisms that contribute to its formation. While for social ecologists nature is real and knowable, this realism is not the same as that of the Cartesian subject but of a knowing subject that is deeply implicated in the same process of world-making. For the anti-essentialists in the humanities and social sciences, biophysical reality certainly exists, but what counts most is the truth claims we make in nature's name and how these truth claims authorize particular agendas that then shape our social and biological being and becoming. Despite the neo-realist approaches of complexity theory, finally, the continued dominance of epistemological realism must be acknowledged; it relies not only on its ability to muster credible forms of knowledge, but also on its many links to power: the link between science, production and technology; the current emphasis on the production of life through the further development of biotechnical rationality; and in the last instance its ability to speak for Western logocentrism, with its dream of an ordered and rational society that most human beings have learned to desire and depend upon – now buttressed by genetically enhanced natures and human beings.

Put differently, positivists are good at providing scientific information about biophysical aspects of nature, yet they are unable to account for the differences among nature–culture regimes, since for them nature is one and the same for all peoples and situations; these differences have biophysical implications that they either miss or are at pains to explain. Constructivists do a good job in terms of ascertaining the representations or meanings given to nature by various peoples, and the consequences or impacts of those meanings in terms of what is actually done to nature (e.g. Slater, 2003 for the case of rainforests). This is very important, yet they usually bypass the question, central to neo-realists and dialecticians, of the ontologically specific character of biophysical reality and this latter's contribution to human societies (e.g. Redclift, 2006). Finally, it is still hard to see how the neo-realism derived from complexity might allow us a different reading of the cultural dimension of nature–culture regimes. Leff's is an initial attempt in this direction. Ingold (2000) also points in this direction with his insistence on the profoundly relational character of reality. Even with the result of processes of individuation, things do not exist in the real world independently of their relations. And knowledge is not merely applied but generated in the course of lived experience, including of course encounters with the environment. In sum, to envision relations between the biophysical and the cultural, including knowledge, that avoid the pitfalls of constructivism and essentialism is not an easy task. This is one of the driving impetuses of the emerging political ecology.

An emerging political ecology? From epistemologies to ontologies

The various waves of deconstruction and discursive approaches of the past few decades brought with them a critique of realism as an epistemological stance. A number of very interesting social theory trends at present entail, implicitly or explicitly, a return to realism; since this is not a return to the naïve realisms of the past (particularly the Cartesian versions, or the realism of essences or transcendent entities), these tendencies might be called neo-realist or postconstructivist. As is often the case when a significantly new approach is being crafted, neo-realist views seem to be springing up worldwide in a broad variety of intellectual and even political terrains – from geography, anthropology and cultural studies to biology, computer science and ecology. Some of the main categories affiliated with this diverse trend include assemblages, networks and actor networks, relationality, non-dualist and relational ontologies, emergence and self-organization, hybridity, virtuality and the like. The trend is fueled most directly by poststructuralism and phenomenology, and in some versions by post-Marxism, actor-network theories (ANT), complexity theory, and philosophies of immanence and of difference; in some cases they are also triggered by ethnographic research with groups that are seen as embodying relational ontologies or by social movements who construct their political strategies in terms of dispersed networks. Taken as a whole, these trends reveal a daring attempt at looking at social theory in an altogether different way – what could broadly be termed 'flat alternatives'. The language used to refer to a host of processes and features is indicative of this aim: flat versus hierarchical, horizontality versus verticality, relational versus binary thinking, self-organization versus structuration, immanence and emergence versus transcendence, enactment versus representation, attention to ontology as opposed to epistemology, and so forth. What follows is a very tentative and partial view of this trend. While they could be said to provide the material for, and contours of, a postconstructivist PE, the trends in question are by no means completely coherent or aiming in the same direction. Moreover, I should stress that there might well be different genealogies to this and to other forms of political ecology at present.[4]

In geography, some of the key interventions are the debates over the past decade on spatial representations (e.g. Pickles, 2004) and 'non-representational theories' (e.g. Thrift, 2007), 'hybrid geographies' (Whatmore, 2002), 'human geography without scale' (Marston et al., 2005, and the ensuing debate in *Transactions of the Institute of British Geographers*, **32** (2), 2007), 'emergent ecologies' in terms of 'rooted networks and relational webs' (e.g. Rocheleau and Roth, 2007), and the shift from dualist to relational ontologies (e.g. Crastree, 2003; Braun, 2008). Again, even within geography these debates cannot be said to relate exactly to the same set of issues, and in some cases they are in tension with each other. Taken together, however, they build up a complex argument about scale, space, place, ontology and social theory itself; 'nature', 'ecology' and 'politics' are often (not always) present in these debates, most potently in Whatmore's and Rocheleau's cases. In these works, there is a renewed attention to materiality, whether through a focus on practice, or relations, networks, embodiments, performances or attachments between various elements of the social and the biophysical domains. The sources, however, are quite varied; some include poststructuralism and phenomenology (in some cases, the latter via anthropologist Tim Ingold's influential work) with attention to practice and engagement with the world, rather than representation. In those works influenced by ANT and Deleuze and Guattari, the emphasis is on ascertaining the production of the real through manifold relations linking human and non-human agents, bridging previously taken-for-granted divides (nature/culture, subject/object, self/other) into processes of productions and architectures of the real in terms of networks, assemblages, and hybrid socionatural formations. Space is no longer taken as an ontologically given but as a result of relational processes.

In *Human Geography without Scale*, for instance, the authors state that most conceptions of scale remain trapped in a foundational hierarchy and verticality, with concomitant problems such as lingering micro–macro and global–local binaries (Marston et al., 2005). An important part of these authors' argument is that these problems cannot be solved just by appealing to a network model; the challenge is not to replace one 'ontological–epistemological nexus (verticality) with another (horizontality)' but to bypass altogether the reliance on 'any transcendent pre-determination' (p. 422; see also the ensuing debate in *Transactions of the Institute of British Geographers*, **32** (2), 2007). This would be achieved by adopting a flat (as opposed to horizontal) ontology that discards 'the centering essentialism that infuses not only the up–down vertical imagery but also the radiating (out from here) spatiality of horizontality' (Marston et al., 2005: 422). Here flat ontology refers to complex, emergent spatial relations, self-organization and ontogenesis. 'Overcoming the limits of globalizing ontologies', these authors conclude, 'requires sustained attention to the intimate and divergent relations between bodies, objects, orders, and spaces' – that is, to the processes by which assemblages are formed; 'sites' become 'an emergent property of their interacting human and non-human inhabitants . . . That is, we can talk about the existence of a given site only insofar as we can follow the interactive practices through their localized connections' (ibid.: 425). Whether all of this amounts to a complete overhaul of the notion of scale remains an open question (see the debate). Rocheleau's proposal, that recent network approaches that refuse binary thinking can help us to understand the world 'as always already networked, already embedded' (Rocheleau and Roth, 2007: 433) contributes to working through the problems in network thinking pointed at by Marston et al.; their attention to ecological dynamics, which is absent in most of their colleagues' work, enables them to make some particularly apposite propositions for PE. In this PE, networks are connected to places and territories – through the counter-intuitive concept of 'rooted networks' – linking up social and natural elements into dispersed and dynamic formations. The challenge, as Rocheleau and Roth see it, is to 'mesh social, ecological, and technological domains in theories and models of rooted networks, relational webs, and self-organized assemblages, all laced with power, and linked to territories across scale' (2007: 436). This is one particular, and cogent, proposal within the PE3 field.

Anthropologist are also busy, and somewhat independently but with increasing and exciting overlaps with the geographical trends just described, at developing novel approaches to nature–culture questions. There are illustrious predecessors to this endeavor, particularly Ingold (2000), Strathern (e.g. 1980) and Descola (e.g. 1986; Descola and Pálsson, 1996). A main thrust is how to study in postconstructivist ways non-Western understandings of 'nature' and 'the environment', and of course of a whole set of other cultural constructions such as 'persons', 'property' and 'the economy'. Besides similar theoretical orientations (ANT, Deleuze and Guattari, phenomenology, and network approaches are main sources, as in geography), ethnographic research with a host of 'non-Western' groups continues to be crucial (with great presence of ethnographies with Melanesian groups; Andean, Amazonian and Canadian indigenous groups; and Australian aborigines). As is well known, ethnographies of socionatural formations are no longer restricted to non-Western contexts; those following ANT approaches, as well as those influenced by Donna Haraway's work, have been particularly prolific in posing new questions and methodologies, although they will not be reviewed here for reasons of space. It should be underscored, however, that taken as a whole the ethnography-based works (largely in anthropology but some in geography and STS) highlight some of the same issues reviewed above but also a particular, different set; among the most discussed are issues of incommensurability, translation, and other forms of communicability among distinct socionatural worlds (e.g. Povinelli, 1995, 2001; Noble, 2007) and of the extent to which these worlds might embody non-modern, alternative-modern, or other-than-modern (e.g. postliberal) socionatural orders (de la Cadena, 2008; Escobar, 2008; Blaser, in press). In this way, the postconstructivist political ecology becomes a *political ontology*, a category for which Blaser (in press) has most clearly advocated. The political implications of these ontology-focused ethnographies are also often dealt with explicitly.

A key emerging category is that of 'relational ontologies' (see also Braun, 2008 for geography). This notion is posed as a way to problematize the commonly accepted modern ontology-based binarisms such as nature (the domain of objects) and culture (the domain of subjects). Some works with indigenous, Afro-descended and other communally oriented groups in South America have focused on this notion. As a category of analysis, 'relational ontologies' signals various issues. First, it constitutes an attempt to develop a way to talk about emergent forms of politics that are not based on homogenized conceptions of indigeneity, race, or essentialized cultures or identities. Second, it is a practice-based concept that calls for ethnographic attention to the distinctions and relations that these groups effect on the vast array of living and non-living entities; the notion points, more than anything, to the fact that indeed many of these groups do not think or act in terms of the proverbial modern binaries. Even the binary 'modern'/'indigenous' exists mostly for the moderns, as indigenous groups are better equipped than moderns to move across socionatural configurations, precisely because they think and act in deeply relational and networked terms. Politically, 'relational ontologies' point to the fact that these ontologies have been under attack for centuries, even more so today with neoliberal globalization's hypernaturalized notions of individuals, markets, rationality and the like; references to Polanyi's notion of ' disembededdness' are sometimes found in these works, with the concomitant cultural–political move to promote re/embedding of person/economy into society/nature. Modernity, in this way, is not only about the suppression of subaltern knowledges, but about the veritable suppression of other worlds, thus calling for making visible and fostering 'worlds and knowledges otherwise' (e.g. Escobar, 2008; Santos, 2007).

In these works, questions of difference at all levels – economic, ecological, cultural, epistemic and ultimately ontological – are of paramount importance, and at this level PE3 is a political ecology of difference, or, again, a political ontology. In this political ontology, there is a decentering of modern politics that is seen as being fostered by indigenous movements and intellectuals themselves. By positing, say, the sentience of all beings and mobilizing this construct politically, and by insisting on the persistence of non-liberal (e.g. 'communal') forms of politics, these movements unsettle the modern arrangement by which only scientists can represent nature and politics can be based on these representations; these groups, on the contrary, assert their right to represent non-human entities through other practices, and to have those practices count as both knowledge and politics (De la Cadena, 2008). A related, yet distinct, recent proposal aims at pluralizing modernity from the perspective of relational thinking; it conceptualizes modernity as multiplicity, hence positing the existence of multiple modernities that are not variations of a single modernity (Grossberg, 2008). A final approach that aims at relational ontologies and postconstructivist realism comes from computer science; it posits the need for ontological pluralism and metaphysical monism (the unity of the world), in what one author calls 'immanence with a vengeance' (Smith, 1996: 373). One way to read the emergence of relational ontologies from the perspective of these various trends is as a 'return of the multiplicities'.

The question of sentience brings me to the last body of work I would like to mention, even if in passing. This refers to the small but possibly growing number of applications of theories of complexity, particularly from biology, to socionatural processes. In these works, the understanding of natural complexity in terms of processes of self-organization, emergence, non-hierarchy, self-similarity and non-linear dynamical processes can provide insights for an altogether different social, or socionatural, theory (e.g. Taylor, 2001; Haila and Dyke, 2006; Escobar, 2008; Leff, 2000). For the biologists, a key message of biological worlds (from neurons to rivers, from atoms to lightning, from species to ecosystems and evolution) is that of self-organization and self-similarity. Some (e.g. Goodwin, 2007) go further to suggest that language and meaning are properties of all living beings and not only of human beings – in other words, that the world is one of pansentience. How do we take this sentience seriously considering that modern epistemes are precisely based on the opposite ontological assumption? The question then becomes: how do we learn to live with/in both places and networks creatively, with the entire array of living and sentient beings? Of course, the idea that material and biological processes could inspire understandings of social life at more than metaphorical levels is bound to be, understandably, resisted by many. One position that could make it more appealing to constructivists is to think of social and biological life in terms of assemblages from a continuum of experience and matter that is both self-organized and other-organized; in this way, there would not be separate biological and social worlds, nature and culture. One could then read the insights of complexity as lessons from one kind of theory to another and not from some pre-given biological realm *per se* (Rocheleau and Roth, 2007; Escobar, 2008).

At the very least, complexity and flat approaches appear as viable proposals to work through two of the most damaging features of modern theory: pervasive binarisms, and the reduction of complexity; like the trends in geography, anthropology and STS reviewed here, they enable the reintroduction of complexity into our intellectual accounts of the real to a greater degree than previous frameworks. While some, perhaps many, of today's social movements also seem intuitively or explicitly aimed at a practice informed by flat conceptions (e.g. self-organizing networks), it remains to be seen how they will fare in terms of the effectiveness of their action (e.g. Zibechi, 2006; Gutiérrez, 2006; Ceceña, 2008 for readings of Latin American social movements from the perspective of autonomous, dispersed and non-state forms of politics). Obviously, there is a need for more empirical and activist-oriented research on particular experiences.

The interest in flat alternatives is, of course, a sign of the times. 'We are tired of trees' – famously denounced Deleuze and Guattari, two of the prophets of this movement in modern social theory; 'We should stop believing in trees, roots and radicles. They've made us suffer too much. All of arborescent culture is founded on them, from biology to linguistics' (1987: 15). What they mean by this is that we need to move away from ways of thinking based on binarisms, totalities, generative structures, pre-assumed unities, rigid laws, logocentric rationalities, conscious production, ideology, genetic determination, macropolitics, and embrace instead multiplicities, lines of flight, indetermination, tracings, movements of deterritorialization and processes of reterritorialization, becoming, in-betweeness, morphogenesis, rhizomes, micropolitics, and intensive differences and assemblages. From biology to informatics, from geography to social movements, from some critical theorists to many indigenous and place-based groups and activists, this is a strong message that can at least be plausibly heard.

Flat alternatives and postconstructivist epistemologies also contribute to putting issues of power and difference on the table in a unique way. If actual economic, ecological and cultural differences can be seen as instances of intensive differences and if, moreover, these can be seen as enactments of a much larger field of virtuality, this means that the spectrum of strategies, visions, dreams and actions is much larger than conventional views of the world might suggest. The challenge is to translate these insights into political strategies that incorporate multiple modes of knowing while avoiding the trap of falling back into modernist ways of thinking, being and doing. It is still too early to say whether a political ecology will coalesce out of these somewhat novel and diverse trends, but there seems to be a great deal of excitement in thinking anew theoretically and politically about difference; from this impetus might indeed emerge a postconstructivist and reconstructivist political ecology.

The political implications of relationality, finally, have been drawn out admirably by Doreen Massey. First, a politics of responsibility is a sequitur of the fact that space, place and identities are relationally constructed. We are all implicated in connections, and we must have an awareness of this fact of such a kind that enables us to act responsibly towards those entities with which we are connected – human and not. Analysis of these 'wider geographies of construction' (Massey, 2004: 11) is central to this awareness. Second, we need to be mindful that the recognition of relationality 'points to a politics of connectivity . . . whose relation to globalization will vary dramatically from place to place' (ibid.: 17); this calls for some sort of ethnographic grounding to that politics (in a broader sense of the term, that is, in terms of a substantial engagement with concrete places and connections). Third, the geography of responsibility that emerges from relationality also leads us to ask: 'What, in other words, of the question of the stranger *without*' (ibid.: 6, italics in the original), of our 'throwntogetherness'? This ineluctably links up to issues of culture, subjectivity, difference and nature. The following quote sums up these notions: 'The very acknowledgement of our constitutive interrelatedness implies a spatiality; and that in turn implies that the nature of that spatiality should be a crucial avenue of inquiry and political engagement' (Massey, 2005: 189). Ultimately, one might add, spatiality is related to ontology. In emphasizing an alternative territoriality, for instance, many movements of ethnic minorities in Latin America are not only making visible the liberal spatiality of modernity (from the nation-state to localities) but imagining power geometries that embed the principle of relationality within them.

Many questions remain to be articulated and addressed, such as: if this reconstitution of PE in terms of three somewhat distinct configurations makes sense, what are the continuities and discontinuities among them, particularly between the second and third PEs? It is not clear how PE3 reconstructs understandings of power and production that were central to PE2, for example. A related question is: how does attention to ontology in PE3 influence our understanding of the role of knowledge, and what other epistemologies might be conceived? Another question: what are the methodological implications of embracing these kinds of epistemological and ontological shifts? These methodologies would have to deal with the types of postconstructivist realism reviewed here but also with the demands posed by relationality; given that most research methodologies operate largely on the basis of subject/object, representation/real distinctions (despite much postmodern reflexivity), the answers to these questions are not straightforward. Another set of questions might deal with how non-academic actors themselves (activists, agriculturalists, seed-savers, multi-species advocates, netweavers of various kinds) deal with some of these issues. How do they do it in their ontological–political practice? Finally, can PE3 ever get to frame issues of sustainability and conservation effectively, given that these notions have been largely shaped by non-constructivist expert knowledge and modernist frameworks? What would it be like to engage in the kinds of ontological design required to bring about the ecological–cultural sustainability of relational socionatural worlds?

Acknowledgments

I would like to thank Dana Powell and Brenda Baletti for detailed comments on the first draft of this chapter. The chapter is part of ongoing conversations with a number of interlocutors, particularly Marisol de la Cadena, Mario Blaser, Dianne Rocheleau, John Pickles and Larry Grossberg.

Notes

1. For well-known statements on political ecology, see the collections by Biersack and Greenberg, eds. (2006); Haenn and Wilk (2005); Paulson and Gezon (2005). See also Brosius (1999); Bryant and Bailey (1997); Rocheleau et al. (1996); Peet and Watts (1996); Schmink and Wood (1987); Martínez-Alier (2002). I should mention that I shall not deal here with the rich debates in Latin American political ecology (or from other parts of the world of which I might be ignorant). There is a continent-wide related but distinct tradition of Latin American political ecology, and also important national developments in many countries (e.g. Mexico, Brazil, Colombia, Argentina). This tradition – it would deserve its own study – would not fit easily into the categories used in this chapter for the Anglo-Saxon works, and unfortunately very little of it has been translated into English. CLACSO's Political Ecology Working Group has been very productive over the past few decades. For recent meetings and publications, see http://www.clacso.org.ar.
2. Oyama provides the following definition from biology: 'By "essentialist", I mean an assumption that human beings have an underlying universal nature that is more fundamental than any variations that may exist among us, and that is in some sense always present – perhaps as a "propensity" – even when it is not actually discernible' (2000: 131).
3. See, e.g. Brosius (1999), Biersack (1999, 2006), Escobar (1999), and Peet and Watts (1996) for reviews of the trends in poststructuralist anti-essentialism in nature studies in anthropology and geography.
4. It is important to mention that flat alternatives and theories of complexity and self-organization have not emerged in a vacuum; the history of their most important antecedents is rarely told, since they pertain to traditions of thought that lie outside the immediate scope of the social sciences. These include cybernetics and information theories in the 1940s and 1950s; systems theories since the 1950s; early theories of self-organization; and the phenomenological biology of Maturana and Varela (1987). More recently, the sources of flat alternatives include some strands of thought in cognitive science and informatics and computing; complexity theories in biology; network theories in the physical, natural and social sciences; and Deleuze and Guattari's 'neo-realism'. Foucault's concept of 'eventalization' resembles recent proposals in assemblage theory. Deleuze and Guattari have inspired some of these developments, including Manuel de Landa's neo-realist assemblage theory (2002, 2006). Finally, it should be mentioned that the logic of distributed networks discussed in many of the trends reviewed here amounts to a different logic of the political, as a number of social movement observers are pointing out; this includes what is called a 'cultural politics of the virtual', understood as the opening up of the real/ actual to the action of forces that may actualize the virtual in different ways (e.g. Terranova 2004; Escobar and Osterweil, 2010; Grossberg, 2008). From the field of computer science, see the persuasive attempt by Smith (1996) to develop a post-representational epistemology. See Escobar (2008: ch. 6) for an extended discussion of some of the aspects discussed in this chapter, including those in this footnote.

References

Biersack, Aletta (1999), 'Introduction: from the "new ecology" to the "new ecologies"', *American Anthropologist*, **101** (1): 5–18.

Biersack, Aletta (2006), 'Introduction', in Aletta Biersack and James Greenberg (eds), *Re-imagining Political Ecology*, Durham, NC: Duke University Press, pp. 3–40.

Biersack, Aletta and James Greenberg (eds) (2006), *Re-Imagining Political Ecology*, Durham, NC: Duke University Press.

Blaser, Mario (in press), *Storytelling Globality: A Border Dialogue Ethnography of the Paraguayan Chaco*, Durham, NC: Duke University Press.

Bookchin, Murray (1986), *Post-scarcity Anarchism*, 2dn edn, Montreal: Black Rose.

Bookchin, Murray (1990), *The Philosophy of Social Ecology*, Montreal: Black Rose.

Braun, Bruce (2008), 'Environmental issues: inventive life', *Progress in Human Geography*, **32** (5): 667–79.
Brosius, Peter (1999) 'Analyses and interventions. Anthropological engagements with environmentalism', *Current Anthropology*, **40** (3): 277–309.
Bryant, Raymond and Sinéad Bailey (1997), *Third World Political Ecology*, London: Routledge.
Castree, Noel (2003), 'Environmental issues: relational ontologies and hybrid politics', *Progress in Human Geography*, **27**: 203–11.
Ceceña, Ana Ester (2008), *Derivas del mundo en el que caben todos los mundos*, Mexico, DF: Siglo XXI/CLACSO.
Crumley, Carole (ed.) (1994), *Historical Ecology. Cultural Knowledge and Changing Landscapes*, Santa Fe: SAR Press.
Cuomo, Chris (1998), *Feminism and Ecological Communities*, New York: Routledge.
De la Cadena, Marisol (2008), 'Taking indigenous politics in its own terms requires an analysis beyond "politics"', unpublished ms, Department of Anthropology, University of California, Davis.
de Landa, Manuel (2002), *Intensive Science and Virtual Philosophy*, New York: Continuum Press.
de Landa, Manuel (2006), *A New Philosophy of Society. Assemblage Theory and Social Complexity*, New York: Continuum Press.
Deleuze, Gilles and Félix Guattari (1987), *A Thousand Plateaus*, Minneapolis, MN: University of Minnesota Press.
Deleuze, Gilles and Félix Guattari (1994), *What is Philosophy?*, New York: Columbia University Press.
Descola, Philippe (1986), *La nature domestique. Symbolisme et praxis dans l'écologie des Achuar*, Paris: Maison des Sciences de l'Homme.
Descola, Philippe and Gísli Pálsson (eds) (1996), *Nature and Society. Anthropological Perspectives*, London: Routledge.
Escobar, Arturo (2008), *Territories of Difference: Place, Movements, Life*, Redes, Durham, NC: Duke University Press.
Escobar, Arturo (1999), 'After nature: steps to an anti-essentialist political ecology', *Current Anthropology*, **40** (1): 1–30.
Escobar, Arturo and Michal Osterweil (2010), 'Social movements and the politics of the virtual: Deleuzian strategies', in Casper Bruun Jensen and Kjetil Rödje (eds), *Deleuzian Intersections: Science, Technology, Anthropology*, New York: Berghahn, Chapter 9.
Goodwin, Brian (2007), *Nature's Due: Healing Our Fragmented Culture*, Edinburgh: Floris Books.
Grossberg, Larry (2008), 'Critical studies in search of modernities', unpublished manuscript, Chapel Hill, NC: University of North Carolina.
Gutiérrez, Raquel (2006), *A desordenar! Por una historia abierta de la lucha social*, Mexico, DF: Casa Juan Pablos/CEAM/Tinta Limón.
Haenn, Nora and Richard Wilk (eds) (2005), *The Environment in Anthropology*, New York: New York University Press.
Haila, Yrjö and Chuck Dyke (eds) (2006), *How Nature Speaks. The Dynamic of the Human Ecological Condition*, Durham, NC: Duke University Press.
Haraway, Donna (2003), *The Companion Species Manifesto*, Chicago, IL: Prickly Paradigm Press.
Haraway, Donna (1997), *Modest_Witness@Second Millennium. FemaleMan._Meets_OncoMouse™: Feminism and Technoscience*, New York: Routledge.
Haraway, Donna (1991), *Simians, Cyborgs and Women. The Reinvention of Nature*, New York: Routledge.
Haraway, Donna (1989), *Primate Visions*. New York: Routledge.
Haraway, Donna (1988), 'Situated knowledges: the science question in feminism and the privilege of partial perspective', *Feminist Studies*, **14** (3): 575–99.
Heidegger, Martin (1977), *The Question Concerning Technology*, New York: Harper and Row.
Heller, Chaia (2000), *Ecology of Everyday Life*, Montreal: Black Rose.
Hess, David (2001), 'Ethnography and the development of science and technology studies', in P. Atkinson, S. Delamont, A.J. Coffey, J. Lofland and L.H. Lofland (eds), *Handbook of Ethnography*, London: Sage, pp. 234–45.
Ingold, Tim (1992), 'Culture and the perception of the environment', in E. Croll and D. Parkin (eds), *Bush Base: Forest Farm*, London: Routledge, pp. 39–56.
Ingold, Tim (2000), *The Perception of the Environment*, London: Routledge.
Laclau, Ernesto and Chantal Mouffe (1985), *Hegemony and Socialist Strategy*, London: Verso.
Leff, Enrique (2002), *Saber Ambiental*, Mexico, DF: Siglo XXI.
Leff, Enrique (1998), 'Murray Bookchin and the end of dialectical materialism', *Capitalism, Nature, Socialism*, **9** (4): 67–93.
Leff, Enrique (1993), 'Marxism and the environmental question', *Capitalism, Nature, Socialism*, **4** (1): 44–66.
Leff, Enrique (ed.) (2000), *La conmplejidad ambiental*, Mexico: Siglo XXI.
Leff, Enrique (ed.) (1986), *Los problemas del conocimiento y la perspectiva ambiental del desarrollo*, México: Siglo XXI.
Levins, Richard and Richard Lewontin (1985), *The Dialectical Biologist*, Cambridge, MA: Harvard University Press.

Marston, Sally, John Paul Jones III and Keith Woodward (2005), 'Human geography without scale', *Transactions of the Institute of British Geographers*, NS **30**: 416–32.

Martínez-Alier, J. (2002), *The Environmentalism of the Poor. A Study of Ecological Conflicts and Valuation*, Cheltenham, UK and Northampton, MA: Edward Elgar.

Massey, Doreen (2005), *For Space*, Los Angeles, CA: Sage.

Massey, Doreen (2004), 'Geographies of responsibility', *Geografiska Annaler*, **86** B (1): 5–18.

Maturana, Humberto and Francisco Varela (1987), *The Tree of Knowledge*, Berkeley, CA: Shambhala, pp. 239–50.

Noble, Brian (2007), 'Justice, transaction, translation: Blackfoot tipi transfers and WIPO's search for the facts of traditional knowledge exchange', *American Anthropologist*, **109** (2): 338–49.

O'Connor, James (1998), *Natural Causes*, New York: Guilford Press.

Oyama, Susan (2006), 'Speaking of nature', in Haila Yrjö and Chuck Dyke (eds), *How Nature Speaks. The Dynamic of the Human Ecological Condition*, Durham, NC: Duke University Press, pp. 49–66.

Oyama, Susan (2000), *Evolution's Eye. A Systems View of the Biology–Culture Divide*, Durham, NC: Duke University Press.

Paulson, Susan and Lisa Gezon (eds) (2005), *Political Ecology across Spaces, Scales, and Social Groups*, New Brunswick, NJ: Rutgers University Press.

Peet, Richard and Michael Watts (eds) (1996), *Liberation Ecologies: Environment, Development, Social Movements*, London: Routledge.

Pickles, John (2004), *A History of Spaces. Cartographic Reason, Mapping and the Geo-Coded World*, London: Routledge.

Povinelli, Elizabeth (1995), 'Do rocks listen? The cultural politics of apprehending Australian aboriginal labor', *American Anthropologist*, **97** (3): 505–18.

Povinelli, Elizabeth (2001), 'Radical worlds: the anthropology of incommensurability and inconceivability', *Annual Review of Anthropology*, **30**: 319–34.

Redclift, Michael (2006), *Frontiers. Histories of Civil Society and Nature*, Cambridge, MA: MIT Press.

Rocheleau, Dianne (1995a), 'Environment, development, crisis and crusade: Ukambani, Kenya, 1890–1990', *World Development*, *23* (6): 1037–51.

Rocheleau, Dianne (1995b), 'Maps, numbers, text, and context: mixing methods in feminist political ecology', *Professional Geographers*, *47* (4): 458–66.

Rocheleau, Dianne (2000), 'Complex communities and relational webs: stories of surprise and transformation in Machakos', paper presented at workshop on 'Communities, Uncertainly and Resources Management', Institute of Development Studies, Sussex, 6–8 November.

Rocheleau, Dianne (2007), 'Rooted networks, webs of relation and the power of situated science: bringing the models back down to earth in Zambrana', unpublished manuscript, Department of Geography, Clark University.

Rocheleau, Dianne and Laurie Ross (1995), 'Trees as tools, trees as text: struggles over resources in Zambrana-Chacuey, Dominican Republic', *Antipode*, *27* (4): 407–28.

Rocheleau, Dianne, Barbara Thomas-Slater and Esther Wangari (eds) (1996), *Feminist Political Ecology*, New York: Routledge.

Rocheleau, Dianne and Robin Roth (2007), 'Rooted networks, relational webs and powers of connection: rethinking human and political ecologies', *Geoforum*, **38**, 433–7.

Saïd, Edward (1979) *Orientalism*, New York: Vintage Books.

Santos, Boaventura de Sousa (2007), *The Rise of the Global Left: the World Social Forum and Beyond*, London: Zed Books.

Schmink, Marianne and Charles Wood (1987) 'The "political ecology" of Amazonia', in P. Little and M. Horowitz (eds), *Lands at Risk in the Third World*, Boulder, CO: Westview Press, pp. 38–57.

Slater, Candace (ed.) (2003), *In Search of the Rainforest*, Durham, NC: Duke University Press.

Smith, Brian Cantwell (1996), *On the Origin of Objects*, Cambridge, MA: MIT Press.

Strathern, Marilyn (1980), 'No nature, no culture: the Hagen case', in C. MacCormack and M. Strathern (eds), *Nature, Culture, and Gender*, Cambridge, UK: Cambridge University Press, pp. 174–222.

Taylor, Mark (2001), *The Moment of Complexity. Emerging Network Culture*, Chicago, IL: University of Chicago Press.

Terranova, Tiziana (2004), *Network Culture*, London: Pluto Press.

Thrift, Nigel (2007), *Non-Representational Theory: Space, Politics, Affect*, London: Routledge.

Whatmore, Sarah (2002), *Hybrid Geographies: Natures, Cultures, Spaces*, London: Routledge.

Winograd, Terry and Fernando Flores (1986), *Understanding Computers and Cognition*, Norwood, NJ: Ablex Publishing Corporation.

Zibechi, Raúl (2006), *Dispersar el poder. Los movimientos como poderes antiestatales*, Buenos Aires: Tinta Limón.

7 Marx's ecology and its historical significance[1]
John Bellamy Foster

Introduction

> For the early Marx the only nature relevant to the understanding of history is human nature . . .
> Marx wisely left nature (other than human nature) alone.
>
> Lichtheim (1961: 245)

Although Lichtheim was not a Marxist, his view here did not differ from the general outlook of Western Marxism at the time he was writing. Yet this same outlook would be regarded by most informed observers on the Left today as laughable. After decades of explorations of Marx's contributions to ecological discussions and publication of his scientific–technical notebooks, it is no longer a question of whether Marx addressed nature, and did so throughout his life, but whether he can be said to have developed an understanding of the nature–society dialectic that constitutes a crucial starting point for understanding the ecological crisis of capitalist society.[2]

Due to mounting evidence, Marx's ecological contributions are increasingly acknowledged. Yet not everyone is convinced of their historical significance. A great many analysts, including some self-styled ecosocialists, persist in arguing that such insights were marginal to his work, that he never freed himself from 'Prometheanism' (a term usually meant to refer to an extreme commitment to industrialization at any cost), and that he did not leave a significant ecological legacy that carried forward into later socialist thought or that had any relation to the subsequent development of ecology. In a recent discussion in the journal *Capitalism, Nature, Socialism*, a number of authors argued that Marx could not have contributed anything of fundamental relevance to the development of ecological thought, since he wrote in the nineteenth century, before the nuclear age and before the appearance of polychlorinated biphenyls (PCBs), chlorofluorocarbons (CFCs) and DDT – and because he never used the word 'ecology' in his writings. Any discussion of his work in terms of ecology was therefore a case of taking 120 years of ecological thinking since Marx's death and laying it 'at Marx's feet' (de Kadt and Engel-Di Mauro, 2001).

My own view of the history of ecological thought and its relation to socialism, as articulated in my book *Marx's Ecology*, is quite different (Foster, 2000a). In this, as in other areas, I think we need to beware of falling into what Edward Thompson called 'the enormous condescension of posterity' (2001: p.6). More specifically, we need to recognize that Marx and Engels, along with other early socialist thinkers, like Proudhon (in *What is Property?*) and Morris, had the advantage of living in a time when the transition from feudalism to capitalism was still taking place or had occurred in recent memory. Hence the questions that they raised about capitalist society and even about the relation between society and nature were often more fundamental than what characterizes social and ecological thought, even on the Left, today. It is true that technology has changed, introducing massive new threats to the biosphere, undreamed of in earlier times. But, paradoxically, capitalism's antagonistic relation to the environment, which lies at the core of our current crisis, was in some ways more apparent to nineteenth- and early twentieth-century socialists than it is to the majority of today's green thinkers. This reflects the fact that it is not technology that is the primary issue, but rather the nature and logic of capitalism as a specific mode of production. Socialists have contributed in fundamental ways at all stages in the development of the modern ecological critique. Uncovering this unknown legacy is a vital part of the overall endeavor to develop an ecological materialist analysis capable of addressing the devastating environmental conditions that face us today.

Metabolism in Liebig and Marx
I first became acutely aware of the singular depth of Marx's ecological insights through a study of the Liebig–Marx connection. In 1862 the great German chemist Justus von Liebig published the seventh edition of his pioneering scientific work, *Organic Chemistry in its Application to Agriculture and Physiology* (first published in 1840 and commonly referred to as his *Agricultural Chemistry*). The 1862 edition contained a new, lengthy and, to the British, scandalous introduction. Building upon arguments that he had been developing in the late 1850s, Liebig declared the intensive, or 'high farming', methods of British agriculture to be a 'robbery system', opposed to rational agriculture.[3] They necessitated the transportation over long distances of food and fiber from the country to the city – with no provision for the recirculation of nutrients, such as nitrogen, phosphorus and potassium, which ended up contributing to urban waste and pollution in the form of human and animal wastes. Whole countries were robbed in this way of the nutrients of their soil. For Liebig this was part of a larger British imperial policy of robbing the soil resources (including bones) of other countries. 'Great Britain', he declared:

> deprives all countries of the conditions of their fertility. It has raked up the battlefields of Leipsic, Waterloo and the Crimea; it has consumed the bones of many generations accumulated in the catacombs of Sicily; and now annually destroys the food for a future generation of three millions and a half of people. Like a vampire it hangs on the breast of Europe, and even the world, sucking its lifeblood without any real necessity or permanent gain for itself.[4]

The population in Britain was able to maintain healthy bones and greater physical proportions, he argued, by robbing the rest of Europe of their soil nutrients, including skeletal remains, which would otherwise have gone into nurturing their own soils, allowing their populations to reach the same physical stature as the English.

'Robbery', Liebig suggested, 'improves the art of robbery'. The degradation of the soil led to a greater concentration of agriculture among a small number of proprietors who adopted intensive methods. But none of this altered the long-term decline in soil productivity. Britain was able to maintain its industrialized capitalist agriculture by importing guano (bird droppings) from Peru as well as bones from Europe. Guano imports increased from 1700 tons in 1841 to 220 000 tons only six years later (Ernle, 1961: 369).[5]

What was needed in order to keep this spoliation system going, Liebig declared, was the discovery of 'beds of manure or guano . . . of about the extent of English coalfields'. But existing sources were drying up without additional sources being found. By the early 1860s North America was importing more guano than all of Europe put together. 'In the last ten years', he wrote, 'British and American ships have searched through all the seas, and there is no small island, no coast, which has escaped their enquiries after guano. To live in the hope of the discovery of new beds of guano would be absolute folly.'

In essence, rural areas and whole nations were exporting the fertility of their land: 'Every country must become impoverished by the continual exportation of corn, and also by the needless waste of the accumulated products of the transformation of matter by the town populations.' All of this pointed to 'the law of restitution' as the main principle of a rational agriculture. The minerals taken from the earth had to be returned to the earth. 'The farmer' had to 'restore to his land as much as he had taken from it', if not more.

The British agricultural establishment, needless to say, did not take kindly to Liebig's message, with its denunciation of British high farming. Liebig's British publisher, rather than immediately translating the 1862 German edition of his *Agricultural Chemistry* as in the case of previous editions, destroyed the only copy in its possession. When this final edition of Liebig's great work was finally translated into English it was in an abridged form under a different title (*The Natural Laws of Husbandry*) and without Liebig's lengthy introduction. Hence the English-speaking world was left in ignorance of the extent of Liebig's critique of industrialized capitalist agriculture.

Nevertheless, the importance of Liebig's critique did not escape the attention of one major figure residing in London at the time. Karl Marx, who was then completing the first volume of *Capital*, was deeply affected by Liebig's critique. In 1866 he wrote to Engels, 'I had to plough through the new agricultural chemistry in Germany, in particular Liebig and Schönbein, which is more important for this matter than all of the economists put together.' Indeed, 'to have developed from the point of view of natural science the negative, i.e. destructive side of modern agriculture', Marx noted in volume one of *Capital*, 'is one of Liebig's immortal merits' (1976: 638).

Marx's two main discussions of modern agriculture both end with an analysis of 'the destructive side of modern agriculture'. In these passages Marx makes a number of crucial points: (1) capitalism has created an 'irreparable rift' in the 'metabolic interaction' between human beings and the earth, the everlasting nature-imposed conditions of production; (2) this demanded the 'systematic restoration' of that necessary metabolic relation as 'a regulative law of social production'; (3) nevertheless the growth under capitalism of large-scale agriculture and long-distance trade only intensifies and extends the metabolic rift; (4) the wastage of soil nutrients is mirrored in the pollution and waste in the towns – 'In London,' he wrote, 'they can find no better use for the excretion of four and a half million human beings than to contaminate the Thames with it at heavy expense'; (5) large-scale industry and large-scale mechanized agriculture work together in this destructive process, with 'industry and commerce supplying agriculture with the means of exhausting the soil'; (6) all of this is an expression of the antagonistic relation between town and country under capitalism; (7) a rational agriculture, which needs either small independent farmers producing on their own, or the action of the associated producers, is impossible under modern capitalist conditions; and (8) existing conditions demand a rational regulation of the metabolic relation between human beings and the earth, pointing beyond capitalist society to socialism and communism (Marx, 1976: 636–9, 1981: 948–50, 959).

Marx's concept of the metabolic rift was the core element of this ecological critique.

The human labor process itself was defined in *Capital* as 'the universal condition for the metabolic interaction between man and nature'. It followed that the rift in this metabolism meant nothing less than the undermining of the 'everlasting nature-imposed condition of human existence' (1976: 290). Further, there was the question of the sustainability of the earth – i.e. the extent to which it was to be passed on to future generations in a condition equal or better than in the present. As Marx wrote:

> From the standpoint of a higher socio-economic formation, the private property of particular individuals in the earth will appear just as absurd as private property of one man in other men. Even an entire society, a nation, or all simultaneously existing societies taken together, are not owners of the earth. They are simply its possessors, its beneficiaries, and have to bequeath it in an improved state to succeeding generations as *boni patres familias* [good heads of the household]. (1981: 911).

The issue of sustainability, for Marx, went beyond what capitalist society, with its constant intensification and enlargement of the metabolic rift between human beings and the earth, could address. Capitalism, he observed, 'creates the material conditions for a new and higher synthesis, a union of agriculture and industry on the basis of the forms that have developed during the period of their antagonistic isolation'. Yet, in order to achieve this 'higher synthesis', he argued, it would be necessary for the associated producers in the new society to 'govern the human metabolism with nature in a rational way' – a requirement that raised fundamental and continuing challenges for post-revolutionary society (Marx, 1976: 637, 1981: 959).

In analyzing the metabolic rift Marx and Engels did not stop with the soil nutrient cycle, or the town–country relation. They addressed at various points in their work such issues as deforestation, desertification, climate change, the elimination of deer from the forests, the commodification of species, pollution, industrial wastes, toxic contamination, recycling, the exhaustion of coal mines, disease, overpopulation and the evolution (and co-evolution) of species.[6]

Marx and the materialist conception of nature
After having the power and coherence of Marx's analysis of the metabolic rift impressed on me in this way, as reflected in my early writings on this subject (Foster, 1999), I began to wonder how deeply imbedded such ecological conceptions were in Marx's thought as a whole. What was there in Marx's background that could explain how he was able to incorporate natural scientific observations into his analysis so effectively? How did this relate to the concept of the alienation of nature, which along with the alienation of labor was such a pronounced feature of his early work? Most of all, I began to wonder whether the secret to Marx's ecology was to be found in his materialism. Could it be that this materialism was not adequately viewed simply in terms of a materialist conception of *human* history, but also had to be seen in terms of *natural* history and the dialectical relation between the two? Or, to put it somewhat differently, was Marx's materialist conception of history inseparable from what Engels (1941: 67) had termed the 'materialist conception of nature'? Had Marx employed his dialectical method in the analysis of both?

The search for an answer to these questions took me on an intellectual journey through Marx's works, and the historical–intellectual context in which they were written, which became *Marx's Ecology* (Foster, 2000a). Let me mention just a few highlights of the story I uncovered – since I do not have the space to explore it all in detail here, and because part of my purpose here is to add additional strands to the story. My account differs from most present-day accounts of Marx's development in that it highlights the formative significance of Marx's doctoral thesis on Epicurus, the greatest of the ancient materialists, and goes on to situate Marx and Engels's lifelong engagement with developments in the natural sciences. This includes Marx and Engels's opposition to the natural theology tradition, particularly as manifested by Malthus, their treatment of Liebig's work on nutrient cycling and its relation to the metabolic rift, and finally their creative encounter with Darwin, coevolution, and what has been called 'the revolution in ethnological time' (Trautmann, 1987: 35 and 220) following the discovery of the first prehistoric human remains.

In most interpretations of Marx's development his early thought is seen as largely a response to Hegel, mediated by Feuerbach. Without denying Hegel's significance I argue that Marx's formative phase is much more complex than is usually pictured. Along with German idealism, Marx was struggling early on with ancient materialist natural philosophy and its relation to the seventeenth-century scientific revolution, and the eighteenth-century Enlightenment. In all of this Epicurus loomed very large. For Kant, 'Epicurus can be called the foremost philosopher of sensibility', just as Plato was the foremost philosopher 'of the intellectual'. Epicurus, Hegel claimed, was 'the inventor of empiric natural science'. For Marx himself, Epicurus was the 'the greatest figure of the Greek Enlightenment' (Foster, 2000a: 49–51).

Epicurus represented, for Marx, most importantly, a non-reductionist, non-deterministic materialism, and had articulated a philosophy of human freedom. In Epicurus could be found a materialist conception of nature that rejected all teleology and all religious conceptions of natural and social existence. In studying Epicurus' natural philosophy, Marx was addressing a view that had had a powerful influence on the development of European science and modern naturalist–materialist philosophies, and one that had at the same time profoundly influenced the development of European social thought. In the Epicurean materialist worldview, knowledge of the world started with the senses. The two primary theses of Epicurus' natural philosophy make up what we today call the principle of conservation: nothing comes from nothing, and nothing being destroyed is reduced to nothing. For Epicureans there was no scale of nature, no set of sharp, unbridgeable gaps between human beings and other animals. Knowledge of Epicurus provides a way of understanding Marx's deep materialism in the area of natural philosophy. His study of ancient and early modern materialism brought Marx inside the struggle over the scientific understanding of the natural world in ways that influenced all of his thought and was deeply ecological in its significance, since it focused on evolution and emergence, and made nature, not God, the starting point. Moreover, Marx's dialectical encounter with Hegel has to be understood in terms of the struggle that he was carrying on simultaneously regarding the nature of materialist philosophy and science.

Darwin had similar roots in natural philosophy, linked to the anti-teleological tradition extending back to Epicurus, which had found its modern exponent in Bacon. We now know, as a result of the publication of Darwin's notebooks, that the reason that he waited so long – 20 years – before making public his theory on species transmutation was that his theory had strong materialist roots, and thus raised the issue of heresy in Victorian England. Darwin's view went against all teleological explanations, such as those of the natural theology tradition. He presented an account of the evolution of species that was dependent on no supernatural forces, no miraculous agencies of any kind, but simply on nature's own workings.

Marx and Engels greeted Darwin's theory immediately as 'the death of teleology', and Marx described it as 'the basis in natural history for our view' (see Foster, 2000a: 196–207 and 212–21). Not only did they study Darwin intensely, they were also drawn into the debates concerning human evolution that followed immediately on Darwin's work, as a result of the discovery of the first prehistoric human remains. Neanderthal remains had been found in France in 1856, but it was the discovery of prehistoric remains that were quickly accepted as such in England in Brixham Cave in 1859, the same year that Darwin published his *The Origin of Species*, that generated the revolution in ethnological time, erasing forever within science the biblical chronology for human history/ prehistory. Suddenly it became clear that the human species (or hominid species) had existed in all probability for a million years or longer, not simply a few thousand. (Today it is believed that hominid species have existed for around 7 million years.)

Many major works, mostly by Darwinians, emerged in just a few years to address this new reality, and Marx and Engels studied them with great intensity. Among these were Charles Lyell's *Geological Evidences of the Antiquity of Man* (1863), Thomas Huxley's *Evidence as to Man's Place in Nature* (1863), John Lubbock's *Prehistoric Times* (1865), Darwin's *Descent of Man* (1871), and a host of other works in the ethnological realm, including Lewis Henry Morgan's *Ancient Society* (1881).

Out of Marx and Engels's studies came a thesis on the role of labor in human evolution that was to prove fundamental. Inspired by the ancient Greek meaning for organ (*organon*) or tool, which expressed the idea that organs were essentially the 'grown-on' tools of animals, Marx referred to such organs as 'natural technology', which could be compared in certain respects to human technology. A similar approach was evident in Darwin, and Marx was thus able to use Darwin's comparison of the development of specialized organs in plants and animals to that of specialized tools (in chapter 5 of *The Origin of Species* on 'Laws of Variation') to help explain his own conception of the development of natural and human technology. The evolution of natural technology, Marx argued, rooting his analysis in *The Origin of Species*, was a reflection of the fact that animals and plants were able to pass on through inheritance organs that had been developed through natural selection in a process that might be called '"accumulation" through inheritance'. Indeed, the driving force of evolution for Darwin, in Marx's interpretation, was 'the gradually accumulated [naturally selected] inventions of living things'.[7]

In this conception, human beings were to be distinguished from animals in that they more effectively utilized tools, which became extensions of their bodies. Tools, and through them the wider realm of nature, as Marx said early on in his *Economic and Philosophic Manuscripts*, became the 'inorganic body of man'. Or, as he was to observe in *Capital*, 'thus nature becomes one of the organs of his [man's] activity, which he annexes to his own bodily organs, adding stature to himself in spite of the Bible'.[8]

Engels was to develop this argument further in his pathbreaking work, 'The Part Played by Labour in the Transition from Ape to Man' (written in 1876, published posthumously in 1896). According to Engels's analysis – which derived from his material-ist philosophy, but which was also influenced by views voiced by Ernst Haeckel a few years before – when the primates, who constituted the ancestors of human beings, descended from the trees, erect posture developed first (prior to the evolution of the human brain), freeing the hands for tool-making. In this way, '*the hand became free* and could hence-forth attain ever greater dexterity and skill, and the greater flexibility thus acquired was inherited and increased from generation to generation. Thus the hand is not only the organ of labor, *it is also the product of labor*' (Engels, 1940: 281; original emphasis).

As a result, early human beings (hominids) were able to alter their relation to their local environment, radically improving their adaptability. Those who were most ingen-ious in making and using tools were most likely to survive, which meant that the evolu-tionary process exerted selective pressures toward the enlargement of the brain and the development of language (necessary for the social processes of labor and tool-making), leading eventually to the rise of modern human beings. Thus the human brain, like the hand, in Engels's view, evolved through a complex, interactive set of relations, now referred to by evolutionary biologists as 'gene-culture co-evolution'. All scientific expla-nations of the evolution of the human brain, Stephen Jay Gould has argued, have thus far been theories of gene-culture co-evolution, and 'the best 19th century case for gene-culture co-evolution was made by Frederick Engels' (Gould, 1987: 111).

All of this points to the fact that Marx and Engels had a profound grasp of ecological and evolutionary problems, as manifested in the natural science of their day, and that they were able to make important contributions to our understanding of how society and nature interact. If orthodoxy in Marxism, as Lukács taught, relates primarily to method, then we can attribute these insights to a very powerful method. But one that, insofar as it encompasses both a materialist conception of natural history and of human (i.e. social) history, has not been fully investigated by subsequent commentators. Behind Marx and Engels's insights in this area lay an uncompromising materialism, which embraced such concepts as emergence and contingency, and which was dialectical to the core.

Marxist ecological materialism after Marx

Engels's *Dialectics of Nature* is known to incorporate numerous ecological insights. But it is frequently contended that Marxism after Marx and Engels either missed out on the development of ecological thought altogether or was anti-ecological and that there were no important Marxian contributions to the study of nature after Engels until the Frankfurt School and Alfred Schmidt's *The Concept of Nature in Marx*, first published in 1962 (Castree, 2000: 14 and Foster, 2001: 465–7). This position, however, is wrong. There were in fact numerous penetrating Marxist contributions to the analysis of the nature–society relation, and socialists played a very large role in the development of ecology, particularly in its formative stages. The influence of Marx and Engels's ideas in this respect was not confined to the nineteenth century.

But it is not just a question of the direct inheritance of certain propositions with respect to nature–ecology. Marx and Engels employed a materialist conception of nature that was fundamental to the major revolutions in the science of their day (as evident in Darwin's theory), and combined it with a dialectic of emergence and contin-gency. A very large part of this was reflected in both socialist and scientific thought in the immediately succeeding generations. Among the socialists (some of them leading natural scientists) who incorporated naturalistic and ecological conceptions into their thinking, after Marx and through the 1940s, we can include such figures as William Morris, Henry Salt, August Bebel, Karl Kautsky, Rosa Luxemburg, V.I. Lenin, Nikolai Bukharin, V.I. Vernadsky, N.I. Vavilov, Alexander Oparin, Christopher Caudwell, Hyman Levy, Lancelot Hogben, J.D. Bernal, Benjamin Farrington, J.B.S. Haldane and Joseph Needham – and in the more Fabian tradition, but not unconnected to Marx and Marxism, Ray Lankester and Arthur Tansley. Bukharin employed Marx's concept of the metabolism of nature and society in his writings, and explicitly situated human beings in the biosphere. 'If human beings', he wrote

> are both products of nature and part of it; if they have a biological basis when their social existence is excluded from account (it cannot be abolished!); if they are themselves natural magnitudes and products of nature, and if they live within nature (however much they might be divided off from it by particular social and historical conditions of life and by the so-called 'artistic environment'), then what is surprising in the fact that human beings share in the rhythm of nature and its cycles? (Bukharin, 2005: 101)

Kautsky in his *The Agrarian Question*, following Liebig and Marx, addressed the problem of the soil nutrient cycle, raised the question of the fertilizer treadmill, and even referred to the dangers of the intensive application of pesticides – all in 1899! Luxemburg addressed ecological problems in her letters, discussing the disappearance of songbirds through the destruction of their habitat. Lenin promoted both conservation and ecology in the Soviet Union, and demonstrated an awareness of the degradation of soil fertility and the breaking of the soil nutrient cycle under capitalist agriculture – the Liebig–Marx problem.

The Soviet Union in the 1920s had the most developed ecological science in the world. Vernadsky had introduced the concept of the biosphere in a dialectical framework of analysis that reaches down to the most advanced ecology of our day. Vavilov used the historical materialist method to map out the centres of the origin of agriculture and the banks of germplasm throughout the globe, now known as the Vavilov areas. Oparin, simultaneously with Haldane in Britain, developed the first influential modern materialist explanation for the origin of life on earth based on Vernadsky's biosphere concept – a theory that was to have an important impact on Rachel Carson's concept of ecology (Foster, 2000a: 241–4; Carson, 1998: 229–30).

Yet this early Marxist ecological thought, or rather the traditions that sustained it, largely died out. Ecology within Marxism suffered something of a double death. In the East in the 1930s Stalinism literally purged the more ecological elements within the Soviet leadership and scientific community – not arbitrarily so since it was in these circles that some of the resistance to primitive socialist accumulation was to be found. Bukharin was executed. Vavilov died of malnutrition in a prison cell in 1943. At the same time in the West, Marxism took an often extreme, avidly anti-positivistic form. The dialectic was seen as inapplicable to nature – a view often associated with Lukács, although we now know that Lukács's position was somewhat more complex.[9] This affected most of Western Marxism, which tended to see Marxism increasingly in terms of a human history severed for the most part from nature. Nature was relegated to the province of natural science, which was seen as properly positivistic within its own realm. In Lukács, Gramsci and Korsch, marking the Western Marxist revolt of the 1920s, nature was increasingly conspicuous by its absence. Nature entered into the Frankfurt School's critique of the Enlightenment, but the nature under consideration was almost always human nature (reflecting the concern with psychology), and rarely so-called 'external nature'. There was no materialist conception of nature. Hence genuine ecological insights were rare.

If an unbroken continuity is to be nonetheless found in the development of socialist nature–science discussions and ecological thought, it survived (though largely unacknowledged) primarily in Britain, where a continuous commitment to a materialist dialectic in the analysis of natural history was maintained. A strong tradition in Britain linked science, Darwin, Marx and dialectics. Although some of the negative features of this tradition, which has been referred to as a 'Baconian strand in Marxism', are well known, its more positive ecological insights have never been fully grasped (Wood, 1959: 145).

Any account of the ecology of British Marxism in this period has to highlight Caudwell, who, although he died at the age of 29 behind a machine-gun on a hill in Spain fighting for the Republic in the Spanish Civil War, left an indelible intellectual legacy. His *Heredity and Development*, perhaps the most important of his science-related works, was suppressed by the Communist Party in Britain due to the Lysenkoist controversy (he was anti-Lysenkoist) and so was not published until 1986.[10] But it contains an impressive attempt to develop an ecological dialectic. Haldane, Levy, Hogben, Needham, Bernal and Farrington – as previously noted – all developed ecological notions (although Bernal's legacy is the most contradictory in this respect). All indicated profound respect not only for Marx and Darwin but also for Epicurus, who was seen as the original source of the materialist conception of nature. The influence of these thinkers carries down to the present day, in the work of later biological and ecological scientists, such as Steven Rose in Britain, and Richard Lewontin, Richard Levins, and the late Stephen Jay Gould in the USA.

Haldane was a deep admirer of the work of British biologist Charles Elton, the great pioneer in animal ecology and ecosystem analysis, whose work strongly influenced Rachel Carson. Referring to the dialectics of nature evident in Elton's ecological invasions analysis (which criticized the use of pesticides and the human transformation of the environment that encouraged such use), Haldane (1985: 137) observed: 'Elton is not so far as I know a Marxist. But I am sure Marx would have approved of his dialectical thinking.' Indeed, for Haldane, the problem of the growing ecological strains brought on by capitalist development made the question of 'back to nature' unavoidable, if somewhat misdirected. A society no longer geared primarily to profits and prestige, he suggested, probably

> should reject a great many artificialities, including stiff collars, bombing, aeroplanes, and high speed motor cars. But we realize that a complete return to nature would mean living without clothes, houses, cookery, or literature. All such slogans as 'back to nature' are meaningless unless we consider the economic system within which the change is to operate, and very often, as in this case, we find that within a better economic system the change would be largely unnecessary. (Haldane, 1938)[11]

Needham was to question the relation between the 'conquest of nature' and social domination. He saw the alienation of nature by class society as the reason that 'the growing pollution of the environment by man's waste-products' was 'hardly recognized as a danger until our own time' (Needham, 1976: 300–301).

Prominent Marxian (and Darwinian) contributions to the understanding of ecology and evolution, building on this same ecological materialist tradition, were later to emerge, as indicated, in the work of such thinkers as Stephen Jay Gould, Richard Lewontin and Richard Levins in the USA, who have advanced dialectical conceptions of nature. As ecologist Richard Levins says of his own development:

> I first met dialectical materialism in my early teens through the writings of the British Marxist scientists J.B.S. Haldane, J.D. Bernal, Joseph Needham, and others, and then on to Marx and Engels. It immediately grabbed me both intellectually and aesthetically. A dialectical view of nature and society has been a major theme of my research ever since. I have delighted in the dialectical emphasis on wholeness, connection and context, change, historicity, contradiction, irregularity, asymmetry, and the multiplicity of phenomena, as a refreshing counterweight to the prevailing reductionism then and now. (Lewontin and Levins, 2007: 367)

Ecology, Lewontin and Levins have insisted, stands not only for the wholeness of life, but increasingly for its alienation as well, due to the ecological depredations of capitalist production. 'For humans ecology is a social ecology' (Ibid.: 203). Hence the rifts in the human metabolism with nature brought on by capitalism require social solutions that are revolutionary in nature.

Materialism and the rise of the ecosystem concept

In order to grasp more fully the complex relation between materialist ecology and historical materialism from the late nineteenth to the early twentieth century, I would like to focus on two figures in Britain who were more Fabian than Marxist, but clearly socialists in the broader sense – namely Ray Lankester (1847–1929) and Arthur Tansley (1871–1955). Ray Lankester taught at University College, London, and Tansley was his student there. Lankester was Huxley's protégé and was considered the greatest Darwinian scientist of his generation. When he was a boy, Darwin and Huxley, who were friends of his father, both played with him. Lankester was also a young friend of Karl Marx and a socialist, though not himself a Marxist. He was a frequent guest at Marx's household in the last few years of Marx's life. Marx and his daughter Eleanor also visited Lankester at his residence in London. Marx and Lankester had in common, above all, their materialism. Marx was interested in Lankester's research into degeneration – the notion that evolution did not necessarily simply go forward – and made an attempt to get Lankester's work published in Russian. Lankester wrote to Marx that he was absorbing 'your great work on Capital . . . with the greatest pleasure and profit'. Lankester was to become one of the leading ecologically concerned thinkers of his time. He wrote some of the most powerful essays that have ever been written on species extinction due to human causes, and discussed the pollution of London and other ecological issues with an urgency that was not found again until the late twentieth century.[12]

Arthur Tansley was the foremost plant ecologist in Britain of his generation and the originator of the concept of ecosystem. He was to become the first president of the British Ecological Society. Tansley was deeply influenced by Lankester, along with the botanist Francis Wall Oliver, in his years at University College, London. Like Lankester, Tansley was a Fabian-style socialist and an uncompromising materialist. And like

Lankester, who wrote a scathing criticism of Henri Bergson's concept of vitalism or the *élan vital*, Tansley directly challenged attempts to conceive evolutionary ecology in anti-materialist, teleological terms.[13]

In the 1920s and 1930s a major split occurred in ecology. In the USA Frederic Clements and others developed the important concept of ecological succession (successive stages in the development of plant 'communities' in a particular region culminating in a 'climax' or mature stage linked to certain dominant species). But in a much more controversial move, Clements and his followers extended this analysis to a concept of super-organism meant to account for the process of succession. This ecological approach inspired other innovations in ecological theory in Edinburgh and South Africa. South African ecological thinkers, led by Jan Christian Smuts, introduced a concept of 'holism' in the ecological realm, most notably in Smuts's book *Holism and Evolution* (1926), which was to lead to modern conceptions of deep ecology. Smuts, who was usually referred to as General Smuts because of his military role in the Boer War (he fought on the side of the Boers), was one of the principal figures in the construction of the apartheid system. How much Smuts himself contributed directly to the development of apartheid may be disputed, but he was a strong advocate of the territorial segregation of the races and what he called 'the grand white racial aristocracy'. He is perhaps best remembered worldwide as the South African general who arrested Gandhi. Smuts was South African minister of defense from 1910 to 1919, and prime minister and minister of native affairs from 1919 to 1924. He was sometimes seen as a figure soaked in blood. When the Native Labour Union demanded political power and freedom of speech, Smuts crushed it with violence, killing 68 people in Port Elizabeth alone. When black Jews refused to work on Passover, Smuts sent in the police, and 200 were killed on his orders. When certain black tribal populations in Bondelwaart refused to pay their dog tax, Smuts sent in planes and bombed them into submission. Not surprisingly, Smuts's ecological holism was also a form of ecological racism, since it was a holism that contained natural–ecological divisions along racial lines.

The legendary opponent of Smuts's holistic philosophy, in the great 'Nature of Life' debate that took place at the British Association for the Advancement of Science meetings in South Africa in 1929, was the British Marxist biologist Lancelot Hogben (who had a position at the University of Cape Town at that time). Hogben not only debated Smuts – opposing his materialism to Smuts's holism, and attacking Smuts for his racist eugenics – but also reportedly hid black rebels fleeing the racist state in a secret compartment in his basement. Another major opponent of Smuts was the British Marxist mathematician Hyman Levy, who, in his *The Universe of Science*, developed a critique of Smuts's holism along similar lines to those of Hogben (Anker, 2001: 41–75 and 118–49; Smuts, 1926; Hogben, 1930; Levy, 1933; and for Smuts's racial views see Smuts, 1930: 92–4).

In 1935 Tansley found himself increasingly at odds with anti-materialist conceptions of ecology that were then gaining influence, and entered the lists against ecological idealism. Tansley wrote an article for the journal *Ecology* entitled 'The Use and Abuse of Vegetational Concepts and Terms' that declared war on Clements, Smuts and Smuts's leading follower in South African ecology, John Phillips. In one fell swoop Tansley attacked the teleological notions that ecological succession was always progressive and developmental, always leading to a climax; that vegetation could be seen as constituting a super-organism; that there was such a thing as a biotic 'community' (with members), encompassing both plants and animals; that 'organismic philosophy', which saw the whole universe as an organism, was a useful way to understand ecological relations; and that holism could be seen as both cause and effect of everything in nature. Smuts's holistic view, Tansley claimed, was 'at least partly motivated by an imagined future "whole" to be realised in an ideal human society whose reflected glamour falls on less exalted wholes, illuminating with a false light the image of the "complex organism"' (Tansley, 1935: 299). This was possibly a polite way of referring to the system of racial stratification that was built into Smutsian holistic ecology.

In combating this type of mystical holism and super-organicism, and introducing the concept of ecosystem in response, Tansley turned to the systems theory utilized in Levy's *The Universe of Science* and at the same time referred to materialist conceptions of dynamic equilibrium in natural systems going back to Lucretius (Epicurus' Roman follower and author of the great philosophical poem *The Nature of Things*). 'The fundamental conception', represented by his new ecosystem concept, Tansley argued, was that of

> the whole system (in the sense of physics), including not only the organism complex, but also the whole complex of physical factors forming what we call the environment of the biome – the habitat factors in the widest sense. Though the organisms may claim our primary interest, when we are trying to think fundamentally we cannot separate them from their special environment, with which they form one physical system. . . . These ecosystems, as we may call them, are of the most various kinds and sizes. They form one category of the multitudinous physical systems of the universe, which range from the universe as a whole down to the atom. (Tansley, 1935: 299)

Following Levy, Tansley emphasized a dialectical conception: 'The systems we isolate mentally are not only included as part of larger ones, but they also overlap, interlock, and interact with one another. The isolation is partly artificial, but it is the only possible way in which we can proceed.'

Rather than seeing ecology in terms of a teleological order, Tansley stressed disruptions to that order. He referred to 'the destructive human activities of the modern world', and presented human beings as an 'exceptionally powerful biotic factor which increasingly upsets the equilibrium of pre-existing ecosystems and eventually destroys them, at the same time forming new ones of very different nature'. 'Ecology', he argued, 'must be applied to conditions brought about by human activity', and for this purpose the ecosystem concept, which situated life within its larger material environment, and penetrated 'beneath the forms of the "natural" entities', was the most practical form for analysis. Tansley's ecosystem concept was, paradoxically, more genuinely holistic and more dialectical than the super-organicism and 'holism' that preceded it, because it brought both the organic and inorganic world within a more complex materialist synthesis (Anker, 2001: 152–6; Tansley, 1935: 303).

The dialectics of the alienation of nature and society

The concept of metabolism was eventually to become crucial to developing the ecosystem analysis arising from Tansley, with leading systems ecologists such as Eugene Odum employing the notion of metabolism to all levels from the cell up to the ecosystem (Odum, 1969). Since Marx was the pioneer thinker to employ this concept in the social relation to nature, tying it to labor and production under capitalism, it is not surprising that a great deal of research by environmental sociologists and others has emerged of late, focusing on his socio-ecological concept of metabolic rift, and using it to explore the major rifts in the biosphere related to: climate change, the destruction of the oceans, problems of the soil, devastation of the forests and so on (Dickens, 2004: 58–90; Clark and York, 2005, 2008; Clausen and Clark, 2005; Clausen, 2007; Mancus, 2007). Other work has investigated the way in which Marx, in line with his metabolism argument, built thermodynamics into the very fabric of his critique of political economy in *Capital*. Marx in this way was to help inspire much of the thinking that has come to characterize ecological economics (a great deal of which was influenced by his work in its early stages). Paul Burkett, in particular, has built on these insights to develop a contemporary Marxist ecological economics (Burkett, 2006; Burkett and Foster, 2006, 2008; Foster and Burkett, 2008).

Some environmental commentators of course persist in claiming that Marx believed one-sidedly in the struggle of human beings against nature, and was thus anthropocentric and anti-ecological, and that Marxism as a whole carried forth this original ecological sin. But there is mounting evidence, as we have seen, of Marx's very deep ecological penetration and of the pioneering insights of socialist ecologists, which has conclusively pulled the rug out from under such criticisms.

What Marx and Marxism have illuminated above all, in this area, are the historic causes of ecological alienation/exploitation in modern systems of class-based production. In *The Grundrisse* Marx observed:

> It is not the *unity* of living and active humanity with the natural, inorganic condition of their metabolic exchange with nature, and hence their appropriation of nature, which requires explanation or is the result of a historic process, but rather the *separation* between these inorganic conditions of human existence and this active existence, a separation which is completely posited only in the relation of wage labor and capital. (Marx, 1973: 489; see also Marx and Engels, 1975: 39–41).

This destructive separation between humanity and nature is not inherent to the human condition, but the product of a given set of alienated social, economic and ecological relations that the world must now transcend.

Notes

1. This chapter is a revised, expanded and updated version of an article that first appeared under the title 'Marx's ecology in historical perspective' in *International Socialism*, **96** (Autumn 2002): 71–86.
2. On the strengths of Marx's ecological analysis see Foster (2000a) and Burkett (1999).
3. Except where otherwise indicated, all the brief quotes from Liebig in the text below are taken from an unpublished English translation of the 1862 German edition of his *Agricultural Chemistry* by Lady Gilbert contained in the archives of the Rothamsted Experimental Station (now IACR–Rothamsted) outside London.
4. The translation of this passage from the introduction to the 1862 edition of Liebig's work follows Marald (2002: 74).
5. For a fuller discussion of Marx's ecological argument and its relation to the nineteenth-century guano trade see Foster and Clark (2003: 186–201).
6. Documentation of Marx's various ecological concerns can be found in Foster (2000a) and Burkett (1999). The problem of local climate change was raised by Engels and Marx in their time (speculation on temperature changes due to deforestation); see Engels's notes on Fraas in Marx and Engels (1999: 512–15).
7. Marx (1971: 294–5); Darwin (1968: 187); Marx (1976: 493); on Marx's use of organic/inorganic see Foster and Burkett (2000: 403–25).

8. Marx (1974: 328, 1976: 285–6). See also Foster and Burkett (2000: 403–25).
9. On the dialectics of nature and ecology in Marx and Lukács, see Foster (2008: 50–82).
10. Lysenkoism was an erroneous doctrine associated with the work of the Russian agronomist Trofim Denisovich Lysenko that de-emphasized genetic inheritance in favor of a notion of the plasticity of the life cycle. For a balanced discussion of Lysenkoism, see Levins and Lewontin (1985: 163–96).
11. See also Foster and Clark (2008a).
12. See the more detailed discussions of Lankester in Foster (2000a: 221–5); and Foster (2000b: 233–5).
13. For biographical information on Tansley see Anker (2001: 7–40). For a much more extensive and detailed discussion of the Smuts–Tansley debate and its relation to Marx's ecology see Foster and Clark (2008b).

References

Anker, Peder (2001), *Imperial Ecology: Environmental Order in the British Empire*, Cambridge, MA: Harvard University Press.
Bukharin, Nicholai (2005), *Philosophical Arabesques*, New York: Monthly Review Press.
Burkett, Paul (1999), *Marx and Nature*, New York: Monthly Review Press.
Burkett, Paul (2006), *Marxism and Ecological Economics*, Boston, MA: Brill.
Burkett, Paul and John Bellamy Foster (2006), 'Metabolism, energy and entropy in Marx's critique of political economy', *Theory and Society*, **35**: 109–56.
Burkett, Paul and John Bellamy Foster (2008), 'The Podolinsky myth', *Historical Materialism*, **16**: 115–61.
Carson, Rachel (1998), *Lost Woods*, Boston, UA: Beacon Press.
Castree, Noel (2000), 'Marxism and the production of nature', *Capital and Class*, **72**: 5–36.
Clark, Brett and Richard York (2005), 'Carbon metabolism', *Theory and Society*, **34** (4): 391–428.
Clark, Brett and Richard York (2008), 'Rifts and shifts', *Monthly Review*, **60** (6): 13–24.
Clausen, Rebecca (2007), 'Healing the rift', *Monthly Review*, **59** (1): 40–52.
Clausen, Rebecca and Brett Clark (2005), 'The metabolic rift and marine ecology', *Organization & Environment*, **18** (4): 422–44.
de Kadt, Maarten and Salvatore Engel-Di Mauro (2001), 'Marx's ecology or ecological Marxism: failed promise', *Capitalism, Nature, Socialism*, **12** (2): 52–5.
Darwin, Charles (1968), *Origin of Species*, New York: Penguin.
Dickens, Peter (2004), *Society and Nature: Changing Our Enviornment, Changing Ourselves*, London: Polity Press.
Engels, Frederick (1941), *Ludwig Feuerbach and the Outcome of Classical German Philosophy*, New York: International Publishers.
Engels, Frederick (1940), *The Dialectics of Nature*, New York: International Publishers.
Ernle, Lord (1961), *English Farming Past and Present*, Chicago, IL: Quadrangle.
Foster, John Bellamy (1999), 'Marx's theory of metabolic rift', *American Journal of Sociology*, **105** (2): 366–405.
Foster, John Bellamy (2000a), *Marx's Ecology*, New York: Monthly Review Press.
Foster, John Bellamy (2000b), 'E. Ray Lankester, ecological materialist: an introduction to Lankester's "Effacement of Nature by Man"', *Organization & Environment*, **13** (2): 233–5.
Foster, John Bellamy (2001), 'Review of special issue of *Capital and Class*', *Historical Materialism*, **8**, 465–7.
Foster, John Bellamy (2008), 'The dialectics of nature and Marxist ecology' in Bertell Ollman and Tony Smith (eds), *Dialectics for the New Century*, Basingstoke, UK: Palgrave Macmillan, pp. 50–82.
Foster, John Bellamy and Paul Burkett (2000), 'The Dialectic of organic/inorganic relations', *Organization & Environment*, **13** (4): 403–25.
Foster, John Bellamy and Paul Burkett (2008), 'Classical Marxism and the Second Law of Thermodynamics', *Organization & Environment*, **21** (1): 3–37.
Foster, John Bellamy and Brett Clark (2003), 'Ecological imperialism', *Socialist Register 2004*, 40: 186–201.
Foster, John Bellamy and Brett Clark (2008a), 'Rachel Carson's ecological critique', *Monthly Review*, **59** (9): 1–17.
Foster, John Bellamy and Brett Clark (2008b), 'The sociology of ecology: ecological organicism versus eco-system ecology in the social construction of ecological science, 1926–1935', *Organization & Environment*, **21** (3): 311–52.
Gould, Stephen Jay (1987), *An Urchin in the Storm*, New York: W.W. Norton.
Haldane, J.B.S. (1938), 'Back to nature', 18 April, in the Haldane Papers, University of London, Box 7.
Haldane, J.B.S. (1985), *On Being the Right Size*, Oxford University Press.
Hogben, Lancelot (1930), *The Nature of Living Matter*, London: Kegan Paul, Trench, Trubner & Co.
Levy, Hyman (1933), *The Universe of Science*, New York: Century.
Levins, Richard and Richard Lewontin (1985), *The Dialectical Biologist*, Cambridge, MA: Harvard University Press.

Lewontin, Richard and Richard Levins (2007), *Biology Under the Influence: Dialectical Essays on Ecology, Agriculture, and Health*, New York: Monthly Review Press.
Lichtheim, George (1961), *Marxism: An Historical and Critical Study*, New York: Praeger.
Liebig, J. (1862), 'Agricultural chemistry', unpublished English translation by Lady Gilbert of the German original contained in the archives of the Rothamsted Experimental Station (now IACR–Rothamsted), Rothamsted, UK.
Mancus, Philip (2007), 'Nitrogen fertilizer dependency and its contradictions', *Rural Sociology*, **72** (2): 269–88.
Marald, Erland (2002), 'Everything circulates: agricultural chemistry and recycling theories in the second half of the nineteenth century', *Environment and History*, **8**: 65–84.
Marx, Karl (1971), *Theories of Surplus Value*, Vol. 3, Moscow: Progress Publishers
Marx, Karl (1973), *The Grundrisse*, New York: Vintage.
Marx, Karl (1974), *Early Writings*, New York: Vintage.
Marx, Karl (1976), *Capital*, Vol. 1, New York: Vintage.
Marx, Karl (1981), *Capital*, Vol. 3, New York: Vintage.
Marx, Karl and Frederick Engels (1975), *Collected Works* Vol. 5, New York: Vintage.
Marx, Karl and Frederick Engels (1999), *MEGA*, IV 31, Amsterdam: Akadamie Verlag.
Needham, Joseph (1976), *Moulds of Understanding*, London: George Allen & Unwin.
Odum, Eugene (1969), 'The strategy of ecosystem development', *Science*, **164**: 262–70.
Smuts, Jan Christian (1926), *Holism and Evolution*, London: Macmillan.
Smuts, Jan Christian (1930), *Africa and Some World Problems*, Oxford: Oxford University Press.
Tansley, Arthur G. (1935), 'The use and abuse of vegetational concepts and terms', *Ecology*, **16** (3): 284–307.
Thompson, E.P. (2001), *The Essential E.P. Thompson*, New York: New Press.
Trautmann, T.R. (1987), *Lewis Henry Morgan and the Invention of Kinship*, Berkeley, CA: University of California Press.
Wood, Neal (1959), *Communism and British Intellectuals*, New York: Columbia University Press.

8 The transition out of carbon dependence: the crises of environment and markets
Michael R. Redclift

Introduction

The environment poses real problems for the social sciences, especially the growing sense of urgency surrounding climate change (Rayner and Malone, 1998; Cock and Hopwood, 1996; Dyson, 2005; Brunnengräber, 2007; Lever-Tracy, 2008, Altvater, 2007). This is partly because some disciplines, among them sociology, have longstanding difficulties with policy agendas (with which they often coevolved historically, and to which they usually offered a critique). In the case of sociology the difficulties were also compounded by the question of naturalism, and the unwillingness to accept what have often seemed facile or insufficient 'biological' explanations of human behaviour (Benton 1994). Other disciplines, notably human geography, have given much more attention to the environmental terrain including climate change, and located it firmly within their domain of interest, in this case the growing field of political ecology (Bryant and Bailey, 1997; Keil et al., 1998; Biersack and Greenberg, 2006).

The way in which the social sciences respond to the climate change agenda is likely to assume more importance in a world where, in principle at least, ways out of carbon dependence and alternatives need to be found. In particular it means revisiting what 'we know', and subjecting environmental knowledges to new and unfamiliar investigations. It means investigating future alternatives to the 'hydrocarbon societies' (Norgaard, 1994) with which we are most familiar, rather as Max Weber investigated unfamiliar 'whole societies' in Antiquity (Norgaard, 1988; Weber, 1991).

In many ways, it can be argued, this quest for an analysis of transitions out of carbon dependence (including more understanding of their ideological and political dimensions) is one that should be heartening for sociologists. The discipline has long been interested in the way in which everyday behaviour is institutionalized and naturalized. In addition, sociology has proved an acute lens through which to explore alternative ways of living and imaginaries, and the way they correspond to and connect with wider human purposes (Kumar, 1978, 1987; Abrams and McCulloch, 1976; Green, 1988). Sociology, and particularly environmental sociology, should be well placed to analyse the social dimensions of carbon dependence and 'decarbonization': the processes through which economically developed societies have grown more dependent on carbon, and the possible routes out of this dependence.

It may be, of course, that to develop this new landscape of sustainability we need to be more familiar with work in other contiguous social science disciplines. This chapter begins by reviewing the major differences and divisions that have come to characterize the discussion of the environment and nature in the social sciences, distinguishing between critical realism and social constructivism. It goes on to review the main intellectual challenges to both positions, and finally argues for a sociological perspective on 'decarbonization' that takes us beyond the current impasse and suggests some areas for theoretical development.

Sustainable development: bringing up an oxymoron

The recent history of sociological concern with the environment begins with the discussion of 'sustainability' and 'sustainable development' in the 1980s. In the wake of the Brundtland Commission Report (WCED, 1987) it was argued in some quarters that economic development ought to be able to accommodate 'sustainability' thinking (Norgaard, 1988; Pearce, 1991). The discussion of development needed to be enlarged and a 'long view' taken of environment–economy relations, which acknowledged a bigger role for future generations and the market (Welford and Starkey, 1996; Murphy and Bendell, 1997). Other critics maintained a more sceptical position towards the easy elision of markets and nature (Redclift, 1987; Adams, 2001; Owens, 1994; McAfee, 1999).

Since the 1990s the formulation that sees no inherent contradiction between sustainability and development has increasingly been called into question. Some critics of 'sustainable development' from the Right have argued that it is an oxymoron, and that economic development cannot accommodate sustainability (Beckerman, 1994; Milbrath, 1994; North, 1995). Others have argued that the concept of sustainable development occludes as much as it reveals, and has served to marginalize distributional issues, poverty and justice (Martínez-Alier 1995; Redclift, 1993; Langhelle, 2000; Page, 2006).

More recent contributions to the debate have argued that both the scientific evidence for global environmental change and increasing globalization (both economic and cultural) suggest that it is possible to 're-tune' development along lines that are less energy and material intensive (Lovins and Hunter, 2000). The emphasis on material throughput and 'dematerialization' has also attracted attention (Fischer-Kowalski and Weisz 1999; Huber, 2000). These positions on the compatibility – or lack of it – between the economy and the environment were influenced by several processes:

(a) Warnings of accelerated ecological losses and degradation at a global scale (the Earth Summits of 1992 and 2002, but also the Millennium Ecosystem Assessment 2005, and the first and second World Conservation Strategies 1983 and 1991). Awareness of existing, and impending, ecological problems stiffened the resolve of some critics to give higher priority to a 'biosphere politics' (Rifkin, 1992).

(b) Neoliberal and structural adjustment policies pursued after the debt crisis (the so-called 'Washington Consensus') effectively marginalized Keynesian economics, which had seen increased public expenditure as a way of managing environmental, as well as social, problems (Lal, 1985; Mawdsley and Rigg, 2003; Onis and Senses, 2005). It had been assumed under neo-Keynesian orthodoxy that increased environmental problems would be matched by increased abatement expenditure.

(c) Climate change politics: the Framework Convention on Climate Change (1992) and the Kyoto Protocol (1997). The growing consensus, which some have labeled 'post-political' (Swyngedouw, 2008), that anthropogenic global warming could galvanize world opinion behind a common policy position.

(d) The development of 'ecological modernization' policies, especially in the developed world, which enable business to benefit from an internalization of environmental externalities (Mol, 2001 and Chapter 4 in this volume).

Despite their obvious resonance, many of these 'real-world' processes have failed to influence academic disciplines, including sociology. For example, the political and social implications of employing the idea of 'sustainability' much more widely than in its original conception have rarely been thought through (Redclift, 2005), and it has been noted how little sociologists have contributed to rethinking the new parameters of climate change (Lever-Tracy, 2008). Similarly, little attention has been given to the implications of rethinking sustainability for governance, security or ideas of justice (Low and Gleeson, 1997, 1998; Harvey, 1996; Swyngedouw and Heynen, 2003). The reasons for this are informative. During the 1970s and 1980s environmental policy and regulation identified *external* risks (wildlife, effluents, etc.) that could be contained or repaired. These risks were seen as *controllable* (Brunnengräber, 2007). There was a strong modernist, Promethean impulse at work in delineating human responsibilities towards nature.

Since 1992, however, this confident, regulatory impulse has been undermined, particularly as the evidence of climate change has increased. Floods, storms, habitat loss and droughts can be seen as immanent to the system (especially the climate system). They are *internal risks.* They were also risks apparently bound up with human profligacy rather than 'natural' limits, with excessive consumption rather than 'carrying capacity' (Redclift, 1996).

At the same time sustainability has also been treated discursively, and its claims subjected to textual deconstruction like any other social proposition or premise. Just as some advocates of sustainability, influenced by neoliberal policies and the hegemony of the market, sought to incorporate the environment into business and corporate planning, so skeptics of a postmodern or poststructuralist persuasion have treated the environment primarily as discursive terrain. Furthermore, doubts about the ability to control the effects of public policy choices have extended to new areas, notably genetics, where 'internal' (biological) nature has found a new footing in the social sciences, and one that parts company with the social sciences' historical ambivalence towards biology (Finkler, 2000; Redclift, 2005).

A post-carbon politics?

> The transition to a low-carbon economy will bring challenges for competitiveness but also opportunities for growth. . .
> Reducing the expected adverse impacts of climate change is therefore both highly desirable and feasible.
>
> (Stern, 2007: xvi)

This quotation from the highly influential report by Lord Stern illustrates the way in which what had previously been viewed as a 'threat' could quickly become an 'opportunity'. The immediate responses to Stern (and the IPCC *Fourth Assessment* of 2007) were effusive and optimistic in tone. One commentator on business and the environment wrote:

> People would pay a little more for carbon-intensive goods, but our economies could continue to grow strongly. . . The shift to a low-carbon economy will also bring huge opportunities. . . Climate change is the greatest market failure the world has seen. (Welford, 2006: 261)

The characterization of climate change as a 'market failure' immediately offers economists and business a lifeline. These brief quotes illustrate the strong teleological drive to much of the work on climate in environmental economics.

But there were also voices that dissented from this rather sanguine account of the converging interests of business and the environment:

> The fundamental victory of late-twentieth-century environmental politics was precisely to highlight and isolate environmental destruction as the integral result of capitalist patterns of production and consumption. If still incompletely, the market has now retaken and recolonised environmental practices. . . The extensive production of nature that has characterized capitalism since its infancy has, since the 1970s, been challenged and increasingly superseded by an intensive production of nature. (Smith, 2007: 26).

As Neil Smith and others have argued, environmental concerns represent not just an opportunity for policy, but an opportunity for capital to employ new technologies in the search for profit. Their critique of capital and nature takes us below the surface of a society unable to manage the deepest contradiction to which it is exposed: relinquishing its dependence on carbon.

'Discourse sustainability'

Radical critiques of the role of 'environmental' capital were only one of several responses to the challenges ahead. The discussion of sustainability had already developed a momentum of its own and, from a sociological perspective, benefited from being grounded in the more familiar terrain of social theory. These discursive accounts I term 'post-sustainability', not because they post-date the achievement of sustainability (a modest goal, indeed) but because, like other 'post-isms', sustainability has travelled a long way since its theoretical conception (Redclift, 2005). The discussion of sustainability is increasingly polarized between those who take an approach grounded in the achievements of science, a broadly critical realist position, and those who approach the environment from the perspective of social constructivism, who locate themselves within a more hermeneutic tradition.

Both positions are sceptical of policy 'agendas'. From a critical realist perspective, we need to begin by identifying the structural conditions responsible for particular environmental problems. While offering advice on these problems is properly the business of the social sciences, most critical realists would deny that their own disciplinary knowledge afforded advantages over that of others – they deny the *primacy* of specialist or 'expert' witnesses. For this reason, in their inquiry critical realists may be reluctant to suggest solutions to problems because they fear that specific policy solutions ignore important larger truths (Proctor, 1998).

The approach of social constructivists is rather different. Like critical realists their approach does not deny the materiality of non-human entities ('nature') but argues that we cannot separate their material existence from our knowledge of them/it. There is no Olympian point from which we gain value-free objective knowledge of the existence of nature, and we never cease to view nature through a social lens.

This approach has been primarily directed towards identifying the ways in which discourses on nature create their own truths (Castree, 2001; Castree and Braun, 2001; Demeritt, 2001). These socially constructed truths help legitimize and facilitate the transformative power with which societies socialize and alter nature. The insights of the 'socionature' thesis rest squarely on poststructuralist thought, especially that of Derrida (Braun and Wainwright, 2001), but defenders have emphasized that this does not necessarily point towards pointless, postmodernist relativism (Demeritt, 2003). The argument is that the social construction of nature thesis emphasizes the discursive aspect of human–nature relations, in the process destabilizing the classic Enlightenment dualisms of nature–society and culture–environment (Proctor, 1998).

The juxtaposition of these two heuristic tendencies, which are different rather than 'opposed', does present some important sociological questions; notably, should we focus on the social processes through which we understand the environment and nature, or should we (as Lever Tracy, 2008 seems to argue) concentrate on, 'listen[ing] to what scientists say about nature. . .'? (ibid.: 459). In addition, appreciating the strength of both critical realist and constructivist positions leaves us with another difficult task. This is to identify the social and cultural implications of changes in materiality, while at the same time examining the effects on materiality of changes in the way it is constructed socially.

The continuing influence of natural science paradigms: complexity theory and 'emergent structures'

Other sociological work in complexity theory undertaken by John Urry (2000) and Manuel Castells (1996) emphasizes the importance for the social sciences of natural science thinking about 'flows', and argues for the changing character and role of (transnational) state power in a network society of flows, fluids and scapes (Spaargaren et al., 2006). Although influential within the discipline this work does not really help us resolve the problem this chapter has set itself: to chart a role for sociology in a 'post-carbon' world. It does not recognize a specific need to address environmental issues as urgent for human survival, or identify the heavy dependence on hydrocarbons as a distinguishing feature of advanced industrial societies.

From a sociological standpoint there are also important implications in the way that different 'environmental knowledges' are being put to use – for example, in predicting extreme weather events, in green labelling of consumer products, in the ethical responsibilities of tourism and consumption generally (Bryant et al., 2008). This renewed use of distinct 'environmental knowledges' is also being deployed in explanations for rising energy and water bills. These examples, often drawn from 'everyday life', benefit from being considered within an interpretive sociological context (Berger and Luckmann, 1966) and the discussion of *doxa* in the work of Pierre Bourdieu (Bourdieu, 1998). Environmental knowledges, in other words, are increasingly used by 'lay' as well as 'expert' opinion, and in support of different groups, against a background of social assumptions and contested claims on society (Yearley, 1996).

These examples illustrate the differences between 'lay' and 'expert' knowledges, but they cannot help us resolve differences about the utility of these knowledges. As 'elite science', environmental knowledge is part of a specialized, esoteric knowledge that can assist, among other things, in offering judgements about the probable consequences of global climate change. However, environmental knowledge is also employed by NGOs, social scientists and others to critique science itself. It is reflexive, and is taken as evidence of the fact that we cannot remove ourselves from the consequences of our own social constructions. The recognition of environmental issues, on this reading, is a socially determined event. Sustainability and environmental discourses thus provide illustrations of the deeply political nature of climate policy and science and need not be subsumed into the 'post-political' policy consensus represented by Stern (Swyngedouw, 2008).

Awareness of our increasing dependence on carbon, and the difficult choices it implies for society, suggests that we are confronted by a challenge in social learning, as much as in policy responsiveness. As we become more dependent on prediction in areas such as climate change, so prediction is increasingly difficult and uncertain: the past is an unreliable guide to the future. The conditions of the natural world are changing so fast that the lessons we learn from 'nature' need to be constantly revisited. In the domain of environmental policy, established markers for the future based on the past are increasingly unworkable (see Bryant, Chapter 12 in this volume). They are historicist, in that future acquisitions of knowledge cannot be predicted from past experiences (Popper, 1957). We are travelling in new and hitherto unexplored territory when we grapple with climate change and other areas such as the new genetics (Finkler, 2000).

Does the acknowledgement of this difference assist in making science and policy more accountable or does it leave us powerless to act? In the remaining sections of this chapter I examine a number of perspectives that throw light on the shared ground of society and nature: environmental governance, ecological modernization and poststructuralist political ecology. The question, then, is to what extent these paradigmatic divisions can be surmounted or developed in charting 'post-carbon' sociology.

Contradictions between changing materiality and changing institutions: environmental governance

> When developing forms of scientific cooperation between the natural and social sciences, the key tasks for the social sciences are to formulate forms of governance that trigger reflexivity by de-routinising social practices, activate human agency and outline possible choices in ways that fit the specific risks dynamic of second modernity. (Spaargaren et al., 2006: 24).

Much of the debate about sociology and nature has proceeded *as if* human institutions endure while the environment changes. But human institutions also change, although rarely in ways that take account of societies' coevolution with nature (Norgaard, 1994). For example, as societies change the problems of sustainability are frequently those of providing access to limited, 'positional goods' (Hirsch, 1976) – the countryside, clean coastlines and uncongested cities. However, as economies develop, these same 'positional goods', to which people expect greater access, suffer from either increasing scarcity or overcrowding. One of the challenges of reducing carbon dependence, then, is to understand the institutional complexes from which materialities gain their legitimacy.

The 'solution' to these problems of material and institutional 'dysfunction' is often described in terms of 'environmental governance'. This is usually invoked in terms of 'improving' governance – either promoting more ethically informed governance or proposing new institutions to do the governing. Interestingly, new environmental regimes, such as the Millennium Ecosystem Assessment (MEA), which was undertaken in 2005, do not provide any insights into how in a 'post-carbon' world governance might change. In place of new ideas about how environmental issues might alter governance, they offer information about the framework of planning, of institutional 'value added', of promises to govern nature. This is another illustration of how thinking on environmental govern-ance has failed to stir sociology or inform policy (Schlosberg, 2004).

It also reveals something of significance about the sociology of environmental 'crises'. The principal innovations in conceptual thinking about the environment and society have arisen because of the scale of likely damage caused by climate change. They examine institutional reforms within the context of material changes. For example, note the way in which disaster studies consider 'emergent structures' within societies in the period just after major disasters, and illuminates the contradictions between disaster and risk 'management' and the trajectories of economic development policy (Pelling, 2003; see also Chapters 11 and 18 by Hannigan and Murphy in this volume). These are situ-ations in which 'normal' or pre-existing structures of governance are often challenged, and provide another example of the way in which changes in materiality can lead to new political and democratic openings.

Ecological modernization

The process through which large-scale capital has incorporated and internalized green policy, in an attempt to widen its market and its appeal, is often referred to as 'ecologi-cal modernization' (Janicke, 1991, Mol, 2001). The concern of advocates of this position is that a self-consciously 'successful' development model, that of northern capitalism, can and should accommodate to the environmental costs that were ignored when the model was first conceived. To some writers there was no inherent problem in pursuing sustainable development within the logic of the market economy. Green capitalism was a possibility *en route* to a reality (Welford and Starkey, 1996). Indeed, for some representa-tives of corporate business, sustainable development was a necessary further stage in the development of capitalism, to be embraced rather than denied.

One of the principal features of 'Agenda 21', the framework for action proposed at the Earth Summit of 1992, was the call for partnerships between business and environmental groups. The Business Council for Sustainable Development, as well as the International Chamber of Commerce, represented the perspectives of global business at Rio. However, the 'official' corporate response to the Rio Conference, representing the views of over 100 international companies, was contained in a publication that was stimulated by the Earth Summit itself. *Changing Course* helped conceptualize the phases through which corporate involvement in the environment had passed: the prevention of pollution in the 1970s, measures to encourage self-regulation in the 1980s and a concern to incorporate sustainability into business practices in the 1990s (Murphy and Bendell, 1997). The 1990s and the period post-Rio were seen as a turning point in the relation between corporate business and the environment, in which environmental concerns (at least in the case of the largest global players) needed to be internalized, and made a central part of corporate governance.

The public stand taken by some large corporations in the 1990s was more visible than previously, and designed to open up new markets, rather than defend existing ones. One example, cited by Adams (2001) in his review of the Rio process, is that of B&Q, the UK hardware chain, which in the mid-1990s argued that the environment was of central concern to shareholders, staff and customers alike. It began to be recognized that the products that customers bought were looked upon as part of the natural environment, as well as the built environment, and a corporate response needed to fully acknowledge this fact. At one level this might lead corporations towards forms of 'green consumerism', which pointed consumers to the environmental standards met by different products, and persuaded companies of the public relations benefits of a 'green' image. At another level were more fundamental questions about the material nature of products and services themselves, and the extent to which 'necessary' environmental costs could be internalized (Ayres and Simonis, 1995).

In some cases large companies sought to establish themselves beyond the boundaries of 'domestic' environmental regulation and stringent controls. Garcia Johnson (2000) shows how some transnational corporations, stimulated by their experiences on the home market, have even sought to 'export' higher environmental standards. 'If multilateral corporations can establish the kinds of rules that favour the technologies and management approaches that they have developed through years of struggle in the United States, they will have an advantage over their competitors from developing countries' (ibid.: 1). Taking as his example that of the US-based chemical industry, Garcia Johnson demonstrates how some companies actively encourage corporate voluntarism in Brazil and Mexico. He argues that spreading good practice in environmental governance is linked with the disadvantaging of Third World companies in global markets.

Critics of corporate 'greening' have sought to distinguish between the rhetoric of corporate environmentalism and the reality. Stephen Bunker (1996), for example, has criticized the so-called 'green Kuznets curve', the view that as economies develop they become more sustainable, and produce less waste. Bunker argues that 'dematerialization', as seen from the vantage point of industrial ecology, is a much more limited process than its advocates acknowledge, suggesting that materially 'lighter' products often have a greater proportional impact on the environment. Cleaner industry in one location can also mean the redistribution of environmental risks to other locations – as suggested in the 'pollution haven hypothesis – and the process of 'greening' industry is neither as transparent nor as disinterested as many corporations avow.

Nature as accumulation strategy

In some respects the willingness to think in terms of categories like 'natural capital' itself constitutes a problem for radical approaches to the environment. The logic and disciplines of the market are a source of potential conflict for Habermas (1981) and other radical social scientists, precisely because they appeared to devalue the intrinsic qualities of nature that placed it apart from market capitalism (Altvater, 1993). On this reading sustainability could not be accommodated to market forces; the circle could not be 'squared'. However, this is precisely what carbon markets, and carbon traders, propose to do. For them, there is no reason why we should not create markets in carbon, simply because it is part of 'nature'.

Other approaches also re-examine Marxist theory and argue for a more pro-ecology interpretation that focuses on different stages in Marx's own intellectual development, and seeks to elaborate on a Marxist position (Foster, 1998, 1999 and Chapter 7 in this volume). In another approach the 'successes' and claims of ecological modernization are addressed squarely, and found wanting (Schnaiberg et al., 2002).

Among the most persuasive Marxist critics of corporate green policy is Neil Smith (2007). Smith argues that, beginning in the 1980s and 1990s, an extraordinary range of new 'ecological commodities' came on line. Ironically, they owe their existence, first and foremost, to the success of the environmental movement in the 1960s and 1970s (Smith, 2007). He sees ecological modernization as 'nothing less than a major strategy for eco-logical commoditisation, marketisation and financialisation which radically *intensifies and deepens* the penetration of nature by capital' (ibid.: 17). He quotes the example of 'wetland credits' in California, which in the 1990s prompted a 'wetland mitigation banking' system in the USA.

Smith suggests that, following Marxist theory, the process of marketization of labour produces scarcity where none existed before – restored wetlands provide exchange value 'under the new conditions of created scarcity'. He goes on to criticize carbon credits for leaving the Costa Rican peasant without a livelihood enhancement:

> whereas the US corporate polluter buying credits contributes not only to continued pollution, but to an intensified accumulation of capital. . . If one takes a wider geographical perspective on wetland mitigation, it is tempting to paraphrase Engels's assessment of 'the housing question': the bourgeoisie has no solution to the environmental problem, they simply move it around. (Smith, 2007: 20)

Taking issue with a constructivist perspective, Smith argues that their mantra 'nature is discursive all the way down' applies today, in a more thorough way, to the *regulation and production of nature*. In his view, 'the market has now retaken and recolonised environmental practices'. The idea of choice and a broad social discussion has become subordinate to 'narrow class control orchestrated through the market' (Smith, 2007: 26).

Smith's essential point is that as nature becomes more subject to the market in 'invis-ible' forms, such as 'commodity futures, ecological credits, corporate stocks, (and) envi-ronmental derivatives', so the process becomes increasingly internalized:

> The extensive production of nature that has characterised capitalism since its infancy has, since the 1970s, been challenged and increasingly superseded by an intensive production of nature. . . a new frontier in the production of nature has rapidly opened up, namely a vertical integration of nature into capital. This involves not just the production of nature 'all the way down', but its simultaneous financialisation 'all the way up'. (Smith, 2007: 31–3)

However, it is not clear that Smith's emphasis on the labour process as a framework for thinking about new venues for accumulation is sufficiently flexible to capture the com-plexities of 'poststructural political ecology' that are most interesting – for example, the mobility of materialities, and new unfolding dimensions of environmental governance and injustice. Foremost among the writers within a 'poststructural political ecology' is undoubtedly Arturo Escobar (1996, and Chapter 6 in this volume).

Poststructural political ecology?
Escobar's position is based on a more reflexive understanding of the conditions prevailing at the geographical margins of global society, such as the Pacific coast of Colombia where he has undertaken fieldwork. As an anthropologist, Escobar brings to our attention the more 'emic' dimensions of behaviour – how people respond is linked to distinct cultural understandings, which should not be universalized. In his ethnographic work Escobar seeks to combine the insights of political ecology with the more discursive approaches reviewed above, suggesting a concern with materiality combined with an interest in its discursive expression, as an instrument or response to the exercise of power.

The approach elaborated by Escobar begins with 'the growing belief that nature is socially constructed',. . . and goes on to explore the discourses of 'sustainable development' and 'biodiversity conservation' in the belief that 'language is not a reflection of reality but *constitutive of it*' (italics in the original). Space, poverty and nature are then seen through the lens of a discursive materialism, suggesting that local cultures 'process the conditions of global capital and modernity' (Escobar, 1996: passim). Escobar argues, like Smith, that capital is entering an 'ecological phase', in which nature is no longer defined as an external, exploitable domain, in the the classic Marxist tradition, but as ostensible self-management and 'conservation'. However, in his view, this is something of an illusion and one that is advanced for economic motives. Capital seeks to use conservationist tendencies to create profit, through genetic engineering for example, and to identify new areas of high profitability, like sourcing biomaterials for pharmaceuticals, which are often outside the traditional domain of finance capital.

This approach significantly qualifies views on the dialectic of nature and capital in several ways. First, the argument is that capitalist restructuring takes place at the expense of production conditions: nature, the body, space. Second, this can take the form of both outright exploitation of nature and *also* 'the sustainable management of the system of capitalized nature'. Third, this, the 'second contradiction' of capitalism, entails deeper cultural domination – even the genes of living species are seen in terms of production and profitability. Fourth, the implication of this is that social movements and communities increasingly face the double task of building alternative productive rationalities while culturally resisting the inroads of new forms of capital into the fabric of nature and society. This 'dual logic' of ecological capital in the North and the South is increasingly complementary, and needs to be viewed as a historical conjunction. What remain to be discovered are the precise forms of political and social resistance that will come to characterize the withdrawal from carbon dependence.

As the quote from the Stern Report at the beginning of this chapter suggests, climate change is now regarded as a 'given', markets are now considered more relevant to policy solutions than ever before, and reduced dependence on hydrocarbons is widely regarded as the single most urgent policy challenge facing us. The evidence of a global economic recession, beginning in autumn 2008 with the so-called 'credit crunch', requires a response that links post-carbon futures to the new financial circumstances.

The economic depression, macroeconomic policy and post-carbon society

General optimism about the economy in the UK during the last decade, and the escalation in property prices, served to discourage saving (Bernthal et al., 2005; Braucher, 2006). At the same time the level of indebtedness had increased, even before the banking crisis of 2008/9. In a society in which increased equity in housing seemed assured, and borrowing was easy (if not cheap), individuals were prepared to buy property to rent and remortgage their homes with apparent alacrity (Tucker, 1991). More disposable income meant enhanced personal consumption, rather than saving, and *sustainable* consumption represented another consumer choice in a buoyant market (see Hinton and Goodman, Chapter 16 in this volume). It was one way in which the citizen, passenger or neighbour could be relabelled as a 'customer', a discursive practice that had grown since the 1980s, and that drew attention to the ubiquity of market relations (Cross, 1993, Cohen, 2003). The interest in sustainable consumption, although always a minority interest, was fuelled by the expansion of credit and market opportunities (Bernthal et al., 2005). It consisted largely of widening consumer choice, and making new or ethical products more available on the market, rather than in narrowing choice to fewer, more sustainable, products and services.

The rise in disposable income, for most consumers, was also driven by increasing female participation in the labour force, facilitating wider social participation for the majority (but not all) of the population (Goodman and Redclift, 1991). This model of rising consumption had also been associated with longer working hours, as Richard Titmuss had argued earlier, to explain the apparent rise of the 'affluent society' in the late 1950s (Titmuss, 1962) and captured more recently in the concept of 'time poverty' (de Graaf, 2003). In addition, of course, the postwar generation of so-called 'baby-boomers', having paid off their mortgages, had surplus income with which to become further indebted, or to pass on to their children. This is in line with regulation theory, which helped to explain the ability of capitalism to stabilize itself in the 1970s and 1980s, but might also help explain the illusion of 'stability' during the long boom of the last decade (Aglietta, 1976, Boyer, 1990, Jessop and Ngai-Ling Sum, 2006). The model of growth at the dawn of the twenty-first century was one of enhanced personal consumption on the basis of negotiated debt.

This 'model' of 'stabilized' debt management and enhanced personal consumption might at first appear at odds with what I have referred to as 'post-carbon' society, but in fact it was quite consistent with the individual-consumer-based policy discourses of the last decade. The increased purchase of consumer goods and services that carry an 'environmental', 'natural' or 'ethical' imprimatur has been bolted on to a loosely regulated market that prioritized individual choice and profitability. The context for most sustainable consumption discourses during the last few years has elements that were consistent with credit expansion and indebtedness, rather than 'self-sufficiency' and deeper green credentials (OECD, 2002). In fact the sustainable consumption discourses were several, and often mutually contradictory throughout the period in which green consumerism has become established (see Hinton and Goodman, Chapter 16 in this volume).

Conclusion

This chapter has argued that the 'contradictions' of thinking about sustainability and development have merged into two policy discourses, both of which can be informed by the social sciences. A realist, science-driven policy agenda has been paralleled by a science-sceptical, postmodern academic discourse. Neither position represents a threat to the other since they inhabit quite different epistemological terrain, and address different audiences. In the process, however, we have seen an enlarged academic debate, and one that closely examines the way environmental language is deployed, while at the same time recognizing that public policy discourses themselves carry weight – so-called 'green consumerism' can reduce the politics of climate change to the size of a green consumer product. The policy debate has proceeded through assumptions about 'choice' and 'alternatives' that have been largely devoid of any critical, structural analysis, and frequently narrow the field of opportunity by assuming that people act primarily as consumers, rather than as citizens (Redclift and Hinton, 2008). There is clearly room for more rigorous sociological analysis.

This chapter has also argued that there are several areas of sociological work that can inform our analysis of the transition from carbon dependence towards more sustainable, lower energy-intensity pathways. One is the investigation of societies as utopias and imaginaries, freed from the heavy burden of 'real-world' policy and practice. In reimagining a future free from carbon dependence we shall need to rethink physical and social infrastructures, and transport and energy production, from the 'supply' side, as well as consumer demand.

Similarly, sociology, by framing environmental policy problems within the context of the understood 'blind' commitments of everyday life, also has the potential to recognize those behavioural commitments, and to address how societies meet 'needs' as well as 'wants'. Rather than speak loftily of the need to 'transform' human behaviour, we could make a start by analysing how current behaviour is tied into patterns and cycles of carbon dependence. There are gains to be made in exploring why and how social and economic structures are *un*sustainable – the real costs of naturalizing social practices that carry important environmental consequences.

Finally, the 'post-carbon'-dependent world will be one of increasingly mobile materialities, in which sustainability needs to be viewed within an increasingly global context. If societies are to manage the transition out of carbon dependence, then the process of 'dematerialization' will have to be examined sociologically. We shall need to know whether waste matter is being reduced, and 'throughput' made more efficient – or simply being dispersed to new spatial locations. We shall need to grapple with scale, as well as materiality, with geography as well as sociology.

The consequences of this debate about the shift from carbon dependence have not benefited from much thoughtful sociological analysis, with a few notable exceptions. The difficulty in separating material evidence for climate change from its discussion has not only spawned 'climate deniers' on the one side, but a fear of democratic accountability and engagement on the other. Perhaps, in the 'new world' of reduced carbon dependence, democracy and governance need to be rethought to take account of new forms of power, and the political economy of the withdrawal from carbon dependence needs to be analysed, rather than evangelized. What may be required is a long view of the society that lies beyond the 'post-politics' consensus, a task to which sociology is well suited, if not willing, to carry out.

References

Abrams, Philip and Andrew McCulloch (1976), *Communes, Sociology and Society*, Cambridge: Cambridge University Press.
Adams, W.M. (2001), *Green Development: Environment and Sustainability in the Third World*, 2nd edn, London: Routledge.
Aglietta, M. (1976), *A Theory of Capitalist Regulation: The US Experience*, London: Verso.
Altvater, E. (1993), *The Future of the Market*, London: Verso.
Altvater, E. (2007), 'The social and natural environment of fossil capitalism', in Leo Panitch and Colin Leys (eds), *Coming To Terms With Nature*, London: Socialist Register, The Merlin Press, pp. 37–59.
Ayres, R.U and U.E. Simonis (eds) (1995), *Industrial Metabolism: Restructuring for Sustainable Development*, Tokyo: UN University Press.
Beckerman, W. (1994), 'Sustainable development: is it useful?', *Environmental Values*, **3**: 191–209.
Benton, E. (1994), 'Biology and social theory in the environmental debate', in Michael Redclift and Ted Benton (eds), *Social Theory and the Global Environment*, London: Routledge, pp. 28–50.
Berger, Peter L. and Thomas Luckmann (1966), *The Social Construction of Reality*, New York: Anchor Books.
Bernthal, M., D. Crockett and R. Rose (2005), 'Credit cards as lifestyle facilitators', *Journal of Consumer Research*, **32** (1): 130–45.

Biersack, A and James B. Greenberg (eds) (2006), *Reimagining Political Ecology*, Durham, NC: Duke University Press.

Bourdieu, Pierre (1998), *Practical Reason: On the Theory of Social Action*, Palo Alto, CA: Stanford University Press.

Boyer, R. (1990), *The Regulation School: A Critical Introduction*, New York: Columbia University Press.

Braucher, J. (2006), 'Theories of overindebtedness: interaction, structure and culture', *Theoretical Enquiries in Law*, **7** (2): 67–83.

Braun, B. and J. Wainwright (2001), 'Nature, poststructuralism and politics', in N. Castree and B. Braun (eds), *Social Nature: Theory, Practice and Politics*, Oxford: Blackwell, pp. 41–63.

Brunnengräber, A. (2007), 'The political economy of the Kyoto protocol', in L. Panitch and C. Leys (eds), *Coming to Terms With Nature*, London: Socialist Register, The Merlin Press, pp. 213–30.

Bryant, R. and S. Bailey (1997), *Third World Political Ecology*, London: Routledge.

Bryant, R., M. Goodman and M.R. Redclift (2008), 'Spaces of intention and the new ethical consumerism', unpublished manuscript, London, King's College.

Bunker, S.G. (1996) 'Raw materials and the global economy: oversights and distortions in industrial ecology', *Society and Natural Resources*, **9**: 419–29.

Castells, Manuel (1996), *The Rise of the Network Society: Vol. 1 of The Information Age: Economy, Society and Culture*, Oxford: Blackwell.

Castree, N. (2001), 'Socialising nature: theory, practice and politics', in N. Castree and B. Braun (eds), *Social Nature: Theory, Practice and Politics*, Oxford: Blackwell, pp. 1–21.

Castree, N. and B. Braun (eds) (2001), *Social Nature: Theory, Practice and Politics*, Oxford: Blackwell.

Cock, Martin and Bill Hopwood (1996), *Global Warning: Socialism and the Environment*, Guildford, UK: Militant Publications.

Cohen, L. (2003), *A Consumer's Republic: The Politics of Mass Consumption in Postwar America*, New York: Vintage.

Cross, G. (1993), *Time and Money: The Making of Consumer Culture*, New York: Routledge.

De Graaf, J. (2003), *Take Back Your Time: Fighting Overwork and Time Poverty in America*, San Francisco, CA: Berrett–Koehler.

Demeritt, D. (2001), 'Being constructive about nature', in N. Castree and B. Braun (eds), *Social Nature: Theory, Practice and Politics*, Oxford: Blackwell, pp. 22–39.

Demeritt, D. (2003), 'What is the "social construction of nature"? A typology and sympathetic critique', *Progress in Human Geography*, **26** (6): 767–90.

Dyson, Tim (2005), 'On development, demography and climate change: the end of the world as we know it', *Population and Environment*, **27** (2): 117–49.

Escobar, Arturo (1996), 'Constructing nature: elements for a poststructural political ecology', in R. Peet and M. Watts (eds), *Liberation Ecologies*, London and New York: Routledge, pp. 46–68.

Finkler, K. (2000), *Experiencing the New Genetics*, Philadelphia, PA: University of Pennsylvania Press.

Fischer-Kowalski, M. and H. Weisz (1999), 'Society as a hybrid between material and symbolic realms: towards a theoretical framework of society-nature interaction', in Lee Freese (ed.), *Advances in Human Ecology*, Vol. 8, Stamford, CT: JAI Press, pp. 215–51.

Foster, J.B. (1998), 'The scale of our ecological crisis', *Monthly Review*, **49** (11): 5–16.

Foster, J.B. (1999), 'Marx's theory of metabolic rift', *American Journal of Sociology*, **105** (2): 366–405.

Garcia Johnson, R. (2000), *Exporting Environmentalism: US Multinational Chemical Corporations in Brazil and Mexico*, Cambridge, MA: MIT Press.

Goodman, D.E. and M.R. Redclift (1991), *Refashioning Nature, Food, Ecology and Culture*, London: Routledge.

Green, J. (1988), *Days in the Life: Voices from the English Underground 1961–1971*, London: Heinemann.

Habermas, J. (1981), 'New social movements', *Telos*, **490**: 33–7.

Harvey, D. (1996), *Justice, Nature and the Geography of Difference*, Oxford: Blackwell.

Hirsch, F. (1976), *The Social Limits to Growth*, London: Routledge.

Huber, J. (2000), 'Towards industrial ecology: sustainable development as a concept of ecological modernization', *Journal of Environmental Policy and Planning*, **2**: 269–85.

IPCC (Intergovernmental Panel on Climate Change) (2007), *Fourth Assessment*, London: DEFRA.

Jänicke, M. (1991), 'The political system's capacity for environmental policy', Berlin: Department of Environmental Politics, Free University Berlin.

Jessop, B. and Ngai-Ling Sum (2006), *Beyond The Regulation Approach*, Cheltenham, UK and Northampton, MA: Edward Elgar.

Keil, R., D. Bell, P. Penz and L. Fawcett (eds) (1998), *Political Ecology: Global and Local*, London and New York: Routledge.

Kumar, K. (1978), *Prophecy and Progress: The Sociology of Industrial and Post-Industrial Society*, Harmondsworth: Penguin Books.

Kumar, K. (1987), *Utopia and Anti-Utopia in Modern Times*, Oxford: Blackwell.

Lal, D (1985), 'The misconceptions of "development economics"', *Finance and Development*, June: 10–13.

Langhelle, O. (2000), 'Sustainable development and social justice: expanding the Rawlsian framework of global justice', *Environmental Values*, **9** (3): 295–323.

Lever-Tracy, Constance (2008), 'Global warming and sociology', *Current Sociology*, **56** (3): 445–66.

Lovins, A. and L. Hunter (2000), *Natural Capitalism: The Next Industrial Revolution*, Snowmass, CO: Rocky Mountain Institute.

Low, N.P. and B.J. Gleeson (1997), 'Justice in and to the environment: ethical uncertainties and political practices', *Environment and Planning A*, **29**: 21–42.

Low, N and B.J. Gleeson (1998), *Justice, Society and Nature: An Exploration of Political Ecology*, London: Routledge.

Martínez-Alier, J. (1995), 'Political ecology, distributional conflicts and economic incommensurability', *New Left Review*, **9** (3): 295–323.

Mawdsley, Emma and Jonathan Rigg (2003), 'The World Development Report Series II: continuity and change in development orthodoxies', *Progress in Development Studies*, **3** (4): 271–86.

McAfee, K. (1999), 'Selling nature to save it? Biodiversity and green developmentalism', *Environment and Planning D*, **17** (2): 48–63.

Milbrath, L.W. (1994), 'Stumbling blocks to a sustainable society: incoherence in key premises about the way the world works', *Futures*, **26** (2): 117–24.

Mol, A. (2001), *Globalisation and Environmental Reform: The Ecological Modernisation of the Global Economy*, Cambridge, MA: MIT Press.

Murphy, D.F. and J. Bendell (1997), *In the Company of Partners: Business, Environmental Groups and Sustainable Development Post Rio*, Bristol, UK: Policy Press.

Norgaard, Richard (1988), 'Sustainable development: a co-evolutionary view', *Futures*, **20** (6): 606–20.

Norgaard, Richard (1994), *Development Betrayed: The End of Progress and a Coevolutionary Revisioning of the Future*, London and New York: Routledge.

North, Richard (1995), *Life on a Modern Planet: A Manifesto for Progress*, Manchester: Manchester University Press.

Onis, Z. and F. Senses (2005), 'Rethinking the emerging post-Washington Consensus', *Development and Change*, **36** (2): 263–90.

Organisation for Economic Cooperation and Development (OECD) (2002), *Towards Sustainable Household Consumption? Trends and Policies in OECD Countries*, Paris: OECD.

Owens, S. (1994), 'Land, limits and sustainability', *Transactions of the Institute of British Geographers*, **19**: 439–56.

Page, Edward (2006), *Climate Change, Justice and Future Generations*, Cheltenham, UK and Northampton, MA: Edward Elgar.

Pearce, David (1991), *Blueprint 2: Greening the World Economy*, London: Earthscan.

Pelling, Mark (2003), *The Vulnerability of Cities: Social Resilience and Natural Disasters*, London: Earthscan.

Popper, Karl (1957), *The Poverty of Historicism*, London: Routledge.

Proctor, J.D. (1998), 'The social construction of nature: relativist accusations, pragmatist and critical realist responses', *Annals of the Association of American Geographers*, **88**, 352–76.

Rayner, Steve and Elizabeth L. Malone (eds) (1998), *Human Choice and Climate Change: Volume One, The Societal Framework*, Columbus, OH: Battelle Press.

Redclift, Michael (1987), *Sustainable Development: Exploring the Contradictions*, London: Routledge.

Redclift, Michael (1993), 'Sustainable development: needs, values, rights', *Environmental Values*, **2**: 3–20.

Redclift, Michael (1996), *Wasted: Counting the Costs of Global Consumption*, London: Earthscan.

Redclift, Michael (2005), *Sustainability: Critical Concepts in the Social Sciences*, 4 vols, London: Routledge.

Redclift, Michael and Emma Hinton (2008), 'Living sustainably: approaches for the developed and developing world', London: Progressive Governance Summit, 4 April.

Rifkin, Jeremy (1992), *Biosphere Politics: A New Consciousness for the New Century*, New York: HarperCollins.

Schlosberg, D. (2004), 'Preconceiving environmental justice: global movements and political theories', *Environmental Politics*, **13** (3): 517–40.

Schnaiberg, Allan, David Pellow and Adam Weinberg (2002), 'The treadmill of production and the environmental state', in A.J.P. Mol and F.H. Buttel (eds), *The Environmental State Under Pressure*, Research in Social Problems and Public Policy Vol. 10, Amsterdam, London and New York: JAI an imprint of Elsevier Science.

Smith, Neil (2007), 'Nature as accumulation strategy', *Socialist Register 2007*, **17**: 16–36.

Spaargaren, G., Arthur Mol and Frederick Buttel (eds) (2006), *Governing Environmental Flows: Global Challenges to Social Theory*, Boston, MA: MIT Press.

Stern, Nicholas (2007), *Report on the Economics of Climate Change: The Stem Report*, London: H.M. Treasury.

Swyngedouw, Eric (2008), 'Post-politics and climate change', paper delivered to King's College, London, Department of Geography.

Swyngedouw, Eric and Nikolas C. Heynen (2003), 'Urban political ecology, justice and the politics of scale', *Antipode*, 898–918.

Titmuss, R. (1962), *Income Distribution and Social Change*, London: Allen & Unwin.

Tucker, D (1991), *The Decline of Thrift in America: Our Cultural Shift from Saving to Spending*, New York: Praeger.

Urry, John (2000), *Sociology Beyond Societies*, London: Routledge.

WCED (World Commission for Environment and Development) (1987), *Our Common Future*, Oxford: Oxford University Press (the Brundtland Report).

Weber, Max (1991), *From Max Weber: Essays in Sociology*, London: Routledge.

Welford, R. (2006), 'The economics of climate change: an overview of the Stern review', *International Journal of Innovation and Sustainable Development*, **1** (3): 260–62.

Welford, R. and R. Starkey (1996), *The Earthscan Reader in Business and the Environment*, London: Earthscan.

Yearley, S. (1996), *Sociology, Environmentalism, and Globalization: Reinventing the Globe*, London: Sage.

9 Socio-ecological agency: from 'human exceptionalism' to coping with 'exceptional' global environmental change

David Manuel-Navarrete and Christine N. Buzinde

Introduction

With the advent of global environmental change, sociology is urged not only to acknowledge the environment, but also to re-examine its own conceptual constructs with regard to socio-ecological dynamics. In this chapter, we reformulate the concept of agency in light of the overwhelming influence that human beings are currently exerting over the Earth's metabolism. The notion of socio-ecological agency is introduced to provide a new understanding of what it means to be human in the global change era. Socio-ecological agency does not shift the locus of agency away from human beings. Agency is still, so to speak, enacted within individual persons. However, it emphasizes the fact that it rarely takes place as an isolated process, and the need to consider people's ongoing interaction with life support structures as well as with social structures. This notion of agency is consistent with Latour's recognition that 'we are never alone in carrying out a course of action' (Latour, 2005). Yet it departs from the flat ontology implied in actor-network theory, which assumes that both embodied consciousness and the entire universe of acting and interacting non-human entities share the same type of agency (Mutch, 2002). That is, socio-ecological agency characterizes human beings as ecological actors, social actors and individuals all at the same time.

One of the main tasks of environmental sociology is to re-evaluate the dualisms of nature–society and realism–constructivism that have been prevalent in sociological research. Catton and Dunlap (1978: 45) were among the first to warn us about the dangers of the so-called 'human exceptionalism paradigm' and its pervasiveness within sociology. These authors advocated a new ecological paradigm for sociology that would recognize human–ecosystem interdependence. Unfortunately, regardless of numerous attempts at formulating concepts, formalisms and approaches for addressing the complex interactive character of social and environmental processes, the emergence of a robust ecological paradigm for sociology is still in the making. The most promising attempts so far are the concepts of 'conjoint constitution' (Freudenburg et al., 1995), and coevolution (Woodgate and Redclift, 1998). These are clearly useful formalisms for understanding environmental problems as both real and knowable physical phenomena brought about by particular practices, which in turn generate material and social consequences for societies themselves. They disclose the limitations of one of the main traits of the modernist project, namely the inclination to slice up reality into ever smaller pieces. However, they have so far fallen short of scrutinizing other pillars of the modernist agenda such as assumptions about progress, nature or human agency. In particular, the notion of analytically independent modern agents is crucial for populating the institutional structures of modern social life: the administrative–bureaucratic state, the capitalist economy and civil society (Emirbayer and Mische, 1998). These assumptions and structures dwell at the heart of modern society and are at the roots of global environmental change.

We argue that reformulating the assumptions regarding human agency in the light of global environmental change has deep implications for both sociology and society at large. The 'human exceptionalism paradigm' is not only the product of sociologists' biases and myths. It responds to the predominance of a worldview through which the biophysical aspects of human existence tend to be perceived as threats and manageable inconveniences, or idealized through pristine notions of nature (Manuel-Navarrete et al., 2006). It is part of well-established cultural paradigms of nature as benign, ephemeral, capricious or perverse/tolerant (Thompson et al., 1990). These worldviews and paradigms have shaped conventional understandings of human agency, in which ecosystems are caricatured as inhospitable and dangerous places, or commoditized as spaces for controlled recreational activities that take us away from our everyday realities of intense socialization. Independent human agents perceive modernity as freeing them from exposure to 'capricious' environmental contingencies, while setting out of sight gruesome realities such as, for instance, the slaughtering of other animals for meat production. Human beings have always been, and will always be, organically embodied, and socio-ecologically embedded. However, during recent centuries a significant part of the world's population has focused its full attention on socialization. We have downplayed the importance of the unavoidable material dimensions of reality and handed them over to science and technology. The paradox is that this disregard has been accompanied by unprecedented levels of consumption of commoditized and processed material goods. As suggested by Woodgate and Redclift (1998: 12):

> [A]s economy, society and social constructions of nature become more complex, we lose sight of, and our affinity with, the external world. This suggests that culture might have as much to do with isolation from external change agents as it has with adaptation to local conditions.

In the extreme, one may argue that we are even de-emphasizing the material reality of our own death: downplaying the fact of its inevitability through medical improvements, anti-ageing products, and all sorts of social and cultural distractions. In such socio-cultural contexts, it is not surprising that sociology too was tempted to de-emphasize materiality.

As the current global environmental crisis is reminding us, ignoring materiality has limits as well as unexpected consequences. Hence environmental sociologists' warnings and concerns are utterly valid. Our argument, however, is that they will fall dramatically short, and may not significantly influence society at large, unless they radically reformulate the assumptions underlying Western science and society regarding agency, and its role in human–nature relations. This radical turn may enable sociology to articulate attractive existential narratives that emphasize new meaningful forms of connecting with socio-ecological realities. Such existential narratives should be capable of informing and enticing new forms of living and socializing. They should bring the connections between consciousness and materiality back into culture. To put it more allegorically, they may raise awareness of our wholeness, and that we human beings already are this wholeness: that we are born into it but have been socialized through modernity out of our awareness of it.

The next section reviews two of the most successful concepts offered so far by

environmental sociology to transcend the human–nature dichotomy: 'conjoint constitution' and 'coevolution'. We build on these two frameworks to develop the notion of socio-ecological agency.

Conjoint constitution

The notion of conjoint constitution was proposed by Freudenburg et al., (1995) to highlight the idea that what are often taken as the separable social and physical aspects of a situation are in fact at each stage conjointly constituted and connected with one another. These authors identified four approaches through which society–environment relationships have been addressed within environmental sociology: (1) analytic separation; (2) analytic primacy; (3) dualistic balance; and (4) conjoint constitution. The first three maintain a neat distinction between the physical and the social dimensions of reality. Only in the fourth approach is this dualism challenged through the view that biophysical facts are significantly shaped by social construction, while at the same time social phenomena are shaped by stimuli and constraints from the biophysical world. Thus, attempting to allocate parts of reality into 'social' and 'physical' categories may contribute as much to confusion as to understanding. Reality is perhaps best understood not in terms of these distinctions, but in terms of their fundamental interconnectedness:

> The relevant challenge is thus not to explore the extent to which one set of factors or the other can be ignored or forgotten, but instead to understand the extent to which each can become a taken-for-granted part of the other – and to realize that it is the taken-for-grantedness itself [. . .] that can lead to ill-advised assumptions about what appear to be 'natural' physical conditions or 'strictly social' factors. (Freudenburg et al., 1995: 372)

Conjoint constitution has an indisputable value for advancing environmental sociology in epistemological terms. Its recognition that the social is inherent in what is usually seen as the physical, just as the physical is often integral to what is perceived as the social, is a positive step in the direction of overcoming the 'human exceptionalism' mirage. The recognition of 'mutual contingency' draws sociologists' attention to the risk of ignoring or overlooking important aspects of a situation, and thus developing 'unrealistically constrained analyses of socially significant questions and problems' (Freudenburg et al., 1995: 388). However, conjoint constitution does not address the implications for society at large of challenging the human–nature dualism. It promotes reflexivity and the betterment of the 'academic mind' (Freudenburg et al., 1996), but misses the opportunity of challenging some of the most deeply entrenched assumptions of modern societies that quite unproblematically situate individual experience into dichotomous space. Through conjoint constitution sociology might be better epistemologically equipped for carrying out its modernist task of grasping reality, but will fall short of challenging the modernist assumptions to be found at the origin of the present global environmental crisis.

Coevolutionary frameworks

The popularity of coevolutionary concepts for describing the reciprocal influence between human beings and their environment is fairly owed to Norgaard (1981, 1994), who was possibly inspired by Boulding's (1978) notions of ecodynamics, integrative systems and the evolutionary interpretation of history. Presently, there is a rapidly growing literature within ecological economics, and other fields, about the coevolutionary character of the relationships between values, knowledge, organization, technology and the environment (Norgaard, 1997). Within this emerging literature coevolution is often presented as a set of framing concepts (e.g. variation, selection, adaptation) that can explain change across interacting systems (Kallis, 2007). Some authors, however, are starting to draw on evolutionary theory in order to develop an overarching framework, or coevolutionary theory, for understanding both natural and social evolution (Winder et al., 2005; Gual and Norgaard, 2008; Hodgson, 2008). The main challenge for this endeavour is to establish the extent to which the 'logical structure of evolution' is equivalent between social and biological phenomena (Farrell, 2007). It is beyond the scope of this chapter to review this body of work. However, from the point of view of environmental sociology, it is worth noting that it is marked by a deep structuralist bias that assumes a rigid causal determinism in social life. The contribution of sociology to this coevolutionary debate has so far been surprisingly meagre. It seems reasonable to think that environmental sociologists have a unique opportunity to transcend the structuralist bias of coevolution. To do so, they should bring to the fore of the debate the universe of meanings, creativity and bewilderment that characterize cognitive systems and human agency. In fact, sociology has been relatively active in questioning unproblematic uses of structure (e.g. Giddens, 1979). As expressed by Sewell (1992: 2):

> What tends to get lost in the language of structure is the efficacy of human action – or 'agency' . . . A social science trapped in an unexamined metaphor of structure tends to reduce actors to cleverly programmed automatons. A second and closely related problem with the notion of structure is that it makes dealing with change awkward. The metaphor of structure implies stability. For this reason, structural language lends itself readily to explanations of how social life is shaped into consistent patterns, but not to explanations of how these patterns change over time.

However, the only significant attempt at outlining a structuralist/constructionist coevolutionary framework in environmental sociology can be found in Woodgate and Redclift (1998), which has unfortunately not produced much in the way of academic progeny. These authors draw on metaphors from systems ecology and evolutionary ecology to explore ecosystems' transformations by human agency, and vice versa. They propose to incorporate an actor-oriented analysis within the coevolutionary framework with the goal of comparing the meanings and values that are attached to social and environmental phenomena by different individuals. This understanding of structure reflects Giddens's (1979) concept of 'duality of structure', indicating that structure arises out of agency as well as providing its context (Woodgate and Redclift, 1998). The link between agency and socio-ecological structures is established by acknowledging that the links between individuals and institutions condition the natural, economic and policy structures, which in turn provide the backdrop to social action, and influence both the development of social choices and the environmental possibilities and constraints. Human agency is conceptualized within this framework as the ways in which different social actors manage and interpret their surrounding environment (in a broad sense). Accordingly, individuals' interpretations and socially generated symbols do not need to be analysed in separation from the material conditions in which they are constructed:

> The social spaces or life-worlds created and experienced by each of these different actors are characterized by specific sets of material and symbolic social relations, which define their structures, and can be located in terms of time–space boundaries. (Woodgate and Redclift, 1998: 15)

Interestingly, after including self-reflexive human agents within the structuralist equation, these authors reach the conclusion that modernity is leading humanity towards a 'coevolutionary *cul-de-sac*' due to the increasing dissociation of dominant values from material realities and the fact that the evolution of these values is increasingly dependent on 'internal [social] games'.

Modernist, structuralist and mutually constitutive notions of agency

Modernism replaced worldviews dominated by literal interpretations of mythologies, as well as the religious ideologization of spirituality, with the agreement on a common material ('natural') reality as a unifying cultural factor (Manuel-Navarrete et al., 2004). Unfortunately, this remarkable achievement came at the cost of confining human agency (and sociology) to the boundaries of individualism and rational self-interest (Emirbayer and Mische, 1998). Arguably, the need to free individuals from the strait jacket of pre-modern worldviews and traditions led to overemphasizing separateness and independence. As a result, a view emerged of isolated individuals, who were completely deprived of meanings arising from either their interplay with ecological and biological processes, or their access to spiritual dimensions.

The relationship of modern agents towards materiality is mostly viewed as mediated by (objective) rationality and (subjective) wants, whereas social agency is often reduced to management, control and the reproduction of established social roles; or through predictable actions and decisions to fulfil material necessities, utilitarian interests (e.g. seeking power, social prestige or socially constructed material rewards) and self-imposed moral imperatives. In this context, it is not surprising that sociologists embraced functionalist and structuralist frameworks to determine and reify social relations while relegating agency to rational choices mediated by compromising means–ends and normative moral imperatives (e.g. Parsons, 1968; Hechter and Kanazawa 1997). The mainstreaming of the concept of stakeholders (individuals, organizations, nation-states) across social sciences signals the zenith of this particular interpretation of agency (see Meyer and Jepperson, 2000 for a critique of interest-based approaches to action).

In recent decades, however, multiple alternative versions of human agency have been surfacing from diverse sociological grounds. These versions share an emphasis on the dual, relational, intersubjective, empowering and self-reflexive dimensions of agency. One of the primordial efforts to reformulate agency as the outcome of creative and innovative individuals is Giddens's 'theory of structuration'. This theory recognizes that structure is better understood as a process with the capacity not only to constrain but also to enable action. As a result, 'knowledgeable' and 'enabled' agents have the power to transform structures if they act together (Giddens, 1984).

Building on Giddens's structuration and Bourdieu's 'theory of practice' (1977), Sewell (1992) describes structures as sets of mutually sustained (virtual) schemas and (actual) resources that empower and constrain social action. Unlike Giddens, Sewell emphasizes the role of materiality in reproducing social structures. Unlike Bourdieu, he explains change as arising from within the operation of structures internal to a society, rather than from events outside the system – that is, from the agents' decisions to transpose new schemas and remobilize the resources that make up the structure. As a result, agency is both constituent of structure and inherent in all human beings (ibid.: 20):

> To be an agent means to be capable of exerting some degree of control over the social relations in which one is enmeshed, which in turn implies the ability to transform those social relations to some degree . . . The specific forms that agency will take consequently vary enormously and are culturally and historically determined. But a capacity for agency is as much a given for humans as the capacity for respiration.

Consequently, even though agency characterizes all persons, its sources and mode of exercise are laden with structurally reproduced differences of power and implicated in collective struggles and resistances.

Sewell's proposal illuminates agents' capacities to 'play around' with schemas (or procedures) and material resources (and the meanings collectively ascribed to them). However, it says little about agents' motivations and actual potential (e.g. introspective or reflexive power) to enact transformations or sustain reproductions, other than saying that these are determined culturally and historically (and thus structurally?). A legitimate question is whether this is not just a more sophisticated version of the structuralist or systemic arguments underlying the notions of coevolution and conjoint constitution outlined in the previous section. That is, to what extent is the agent defined as reactive to, or a mere product of, the spatio-temporal and socio-material coevolution of structure. The acknowledgement of the mutual constitution of structure and agency should not lead to the structuration of agency. There must be a moment or a degree in which the agent is freed from, or transcends, structure in order to make social creativity possible. This is crucial in the context of the present global environmental crisis because this context will demand a radical transformation of the structures of modernity that have led us into the crisis in the first place. A key question is then: how can this structural transformation possibly occur if agency is so highly conditioned by the reproduction of these same structures? Are our reactions to the changes that we are inflicting on the planet the only chance to provoke structural transformations or does human agency undergo such structural transformations in proactive, rather than merely reactive, terms?

The main argument of this chapter is that the chances of overcoming the global environmental crisis would be much greater if the mutual co-creation of material and social structures were mediated by a self-reflexive, or transcendental, form of agency enacted by individuals in their interaction with not only society and the environment, but also with themselves: with their inner worlds. Therefore the crucial questions for environmental sociology are: does this kind of agency actually exist? Can it be created or promoted? Is agency limited to the transposition of existing schemas into new contexts (as Sewell suggests) or it is conceivable that agents can suddenly start off brand new schemas not conditioned by past structures? We argue that these key questions can be effectively addressed through the notion of socio-ecological agency.

Socio-ecological agency in the anthropocene
Environmental sociology has mostly focused on overcoming the dichotomy between material and social systems. It has been argued that this dividing line is an intellectual construct that can be analytically convenient in the proper circumstances. However, the profuse reification of this illusory divide by society at large is a threat to the planet's life support systems. Presently, human beings are capable of altering the composition of the atmosphere, modifying the earth's nutrient cycles and causing major biodiversity extinctions. For the first time we are not only the agents of social change and

ecosystem change at the local level, but also the main agents affecting the dynamics and evolution of the global environment. This unprecedented power suggests a new type of agency that goes far beyond the discussion of how individuals affect social structures. We argue that the task of transcending the human–nature divide set by environmental sociology requires thinking in terms of a novel form of human agency, which we call socio-ecological agency. The term socio-ecological does not mean that agency is shifted away from human beings. It is still, so to speak, enacted within the individual person. However, it emphasizes both the idea that human agency rarely takes place as an isolated process and the need to consider our influence on life support structures as well as social structures. Yet, does this twist in meaning necessitate the coinage of a brand new term? Why is it that the global environmental crisis cannot be properly addressed through the conventional analytic construct of 'human agency'? How can this empirical rupture be justified?

To start answering these questions, it is crucial to notice that global environmental change entails a new type of material constraint. Modernist conceptions of agency have undoubtedly considered material constraints. We should first note, however, that these constraints were usually related to depletion of resources or degradation of local (i.e. localized) environmental services; second, that local societies confronted with self-inflicted environmental threats were arguably never as aware as we are now of the damage that their actions were about to inflict upon themselves; and third, that they could often count on the possibility of migrating elsewhere. On the contrary, the present emerging 'socio-ecological agents' have the task ahead of dealing with self-imposed material constraints, which surface from a clear awareness about self-inflicted threats (e.g. climate change) and with no place else to go to avoid these threats. Additionally, it is important to note that such voluntary limits are not only to be adopted by individuals and specific societies, but they must be embraced by humanity as a whole. In other words, it is of little use if only some individual agents or specific collectives manage to self-constrain their consumption of, for example, fossil fuels. In the end they might be equally, or even more, affected than anyone else by global climate change.

It might be argued that the scaling up of environmental constraints we have described does not justify the claim for a new type of agency. It is conceivable that through conventional human agency, modern individuals are eventually capable of transforming social structures at a global scale in order to self-impose the necessary constraints. Yet we argue that global environmental change forces us to address a more fundamental question, namely how the need to become stewards of the planet is going to transform the nature of individual human identities. We contend that this type of transformation is unlikely to happen as merely the outcome of our perceived self-interest or moral imperatives. Rather, it is likely to emerge from a radical realization about the reciprocity and double directionality that exists between humanity and the planet as a whole, including our increasing ability to influence the genetic make-up of life. This is precisely the main point that environmental sociology is trying to put forward, namely the mutual co-creation between environment and society, which departs at one extreme from unidirectional deterministic relations through which genetic, ecological or social structures may be seen as determining agency (Sewell, 1992; Redclift, 2001; Judkins et al., 2007). At the other extreme of unidirectional thinking, we may find chimeras of human agency entirely determining these structures through social or genetic engineering. An example is what Finkler (2000: 3) calls the 'hegemony of the gene that leads to the medicalization of kinship'.

While it is dubious that unidirectional explanations can entirely account for historical nature–human relations, such explanations will become increasingly inadequate and incomplete in the context of global environmental change. The implications of acknowledging the multidirectional relationships between materiality and cognition are paramount for human identity and agency, as well as for our grasping of the origins of life on Earth. For instance, the era of Earth stewardship challenges creationist identities assuming that the planet was formed and then human beings were quite unproblematically put on it to socialize according to a written code. It also challenges evolutionist identities postulating that life and self-awareness mysteriously emerged stochastically, or as the result of highly improbable contingencies. These rather improvised explanations are outmoded by the palpable verification that human beings are a planetary species (i.e. cannot exist outside the planet in their material form), while at the same time the earth has become a human planet (i.e. dramatically shaped by human beings, and inevitably so?). Traditional assumptions about the origins of life and cognition need to be challenged, and environmental sociology is in a good position to do it. In the following paragraphs we argue that socio-ecological agency may become a means through which a much-needed globalized form of identity based on human–planet reciprocity can be enacted.

In order to make a more convincing argument for the need to rethink human agency in socio-ecological terms, we shall discuss three of its main aspects: first, the essential role that reflexivity and meaning-making processes play in its conceptualization; second, the consideration of individual, social and material forms of agency as interconnected aspects of socio-ecological agency; and third, the implications of socio-ecological agency in terms of the construction of the fundamental myths and stories about the origin of life on Earth and the emergence of human beings, self-awareness and cognition.

A convenient starting point to explore socio-ecological agency is reflexivity, which becomes the processes through which the individual makes sense of her/his own transient life in the context of a living planet. Individual agents are constantly reflecting and creating meanings about their own relationship with material and social processes and structures. However, the fact that human beings are having an unprecedented influence on the earth's metabolism, of which they are an integral part, leads to a much broader conception of agency far beyond their individuality and immediate sociocultural context. Therefore socio-ecological agency requires an understanding of reflexivity that highlights the fact that in any interaction with the 'external world', we are simultaneously disclosing something about ourselves. Socio-ecological reflexivity entails a critical stance which challenges both the traditional scientific ideal of objective inquiry and the modern ideal of a clear-cut separation between individuals, social structures and the environment.

Beck et al. (1994) identify reflexivity as an organizing systemic principle in late modernity. 'Reflexive modernization' refers to a recursive turn of modernity upon itself. This involves the emergence of a collective form of self-reflection about our shared identity as human beings, which was not previously available to us. Linearity and the following of rules, in consonance with a set of pre-established roles, characterized the functioning of pre-reflexive modern individuals and institutions (e.g. family, ethnic group and the state). These institutions are now in crisis, and the functions that were once taking place at the interface of institution and role are now taking place much closer to the subject.

Unidirectional rules and roles are progressively being denormalized in the light of non-linear reflexivity. Yet the outcome is neither chaos nor irrationality. Instead, the outcome is a reorganization in which the subject relates to institutions by being reflexive rather than by the strict following of rules and roles. Reflexive modernity calls for people's willingness to learn, to be self-reflexive and question themselves, to seek wisdom, to be accepting of other perspectives and consider what they can learn from them, and to trust others in this process of mutual re-examination. Thus the search for personal meanings takes precedence over the unidirectional performance of function or the reproduction of social roles and structures.

Socio-ecological reflexivity entails an ongoing understanding of the multidirectional interdependence between inner world (e.g. dreams, fantasies, emotional responses) and outer world (e.g. social and biophysical phenomena). Meaning is the 'substance' linking the intrapersonal (e.g. a particular trajectory unique to a person) with other beings and with some kind of 'organic wholeness' (Bateson, 1987; Young-Eisendrath and Miller, 2000). Persons are not bounded, unique, cognitively integrated entities; nor are they constructed only by social discourses. This alternative position suggests a permeable boundary between inner and outer that allows (1) the existence of an inner identity that gives rise to powerful internal thoughts, feelings and tendencies to act in a certain way, and (2) a continuous actualization of such identity through the person's interaction with the extra-personal in the process of mutual co-creation (Varela et al., 1991).

In the context of the current environmental crisis, reflexivity is required to question how individual and social values and worldviews affect our ways of interacting with ecosystems and how this interaction, in turn, affects our own sustainability and well-being. This implies shifting the focus from unidirectional management and decision-making towards making sense of the relational matrix within which individuals, social systems and ecosystems coevolve. Coercion aside (i.e. when free of differentials in status or power), we influence each other through the stories we tell. Socio-ecological agency requires a commitment to learning to learn, opening ourselves to other perspectives and, more importantly, to the observation of our personal experience of the world around us (Wenger, 1998). Even though each individual interprets reality in a unique way, the process of interpretation is somehow co-created through interactions with others and the environment. This 'opening up' makes people aware of the misplaced trust that they have put in the dominant social structures of their time, structures that, eventually, have instilled in individuals a value system that is entirely out of line with any consideration for human–nature interdependence.

The second vital aspect of socio-ecological agency is the consideration of material, social and individual agencies. The notion of material agency is gaining currency within natural sciences due to the spectacular development of theories concerning self-organizing systems and, in particular, Prigogine's theory of dissipative structures. These theories show that matter and life are capable, within the limits of deterministic physical laws, of producing new patterns of organization and 'doing things' (typical examples include tornadoes and hurricanes). They evolve towards higher complexity, are path-dependent (i.e. have a history), and exhibit characteristics that are usually attributed to society and the human mind. These realizations blur the boundaries between the material, social and cognitive by rendering the possibility of characterizing all of them in terms of self-organizing open systems. By definition a system appears to have an identity and to 'do something' either actively or passively. Open systems are characterized by having an environment that provides their context. As described in Kay and Boyle (2008), complex self-organizing systems, unlike mechanical systems, can change their internal structure. As a consequence, 'different relationships and processes can develop, and the system can change its repertoire of behaviour. In short, the system can change its organization through internal agency' (ibid.: 53). This is not to say that the agency of material and biological systems is equivalent to volitional human agency. However, socio-ecological agency involves understanding, and a more active consideration of, physical and biological processes, including their unfolding and evolution.

The point is not to prescribe a moral code for regulating conflicts between different types of agencies. Every individual and every society has to work this out for itself, as well as collectively. However, socio-ecological agency suggests the promotion of curiosity, creativity, and non-exploitative and non-instrumental interaction in order to let a socio-ecological consciousness unfold (Goodwin, 1998; Castro-Laszlo, 2001). The overwhelming power that humanity has achieved over the planet has to be matched with a higher sense of responsibility and significant attention towards one's own life:

> To survive in this world, and to live fully and well, one must be attentive. To impose agendas on the world – ethical, political, economic, scientific – is, to some extent, to cease to pay attention, it is to organize one's perception of the world according to the dictates of the mode of control. (Hester et al., 2000: 281)

As a corollary, acknowledging and understanding the essence and functioning of material and social agency provides both a source of meaning for the consciousness of the socio-ecological agent, and inspirational guidance for his/her external interaction with the collective and material. This draws a stark contrast with the narrower understanding of human agency as independent actions involving volition and the decision to act or refrain from acting.

The third fundamental dimension of socio-ecological agency addresses its implications for our existential stories about the origin of life on Earth and about the emergence of human beings, self-awareness and cognition. As a warning, this point does not easily fit the confines of most sociological theoretical discussions, but it is crucial in understanding the role of environmental sociology in the exceptional present situation marked by global environmental change. Our main argument is that we need to construct new, negotiated stories that transcend both anthropocentric forms of creationism (as in Christianity) and naturalistic evolutionism (based on the idea of a single reality). The alternative is to encourage every socio-ecological agent to engage in the task of constructing their own existential story from their unique position in the world (i.e. their unique awareness about our ability to act upon socio-ecological structures and, in turn, be acted upon by them). The quality of these emerging individual stories is to be evaluated in the context of the evolutionary crossroads that humanity faces, rather than in terms of their (prophetic or natural) 'Truth'. The role of science in general would be to facilitate communication, translation and coherence among these continuously forming narratives without imposing its own perspective, but ensuring that the dialogue does not become a cacophony of 'voices' all claiming to have got it right (Thompson et al., 2006). Social sciences would evaluate the consequences of the narratives in terms of equity, solidarity and power relations, while environmental sociology would assess their implications for the making of nature–society interrelations.

The daunting task of negotiating a pluriverse of existential stories constructed by single 'socio-ecological agents' may seem insurmountable and rather unfeasible at the present time. Nonetheless, for the task to commence, we first need to have in place some kind of socio-ecological identity, a reasonable precondition for enacting socio-ecological agencies. One may speculate that the challenges posed by global environmental change may already be pushing in this direction. However, what we appear to have at the moment is a mosaic of traditional religious and cultural existential narratives barricaded in against the overwhelming progress of a Western-branded naturalism that has been caricatured as follows:

> [W]e all live under the same biological and physical laws and have the same fundamental bio-logical, social, and psychological makeup. This, you have not understood because you are pris-oners of your superficial worldviews, which are but representations of the reality to which we, through science, have privileged access. But science is not our property; it belongs to mankind universally! Here, partake – and with us you will be one. (Latour, 2004: 458).

Independently of whether this naturalistic argument is right or wrong, we have to ask what it offers in terms of finding ways of co-creating the planet sustainably. Does its uniform power preclude the kind of radical structural changes that the present global situation seems to be demanding? Is not the present situation precisely an outcome of the modernist notion of 'fundamental biological, social, and psychological makeup'? What room does it leave for alternative existential narratives that are not based on fundamentalist divisions between human beings and nature?

It is true that the negotiation of existential stories constructed by 'socio-ecological agents' might be easily dismissed as pure relativism. We admit that it is extremely radical in that it demands a blank slate and implies a highly problematic process of negotiation. However, it is not pure relativism. Instead, we would argue that it brings about a new form of constrained relativism (Thompson et al., 2006). In fact, it adds to the 'structural voices' proposed by Thompson et al. the meaning-making dynamics of human (socio-ecological) agency. That is, the constraint originates in the need to construct internally meaningful journeys in interaction with the socio-ecological realities of one's own time. The notion of the personal journey of discovery played an important role in pre-modern cultures and religions. Before globalization, these journeys often consisted of meaning-ful interactions of the individual with the local socio-ecological reality of his/her group or country. Eventually the journey started increasingly to venture outside local realities in actuality (through travelling), or figuratively (through narratives about the journeys of heroes and explorers). This has been one of the key mechanisms by which traditional (and modern) cultures, myths and religions have been constructed. Thus the novelty we are proposing is that the present circumstances demand that we expand this process and scale it upwards to the level of a global planet in peril.

Conclusions

Social science has tended to conceptualize human agents as either individualist/calculative, or abiding by categorical moral rules. Accordingly, the social world is seen as the product of conflicting actions and decisions emanating from independent agents pursuing their individual goals and preferences. Within this dominant perspective, institutions are often taken as a given, sent to the background, and reduced to sources of incentives or constraints for action. Following efforts to reconcile the utilitarian – normative dichotomy, a more relational understanding emphasizing the co-creation between agency and sociocultural structures is emerging. The basic tenet of this relational approach is that social structures condition agencies while individual agents may choose to either reproduce or transform these structures.

In this chapter we have argued that sociology will require a far broader paradigm of human agency if it aspires to contribute with relevant insights to the challenges of the global environmental change era. The new socio-ecological agent departs from modernist agency as much as the latter departed from medieval conceptions. It entails a new creation story about where we come from, who we are as human beings, and what our future possibilities will be. Rethinking 'where we come from' in this era leads to conceiving of individuals, society and the whole planetary system as co-created. Human beings are the product of, and are constrained by, the planet's identity. The 'miracle' of cognition is nothing other than an inevitable emergent property resulting from coevolutionary dynamics within the earth. 'Who we are' is reformulated by the fact that through cognition we are now capable of dramatically altering and shaping these coevolutionary dynamics. Therefore global environmental change is forcing us to redefine our agency in terms of global stewardship. The transition from modern agency to socio-ecological agency is just starting as human beings' identities rise beyond the constraints of specific social structures and boundaries. It is beyond the scope of this chapter to speculate about the future possibilities that this new form of agency will bring. Yet it is reasonable to expect future social structures to be based on co-responsibility rather than on ideological confrontations and the pursuit of individual privileges. The imminent collapse of the neoliberal global project suggested by the current financial crisis argues for the construction of alternative global narratives and social patterns that allow humanity to build new forms of coexistence, while at the same time facing up to the challenges of the global environmental crisis. This chapter has suggested that sticking to modernist conceptions of agency can only generate narratives and patterns that, while possibly buying some time, will eventually dig us deeper into the environmental crisis. Our only chance may be to emphasize narratives and patterns based on increased recognition of the bonds between human beings and the planet as a whole. The origin and possibility of these narratives and patterns entails embracing a socio-ecological sort of agency.

References

Bateson, G. (1987), 'Men are grass: metaphor and the world of mental process', in W.I. Thompson (ed.), *Gaia: A Way of Knowing. Political Implications of the New Biology*, Great Barrington, MA: Lindisfarne Press, pp. 37–47.

Beck, U., A. Giddens and S. Lash (1994), *Reflexive Modernization: Politics, Tradition and Aesthetics in the Modern Social Order*, Cambridge: Polity Press.

Boulding, K. (1978), *Ecodynamics: A New Theory of Societal Evolution*, Beverly Hills, CA: Sage.

Bourdieu, P. (1977), *Outline of a Theory of Practice*, Cambridge: Cambridge University Press.

Castro-Laszlo, K. (2001), 'Learning, design, and action: creating the conditions for evolutionary learning community', *System Research and Behavioral Science*, **18**: 379–91.

Catton, W.R. Jr and R.E. Dunlap (1978), 'Environmental sociology: a new paradigm', *The American Sociologist*, **13**: 41–9.

Emirbayer, M. and A. Mische (1998), 'What is agency?', *American Journal of Sociology*, **103**: 962–1023.

Farrell, K.N. (2007), 'Living with living systems: the co-evolution of values and valuation', *International Journal of Sustainable Development and World Ecology*, **14**: 14–26.

Finkler, K. (2000), *Experiencing the New Genetics: Family and Kinship on the Medical Frontier*, Philadelphia, PA: University of Pennsylvania Press.

Freudenburg, W.R., S. Frickel and R. Gramling (1995), 'Beyond the nature/society divide: learning to think about a mountain', *Sociological Forum*, 10, 361–392.

Freudenburg, W.R., S. Frickel and R. Gramling (1996), 'Crossing the Next Divide: A Response to Andy Pickering', *Sociological Forum*, **11**, 161–75.

Giddens, A. (1979), *Central Problems in Social Theory: A Positive Critique of Interpretive Sociologies*, London: Macmillan.

Giddens, A. (1984), *The Constitution of Society: Outline of the Theory of Structuration*, Berkeley, CA: University of California Press.

Goodwin, P. (1998), 'Hired hands or local voices: understandings and experiences of local participation in conservation', *Transactions of the Institute of British Geographers*, **23**, 481–99.

Gual, M.A. and R.B. Norgaard (2008), 'Bridging ecological and social systems coevolution: a review and proposal', *Ecological Economics* doi:10.1016/j.ecolecon.2008.07.020.

Hechter, M. and S. Kanazawa (1997), 'Sociological rational choice theory', *Annual Reviews in Sociology*, **23**: 191–214.

Hester, L., D. McPherson, A. Booth and J. Cheney (2000), 'Indigenous worlds and Callicott's land ethic', *Environmental Ethics*, **22**: 273–90.

Hodgson, G.M. (2008), 'Darwinian coevolution of organizations and the environment', *Ecological Economics*, doi:10.1016/j.ecolecon.2008.06.016.

Judkins, G., M. Smith and E. Keys (2007), 'Determinism within human–environment research and the rediscovery of environmental causation', *Geographical Journal*, **174**: 17–29.

Kallis, G. (2007), 'Socio-environmental co-evolution: some ideas for an analytical approach', *The International Journal of Sustainable Development and World Ecology*, **14**: 4–13.

Kay, J.J. and M. Boyle (2008), 'Self-organizing, holarchic, open sytems (SOHOs)', in D. Waltner-Toews, J.J. Kay and N.-M. E. Lister (eds), *The Ecosystem Approach: Complexity, Uncertainty and Managing for Sustainability*, New York: Columbia University Press, pp. 51–78.

Latour, B. (2004), 'Whose cosmos, which cosmopolitics?: Comments on the peace terms of Ulrich Beck', *Common Knowledge*, **10**: 450–62.

Latour, B. (2005), *Reassembling the Social: An Introduction to Actor-Network-Theory*, Oxford and New York: Oxford University Press.

Manuel-Navarrete, D., J.J. Kay and D. Dolderman (2004), 'Ecological integrity discourses: linking ecology with cultural transformation', *Human Ecology Review*, **11**: 215–29.

Manuel-Navarrete, D., S. Slocombe and B. Mitchell (2006), 'Science for place-based socioecological management: lessons from the Maya forest (Chiapas and Petén)', *Ecology and Society*, **11** (1): article 8.

Meyer, J.W. and R.L. Jepperson (2000), 'The "Actors" of modern society: the cultural construction of social agency', *Sociological Theory*, **18**: 100–120.

Mutch, A. (2002), 'Actors and networks or agents and structures: towards a realist view of information systems', *Organization*, **9**: 477–96.

Norgaard, R.B. (1981), 'Sociosystem and ecosystem coevolution in the Amazon', *Journal of Environmental Economics and Management*, **8**: 238–54.

Norgaard, R.B. (1994), *Development Betrayed: The End of Progress and a Coevolutionary Revisioning of the Future*, London and New York: Routledge.

Norgaard, R.B. (1997), 'A coevolutionary environmental sociology', in M.R. Redclift and G.R. Woodgate (eds), *The International Handbook of Environmental Sociology*, Cheltenham, UK and Lyme, USA: Edward Elgar, pp. 158–68.

Parsons, T. (1968), *The Structure of Social Action*, New York: Free Press.

Redclift, M. (2001), 'Environmental security and the recombinant human: sustainability in the twenty-first century', *Environmental Values*, **10**: 289–99.

Sewell, W.H.J. (1992), 'A theory of structure: duality, agency, and transformation', *American Journal of Sociology*, **98**: 1–29.

Thompson, M., R. Ellis and A.B. Wildavsky (1990), *Cultural Theory*, Boulder, CO: Westview Press.

Thompson, M., M. Verweij and R.J. Ellis (2006), 'Why and how culture matters', in R.E. Goodin and C. Tilly (eds), *The Oxford Handbook of Contextual Political Analysis*, Oxford and New York: Oxford University Press, pp. 319–40.

Varela, F.J., E. Thompson and E. Rosch (1991), *The Embodied Mind: Cognitive Science and Human Experience*, Cambridge, MA: MIT Press.

Wenger, E. (1998), *Communities of Practice: Learning, Meaning, and Identity*, Cambridge, UK: Cambridge University Press.

Winder, N., B. McIntosh and P. Jeffrey (2005), 'The origin, diagnostic attributes and practical application of co-evolutionary theory', *Ecological Economics*, **54**: 347–61.

Woodgate, G.R. and M.R. Redclift (1998), 'From a "sociology of nature" to environmental sociology: beyond social construction', *Environmental Values*, **7**: 3–24.

Young-Eisendrath, P. and M.E. Miller (2000), 'Beyond enlightened self-interest', in P. Young-Eisendrath and M.E. Miller (eds), *The Psychology of Mature Spirituality: Integrity, Wisdom, and Transcendence*, London and Philadelphia, PA: Routledge, pp. 11–20.

10 Ecological debt: an integrating concept for socio-environmental change
Iñaki Barcena Hinojal and Rosa Lago Aurrekoetxea

Seeking to define the ecological debt

The concept of ecological debt originated in the written literature and the contributions made by the popular movements of the South, specifically the Institute of Political Ecology of Chile on the occasion of the Rio de Janeiro Summit (1992). Since then, it has come to be used in other geographical areas, and it has moved from the associative field and the social movements to the academic and institutional spheres. Unlike other sister concepts, such as the 'ecological footprint' (Wackernagel and Rees, 1996) or 'ecological space' (Spangenberg, 1995), which emerged in university research circles and were later popularized through publications and the mass media, the concept of ecological debt has followed an inverse path, moving from the bottom to the top. Our aim is that 'ecological debt' should play a role as relevant as that of the concepts of 'ecological footprint' and 'space', since both were enthusiastically received by environmental activism (WWF and Friends of the Earth), and such indicators are now taken into account by governments and institutions in public environmental policies from the local level to the United Nations.

The prevailing economic system 'externalizes' the social and environmental impacts it provokes; it does not recognize them as its own or as something inherent in its economic model. The ecological debt is intended to help in developing new theories that argue for 'internalizing' these impacts, making them one of the basic axes of a new paradigm that will put a stop to the deterioration of the planet.

Ecological debt is the debt contracted by the world's wealthiest nations with the other countries of the planet as a result of the historical and present-day pillage of natural resources, exported environmental impacts and the free use of the global environmental space for waste disposal. It reflects what the North owes the South because of that plundering, which originated in the colonial period and has continued to grow (Observatorio de la Dueda en la Globalización, 2003). Today its characteristics are not only economic but also social and environmental, making it perfectly objective.

In any case, ecological debt is a concept whose definition is more complex and difficult than those of the 'environmental footprint' or 'space'. In the last decade, several definitions have been proposed, some proceeding from the ecology movement and others from academic spheres. For example, Aurora Donoso (Acción Ecológica – Ecuador), at the Popular Forum in Bali, before the Johannesburg Summit, defined ecological debt as

> the responsibility held by the industrialised countries and their institutions, banks, political and economic corporations for the gradual appropriation and control of the natural resources, and for the destruction of the planet caused by their models of production and consumption . . . A debt that includes the appropriation of the absorption capacity of the planet and the atmosphere, polluted by their greenhouse gases. (Donoso, 2002)

Ecological debt, according to Martínez-Alier (2004), is the debt accumulated by the countries of the North towards the countries of the South in two ways: in the first place, the export of primary products at very low prices, that is to say, prices that take no account of the environmental damage caused in the place of extraction and processing, nor of pollution at a global level; in the second place, by the free or very cheap occupation of environmental space – the atmosphere, the water, the land – through the dumping of production wastes. Its conceptual foundation is based on the idea of environmental justice, since if all the inhabitants of the planet have the right to the same quantity of resources and to the same portion of environmental space, then those who use more resources or occupy more space have a debt towards the others.

Other authors, searching for a broader definition, have argued that ecological debt is the debt accumulated by the wealthy countries of the North with respect to the countries of the Third World due to the pillage of resources, unfair trade, environmental damage and the free occupation of environmental space for depositing their wastes (Martínez-Alier et al., 2002).

Everybody knows and understands what we are talking about, but, bearing in mind that intellectual and academic contributions on ecological debt have been scarce, it is especially important to offer an understandable and communicable definition – one that will be credible and deal with something significant to people.

Sharing this concern, and as part of an effort to calculate the ecological debt of their country, Belgium, a group of researchers at the Centre for Sustainable Development of the University of Ghent drew up the following definition:

> The ecological debt of a country consists of: (1) the environmental damage caused by a country X in other countries, or in areas of jurisdiction of other countries, as a result of its model of production and consumption; and/or (2) the ecological damage caused historically by a country X in ecosystems outside its national jurisdiction as a result of its model of production and consumption; and (3) the use or exploitation of ecosystems, or of goods and services of ecosystems, over the course of time by a country X, at the expense of the equitable rights over those ecosystems of other countries or individuals. (Paredis et al. 2004: 48–9)

This definition is still in its initial phase and will continue to be developed, but it puts into relief a series of options and decisions that must be borne in mind when specifying the concept. 'Who owes whom?' is the leitmotiv used by the grassroots and ecologist movement to give sociopolitical expression to the economic and environmental inequalities that they denounce (Ekologistak Martxan, 2005). However, providing an answer to such an open question can turn out to be a hard task, one requiring a suitable, scientifically verifiable methodology and a deep moral and political resolve.

Ecological debt is no less a debt just because it is not reflected in contracts. It is at the same time both public and private, but it seems more important to stress the public debt, in order to refer in the first place to the responsibility of our countries and governments, rather than to call normal citizens to account. This does not exclude the search for greater precision and depth in its development, whether in the category of ecological damage (pollution, exhaustion, degradation etc.), or in the specification of its temporal and spatial dimension (global, continental, regional, local), or in the characterization of the debtors and creditors (states, present and future generations, social classes, transnational companies etc.), or in its physical or monetary quantification (see Box 10.1).

BOX 10.1   ELEMENTS FOR QUANTIFYING ECOLOGICAL DEBT

Environmental damage: pollution, degradation, extinction
Spatial level of damage: global, continental, national, regional, local
Type of ecosystem and ecosystem services
Equity rights: several interpretations for different types of ecosystems and services
Actors (creditors and debtors): countries, present and future generations, social classes, enterprises
Quantification: physical units or monetary accounts
Time: different time periods to be considered

Source: Adapted and developed from Paredis et al. (2004).

As can be seen in Figure 10.1, the emergence of the concept of ecological debt is linked to numerous disciplines and is based on previously established methodologies for measuring and calculating the factors that contribute to the debt. Hence, bearing in mind that 'ecological debt' is rooted in, and nourished by, different disciplines, we can say that it

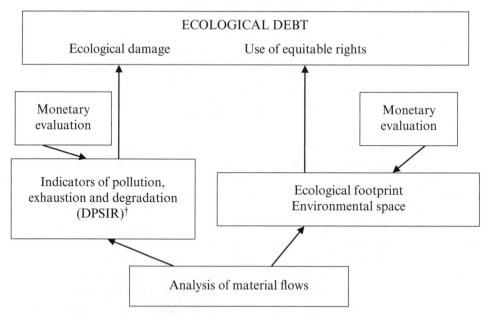

Note: † DPSIR (driving forces–pressures–state–impacts–responses) is a commonly employed framework for assessing and managing environmental problems.

Source: Paredis et al. (2004).

Figure 10.1   Calculating ecological debt

Table 10.1   A comparison of ecological debt: Canada and Bangladesh

Country	Ecological footprint (ha/person)	Carrying capacity (ha/person)	National deficit (ha/person)	Sustainable deficit (ha/person)
Canada	8.84	14.24	−5.40	7.04
Bangladesh	0.53	0.30	0.23	−1.27

Source: Russi et al. (2006).

has resulted from a series of contributions, or different and diverse viewpoints, that are mutually complementary, and without which it would be unthinkable or inconceivable. That is, this concept is as much based on the idea of the 'carrying capacity' of Earth's ecosystems and systems of biophysical accounting, such as the ecological 'footprint' or 'space', as on the analysis of material flows. It is a new concept that is directly related to the critical viewpoint of ecological economics, which links the economic dynamics among countries with environmental interaction; to environmental justice and human rights and theories of historical injustices and restitution; to other fields such as political ecology, which Martínez-Alier defines as the study of distributive ecological conflicts; or to the 'eco-colonialism' of Agarwal and Narain (Paredis et al. 2004: 74).

The 'ecological footprint' measures the quantity of land (and water) needed to sustain a specific mode of production and consumption, and this is compared with the carrying capacity of a specific territory and with the average carrying capacity of the planet, to provide a measure of the ecological deficit between the ideal and the real: the ecological debt. A large and sparsely populated country like Canada, for example, had a carrying capacity of 14.24 ha/per capita in 2002, and although its ecological footprint was only 8.84 ha/person, the latter figure was far above the sustainable global average (1.8 ha/person); even so, from this perspective, Canada can be considered an ecological creditor. The opposite occurs in a relatively small and overpopulated country like Bangladesh: although it has a footprint of only 0.53 ha/person and is a long way from the sustainable global average, its carrying capacity was only 0.30 ha/person (see Table 10.1).

We thus find an ecological debt of −5.40 ha/person in the Canadian case, and 0.23 in the Bangladeshi case, figures that express very different and contradictory socio-ecological realities. The ecological debt, as Joan Martínez-Alier would put it, refers to the 'carrying capacity expropriated' by some countries and societies at the expense of others.

In the case of environmental space, instead of combining all the parameters (agricultural land, pasture, forest, sea, built-up area and CO_2 absorption capacity) into a single factor, the area of land needed to sustain a given population, five factors – energy, non-renewable raw materials, agricultural land, wood and water – are calculated for each country and compared with the global averages for each.

This type of indicator, together with calculation methodologies like the analysis of material flows (Naredo and Valero, 1999) or the DPSIR model (driving force–pressure–state–impact–response) utilized by the European Environment Agency or Eurostat, lays the foundations for a multidisciplinary approach to obtaining a complex calculation.

In any case, the need for measurement can lead us to both a physical calculation and the translation of such physical magnitudes into a monetary debt. Conscious that monetary quantification is biased and that it is not a central concern of the social movements working for recognition of the ecological debt, the use of economic figures can on occasion serve, in a globally monetarized world, as a graphic form for representing environmental damage and, above all, as an evaluative element that counteracts the frequently paid foreign debt. As Joan Martínez-Alier explains for the Latin American case, if the region's total foreign debt were $700 000 million dollars in 1991, that would be the equivalent to the costs of reducing the carbon debt of the industrialized countries in a mere 12 years, at a rate of $60 000 million dollars annually (Martínez-Alier, 2004: 293). Or for the case of Ecuador, if we consider an element such as unequal exchange, both ecological and economic, the ecological debt generated in favour of the country annually (approximately $6500 million) is equivalent to a third of its total foreign debt (Villalba, 2008).

How to quantify the ecological debt
Giving a monetary value to the ecological debt as a whole is a complex question (Barcena et al., 2009). In the first place, there are difficulties due to the great quantity of environmental damage done from the colonial period up to the present, making it impossible to quantify and evaluate all of this. A first attempt at clarification would be to distinguish between the mechanisms generating that debt (pillage of resources, loss of sovereignty in food, unequal exchange in trade, unequal use of the global environmental space etc.) and its components (carbon debt, biopiracy, export of wastes, environmental liabilities and externalities etc.).

In the second place, the complexity of relations between ecosystems and human society makes it difficult to determine exactly the consequences of environmental damage. The interactions between the elements of the natural and the social systems can greatly amplify a disturbance in the initial balance and lead to irreversible and unforeseeable changes. Pollution is transmitted and accumulated throughout the food chain, and the risk is increased by many factors that at times interact and often have long-term effects. It is therefore very difficult to isolate the effect of each polluting element and to establish a linear relationship of cause and effect.

In the third place, monetary evaluation can reflect only a part of the losses associated with the ecological debt, while ignoring many other aspects of the losses. For instance, economists employ several methods to estimate the economic value of a human life, using for example the opportunity cost of work lost or the cost of life insurance policies. These evaluations reflect only a part of the losses associated with a death, while many other aspects cannot be expressed in monetary language at all. Besides, these estimations are questionable as they depend on income (the death of a professional is more expensive than that of a labourer).

For all these reasons, it is not possible to compensate for more than a minimal part of the ecological debt. In many cases, communities adversely affected by a company refuse to discuss the sum of money they should be offered. However, in the business and institutional field it can be more effective to talk in a quantitative and monetary language. For example, contrasting parts of the ecological debt, expressed in monetary values, with the foreign debt can be useful for demonstrating that the latter has been amply 'paid', and that it is the North that is indebted to the South and not vice versa. Besides, the monetary evaluation of environmental damage is useful in a judicial context: monetary compensation for damage may be the only way for the victims to receive at least something and for the guilty party to be punished, as well as providing a deterrent effect that prompts companies to take precautions to reduce the risk of accidents.

In any case, a debt is an acquired responsibility, an obligation towards others, which in our case proceeds from excess or overutilization of something belonging to others, or held in common with them. This takes us from the economy to the fields of philosophy and law, to the definitions of environmental justice, equitable rights and national sovereignty over resources, and also to the natural sciences for determining the sustainable use of resources and the carrying capacity of ecosystems.

Monetary compensation is therefore not the only way of evaluating the ecological debt: methods of physical quantification should and must be preferentially employed. Some of the indicators that can be used are those obtained from the Analysis of Material Flows (e.g. Eurostat, 2001), a methodology that consists in calculating the weight of all the materials that enter and leave an economic system. The flow of materials is not a direct indicator of pollution (a gram of mercury pollutes more than a ton of iron), but it can give an idea of the physical dimensions of an economy. Using this methodology, we can observe that while from the monetary point of view European imports are roughly equal to exports, in terms of weight Europe imports approximately four times more than it exports (Giljum and Hubacek, 2001, cited in Giljum, 2004). In Latin America, by contrast, as much as six tons is exported for each ton imported (Vallejo, 2006a, 2006b); hence it is abundantly clear that Latin America is situated among the ecological creditors and the EU is among the debtors.

This means that European exports are much more expensive than its imports: the income obtained from the sale of a ton of exported goods can be used to buy four tons of imported goods. That is why the countries of the South, due to poverty and the foreign debt, find themselves motivated to sell a growing volume of primary goods, such as fossil fuels, metals, minerals etc., which produce a great deal of pollution and little wealth at the site of extraction and processing, while the countries of the North specialize in final products, which are more expensive and less polluting.

Turning now to the field of responsibilities, the ecological debt obliges us to talk of creditor and debtor agents. The latter can be public and/or private, state administrations and/or companies, as well as certain consumer classes in both the wealthy and impoverished countries. Who are the creditors of the debt? In the ranks of those who should receive compensation, we find states and social collectives – indigenous, farmers' and women's groups – as well as the future generations who will be deprived of resources or affected by ecological problems inherited from an inappropriate and selfish management of natural ecosystems by past generations. Such is the case of the debt acquired through the abusive use of the atmosphere for the dumping of greenhouse gases, which have led to climate change.

Content of the ecological debt

We now set out to explain some of the possible contents of the so-called ecological debt, concentrating, without any pretension to be exhaustive, on those elements that seem most relevant and on which most work has been done. At the same time, it must be recognized that there are other areas, such as the debt contracted through the loss of sovereignty in food, towards which attention should be directed.[1]

Here, following in the steps of Acción Ecológica (Ecuador) and of Joan Martínez-Alier, we propose four elements, or domains, where the ecological debt can be evaluated. These are: carbon debt, biopiracy, waste export and environmental liabilities.

Carbon debt

Scientists, especially after the presentation in Paris (December 2006) of the *Fourth Assessment Report* of the Intergovernmental Panel on Climate Change (IPCC), are now agreed that the build-up of gases caused by the use of fossil fuels is causing an increase in global mean temperatures. This has potentially disastrous consequences, such as a rise in sea level, the melting of the glaciers, increase in desert areas, reduction of agricultural yield, loss of plant and animal species and an increase in extreme meteorological events (see Parks and Roberts, Chapter 19, and Murphy, Chapter 18, in Part II of this volume). Recently, the report prepared by Lord Stern,[2] Economic Adviser to the UK Government and former chief economist of the World Bank, has had a strong social and political impact through its affirmation that the annual economic cost of climate change could be between 5 and 20 per cent of global GDP, and by comparing it to the economic costs of the two world wars and the subsequent reconstruction efforts.

These harmful effects will befall all inhabitants of the planet. But it is the countries of the South that will be most affected by anthropogenic climate change (Simms, 2005). This is for three reasons: first, because the areas most subjected to hurricanes, flooding and desertification are located in the countries of the South; second, because the impoverished countries have less resources available for defending themselves against these phenomena; and, third, because their economies are based to a larger extent on the primary sector, which will be the most damaged.

On the other hand, the causes of the greenhouse effect are to be found principally in the great consumption of fossil fuels by the rich countries (see Parks and Roberts, Chapter 19 in Part II of this volume). As a result, the countries of the North, whose economic development and welfare are based on a highly intensive use of the energy sources responsible for the emission of greenhouse gases, are debtors towards the countries of the South. That part of the ecological debt is called the carbon debt (Dillon, 2000).

Calculation of the portion of the ecological debt corresponding to the carbon debt involves approximations and ambiguities for three reasons. First, there is no agreement among scientists on the quantity of anthropogenic greenhouse gases that might be considered acceptable, due to the complexity of atmospheric phenomena. It is not known by how much the temperature of the earth will rise as a result of the increase in the concentration of greenhouse gases in the atmosphere. Second, the increase in the temperature of the earth will have unforeseeable consequences because the network of interrelations and feedbacks among the different components of the ecosystems could amplify the effects. Finally, a fictitious price must be used in estimating the monetary value of the carbon debt, and this figure will always be open to criticism, as there are different methods for its calculation, each of which produces a different result (Encina and Barcena, 2006).

The IPCC calculates that, in the future, an increase of 2.5 °C in the temperature would mean a cost of between 1.5 per cent and 2 per cent of world GDP, as stated in the *Third Evaluation Report* (2001).[3] The German Institute for Economic Research (DIW)[4] has concluded that an increase in world temperature of only 1 °C would give rise to losses of over €1.5 trillion per year in the world economy from 2050 onwards, which would mean between €5 and €181 per tonne of CO_2 emitted, with an average value of €58 per tonne (tCO_2).

The European Commission, which seeks to play the role of leader in global climate change policies, has made a proposal to place a value on each tonne of CO_2, with the aim of penalizing at that cost those emitters who exceed the assigned quotas in the Internal Market of CO_2 emissions – a cost that will be €100 per tCO_2.[5]

According to the IPCC, in order to maintain stable levels of CO_2 in the atmosphere, emissions should be reduced to 3.33 Gigatonnes[6] of carbon (GtC) per year. If we take 6 GtC, the baseline emissions level used in the Kyoto Protocol (1990), and calculate the excess emissions in that year, we can see that in 1990 the excess was 2.65 GtC, which is equivalent to 9.805 GtCO_2.[7]

If carbon debt is simply calculated as the product of excess CO_2 emissions and the price per tonne of CO_2 (tCO_2) in Euros, then using the DIW average figure of €58/tCO_2, the global carbon debt in 1990 would have been €568.7 billion, while using the European Commission price of €100/tCO_2 it would have been only just short of one trillion euros: €980.5 billion.

This monetary measure enables us to compare the environmental footprint inflicted on the planet, the effects of which are felt disproportionately by the countries of the South, with the economic impact and profits that are generated in the North; the picture thus revealed is totally asymmetric. For example, the ecological debt figure calculated using the EU CO_2 price is €980 billion for 1990 alone, which compares with a total accumulated external debt for Latin America of around €700 billion in 1991 (Martínez-Alier, 2004). Thus, in just one year, the ecological debt incurred by the world's wealthiest countries was sufficient to repay the total accumulated external debt of Latin America, leaving a further €280 billion of ecological debt.

Alternatively, we might calculate the carbon debt generated by a transnational company like the Spanish petroleum conglomerate Repsol. In 2001 alone, Repsol acquired a carbon debt of €650 million, with its total debt today standing at approximately €2 billion.[8]

Finally, it can be seen that the logic underlying the concept of the ecological debt is different from that which inspires the Kyoto Protocol. In fact, the Kyoto Protocol assigns quotas for the reduction of emissions on the basis of 1990 emissions: whoever polluted the most in 1990 will have more right to pollute in the future. As Lohmann (2001) has observed, 'the Kyoto Protocol creates more monetary *goods* than any other treaty in history'. In contrast, the idea of ecological debt implies that all the inhabitants of the planet should have the right to the same quantity of emissions, irrespective of where they were born; hence whoever pollutes more than their corresponding quota is a debtor towards humanity.

Biopiracy

There is another part of the ecological debt that derives from the intellectual appropriation and commercial utilization of ancestral knowledge relating to seeds, the use of medicinal plants and other knowledge of the peasantry and indigenous peoples, knowledge on which biotechnology and modern industrial agriculture are based. This is known as biopiracy.

The characteristics of plant and animal species are the product of their continuing interaction over time with their physical surroundings, with each other and with human beings. For thousands of years indigenous and peasant communities have selected species for use as food, fibre and medicinal products, and through that interaction they have changed the characteristics of the natural species, creating different varieties with properties that are known to only a few. This knowledge is of great value to pharmaceutical, biotechnological and agricultural companies, which use it to obtain income. And in the majority of cases they do not pay, or pay very little, to the local populations that are the authentic owners of that knowledge.

As Vandana Shiva says, biodiversity has always been a local communitarian resource:

> A resource is common property when there is a social system that assures its utilisation adapted to criteria of justice and sustainability. That implies combining the rights and responsibilities of the users, combining utilisation with conservation and the existence of a sense of cooperation with nature in productive activity and a spirit of mutual interchange amongst members of the community. (Shiva, 2001: 90–91)

All the species that inhabit the earth carry information about themselves in their cells. Their characteristics have resulted from thousands of years of evolution. Human populations and cultures have coevolved with plant and animal species (principally selecting species for their use), adapting their characteristics to suit their purposes and in the process adapting their cultures to accommodate the needs of the crop and livestock varieties they have bred. They are, thus, the *de facto* owners of the knowledge of the varieties they have created.

Regrettably, there are numerous examples of biopiracy in the world. One involves the neem or nim tree (*Azarichdita indica*), which originates in India where it has been used for thousands of years to derive food, pharmaceutical and cosmetic products. Nonetheless, the products of the neem and the knowledge of its many properties have been patented by certain researchers and multinationals of the North, who obtain considerable income from this without any recompense for the people of India (see Ambrose-Oji, Chapter 20 in Part II of this volume).

We find another case of biopiracy in Peru, where the company Liofilizadora del Pacífico commercializes the Amazonia liana 'cat's claw' (*Uncaria tomentosa*), traditionally used against arthritis, rheumatism and diabetes. The company envisages giving the indigenous community of the Ashaninkas a mere 0.2 per cent of the income, in payment for the work done cultivating the plants and not for the knowledge contributed, as the company itself recognizes: 'For hundreds of years this remarkable herb has been used by the Indian Natives of the Peruvian Rain Forest to cure cancer, arthritis, gastritis, ulcers and female hormonal imbalances. Study has determined that this herb contains a wealth of beneficial phytochemicals and alkaloids, proanthoncyanidins, polyphenols, triterpines, and plant sterols.'[9]

In this way, 'intellectual property rights' reward solely the creativity of the laboratories, that is, they are a further tool for extending the territory of the market economy. Is application of the logic of the market a guarantee of biodiversity? What is the just price that a community should receive for its contribution to the creation of a modern medicine derived from the natural resources of its ancestors and its present-day members? How much should a Mexican peasant pay a multinational for the seed of an 'improved bean' if the latter was discovered in his field? Should price be related to ends? Is the end of seeking company profits the same as when a vaccine is bought by a humanitarian organization or a state for social ends?

Waste export
The industrial system produces a huge quantity of waste, with different degrees of toxicity. Treatment of that waste is a very costly process, whose price depends on the environmental regulations of the country where this is carried out. For that reason, the companies of the North find it convenient to export their toxic waste to countries where environmental legislation is less strict and where fewer safety measures are required, so that disposing of waste is less costly.

One example is the transport of electric and electronic waste. In recent years, about 80 per cent of electric and electronic appliances collected in the USA for recycling have been exported to China, India and Pakistan, where they are treated in conditions that are highly dangerous to human health: open-air incineration, creation of acid-waste pools, uncontrolled dumping in rural areas. According to a study by the Environmental Protection Agency of the USA, it is ten times cheaper to send a VDU screen to Asia for recycling than for this to be done in the USA.

In the opinion of Lawrence Summers, Vice President for Development, World Bank, President of Harvard University, US Secretary of the Treasury (1999–2000), and subsequently a member of Barack Obama's government, this is something that we should consider only natural. In his own words: 'I think that the economic logic of disposing of toxic waste in poorer areas is flawless, and it is necessary to recognize this' (cited in Barcena, 2004).

According to Filartiga and Agüero Wagner (2000), toxic garbage refers to

> any residue, waste, mud, liquid or any other disposable material that due to its quantity, concentration or physical, chemical or infectious characteristics can cause, or significantly contribute to, an increase of serious and irreversible diseases, or temporary disability; or that presents an immediate or potential risk for the health of people and the environment when it is treated, stored, transported or disposed of in an inappropriate or inconvenient way.

The wealthy nations generate an enormous quantity of toxic residues that it is either impossible or extremely expensive to recycle. In a generalized way, the solution adopted is to export this to countries with fewer economic resources that have 'softer' or 'more flexible' legislation.

The 'Basle Agreement for the control of transnational movements of dangerous toxic waste and its elimination' was adopted in 1989 and came into effect in 1992; to date it has been signed by 149 countries. This Agreement was initially criticized by environmentalist groups that believed it would be incapable of imposing an effective prohibition on the massive exportation of waste to impoverished countries with much weaker environmental legislation. In 1995, an amendment was passed that prohibited any type of export of polluting materials to those countries, but it came into effect with the signature of only 62 of the countries that had signed the Agreement at that time. The fact that the USA, the main producer of toxic garbage in the world, has still not signed the Agreement limits its scope appreciably.

In spite of the agreements and, above all, because of the failure to sign the clause categorically preventing the export of waste to impoverished countries, such practices continue to be carried out today. These practices include the scrapping of ships, the recycling of electric and electronic devices, the incineration of plastic, the creation of acid pools and uncontrolled dumping in the rural areas of countries with weaker legislation.

The world's wealthiest nations produce close to 80 per cent of the 400 million tonnes of toxic garbage generated in the world each year, and they export 10 per cent of this, the greater part of it to impoverished countries with great economic needs. Due to this export of waste, the wealthy countries have acquired a debt to the impoverished countries that must be recognized and paid. It is difficult to quantify this debt, but the cost to a 'developed' economy for the recycling and disposal of solid residues and polluted water can be calculated, in both monetary and energy terms. However, we must realize that the flexibility of norms and restrictions of the countries with fewer economic resources, aimed at attracting foreign investment, also has to be explained by the interest of the polluting countries in maintaining their level of economic growth and increasing the profitability of their productive processes.

Environmental liabilities
The term 'environmental liability' derives from economic language. In company accounting, liabilities are the set of debts and taxes that reduce assets. Used in environmental terms, the term refers to the set of uncompensated environmental damages transferred to the collective by companies due to incidents during their everyday activities, as well as to the unsustainable use of resources. Thus we can define environmental liabilities as 'the set of environmental damages, in terms of contamination of the water, the soil, the air, the deterioration and exploitation of resources and ecosystems, produced by a firm, during its normal working or through unforeseen accidents, over the course of its history'.

When a company causes damage to a collective, the moral responsibility is clear, but the legal responsibility depends on the legislative system. Often, the legal context of the countries of the South means that companies do not consider environmental damages as costs (or consider them to be low-order costs), they thus have little incentive to reduce such damages. That is why it is necessary to create effective international legislation on environmental responsibility, something that is still widely insufficient. In fact, the demand for responsibility is a strong incentive to reduce environmental damages, since it makes possible a partial internalization in company accounting of the costs and environmental risks, with the result that environmental resources are not considered as free goods.

During 30 years of activity in Ecuador, the US transnational petroleum company Texaco extracted 1500 million barrels of crude oil from the country, built 22 petrol stations and drilled 339 wells in an area of 442 965 ha. It dumped an (uncalculated) number of tonnes of toxic material and maintenance waste, derived from the extraction processes, and more than 19 000 million gallons of production water were polluted with hydrocarbons and heavy metals. Accidental spillages were frequent, calculated at approximately 16.8 million gallons of liquid deriving from the production processes. At its 200 burners, it daily flared off two million cubic metres of gas (producing acid rain, dioxins etc.) and it constructed 500 km of road and pipeline.

The malnutrition resulting from the pollution and from the destruction of resources in the area is the highest in the country. The cases of cancer are the most numerous in the country and are increasing; besides, the construction of petrol towns meant the extinction of the Tetete culture.

Who owes whom? A very useful question

A simple mathematical equation raises a highly alarming ethical issue. If all the people on the earth had a level of consumption similar to that of the 'developed' economies (using the same level of resources and generating the same waste), the global economy would need access to five or six more earths. Ecological debt is a concept that can be very useful for understanding the underlying problems from a historical, political, social, ecological, economic and even cultural point of view. It enables graphic form to be given to the permanent state of conflict and the increasing debts to humanity. Linking everyday habits – such as meals – with a global analysis can be educational. 'The generation of an ecological debt and the loss of sovereignty in food are closely linked and often associated to monoculture exports . . . We must turn the spotlight on the analysis of importation in order to change the effects of exportation' (Garcia, 2005).

Ecological debt implicitly refers to other concepts, such as environmental justice, social ecology and the environmental space. That is why it is a concept that, in an integral way, introduces, explains and responds to the model of capitalist globalization. It includes both equity and ecology, and confronts the dominant system in a geographical, transversal, intergenerational and multidisciplinary way.

According to José Manuel Naredo, the unceasing search for that myth called economic growth is what is promoting the progressive exploitation and human use of the biosphere, the terrestrial crust, the hydrosphere and the atmosphere, together with the expansion of settlements and infrastructures, at rates far higher than that of demographic growth. These are leaving their mark in obvious territorial deterioration, such as the occupation of better-quality agricultural land for extractive, urban–industrial uses and the provision of infrastructures, the reduction of the surface area of forests and other ecosystems of great biological diversity and landscape interest, the advance of erosion, fires and the loss of vegetation cover etc. (Naredo, 2006).

It can be seen that the concept of ecological debt leads to a multidisciplinary study in order to obtain a complex calculation that attempts to reflect the imbalances and injustices deriving from a system of unlimited economic growth, which, besides being an irrational myth, produces inequalities and generates unacceptable socio-environmental risks for humanity.

In summary, ecological debt is a synthetic and efficient conceptual tool for speaking of the injustice in North–South relations and for trying to obtain:

- *Recognition* of the imbalance in the use of natural resources and the pollution produced, aided by indicators such as carrying capacity, environmental space and ecological footprint, which reproduce the unsustainability of our model of production and consumption in a concise and graphic way.
- *Prevention*, that is, a series of environmental and economic policies that would prevent the production of fresh debt; the issuing of regulations that would put a brake on the squandering of ecosystems and seek reparations for the social and ecological damages inflicted.

- *Reparation*, both monetary and political, for the debt acquired, while accepting that a large part of the natural and social deterioration cannot be undone: it is irreversible and cannot be compensated for.
- *Compensation* (as far as this is possible) for the debt already incurred and abolition of the South's foreign debt. This would mean a commitment to pay for recognized abusive and undue use, and a willingness to accept such compensation.

Finally, while this new concept of ecological debt has potential, it also has problems. It is still not clear how legal principles such as 'polluter pays' or 'common but differentiated responsibility' will represent a sufficient link or legal motive for there to be international recognition of this concept. It is a concept that, as well as considering the present, looks back on the economic and ecological relations of previous decades, which for many sociopolitical actors constitutes a hindrance, since the search for environmental sustainability tends basically to look to the future.

Among its virtues, this new concept entails both a new instrument of political economy and a nexus of union that contributes solutions to both the problem of the South's foreign debt and climate change, and to the ecological restructuring of our societies in the search for sustainability. Attempting to observe energy flows at the same time as those of international trade, and to be able to relate them to international cooperation for development, means a new attitude that could induce a change of behaviour.

Notes

1. See 'Deuda y Soberanía Alimentaria [Debt and Sovereignty in Food]', in Ortega (2005), pp. 99–115.
2. Available at http://www.hm-treasury.gov.uk/sternreview_index.htm, last accessed 14 May 2009.
3. Available at http://www.ipcc.ch/ipccreports/assessments-reports.htm, last accessed 15 May 2009.
4. Special dossier on climate change: 'We either act now or we pay the consequences', available at http://ec.europa.eu/environment/news/efe/climate/index_en.htm, last accessed 15 May 2009.
5. 'Directive of the European Parliament and of the Council establishing a scheme for greenhouse gas emission allowance trading within the Community and amending Council Directive 96/61/EC', version presented by the Commission 2001/0245 (COD).
6. 1 Gigatonne = 1 000 000 000 tonnes.
7. Each tonne of CO_2 contains 0.27 tonnes of carbon.
8. Source: www.ecologistasenaccion.org.
9. http://www.perumarketplaces.com/esp/ficha_producto0.asp?Prod=13294&sector=298, last accessed 15 May 2009.

References

Barcena, I. (2004), *Euskal Herria nora zoaz? Retos sociales y ambientales para la sostenibilidad*, Bilbao: Ekologistak Martxan.
Barcena, I., R. Lago and U. Villalba (2009), *Energía y Deuda Ecológica. Transnacionales, cambio climático y alternativas*, Barcelona: Icaria.
Dillon, J. (2000), 'Ecological debt: South tells North "time to pay up"', *Economic Justice Report*, **XI** (3), September.
Donoso, Aurora (2002), 'An alliance to stop the destruction of Southern peoples' livelihoods and sustainability', speech delivered at the Indonesian People's Forum, 24 May–05 June, Bali, Indonesia.
Encina, J. and I. Barcena (2006), *Democracia Ecológica. Formas y experiencias de participación en la crisis ambiental*, Sevilla: UNILCO.
Ekologistak Martxan (2005), *La Deuda ecológica de Euskadi. Nuestro modelo energético y la Amazonía Ecuatoriana*, Bilbao: Ekologistak Martxan.
Eurostat (2001), *Economy-wide Material Flow Accounts and Derived Indicators – A Methodological Guide*, Luxembourg: Office for Official Publications of the European Communities.
Filartiga Joel and Luis Agüero Wagner (2000), *Apocalipsis Geo-Ambiental. El Imperialismo ecológico*, available at: http://www.quanta.net.py/userweb/apocalipsis/index.html, last accessed 15 May 2009.

Garcia, Ferrán (2005), 'Nos comemos el mundo: Deuda Ecológica y soberanía alimentaría', in *Revista Pueblos*, 15 September, available at http://www.revistapueblos.org/spip.php?article268, last accessed 15 May 2009.

Giljum, S. (2004), *Biophysical Dimensions of North–South Trade: Material flows and Land Use*, Vienna: University of Vienna, PhD thesis.

Lohmann, L. (2001), 'Democracy or carbonocray? Intellectual corruption and the future of the climate debate', Corner House Briefing No. 24, UK.

Martínez-Alier, J., A. Simms and L. Rijnhout (2002), 'Poverty, development, and ecological debt', pamphlet.

Martínez-Alier, J. (2004), *El ecologismo de los pobres. Conflictos ambientales y lenguajes de valoración*, Barcelona: Icaria–FLACSO.

Naredo, J.M. and A. Valero (eds) (1999), *Desarrollo económico y deterioro ecológico*, Madrid: F. Argentaria y Visor Distrib.

Naredo, J.M. (2006), *Raices económicas del deterioro ecológico y social. Más allá de los dogmas*, Madrid: Siglo XXI.

Observatorio de la Deuda en la Globalización (2003), *Deuda ecológica: ¿quién debe a quién?*, Barcelona: Colectivo de difusión de la deuda ecológica, ODG, Icaria editorial.

Ortega M. (ed.) (2005), *La Deuda Ecológica Española. Impactos ecológicos y sociales de la economía española en el extranjero*, Colección Pensamiento Global, Llerena, Badajoz, España: Muñoz Moya Editores y Secretariado de publicaciones Universidad de Sevilla.

Paredis, E. et al. (2004), *Elaboration of the Concept of Ecological Debt*. Center for Sustainable Development (CDO), Ghent University, Belgium.

Russi, D., T. Kucharz and I. Barcena (2006), 'Deuda ecológica: un concepto integral en la lucha contra la globalización capitalista', in J. Encina and I. Barcena (eds) *Democracia Ecológica. Formas y experiencias de participación en la crisis ambiental*, Sevilla: UNILCO.

Shiva, V. (2001), *Biopiratería. El saqueo de la naturaleza y el conocimiento*, Barcelona: Icaria.

Simms A. (2005), *Ecological Debt. The Health of the Planet and the Wealth of Nations*, London: Pluto Press.

Spangenberg, J.H. (1995), *Towards Sustainable Europe. A Study from the Wuppertal Institute for Friends of the Earth Europe*, Luton, UK and Brussels: FoE Publications Ltd.

Vallejo, M.C. (2006a), *La estructura biofísica de la economía ecuatoriana: el comercio exterior y los flujos ocultos del banano*, Quito, Ecuador: Abya-Yala FLACSO Ecuador.

Vallejo, M.C. (2006b), 'Estructura biofísica de la economía ecuatoriana: un estudio de los flujos directos de materiales', *Revista Iberoamericana de economía ecológica*, **4**: 55–72.

Villalba, Unai (2008), *El concepto de deuda ecológica y algunos ejemplos en Ecuador*, Bilbao: Jornadas de Economía Crítica.

Wackernagel, M. and W. Rees (1996), *Our Ecological Footprint. Reducing Human Impact on the Earth*, Philadelphia, PA: New Society Publishers.

11 The emergence model of environment and society
John Hannigan

Introduction
In mid-September 2008, world financial markets were rocked by a steady succession of shocks: the collapse of rescue attempts and subsequent filing for bankruptcy of Lehman Brothers Holdings Inc., the fire sale of Merrill Lynch & Co. to Bank of America Corp., the US government bailout of insurance giant American International Group Inc., and finally, a mortgage 'bailout' plan proposed by US Treasury Secretary Henry Paulson that could end up costing taxpayers $750 billion or more. Writing in the Canadian daily newspaper, *The National Post*, chief business correspondent Theresa Tedesco observed that old game plans had been rendered irrelevant and new standards of panic established. 'Clearly', Tedesco opined, 'this is one financial crisis that doesn't come with a playbook.' Tedesco's comments apply equally well to the environmental challenges of the early twenty-first century, whose 'playbook' is similarly missing in action.

In this chapter, I propose a sociological approach to the society–environment relationship that spotlights elements of novelty, uncertainty, emergence, improvisation and social learning. My goal here is neither to explain the origins of the environmental 'crisis', as did a critical mass of seminal thinking in environmental sociology in the 1970s and 1980s, nor to identify and assess the most effective mechanism of environmental reform or improvement, the object of much recent work (see Buttel, 2003). Rather, I aim to frame the study of nature, society and the environment within an interactionist tradition in sociology, as it first developed at the University of Chicago under the guidance of Herbert Blumer and Robert Park, and later flourished in the 1960s in the work of Lewis Killian, Tamotsu Shibutani, Ralph Turner, Anselm Strauss and others. This 'emergence' approach further evolved in the 1970s and 1980s in a series of studies of community emergencies and collective behaviour at the Ohio State University Disaster Research Center.[1] More recent strands of emergence theory can be identified in the literature on social movement identity formation, on social learning in an environmental context, in Beck's 'risk society' thesis, in the construction of 'social arenas', and, most recently, in the 'sociology of environmental flows'.

Nearly three decades ago, Dunlap and Catton (1979: 253–4) observed that the 'disciplinary traditions inherited from George Herbert Mead, W.I. Thomas and other symbolic interactionists predispose sociologists to recognize only the "symbolic" or "cognitive" level of interaction'. For their part, Dunlap and Catton were eager to emphasize the 'non-symbolic' levels of interaction, that is, the direct effects on human beings of harmful environmental conditions such as pollution and soil erosion. Given the nature of their mandate, an emphasis on meaning and perception was not to be encouraged. Later on, of course, these 'levels of interaction' were respectively represented in the 'realist' (non-symbolic) and 'social constructionist' (symbolic) approaches to environment and society.

A quarter-century later, Riley Dunlap (2002) returned to and expanded on this point. Dunlap identifies two major traditions in sociology that have contributed to the discipline's tendency to ignore the biophysical environment. The first of these is the 'Durkheimian anti-reductionism taboo', with its emphasis on social rather than psychological facts and a concomitant 'sociological rejection of biological and physical variables as potential explanations of social phenomena' (ibid.: 332). A second tradition, the 'social definition perspective', was inherited from Max Weber and elaborated by Mead, Cooley, Thomas and others. Dunlap cites the urbanist, Harvey Choldin, and Samuel Klausner, a sociologist and clinical psychologist who was one of the first scholars to use the term 'environmental sociology', to the effect that this definitional approach rendered the physical properties of a situation largely irrelevant and unimportant for social life.

One relatively recent attempt to reconcile the physical and the symbolic can be found in an article in *The American Sociologist* by Kroll-Smith et al. (2000). These authors begin by noting the ongoing debate in environmental sociology between 'two *ontologically* [italics in the original] distinct realities' (p. 45). They point out that this dispute is generic to the discipline. Its core is between those 'who believe in the sociological significance of things that exist independent of human perception and those who believe that the act of perception must be the starting point of sociology' (p. 46).

Kroll-Smith et al. suggest that sociologists think about environments in the course of their empirical work in very different ways. Specifically, three different 'stances' can be identified: the legislative, the social subjectivist and the symbolic realist. The first one of these 'places the sociological investigator in the normative role of defining the qualities of environments and their relationships to social and cultural processes' (p. 48). Allan Schnaiberg adopts this stance in his seminal book *The Environment* (1980), as does William Catton in *Overshoot* (1982), his apocalyptic warning about the consequences of exceeding our planet's 'carrying capacity'. The 'social subjectivist stance' requires the researcher to observe and record how groups and communities assign meanings to environmental risks and crises. Classic case studies undertaken from this perspective include Adeline Levine's (1981) book *Love Canal* and Brown and Mikkelsen's (1977) research on Woburn, Massachusetts. Kroll-Smith and his colleagues propose that we adopt a 'symbolic realist' stance that 'encourages a simultaneous consideration of the physical and symbolic properties of environments, attempting to avoid the seductive call to privilege one or the other' (2000: 58). This position is most clearly discernible in some of Freudenburg and Gramling's work from the mid-1990s on offshore drilling around the Gulf Coast and off the coast of California (Freudenburg and Gramling, 1994; Gramling, 1996). Kroll-Smith et al. make a sound case for adopting this strategy; however, in the concluding paragraph of the article they acknowledge that 'the legislative and subjectivist stances will continue to dominate the field' (2000: 59).

In this chapter, my intent differs from that of Kroll-Smith and his co-authors. Rather than manifestly attempt to synthesize the physical and the symbolic, I argue that the interactionist perspective is far more useful in analysing the society–environment relationship than most environmental sociologists have heretofore recognized. Emergence theory, as I develop it here, combines structure and action in a manner that classic symbolic interactionism did not always do. First of all, both individuals and collectivities are treated as capable of acting (see Maines, 1993: xiv). Second, emergence suggests a solution to 'Mead's quest for an answer to the question of how order and change can occur simultaneously' (Maines, 1977: 243).

In identifying this approach as 'theory', I mean to convey the idea of an overarching narrative–interpretive framework that revolves around the concept of emergence. This is consistent with Marshall's (1998) definition of theory as 'an account of the world which goes beyond what we can see or measure' and 'embraces a set of interrelated definitions and relationships that organizes our concepts of and understanding of the empirical world in a systematic way'. In its first three decades, environmental sociology has recognized a handful of major accounts or narratives. One of these pivots on the notion that the unfettered forces of runaway capitalism and consumerism have seriously imperilled nature and the environment. Another divides the world into those who embrace forward-looking 'ecological' values and those who continue to cling to a selfish, traditional human-centred, worldview. A third retells the environmental story primarily in terms of institutional injustice and racism. An 'emergent' narrative, by contrast, visualizes a human odyssey to cope with an increasingly complex, uncertain and dangerous world through improvisation, boundary ordering and social learning. In this, it parallels the processes of collective redefinition and organizational adaptation that characterize mass and group response to social crisis and disaster.

Collective behaviour, social movements and emergence theory
Within the disciplines of sociology and social psychology, the emergence of symbolic interactionism as a distinct perspective can be traced to the work of John Dewey, Charles Horton Cooley, William I. Thomas, Florian Znanieki and George Herbert Mead (Manis and Meltzer, 1972: xi). Most accounts name Mead as its chief architect, although Anselm Strauss (1993) recalls that Dewey's writing was rather more influential. After the 1930s, symbolic interactionism split into two camps: the 'Chicago School' led by Herbert Blumer, and the Iowa School championed by Manford Kuhn. It is the former stream that is more relevant to the discussion of emergence and the environment that I have undertaken in this chapter.

Standard to most interactionist explanations is the idea that the social situations in which we find ourselves are both recurrent and predictable. In a theory text published before his environmental turn, Catton (1966: 235) attributes this to an 'axiom of inertia' which holds that 'a pattern of social behavior will continue to manifest itself at unaltered rates unless some social force modifies the pattern or rate' (McPhail, 1969: 445). How we define a situation and choose to act is determined by the socialization process, which instills a set of shared meanings and normative expectations. In some situations, of course, there may be competing definitions and potential courses of action, but these are drawn from a familiar repertoire.

But what happens when we enter into a situation in which there are no firm normative and definitional guideposts or those that exist are ambiguous or contradictory? Starting in the 1950s and 1960s, a handful of American sociologists, most with backgrounds in Chicago School symbolic interactionism, began systematically to address this question with specific reference to those social phenomena classified as 'collective behaviour'.

At that time, the orthodox explanation was that collective behaviour occurred *outside* the reach of established categories of social structure. For example, in their text *Collective Dynamics* (1961: 13), Kurt and Gladys Lang insist that 'the spontaneous evolution of a collective system of behavior cannot be approached by studying its structure'. In any collective behaviour episode, they observe, the participants are 'governed only by the barest elements of tradition and convention', and lack any common goals, lines of authority, formal division of labour, or established ways of recruiting new members.

Breaking with this view, Lewis Killian and Ralph Turner proposed an 'emergent norm' approach to collective behaviour. Emergent norm theories see collective behaviour 'as regulated by a social norm which arises in a special situation' (Turner, 1964: 384). Turner and Killian (1957) argued that people thrust into settings where traditional normative/ cultural directions or guidelines are confusing or silent collectively try to make sense of things and create meanings to guide their behaviour. Central to this is the role of 'key-noters', charismatic innovators who suggest a course of action that is enthusiastically taken up by the crowd or other collectivity and becomes the nucleus of a reformulated consensus.

Rather than subscribe to the notions of 'contagion' and 'collective excitement' that inform Blumer's model of crowd behaviour, the state of the art in collective behaviour theory at that time, Turner and Killian accounted for the tendency of crowds or publics to obediently fall into line behind the keynoter by turning to the classic studies of small group interaction by Asch (1951), Lewin (1958) and Sherif (1936). These researchers revealed the intensity of pressures towards uniformity that form in ambiguous situations. Just as experimental laboratory subjects find it difficult to resist group pressures towards conformity, even where they clearly disagree with others' assessments, members of a crowd often feel reluctant to oppose a suggested course of action. Dissenters soon realize that 'they must either suppress their views or withdraw from the scene' (Shibutani, 1966: 145).

The revised patterns of coordinated behaviour that so emerge are neither totally new nor spontaneous, but rather comprise a new and different sequencing of the component behaviours, whether they be 'preparing and hurling a Molotov cocktail, taking an item from a store and walking out with it [i.e. looting], or walking out of a classroom' (McPhail, 1969: 447).

Another influential contributor to this early version of emergence theory was Tamotsu Shibutani. As a young Japanese American during the Second World War, Shibutani, together with his family, had spent some time in a relocation centre (i.e. internment camp) in the San Francisco Bay Area. One thing that he noticed was the proliferation of rumours, both during and in the aftermath of the confinement. In his aptly named book *Improvised News: A Sociological Study of Rumor* (1966), Shibutani argued that in situations such as this, when the normal channels of communication are disrupted or suspended, people utilize informal channels in order to make sense of what is going on. One popular alternative channel is the rumour. Rumours are especially prone to emerge 'after environmental changes to describe related events that are not immediately visible, to provide details, to explain anything that is not obvious, and to predict other occurrences' (Shibutani, 1966 p.37). Thus, rather than being uniformly dysfunctional or damaging, rumours are an important part of the process of collective definition (or redefinition) and 'result from a cognitive effort to order an unclear reality in an intelligible way' (Marx and McAdam, 1994: 30).

Initially, emergent norm theory was mainly concerned with social process rather than with structure, and featured the empirical prototype of the acting crowd. In subsequent versions, however, the scope of emergence was expanded to include other forms of collective behaviour, including fads and social movements. Sociological analysts now began to consider the possibility of emergent relationships, structures and patterns of authority. For example, in analysing the dynamics of a student walkout from one of his undergraduate sociology classes, Clark McPhail (1969) concluded that participation in new lines of coordinated behaviour requires the emergence of new social relationships among the acting units.

This expanded repertoire of emergent phenomena during collective behaviour episodes was systematically explored in the late 1960s and early 1970s at Ohio State University's Disaster Research Center (DRC). Enrico (Henry) Quarantelli, one of the Center's co-founders had done his doctoral work in sociology at the University of Chicago in the 1950s. His master's thesis was on panic. One of Quarantelli's articles from the mid-1960s (Quarantelli and Cooper, 1966) was an attempt to apply a key Meadian notion on the relationship between self-conception and social others to an empirical case, the professionalization of dental students. At DRC, he joined forces with co-director Russell Dynes, whose interests lay more in the area of social organization and social change. Together, they proposed a framework for studying human behaviour in the aftermath of community disasters such as floods, tornadoes and hurricanes that combined organizational and collective behaviour perspectives and identified emergent elements (Dynes and Quarantelli, 1968). In a typology that appears in his well-known book *Organized Behavior in Disasters* (1970), Dynes proposed that normatively guided responses during and in the aftermath of emergency situations can include changes in both tasks and structure. Where both of these are present, you have an 'emergent organization'. In other situations, an organization might carry out the same tasks during the disaster period as it normally does but expand its structure (an expanding organization) or keep the same structure but engage in different tasks (an extending organization).

In 1973 Dynes and Quarantelli edited a special issue of the *American Behavioral Scientist* that featured the empirical work of their doctoral students on organizational change and group emergence during the urban civil disturbances (riots) of the 1960s. Among the phenomena studied were rumour control centres, human relations commissions and interfaith emergency centres. Subsequently, several DRC alumni published articles that pushed the limits of emergence theory even further.

Dennis Wenger (1978) identified four emergent forms that characterized community structural adaptations in a disaster setting: emergent values and beliefs, emergent normative structures, emergent organizational structures; and emergent power structures. Wenger's article combines some theoretical perspectives from the collective behaviour literature with insights from the study of community integration and conflict. In brief, he notes that disaster agents such as earthquakes, tornadoes and hurricanes have the capacity to cast the affected community into a 'crisis' condition or state. What permits this is the inability of the traditional, institutional structure to cope with and respond to the demands on the local system. As a result, an emergent disaster structure temporarily develops with new and revised values and beliefs, norms, organizations and organizational linkages, and an altered resource base and loci of power. A disaster, therefore, creates a crisis condition 'for which the traditional, institutionalized structure of the community is collectively defined as an inadequate guide to behavior' (1978: 39).

Wenger raises some provocative questions about the nature of emergence, crisis and the state. He argues that this suspension of routine structural patterns and activities in favour of emergent structures and solutions has some negative consequences in the long term. After the emergency period, the prior power structure is reinstated, often in strengthened form. Sometimes local autonomy has been eroded, as national and regional agencies and social actors gain a toehold. More pluralistic and democratic decision-making channels that thrived before the disaster crisis find it difficult to re-emerge. The situation of New Orleans several years after the crisis created by Hurricane Katrina is one recent and dramatic illustration of this.

This 'emergence' paradigm never found its way from the sociology of disasters into environmental sociology. While Dunlap and Catton (1979: 258–9) include 'natural hazards and disasters' as one of five main areas of research in environmental sociology, they explicitly reject 'disaster research' of the type being conducted at DRC as unhelpful. Citing Quarantelli and Dynes's (1977) review of the disaster field that appeared in the same journal (*Annual Review of Sociology*) two years earlier (in which the authors discuss emergence), Dunlap and Catton (1979: 259) observe that 'the focus of such research has been on the social impacts of disasters per se, and a consideration of physical causes (or physical consequences) has been eschewed'. While acknowledging that traditional disaster research 'may serve to establish useful empirical generalizations about human response to "stressful situations"', they complain (rather unfairly, I think) that 'it has diverted sociological attention from human efforts to avoid natural disasters', something research by environmental sociologists promises to set right. Whereas disaster researchers 'examined responses to location and time-specific events that cause serious disruptions in social order' (Omohundro, 2004: 7), environmental researchers took a longer-term view.

While Turner and Killian's treatment of emergence was originally directed towards the situation of the acting crowd, subsequently they began to consider the emergent dimensions of social movements and social movement organizations. The key element here is a revised sense of justice/injustice, which 'is central to the dual and interrelated processes of reconceiving reality and revising social norms' (Turner, 1981: 9) and continuously 'motivates and crystallizes with the development of the movement' (Turner and Killian, 1987: 243). In one noted laboratory study from this same era, Gamson et al. (1982) explored how encounters with unjust authority produced an emergent sense of opposition. The researchers identified four classes of protest activity: reframing; divesting acts; loyalty building; and internal conflict management.

Another important emergent element in social movements is collective identity formation, related to but conceptually and empirically different from the formulation of personal identities. Turner and Killian's treatment of the process of forging new collective movement identities is remarkably similar to that proposed a decade later by the French and Italian 'new social movement' theorists (Tarrow, 1988), most notably the Italian sociologist/psychotherapist Alberto Melucci (Hannigan, 1990). In conceptual language strongly evocative of symbolic interactionism, Melucci (1989) described a social movement as a composite action system wherein individuals act collectively to construct their action by defining in cognitive terms new possibilities and limits. Specifically addressing the formation of emergent identities, Melucci (ibid.: 25) concluded that constructing collective movements involves three interwoven activities: 'formulating cognitive frameworks, activating interpersonal relationships, and making emotional investments'.

Emergence and the environment
In his perceptive chapter for the first edition of *The International Handbook of Environmental Sociology* (reprinted as Chapter 2 in the current volume), Fred Buttel (1997) wrote that environmental sociology's most influential theories were those that demonstrated how societal institutions 'contained intrinsic dynamics toward environmental degradation' (ibid.: 43–4) and, accordingly, environmental change 'came to be seen as being virtually coterminous with environmental destruction' (ibid.: 44). In proposing an 'emergent' model of environment and society I neither intend to downplay the seriousness of that threat, nor to suggest that massive 'environmental improvement' is inevitably in the pipeline. Rather, I have tried to embrace Buttel's suggestion that 'environmental sociology must diversify its conception of the environment beyond the processes of scarcity and degradation' (ibid.). In applying some useful insights from the collective behaviour and social movements literature to the sociology of the environment, several key concepts can be identified: uncertainty, improvisation and social learning.

Uncertainty
In what has become a classic in the field of economic forecasting, F.H. Knight (1921) distinguished between risk and uncertainty. The former, Knight observed, refers to randomness with knowable probabilities, while the latter describes randomness with unknowable probabilities. 'A pervasive sense of uncertainty or indeterminacy is a crucial component of emergence theory because it strands people in a kind of twilight zone without the benefit of a firm set of cognitive or interpretive guidelines' (Hannigan, 2006: 149).

One especially helpful discussion of the nature of uncertainty can be found in the literature on the sociology of organizations. In the 1970s and 1980s, an 'organization–environment interaction' perspective attracted considerable attention among organizational scholars. Environment here doesn't denote the natural or built environment. Rather, it refers to the set of opportunities and constraints that surround an organization and supply it with or deny it required resources. Organizational environments are classified on the basis of being either placid (certain) or turbulent (uncertain). The former demands an organizational structure that is relatively simple, centralized and hierarchical, while the latter requires one that is complex, decentralized and flexible. This 'contingency' approach specifies that an organization both mirrors its environment and strategically adapts to it (Collins 1988: 48–81). In his final monograph, *Continual Permutations of Action* (1993), the symbolic interactionist Anselm Strauss identifies two 'classes' of environmental uncertainties or contingencies. The most obvious, he says, consists of conditions ordinarily considered as 'external' to the course of action, in particular those that are economic, political, organizational, cultural, physiological, geological or climatic. A 'less obvious source of powerful contingencies', he observes, is 'the course of action itself', with its many unanticipated consequences (Strauss, 1993: 36).

Working within this organization–environment interaction paradigm, Milliken (1987) proposed three types of perceived uncertainty about the external environment of the organization. In the case of 'uncertainty about the state of the environment', there is an incomplete understanding of how components of the environment may be changing, including the nature of their interrelationships. 'Effect uncertainty' refers to an inability to predict what the nature of the impact of a future state of the environment or environmental change will be on the focal organization. 'Response uncertainty' involves a lack of knowledge of possible response options and an inability to predict the likely consequences of a response choice.

Milliken's typology applies equally well to the environment–society nexus. As Wynne (2002: 471–2) observes, 'the relationship between nature and the environment is becoming progressively more complex and indeterminate, especially as science steadily loses its traditional role as a reliable and trustworthy guide'. While it is true that our toolkit of basic and applied science has grown immeasurably, this has been 'accompanied by massive growth in the contingencies resulting from this development' (Richter et al., 2006: 3). Scientific uncertainty has become so pervasive, Freudenburg et al. (2008: 2) note, that 'the outcomes of scientific/technological controversies may depend less on which side has "the best science" than on which side enjoys the benefit of the doubt in the face of scientific ambiguity'.

Improvisation

Another important concept here is improvisation. As Shibutani (1966) pointed out many years ago, social actors who find themselves in a situation where they are cut off from normal, everyday channels of communication spontaneously find alternative ways of seeking out, assembling and passing on information. To underline this point, he labelled rumours as 'improvised news'. Ray Murphy (2004 and Chapter 18 in this volume) makes a similar point in describing the human response to an ice storm that crippled parts of Eastern Canada and the USA in 1998. In a situation where the power grid had been knocked out, residents were forced to improvise in order to secure heat and light. Murphy characterizes the relationship between nature and society as resembling a dance where either partner may choose to take the lead. Extreme events such as the ice storm can be thought of as being 'prompts' from nature that compel us to improvise and choreograph a response. However, this improvisational process is by no means restricted to short-duration, high-impact emergencies such as floods, tornadoes, hurricanes, tsunamis and fires. Longer-term environmental threats – droughts, deforestation and global climate change – also require coping strategies that are both innovative and interactive.

In an Internet essay entitled 'Emergent improvisation', Susan Sgorbati (2005) provides an intriguing meditation on how this process operates. By emergent improvisation Sgorbati means 'the ordering or structuring of forms in the present moment that does not involve an exterior agent or outside director'. Her inspiration here is the emergent property of self-organization in natural living systems, something that she applies to dance and music improvisation. According to Sgorbati, there are three key concepts that link emergent improvisation to the science of complex systems: 'self-organization' (the ordering and structuring of people or entities that do not have a choreographer); 'emergence' (the process by which some new form, ordering, pattern or ability arises to move something towards the creation of another idea; and 'complexity' (a structuring at the edge of chaos that leads to the creation of a new property or outcome) (ibid.).

Social learning

A third concept is 'social learning' – a process of collective reflection that informs and directs collective action. As such, it echoes Habermas's notion of 'communicative action' whereby social conflict is resolved through negotiation and forging a consensus.

The concept initially surfaced in social psychology, where it denoted individual learning based on the imitation of role models (see Bandura, 1977). Subsequently, public policy analysts in the UK borrowed the term, bringing it to bear on a wide range of topics related to macroeconomic policy (Greener, 2001) and economic policy-making (Hall, 1993). The concept also found a nesting place in the literature on 'communities of practice' (Wegner, 1998; Van Wynsberghe, 2001).

Social learning first achieved currency in environmental studies through the efforts of the American political scientist Lester Milbrath. Milbrath (1989) employed the term in an unabashedly normative fashion. Social learning (or 'social re-learning' as he preferred to call it) was the means, he predicted, whereby human beings would inevitably make the transition from a value system based on the dominant social paradigm (DSP) to one rooted in the new ecological paradigm (NEP). Nature itself, especially global climate change, was likely to be 'the most insistent and persistent teacher' (1989: 376). A more contemporary proponent of the benefits of social environmental learning is Robert Brulle, a critical theorist in the mode of Habermas. Brulle argues that social learning about the environment has been stifled as a result of interference from the institutions of capitalism and the bureaucratic state, and by the failure of mainstream American environmentalism to speak with a clear, unified voice and democratically involve the citizenry. Social learning, he notes, depends on the creation both of alternative worldviews and social institutions that can translate and convey these into the public sphere (Brulle, 2000).

In recent years, much of the writing about social environmental learning has been more applied and policy specific. For example, Mostert et al. (2007) carried out ten case studies of participatory river-basin management in Western and Southern Europe that emphasize the importance of collaboration, organization and learning. The researchers identified 71 factors fostering or hindering social learning which they grouped into eight themes: the role of stakeholder involvement; politics and institutions, opportunities for interaction, motivation and skills of leaders and facilitators, openness and transparency; representativeness, framing and reframing; and adequate resources. While they discovered ample evidence of social learning, Mostert and his co-researchers also found many instances in which it was limited or absent. Resistance was especially sharp in complex organizational settings and in controversial cases in which it does not occur naturally. In such cases, they caution, power differentials need to be addressed and strategies other than collaboration may be required, such as legal action or lobbying.

Social learning, the collective acquisition of knowledge in the context of uncertainty, is an emergent process, just as rumours are in collective behaviour episodes. Lipschutz (1996: 64) underscores this, characterizing it as a 'deliberate, incremental process of achieving consensual knowledge as it proceeds in the absence of absolute truth'. Inevitably, it is laden with arguments, uncertainties and contradictions. Wynne (1992: 293) makes much the same point when he observes that social learning 'has no preordained or guaranteed direction; indeed, it needs recognition of the *indeterminacy* of values, identities, and knowledges in order to be possible' (italics in the original).

Emergent environmental forms
In so far as we live in a world enveloped by an escalating environmental uncertainty that unconditionally demands a strong measure of emergence, improvisation and social

learning, several questions immediately arise. What type of emergent phenomena can be identified? Which of these is most likely to be associated with each of the three types of perceived uncertainty about the environment identified by Milliken (1987)? In this section of the chapter, I focus specifically on two of these: emergent structures and associations, and the emergent framing of technological risks.

Emergent structures and associations

While there is no perfect consensus, most accounts of environmentalism begin in the late nineteenth century with the rise of the conservation movement. As Frank (1997) has documented, this initially assumed a 'humanitarian' form but over the course of the twentieth century increasingly took on a 'scientific' form. Consistent with the 'contingency' model of organizations, nature protection responded to macro-level changes in world politics and culture, passing through three main stages of global institutionalization: change in world culture; change in world organization; and change in nation-state politics. Many of these new organizations and structures were formal and 'recipe-like' (Frank, 2002: 49) and resided within the institutional boundaries of science, industry and government, but some displayed a more emergent character, 'germinating and growing outside in civil society' (Hannigan, 2006: 150).

Within the institutional field, one of the more interesting recent developments is the appearance of 'emerging boundary organizations'. These thrive at the threshold between science and public policy, especially where this boundary is blurred. According to Guston (2001), emergent boundary organizations are distinguished by three criteria. First, they stabilize the relations between science and non-science through the creation of patents, model research agreements, computer models and other 'boundary objects and standardized packages'. Second, boundary organizations require input from actors from both edges of the boundary as well as professionals who intervene in a mediating role. Third, boundary organizations are answerable to two relatively different masters: the communities of science and politics.

There is a rapidly expanding corpus of empirical studies of emergent boundary organizations. Agrawala et al. (2001) report on the history of the International Research Institute for Climate Prediction (IRI), a boundary organization created in 1996 to help coordinate, implement and evaluate research on seasonal climate variations and their impacts. The IRI operates in the boundary space between climate modelling and forecasting and global agriculture and politics.

White et al. (2008) examine the problems and prospects associated with the boundary-ordering process among water managers in Phoenix, Arizona. Drawing on in-depth interviews, the researchers identify two perspectives: a traditional rational, linear model with distinctive boundaries between science and policy-making; and a perspective with more fluid boundaries that features the co-production of science and policy. In analysing this latter perspective, White and his colleagues specifically address several of the components of my emergence model of environment and society. One central topic in their interviews with water managers was 'the identification, communication, management and reduction of uncertainty' (2008: 237). Uncertainty here derived from multiple sources: the inaccuracy and incompleteness of records measuring river flows, precipitation levels and drought; the lack of knowledge about the long-term effects of climate change; and a host of doubts about various demographic, economic and political issues.

Nevertheless, managers described uncertainty as inescapable but manageable. Echoing Shackley and Wynne (1996), the authors observe that uncertainty serves as a boundary-ordering device and provides a bridge for communication. Another key concept is social learning, which together with social capital is deemed to be vital to reconciling science and policy priorities. As with Mostert et al.'s (2007) findings on participatory river-basin management (see above), power differentials shape outcomes here, with political considerations associated with local economic growth and development being especially salient.

Outside the institutional sphere, environmentalism has spawned a number of emergent structural and associational forms. While long-established conservationist groups (Sierra Club, Audubon Society) most closely resembled 'extending organizations' (Dynes, 1970), maintaining the same basic structure but embracing new issues and, sometimes, engaging in new tasks, a more recent generation of environmental organizations (Greenpeace, Friends of the Earth) looked quite different, with their activist teams boarding whaling ships or climbing toxic smokestacks, video camera in hand. This was even more evident with grassroots environmentalism. When Lois Gibbs first mobilized her neighbours in the Love Canal Homeowners' Association to seek answers and remedial action concerning the health effects of the chemical wastes buried 30 years before in their backyards, they were innovating by the seat of their pants, both organizationally and strategically. Later on, Gibbs diffused this model to hundreds of similar communities through the Washington-based Citizens' Clearinghouse for Hazardous Wastes. This same emergent organizational dimension characterized the experience of the grassroots groups that spontaneously arose to battle toxic landfills, garbage incinerators and the like in low-income, non-white rural and urban communities in the Southern and Western USA and which collectively became known as the environmental justice movement. Not only did these GEJOs (grassroots environment justice organizations) derive their discursive tone from a different source, the civil rights movements of the 1960s (Kebede, 2005), they were also held together organizationally by a number of 'decentralized, loosely-linked, networks of umbrella groups, newsletters and conferences' (Higgins, 1993: 292) rather than the 'top-down, professionalized configuration typical of mainstream environmentalism' (Hannigan, 2006: 50). Elsewhere in the world, grassroots citizens' movements such as the Chipko Movement (India) and the Greenbelt Movement (Kenya) collectively reinvent new forms of oppositional structure.

Emergent framing of new technological risks
In an uncertain world in which the existing playbook has limited value, the process of assessing and prioritizing risk is necessarily unstable and emergent. This is especially the case when considering the public perception of risk. One arena in which this is especially evident is that of risk perceptions of new technologies such as carbon capture and storage, genetically modified organisms, and food and nanotechnology. In Europe, a critical mass of social scientific studies has been undertaken that focus on public awareness of and engagement with 'emergent' sustainable energy technologies.

Flynn et al. (2006) examine the case of hydrogen energy and the possibility of a hydrogen economy, around which there is 'considerable scientific uncertainty and relatively little public awareness'. The authors observe that hydrogen-based technologies currently exist only in the form of prototypes or at the laboratory stage. Although hydrogen's chemical qualities are well known, its use as an energy carrier is largely untested and undeveloped. While its public health effects appear to be minimal, hydrogen's safety and environmental impacts may be much greater, especially at the production stage.

In cases such as this, the relationship between experts and the public is much like that described by Murphy (2004) as existing between nature and society – a type of interactive 'dance'. Citing Wolfe et al. (2002), Flynn et al. (2006) caution readers that this must necessarily take the form of 'a deliberative process of dialogue between experts and laypeople'. They conclude that the framing of risks associated with uncertain new technologies cannot be divorced from their cultural and ideological context and are 'subject to change as experience of the emergent technology unfolds'.

On an everyday basis, the framing and perception of risk is a product of historical legacy and interpretive context (Heimer, 1998). Drawing on a case study of Flammable (its actual name), an Argentine shantytown, Auyero and Swistun (2008) explain the rather dismaying tendency of residents to remain confused about the sources and effects of health-threatening local pollution as being the product of two processes: the 'relational anchoring' of risk perception and the 'labour of confusion' generated by powerful outside actors. The former refers to the tendency of locals selectively to screen out and downplay negative perceptions of risk when the toxic contamination is slow and gradual and doesn't disrupt people's daily routines. The latter has a decisive effect in creating shared (mis)understandings, in so far as it magnifies the sense of 'toxic uncertainty'. When petrochemical companies deny that a threat exists, state officials prevaricate and avert their gaze and local physicians give conflicting advice, uncertainty and confusion reign.

These findings are relevant to the collective framing and perception of new technological risks. To begin with, these issues are usually technically difficult to understand and may appear remote from everyday routines. Furthermore, the 'labour of confusion' discussed by Auyero and Swiston is well documented in the risk society. Cable et al. (2008) point out that government, corporations and physicians frequently dispute citizens' claims of illnesses caused by exposures to risky and complex production technologies. Data from their study of contested illness claims by nuclear weapons workers at the federal Oak Ridge Nuclear Reservation in Tennessee indicate that authorities took advantage of their privileged access to institutional and organizational resources to gain tactical leverage and manufacture an ambiguous climate for public discourse.

Concluding note

Throughout the years, sociological criticisms of symbolic interactionism have periodically touched on its alleged astructural bias, neglect of politics, and blindness to the constraining characteristics of class hierarchies and power constellations (see Maines 1977: 236–7). Critics might well be expected to make a similar complaint about an emergence approach to environmentalism and the environment.

Throughout this chapter, I have attempted to show that emergent structures and processes most certainly do not materialize in a power vacuum. In considering how technological risks are framed and presented to the public, for example, I introduced Auyero and Swiston's concept of the 'labour of confusion' to describe how powerful institutional actors sometimes deliberately fan the flames of uncertainty and ambiguity. In several of the papers cited above, the authors caution that power differentials cannot be ignored, for example in the potential for success of participatory river-basin management (Mostert et al., 2007) or the successful development of an emerging boundary organization in Phoenix, Arizona to deal with water supply issues (White et al., 2008). Bill Freudenburg and his colleagues recently introduced the concept of SCAMs (scientific certainty argumentation methods) to explain how organized industries and interest groups exploit the ambiguity or incompleteness of scientific evidence and derail attempts at regulation (Freudenburg et al., 2008). Our engagement with nature and the environment, then, may be characterized by emergent elements of improvisation, social learning and collective redefinition, but this is always leavened by structures of power and control.

Note

1. The Disaster Research Center was established at Ohio State University in 1963 and moved to the University of Delaware in 1985.

References

Agrawala, S., K. Broad and D.H. Guston (2001), 'Integrating climate forecasts and societal decision making: challenges to an emergent boundary organization', *Science, Technology, & Human Values*, **26** (4): 454–77.
Asch, S.E. (1951), 'Effects of group pressure upon the modification and distortion of judgement', in H. Guetzkow (ed.), *Groups, Leadership and Men*, Pittsburgh, PA: Carnegie Press, pp. 177–90.
Auyero, Javier and Debora Swistun (2008), 'The social production of toxic uncertainty', *American Sociological Review*, **73**: 357–79.
Bandura, A. (1977), *Social Learning Theory*, Englewood Cliffs, NJ: Prentice-Hall.
Brown, Phil and Edwin Mikkelsen (1977), *No Safe Place: Toxic Waste, Leukemia and Community Action*, Berkeley, CA: University of California Press.
Brulle, Robert J. (2000), *Agency, Democracy and Nature: The US Environmental Movement from a Critical Theory Perspective*, Cambridge, MA: MIT Press.
Buttel, F.H. (1997), 'Social institutions and environmental change', in Michael Redclift and Graham Woodgate (eds), *The International Handbook of Environmental Sociology*, Chetenham, UK and Lyme, USA: Edward Elgar, pp. 40–54.
Buttel, F.H. (2003), 'Environmental sociology and the exploration of environmental reform', *Organization & Environment*, **16** (3): 306–44.
Cable, Sherry, Tamara Mix and Thomas E. Shriver (2008), 'Risk society and contested illness: the case of nuclear weapons workers', *American Sociological Review*, **73**: 380–401.
Catton, W.R. Jr (1966), *From Animistic to Naturalistic Sociology*, New York: McGraw-Hill.
Catton, W.R. Jr (1980), *Overshoot: The Ecological Basis of Revolutionary Change*, Urbana, IL: University of Illinois Press.
Collins, Randall (1988), *Theoretical Sociology*, San Diego, CA: Harcourt Brace Jovanovich.
Dunlap, R.E. (2002), 'Environmental sociology: a personal perspective on its first quarter century', *Organization & Environment*, **15** (1): 10–29.
Dunlap, R.E. and W.R. Catton Jr (1979), 'Environmental sociology', *Annual Review of Sociology*, **5**: 243–73.
Dynes, R.R. (1970), *Organized Behavior in Disasters*, Lexington, MA: D.C. Heath and Co.
Dynes, R.R. and E.L. Quarantelli (1968), 'Group behavior under stress: a required convergence of organizational and collective behavior perspectives', *Sociology and Social Research*, **52**: 416–28.
Flynn, Rob, Paul Bellaby and Mriam Ricci (2006), 'Risk perception of an emergent technology: the case of hydrogen energy', *Forum: Qualitative Social Research*, **7** (1): Article 19, January, http://nbn-resolving.de/urn:nbn:de:0114-fqs0601194, 20 April 2009.
Frank, D.J. (1997), 'Science, nature and the globalization of the environment, 1870–1990', *Social Forces*, **76**: 409–35.
Frank, D.J. (2002), 'The origins question: building global institutions to protect nature', in A.J. Hoffman and M.J. Ventresca (eds), *Organizations, Policy and the Natural Environment*, Stanford, CA: Stanford University Press, pp. 41–56.
Freudenburg, William R. and Robert Gramling (1994), 'Bureaucratic slippage and failures of agency vigilance: the case of the environmental studies program', *Social Problems*, **94** (1): 89–114.
Freudenburg, William R., Robert Gramling and Debra J. Davidson (2008), 'Scientific certainty argumentation methods (SCAMs): science and the politics of doubt', *Sociological Inquiry*, **78** (1): 2–38.

Gamson, W.A., B. Fireman and S. Rytina (1982), *Encounters With Unjust Authority*, Homewood, IL: The Dorsey Press.

Gramling, Robert (1996), *Oil on the Edge*, Albany, NY: SUNY Press.

Greener, I. (2001), 'Social learning and macroeconomic policy in Britain', *Journal of Public Policy*, **21**: 133–52.

Guston, D.H. (2001), 'Boundary organizations in environmental policy and science: an introduction', *Science, Technology, & Human Values*, **26** (4): 399–408.

Hall, P.A. (1993), 'Policy paradigms, social learning and the state: the case of economic policymaking in Britain', *Comparative Politics*, **25**: 275–96.

Hannigan, J. (1990), 'Emergence theory and the new social movements: a constructivist approach', paper presented at the World Congress of Sociology, section on Collective Behavior and Social Movements, Madrid, 12 July.

Hannigan, John (2006), *Environmental Sociology*, 2nd edn, London and New York: Routledge.

Heimer, C. (1998), 'Social structure, psychology and the estimation of risk', *Annual Review of Sociology*, **14**: 491–519.

Higgins, R.R. (1993), 'Race and environmental equity: an overview of the environmental justice issue in the policy process', *Polity*, **26** (2): 281–300.

Kebede, A. (2005), 'Grassroots environmental organizations in the United States: a Gramscian analysis', *Sociological Inquiry*, **75** (1): 81–108.

Knight, F.H. (1921), *Risk, Uncertainty and Profit*, Boston, MA: Houghton Mifflin.

Kroll-Smith, Steve, Valerie Gunter and Shirley Laska (2000), 'Theoretical stances and environmental debates: reconciling the physical and the symbolic', *The American Sociologist*, **31**: 44–61.

Lang, Kurt and Gladys Lang (1961), *Collective Dynamics*, New York: Thomas Y. Crowell Company.

Levine, Adeline G. (1981), *Love Canal: Science, Politics and People*, Lexington, MA: Lexington Books.

Lewin, Kurt (1958), 'Group decision and social change', in E.M. Maccoby, T.M. Newcomb and E.L. Hartley (eds), *Readings in Social Psychology*, 3rd edn, New York: Holt, Rhinehart and Winston, pp. 197–211.

Lipschutz, R.D. (1996), *Global Civil Society and Global Environmental Governance: The Politics of Nature from Planet to Planet*, Albany, NY: SUNY Press.

McPhail, Clark (1969), 'Student walkout: a fortuitous examination of elementary collective behavior', *Social Problems*, **16** (4): 441–55.

Maines, David (1993), 'Foreword', in Anselm L. Strauss, *Continual Permutations of Action*, New York: Aldine De Gruyter, pp. xiii–xv.

Maines, David (1977), 'Social organization and social structure in symbolic interactionist thought', *Annual Review of Sociology*, **3**: 235–59.

Manis, Jerome G. and Bernard N. Meltzer (1972), 'Preface to the first edition', in J.G. Manis and B.N. Meltzer (eds), *Symbolic Interaction: A Reader in Social Psychology*, 2nd edn, Boston, MA: Allyn & Bacon, pp. xi–xiii.

Marshall, Gordon (1998), *Oxford Dictionary of Sociology*, Oxford and New York: Oxford University Press.

Marx, Gary and Doug McAdam (1994), *Collective Behavior and Social Movements: Process and Structure*, Englewood Cliffs, NJ: Prentice-Hall.

Melucci, Alberto (1989), *Nomads of the Present: Social Movements and Individual Needs in Contemporary Society*, Philadelphia, PA: Temple University Press.

Milbrath, L.W. (1989), *Envisioning a Sustainable Society: Learning Our Way Out*, Albany, NY: SUNY Press.

Milliken, Frances J. (1987), 'Three types of perceived uncertainty about the environment: state, effect and response uncertainty', *The Academy of Management Review*, **2** (1): 133–43.

Mostert, Erik, Claudia Pahl-Wostl, Yvonne Rees, Brad Searke, David Tabara and Joanne Tippett (2007), 'Social learning in European river-basin management: barriers and fostering mechanisms from 10 river basins', *Ecology and Society*, **12** (1): http://www.ecologyandsociety.org/vol12/iss1/art19/, 20 April 2009.

Murphy, Raymond (2004), 'Disaster or sustainability: the dance of human agents with nature's actants', *The Canadian Review of Sociology and Anthropology*, **41** (3): 249–66.

Omohundro, Ellen (2004), *Living in a Contaminated World: Community Structures, Environmental Risks and Decision Frameworks*, Aldershot, UK: Ashgate.

Quarantelli, E.L. and Joseph Cooper (1966), 'Self conceptions and others: a further test of Meadian hypotheses', *The Sociological Quarterly*, **7** (3): 269–84.

Quarantelli, E.L. and R.R. Dynes (1977), 'Response to social crisis and disaster', *Annual Review of Sociology*, **3**: 23–49.

Richter, Ingo K. Sabine Berking and Ralf Müller-Schmid (2006), 'Introduction', in Ingo K. Richter, Sabine Berking and Ralf Müller-Schmid, *Risk Society and the Culture of Precaution*, Basingstoke, UK: Palgrave Macmillan, pp. 1–18.

Schnaiberg, Allan (1980), *The Environment: From Surplus to Scarcity*, New York: Oxford University Press.

Sgorbati, Susan (2005), 'Emergent improvisation', essay by Susan Sgorbati, http://www.emergentimprovisation.org/essay.html, 20 April 2009.

Shackley, S. and B. Wynne (1996), 'Representing uncertainty in global climate change science and policy: boundary-ordering devices and authority', *Science, Technology, & Human Values*, **21**, 275–302.

Sherif, M. (1936), *The Psychology of Social Norms*, New York: Harper.

Shibutani, Tamotsu (1966), *Improvised News: A Sociological Study of Rumor*, Indianapolis, IN: Bobbs-Merrill.

Strauss, Anselm (1993), *Continual Permutations of Action*, New York: Aldine De Gruyter.

Tarrow, Sidney (1988), 'National politics and collective action: recent theory and research', *Annual Review of Sociology*, **14**: 421–40.

Tedesco, Teresa (2008), 'Crisis comes without a playbook', *National Post* (Toronto), 18 September, p. A6.

Turner, Ralph H. (1964), 'Collective behavior', in Robert L. Faris (ed.), *Handbook of Modern Sociology*, Chicago, IL: Rand McNally & Company, pp. 382–425.

Turner, Ralph H. (1981), 'Collective behavior and resource mobilization as approaches to social movements: issues and continuities', *Research in Social Movements, Conflict and Change*, **4**: 1–24.

Turner, Ralph H. and Lewis M. Killian (1957; 3rd edn 1987), *Collective Behavior*, Englewood Cliffs, NJ: Prentice-Hall.

Van Wynsberghe, R. (2001), 'Organizing a community response to environmental injustice: Walpole Island's Heritage Centre as a social movement organization', *Research in Social Problems and Public Policy*, **8** ('The Organizational Response to Social Problems'), ed. S.W. Hartwell and R.K. Schutt, pp. 221–43.

Wegner, E. (1998), *Communities of Practice: Learning, Meaning, Identity*, Cambridge, UK: Cambridge University Press.

Wenger, D. (1978), 'Community response to disaster: functional and structural alterations', in E.L. Quarantelli (ed.), *Disasters: Theory and Research*, London: Sage, pp. 17–47.

White, Dave D., Elizabeth A. Corley and Margaret S. White (2008), 'Water managers' perceptions of the science–policy interface in Phoenix, Arizona: implications for an emerging boundary organization', *Society & Natural Resources*, **21** (3): 230–43.

Wolfe, Amy K., David J. Bjornstad, Russell Milton and Nichole D. Kerchner (2002), 'A framework for organizing dialogues over the acceptability of controversial technologies', *Science, Technology, & Human Values*, **27** (1): 134–59.

Wynne, Brian (1992), 'Risk and social learning: reification to engagement', in Sheldon Krimsky and Dominic Golding (eds), *Social Theories of Risk*, Westport, CT: Praeger, pp. 275–97.

12 Peering into the abyss: environment, research and absurdity in the 'age of stupid'
Raymond L. Bryant

Introduction

In a world of runaway climate change, apocalyptic capitalism and endemic political hand-wringing, scholars need new concepts to make sense of the contemporary human predicament. In doing so, they must endeavour to grasp the sheer oddity of that predicament. How even to begin to comprehend, for example, the logical yet illogical thinking behind such things as green munitions (bombs that harm people, not the environment), celebrity conservationism (the rich and famous 'save' nature from a global political economy that they helped to create), the public bailout of banking bosses in the latest global recession (taxpayers reward bankers for catastrophic failure) or food neocolonialism (wealthy oil-rich countries safeguard food supplies by depriving poor farmers of productive land in the South)? Or what of the relationship between the ever-more strident scientific and environmentalist calls for immediate action to avert climate catastrophe on the one hand, and the more or less business-as-usual approach to the issue shown by most politicians and publics alike?

This chapter argues that an approach based on a theory of absurdity might just do the trick here. That theory situates the current human predicament in a wider perspective, seeing it not so much as the absence and/or presence of 'rational' thought *per se*, but rather as the manifestation of a more fundamental (and hence less 'fixable') lack of coherence and reasonableness in human thought and its ability to grasp an elusively alien world. In this view, the human fate is one indelibly shaped by illogical, ludicrous and grotesque behaviour. Absurdity emerges in the dawning consciousness of humanity that successive crises and predicaments can never be resolved via 'knowledge fixes', let alone via baseless mantras of hope.

The following discussion aims to introduce the reader to an approach based on absurdity theory providing at least an initial sense of what this might mean for research in what has been dubbed by filmmaker Franny Armstrong the 'age of stupid'. It first briefly sets out a theory of absurdity drawn from the work of Franz Kafka, Albert Camus and Samuel Beckett. Next, it adapts that theory to better address the 'slow collective suicide' of humanity under fast capitalism, providing a short case study of the role of Christmas in that act of violence. The oddity of contemporary academic life and the need for 'reflexive absurdity' as a basis for research is canvassed. The conclusion summarizes the core argument.

We have never been logical

We have certainly been forewarned. Efforts to dramatize worsening human–environment relations become ever-more intensive as scientists and artists beg, plead, scold, cajole, shame, condemn, harangue and reason with politicians and public alike in an attempt to effect a paradigm shift in social practice. Warnings of climate catastrophe appear on a daily basis even as apocalyptical activism seems to have less and less social traction.

Take the recent case of the well-publicized docudrama *The Age of Stupid*, made on a shoestring budget by Franny Armstrong, best known for working on the classic documentary *McLibel*. The new film is explicitly designed to shock the human species out of its 'suicidal' state of being, notably through a stinging post-apocalypse lament by an elderly survivor (played by Pete Postlethwaite), who wonders why humanity had not acted when it still had the chance to avert climate catastrophe. The film was showcased through a 'people's premiere', with its London showing beamed to 65 cinemas around the world. Armstrong hoped the film would be seen by at least 250 million people in the lead-up to the crucial UN climate meeting in Copenhagen in December 2009 – as part of the campaign to force the world's leaders into adopting a radical new course of urgent action (Vidal, 2009). While there is much that is commendably refreshing about the film and its making, it is most unlikely to achieve its highly ambitious aim: to effect urgent and dramatic change. After all, what grounds are there for success when the film's illustrious predecessor – Davis Guggenheim's award-winning film *An Inconvenient Truth* featuring the former US Vice President Al Gore (and the associated best-selling book, Gore, 2006) – caused barely a ripple in the way in which politics and economics have happened around the world over the past few years? Meanwhile, a parallel gathering of the world's leading climate scientists in March 2009 in Copenhagen (designed to update the science before the December 2009 UN meeting) served only to highlight how climate catastrophe is now all but unavoidable, given the existing build-up in emissions – raising the spectre of a self-fulfilling prophecy (Monbiot, 2009).

A big part of the problem with this sort of campaigning seems to be an underlying expectation of 'rational' behaviour whereby appeals put reason on to a supreme pedestal and hence might be construed by some as 'disingenuous attempts to keep something like God alive in the midst of a secular culture' (Rorty, 1999: xxix). If only people are confronted at every turn with the 'facts' of climate science, if only people can be shaken from their stupor via hard-hitting 'infotainment', if only people can be brought to personal and collective reflection on the links between their behaviour and climate catastrophe, then things will improve as positive change occurs. Yet such great expectations collide with the seemingly perverse illogic of human–environmental interaction that defies easy explanation let alone remedy. The monstrosity of it all is ultimately overwhelming.

This is where a theory of absurdity comes in. In origin, it is a theory of alienation steeped in European philosophy going back to Descartes, if not before, combining three key elements: (1) an inquiry into the meaning of existence; (2) an ontology based on a subject–object dualism; and (3) a rejection of belief in ultimate certainties, notably those based on an affirmation of God. Following a nineteenth century in which philosophical reflection (Nietzsche), economic transformation (Marx) and scientific advance (Darwin) chipped away at faith-based certainties underpinning social life, the stage was set for a twentieth-century florescence of theorizing about the absurd (Sagi, 2002). Two world wars featuring mass murder on an unprecedented scale provided more immediate inspiration; these wars revealed the rotten fruit of modernism – 'rational' principles of management and production led both to the Model-T Ford and the Nazi concentration camps.

Such grotesquery prompted a group of European thinkers, writers and playwrights to investigate and, in some cases, to embrace the absurd. For some, philosophical inquiry dissected the problematic bases of understanding 'being' in a purportedly rational and modern world (Husserl, Heidegger) even while shying away, ultimately, from the 'abyss' of the absurd. In contrast, the writing of Franz Kafka revelled in that abyss, describing an unknowable world in which isolated individuals experience existential anguish, confusion and despair before succumbing to their inevitable and meaningless death (Preece, 2002). For example, in *The Trial*, the main character, Joseph K, is arrested, tried and convicted for a crime of which he has no knowledge, and which the authorities never explain to him. Hope, incomprehension, then consciousness and tragedy all come together in the final terrifying passage of the book:

> With a flicker as of a light going up, the casements of a window were suddenly flew open; a human figure, faint and insubstantial at that distance and that height, leaned abruptly far forward and stretched both arms still farther . . . Was help at hand? Were there arguments in his favor that had been overlooked? Of course there must be. Logic is doubtless unshakable, but it cannot withstand a man who wants to go on living. Where was the Judge whom he had never seen? Where was the High Court, to which he had never penetrated? He raised his hands and spread out all his fingers.
>
> But the hands of one of the partners were already at K's throat, while the other thrust the knife deep into his heart and turned it there twice. With failing eyes K could still see the two of them immediately before him, cheek leaning against cheek, watching the final act. 'Like a dog!' he said; it was as if the shame of it must outlive him. (Kafka, 1969: 286)

The characteristic strangeness and enigmatic qualities of such writing are captured in the expression that became posthumously associated with his name: Kafkaesque (Preece, 2002). To describe some situation as Kafkaesque is to evoke a world that is unknowable despite the best efforts of the individual to do so, a world without reason in which causality can never be known, and a world where uncertainty and futility go hand in hand unto a person's inevitable death.

Yet for Albert Camus, the French novelist and essayist, Kafka's brilliant dissection of the absurdity of life was nonetheless flawed inasmuch as it retained a will to live based on hope – neatly illustrated in the above quote from *The Trial*. Hope was an unwelcome guest in the world of the absurd, as Camus sought to demonstrate in his theory of absurdity set out in a landmark essay, 'The myth of Sisyphus', first published in French in 1942 and in English in 1955 (Camus, 1955). In that essay, Camus paints a bleak picture of a futile human quest for reason in an unintelligible world devoid of eternal truth, with absurdity arising precisely from the incompatibility of the two (Hanna, 1958). It follows from this that there can be no hope of a better future in this world: he is indeed a 'witness of decline' (Braun, 1974). Nor can there be any meaningful ethics. It is an isolated and lonely vision of humanity based on the individual as 'the sole ontological and epistemic foundation of existence' (Sagi, 2002: 1). Making a comparison between the plight of Sisyphus and the common working man of his day, Camus sees the pointless toil of the former – condemned by the gods to roll a rock to the top of a mountain only to see it tumble down the slope again so that Sisyphus must repeat his labour for eternity – as an apt metaphor for the futility of everyday modern life. Interestingly, being conscious of this cruel fate is not a recipe for suicide. Instead, the essential contradiction of life must be lived, without hope, with a recompense of sorts coming in the form of freedom, passion and perhaps even joy. As Sisyphus trudges down the mountain, behind his falling rock, he is supremely conscious of his situation via a lucidity that is simultane-ously 'his torture' as well as 'his victory' – a descent thus performed often 'in sorrow' but also sometimes 'in joy' because whatever the torment, he knows that 'his fate belongs to him'. It is indeed *his* rock (Camus, 1955; Sagi, 2002).

The theory of the absurd received its most famous airing in the context of the Theatre of the Absurd, an avant-garde arts movement that burst on to the international stage in the 1950s led by the likes of Samuel Beckett and Eugene Ionesco (Esslin, 1973). As with Kafka and Camus before them, these dramatists painted a strange world of purposeless existence, grotesque, irrational and even funny behaviour, as well as deep pessimism borne of an inability ultimately ever to understand the human predicament (Demastes, 1998). Plays such as *Rhinoceros* and *The Bald Soprano* by Ionesco, and *Waiting for Godot* and *Endgame* by Beckett baffled and (initially) alienated audiences with their lack of a plot and anything resembling 'substance'.

Having generated much media and scholarly attention in the 1950s and 1960s, the theory of the absurd fell from grace thereafter (Braun, 1974), albeit the 'absurd hero' continued to flourish in some literary sectors (Galloway, 1981; Cornwell, 2006). For some, the rejection of ethics and hope in favour of a tryst with death and despair posed an insurmountable problem to purposive action designed to change the world (Hochberg, 1965; Trundle and Puligandla, 1986). Indeed, the rise of social movements and NGOs in the West from the early 1960s – notably addressing environmental, racial and feminist issues – can be thought of as one sustained institutional rejection of the apparent message of gloom associated with the absurdist school of thought (Wapner, 1996; Bryant, 2009). Seemingly, this struggle would not have been mounted in the absence of hope wed to belief in change for the better: civil rights, gender equality, or environmental improvement. If these activists could speak to Beckett et al., they would probably say in the now legendary phrase of Barack Obama: 'yes, we can!' The rejection of pessimism was unevenly paralleled in the arts, as dramatists such as Tom Stoppard through plays such as *Rosencrantz and Guildenstern are Dead* were seen to articulate a 'post-absurdity' philosophy (Freeman, 1996).

Of late, though, optimism seems to have largely run out. The institutionalization of hope via social movements and NGOs appears to be crumbling, as activist warnings of impending catastrophe go unheeded: 'the continued marginalisation of environmental considerations by policy elites fuels the rumblings of discontent and disappointment within the movement' (Carter, 2007: 169). Which activist today could fail to see the parallels between their endless campaigning for fundamental social change and poor old Sisyphus trudging up and down the mountain for eternity? Who can fail to spot the parallels between the ashen-faced men and women who congregate ineffectually at international summits (notably at Stockholm in 1972, Rio de Janiero in 1992, and Johannesburg in 2002: for contrasting analyses, see Middleton and O'Keefe, 2003; Kjellen, 2008) and Beckett's two characters milling aimlessly around the stage in *Waiting for Godot*? If ever there was a time for the re-emergence of a theory of absurdity in order to 'make sense' of what was happening in the world, then arguably that time is now.

Revisiting Camus: slow collective suicide under fast capitalism
Building on Nietzsche, Camus described a human fate that was indelibly shaped by illogical, ludicrous and grotesque behaviour in the absence of a world shaped by a unified

religious or metaphysical meaning. At the same time, Camus suggests that absurdity arises precisely from the disjuncture between a human being and the outside world, and his/her recognition of an ultimate inability to know that world with any certainty – and hence, not so much because that outside world is itself absurd. Absurdity is thus based in the very subject–object dualism that is said to reside at the heart of the human condition (Camus, 1955; Trundle and Puligandla, 1986).

Yet this theory of absurdity, which is borne of the human-engineered cataclysm of the mid-twentieth century, is in some respects dated (partly acknowledged in late Camus, see Sagi, 2002). It is not so much that the will to engineer things and people (based on a quest to know and control) has gone out of humankind. To the contrary, it has advanced to such an extent that today it is busy re-engineering the very bases of life – from the tiniest molecules to entire life-support systems on Earth (Haraway, 1991). In the process, new uncertainties have joined the old – as a whole host of threats and dangers work their way through the hybrid 'socionatures' and 'actor networks' of the contemporary era (Braun and Castree, 1998; Hinchliffe, 2007). At the same time, there is increased popular awareness of the unseen dangers posed by the 'risk society' in an era of 'reflexive modernity' (Beck, 1992).

From such insights, emerging notably from poststructural thinking since the 1980s, two observations can be made in relation to a theory of absurdity. First, and to modify Camus, absurdity is also embedded today in the 'outside world' in so far as old dualisms crumble or their borders become blurred in both thought and practice (Latour, 1993). However, such a rapprochement leads to more, not less, incomprehensibility, as the grotesque and illogical become pervasive. In a sense, and as a result of the cumulative effects of human actions, the whole world is 'on trial' alongside Joseph K. Absurdity thus needs to be recast as being simultaneously a matter about the limits of human knowledge in a world shorn of metaphysical truth and the outcome of human actions that transform the very basis of life on this planet but in unpredictable ways: 'attempts to order will provide conditions for disorder' (Hinchliffe, 2007: 122).

Second, the question of suicide explored by Camus needs to be reconsidered in light of the previous point about the 'escape' of absurdity from the confines of Cartesian dualism ('I' versus 'the world') and outwards to 'the world'. In 'The myth of Sisyphus', Camus rejects the option of suicide in the face of a hopeless and frustratingly unknowable world (at least concerning the 'big' questions that shape human existence and life in general), insisting that the individual, like Sisyphus, must continue to live his or her life within the narrow confines of what little can be known and accept the inevitability of limits on the human desire to know (Camus, 1955). Reconcile yourself to life as it is and you may find peace, even happiness. And yet the breakdown of the dualism noted above as a result of human action and thought – with ever-more dire consequences for life on Earth – alerts us to an unintended set of consequences that suggests, in turn, that humanity as a collective enterprise is ignoring the admonition of Camus that we should all 'live life'. Indeed, and based on mounting evidence all around us (climate change being the most vivid example nowadays), it becomes possible to describe the present human trajectory as one characterized by 'slow collective suicide'. Further, this trajectory is perfectly visible to most people today thanks to saturated media coverage of the world's growing 'environmental crisis' – everyday life now takes place against the backdrop of Arctic/Antarctic ice sheets crashing into the ocean as glacier retreat becomes a proxy 'measure' for impending doom (Orlove et al., 2008). This condition of slow collective suicide, which is the flipside of 'fast capitalism' (Agger, 2004) and 'turbo consumerism' (Honore, 2004), sets up a paradox: people individually continue to live their lives in a 'normal' manner despite the anxiety and uncertainty that surrounds and threatens to engulf them (thereby accepting Camus' enjoinder to the individual to reject suicide), but in doing so, and via the 'unseen hand of the market', they embark inexorably and perhaps inevitably on the path to collective suicide (an unforeseen situation that ultimately seems to undermine the very foundations of Camus's position on suicide; see also Lovelock, 2009).

Let me now provide a short example to illustrate these arguments and thereby put some empirical flesh on the bones. At the same time, this is an opportunity to demonstrate how analysis based on a theory of absurdity can proceed, and with what effects. That example is the problem of Christmas and its curious role as the world's greatest annual environmental disaster.

Kamikaze Christmas

At the heart of fast capitalism is a phenomenon called 'Christmas' – an annual event that profoundly shapes the rhythm of both production and consumption around the world. Since the mid-nineteenth century, the staging of Christmas has become an ever-more elaborate affair, thereby creating a powerful combination of public faith-based assertiveness and carefully honed commercial enterprise (Miller, 1993; Horsley and Tracy, 2001). On the one hand, the elevation of Christmas to a status as *the* major Western religious event can be seen as one way in which the church sought to see off the multifaceted threat to its authority arising from philosophy (Nietzsche), economic transformation (Marx) and natural science (Darwin) noted above, even as it went on the offensive harvesting new souls for God's purpose under the rubric of an advancing colonialism. Emerging doubts about the traditional place of humanity in the world and the ultimate meaning of life were to be quashed via a strategy in which Christianity would hitch its fate to the growing power of economic capitalism, albeit with contradictory results (Comaroff and Comaroff, 1986). The consumption of religion and the consumption of objects in everyday life would thus be entwined (Miller, 1993).

On the other hand, embedding Christmas at the heart of capitalism was a key profit-boosting means by which capitalists sought to stabilize conditions of production in what seemed to be an inherently unstable economic system (what Joseph Schumpeter, [1942] 1975 later described as 'creative destruction'). While not eliminating in the least the booms and busts that have continued to plague capitalism to the present day, the strategy did serve to make that economic system increasingly dependent on the Christmas season. Good economic times became closely associated (albeit not synonymous) with a successful Christmas season comprising of three main parts: the long build-up stretching through the autumn and early winter; the immediate Christmas holiday; and the post-Christmas sales (Basker, 2005). The consumption of objects in everyday life thus came to revolve around rituals of purchase, gift-giving and consumption, notably concentrated in a late December hyper-festival that was cloaked in religious garb (Connelly, 1999; Horsley and Tracy, 2001; Whiteley, 2008).

Here, then, we have a hitherto rather modest seasonal festival turned into a critical worldwide event at the interface of capitalism and Christianity. In its own way, Christmas, too, reflects an institutionalization of hope – albeit a multifaceted hope reflecting a wide array of individual circumstances (including love, desire, guilt, self-esteem), economic imperatives (notably to make a profit or to keep one's job), and faith- (as well as non-faith-) based aspirations. Its success can thus be 'measured' variously in terms of the 'quiet' humming of machines producing millions of items for Christmas purchase, the not-so-quiet unwrapping of gifts and associated 'Christmas cheer', and extra-ordinary levels of attendance at Christmas mass.

And yet, if hope springs eternal from the midst of Christmas, it has but a hollow and ephemeral ring to it. Manufactured good cheer is, in the end, manufactured after all. Disappointment soon follows: gifts are put to one aside or thrown away, fast follows feast in the business world, and many churches resume their (usually lower) normal attendance levels. Indeed, and following Camus, the entire Christmas experience does not seem to fill the terrifying void of a world in which old certainties are gone. Just as consumption is a weak political tool in battles against global injustice (Bryant and Goodman, 2004), so too it is not up to the even larger task of mending the rupture in traditional metaphysical certainties that notably followed the publication in 1883 of Nietzsche's radical thesis that 'God is dead'. To the contrary, the orgy of consumption that is Christmas further undermines the quest for certainty by the 'truth-seeking' individual by socially validating and prioritizing mindless and trivial action instead of deeper and more sustained reflective thought (Pollay, 1987). Sermons at Christmas Mass scarcely succeed in this latter endeavour either and, in any event, are a mere blip on the scale of time compared with that devoted to preparing for, enacting and clearing up after consumption (Horsley and Tracy, 2001).

Worse still, Christmas is at the centre of human efforts that have radically and irrevocably transformed the 'outside world'. When viewed from the vast expanse of time, the event we call Christmas is best understood as the world's greatest annual environmental disaster (Bryant, 2008). If fast capitalism has been the key driving force behind the increasingly severe environmental catastrophes that scientists and activists alike warn that we face on Earth, then Christmas is the focal point – a benchmark event that is ultimately productive of the grotesque, illogical and monstrous ingredients that make up our contemporary absurd world. On the one hand, it is the lodestar of conspicuous consumption – an annual invitation to excess (Pollay, 1987; Horsley and Tracy, 2001) and distinction making (Bourdieu, 1984). On the other hand, it is a powerful stimulus package for year-round environmentally damaging inconspicuous consumption in the form of enhanced everyday use of energy, water and other ecological services (Shove and Warde, 2002), as well as heightened waste disposal (Redclift, 1996; Dauvergne, 2008). At the same time, Christmas is also at the heart of the paradox mentioned earlier: it is simultaneously a global celebration of the individual will to live and a global enactment of the slow collective suicide that is killing the human species along with many other species on Earth.

Scholarship and reflexive absurdity

The scholar faces a difficult task in a world thus understood. As with Camus's Sisyphus, he or she must navigate life without religious or metaphysical certainty, without hope, and (perhaps most cruelly) with clear but unknown limits to his or her ability to know. Yet the work of the scholar is no less important for its loss of the romanticisms of the academy – such as the currently hegemonic idea that all research must be readily identifiable as 'useful', and typically only then in an applied policy sense.

Instead, the scholar needs to become engaged in what might be termed 'reflexive absurdity' – a situation whereby a researcher is conscious of the absurdity of the human predicament, seeks to carefully analyse the conditions of such absurdity, and reflects on his or her part in living under while contributing to conditions of absurdity.

To embark on this task is to begin by recognizing how absurd the academic life is – typically unreflective, ceaseless, and ultimately meaningless. This condition is particularly acute at the present juncture given the pre-eminence of an audit culture comprising ever-higher and arbitrary numerical targets (students taught, publications achieved, income generated, forms completed), individualized performance evaluations, information processing rather than intellectual reflection, and the measurement of everything coupled with the understanding of virtually nothing except perhaps the process of measurement itself (Castree, 2006; Shore, 2008). Yet the absurd academic life is not completely reducible to an outcome of the neoliberalization of the university sector. There is too, for instance, the deployment of modern technology – above all the personal computer – in academic life that has enabled a rapid leap in the 'productivity' of the individual scholar via cut-and-paste writing and salami-slice publishing (Luey 2002). The result is the rapid bloating of CV publication lists, thereby providing even more fertile ground for the competitive quest for distinction by *Homo academicus* (Bourdieu, 1990).

There is also a need to recognize how academic life makes its own important contribution to the transformation of the 'outside world' and the associated slow collective suicide discussed above. For one thing, the research endeavour often directly contributes to environmental degradation. This impact is not negligible – involving, as it usually does, much travel to and from fieldwork sites scattered around the world, much production of paper, more travel to and from conferences and workshops, and so on (Upham and Jakubowicz, 2008). Moves to introduce carbon-offsetting schemes (such as through the American College and University Presidents Climate Commitment initiative) are hardly a comprehensive solution either (Buytaert, 2007) and are, at best, a 'last resort' (Milmo, 2008). For another thing, success in academia (like in a number of other professions) is seemingly positively correlated with the size of one's CO_2 footprint. Famous professors thus criss-cross the world at 39 000 feet like leading celebrities, entrepreneurs and politicians – ever tempted by that new distinguished international speaking invitation or research project – with nary even a thought usually given to alternatives such as video conferencing (Hobson, 2007). Systemic pressures thus tend to reward relative environmental failure (the 'migratory' academic) even as they usually punish relative environmental 'sustainability' (the 'sedentary' academic). This situation is fundamentally at odds with the root-and-branch rethink of both professional and personal lives that many are now saying is essential (Hobson, 2008).

It is not that the academic does not reflect, from time to time, on some or even many of these processes, or how they might connect him or her to the very processes sometimes described in their work. Yet, *pace* Camus's Sisyphus, academic moments of realization are as profound as they are usually fleeting, before 'normal' mechanical life resumes with its targets, its logistics and its distinctions.

Conclusion
This chapter has explored an approach to understanding the current human predicament based on a theory of absurdity. It was suggested that such an approach affords impor-

tant insights into that predicament and the perverse illogic of human–environmental interaction that underpins it. Shorn of the cruel false promise of hope, and misguided discourses of 'positive' thinking, absurdity theory holds out instead the stark promise of discomfiting but nonetheless lucid consciousness about the absurd life that human beings live. Like Kafka's Joseph K, being is to be endured in a world without reason until the ultimate and terrifying end.

Yet in such endurance resides the kernel of something else, something precious. As Camus suggests, it is not the residual glimmer of hope that Joseph K mistakenly believed in. Instead, it is a freedom borne of a mind no longer fettered by hopes for a better future, including his or her place in eternity. Indeed, being conscious of the cruel fate awaiting every individual is not a recipe for personal suicide – which, after all, is an act partly reflective of crushed hope. Instead, the essential contradiction of life must be lived, without the comforting myth of hope, with a possible recompense of sorts coming in the form of freedom, passion and perhaps even joy. As Sagi (2002: 2) notes, 'paradoxically, the person who embraces the absurd is the one who attains self-acceptance . . . the individual who lives the absurd realizes human existence to the full, and is therefore happy'.

That freedom is precious precisely because it reflects a hard-won and painful realization of the limits of knowledge and hence of the limits of what humanity can do in an absurd world. Yet there is an ultimate paradox here: armed with a freedom from hope and the associated knowledge fix, the individual can go forth and seek to live his or her life in a manner that can begin to unravel some (but not all) of the damage that the human species has done to the planet as part of a life that firmly rejects suicide, including the path of slow collective suicide that our species has embarked on. It will probably not be enough, but it is better than nothing.

References

Agger, B. (2004), *Speeding Up Fast Capitalism*, Boulder, CO: Paradigm Publishers.

Basker, E. (2005), 'Twas four weeks before Christmas: retail sales and the length of the Christmas shopping season', *Economics Letters*, **89** (3): 317–22.

Beck, U. (1992), *Risk Society: Towards a New Modernity*, trans. M. Ritter, London: Sage.

Bourdieu, P. (1984), *Distinction: A Social Critique of the Judgement of Taste*, trans. R. Nice, Cambridge, MA: Harvard University Press.

Bourdieu, P. (1990), *Homo Academicus*, Oxford: Polity Press.

Braun, B. and N. Castree (eds) (1998), *Remaking Reality: Nature at the Millennium*, London: Routledge.

Braun, L. (1974), *Witness of Decline: Albert Camus, Moralist of the Absurd*, Rutherford, NJ: Fairleigh Dickinson University Press.

Bryant, R.L. (2008), 'Christmas as the world's greatest annual environmental disaster: geographies of seasonal consumption', paper presented at the Arts and Humanities Research Council workshop 'Not Just for Christmas', Glasgow School of Art, 17 July.

Bryant, R.L. (2009), 'Born to be wild? Nongovernmental organisations, politics and the environment', *Geography Compass*, **4** (3): 1540–58.

Bryant, R.L. and M. Goodman (2004), 'Consuming narratives: the political ecology of "alternative" consumption', *Transactions of the Institute of British Geographers*, **29** (3): 344–66.

Buytaert, W. (2007), 'Carbon offset schemes are of questionable value', http://environmentalresearchweb.org/cws/article/opinion/30246, accessed 10 April 2009.

Camus, A. (1955), *The Myth of Sisyphus, and Other Essays*, New York: Knopf.

Carter, N. (2007), *The Politics of the Environment: Ideas, Activism, Policy*, 2nd edn, Cambridge: Cambridge University Press.

Comaroff, J. and J. Comaroff (1986), 'Christianity and colonialism in South Africa', *American Ethnologist*, **13** (1): 1–22.

Connelly, M. (1999), *Christmas: A Social History*, London: I.B. Tauris.

Castree, N. (2006), 'Research assessment and the production of geographical knowledge', *Progress in Human Geography*, 30 (6), 747-82.

Cornwell, N. (2006), *The Absurd in Literature*, Manchester: Manchester University Press.

Dauvergne, P. (2008), *The Shadows of Consumption: Consequences for the Global Environment*, Cambridge, MA: MIT Press.

Demastes, W. (1998), *Theatre of Chaos: Beyond Absurdism, into Orderly Disorder*, Cambridge: Cambridge University Press.

Esslin, M. (1973), *The Theatre of the Absurd*, Woodstock, NY: Overlook Press.

Freeman, J. (1996), 'Holding up the mirror to mind's nature: reading *Rosencrantz* "beyond absurdity"', *The Modern Language Review*, **91** (1): 20–39.

Galloway, D. (1981), *The Absurd Hero in American Fiction: Updike, Styron, Bellow, Salinger*, Austin, TX: University of Texas Press.

Gore, A. (2006), *An Inconvenient Truth: The Planetary Emergence of Global Warming and What We Can Do About It*, London: Bloomsbury.

Hanna, T. (1958), *The Thought and Art of Albert Camus*, Chicago, IL: H. Regnery.

Haraway, D. (1991), *Simians, Cyborgs, and Women: The Reinvention of Nature*, London: Free Association Books.

Hinchliffe, S. (2007), *Geographies of Nature: Societies, Environments, Ecologies*, London: Sage.

Hobson, K. (2007), 'So we are all environmentalists now?', *Geoforum*, **38** (6): 546–8.

Hobson, K. (2008), 'Reasons to be cheerful: thinking (sustainably) in a climate changing world', *Geography Compass*, **2** (1): 199–214.

Hochberg, H. (1965), 'Albert Camus and the ethic of absurdity', *Ethics*, **75** (2): 87–102.

Honore, C. (2004), *In Praise of Slow*, London: Orion.

Horsley, R. and J. Tracy (eds) (2001), *Christmas Unwrapped: Consumerism, Christ, and Culture*, Harrisburg, PA: Trinity Press International.

Kafka, F. (1969), *The Trial*, trans. by E.M. Butler, first published in 1937, New York: Vintage Books.

Kjellen, B. (2008), *A New Diplomacy for Sustainable Development: The Challenge of Global Change*, London: Routledge.

Latour, B. (1993), *We Have Never Been Modern*, Hemel Hempstead, UK: Harvester Wheatsheaf.

Lovelock, J. (2009), *The Vanishing Face of Gaia: A Final Warning*, London: Allen Lane.

Luey, B. (2002), *Handbook for Academic Authors*, 4th edn, Cambridge: Cambridge University Press.

Middleton, N. and P. O'Keefe (2003), *Rio plus 10: Politics, Poverty and the Environment*, London: Pluto Press.

Miller, D. (ed) (1993), *Unwrapping Christmas*, Oxford: Oxford University Press.

Milmo, C. (2008), 'Schemes to offset carbon "overpriced and unfair"', *The Independent*, 25 August.

Monbiot, G. (2009), 'If we behave as if it's too late, then our prophecy is bound to come true', *The Guardian*, 17 March.

Orlove, B., E. Wiegandt and B.H. Luckman (eds) (2008), *Darkening Peaks: Glacier Retreat, Science, and Society*, Berkeley, CA: University of California Press.

Pollay, R.W. (1987), 'It's the thought that counts: a case study in Xmas excesses', *Advances in Consumer Research*, **14** (1), 140–43.

Preece, J. (ed) (2002), *The Cambridge Companion to Kafka*, Cambridge: Cambridge University Press.

Redclift, M. (1996), *Wasted: Counting the Costs of Global Consumption*, London: Earthscan.

Rorty, R. (1999), *Philosophy and Social Hope*, London: Penguin.

Sagi, A. (2002), *Albert Camus and the Philosophy of the Absurd*, trans. by B. Stein, Amsterdam: Rodopi.

Schumpeter, J. ([1942] 1975), *Capitalism, Socialism and Democracy*, New York: Harper.

Shore, C. (2008), 'Audit culture and illiberal governance: universities and the politics of accountability', *Anthropological Theory*, **8** (3): 278–98.

Shove, E. and A. Warde (2002), 'Inconspicuous consumption: the sociology of consumption, lifestyles and the environment', in R.E. Dunlap, F.H. Buttel, P. Dickens and A. Gijswijt (eds), *Sociological Theory and the Environment: Classical Foundations, Contemporary Insights*, Lanham, MD: Rowman & Littlefield, pp. 230–51.

Trundle, R. and R. Puligandla (1986), *Beyond Absurdity: The Philosophy of Albert Camus*, Lanham, MD: University Press of America.

Upham, P. and S. Jakubowicz (2008), 'Aircraft dominance in the transport-related carbon emissions of business school students', *Journal of Transport Geography*, **16** (1): 73–6.

Vidal, J. (2009), 'The people's premiere', *The Guardian*, 28 February.

Wapner, P. (1996), *Environmental Activism and World Civic Politics*, Albany, NY: SUNY Press.

Whiteley, S. (ed) (2008), *Christmas, Ideology and Popular Culture*, Edinburgh: Edinburgh University Press.

PART II

SUBSTANTIVE ISSUES FOR ENVIRONMENTAL SOCIOLOGY

Editorial commentary
Graham Woodgate

Many of the concepts and theories discussed in the contributions to Part I of this book reappear in the eight chapters that comprise Part II, framing discussions of the substantive issues with which this part of the book is concerned. Clearly, it would not have been possible to invite contributions dealing with the full range of issues that attracts the attention of environmental sociologists at the beginning of the twenty-first century, but we hope that what follows gives a flavour of some of the most significant.

We begin with Ted Benton's 'Animals and us' (Chapter 13), which deals with the philosophical issue of the relationship between human beings and animals. He begins by noting the longstanding dominance in Western societies of a dualistic view, which associates human beings with characteristics such as 'rationality, language, moral autonomy, creativity, love of beauty' etc., in contrast to all other animals, which are considered to lack them and also to embody unwanted human characteristics such as brutality. There are, however, as Benton points out, alternative views based on the experiences of those who, in the course of their lives, have formed close relationships with animals and taken on a duty of care for their well-being. Such experiences and sentiments have been one of the motivational sources for militant campaigning activity against various sorts of perceived abuse of animals and, more recently, armed with more sophisticated philosophical arguments, powerful critiques of our 'whole form of social existence as grounded in violent abuse of other species'.

From this point of departure, Benton reviews the bases in utilitarian and rights theory of the case for an enhanced moral status for animals. In both traditions the argument on behalf of animals works by extending an established moral theory across the species boundary so that any shortcomings in their application to human beings automatically tell against their extension to encompass other animals. Thus the powerful arguments against utilitarianism, not least its focus on ends rather than means (its consequentialism), lead Benton to look more closely at the case for animal rights and to argue that a universalistic concept of 'basic' rights can serve as the starting point for 'a much more "relationship-sensitive" and context-specific critical examination of "actually existing" human practices', in terms of our social relationships and in relation to other animals.

The radical critique of human rights discourse posits that rights are required only because of the competitive antagonism that is 'built into the very fabric of economic, cultural and political existence' under the current phase of globalizing free market capitalism. Drawing on this critique, 'What if', asks Benton, 'instead of promoting individualized "entrepreneurialism" and competitive achievement, the prevailing culture valued collaboration, mutual recognition, solidarity and compassion?' His response, while accepting that such a position is easily criticized as 'pie-in-the-sky' utopianism, is that in acknowledging the incontrovertible evidence that our current form of socioeconomic organization is 'already degrading crucial global life-support systems in ways that may be irreversible', we should be prompted to develop moral codes that aim to promote social justice and maintain ecological integrity. In conclusion, while accepting that 'a more socially and ecologically nuanced concept of rights' may be important, in the context of humanity's ubiquitous impact on global ecosystems and threats to biodiversity there is an urgent need for a range of other moral concepts and rules to regulate our relations with the non-human world – concepts and rules perhaps for the conduct of Manuel-Navarrete and Buzinde's reflexive socio-ecological agents (see Chapter 9 in Part I).

In the context of free market capitalism, however, many of humanity's interactions with nature and attempts to ameliorate environmental impact are expressed through markets. Ecological modernization, environmental information dissemination and the development of markets for 'sustainable' products form the basis of currently dominant recipes for environmental reform. The primary source of information for sustainable development is modern science and, in Chapter 14, Steven Yearley considers the relationship between science and the environment at the beginning of the twenty-first century.

In Yearley's contribution to the first edition of this handbook, he illuminated the contemporary situation, in which science was both damned for its role in the production of environmental problems and acclaimed for its contribution to their identification and solution. Some 12 years later, he claims, 'virtually everyone has come round to the idea that science is the authoritative way to speak about the environment'. At the same time, however, 'despite science's foundation in factual evidence and scientists' pursuit of objectivity', Yearley points out that influential public voices are still able to 'sustain disagreements about what scientists know and what the scientific evidence about the natural environment means'. In Chapter 14 of this second edition Yearley investigates these two issues in relation to climate change and genetically modified organisms (GMOs).

With regard to the first phenomenon, he notes that the science of global climate change has manifested several unprecedented and fascinating features. First, a novel form of organization has been created in order to foster the production of more authoritative information based on the synthesis of different disciplinary perspectives – the Intergovernmental Panel on Climate Change (IPCC). Critics of the IPCC have focused not only on their disagreements with the assertions of the Panel's researchers, but also on supposed weaknesses in the IPCC system itself. In contrast to their past challenges to scientific 'evidence', however, NGOs and environmental campaigners have found themselves 'defending the objectivity of scientists' published findings, of speaking up for peer review, and of countering the IPCC's critics'.

The case of GMOs displays very different characteristics and dynamics. Environmental groups disagree with the majority of established scientists and, especially in Europe, there has been widespread sabotage of GM field trials. The chief question underlying these disputes over GMOs has been: how do we guarantee the safety of novel and unprecedented materials? Despite strong opposition in Europe, the push for GM agriculture has not abated. With growing interest in biofuels and renewed concern over food security in the wake of recent food price crises, Yearley predicts that 'the pressure to introduce GM and related innovations in agriculture will intensify'. Whether supporting or contesting the pronouncements of science, the close ties between the strategies of environmental groups and scientific knowledge have clear implications for the way that we conceive of such organizations, underlining the vital contribution to environmental sociology provided by the sociology of scientific knowledge.

In Chapter 15, Maria Kousis documents and analyses the diverse strategies and tactics employed by environmental movements in relation to GM agriculture and nanotechnology in more detail, testing recent claims concerning significant differences in their character and practices in the twenty-first century. In relation to the organizational geography of activists, NGOs and targets, there is a perceived shift from local, national and regional spheres to the international and global, while in relation to claims-making activities, the incorporation of new information and communications technologies has been highlighted. These shifts are confirmed by Kousis's analysis, as are likely future social movement trajectories including a slower and less extensive shift towards more international and global configurations and, in large-scale social movements such as Greenpeace and Friends of the Earth, the increasing dominance of professional social movement entrepreneurs, NGOs and links with authorities. The expanding scale, professionalization and articulation with government agencies come at a price, however: elements of local and regional claims making that cannot be co-opted into international activism are left behind. Finally, and in line with Yearley's observations, Kousis's analysis suggests that the relationship between environmental activists and scientists may shift attention to alternative future strategies of technological innovation.

Maintaining the focus on the dynamics of environmental reform, Chapter 16 considers developments surrounding the issue of sustainable consumption (SC) and the role of 'information' and policy in promoting behavioural change among consumers. Emma Hinton and Michael Goodman begin their essay with a brief review of international and UK policy surrounding sustainable consumption, preparing the ground for their analysis of the important but contentious role of 'information' and how it imposes 'responsibilization' for sustainability onto the figure of the consumer in the spaces of the 'everyday'. From here, they explore the links between SC and ecological modernization and the associated product-focused pathways to SC that constitute much of the current policy focus. Besides official, policy-based attempts at promoting 'ecological modernization' through sustainable consumption, Hinton and Goodman also discuss several important 'alternatives' to these more mainstream approaches portrayed by discourses surrounding voluntary simplicity, (re)localized economic systems and the emerging concept of 'hedonic' consumption.

Chapter 16 concludes with a short consideration of SC in the context of the financial crisis and economic recession that have marked the final years of the first decade of the twenty-first century, a context in which 'simplicity' might become less voluntary and more a product of necessity. Hinton and Goodman conclude that the 'new economic climate, coupled with increasing popular concern over climate change and peak oil, in combination with renewed policy commitments in support of sustainable consumption, could open up new opportunities for the discourses around SC to be refocused on to the continuing multi-scale inequalities of lifestyles and livelihoods across the globe'.

The globalization of free market capitalism and its impacts on social justice and ecological integrity are taken up in Wolfgang Sachs's contribution in Chapter 17. Sachs begins by pointing out that 250 years ago there was very little difference between China and Britain in terms of their level of economic development and that 'Industrial society would not exist in today's shape, had not resources been mobilized from both the expanse of geographical space and the depth of geological time'. The Euro-Atlantic development model that began with the Industrial Revolution in Britain has produced both social and biophysical injustices. Notwithstanding the adoption and proclamation of the Universal Declaration of Human Rights in 1948, the idea that 'all human beings are born free and equal in dignity and rights' remains an ideal rather than a reality. At the same time, and with a clear link to social injustice, capitalist development has resulted in a substantial and growing ecological debt (e.g. Barcena Hinojal and Lago Aurrekoetxea, Chapter 10 in this volume).

Where Benton promotes the development of a more socially and ecologically nuanced concept of rights and the development of additional moral concepts and rules for governing human behaviour in a future 'more-sustainable' society, Sachs demands a move to Kantian ethics where the focus is on our duties rather than our rights, with a basic duty not to allow our own development to infringe on the development possibilities of others. From the Kantian perspective, resource justice demands sustainable consumption, the eradication of ecological debt and a fair sharing of environmental space. To achieve this requires that North and South follow different trajectories: citizens of the global North must reduce their consumption considerably to provide the environmental space for those of the global South to attain levels consistent with at least a minimal, 'dignity line' of consumption.

The globalization of the Euro-Atlantic development model has, by common consensus, led to a rapid accumulation of greenhouse gases in the upper atmosphere and the emergence of global warming. Global warming is now strongly associated with increasing frequency and intensity of extreme hydrometerological events such as tropical storms, floods, droughts, heat waves and freezing. But what exactly is the relationship between such hazards and the human disasters in which they all too often result? This is the starting question for Raymond Murphy's contribution to this handbook (Chapter 18).

Disaster research uses retrospective analysis of the actualization of risk in order to learn lessons that may help to prevent, mitigate and/or adapt to hazards in the future. Murphy's chapter expands on disaster research methodology with the goal of elaborating a categorization of risks associated with environmental hazards. Environmental hazards can be perceived or unperceived. If unperceived, this can either be because they are unforeseeable or because they are unacknowledged due to social, cultural or economic practices. When perceptions, acknowledgement and the referent correspond, the risk is detected and addressed. 'Correspondence also occurs when there is no disturbance of nature imminent and no perception of risk, hence perceived, acknowledged safety prevails.' Finally, when perceptions of a hazard are acknowledged, but no disturbance of nature is immanent, a situation of 'unperceived safety' exists.

Murphy's essay uses historical case studies to illustrate unperceived risk, unacknowledged risk, perceived acknowledged risk, unperceived safety (false risk discourse) and their consequences for human populations, before addressing the question of whether risk is actually reduced by modern expert systems. His findings suggest that such systems 'cut both ways: they have improved robustness and resilience when confronted with disturbances of nature yet have promoted risk-taking and in some cases increased vulnerability when a disturbance exceeded predictions'. What his analysis of the consequences of the various types of risk discourse demonstrates is that 'the analysis of risk must not be reduced to the study of perceptions torn out of their dynamic biophysical context'. Extrapolating from the specified environmental hazards that he uses to exemplify the different types of risk discourse, Murphy's final move is to consider the implications of his findings for the ways in which we might deal with the, as yet incompletely specified, risks of global warming.

Of course mitigation and adaptation to climate change are likely to require unprecedented levels of cooperation, which, despite the many years of international negotiations, is still notable largely by its absence. In Chapter 19, Bradley Parks and Timmons Roberts seek to elucidate the reasons why this might be so. In short, and in concert with the views expressed by other contributors to this volume (e.g. Sachs, Chapter 17 and Barcena Hinojal and Lago Aurrekoetxea, Chapter 10), their answer is 'inequality'. According to Parks and Roberts, three broad types of inequality have figured prominently in international climate change negotiations: climate-related inequality (culpability, vulnerability and expected role in clean-up); inequality in international environmental politics; and inequality in international economic regimes. While these inequalities are left unaddressed, suggest Parks and Roberts, the prospects for mutually beneficial cooperation remain limited.

The main body of Chapter 19 is devoted to describing these inequalities and explaining how their existence, and the less-industrialized world's reaction to them, has made it more difficult for rich and poor nations to forge a post-2012 global climate pact. The authors conclude by providing a number of historical examples that illustrate how countries with highly disparate worldviews, causal beliefs, principled beliefs and policy positions have resolved their differences and cooperated on issues of mutual interest, which may provide lessons for the 'crafting an effective post-2012 global climate regime'. This will, they emphasize, 'require unconventional – and perhaps even heterodox – policy interventions'.

The world's forests play a key role in global carbon cycles: 'natural forests' represent a storehouse of carbon, while productive plantation forestry can sequester or remove carbon from the atmosphere. However, the role of forests in climate change mitigation is just one of the numerous calls being made on these most complex of ecosystems at the beginning of the twenty-first century. As well as acting as global carbon storehouses and sinks, forests are, as noted by Bianca Ambrose-Oji in Chapter 20, essential to the survival of forest-dependent communities; they mediate local and regional weather systems; they are a store of genetic diversity; they provide traditional and novel sources of energy, food and fibre; they affect local hydrological systems; and they can improve living spaces and quality of life through greening and cooling in urban microclimates.

Ambrose-Oji's essay is the final contribution to Part II of the book and provides an overview of the important trends in the history and development of international forestry, linking them to parallel developments in environmental sociology. Drawing on Fred Buttel's identification of four central foci for environmental sociology – social movements; state regulation; ecological modernization; and international environmental governance – Ambrose-Oji examines the extent to which the same concerns and the different approaches to addressing them have been incorporated into international forestry scholarship and practice.

The influence of growing global concern over the fate of tropical forests in the 1980s led to calls for their conservation in pursuit of Northern interests in novel genetic materials and climate change mitigation, while Southern forest nations sought to protect their development rights and local forest-dependent communities struggled to maintain access to livelihood resources. As result, the demand was for foresters and conservation professionals to identify and implement methods of forest management that would protect natural forests and biodiversity while continuing to meet national and local development aims (see Haenn's essay on integrated conservation/development in the tropical dry forest of Campeche, Mexico in Chapter 26).

In coming to terms with the need to incorporate people and society into analytical and practical management frameworks, international forestry discourse became dominated by a series of sharply polarized debates concerning the most important social factors to be considered in serving multiple and competing interests. Mirroring Buttel's four key foci within environmental sociology, forestry discourse, suggests Ambrose-Oji, can be divided into four areas of interest: 'knowledge, power and indigenous resistance movements; community and social forestry emphasizing the structural interface between community and state regulation; the application of economic value to forests; and the integrative sustainable livelihoods framework'. Chapter 20 illuminates these overlapping areas of interest and links them to contemporary debates in environmental sociology.

Ambrose-Oji concludes her contribution by looking at what environmental sociology might have to offer our understanding of the relationships between forestry and society in the future. In doing so she reinforces a number of points raised by her fellow contributors to Part II of this book and presages some of the points to emerge in Part III. Emerging themes in contemporary international forestry include: 'the information and knowledge needs for effective management of globalized socio-environmental systems; the tension between market-based and regulatory governance of the global forest commons and global risk in an age of increasingly unpredictable ecologies; and the need to recognize and incorporate social and cultural resilience within forest tenure and management systems'. Risk society, political ecology and ecological modernization all offer prospects for understanding the way forests will be viewed or utilized as environments, but their well-rehearsed arguments need to move further forward to take account of social nature and the insights of global change science. 'Regardless of the switch of attention away from the rainforest campaigns of the late 1980s and 1990s', Ambrose-Oji affirms that 'forests will remain iconic resources and landscapes in globalizing environments and the brave new world of changing global climate and ecological agency'.

13 Animals and us
Ted Benton

Introduction: dualism and its critics

In Western societies the dominant view of the relationship between human beings and animals has been to make a strong distinction between the two: human beings have been contrasted with animals, with highly valued qualities such as rationality, language, moral autonomy, creativity, love of beauty and so on attributed to human beings, while animals have been seen as not just lacking in these qualities, but as also embodying unwanted human traits such as 'brutality' and 'bestiality' (see Midgley, 1979). However, this has never been the only available way of thinking and feeling. Traditional farmers, pet-keepers and naturalists, among others, have generally found themselves forming close ties with other species, have often recognized strong similarities and accepted responsibility for the well-being of these 'others'. Sometimes, especially since the latter part of the nineteenth century, such experiences have formed one of the motivating sources for militant campaigning activity against various sorts of perceived abuse of animals (including birds). In recent decades, and especially in the richer countries, there has been a resurgence of such militant action, now armed intellectually with powerful philosophical arguments, and often calling into question not just this or that abuse, but denouncing our whole form of social existence as grounded in violent abuse of other species.

Though treated with deep suspicion, and even outright hostility by the mainstream communications media and political 'establishment', the wider, more generous sentiments underlying the animal rights and welfare campaigners clearly evoke broad public sympathy. However, the arguments in favour of an enhanced moral status for animals have not gone unchallenged. Most commonly the critics of animal rights and liberation reassert the depth of the morally significant difference between human beings and animals. Why do protesters campaign for better treatment of animals when the world contains so much human oppression and suffering? Philosopher Peter Carruthers made the point unequivocally: 'I regard the present popular concern with animal rights in our culture as a reflection of moral decadence' (Carruthers, 1992: xi).

However, the sort of approach I'll be developing here suggests that, if we combine insights from modern life sciences and social sciences with philosophical thinking, the neat opposition between the human and the animal that is implicit in the thought of Carruthers and other critics can't be sustained. The lives of human beings and animals share so much, and are so indissolubly intertwined, that counterposing animal to human well-being in this way is very hard to justify. If we consider the plight of animals used in vivisection or in 'factory' farming, for example, there are close parallels between the treatment of animals in these institutional systems with widely criticized treatments of human beings in oppressive labour regimes in factory production. The reduction of human beings to the status of commodities, and the 'alienation' of their life activity by loss of autonomy and distortion of their life pattern by physically and mentally degrading conditions and confinement, is arguably paralleled by the treatment of animals in the intensive production regimes of large sectors of the meat industry, or by the use of captive animals in invasive experimental programmes imposed on them for a wide variety of human purposes. Of course, there are differences – in many systems factory workers lease out their labour-time for limited periods, and have some time for rest, recreation and reproduction (in this respect the situation of animals in these regimes is closer to human slavery). But even here, many critics of these systems of production would point to the ways that even 'free time' is strongly constrained, and often degraded, by the necessities of working life. In both sorts of regime, political pressure over many decades has brought some amelioration, with at least some degree of regulation of conditions of work, in the human case, and of the range of acceptable treatment, and requirements of justification, in the case of animals (see Lyons, 2008).

But there are other ways in which human well-being is intertwined with that of animals. The emergence of large-scale concentrations of power in transnational companies in agribusiness and food production and processing (see, e.g., Goodman and Redclift, 1991) has implications for global justice in food distribution, environmental degradation and human health. The new biotechnologies, especially 'genetic engineering', give cause for a number of legitimate concerns in addition to their implications for animal welfare. These points are perhaps simply indications of the more fundamental commonality between human beings and (other) animals – that, as what Marx called 'active natural beings', we can live only by constant practical interchange with the rest of nature. We, both human beings and animals, are organic, needy beings who depend on what the rest of nature provides as the ultimate condition of our survival.

Some of these connections might be accepted by a sceptic such as Carruthers. Where attention to welfare has payoffs for human well-being (as, arguably, in some cases of vivisection), presumably even Carruthers would think it morally justifiable. However, the moral sentiments of the social movement activism in defence of animals are quite different from this 'instrumental' orientation to animal well-being. Most often, activism is motivated by compassion for the suffering of fellow sentient beings (see Benton and Redfearn 1996). The parallels I suggested above, between exploitative and alienating conditions imposed on human beings and those suffered by captive animals, would make no sense except on the assumption that the non-human animals involved are, indeed, sentient beings, with ends, preferences, and a capacity to suffer harm and experience well-being. If it makes no sense to apply these concepts to non-human animals, then, it might seem, the ontological basis for moral concern is simply absent. The protesters and their supporters would be, perhaps, well-meaning, but they would appear to be deluded by a mistakenly anthropomorphic view of animals.

So there is no escaping the thorny question of the psychological status of non-human animals. As is well known, Western philosophical traditions have tended to attribute a unique and elevated status to the human species, and, in general, the main means by which this has been accomplished has been some form of human/animal contrast: attributes supposedly peculiar to human beings become definitive of our superior status within the order of nature, or of our elevation above it. The mark of distinction might be possession of an immortal soul, autonomous will, reason, language, or even sentience itself, as in Descartes's famous view of animals as automata.

Within the Western traditions, perhaps the most powerful challenge to this dualistic opposition between human beings and animals came with Darwin's version of evolutionary thinking. In a striking passage of his 'Species notebook' he writes:

> Animals – whom we have made our slaves we do not like to consider our equals. – Do not slave-holders wish to make the black man other kind? – Animals with affection, imitation, fear of death, pain, sorrow for the dead – respect . . .. The soul by consent of all is superadded, animals not got it, not look forward if we choose to let conjecture run wild, then animals our fellow brethren in pain, disease, death, & suffering & famine; our slaves in the most laborious work, our companions in our amusements. they may partake, from our origin in one common ancestor we may be all netted together. (Darwin [1837] 1987: 228–9)

In this very dense passage, Darwin links together his conjecture that human beings and other animals have a common ancestry with a series of observations of commonalities in the life experience of human and non-human species, as well as noting forms of social relatedness across species boundaries. We have in common a whole range of vulnerabilities to harms, in virtue of our organic constitutions and associated psychological capacities and dispositions. We establish social relations with animals through both enslavement of them and taking them as 'companions' in our amusements. Finally, Darwin even postulates a parallel between the racist ideologies that legitimate slavery within the human species, and the human–animal dualism that legitimates the 'slavery' imposed by human beings on other species. Darwin clearly thought that a deep revaluation of the moral character of our relations to other animals followed from his evolutionary thesis and related observations of animal behaviour.

Philosophical arguments: utilitarianism

Even though, as I claimed above, spontaneous sentiments of compassion are an important motivation for activism, it is also true that the recent growth of activism has been – to an unusual extent – influenced by the writings of academic philosophers. The most influential of these writings have taken the form of extensions beyond the human species boundary of moral theories that are already well established. In general, the argument has been: if human beings are worthy of moral consideration, then so must be non-human animals that share with us the relevant characteristics that make us worthy of consideration. Two main approaches – utilitarianism and liberal rights theory – both make use of Darwinian ideas in making their case.

The leading philosopher who uses utilitarian theory to make the case for animals is Peter Singer (see, e.g., Singer, 1990). The 'classic' nineteenth-century version of utilitarianism is an attempt to put moral judgements on an objective basis by calculating the consequences of actions (or moral rules) for the sum total of pleasures or pains among those affected by them. Peter Singer argues that the similarities between vertebrate central nervous systems, together with the evolutionary advantages conferred by sentience, make it unlikely that vulnerability to pain is a uniquely human attribute. This, in addition to the common observation of cross-species similarities in behavioural expressions of pain, gives us strong theoretical and empirical grounds for thinking that the capacities to suffer pain and experience pleasure are widely shared across species boundaries. If this is so, then (non-human) animals clearly qualify to be included in the utilitarian calculus. Indeed, this was already proclaimed by the leading utilitarian philosopher, Jeremy Bentham, in his much-quoted dictum to the effect that animal rationality was beside the point. For him, the question was 'Can they suffer?' (Bentham [1789] 1948).

Of course, the utilitarian tradition has become both more diverse and more sophisticated since Bentham's day, so, for example, some latter-day utilitarians would speak of satisfaction or non-satisfaction of preferences in place of pleasure and pain. So, if we used this version of utilitarianism, animals could be included in the moral community only if non-human animals could be truly said to have preferences. To judge from the adverts, the manufacturers of pet foods assume this to be uncontroversial among their customers.

It is, therefore, not surprising that the utilitarian tradition has taken the lead in advocacy of a positive moral standing for non-human animals. However, there are some serious problems with utilitarian moral theory quite independently of its application to animals. The first of these is that what is morally important in human life cannot easily be reduced to pleasure and pain. Some pleasures may be deemed good, others evil, while pain may be suffered for fine or noble purposes. While there may be substantive moral disagreement about these judgements, it is clear that the relation between good and evil, on the one hand, and pleasure and pain, on the other, is a contingent one. Similar considerations apply to 'preference-utilitarianism': what is good is not *necessarily* what is preferred (neoclassical economics notwithstanding).

A second longstanding objection to utilitarianism is closely related to the first. It is that the quantitative focus of the doctrine limits its capacity to acknowledge qualitative differences among pleasures, or preferences. Different pleasures differ not just in amounts – intensities, durations and so on – but also in kind, or quality. How many bars of a Mahler symphony are equivalent to a good meal? But the ability to subject pleasures, pains and preferences to moral evaluation, and to make qualitative discriminations, seems to be closely bound up with the culturally mediated, or shaped, character of human experience. Interestingly, it seems that these two objections to utilitarianism might carry less weight when it is applied to other animals since they (arguably) don't have the ability to make moral judgements for themselves. However, to argue in this way would weaken the utilitarian case for animal liberation as this depends on the assumption that human and animal suffering are similar in kind, and that each counts equally in utilitarian moral calculations.

There is another quite standard argument against utilitarian moral theory, one that has tended to be the most prominent in the debate about the moral standing of animals. This is the objection to the theory as a version of 'consequentialism'. Consequentialists deny that the moral character of an act, or a proposed rule of conduct, is inherent in the act or rule itself. Rather, we can decide on the rightness or wrongness of an act or rule only by measuring or estimating its consequences. One uncomfortable implication of consequentialism is that it appears to allow that it would be right to mistreat an innocent individual if it could be shown that some aggregate benefit could be achieved by it. This cuts against very widespread moral intuitions that it is wrong to punish the innocent, no matter what the consequences, that some forms of treatment, such as torture and enslavement, are simply unacceptable, and cannot be justified in any circumstances. This has become a very topical issue in relation to attempts to defend the imprisonment of suspected terrorists without due legal process, or to justify torture in cases where information so gained might save many lives.

Philosophical arguments: rights theory

The intuition that morality or immorality is not just a matter of consequences, but may be inherent in the very nature of an act, finds justification in another influential tradition of moral theory. The most frequently cited source of this tradition is the great eighteenth-century German philosopher, Immanuel Kant. Central to this way of thinking is the importance of the integrity of autonomous individuals, who are authors of their own ends, or purposes, and should never be treated solely as means to the ends of others. One way of grounding this moral view is to say that individuals have basic, or 'natural', rights to respectful treatment in virtue of their 'inherent value'. Tom Regan is the leading advocate of this version of non-consequentialist, or 'deontological', moral theory in the 'animals' debate. At first sight, this seems to be a most unpromising approach. Unlike utilitarianism, the 'rights' tradition imposes quite stringent conditions on the kinds of being that can be allowed into the moral universe. Kant's concept of autonomy, for example, presupposed a being rational enough to recognize its contemplated actions as falling under universal principles, and capable of acting in accordance with those principles, against the pull of contingent desires and preferences. To make such a concept stretch across the species boundary would be a tall order!

Tom Regan solves this problem by way of a crucial distinction between moral agents and moral patients. Something like Kant's account of autonomy would be needed to characterize full moral agency. Only moral agents in that sense are bearers of moral responsibility for their actions. Since there are close conceptual ties between the necessary rational capacities, language use and full moral agency, it seems reasonable to accept that only individuals of the human species are moral agents. Of course, there may have been other hominids with such capacities, and, indeed, it may yet be discovered that other living species share them. Certainly research on other primates and some marine mammals has already produced results that have challenged human uniqueness in these crucial respects. This has led, for example, to increasing acceptance of the claim that our closest primate relative should be accorded something similar to the moral and legal protections supposedly enjoyed by human beings. The Great Apes Project is the leading organization advancing this cause. But even if this were accepted, it would justify the inclusion of only a small group of species into the 'family' of morally significant beings – the vast majority of animals of other species would still be given no moral standing.

Regan's view (1988, *inter alia*) is that there are no good reasons for limiting the class of beings entitled to moral consideration to those (i.e. moral agents) who can bear moral responsibility. For Regan, there is a wider class of living beings who, along with full moral agents, possess 'inherent value'.

A sufficient (but not necessary) condition for possession of inherent value is to be a 'subject of a life'. Although it includes sentience, this criterion is more demanding than the utilitarian doctrine. To count as subjects of a life, individuals must have preferences, purposes, some sense of self-identity through time, and enough capacity to be harmed or benefited by the actions of others to be said to have 'interests'. Regan's claim is that mammals above the (seemingly rather arbitrary) age of one satisfy this criterion, and so must be held to possess 'inherent value' in the required sense, even though they do not count as full moral agents (can't be held morally responsible for their actions, for example). But there are also human beings to whom this applies – some psychologically damaged or mentally ill adults, infants and, perhaps, others.

All those beings who are in the required sense 'subjects of a life', whether human or non-human, but are not full moral agents, are defined as 'moral patients'. Since moral patients have inherent value (have their own purposes, preferences etc.) they, like moral agents, should not be treated merely as means to the ends of others. Moral agents, therefore, should treat them with respect, refrain from harming them, etc. In other words, moral patients have a moral claim on moral agents to treat them in certain ways – they can properly be said to possess 'rights'.

So, if the concepts of 'subject of a life' and 'inherent value' can be stretched beyond the species boundary to apply to individuals of other animal species, then (many) non-human animals can properly be said to have rights.

Regan's advocacy of rights is designed to give a more morally powerful and unconditional protection to animals than utilitarianism can offer. It rules out ill-treatment as an abuse of rights, not dependent on calculations of aggregate costs and benefits, and it rules out the use of animals as mere means to human ends. So the protection given (in theory, at least) is a more powerful and unconditional one than that offered by utilitarianism, but it has several disadvantages. One is that it offers no protection to individuals of the many species (reptiles, amphibians, fish, invertebrates of myriad forms etc.) for whom the case for 'subject of a life' status would be very difficult to make. Of course, this might not be taken as a disadvantage – perhaps these beings are not entitled to respectful treatment. I'll return to this later in the chapter.

Moral agents and moral patients

A more central difficulty has to do with the concept of moral patient itself – and related ideas such as 'inherent value' and 'subject of a life'. At least the utilitarian view that human beings and individuals of many other species can suffer harm is unlikely to be very controversial now. However, those who dispute that non-human beings have the various powers and capacities that go to make up 'subjecthood' have more of a case. R.G. Frey, for example, has argued that to have preferences one must also have beliefs about the objects of those preferences. Beliefs, in turn, are always beliefs that something is the case. Since only a being with the capacity for language could be properly said to have beliefs, only such a being could have preferences (see Frey, 1980, 1983). M.P.T. Leahy (1991) also (mis)uses a version of the later philosophy of Wittgenstein as grounds for denying that psychological capacities can be coherently applied to non-participants in human 'language games' (see Benton, 1993: ch. 3). More cautiously, Peter Carruthers introduces the idea of non-conscious mental states in questioning whether animal experience is sufficiently like human experience to justify the extension of moral concern to them.

Regan offers a 'cumulative' argument against such sceptics. This draws upon the authority of Darwinian evolutionary theory, but also takes common-sense beliefs and language as a touchstone. We ordinarily do refer to the cat as wanting to get closer to the fire, or the dog as wanting to go for a walk, for example. Of course, we could be wrong in speaking and thinking in this way. We might simply be sentimentally projecting our human attributes on to other species, rather as children attribute thoughts and feelings to their dolls and other toys. Regan's response is to argue that the onus is on those who would reject these ways of thinking about other animals to show that other ways of adequately characterizing animal activity without reference to their sentience or conscious states can be devised. So far, he claims, the programmes that have tried to do this – whether behaviourist psychology or neurophysiology – have signally failed. On the contrary, it might be added that research on the lives of animals in their natural habitats, as well as much psychological research on captive animals, has revealed complexities and flexibilities in their modes of life that render such reductive programmes ever-more implausible.

Although, as Regan admits, the case for attributing 'subject of a life' status to (some) non-human animals is not conclusive, it is certainly well grounded. The reasonableness of this case will be assumed in the rest of this chapter. But to accept that individuals of at least some non-human species can properly be regarded as 'subjects of a life' is still some way from accepting that they have moral standing in their own right – let alone one that is equal to that of human 'moral patients'. One problem is Regan's concept of 'inherent value'. This idea is questionable in several ways, notably that it is hard to make sense of something having value 'in itself' independently of others who value it. But we don't need to go into the complex philosophical issues raised by this. It seems that the main argument of Regan's advocacy of animal rights can be restated without using this disputed idea.

Both Regan and Singer make use of examples of human individuals who lack full moral agency, such as very young infants, and seriously mentally retarded or psychologi-cally disabled adults. Regan includes these groups of human beings along with fully able animals in the category 'moral patients'. Very few people will deny that such groups of human beings lack moral standing – indeed, as I shall argue later, their very vulnerability makes the assertion of their rights particularly important. If this is simply accepted as given (without need to justify it by means of dubious constructs such as 'inherent value'), then the onus is on anyone who refuses to accept non-human animals as having positive moral standing to show what morally relevant characteristics distinguish animals from human moral patients. The mere fact of species difference will not do as this would be comparable with racism or sexism, ideologies in which morally irrelevant characteristics such as skin colour or details of anatomy are used as a basis for discrimination.

Of course, some may wish to deny that human moral patients such as the very severely mentally handicapped do have positive moral standing, and if so, this would divert the argument from one about animal rights to one about the justification for moral precepts in the human case. However, it seems unlikely that anyone initially not inclined to assign a positive moral status to human moral patients would be convinced by the simple device of attributing to them the somewhat mysterious property of inherent value. There are, of course, numerous attempts in the literature to identify differences between non-human animals and human infants, the deeply psychologically damaged and so on, but few, if any, that rise to the challenge by denying moral status to human moral patients.

Although there is not space here to do the subject justice, it seems to me that there are, indeed, very significant differences between the different kinds of human moral patients, both among themselves, and between them and non-human animals. Some of these dif-ferences are clearly morally significant. However, it is quite another thing to show that these differences are of an order, and have a patterned distribution, such that the bound-ary of appropriate moral concern coincides exactly with the species boundary at every point. Once the distinction between moral patients and moral agents is accepted, so that we recognize that beings, of whatever species, that are incapable of full moral agency may still be proper objects of moral concern, there is little to prevent the inclusion of animals within the scope of human morality. Attempts to persist in this increasingly take on the appearance of defensively motivated 'special pleading'.

So, while, again, the case is far from conclusive, it is nevertheless reasonable, and well grounded, both empirically and philosophically, to recognize the individuals of at least some non-human animal species as proper objects of moral concern. This far, it seems to me, the case on behalf of animals is well made. However, what remains to be considered, if we accept that animals do have positive moral status, is just what that moral status is. Since, for both the utilitarian and the rights view, the argument on behalf of animals works by extending an established moral theory across the species boundary, a weakness in either theory in its application to the human case will, *a fortiori*, tell against it as a theory of the moral status of animals. Since there are powerful arguments against the utilitarian position, in particular the familiar implications of its consequentialism, I shall focus, in the rest of this chapter, on the case for rights.

Why rights and *what* rights?

So far most of the debate about animal rights has focused on the question: 'Are non-human animals the sort of being to whom it makes sense to attribute rights?' This is, indeed, a relevant and important question. However, it is not the only relevant and important question to be asked in this area. There are, of course, philosophical sceptics for whom it makes no sense to attribute rights even to human beings, particularly the sort of 'basic' rights (a notion closely related to alleged 'natural' rights) upon which Regan's argument rests. My provisional assumption here is that these sceptics are mistaken, and that some notion of 'basic' or 'natural' human rights is defensible. But even on this assumption, we may still ask: 'What is the point or purpose of assigning and respecting rights?' Once we have an answer to this, the next question that arises is: 'What kinds of being stand in need of rights, and in virtue of what do they need them?'

Finally, these questions take us on to a further set of considerations about rights that have typically been raised by radical critics from the Left, from socialists, feminists and communitarians of various stripes. These considerations bring into the picture the social relations, especially power relations that hold between the individuals who are assigned rights. Can the purposes for which rights are assigned be achieved in the case of those with insufficient social power to exercise them? More fundamentally, is it only because of the persistence of (alterable) social relations of mutual competitiveness, self-interest and unequal power that individuals need rights in the first place (see Benton, 2006)? My central argument will be that since these are questions of importance for the discourse of *human* rights, the recognition of animals as possible holders of rights suggests that they will also have an important bearing on the *animal*-rights debate.

This brings us to the edge of a very tangled web of arguments and issues that cannot be settled in the space of one short chapter. Still, we can take the issues just a little further. Let us deal, first, with the question of whether non-human beings can qualify as (basic) rights-holders (assuming human beings can). To the extent that at least some non-human animals have purposes and preferences of their own, are able to benefit, and are vulnerable to suffering at the hands of moral agents, they, like human moral patients, can be said to have an interest in respectful treatment. If the analogy with human moral patients holds, they have a justified moral claim to such treatment, and it is a moral obligation on the part of the relevant human moral agents to answer the claim. This is all that is required, on the concept of rights that Regan adopts.

Even accepting this rather 'thin' concept of rights, however, there are problems. The first problem concerns a long-held philosophical view that there is a 'symmetry' between rights and obligations: that wherever there is a right there must be a correlative obligation to respect it on the part of another (or others), and vice versa. I have already accepted the case for obligations on the part of moral agents towards moral patients of other species. But do obligations always confer correlative rights? One way of thinking about this is to ask whether, and when, attributing a right is doing anything over and above the attribution of the correlative obligation. When Regan and others appeal to their readers' acknowledgement of the rights of human moral patients, they do, indeed, tap into an established usage. However, it is arguable that these rights-attributions amount to no more than could be said by simply specifying the obligations that the fully abled have to their immature or unfortunate fellow beings: to protect them, or care for them. Seen in this light, the case for animal rights in this rather narrow sense may not seem too controversial.

Vulnerability or self-determination?
Another line of criticism of animal-rights claims – not far removed from Carruthers's view – is that the often-used comparison between animal liberation, and the liberation struggles of women, African Americans and colonized people, is to devalue the latter ones. Above all these have been expressions of self-assertion, in which rights are, centrally, claims for self-definition and self-determination. These moral claims do, indeed, entail moral obligations on the part of others, but what those obligations might be could not be established independently of the active claims-making activities of those demanding recognition. Provisionally, I shall mark this distinction with the terms 'active' and 'passive'. Passive rights-holders are the subjects of moral obligations on the part of moral agents, while active rights-holders are also entitled to contribute to the processes of establishing what those obligations are and how they are to be implemented. Although suffering many kinds of material deprivation, social disadvantage and lack of esteem has played its part in fuelling these social struggles, their aims go beyond the requirement for ameliorative reform. To be a mere recipient of the benevolence of others would not merely fall short of the rights that are claimed, but would itself be an instance of their denial – of paternalistic condescension.

This difference between active and passive rights does seem to mark out a significant moral boundary, more or less coextensive with the distinction between moral agents and moral patients. While passive rights may be attributed, as Regan argues, to all 'subjects of a life', active rights do seem to require a range of conceptual and other cultural capacities possessed only by moral agents. If we now take into account the point of attributing rights, we can see a case for both sorts of rights. The moral force of attributing rights to moral patients is now clear. Since, by definition, moral patients are incapable of making claims on their own behalf, they are likely to be particularly vulnerable, compared with individuals who do have this ability. They stand in need of a moral agent who will accept the obligation to speak and act on their behalf. We might speak here of passive rights as 'vulnerability rights'. However, for moral agents, their capacity for self-definition and self-determination implies that what counts as their welfare cannot be fully known independently of their own active participation in defining it. Moreover, the relevant human liberation movements provide evidence that recognition and preservation of their own powers of self-definition and self-determination are likely to figure centrally as elements in the substantive views of their welfare that they advance as rights-claims. The active rights claimed by human agents who demand full recognition of their status we might call 'self-determination rights'.

This does seem to suggest that even if we accept (as I do) the case for recognition of vulnerability rights for non-human animals, they may still not qualify for self-determination rights, since they (in general) do not possess the relevant cultural, linguistic and conceptual abilities. However, this might be seen as a kind of 'speciesist' special pleading. Culture, language and the rest just happen to be part of our evolved species-character. Other species, too, have their distinctive character, mode of life and associated needs. For them, the analogue of self-determination rights might simply be the opportunity to live the life appropriate to their species, without the distortions or deprivations imposed by human social practices of incarceration or habitat destruction.

Rights and communities
Yet another line of criticism of the case for animal rights advanced by Regan derives from a rather different way of thinking about rights in the human case. This alternative approach – 'communitarianism' – objects to the attempt to assign moral rights to individuals independently of the social relations and form of community to which they belong. This sort of approach would be inclined to reject the idea of 'natural' rights in the human case, and so also the related concept of 'basic' rights that Regan assigns to non-human animals. For this tradition, rights and responsibilities are socially established norms governing interaction in actually existing communities. As animals cannot be members of human communities, the attribution of rights to them makes no sense. Rights and responsibilities that flow in this way from actual social relations and practices are called by Regan 'acquired' rights, and he seems to give them little consideration as protections for non-human beings. However, they may have more to offer than either the communitarians or Regan seem to suspect. In any case, the communitarian way of thinking about rights has at least one rather important limitation: it makes it very difficult to grasp the importance of the role of rights-claims in challenging the patterns of rights and obligations that prevail in a community: 'natural' or 'basic' rights-claims point to moral requirements that are *not* being met in a given social order, but *should* be. The historical contribution of such rights-claims to struggles that have brought about progressive historical change in favour of justice for oppressed, exploited or stigmatized groups is very considerable. This is the point of making comparable claims on behalf of non-human animals.

Rights and relations
However, the communitarians do have a point – several, in fact! The concept of rights that Regan makes use of belongs to a long tradition of 'liberal' rights that, in its classic versions, relied on a narrow conception of personal identity and individual autonomy, such that 'basic interests' could be understood as bodily integrity, freedom of thought and association, autonomous pursuit of happiness and so on. What this conception of the individual and her needs tended to leave out of account were the social and emotional needs associated with one's place in a network of relations. It also tended to be assumed

that individual autonomy was something 'given' – something that could just be taken for granted, with rights required only to protect people from abuses or unjustified constraints on their free choices. In both these respects, this narrow, 'negative' concept of rights is limited in its relevance to non-human animals.

Most species that have been incorporated into human society through domestication, as 'companion' animals, or as sources of food, clothing, labour or entertainment are social animals. For many of them, domestication depends on transposing at least some of their social dispositions into learned patterns of interaction with human beings. In other cases, as, for example, traditional animal husbandry, the social bonds formed among the animals themselves are used in regulating their behaviour for human purposes. In each of these sorts of case, recognizing and respecting the social and emotional needs of the animals would be required by any adequate concept of 'rights' – beyond simply ensuring they had enough food and water, and so on. Again, the assumption that all individuals have the autonomy necessary to pursue their well-being unless interfered with by others, clearly untenable for human 'moral patients' (such as infants, the severely psychologically ill and others), is even less applicable to non-human animals trapped in dependency relations with human beings. What is required in both sorts of case are 'positive' rights that impose on others the obligation not just to avoid harming, but to actively intervene to enable dependent others to meet such needs as they have. In other words, for dependent beings, failure to respect their rights may take the form not only of direct abuse, but also of *failure* to act – neglect.

As soon as we start to take relationships seriously in thinking about rights – as evidenced by the above paragraph – the difficulty in specifying rights and obligations in abstraction from specific social contexts becomes clear. So, while we may be convinced by Regan's argument that any subject of a life, whether human or animal, may be worthy of moral consideration, this gives surprisingly little direct guidance about just what this requires in the form of specific rules of action, and to whom such responsibilities are to be assigned. Do we have an obligation to come to the aid of a wild animal under attack from a predator? Should we take account of the interest of populations of wild animals in planning decisions that affect their habitats? Is pet-keeping an infringement of an animal's rights? Is there a moral difference between 'factory' farming and traditional methods of animal 'husbandry' for meat? Many people, for example, would hold that pet-owners or keepers of zoo animals have a moral responsibility for the welfare of their animals while denying any such responsibility on the part of a passer-by to rescue a wild animal from a predator. Some would argue more fundamentally that institutions such as zoos and pet-keeping are intrinsically unacceptable. At least part of the moral argument in these cases would be grounded in the moral character and implications of the different animal/human relationships involved, independently of the assumed status of the animals as 'subjects of a life'. This begins to suggest that what Regan tends to dismiss as 'acquired' rights have more relevance than might be thought. Perhaps an abstract and universalistic concept of 'basic' rights can serve as the starting point for a much more 'relationship-sensitive' and context-specific critical examination of 'actually existing' human practices in relation to other animals.

The radical critique of (liberal) rights
Finally, there are some considerations that derive from a long-established radical critique of liberal rights – often associated with Marx, but shared by other critical traditions

including other versions of socialism, anarchism and feminism. There is too little space in this chapter to explore these issues in detail (see the more extended treatment in Benton, 1993). One strand in this radical critique is to point out that when equal rights are attributed to all individuals in a society that is characterized by very deep inequalities in wealth and power, there is a huge gap between abstractly 'having' a right, on the one hand, and being able to *exercise* it, on the other. The law may recognize the equal rights to own property of the rich man and the beggar, but in reality it protects the actual property of the rich man against the interests of the property-less. Again, 'equality under the law' is a fine proclamation, but it is more likely to benefit those who can afford a good barrister.

One way of addressing this radical criticism has been to broaden the preferred concept of rights to include social, economic and cultural rights, and, associated with this, to introduce reforms to compensate for inequalities: socialized systems of health care 'free at the point of need', trade union recognition, legal aid and so on. Similar reforms, much more limited in scope, and enforced more unevenly, of course, have been introduced to ameliorate some aspects of the treatment of animals in confinement (see Lyons, 2008). But the radical critique points to the partial and uncertain character of these compensatory reforms, even when they address the complaints of oppressed, exploited or otherwise disadvantaged human beings. Where poor working and residential environments and economic uncertainty increase the likelihood of serious illness, and of premature death, free health care is only a partial remedy. Nation-states possess coercive power that can be used to destroy or subvert trade union organization. When public spending is under pressure for other projects, resources for legal aid may take second place. And so on.

So, the radical critique continues, perhaps the demand for rights arises only because we live in a certain sort of society – one in which competitive antagonism is built into the very fabric of economic, cultural and political existence. A society that rewards competitive performance and punishes 'failure' is one in which we might expect individuals to adopt a narrowly focused view of self-identity and interest, and devote most of their efforts to securing it. What if, instead of promoting individualized 'entrepreneurialism' and competitive achievement, the prevailing culture valued collaboration, mutual recognition, solidarity and compassion? What if the enjoyments of convivial relationships with each other were valued over the pressure to consume in a never-ending spiral of acquisition of material goods? If such a society were possible, people would, surely, spontaneously recognize one another's needs, without having to be constrained or coerced into doing so by the law or by authoritative moral rules.

Of course, it would be easy to write off these thoughts as pie-in-the-sky utopianism. For many people, it is impossible to imagine a possible future beyond our current phase of globalizing free market capitalism. Difficult to imagine it certainly is – and even more difficult to envisage the process of change itself. But, on the other side of the argument is the stark warning that this form of socioeconomic organization is already degrading crucial global life-support systems in ways that may be irreversible. Its profound and contested injustices, and the military confrontations they generate, combine with its ecological crisis to suggest this is a way of (dis)organizing our relations with each other and the rest of nature that has little future. But on the smaller scale, anyone who has lived through the privatization or commercialization of a public service will have first-hand experience of the destruction of wider identifications, of the withering of benevolence and solidarity that accompanies the imposition of performance indicators, performance-related pay, job insecurity and enhanced differentials. Clearly, the balance of antagonism and mutual benevolence is deeply affected by institutional forms and can sometimes be altered very quickly.

Utopian thoughts and moral futures
So, to conclude, let us at least speculate on the possibility of a more benign, cooperative and compassionate future society. In some versions of utopia, competitiveness is over-come by first overcoming scarcity: if there is enough for all, then what reason is there to compete? But this argument lacks conviction – our own society has, at least in the rich countries, greater abundance than any in history, but it is certainly no less competitive. In any case, our recognition of the way our own society presses against its ecological limits should teach us that any future society would need to devise rules by which it lived within its ecological means. Perhaps in any society, however benevolent, we would still require rules to govern our just share in the necessary work, and in the enjoyment of its results. The difference might be that in a more generous, convivial and collaborative culture these rules would go with rather than against the spontaneous 'moral sentiments' of the citizenry, and so be more effective in fulfilling their purpose.

But what might such an alternative society mean for our relationships with other species? The argument so far has suggested that where animals of other species are brought within the frame of human societies, new forms of moral obligation to them emerge by that fact. Where animals, either through long historical processes of selec-tive modification or by elimination of their former habitat, have become dependent on human social life, then it is arguable that positive obligations of care on the part of indi-viduals or of communities follow. Again, as argued above, the obligations here are likely to include provision for the meeting of relational and emotional needs, according to the specific character and mode of life of the species concerned.

But only a small number of species has been subjected to domestication, while many others have a range of more-or-less distant or contingent relationships to human social life – from semi-domesticated herbivores, through species that have adapted to human habitation as scavengers or commensals, to 'wild' species that continue to survive in rem-nants of natural and semi-natural habitat. How far might the allocation of rights beyond the species boundary apply to this range of other species?

If, as I suggested above, there are good reasons for thinking that any form of human social life would continue to be bounded by ecological constraints, with the consequent necessity for some rules governing allocation by rights and justice, these considerations must also cover non-human animal populations. In fact, since what human beings treat as their own 'habitat requirements' have progressively transformed, and often completely destroyed, the actual habitats of almost all other species on earth, these considerations are raised rather acutely. In the case of 'livestock' animals, fulfilling the responsibility to enable them to live according to their species-specific modes of life would entail much more extensive agricultural systems than those now established in most parts of the world. That would, in turn, entail much more restraint on the part of human populations in their land-use strategies.

But, at this point, moral consideration of 'wild' populations becomes relevant. Even someone convinced by the arguments of both utilitarians and rights-theorists that

vegetarianism is morally required will surely accept that the growing of sufficient vege-
table food will itself have ecological effects. Large areas of land will still be required
for the growing of food for human beings that might otherwise have sustained large
populations of herbivorous animals, and their predators. It is also hard to imagine how
such purely arable systems could operate without some method of *prima facie* rights-
infringing pest control.

The philosophy of animal rights seems not well placed to deal with these issues. On the
face of it, a 'non-interference' view of rights, with its liberal assumption of autonomy as
'given', might seem particularly appropriate in relation to animals in the wild. It would
also be consistent with a deep green ethic in favour of the preservation of 'wilderness'.

But it is a measure of the overwhelming significance of the human impact on the contemporary world that the preservation of wilderness is now a moral and political issue. In
a real sense, there are no 'wild' animal populations left. Such habitat as is not yet directly
under human management is largely so because of socially agreed and enforced restraint.
So, unqualified, the demand not to interfere is insufficient. How are the individual rights
of wild animals not to be interfered with to be balanced against the rights of 'livestock'
animals to sufficient grazing land, and the rights of human populations to grow and
protect their crops, establish settlements and so on? An undifferentiated concept of rights
does seem inadequate to provide decision procedures that would respect the complexity
of these questions.

Perhaps more seriously for the rights view, moral issues arise in this context upon
which the concept of rights seems to have little or no purchase at all. For example,
widely shared moral intuitions, even enshrined in international conventions, place a high
significance on preserving diversity of living species. On this view, protecting habitat
from 'development' might be justified in terms of the vulnerability of a species to extinction, rather than in terms of the well-being of whatever individual animals happened to
live there. More seriously still, most greens and other environmentalists would accept
a responsibility towards an immense diversity of species, including plant species, the
individuals of which do not even come close to satisfying Regan's 'subject of a life' criterion. Of course, Regan offers this as a sufficient condition for moral considerability,
not a necessary one. So it remains open that we should develop a range of other moral
concepts and rules to regulate our relations with the non-human world. This would not
deny that there is important work for the concept of rights to do, but it would entail an
acknowledgement that there is a great deal of morally necessary work that even a more
socially and ecologically nuanced concept of rights cannot do. Now, more than ever, this
is an urgent moral demand.

References

Bentham, J. ([1789] 1948), *The Principles of Morals and Legislation*, New York: Hafner.
Benton, E. (1993), *Natural Relations: Ecology, Animal Rights, and Social Justice*, London: Verso.
Benton, E. (2006), 'Do we need rights? If so, what sort?' in L. Morris (ed.), *Rights: Sociological Perspectives*.
    Abingdon, UK and New York: Routledge, pp. 21–36.
Benton, E. and S. Redfearn (1996), 'The politics of animal rights. Where is the left?', *New Left Review*, **215**:
    43–58.
Carruthers, P. (1992), *The Animals Issue: Moral Theory in Practice*, Cambridge: Cambridge University Press.
Darwin, C. ([1837] 1987), *Charles Darwin's Notebooks 1836–1846*, in P.H. Barrett, P.J. Gautrey, S. Herbert, D.
    Kohn and S. Smith (eds), British Museum (Natural History)/ Cambridge University Press, (Notebook B).
Frey, R.G. (1980), *Interests and Rights: The Case Against Animals*, Oxford: Clarendon Press.

Frey, R.G. (1983), *Rights, Killing and Suffering*, Oxford: Blackwell.
Goodman, D. and M. Redclift (1991), *Refashioning Nature: Food, Ecology, and Culture*, London and New York: Routledge.
Leahy, M.P.T. (1991), *Against Liberation: Putting Animals in Perspective*, London: Routledge.
Lyons, D. (2008), 'The rights of others', *Green World*, **62**: 14.
Midgley, M. (1979), *Beast and Man*, Brighton, UK: Harvester.
Regan, T. (1988), *The Case for Animal Rights*, London: Routledge.
Singer, P. (1990), *Animal Liberation*, 2nd edn, London: Jonathan Cape.

14 Science and the environment in the twenty-first century
Steven Yearley

Introduction

According to Simon Caldwell of the popular right-leaning UK newspaper *The Daily Mail* – drawing on advance information about the pontiff's message for the New Year's 'World Day of Peace' for 2008 – the Pope 'said that while some concerns [over climate change] may be valid it was vital that the international community based its policies on science rather than the dogma of the environmentalist movement' (*Daily Mail*, 13 December 2007). Although the disinterested observer might find many aspects of Caldwell's exegetical work on the Pope's text rather odd,[1] the most interesting point here is that *The Daily Mail* lauds the Pope for putting science first when thinking about climate change. Earlier in 2007, former US Vice President Al Gore had shared the Nobel Peace Prize and seen his film on global warming, *An Inconvenient Truth*, win two Academy Awards. If even the Pope – presumably still an enthusiast for dogma in many areas of life – thinks we should put science before dogma when it comes to the environment, and if a right-wing newspaper praises him for thinking this, while at the same time left-liberal Al Gore successfully draws the world's attention to inconvenient facts underscored by scientific research, then there might appear to be a broad consensus about the relationship between science and the environment in the twenty-first century.

But as soon as one reads further into Caldwell's piece, one realizes that the world has not grown eerily harmonious. The dogma that *The Daily Mail* columnist was seeking to bypass was the 'dogma' of global climate change to which – in his view – environmentalists such as Gore are unreasonably attached. In substantive terms there are few surprises in his article. But what these remarks by the Pope and their treatment by the columnist do indicate is the following. First, by the opening decade of the twenty-first century, virtually everyone has come round to the idea that science is the authoritative way to speak about the environment. More than almost any other public policy issue, the environment is framed and interpreted though the discourse of scientific knowledge and scientific evidence (see Yearley, 2005: 113–43). Second, despite science's foundation in factual evidence and scientists' pursuit of objectivity, influential public voices manage to sustain disagreements about what scientists know and what the scientific evidence about the natural environment means. This chapter will investigate these two issues in relation to the key meeting points for science and environment at the start of the twenty-first century: climate change and genetically modified (GM) agriculture.

Climate-change protests and proofs

At first sight, the issue of climate change resembles numerous other environmental controversies that sociologists have studied. But I shall demonstrate below that it stands out, both because of the way it gave rise to innovations in the production and certification of scientific knowledge, and because of the novel positions into which it led environmental non-governmental organizations (NGOs).

At the outset, the situation looked familiar. A claim about a putative environmental problem was first raised by scientists and taken up and amplified by the media and environmental groups; in time a policy response followed. As is well known, meteorologists – already aware that the climate had undergone numerous dramatic fluctuations in the past – began in the second half of the twentieth century to offer ideas and advice about the possibility of climate changes affecting our civilization in the longer term (see Boehmer-Christiansen, 1994a; Edwards, 2001). Although sceptics like to point out that initial warnings also included the possibility that we might be heading out of an interglacial warm period into ice-age cold, as early as the 1950s there was a focus on atmospheric warming (Edwards, 2000). As such climate research was refined, largely thanks to the growth in computer power in the 1970s and 1980s, the majority opinion endorsed the earlier suggestion that enhanced warming driven by the build-up of atmospheric carbon dioxide was the likelier problem. Environmental groups are reported to have been initially wary of mobilizing around this claim (Pearce, 1991: 284) since it seemed such a long shot and with such high stakes. With acid rain then on the agenda as the leading atmospheric problem and many governments active in denying scientific claims about this effect, it seemed far-fetched to warn that emissions might be sending the whole climate out of control.

Worse still, at a time when environmentalists were looking for concrete campaign successes, the issue seemed almost designed to provoke and sustain controversy. The records of past temperatures and particularly of past atmospheric compositions were often not good and there was the danger that rising trends in urban air-temperature measurements were simply an artefact: cities had simply become warmer as they grew in size. The heat radiating from the sun is known to fluctuate, so there was no guarantee that any warming was a terrestrial phenomenon due to 'pollution' or other human activities. Others doubted that additional carbon dioxide releases would lead to a build-up of the gas in the atmosphere since the great majority of carbon is in soils, trees and the oceans, so sea creatures and plants might simply sequester more carbon. And even if the scientific community was correct about the build-up of carbon dioxide in the atmosphere, it was fiendishly difficult to work out what the implications of this would be: it was unclear how much warming might result and how the impacts would be distributed across regions and continents.

Policy responses in the 1980s were generally limited, with most politicians responding to the warnings from the scientific and NGO communities with calls for more research. One significant outcome of this support for research was the setting up in 1988 of a new form of scientific organization, the Intergovernmental Panel on Climate Change (IPCC) under the aegis of the World Meteorological Organization and the United Nations Environment Program. The aim of the IPCC was to collect together the leading figures in all aspects of climate change with a view to establishing in an authoritative way the nature and scale of the problem and to identify candidate policy responses. This initiative was accorded substantial political authority and was novel in significant ways. Among its innovations were the explicit inclusion of social and economic analyses, alongside the atmospheric science, and the involvement of governmental representatives in the agreeing and authoring of report summaries: 'While by no means the first to involve scientists in an advisory role at the international level, the IPCC process has been the most extensive and influential effort so far' (Boehmer-Christiansen, 1994b: 195).

As is widely known, the IPCC has met with enormous success (the IPCC shared the 2007 Nobel Peace Prize with Gore), but also with determined criticism. At one end there have been scholars and moderate critics who have concerns about the danger that IPCC procedures tend to marginalize dissenting voices and that particular policy proposals (such as the IPCC-supported Kyoto Protocol) may not be as wise or as cost-effective as proponents suggest (see for example Prins and Rayner, 2007 and, for a review, Boehmer-Christiansen, 2003). There are also very many consultants backed by the fossil-fuel industry who are employed to throw doubt on claims about climate change (Freudenburg, 2000 offers a discussion of the social construction of 'non-problems'); these claims-makers have entered into alliance with right-leaning politicians and commentators to combat particular regulatory moves as detailed by McCright and Dunlap (2000; 2003; see also Dunlap, Chapter 1 in Part I of this volume). Informal networks, often web-based, have been set up to allow 'climate change sceptics' to exchange information, and they have welcomed all manner of contributors, whether direct enemies of the Kyoto Protocol or more distant allies such as opponents of wind farms or conspiracy theorists who see climate change warnings as the machinations of the nuclear industry.

Gifted cultural players, including Rush Limbaugh and the late Michael Crichton, waded into this controversy too, with Crichton's 2004 novel *State of Fear* having a technical appendix and an author's message on the errors in climate science. In his book Crichton even went so far as to offer his own estimate of the rate of global warming (0.812436 degrees for the warming over the next century; 2004: 677). Crichton and others have concentrated not only on the scientific conclusions (and their disagreements with them) but have looked at putative explanations for the persistence of error in 'establishment' science and much of the media, which I shall return to shortly. At the same time, mainstream environmental NGOs have tended to argue simply that one should take the scientists' word for the reality of climate change, a strategy about which they have clearly been less enthusiastic in other cases (Yearley, 1993: 68–9).

The rhetorical difficulties of doing this were already foreshadowed in the strategy of Friends of the Earth (FoE) in London nearly 20 years ago; campaign staff working on climate change issues were disturbed by a programme aired on the UK's Channel 4 television in the 'Equinox' series in 1990, and subsequently broadcast in other countries, that sought to question the scientific evidence for greenhouse warming. The programme even implied that scientists might be attracted to make extreme and sensational claims about the urgency of the problem in order to maximize their chances of receiving research funding. The programme was criticized in the 'campaign news' section of the FoE magazine, *Earth Matters*. An unfavourable comparison was drawn between the sceptical views expressed in the programme and the conclusions of the IPCC, with whose scientific analysis FoE was generally in agreement. FoE's article invoked the weight of 'over 300 scientists [who] prepared the IPCC's Science Report compared to about a dozen who were interviewed for Equinox'.[2] When apparently well-credentialled scientists are seen to disagree, it is very difficult for environmentalists to take the line that they are simply in the right. It seems like a reasonable alternative to invoke the power of the majority. But, of course, this remedy cannot always be adopted since in many areas where environmentalists believe themselves to be factually correct (as over GMOs, see below), they have been in the scientific minority, at least initially. In March 2007, UK's Channel 4 repeated this attention-seeking strategy, broadcasting a programme unambiguously entitled *The Great Global Warming Swindle*. The argumentational response of NGOs and green commentators was essentially the same: we should trust the advice of the great majority of well-qualified scientists who accept the evidence of climate change. Environmental groups looked to invoke the possible vested interests of the critics in order to make sense of the programme makers' and contributors' continued scepticism. This argumentational strategy has also been adopted in street protests, where new groups such as Rising Tide invoke the power of peer-reviewed science in their campaigns against airport expansions and coal-fired power stations.

In the relationship between the IPCC – indeed the whole climate change regulation community – and its critics, not only the science but the various ways in which the science is legitimated have come under attack (see Lahsen, 2005). Critics have been quick to point to the supposed vested interests of this community. Its access to money depends on the severity of the potential harms that it warns about; hence – or so it is argued – it inevitably has a structural temptation to exaggerate those harms. As it was working in such a multidisciplinary area and with high stakes attached to its policy proposals, the IPCC attempted to extend its network widely enough so as to include all the relevant scientific authorities; it was important that the IPCC should not be dominated by, say, meteorologists alone or by atmospheric chemists. But this meant that the IPCC ran into problems with peer reviewing and perceived impartiality: there were virtually no 'peers' who were not already within the IPCC. Conventional peer reviewing relies on there being few authors and many (more or less disinterested) peers; the IPCC effectively reversed this situation. When just one chapter in the 2001 *Third Assessment Report* has ten lead authors and over 140 contributing authors,[3] then it is clear that this departs from the standard notions of scientific quality control.

The IPCC is alert to this problem and has introduced various innovations in the way that refereeing and peer review are organized. Nonetheless, in public the IPCC tends to respond to challenges using the classic script of 'science for policy' (Yearley, 2005: 160–62); the IPCC legitimates itself in terms of the scientific objectivity and impartiality of its members. But critics were able to point out that the scientific careers of the whole climate change 'orthodoxy' depend on the correctness of the underlying assumptions. Moreover, the IPCC itself selects who is in the club of the qualified experts and thus threatened to be a self-perpetuating elite community (this line of attack is described in Boehmer-Christiansen, 1994b: 198). This was exactly the point that Crichton picked up. Many of his speeches and articles are available on his website, alongside a very specific demand that the work not be reproduced. Therefore, without quoting him, his principal argument is that the key requirements are a form of independent verification for claims about climate change and the guarantee of access to unbiased information.

However well (or tendentiously) meant, this is clearly an unrealistic demand since there is no one with scientific skills in this area who could plausibly claim to be entirely disinterested. There is no Archimedean point to which to retreat and environmental groups will correctly claim that such demands for a review are primarily ways to post-pone taking action. Crichton further muddies the water by proposing to offer his own estimate of future climate change to six decimal places. Although his ridiculous precision clearly signals some jocular intent, the idea that even he (a medic turned popular author) can offer a temperature-change forecast implies that there are lots of people in a position to make independent judgements in this matter. By contrast, there are rather few, and a central challenge for campaigners, the serious media, scientists themselves and the public is to distinguish between those who can credibly comment and those who cannot. In the UK the BBC has publicly rehearsed its internal debates over how climate change is presented: until 2008 the topic was generally treated as in need of 'balance' with adherents of 'pro' and 'anti' views frequently paired. Increasingly, the topic is treated as decisively concluded.

Although they have found it hard to participate in the central scientific debate and have been obliged to take up the (for them) unusual position of defending the correctness of mainstream science, environmental action groups have found other activities that they have been able to pursue. For example, in the USA they were active under the Republican Administration that dominated the first decade of the twenty-first century in trying to identify novel ways to press the government to change its position on climate change aside from simply bolstering the persuasiveness of climate science and seeking to rebut the claims of critics such as Crichton. Thus in 2006 the Center for Biological Diversity (CBD), the Natural Resources Defense Council and Greenpeace learned that their inventive use of the Endangered Species Act to sue the US government for protection of polar bears and their habitat in Alaska had won concessions from the government. In its campaigning, the CBD had argued that oil exploration in the far north would harm polar bears and their hunting grounds; but they also suggested that ice melting caused by global warming was responsible for additional habitat loss and harms to bears, who need large expanses of solid ice in spring for successful hunting.[4] Potentially the Endangered Species legislation could force the government to examine the impact on polar bears of all actions in the USA (such as energy policy), not just activities local to polar-bear habitat. By early 2009 the new Obama Administration had encouraged a review of policy on this issue, and in April of the same year the Environmental Protection Agency (EPA) announced that CO_2 emissions would henceforth be treated as hazardous air pollution under the Clean Air Act.[5] Nonetheless, the full polar-bear gambit was resisted, and George W. Bush's controversial decision to prohibit the relevant federal bodies from considering whether practices outside the polar bear's territory are affecting its chances for survival was retained.

In the case of climate change, environmental NGOs have been stuck in a dilemma. What they see as the world's leading environmental problem is fully endorsed by the mainstream scientific community. Indeed, in January 2004 the then UK government's chief scientific adviser Sir David King gave his judgement that climate change posed a greater threat than terrorism.[6] Their principal efforts have accordingly been directed at restating and emphasizing official findings, finding novel ways to publicize the message and to counter the claims of greenhouse-sceptics. The difficult part of the dilemma is that such statements in favour of the objectivity of the scientific establishment's views mean that it is harder to distance themselves from scientists' conclusions on other occasions without appearing arbitrary or tendentious.

To summarize this section, the science of global climate change has manifested several unprecedented and fascinating features. First, a novel form of organization – the IPCC – has been created to try to synthesize all the disciplinary perspectives on this enormously complex topic. But critics have focused not only on their disagreements with particular assertions of the IPCC researchers, but also on supposed weaknesses in the IPCC system itself. NGOs and environmental campaigners have found themselves in the unusual position of defending the objectivity of scientists' published findings, of speaking up for peer review, and of countering the IPCC's critics, while – at the same time – urging governments to go much faster in responding to the IPCC's scenarios and policy prescriptions.

Genetic modification and GM plants and foods

The case of genetically modified (or genetically engineered) organisms was just the opposite of climate change in the sense that environmental groups were, at the height of the campaign, out of line with the views of the scientific establishment. The dynamics of the issue were accordingly very different. In this instance the principal issues concerned safety and safety-testing. Here was a new product, whether GM crop, animal or bacterium, that needed to be assessed for its implications for consumers and the natural environment.

Of course, all major industrialized countries had some established procedures for the safety-testing of new foodstuffs. But the leading question was how novel GM products were taken to be. For some, the potential for the GM entity to reproduce itself or to cross with living relatives in unpredictable ways suggested that this was an unprecedented form of innovation that needed unprecedented forms of caution and regulatory care. On the other hand, industry representatives and many scientists and commentators claimed that it was far from unprecedented. People had been introducing agricultural innovations for millennia by crossing animals, allowing 'sports' to flourish and so on. Modern (though conventional) plant breeding already used extraordinary chemical and physical procedures – including radiation treatment – to stimulate mutations that might be beneficial. On this view, regulatory agencies and agricultural systems were already well prepared for handling innovations in living, reproductive entities. And, as Jasanoff points out (2005: 49) the ground for the regulatory battle was prepared to a large degree in the USA, where the courts had endorsed the regulators' decision that it was products (particular foods or seeds and so on) and not processes (the business of genetic modification) that should be the heart of the test (see also Kloppenburg, 2004: 132–40).

GM crops were first certified in the USA, where they passed tests set by the Department of Agriculture, the Food and Drug Administration and the Environmental Protection Agency. Although an early product, the Flavr Savr (*sic*) tomato found little acceptance on the market, success came with GM corn (maize), soy beans, various beets and canola (rape). Essentially, the typical GM versions of these crops offered two sorts of putative benefits: either the crops had a genetic resistance to a pest or they had a tolerance to a particular proprietary weedkiller. The potential advantages of the former are rather evident (even if there is a worry about pests acquiring resistance); the supposed benefits of the latter are more roundabout.[7] The idea is that weedkiller can be used at a later stage in the growing season since the crops are immune. Weeds can be killed off effectively with minimal spraying. Companies also benefit, of course, since farmers are obliged to buy the weedkillers that match the seeds and this may even extend the period of market protection beyond the expiry of patents.

European companies were not far behind their US counterparts in bringing these products to market, but European customers were far less accepting of the technology than those in North America. Two particular issues are of interest here: first, there is the question of why responses differed so much between European and North American polities. The other issue concerns the conflict between the competing regulatory logics available.

To begin with the latter, it is clear that European regulators tended to be more precautionary about this technology than US officials. But examination of the precautionary principle in practice indicates that the principle itself does not tell the regulator exactly how precautionary to be (Levidow, 2001; see also Marris et al., 2005). Arguments about the regulatory standard have simply switched to arguments about the meaning of precaution (see also Dratwa, 2002). Discordant interpretations of precautionarity have taken a more precise form in disputes over the standard known as 'substantial equivalence'. As Millstone et al. pointed out in a contribution to *Nature* (1999), in order to decide how to test the safety of GM food, one needs to make some starting assumptions. Precisely because GM crops are – by definition – different from existing crops at the molecular level, one needs to decide at what level one will begin to test for any differences that might give cause for concern or even rule out the new croptechnology. According to Millstone et al.:

> The biotechnology companies wanted government regulators to help persuade consumers that their products were safe, yet they also wanted the regulatory hurdles to be set as low as possible. Governments wanted an approach to the regulation of GM foods that could be agreed internationally, and that would not inhibit the development of their domestic biotechnology companies. The FAO/WHO [UN Food and Agriculture Organization/World Health Organization] committee recommended, therefore, that GM foods should be treated by analogy with their non-GM antecedents, and evaluated primarily by comparing their *compositional data* with those from their natural antecedents, so that they could be presumed to be similarly acceptable. Only if there were glaring and important compositional differences might it be appropriate to require further tests, to be decided on a case-by-case basis. (1999: 525; italics added)

Regulators and industry agreed on a criterion of substantial equivalence as the means for implementing such comparisons.

By this standard, if GM foods are compositionally equivalent to existing foodstuffs, they are taken to be substantially equivalent in regard to consumer safety. Thus GM soy beans have been accepted for consumption after they passed tests focusing on a 'restricted set of compositional variables' (1999: 526). However, as Millstone et al. argue, with just as much justification, regulators could have chosen to view GM foodstuffs as novel chemical compounds coming into people's diets. Before new food additives and other such innovative ingredients are accepted, they are subject to extensive toxicological testing. These test results are then used very conservatively to set limits for 'acceptable daily intake' (ADI) levels. Of course, with GM staples (grains and so on), the small amounts that would be able to cross the ADI threshold would be commercially insufficient. But safety concerns would be strongly addressed. These authors' point is not that GM foods should be treated as food additives or pharmaceuticals, but that the decision to introduce the substantial equivalence criterion is not itself based on scientific research. That decision is the basis on which subsequent research is done. For proponents of the technology, substantial equivalence is a straightforward and common-sense standard. But the standard conceals possible debate about what the relevant criteria for sameness are. As Millstone et al. point out, for other purposes the GM seed companies are keen to stress the distinctiveness of their products. GM material can be patented only because it is demonstrably novel. How then can one be sure that it is novel enough to merit patent protection but not so novel that differences beyond the level of substantial equivalence may not turn out to matter a decade or two into the future?

This issue was also at the heart of the UK's widely publicized 'Pusztai affair'. Pusztai was employed as a research scientist at a largely government-funded research establishment near Aberdeen in Scotland and was part of a team examining ways of testing the food safety of GM crops. He and others were concerned that compositionally similar foodstuffs might not have the same nutritional or food-safety implications. The experiments for which he became notorious were conducted on lab rats, to whom he fed three kinds of potato: regular potatoes, non-GM potatoes with a lectin from snowdrops added; and potatoes genetically modified to express the snowdrop lectin. Lectins are a family of proteins, some of which are of interest for their possible insecticidal value; it is also known that some lectins (for example those in ordinary red kidney beans) can cause problems when eaten. His results suggested that the rats fared worse in terms of their uptake of nutrition on the GM lectin-producing potatoes than on the other samples, possibly implying that it was not the lectins that were causing the problem but some aspect of the business of genetic modification itself.

As Eriksson (2004) has detailed, this controversy unravelled in a surprising way. Pusztai announced his results in a reputable UK television programme in 1998, apparently intending not to argue against GM *per se* but to assert that more sophisticated forms of testing would be needed to address safety concerns fully – exactly the kinds of testing that he and colleagues might have been able to perform. But the headline message that came over was that GM foods might cause health problems when eaten. In a muddled and confusing way, Pusztai's conclusions came to be criticized by his own institute and he was ushered into retirement. The ensuing controversy and hasty exercise in news management signally failed to concentrate on his findings and the details of his experimental design. Instead people lined up around the conduct of the controversy itself, either championing Pusztai as a whistle-blowing researcher who was unjustly disciplined by his bosses for publicizing inconvenient findings, or dismissing him as a sloppy scientist who rushed into the public gaze with results that were unchecked and unrefereed. On the face of it, it is a curious sociological phenomenon that such important studies have barely been repeated, even if the 'Pusztai affair' lives on within the wider debate and on line.

Procedural errors by the manufacturers and suppliers have also attracted a great deal of attention. No matter how emphatic the assurances have been that the new plant technologies are well tested and well regulated, there has been a series of problems that indicate how hard it is to exercise comprehensive control over seeds and genes. Corn (maize) approved only for animal rations ended up in human foodstuffs, for example, while traits engineered into plants arose in wild relatives. The key analytical point here is that these difficulties continue to throw up problems of what is to count as a reasonable test in such open-ended and far from comprehensively understood contexts. Moreover, such difficulties pose interesting challenges for one popular governmental and commercial strategy for managing the horrors of GMOs: the idea that there should be labelling and strict traceability. But of course any reassurance from labelling and traceability relies on the adequacy of routine methods for identifying, tracing and containing the technology and all of these points have been disputed (see Klintman, 2002; Lezaun, 2006).

The second major question to be raised by this environmental controversy has been the precise reasons for public resistance and consumer anxiety.[8] Actors within the controversy have clearly faced the same question but they have tended to answer in asymmetrical ways. Proponents of the technology tend to blame public anxieties on scare tactics and protectionism, while its opponents see corporate greed combated by the perspicacity of the public. Adopting a more symmetrical approach, one can point to three principal factors. First, Europeans were being offered this new food technology in the wake of the BSE (bovine spongiform encephalopathy) or 'mad-cow' controversy. The changes in the food-processing procedures that are now thought to have created the conditions for the release and spread of the mad-cow prions had been pronounced safe by the same regulatory authorities as were now offering assurance about GMOs. Particularly in the UK, the government initially insisted that the best scientific advice was that there was no danger to human beings from the affected beef; subsequently in 1996 they announced a sudden change of mind. Thus the fact that GMOs were being pronounced safe by the regulatory authorities and by governmental advisers could easily be shrugged off and viewed with distrust. Events such as the Pusztai affair were drawn on to intensify this feeling that the scientific establishment was not to be trusted. Moreover, the average consumer saw little benefit in the new crops, which were intended to boost production and – perhaps – lessen agrochemical use. In the absence of persuasive and comprehensive assurance, there was also a question about how ordinary citizens made dietary decisions and carried on their lives (see also Tulloch and Lupton, 2003). In the UK, for example, the reputable supermarkets moved to institutionalize the reassurance that governmental agencies failed to provide (see Yearley, 2005: 171–4). Jasanoff (1997) had noted a similar response by major UK food retailers in the case of BSE.

Another explanatory factor resulted from the fact that the European landscape is decisively shaped by centuries of agricultural practice. Natural heritage and farming are inseparable. Thus there was concern from environmentalists, and even from official nature-protection bodies and from countryside groups, about the effect of this new technology on wildlife. Campaign organizations tended to allow these first two considerations to merge into each other with – for example – Greenpeace activists turning up to sabotage trial-planting sites in the UK dressed in protective suits (Yearley, 2005: 173–4), as though mere contact with GM plant stems and leaves might be injurious. Particularly in France, this concern with safeguarding the countryside was allied to a third explanatory issue: a desire to protect traditional rural lifestyles in the face of the perceived threats of globalization and economic liberalization. These new technologies were viewed as further evidence of US attempts to penetrate and reshape the European agricultural market and to 'McDonaldize' European culture.

This last point came to be reflected in the unfolding trade conflict over GM foods and seeds. In 2003 the USA, Canada and Argentina filed a complaint at the World Trade Organization (WTO) against the EU over alleged EU trade restrictions on GM food and agricultural products. The environmental and health impacts of genetically modified organisms (GMOs) had been debated for around a decade at this stage. US companies and politicians urged that European resistance to GM imports should be overruled by the WTO, arguing that there was no scientific evidence of harm arising from GM food and crops, since these products had all passed proper regulatory hurdles in the US system and, more importantly, the corresponding regulations inside the EU too.

European environmental and consumer advocates argued, by contrast, that the US-style testing had not been precautionary enough and that proper scientific tests would require much more time and more diverse examinations than had been applied in routine US trials and in their EU counterparts.

The distinctive difficulty in this case is that, by and large, the official expert scientific communities on opposing sides were taking diametrically opposing views. In the USA, the conceptualization of the issue was primarily this: all products have potential associated risks and the art of the policy-maker is to ensure that an adequate assessment of risk and of benefits is made. European analysts were more inclined to argue that the very risk framework itself left something to be desired since the calculation of risk necessarily implies that risks can be quantified and agreed (see Winickoff et al., 2005). In the case of GM crops, so the argument went, there was as yet no way of establishing the full range of possible risks, including risks to environmental quality or to biodiversity, so no 'scientific' risk assessment could be completed.

Within their separate jurisdictions, each of these opposing views could be sensibly and more or less consistently maintained. In the USA, the new technology was widely adopted and within the EU it was broadly resisted. However, the differing views appear to be tantamount to incommensurable 'paradigms' for assessing the safety and suitability of GM crops. And the key difficulty was that there is no higher level of scientific rationality or expertise to which appeal could be made to say which approach is correct. The WTO does not have its own *corps* of 'super-scientists' to resolve such issues. On the contrary, the WTO introduces no new empirical evidence but assesses the arguments in a judicial manner.

Observers of the WTO considered that its dispute settlement procedures, although supposedly neutral and merely concerned with legal and administrative matters, tacitly favoured the US paradigm since the WTO's approach to safety standards emphasizes the role of scientific proofs of safety and, in past rulings, 'scientific' had commonly been equated with US-style risk assessment (see Busch et al., 2004). This case, which broadly favoured the US point of view, may thus not only have affected policy towards GMOs but set a highly significant precedent for how disputed scientific views are handled before the WTO.

The final way in which the GM case has been of great sociological interest is because of the willingness of governments, particularly in Europe but also for example in New Zealand, to initiate various public consultations over the introduction of the technology (Walls et al., 2005). In this case a key consideration in Europe and the Antipodes was the explicit attempt to combat public disquiet by being seen apparently to listen to the public. However, Horlick-Jones et al. (2004) – who carried out an external assessment of the UK 'GM Nation' exercise that ran alongside the exercise itself – pointed out that it was difficult to get an 'authentic' consultation since participants were self-selecting and the process was shaped by its instigators, not by the participants. On a smaller scale, Harvey (2009) undertook a participant observation study of a subset of the GM Nation groups. He not only confirmed that participants seemed unclear about their relation to policy-making over GMOs; he also focused on participants' experience of the exercise and on the kinds of topics they opted to talk about. He noted that the discussion often turned on scientific information. Given a more or less free rein, he observed, participants chose to argue about such issues as safe planting distances, the impact of GM crops on beneficial insects and so on, and were thus caught in endless and frustrating debates that they were typically unable to resolve in the context of the meetings.

In the UK, alongside the GM Nation exercise, the government also held a series of farm-scale trials – conducted on volunteered farmland – to test the environmental and practical implications of the new technology. Initially these trials were treated by anti-GM campaigners as bogus; they were thought to have been set up so as to more or less guarantee success. Accordingly Greenpeace and other groups attempted to disrupt the trials (see Yearley, 2005: 173–4). But by 2005, when the trial results finally came to be announced, it was reported that GM cultivation had demonstrated a negative effect on wildlife in some cases. It was not that the GM material itself was harmful but that the weedkilling was so effective that wildlife was deprived of weeds, seeds and other food.

Overall, therefore, the GM controversy, though it ran in parallel with the climate debate, had a strongly contrasting character. It saw environmental campaigners once again take their claims outside the law; some were jailed for damaging property. Environmental groups were at odds with the majority of established scientists and there was widespread sabotage of what were designed to be 'experimental tests'. The merits of peer review were seldom trumpeted in this case. But although the GM controversy in many ways resembled the kind of environmental activism of earlier decades, there are reasons to think that the pattern will persist. For one thing, although GM crops have suffered a major setback in Europe and a few other countries (including ones that sell chiefly to Europe), the push for GM agriculture has not abated. The Chinese authorities are facing the dilemma of whether to allow GM rice and their decision will be particularly significant, both because of the size of the market affected and because this will become the first GM staple food. As food security and the possibility of widespread growing of crops for fuel rise up the policy agenda in this century, the pressure to introduce GM and related innovations in agriculture will intensify. Furthermore, exactly the same 'logic' as in the case of GM crops surrounds the more high-tech areas of nanotechnology[9] and synthetic biology. In both instances the chief question is: how does one guarantee the safety of novel and unprecedented materials? As the GMO case amply illustrated, there is likely to be no agreed answer to this deep question.

Conclusion

As we saw at the outset, there is now widespread acceptance that scientific evidence and reasoning lie at the heart of environmental decision-making. Governments, companies and NGOs dedicate immense resources to developing their positions around such evidence. But in the most contentious cases that have characterized early twenty-first-century environmental policy, the links between scientific evidence and environmental options are far from unanimously agreed. Climate change 'sceptics' continue to propagate their views in face of scientific and NGO opinion, while European NGOs – so taken with scientific proof in the case of global warming – seem to resist establishment scientific opinion over GMOs. In charting their way through these complex issues, the main 'players' have become very sophisticated about mounting and defending arguments over science, contesting not just the data and the theories but adopting stances on experimental protocols, peer review, scientific judgement and the minutiae of scientific practice.

But equally, it is clear that the chief issues are not argued out exclusively over science – even if they cannot but feature scientific claims. Science alone cannot resolve these questions. Scientific research cannot tell one how precautionary to be or to what extent 'natural' genomes should be manipulated through radiation treatment or gene insertion. Indeed, the situation is even more complex than this implies, since scientific arguments are themselves often framed within broader judgements. Thus, as we saw above, the key question of substantial equivalence between GM crop products and non-GM ones became the *basis* for scientific comparisons but could not itself be 'proven' in scientific terms. Similar issues arise (for example over how clouds are to be analysed) in the modelling on which much climate science depends. Provisional agreements over such matters are the starting points for scientific work, not the outcome of scientific deduction.

Given the role of extra-scientific considerations in assessing environmental topics and given that scientific procedures themselves may depend on agreements over principles such as substantial equivalence – given, in other words, that there are pivotal questions that cannot be answered in technical terms alone – methods of public engagement will likely continue to be an important resource for making environmental decisions. Done badly, such exercises can promote public distrust and unease. But done well, they may help to generate enduring agreements over critical matters that cannot be answered in scientific or technical terms alone. It seems likely, for example, that current proposals to increase the use of nano-materials and radical initiatives to combat climate change through so-called 'geo-engineering' (adding materials to the atmosphere to reflect sunlight or spreading fertilizers in the seas to promote plants that sequester carbon) will both benefit from innovative and sensitive public-engagement exercises.

Finally, the evidence of the close ties between scientific knowledge and the strategies of environmental groups provided in this chapter has clear implications for the way that sociologists conceive of such organizations. Sociologists are still very inclined to treat such organizations as though the choice were to conceptualize them either as bottom-up social movements or as lobby organizations (see the systematic and well-documented material in Markham, 2008). But there is an additional dimension: environmental organizations have to develop an approach to science too, and this is often the characteristic that sets them apart from other kinds of movement and lobby organizations. The sociology of the environment cannot but also be a sociology of science.

Notes

1. Out of a sense of fairness, I should also – very briefly – clarify what His Holiness actually said and highlight the differences between his text and the *Mail*'s account. The Pope was warning about putting environmental objectives ahead of spiritual/ethical ones; he did not use the term 'dogma' or even speak of science in general. Furthermore, only a few weeks previously it had been reported that 'Vatican City has become the first fully carbon-neutral state in the world, after announcing it is offsetting its carbon footprint by planting a forest in Hungary and installing solar panels on the roof of St Peter's Basilica in Rome', *The Independent*, 22 September 2007.
2. There was no author given for this report in *Earth Matters*, Autumn/Winter 1990: 4.
3. My example is chapter 2, 'Observed climate variability and change'.
4. According to the CBD website: '"Short of sending Dick Cheney to Alaska to personally club polar bear cubs to death, the administration could not have come up with a more environmentally destructive plan for endangered marine mammals", said Brendan Cummings, ocean program director of the Center. "Yet the administration did not even analyze, much less attempt to avoid, the impacts of oil development on endangered wildlife".' See http://www.biologicaldiversity.org/swcbd/press/off-shore-oil-07-02-2007.html, accessed 15 May 2009.
5. See the coverage in the *New York Times* (18 April 2009, p. A15).
6. 'US Climate Policy Bigger Threat to World than Terrorism' was the headline in the UK newspaper *The Independent* (9 January 2004).

7.   Such resistance can arise without genetic modification (e.g. 'naturally' pesticide-resistant crop strains are in use in Australia), although this is held to be usually a multi-gene characteristic and thus possibly not identical to GM pesticide resistance.
8.   Some analysts sought to identify actors' positions not in order to explain them but to try to get them to agree on 'least-worst' ways forward: see Stirling and Mayer (1999) and, for comment, Yearley (2001).
9.   On environmental movements and nanotechnology, see Kousis, Chapter 15 in this volume.

References

Boehmer-Christiansen, Sonja (1994a), 'Global climate protection policy: the limits of scientific advice, Part 1', *Global Environmental Change*, **4**: 140–59.
Boehmer-Christiansen, Sonja (1994b), 'Global climate protection policy: the limits of scientific advice, Part 2', *Global Environmental Change*, **4**: 185–200.
Boehmer-Christiansen, Sonja (2003), 'Science, equity, and the war against carbon', *Science, Technology and Human Values*, **28**: 69–92.
Busch, Lawrence, Robin Grove-White, Sheila Jasanoff, David Winickoff and Brian Wynne (2004), Amicus Curiae Brief Submitted to the Dispute Settlement Panel of the World Trade Organization in the Case of 'EC: Measures Affecting the Approval and Marketing of Biotech Products', 30 April.
Crichton, Michael (2004), *State of Fear*, London: HarperCollins.
Dratwa, Jim (2002), 'Taking risks with the precautionary principle: food (and the environment) for thought at the European Commission', *Journal of Environmental Policy and Planning*, **4**: 197–213.
Edwards, Paul N. (2000), 'The world in a machine: origins and impacts of early computerized global systems models', in Agatha C. Hughes and Thomas P. Hughes (eds), *Systems, Experts, and Computers: The Systems Approach in Management and Engineering, World War II and After*, Cambridge, MA: MIT Press, pp. 221–54.
Edwards, Paul N. (2001), 'Representing the global atmosphere: computer models, data, and knowledge about climate change,' in Clark A. Miller and Paul N. Edwards (eds), *Changing the Atmosphere: Expert Knowledge and Environmental Governance*, Cambridge, MA: MIT Press, pp. 31–65.
Eriksson, Lena (2004), *From Persona to Person: The Unfolding of an (Un)Scientific Controversy*, Cardiff University, PhD thesis.
Freudenburg, William R. (2000), 'Social constructions and social constrictions: toward analyzing the social construction of "the naturalized" as well as "the natural"', in Gert Spaargaren, Arthur P. J. Mol and Frederick H. Buttel (eds), *Environment and Global Modernity*, London: Sage, pp. 103–19.
Harvey, Matthew (2009), 'Drama, talk, and emotion: omitted aspects of public participation' *Science, Technology, & Human Values*, **34** (1): 139–61.
Horlick-Jones, Tom, John Walls, Gene Rowe, N.F. Pidgeon, W. Poortinga and Tim O'Riordan (2004), 'A deliberative future? An independent evaluation of the *GM Nation?* Public debate about the possible commercialization of transgenic crops in the UK, 2003', Understanding Risk Working Paper 04-02, Norwich, UK: Centre for Environmental Risk.
Jasanoff, Sheila (1997), 'Civilization and madness: the great BSE scare of 1996', *Public Understanding of Science*, **6**: 221–32.
Jasanoff, Sheila (2005), *Designs on Nature*, Princeton, NJ: Princeton University Press.
Klintman, Mikael (2002), 'The genetically modified food labelling controversy', *Social Studies of Science*, **32** (1): 71–92.
Kloppenburg, Jack Ralph (2004), *First the Seed: the Political Economy of Plant Biotechnology*, 2nd edn, Madison, WI: University of Wisconsin Press.
Lahsen, Myanna (2005), 'Technocracy, democracy and US climate politics: the need for demarcations', *Science, Technology, & Human Values*, **30** (1): 137–69.
Levidow, Les (2001), 'Precautionary uncertainty: regulating GM crops in Europe', *Social Studies of Science*, **31**: 845–78.
Lezaun, Javier (2006), 'Creating a new object of government: making genetically modified organisms traceable', *Social Studies of Science*, **36**: 499–531.
McCright, Aaron M. and Riley E. Dunlap (2000), 'Challenging global warming as a social problem: an analysis of the conservative movement's counter-claims', *Social Problems*, **47**: 499–522.
McCright, Aaron M. and Riley E. Dunlap (2003), 'Defeating Kyoto: the conservative movement's impact on US climate change policy', *Social Problems*, **50**: 348–73.
Markham, William T. (2008), *Environmental Organizations in Modern Germany: Hardy Survivors in the Twentieth Century and Beyond*, Oxford: Berghahn.
Marris, Claire, Pierre-Benoit Joly, Stéphanie Ronda and Christophe Bonneuil (2005), 'How the French GM controversy led to the reciprocal emancipation of scientific expertise and policy making', *Science and Public Policy*, **32** (4): 301–8.

Millstone, Erik, Eric Brunner and Sue Mayer (1999), 'Beyond "substantial equivalence"', *Nature*, **401**: 525–6.

Pearce, Fred (1991), *Green Warriors: the People and the Politics Behind the Environmental Revolution*, London: Bodley Head.

Prins, Gwyn and Steve Rayner (2007), 'Time to ditch Kyoto', *Nature*, **449** (25): 973–5.

Stirling, Andy and Sue Mayer (1999), *Re-Thinking Risk: A Pilot Multi-Criteria Mapping of a Genetically Modified Crop in Agricultural Systems in the UK*, Brighton, Sussex: Science Policy Research Unit.

Winickoff, David, Sheila Jasanoff, Lawrence Busch, Robin Grove-White and Brian Wynne (2005), 'Adjudicating the GM food wars: science, risk and democracy in world trade law', *Yale Journal of International Law*, **30**: 81–123.

Tulloch, John and Deborah Lupton (2003), *Risk and Everyday Life*, London: Sage.

Walls, John, Tee Rogers-Hayden, Alison Mohr and Tim O'Riordan (2005), 'Seeking citizens' views on GM crops: experiences from the United Kingdom, Australia, and New Zealand', *Environment*, **47** (7): 22–36.

Yearley, Steven (1993), 'Standing in for nature: the practicalities of environmental organisations' use of science', in Kay Milton (ed.), *Environmentalism: the View from Anthropology*, London: Routledge, pp. 59–72.

Yearley, Steven (2001), 'Mapping and interpreting societal responses to genetically modified food and plants – essay review', *Social Studies of Science*, **31**: 151–60.

Yearley, Steven (2005), *Cultures of Environmentalism: Empirical Studies in Environmental Sociology*, Basingstoke, UK: Palgrave Macmillan.

15 New challenges for twenty-first-century environmental movements: agricultural biotechnology and nanotechnology

Maria Kousis[1]

Introduction

In the past 30 years, the application of new biotechnologies, especially those related to agricultural production and food, have led to sustained concerns and mobilizations by very diverse groups and networks, most of which are linked to environmental movements across the globe. Recent breakthroughs in nanotechnology have now led to new products entering the market that have raised some concerns. Sustainability, therefore, is no longer only a matter of protecting environmental resources, but increasingly involves engineering new environments (Redclift, 2001) that give rise to contested discourses.

A new biological frontier of civil society enters the twenty-first century, as the technologies that had been developed to exploit natural resources are increasingly giving way to technologies altering the nature of biotic resources[2] and transforming environments (Redclift, 1987: 17 and 2006: 130). New social movements are part of this frontier. According to Charles Tilly (2004: 97–8), social movements in the early twenty-first century are marked by significant changes compared to those in the twentieth. They are more internationally organized, in terms of activists, non-governmental organizations (NGOs) and visible targets (e.g. multinational corporations and international financial institutions), while they have integrated new technologies into their organizing and claim-making performances. Tilly (2004: 153–7) proposes four 'scenarios' for future routes in social movements (SMs) during the remaining part of the twenty-first century, focusing on internationalization, democracy, professionalization and triumph. First, he envisages a slower, less extensive and less complete net shift away from local, regional and national SMs towards more international and global configurations that is likely to continue for decades. Second, he argues that some democratic decline will take place in major existing democracies but substantial democratization is expected in such undemocratic countries as China. A decline of democracy is likely to depress different types of large-scale SMs, but could allow enclaves of local and regional SM activity where democratic institutions persist. Third, he suggests that professional SM entrepreneurs, NGOs and links with authorities will increasingly dominate in large-scale SMs while at the same time abandoning portions of local and regional claim-making that they cannot co-opt into international activism. Finally, he views as exceedingly unlikely the possibility of SM triumph as envisaged in the ultimate aims of SMs.

Are the organized oppositions to agricultural biotechnology and the recently developing concerns about nanotechnologies part of the environmental movements? In what ways are they challenges for twenty-first century environmental movements? Do they introduce new issues to the environmental movement? This chapter aims to address these issues on the basis of related works and to point out future directions for SM research.

Defining environmental movements and their opportunity structures

Tilly (1994: 7, 18) defines social movements as sustained challenges to power-holders in the name of interested populations, which appear in the form of professional movements, *ad hoc* community-based, or specialized movements, and communitarian, unspecialized movements, that give rise to a new community.[3] Tilly's classification is similar to those on environmental movements offered by environmental sociologists (Humphrey and Buttel, 1982; Gould et al., 1996; Dunlap and Mertig, 1991; Jamison, 2001; Schlosberg and Bomberg, 2008). Their views converge on three basic forms of the environmental movement: formal environmental movement organizations; grassroots, community-linked groups; and radical, highly committed ecological groups. Movement participants, whether they take direct or indirect action, in general call for power-holders to take crucial measures to address their claim and redress the situation (Tilly, 1994). Professional environmental organizations, to which millions of supporters are merely donors, may have a longer history than the other two types, but diverge from the expected appearance of social movement organizations, given the bureaucratic organization and lobbying strategies visible in conservation and preservation associations.

Students of social movements need to distinguish between the basis and the campaign of a social movement. The bases of social movements range from movement organizations, networks, participants to accumulated cultural artefacts, memories and traditions. A movement campaign involves a sustained public and collective challenge to those in power in the name of a population living under those in power (Tilly and Tarrow, 2006: 192).

The importance of integrating new technologies into social movements' organizing and claim-making performances has recently been pointed out (Tilly, 2004). The Internet has become an important tool that activist organizations and networks recognize and use to promote their aims at the global level (Smith and Fetner, 2007).

Transnational networks, cooperations and strategies have emerged as a response to a growing need to face global problems, and may take a wide variety of forms. Environmental NGOs at the international level undertake lobbying, or educational and administrative activities. Since the 1980s, these NGO activities are reflected in processes, strategic interactions and their transformative effects (Princen and Finger, 1994; Young, 1999). Transnational associations cultivate group identities beyond national states (Smith and Fetner, 2007), encouraging people, for example, to emphasize their political views (such as GMO-free Balkans by Balkan Network) over political nationalities. Transnational mobilizing structures play an increasingly important role in the global political system (Tilly, 2004; Tarrow, 2005; Smith and Fetner, 2007). Studies have been increasingly focusing on transnational environmental NGO networks and advocacy coalitions at the global level (e.g. della Porta and Tarrow, 2005).

Recent case studies on participatory governance in the 'politics of life',[4] including those related to GM crops and food, point to three strategies of increasing importance (PAGANINI, 2007: 28). First, public participation by diverse groups of actors has been taking place in the polity process through formal or informal means. Second, scientific research has been moving away from a closed, technocratic discourse towards one enabling participation. Finally, discourses about ethics and emotions have made a significant appearance. Being more technocratic and elitist structures, ethics committees are not directly linked with social activism; nevertheless, they have facilitated opening up debates and making them visible to broader audiences. This also occurred with scientific advisory committees, which turned into forums for public participation, as in the UK food-safety case (PAGANINI, 2007; Gottweis et al., 2008).

Opportunities and constraints
Overall, the development of the environmental movement may be attributed to differences in political, economic and socio-historical cultures/contexts. For example, the 'stark contrast between the American Winner-take-all electoral system and West Germany's partially proportional system of representation probably accounts for the very different development histories of the American and West German environmental movements' (McAdam et al., 1996: 12). Key differences between the US and West German anti-nuclear movements are also attributed to the different national political contexts (ibid.: 18). Environmental movements are also influenced by new opportunities offered by European integration (see Carmin, Chapter 25 in Part III of this volume) or globalization processes. Environmental activists have pursued their goals through the European Court and the European Parliament, taking advantage of new opportunities in the form of emerging EU structures (Marks and McAdam, 1996), which shifted power away from the nation-state (Kousis and Eder, 2001; Kousis, 2001, 2004).

Since the 1980s, a more transnational environmentalism (Kiefer and Benjamin, 1993; Finger, 1992; Lewis, 2000) has been facing international opportunities and constraints in the form of neoliberal economic and sustainable development policies and practices. In the 1990s, international economic opportunities and constraints were increasingly reflected in the growing commercialization and privatization of R&D activities, as well as in an entrepreneurial approach to science and technology, especially in the USA and the EU (Jamison, 2001; Kousis, 2004).

At the same time, new opportunities and constraints have also been created for environmental activists and concerned publics in Eastern European and former Soviet Union countries, as well as China (see, e.g., Yanitsky, 1999; Rinkevicius, 2000; Ovcearenco, 2006; Ho et al., 2006).

The relationship between environmental movements and sustainable development or ecological modernization has been studied only since the mid 1990s, pointing to competing frames of sustainable development, which follow either economic development or modernization orientations on the one hand, or those of environmental and new social movement contenders on the other. Such studies also note the institutionalization and professionalization of the environmental movement (Kousis, 2004). The role of biotechnology and nanotechnologies has not yet been explored in the context of ecological modernization or sustainable development.

Environmental organizations not only adopt ecological modernization or sustainable development alternatives (van der Heijden, 1999; Brand, 1999) on the basis of their cultural identities.[5] They also mobilize their expertise and often compete to seize the economic opportunities offered in the wider context of international and national economic policies targeting sustainability objectives.[6] Following this opportunity spiral, new types of organizations are created at the same time,[7] which are more exclusively oriented to consulting activities and advising business firms (Kousis, 2004).[8]

Anti-GMO environmental movement(s) in the making

International commercial techno-science developing in the 1980s gave rise to GM products and prospects, with very different responses from social actors. Movement claims concern the relationship between nature and society, defining sustainability and sustainable livelihoods, the public accountability of science and redefining democracy in the era of neoliberal globalization (Brooks, 2005).

Movements opposing GMOs affected the biotechnology sector and its trajectory of technological change, contributing to an emerging shift towards re-regulation of the technology and the industry (Schurman and Kelso, 2003; Eaton, 2009). They pressured the EU as well as the USA to consider regulation seriously, imposed high economic costs on the industry and created new supranational regulatory regimes for GMOs. Such critiques and their impacts, however, should turn the attention of the anti-GMO movements to their relations with scientists concerning alternative scientific strategies for the future (Buttel, 2005).

What is the relationship between the environmental movement and the more recent, anti-GMO movements – as they are referred to in the related literature? Recent work offers new evidence on this relationship by placing anti-GMO activism in the wider context of contemporary, online environmental activism. Especially during the past decade or so, active and established environmental groups and organizations have been integrating new technologies in their organizational tactics through the construction and operation of websites. These online profiles of the wider environmental activist structures have recently been the focus of study.

In their encompassing and novel analysis of 161 grassroots, transnational and advocacy online environmental organizations, Ackland and O'Neil (2008) distinguish three 'thematic' groups. The most prominent is the 'environmental–global', with 92 sites on issues such as climate change, forest and wildlife preservation, nuclear weapons and sustainable trade. The second in frequency is the 'environmental–bio' group of 47 sites related primarily to genetic engineering/biotechnology, biopiracy, patenting, but also to organic farming issues. The third group, 'environmental–toxic', consists of 23 sites mainly addressing pollutants and issues of environmental justice (Ackland and O'Neil, 2008; O'Neil and Ackland, 2008).

Out of the 161 online environmental organizations and groups, almost half are US-based, about one-fifth originate in the UK, while the country of origin for the rest is spread across Northern and Southern countries. The environmental–bio group that has more recently entered the movement has a slight lead in nanotech content on its sites (Ackland and O'Neil 2008; O'Neil and Ackland, 2008).

The sections that follow aim to offer a general overview of the roots and development of anti-GMO environmental movements in regions of the global South and the global North, as well as a portrayal of the major issues which they have raised, based on the related literature.

Global South

In its earlier period, the green movement in the South mounted resistance to Northern development schemes or ecosystem-disturbing activities promoted by international actors with First World links (Finger, 1992), or by foreign producers who entered Southern regions in order to exploit local resources or local labour (Redclift, 1987; Faber, 1992;

Shiva, 1992). At the start of the twenty-first century, Southern environmental resistance was expected to increase in view of economic globalization, with subsequent responses from market and policy actors, the professionalization of the environmental movement and its linking/collaboration with other civil-society actors (Dwivedi, 2001).

Struggles over GM crops began in the South during the early 1980s, almost simultaneously, and to an extent with similar concerns to North American activists. Their critique focused on corporate domination of agro-food systems and the related patents and proprietary initiatives (Buttel, 2005). The activists, who had been opponents of the Green Revolution and international agencies such as the World Bank and US Agency for International Development (AID), argued that GM crops developed by 'big ag', rich peasants and agribusiness interests would be another significant force for the further destabilizing of Southern inequalities imposed by Western technologies and development schemes (Shiva, 2000; Powell, 2001; Schurman and Kelso, 2003; Buttel, 2005: 314).

Indigenous people and their international supporters oppose GMO policies and initiatives by Western researchers and industries who explore Southern biological resources to find useful genetic and biological material. Bioprospecting is viewed as biopiracy or the plundering of natural resources and related knowledge of developing countries by powerful industrial interests (Takeshita, 2001; see also Barcena Hinojal and Lago Aurrekoetxea, and Ambrose-Oji, Chapters 10 and 20 in this volume).

During the 1990s, progressive Southern NGOs aimed for an alternative to 'bio-imperialism' via their proposed 'biodemocracy' approach, which also entails opposition both to biotechnology as a tool to maintain biodiversity and to the adoption of intellectual property rights as the mechanism for protecting local resources and knowledge (Escobar, 1998: 59–60). Advocating collective rights concerning shared knowledge and resources, these transnational networks contest positivist science, the market and individual property, enacting a cybercultural politics of importance for the defence of place (Escobar, 1998).

In the late 1990s, resistance to neoliberal economic globalization included the campaign against GMOs and the penetration of transnational agribusiness, coordinated in 1999 by the People's Global Action network, including hundreds of Indian farmers and members of the Landless Movement of Brazil (Woodgate et al., 2005). Another campaign during the same period in India brought together a variety of non-institutionalized grassroots movements mounting resistance to the privatization of public goods via the WTO's Trade Related Intellectual Property Rights (TRIPs), such as that by Pattuvam's farmers. They claimed collective ownership over all genetic resources within their jurisdiction by registering local plant species in local names and denying the possibility of corporate patents applying to these resources (Shiva, 1997, cited in Jamison and Kousis, 2005).

In the Philippines, bottom-up social resistance to US, Japanese and EU GMO trade is organized as an epistemological struggle by a network of farmers, MASIPAG, with links to international network partners. Opposing US 'patents on life' and the corporations promoting them, they resist regimes of intellectual property (IP) and advocate a normative farmers' rights framework to make IPs obsolete (Wright, 2008). In Ecuador, land conflicts between landlords and tenants have been intensified in view of an intensive biotechnology-related frontier of agricultural products linked to international exchange and global trade (Redclift, 2006).

Southern opposition to GMOs, by groups such as BioWatch South Africa, the Tamil

Nadu Women's Forum in India, and the New Agriculture Movement in Bangladesh, centres on issues related to the appropriation of traditional knowledge and biological resources by Northern corporations (Schurman and Kelso, 2003; Hindmarsh, 2004). Their actions include engaging in critical multilateral negotiating bodies and forums such as the UN Convention on Biodiversity and the UN Cartagena Protocol on Biosafety (Schurman and Munro, 2003).

In an attempt to explore issues on the 'science of environmental justice', recent research focuses on the ways in which indigenous people across the globe are facing and confronting biocolonialism linked to the genetics revolution (Di Chiro, 2007). Environmental justice issues related to IPR and the spread of GMOs are raised, for example, by Latin American activists such as campesino and indigenous people's movements in countries growing maize as well as other crops. IPRs continue to be viewed by these groups as well as their international supporters as a form of colonialism or, at least, a commodification of knowledge rights (Newell, 2008). Aiming towards food security and food sovereignty, the network Via Campesina is involved in the World Social Forum as well as in international campaigns opposing transnational corporation (TNC) control of agriculture and the related patenting and biopiracy, free trade in agricultural produce, and the use of hormones and transgenics. More recently, they have voiced concerns over 'sound science' and corporate accountability (Newell, 2008).

Global North
In a brief comparison of the US and European environmental movements in the late 1980s, they appeared as embracing 'groups ranging from conservative or at least moderate conservation organizations to radical organizations that are not averse to direct confrontations with the government' (Klandermans and Tarrow, 1988: 19). However, differences in orientations as well as in the histories of the two continents led to diversifications of the environmental movements in the USA and the EU.

Concern over new biotechnology and its agricultural applications first appears during the late 1970s in the USA and Canada (Schurman and Kelso, 2003; Buttel, 2005). The core of arguments by these first activists relied more on social or social-scientific and ethical themes and less on scientific and environmentally oriented frames (Buttel, 2005). These are reflected in critiques of corporate control over agro-food systems by Jeremy Rifkin and his Foundation on Economic Trends, Pat Mooney, Cary Fowler and Hope Shand from the Rural Advancement Fund International (RAFI) and Jack Doyle at the Environmental Policy Institute in Washington, DC (Schurman and Munro, 2003).

By the late 1990s, US activist groups opposing new biotechnology in agriculture were diverse in the types of constituents and action forms, as well as in their frames (Reisner, 2001 in Jamison and Kousis, 2005). According to Reisner (2001: 1392–8), groups and networks that actively resist and oppose GM crops and food include the following:

- *Food and agricultural groups* include consumer and sustainable agriculture advocates, with a strong presence of the Pesticide Action Network (North American) and Mothers for Natural Law.
- *Environmental groups*, especially the Turning Point Coalition (TPC), include Citizens' Clearinghouse for Hazardous Wastes, Earth First!, Earth Island Institute, Environmental Action, Friends of the Earth, Greenpeace and the Green Party.

- *Anti-corporate health and consumer groups* such as the Organic Consumers' Association express concerns about the unintended health and environmental consequences of GM food.
- *Science-based groups* include Physicians for Social Responsibility and the Union of Concerned Scientists. Both of the more recent groups, the Campaign for Responsible Transplantation and the Council for Responsible Genetics (CRP), provide resource materials and information, such as the bimonthly *GeneWatch*.
- *Left-Labor groups* joined the TPC and the majority of left-labour advocacy groups, including AFL–CIO, Democratic Socialists of America and the International Forum on Globalization, have taken a position against GM foods.
- All of the *animal rights organizations* formally expressed opposition to GMOs, yet have not been very active.
- Finally, of all the *racially and ethnically based advocacy groups* only the Native American Rights Fund took a public position against GM plants (Reisner, 2001).

Canadian anti-GM activism usually appears in coalitions such as the one by farm, consumer, health, environmental and industry organizations opposing Monsanto's attempts to commercialize GM in 2001. The main discourse of a 2001 coalition, which was mostly led by rural and agricultural groups, centred on market acceptance, environmental risk, and the lack of transparency and democratic processes in biotechnology regulation and policy – where farmers' production-oriented claims existed simultaneously with consumer discourses (Eaton, 2009).

Opposition to GMOs has been very different across EU member states. Yet the European anti-GMO campaigns have been considered of high importance. The first wave of European protest campaigns took place between 1996 and 1997 (when the first shipments of GM corn and soybeans arrived in the EU), while the 1995–97 period witnessed anti-GMO campaigns targeting the EU (possibly due to the involvement of transnational environmental organizations), its national governments and the food industry (Kettnaker, 2001). Greenpeace and other professional environmental organizations took part in most protest actions. Fusing domestic and transnational activism, the anti-genetic seed campaign in Western Europe was launched by a loose coalition among environmental, consumer and public health organizations, with the flexibility to shift actions from one institutional venue to another, from the national to the EU level (Tarrow, 2005: 175–6).

In the UK, in 1998, environmental activists disrupted field trials of GM crops. The newly announced field trials provoked more direct action and the founding of 'GenetiX Snowball' (Reynolds et al., 2007). Since the late 1990s, environmental activists such as those involved in the GenetiX Snowball campaign aimed for labelling, the promotion of consumer rights and an 'epistemic consumer' (Lezaun, 2004: 55).[9] Innovative direct actions of crop destruction by anti-GMO activists were also performed in the fields, aiming towards encouraging a more precautionary approach (Szerszynski, 2005). Activists linked with organizations such as Greenpeace and Friends of the Earth opposed biotechnology in agriculture, shifted the locus of resistance from the country to the city, from the farm to the supermarket, and from the decontamination of the fields to confiscation of GM foods (Lezaun, 2004).

In Spain, during the mid-1990s, national-level environmental organizations organized for the first time consumer boycotts of goods or companies in their campaigns against GM food (Jimenez, 2003). In Greece, although governments have adopted a precautionary, anti-GMO stance since the moratorium, activist networks nevertheless developed at different levels, targeting the state and multinational actors, with the aim of expanding beyond national borders and participating in the promotion of GM-free Balkans (Reynolds et al., 2007).

During the decade 1988–97 in Germany, only a minority of environmental protest groups opposed genetic engineering, taking place at levels comparable to transport and nature conservation protest (Rucht and Roose, 2003). During the same period, 14 mass protests involved more than 100 000 people – but the collection of signatures was the predominant form of protest. In 1994, one of these involved the collection of 550 000 signatures as an appeal to stop the production and circulation of GM food (Rucht and Roose, 2003: 90). In general, the environmental movement in Germany lost its distinct profile and identity due to its specialization and fragmentation in different issue areas, the increasing ties with non-movement organizations, the acceptance of funding from industry and administrative agencies, as well as the increasing role of green parliamentary politics (ibid.: 82).

Since the late 1990s, agricultural organizations in Spain have become active in protest against GM crops, also through their collaborations with environmental organizations (Jimenez, 2003). In the more recent period, coexistence schemes remain highly contested, while the related technical measures are difficult to apply. In Spanish Catalonia and Aragon, the implementation of coexistence measures failed to resolve previous conflicts, while producing new ones through the individualization of choice and impacts (Binimelis, 2008).

In Denmark, discourses of concern by the public were divided into three ideal-typical categories, i.e. 'social', 'economic' and 'cultural', based on focus-group analysis (Lassen and Jamison, 2006: 11–12). Influenced by media, environmental NGOs and green parties, 'social concerns' address environmental and health risks, focusing on issues of uncertainty. Affected by economic structures and interests, 'economic concerns' are usually expressed as costs and benefits to the economy. They refer to both the threats and opportunities of the new technologies and include 'political-economic concerns' related to issues of corporate power and responsibility, commercialization of research, and the links between science and business. In view of the fact that the new biotechnologies are developed in the USA and exported to Europe, this discourse has a resonance in countries like Denmark that is not found in the USA. Finally, 'cultural concerns' focus on ethical and moral issues, and in Denmark, they not only refer to human rights but also to natural and animal rights (Lassen and Jamison, 2006: 11–12). It has been suggested that in contrast to lay people's discourses, all three of the above discourses are framed in narrower terms by policy-makers, scientists, business people and other promoters (ibid.: 26).

A comparative account of the conflict over GMOs in food and agriculture in the UK and Greece, between 1990 and 2006, reveals contrasting responses, with Greenpeace playing an active role, especially in Greece. While Greece was among the EU member states that led to the moratorium and banned GM varieties in its territories, the UK government took a pro-GM position, attempting to manage the GMO issue at the societal and environmental level. A more united view among civil society and the state was maintained in Greece, opposing GM agriculture and food. By contrast, a much more polarized situation was sustained in the UK, one that was not even overcome by a massive state-initiated public participation scheme in 2003, GM Nation (Reynolds et al., 2007).

Comparing Austrian and French GMO opposition, Seiffert (2008) finds that Austrian farmers protected by the Austrian state play a passive role compared to the contentious French farmers, led by their farmers' union and its spokesman Jose Bove to spectacular protest such as the destruction of GM crops and confrontational actions as part of the anti-globalization movement. Greenpeace and Global 2000 support and participate in such opposition against Northern GMO policies. The importance of political opportunity contextual factors is vital in explaining the differences in the two countries' GMO opposition (Seiffert, 2008).

Three major types of European-wide, anti-GMO protest events occurred: protest targeted at EU institutions, protest against European-level firms (e.g. Monsanto Europe), and solidarity between social movement organizations in different states – such as Italian Greenpeace activists supporting the French activist Jose Bove (Ansell et al., 2006: 115–19). The relative success of the anti-GMO coalition is attributed to 'an unusual confluence of political and international factors following the BSE affair'; however, it also illustrates that Europe is developing into a multi-level polity (Tarrow, 2001: 243).

Are the European anti-GMO transnational and national protest campaigns a 'preview of future transnational social movements, or an exception to the norm of "domestication" produced by the European valence of food-related issues after the Mad Cow crisis and the fact that the main producer of GMOs is the superpower across the sea' (Tarrow, 2001: 243)? According to Tarrow (2001: 239), this will depend on whether the same patterns are observed for other protest campaigns.

In their cross-national analysis, Ansell et al. (2006) also point out that the European anti-GMO movement is both territorially and functionally differentiated. They assert that the anti-GMO movement can be seen as a European movement given its multi-level organization at national and EU levels. Although it covers a wide array of interests and claims, and includes environmental and consumer groups, farmers and development organizations, it has been successful in mobilizing at the EU level. Following the mad-cow/BSE crisis and the emergence of the anti-globalization movement, it framed GMOs as a threat to biodiversity and farmer autonomy and an inadequately regulated food-safety issue. It is composed of four types of groups: (a) national constituencies at the nation-state level; (b) national constituencies with both nation-state and European branches; (c) international constituency and based in Brussels (FoE, CPE, BEUC etc.); and (d) transnational constituency with both nation-state and European branches, e.g. Greenpeace (Ansell et al., 2006).

Bernauer and Meins (2003: 643) argue that 'the regulatory outcome in the EU can be traced back to nongovernmental organizations' (NGOs) increased collective action capacity due to public outrage, an institutional multilevel environment favorable to anti-biotechnology NGO interests and a disintegration of the producer coalition due to NGO campaigns and differences in industrial structure'. By contrast, lower public demands and a different institutional environment in the USA excluded similar NGOs from the related policy-making area (Jamison and Kousis, 2005).

The economic, organizational and cultural characteristics of industry structures can explain the effectiveness of the EU's opposition to GMOs (Schurman, 2004). One such alternative argument focuses on anti-GMO variations within the EU's national settings, arguing that moving back to national settings sheds light on how the presence of an alternative food-production regime, such as organic farming, and its political organization shape the depth, breath and strength of oppositions to GMOs (Kurzer and Cooper, 2007). Networks for environmentally responsible food oppose agricultural biotechnology and chemical agriculture, aiming for the consumption of healthy food (Lockie et al., 2007).

The European challenge to GMOs varied at the member-state level, especially after the 1999 *de facto* moratorium (led by Austria, Denmark, France, Greece, Italy and Luxemburg) that stopped the commercialization of GM agro-food products in the EU until 2004. After the moratorium, several member states of the EU who defined harm in a broader manner attempted to prohibit GMO-related products in their countries. Industry also responded differently. In 2004, Monsanto announced that it would 'discontinue breeding and field level research of [transgenic] Roundup Ready1 wheat' (Eaton, 2009: 256).

Following the end of the moratorium, large environmental NGOs (e.g. Greenpeace and Friends of the Earth Europe) called for wider precautionary approaches by linking harm to sustainable development, collaborated with regional authorities on initiatives leading to the declaration of 'GM-free zones' within the EU, and demanded consumer choice (e.g. labelling, monitoring and traceability) and coexistence alternatives (Devos et al., 2008; Levidow and Boschert, 2008). Aiming to offer farmers free choice and mediate policy conflicts over GM crops, the EU developed a policy framework for coexistence between GM, conventional and organic crops. This initiative, however, evolved into another arena for contending agricultural systems (Levidow and Boschert, 2008).

According to Devos et al. (2008), such pressures by diverse transnational networks led, first, to the restyling of EU legislation with two legal openings, the consultation of an ethics committee and the imposed labelling given ethical/religious concerns, as well as one implicit link to ethics, i.e. the adoption of the precautionary principle to deal with uncertainties. Second, they led to the restyling of science communication and public engagement with science. These changes aimed for the restoration of public and market confidence by clarifying and accommodating different values and ideals in decision-making and enhancing public accountability and democratizing expertise. The new challenge faced by regulatory authorities is the implementing of an integral sustainability evaluation (Devos et al., 2008).

Comparing politics of life in Australia and New Zealand, recent analysis challenges conventional notions of centre and periphery, global and local, international and national, reflecting on future civic trajectories for science-related good governance (Hindmarsh and Du Plessis, 2008). A more technocratic Australian response to GM food and fibre is found, in contrast to New Zealand's emphasis on civic input. New Zealand features state-facilitated civic engagement while Australia witnessed sustained resistance, yet not enhanced civic engagement (Hindmarsh and Du Plessis, 2008).

Summary
With the establishment of neoliberalism during the late 1980s and early 1990s in OECD countries, Russia, and especially in North America, where key decisions were taken, a notable decrease in the social justice critique is visible, concerning GMO-related agribusiness domination and the subsequent social inequalities (Buttel, 2005: 315).

It was during the late 1990s, however, that a discursive shift away from social justice and towards the environmentalization of GMO opposition took place, mainly in the global North, as promoted by activists including those of Greenpeace and Friends of the Earth. This can be seen as a result of (a) the impact of the 1992 Rio Earth Summit, (b) the 1999 'Seattle' protests against WTO, mostly carried out by environmental activists, (c) heightened European concerns after the BSE scandal, (d) the establishment, transnationalization and environmental movement alliances with power, as well as (e) the vulnerability of the US and global regulatory systems to critique and their susceptibility to movement critique (Buttel, 2005: 315; Levidow, 2001).

Anti-GMO claims in the global South emphasize environmental justice issues, aiming towards food security and food sovereignty. IPRs continue to be viewed as a form of colonialism or, at least, a commodification of knowledge rights (Newell, 2008).

Northern opposition to GMOs adopts discursive frames concerned with moral, cultural, material, health and environmental issues while engaging in actions such as lobbying, regulatory and policy disputes (related, e.g., to food labelling), political consumption, public education and consciousness-raising, or destruction of crops (Schurman and Kelso, 2003).

Southern as well as Northern GMO opposition also embraces issues related to the science of environmental justice and 'sound science' (Newell, 2008; Frickel, 2004). Such science activism may take one of the following forms: environmental boundary organizations; scientific associations, public-interest science organizations; and grassroots support organizations, which have the expert knowledge to anticipate reactions from powerful institutional challengers (Frickel, 2004: 455). For example, the Ecological Society of America's Public Affairs Office gave ecological science a voice on Capitol Hill and in federal agencies by issuing congressional briefs and statements on GM foods (ibid.).

More recent concerns voiced by the global North focus on future challenges of new technologies and environmental activism. Mobilization frames in the 2004 European Social Forum[10] sessions on science and genomics focus on justice as well as science-related issues. In the better-attended science session mobilization frames focused first on North–South justice issues concerning control over biological material and resources as well as respect for sociocultural differences, second on the promotion of diverse, proactive public participation via lobbying and civil-society initiatives and, finally, on public education and lobbying. The same frames ranked differently for the genomics session, with the promotion of diverse, proactive public participation via lobbying and civil-society initiatives ranking first, followed by direct action, North–South justice and, finally, public education and lobbying (Welsh et al., 2007).

GMOs are also making their appearance in Russia, Ukraine, Belarus and Moldova, raising concerns in civil society, reflected in campaigns by environmental organizations, legislative changes and media attention (Ovcearenco, 2006). For example, Greenpeace-Russia has been active in the campaigns opposing GMOs, reflected in the collection of 5400 signatures requesting a ban on GMOs in infant food (Greenpeace, 2007).[11]

Nanotech: entering the environmental claims repertoire?
Nanotech innovations are expected to revolutionize everyday life in the coming decades; hence the urgent need for a deeper understanding of the viewpoints of the different

communities of interest via a precautionary approach (Petersen, 2009). In this context a number of works address the role of social science and its prospective agendas (Macnaghten et al., 2005; Ebbesen, 2008). Furthermore, recent research (Kjølberg and Wickson, 2007) on the literature related to the social and ethical interactions with nano-tech (SEIN) distinguishes four research foci. Governance issues rank first (40 per cent), with concerns about processes and institutions for decision-making, regulation, legislation and public engagement. The remaining three research foci relate to perception, science and philosophy issues.

According to recent work, the governance gap is significant in the shorter term for passive nanostructures of high exposure rates currently in production, while it is very important for the several 'active' nanoscale structures and nanosystems expected to enter the market in the near future, with potential impacts on human health, the environment and sociocultural contexts (Renn and Roco, 2006).

Although recent works by social scientists stress the difficulties in predicting the effects of the new nanotechnologies, they expect that significant social impacts will arise in the areas of health and medicine, as well as in power issues between citizens and government and citizens and corporations (Sparrow, 2009; Ebbesen, 2008). Recent work by Environmental Defense (a US NGO) points out that nanotechnology is already reaching the market in a wide variety of consumer products, while existing regulatory tools and policies that adequately protect human health and the environment are limited (Balbus et al., 2007).

Environmental NGOs, as well as industry, government and scientist agencies, make variable efforts to apply lessons from the previous technology conflicts, especially those related to GMOs, to address dilemmas raised by the application and use of nanotechnology (Schirmer, 2004; Kearnes et al., 2006). For example, dialogue processes in the UK run by the government encourage academia, the media, NGOs such as Greenpeace and Demos, and other stakeholders to participate, focusing on collaboration (Bowman and Hodge, 2007). Such dialogues vary among Northern countries and occur across different scientific, commercial, NGO and other communities.

Nanotechnology policy processes have been influenced by their historical context and political and industry opportunities. This is apparent in Germany and the UK, which have been affected by the integration of the precautionary principle into EU regulatory policy over the past two decades, in contrast to the lack of legal status given to the principle in the USA and Australia, where governments primarily framed nanotechnology policy discourse, including dialogue, within the contexts of research funding and economic benefits (Bowman and Hodge, 2007).

Although global justice movements have shown limited interest in nanotechnology, it has been argued that variants of the 'old', 'new' and newer waves of global social movements show differential discursive frames on the new technology. Labour and social-democratic movements are largely supportive, but also concerned about occupational safety. Environmental organizations are concerned with the environmental impacts of the technology, while neglecting social justice issues. Among the environmentalists, there are NGOs with a market-oriented perspective towards developing nanotechnology. Finally, the smaller and newer groups of global activists take up global justice and economic disparities issues, viewing nanotechnology as one more example of corporate expansionism (Jamison, 2009: 9–13).

Activist environmental groups compete in online networks in the form of hyperlinks ('hyperlink capital') and control over the terms of the debate via framing strategies (Ackland and O'Neil, 2008; O'Neil and Ackland, 2008). An innovative analysis of online environmental activist groups and networks uses hyperlink and content analysis to examine the symbolic and organizational dimensions of online contestation (Ackland and O'Neil, 2008, O'Neil and Ackland, 2008[12]). They show that when it comes to the issue of nanotechnology, the environmental–bio/biotechnology online groups are more likely to focus on the new issue of nanotechnology than the more established environmental–global and environmental–toxic groups. This difference goes beyond the parallel concerns about biotech products. The web analysis suggests that by taking up the nanotech issue, the environmental–bio group shows its ability to identify the new field – as reflected in the ETC Group's[13] (bio, Canada) leading position amongst all the seed sites and its framing of the potential risks of nanotechnology with the new terms 'atomtech' and 'nanotoxicity' (Ackland and O'Neil, 2008; O'Neil and Ackland, 2008). Following ETC, three other groups have a leading role in the nanotechnology opposition: Organic Consumers (bio, USA), Environmental Defense (global, USA) and Greenpeace UK (global, UK) (Ackland and O'Neil, 2008; O'Neil and Ackland, 2008).

Similar evidence is provided by another analysis at the website level (Huey, 2005), showing RAFI (Rural Agriculture Foundation International – now the ETC Group) as the primary proponent of the anti-nanotechnology discourse, while being simultaneously the anti-agricultural biotechnology site with the highest number of links. PureFood (now Consumers' Union) and Greenpeace appear second in this analysis. All three organizations are found to represent three anti-GMO frames: the rights frame, the health safety frame, and the environmental risk frame. Friends of the Earth, the Soil Association, GeneWatch (Cambridge, MA), Union of Concerned Scientists, Center for Food Safety (Washington, DC) are also among the organizations opposing agricultural biotechnology and nanotechnology (Huey, 2005).

With offices in Ottawa, Canada (headquarters), Carrboro, USA and Mexico City, ETC has been active for almost three decades, advocating on global issues including the conservation of agricultural biodiversity and food security and on impacts of new technologies on the rural poor.[14] Since the 1980s they have engaged in research, education and social action on issues related to agricultural biodiversity, biotechnology, intellectual property and community knowledge systems. In the 1990s, they expanded their repertoire by including social and environmental concerns related to biotechnology, biopiracy and human genomics and, in the late 1990s, to nanotechnology (ETC, 2004).

Focusing on three NGOs that participated actively in the nanotechnology and nanoscience discourse, Schirmer (2004) finds through her qualitative analysis that, although different in size, type and orientation, the ETC Group, GeneWatch UK and Greenpeace all aim towards a socially responsible nanotechnology.

Conclusion

The account at hand attests to a number of findings. These centre on the character of the anti-GMO movement itself, its future and its expansion to novel and salient issues. To begin with the movement itself, following Tilly's (1994) definition, the sustained resistance towards agricultural biotechnology and its products, especially by the wide variety of EU and Southern groups and networks in the past two decades, can be seen as a variant of the environmental movement, given its sustained challenges as well as the acknowledged impacts that it has had on regulatory and market spheres at national and international levels. Although there are signs of activism, a similar sustained opposition against nanotechnology is not visible and, thus far, no social movement has been formed in relation to nanotechnology.

The movement against agricultural biotechnology and its products in the early twenty-first century, following other social movements of its era (Tilly, 2004), is more internationally organized, in terms of activists, organizations, networks and visible targets, while it has integrated new technologies into its organizing and claim-making performances. It is a movement that reflects the transnational contention linking activists to one another, to states, and to international institutions (Tarrow, 2005: 25).

Hence the anti-GMO movement is a new prototype of the environmental movement, rather than an exception or a deviant case of a social movement.[15] Given its focus on new technological breakthroughs and their novel ways of engineering environments in the twenty-first century, this new prototype of the environmental movement appears increasingly to incorporate specific nanotechnology concerns in its claim-making repertoires, as shown by Ackland and O'Neil (2008). A deeper understanding of the development of the anti-GMO movement and its future could be achieved through the study of political and economic opportunities and constraints, as well as the related cultural discourses. More work is needed in both areas.

What are likely to be the trends of the environmental movement opposed to agricultural biotechnology and the rising concerns on nanotechnology during the remaining part of the twenty-first century? This work can offer preliminary reflections on three of Tilly's (2004) four 'scenarios' on the future of social movements: those related to internationalization, to democracy and to professionalization. First, the internationalization of the anti-GMO movement thus far appears to follow Tilly's vision of a slower, less extensive and less complete net shift away from local, regional and national social movements toward international and global. The pace and intensity of this internationalization, however, varies between the global South and the global North, as well as within the North. Although evidence is very limited, following Tilly's expectation, the movement against agricultural biotechnology may also be influenced by some democratic decline in major existing democracies, but notable democratization in undemocratic countries. There is a lack of related studies on this area of high priority. Finally, for the movement against agricultural biotechnology, as Tilly foresees, professional social movement entrepreneurs, NGOs and links with authorities will increasingly dominate, while at the same time abandoning portions of local and regional claim-making that they cannot co-opt into international activism. This is especially visible with such professional organizations as Greenpeace, Friends of the Earth, GeneWatch and the ETC Group.

In addition to these more general trends that are likely to occur in the future of the anti-GMO movement, this chapter points to new issues brought forth by sustained opposition to agricultural biotechnology and its products. Science has increasingly come to be of vital importance for environmental movements of the twenty-first century, as shown in new biotechnology products or current anti-GMO concerns about nanotechnologies. This is reflected in recent works focused on the efforts to organize expert-activists. As Frickel (2004) points out, the emergence of new science-oriented organizations and the politicization of existing ones are indicative of the emergence of a culture of environmental research-oriented professional activism. Furthermore, the relationship between environmental activists and scientists may also shift attention to alternative future strategies of technological innovations (Buttel, 2005; Jamison, 2009).

Beyond the classical environmental claims repertoire, however, the entrance of bio-technology and nanotechnology issues has extended the environmental discourse to include ethical issues in ways that would not have been foreseen even a decade ago, in both the global South as well as the global North.

Notes

1. I am grateful to Michael Redclift and Graham Woodgate for their encouragement in writing this chapter and their very helpful comments. Sincere thanks to Kathrin Braun and Bronislaw Szerszynski for their constructive comments. I am also grateful to Andrew Jamison for his insightful observations and suggestions. Any remaining flaws are my own. This work has been inspired primarily by my participation in the PAGANINI project (Participatory Governance and Institutional Innovation, EC, DGXII, Contract No. CIT2-CT-2004-505791, http://www.univie.ac.at/life-science-governance/paganini/). Special thanks to Bronislaw Szerszynski and Herbert Gottweis for the invitation and collaboration in the GM Food Work Package, as well as to Larry Reynolds and the other members of the team.
2. Biotic resources are the biological resources that depend on land and comprise the ecosystems of other places (plant and animal life); these have increasingly become elements of international exchanges (Redclift, 2006: 130 and 1987: 17).
3. Electoral competitions are excluded under this definition since parties do not challenge the system but work within it.
4. '"Politics of life" refers to dimensions of life that are only to a limited extent under human control, or else where the public has good reasons to suspect that there are serious limitations to socio-political control and steering. Also, 'politics of life' areas are strongly connected to normative, moral and value-based factors, such as a sense of responsibility towards non-human nature, future generations and/or one's own body' (PAGANINI, 2007: 6).
5. As described by Jamison (2001), and Rinkevicius (2000).
6. These organizations may carry out environmental impact assessment (EIA), cost–benefit analysis, resource accounting, ecolabelling, and risk assessment.
7. Such as the 'Natural Step' in Sweden with branches in the UK and USA – see Dekker et al., in Jamison (2001: 95).
8. Not all environmental organizations seek or take these opportunities. According to Brand (1999), faith in ecological modernization initiatives appears to subside.
9. An 'epistemic' consumer is 'an actor whose competencies and behavior are defined in terms of "understanding" the issues – or, more frequently, not understanding them – and whose fundamental demand, precisely because he does not understand, is an abstract "right to know", to be satisfied through product labelling' (Lezaun, 2004: 55).
10. Following the World Social Forum.
11. See http://www.greenpeace.org/russia/en/news/5400-people-demand-a-ban-on-ge, last accessed 1 June 2009.
12. See also http://voson.anu.edu.au/papers.html, last accessed 1 June 2009.
13. Former Action Group on Erosion, Technology and Concentration; ETC since 2001.
14. www.etcgroup.org.
15. I thank Kathrin Braun for her help on this point.

References

Ackland, Robert and Mathieu O'Neil (2008), 'Online collective identity: the case of the environmental movement', Australian Demographic and Social Research Institute Working Paper No. 4, The Australian National University.
Ansell, Christopher, Rahsaan Maxwell and David Sicurelli (2006), 'Protesting food: NGOs and political mobilization in Europe', in Christopher K. Ansell and David Vogel (eds), *What's the Beef?: The Contested Governance of European Food Safety*, Cambridge, MA: The MIT Press, pp. 97–122.
Balbus, John M., Karen Florini, Richard A. Denison and Scott A. Walsh (2007), 'Protecting workers and the environment: an environmental NGO's perspective on nanotechnology', Special issue: Nanoparticles and Occupational Health, *Journal of Nanoparticle Research*, 9: 11–22.
Bernauer, Thomas and Erika Meins (2003), 'Technological revolution meets policy and the market: explaining

cross-national differences in agricultural biotechnology regulation', *European Journal of Political Research*, **42** (5): 643–83.

Binimelis, Rosa (2008), 'Coexistence of plants and coexistence of farmers: is an individual choice possible?', *Journal of Agricultural and Environmental Ethics*, **21**: 437–57.

Bowman, Diana M. and Graeme A. Hodge (2007), 'Nanotechnology and public interest dialogue: some international observations', *Bulletin of Science, Technology & Society*, **27** (2): 118–32.

Brand, Karl-Werner (1999), 'Dialectics of institutionalization: the transformation of the environmental movement in Germany', *Environmental Politics*, **8** (1): 35–58.

Brooks, Sally (2005), 'Biotechnology and the politics of truth: from the Green Revolution to an evergreen revolution', *Sociologia Ruralis*, **45** (4): 360–79.

Buttel, Frederick H. (2005), 'The environmental and post-environmental politics of genetically modified crops and foods', *Environmental Politics*, **14** (3): 309–23.

della Porta, Donatella and Sidney Tarrow (2005), *Transnational Protest and Global Activism*, Lanham, MD: Rowman & Littlefield.

Devos, Yann, Pieter Maeseele, Dirk Reheul, Linda van Speybroeck and Danny De Waele (2008), 'Ethics in the societal debate on genetically modified organisms: a (re)quest for *Sense and Sensibility*', *Journal of Agricultural and Environmental Ethics*, **21**: 29–61.

Di Chiro, Giovanna (2007), 'Indigenous peoples and biocolonialism: defining the "science of environmental justice" in the century of the gene', in Ronald Sandler and Phaedra C. Pezzullo (eds), *Environmental Justice and Environmentalism: The Social Justice Challenge to the Environmental Movement*, London: MIT Press, pp. 251–83.

Dunlap, Riley E. and Angela G. Mertig (1991), 'The evolution of the US environmental movement from 1970 to 1990: an overview', *Society and Natural Resources*, **4** (3): 209–18. (Special Issue: Two Decades of American Environmentalism: The US Environmental Movement, 1970–1990).

Dwivedi, Ranjit (2001), 'Environmental movements in the global South', *International Sociology*, **16** (1): 11–31.

Eaton, Emily (2009), 'Getting behind the grain: the politics of genetic modification on the Canadian Prairies', *Antipode*, **41** (2): 256–81.

Ebbesen, Mette (2008), 'The role of the humanities and social sciences in nanotechnology research and development', *Nanoethics*, **2**: 1–13.

Escobar, Arturo (1998), 'Whose knowledge, whose nature? Biodiversity, conservation, and the political ecology of social movements', *Journal of Political Ecology*, **5**: 53–82.

ETC (2004), *Down on the Farm: The Impact of Nano-scale Technologies on Food and Agriculture*, Ottawa, Canada: ETC Group, available at http://www.etcgroup.org/en/materials/publications.html?pub_id=80, last accessed 29 May 2009.

Faber, Daniel (1992), 'Imperialism, revolution, and the ecological crisis of Central America', *Latin American Perspectives*, **19** (1): 17–44.

Finger, Matthias (1992), *The Green Movement World Wide*, London: JAI Press.

Frickel, Scott (2004), 'JUST SCIENCE? Organizing scientist activism in the US environmental justice movement', *Science as Culture*, **13** (4): 449–69.

Gottweis, Herbert, Kathrin Braun, Yrjö Haila, Maarten Hajer, Anne Loeber, Ingrid Metzler, Larry Reynolds, Susanne Schultz and Bronislaw Szerszynski (2008), 'Participation and the new governance of life', *BioSocieties*, **3** (3): 265–86.

Gould, Kenneth, A., Allan Schnaiberg and Adam S. Weinberg (1996), *Local Environmental Struggles: Citizen Activism in the Treadmill of Production*, Cambridge, UK: Cambridge University Press.

Greenpeace (2007), 'Stop experiments on kids!', http://www.greenpeace.org/russia/en/press/releases/stop-experiments-on-kids, last accessed 17 September 2009.

Hindmarsh, Susan (2004), 'Resistance in Asia: voices of a people's caravan', in Richard Hindmarsh and Geoffrey Lawrence (eds), *Recoding Nature: Critical Perspectives on Genetic Engineering*, Sydney: The University of New South Wales Press, pp. 206–19.

Hindmarsh, Richard and Rosemary Du Plessis (2008), 'The new civic geography of life sciences governance: transitions and trajectories in Australia and New Zealand', *New Genetics and Society*, **27** (3): 175–80.

Ho, Peter, Eduard B. Vermeer and Jennifer H. Zhao (2006), 'Biotechnology and food safety in China: consumers' acceptance or resistance?', *Development and Change*, **37** (1): 227–53.

Huey, Tina Andersen (2005), 'Thinking globally, eating locally: website linking and the performance of solidarity in global and local food movements', *Social Movement Studies*, **4** (2): 123–37.

Humphrey, Craig, R. and Frederick H. Buttel (1982), *Environment, Energy and Society*, Malabar, FL: Krieger Publishing Company.

Jamison, Andrew (2001), *The Making of Green Knowledge. Environmental Politics and Cultural Transformation*, Cambridge, UK: Cambridge University Press.

Jamison, Andrew (2009), 'Can nanotechnology be just? On nanotechnology and the emerging movement for global justice' (under review in *Nanoethics*), available at http://people.plan.aau.dk/~andy/other_texts_on_ the_net.htm, accessed 5 May 2009.

Jamison, Andrew and Maria Kousis (2005), 'Dilemmas of deliberation: biotechnology and the environmental movement,' paper presented in the ECPR annual sessions, Workshop no. 16, 'Mapping Biopolitics: Medical-Scientific Transformations and the Rise of New Forms of Governance', Granada, Spain, 12–17 April.

Jimenez, Manuel (2003), 'Spain', in Christopher Rootes (ed.), *Environmental Protest in Western Europe*, Oxford: Oxford University Press, pp. 166–99.

Kearnes, Matthew, Robin Grove-White, Phil Macnaghten, James Wilson and Brian Wynne (2006), 'From bio to nano: learning lessons from the UK agricultural biotechnology controversy', *Science as Culture*, **15** (4): 291–307.

Kettnaker, Vera (2001), 'The European conflict over genetically-engineered crops', in Doug Imig and Sidney Tarrow (eds), *Contentious Europeans*, Lanham, MD: Rowman & Littlefield, pp. 205–32.

Kiefer, Chris and Medea Benjamin (1993), 'Solidarity with the Third World: building an international environmental-justice movement', in Richard Hofrichter (ed.), *Toxic Struggles: The Theory and Practice of Environmental Justice*, Philadelphia, PA: New Society Publishers, pp. 1226–36.

Kjølberg, Kamilla and Fern Wickson (2007), 'Social and ethical interactions with nano: mapping the early literature', *NanoEthics*, **1** (2): 89–104.

Klandermans, Bert and Sidney Tarrow (1988), 'Mobilization into social movements: synthesizing European and American approaches', in Bert Klandermans, Hanspeter Kriesi and Sidney Tarrow (eds), *From Structure to Action: Comparing Social Movement Research Across Cultures*, London: JAI Press, pp. 1–38.

Kousis, Maria (2001), 'Competing claims in local environmental conflict in Southern Europe', in Klaus Eder and Maria Kousis (eds), *Environmental Politics in Southern Europe: Actors, Institutions and Discourses in a Europeanizing Society*, Dordrecht, The Netherlands: Kluwer, pp. 129–50.

Kousis, Maria (2004), 'Economic opportunities and threats in contentious environmental politics: a view from the European South', Special Issue on Contentious Politics and Social Change, *Theory and Society*, **33**: 393–415.

Kousis, Maria and Klaus Eder (2001), 'EU policy-making, local action, and the emergence of institutions of collective action', in Klaus Eder and Maria Kousis (eds), *Environmental Politics in Southern Europe: Actors, Institutions and Discourses in a Europeanizing Society*, Dordrecht, The Netherlands: Kluwer, pp. 3–23.

Kurzer, Paulette and Alice Cooper (2007), 'What's for Dinner? European farming and food traditions confront American biotechnology', *Comparative Political Studies*, **40** (9): 1035–58.

Lassen, Jesper and Andrew Jamison (2006), 'Genetic technologies meet the public: the discourse of concern', *Science, Technology, & Human Values*, **31** (1): 8–28.

Levidow, Les (2001), 'Precautionary uncertainty: regulating GM crops in Europe', *Social Studies of Science*, **31** (6): 842–74.

Levidow, Les and Karin Boschert (2008), 'Coexistence or contradiction? GM crops versus alternative agricultures in Europe', *Geoforum*, **39**: 174–90.

Lewis, Tammy (2000), 'Transnational conservation movement organizations: shaping the protected area systems of less developed countries', *Mobilization*, **5** (1): 103–21.

Lezaun, Javier (2004), 'Genetically modified foods and consumer mobilization in the UK', *Technikfolgenabschatzung-Theorie und Praxis*, **3** (13): 49–56.

Lockie, Stewart, Kristen Lyons, Geoffrey Lawrence and Darren Halpin (2007), *Going Organic: Mobilizing Networks for Environmentally Responsible Food Production*, Cambridge, UK: CABI Bioscience.

Macnaghten, Phil, Matthew, B. Kearnes and Brian Wynne (2005), 'Nanotechnology, governance, and public deliberation: what role for the social sciences?', *Science Communication*, **27**: 268–91.

Marks, Gary and Doug McAdam (1996), 'Social movements and the changing structure of political opportunity in the European Union', *West European Politics*, **19**: 249–78.

McAdam, Doug, John D. McCarthy and Meyer N. Zald (eds) (1996), *Comparative Perspectives on Social Movements: Political Opportunities, Mobilizing Structures and Cultural Framings*, Cambridge, UK: Cambridge University Press.

Newell, Peter (2008), 'Contesting trade politics in the Americas: the politics of environmental justice', in David V. Carruthers (ed.), *Environmental Justice in Latin America: Problems, Promise and Practice*, London: MIT Press, pp. 49–73.

O'Neil, Mathieu and Robert Ackland (2008), 'Competition in an online environmental social movement', Australian Demographic and Social Research Institute Working Paper No. 5, The Australian National University.

Ovcearenco, Albina (2006), 'Chapitre 4. La réglementation des organismes génétiquement modifiés dans les pays d'Europe de l'Est. Développement pendant la période transitoire de 1991–2001 et à l'heure actuelle', *Journal International de Bioéthique*, **17** (3), available at http://www.cairn.info/resume.php?ID_ ARTICLE=JIB_173_0065#, last accessed 29 May 2009.

PAGANINI (2007), Summary Report of the PAGANINI project, 'Participatory Governance and Institutional

Innovation: The New Politics of Life', Department of Political Science, University of Vienna, Austria. Available at http://www.univie.ac.at/LSG/paganini/, last accessed 29 May 2009.

Peterson, Alan (2009), 'Introduction: the ethical challenge of nanotechnologies', *Bioethical Inquiry*, **6**: 9–12.

Powell, Walter W. (2001), 'Networks of learning in biotechnology: opportunities and constraints associated with relational contracting in a knowledge-intensive field', in Rachel Dreyfuss, Diane L. Zimmerman and Harry First (eds), *Expanding the Boundaries of Intellectual Property*, Oxford: Oxford University Press, pp. 251–66.

Princen, Thomas and Matthias Finger (1994), *Environmental NGOs in World Politics*, London: Routledge.

Redclift, Michael (1987), *Sustainable Development: Exploring the Contradictions*, London: Methuen.

Redclift, Michael (2001), 'Environmental security and the recombinant human: sustainability in the twenty-first century', *Environmental Values*, **10**: 289–99.

Redclift, Michael (2006), *Frontiers: Histories of Civil Society and Nature*, London: MIT Press.

Reisner, Ann Elizabeth (2001), 'Social movement organizations' reactions to genetic engineering in agriculture', *American Behavioral Scientist*, **44** (8): 1389–404.

Renn, Ortwin and Mihail C. Roco (2006), 'Nanotechnology and the need for risk governance', *Journal of Nanoparticle Research*, **8**: 153–91.

Reynolds, Larry and Bronislaw Szerszynski, with Maria Kousis and Yannis Volakakis (2007), Work Package 6: GM-Food: The Role of Participation in a Techno-Scientific Controversy, 'Participatory Governance and Institutional Innovation', European Commission, 6th Framework, STREP, Coordinated by Herbert Gottweis, available at http://www.univie.ac.at/LSG/paganini/, last accessed 29 May 2009.

Rinkevicius, Leonardus (2000), 'Ecological modernization as cultural politics: transformations of civic environmental activism in Lithuania', *Environmental Politics*, **9** (1): 171–202.

Rucht, Dieter and Jochen Roose (2003), 'Germany', in Christopher Rootes (ed.), *Environmental Protest in Western Europe*. Oxford: Oxford University Press, pp. 80–108.

Schirmer, Janine (2004), 'Nanotechnology in context: science, non-governmental organisations and the challenge of communication', MA thesis, The European Inter-University Association on Society, Science and Technology. http://www.esst.uio.no.

Schlosberg, David and Elizabeth Bomberg (2008), 'Perspectives on American Environmentalism', *Environmental Politics*, **17** (2): 187–99.

Schurman, Rachel (2004), 'Fighting "Frankenfoods": industry opportunity structures and the efficacy of the anti-biotech movement in Western Europe', *Social Problems*, **52** (2): 243–68.

Schurman, Rachel and Dennis Doyle Takahashi Kelso (eds) (2003), *Engineering Trouble: Biotechnology and its Discontents*, Berkley, CA: University of California Press.

Schurman, Rachel and William Munro (2003), 'Making biotech history social resistance to agricultural biotechnology and the future of the biotechnology industry', in Schurman, Rachel and Dennis D. Kelso (eds), (2003) *Engineering Trouble: Biotechnology and its Discontents*, Berkeley, CA: University of California Press, pp. 111–29.

Seiffert, Franz (2008), 'Consensual NIMBYs, contentious NIABYs: explaining contrasting forms of farmers' GMO opposition in Austria and France', *Sociologia Ruralis*, **49** (1): 20–40.

Shiva, Vandana (1992), *Biodiversity: Social and Ecological Consequences*, London: Zed Books.

Shiva, Vandana (1997), *Biopiracy. The Plunder of Nature and Knowledge*, Boston, MA: South End Press.

Shiva, Vandana (2000), *Stolen Harvest: The Hijacking of the Global Food Supply*, Boston, MA: South End Press.

Smith, Jackie and Tina Fetner (2007), 'Structural approaches to social movements', in Conny Roggeband and Bert Klandermans (eds), *Handbook of Social Movements across Disciplines*, New York: Springer, pp. 13–57.

Sparrow, Robert (2009), 'The social impacts of nanotechnology: an ethical and political analysis', *Bioethical Inquiry*, **6**: 13–23.

Szerszynski, Bronizlaw (2005), 'Beating the unbound: political theatre in the laboratory without walls', in Gabriella Giannachi and Nigel Stewart (eds), *Performing Nature: Explorations in Ecology and the Arts*, Frankfurt and New York: Peter Lang, pp. 181–97.

Takeshita, Chikako (2001), 'Bioprospecting and its discontents: indigenous resistances as legitimate politics', *Alternatives: Global, Local, Political*, **26**: 259–82.

Tarrow, Sidney (2001), 'Contentious politics in a composite polity', in Doug Imig and Sidney Tarrow (eds), *Contentious Europeans*, Lanham MD: Rowman & Littlefield, pp. 233–51.

Tarrow, Sidney (2005), *The New Transnational Activism*, Cambridge: Cambridge University Press.

Tilly, Charles (1994), 'Social movements as historically specific clusters of political performances', *Berkeley Journal of Sociology*, **38**: 1–30.

Tilly, Charles (2004), *Social Movements, 1768–2004*, London: Paradigm Publishers.

Tilly, Charles and Sidney Tarrow (2006), *Contentious Politics*, London: Paradigm Publishers.

Van der Heijden, Hein-Anton (1999), 'Environmental movements, ecological modernization, and political opportunity structures', *Environmental Politics*, **8** (1): 199–221.

Welsh, Ian, Alexandra Plows and Robert Evans (2007), 'Human rights and genomics: science, genomics and social movements at the 2004 London Social Forum', *New Genetics and Society*, **26** (2): 123–35.

Woodgate, Graham, Bianca Ambrose-Oji, Ramón Fernandez Duran, Gloria Guzman and Eduardo Sevilla Guzman (2005), 'Alternative food and agriculture networks: an agroecological perpsective on responses to economic globalization and the "new" agrarian question', in Michael R. Redclift and Graham R. Woodgate (eds), *New Developments in Environmental Sociology*, Cheltenham, UK and Northampton, MA: Edward Elgar, pp. 586–612.

Wright, Sarah (2008), 'Locating a politics of knowledge: struggles over intellectual property in the Philippines', *Australian Geographer*, **39** (4): 409–26.

Yanitsky, Oleg (1999), 'The environmental movement in a hostile context', *International Sociology*, **14** (2): 157–72.

Young, Zoe (1999), 'NGOs and the global environmental facility: friendly foes?', special issue, *Environmental Politics*, **8** (1): 243–67.

16 Sustainable consumption: developments, considerations and new directions
Emma D. Hinton and Michael K. Goodman

Introduction

In 1997, when the first edition of this handbook was published, academic engagement with the notion of sustainable consumption (SC) was limited. Since then, academics from across the disciplines of human geography, environmental psychology, industrial ecology and ecological economics have undertaken a wealth of new research and writing in this field. Moreover, there have been novel developments in international and national policies surrounding SC, in practitioner-based approaches to various forms of advocacy, and in global political economies that have the potential to greatly alter the SC playing field. In short, consumption as a growing form of 'green governmentality' (Rutherford, 2007) – in addition to how SC itself is and should be governed – has become a key interest throughout much of the relatively well-off 'society of consumers' (Bauman, 2007) in the industrial North, and for many (e.g. *Local Environment*, 2008), is deeply marred by the continuing inequalities inherent in its uptake.

This chapter focuses on describing many of these developments, beginning with a brief contextualizing review of international and UK policy surrounding SC. Two sections follow from here: the first is on the important but contentious role that 'information' plays in SC networks and how this imposes the 'responsibilization' for sustainability onto the figure of the consumer in the spaces of the 'everyday'. The second section explores the links between SC and ecological modernization and the associated product-focused pathways to SC that constitute much of the current policy focus. Next, we discuss several important 'alternatives' to these more mainstream approaches in the discourses around voluntary simplicity, (re)localized economic systems and the emerging concept of 'hedonic' consumption, the last building on consumers' self-interests in developing more environmentally and socially friendly lifestyle choices. We then consider several different ways designed to quantify the progress to SC through, for example, the vastly popular processes of carbon 'footprinting' of one's personal consumption and lifestyle behaviours. We conclude with a short consideration of the current and impending economic recession in the context of SC; here 'simplicity' might become less voluntary and more a product of necessity. At the same time, this new economic climate, coupled with increasing popular concern over climate change and peak oil, in combination with renewed policy commitments in support of sustainable consumption, could open up new opportunities for the discourses around SC to be refocused on the continuing multi-scale inequalities of lifestyles and livelihoods across the globe.

Exploring sustainable consumption

So, what *is* SC? Is it choosing to purchase fair trade coffee and bananas? Is it about installing compact fluorescent lightbulbs to reduce energy usage and, as importantly, household bills? Is it about buying recycled paper and recycling your waste? Is it perhaps about riding your bike to work instead of driving *even* that hybrid car? Is it about buying 'local'? Or maybe it's about buying carbon offsets for your vacation flight? Or, could it perhaps be about the purchase and consumption of fewer things or even *no thing(s)* as a wider lifestyle choice?

In many ways, SC is about all of these practices and approaches in that it criss-crosses and works through a multitude of consumption-related behaviours and scales; this is particularly true given the rather 'slippery' and open nature of what has counted as 'sustainability' over time. In essence, however, SC might be regarded, on the one hand, as the attempt to *reduce* the enviro-social impacts of consumption through, for example, less or 'different' forms of consuming or more efficient use of what one already consumes. On the other hand, SC can also be about *increasing* the impacts of consumption through the support of environmental and socially related 'alternative' causes such as fair trade. In some cases, the rationale for SC encapsulates both desires: shopping for locally produced foods is about both avoiding/reducing the carbon footprint of internationally sourced supermarket foods, and supporting local businesses and local farmers so that they stay in business. Furthermore, the scale of SC activities can incorporate entities from whole economic sectors, to corporations, to municipalities, to communities, all the way down to the level of individual consumers on their way to becoming 'responsible' (Hughes et al., 2008; Lawson, 2007; see also Raghuram et al., 2008) 'ecological citizens' (Seyfang, 2005, 2006) through their now altered (non-)buying habits.

Yet, one of the overarching components of SC is its (purported) ethical character and characteristics. Thus SC might be seen as the desire to do 'good' or 'right' by the environment, others and even one's self by doing less, 'differently', and/or more through the act of *consumption* and as *consumers*. Contextualized in the midst of the wider 'moral' turn in the social sciences (e.g. Held, 2006; Smith, 2000; Whatmore, 2002), several have commented on the role of consumption in working to develop a more 'moral economy' (Goodman, 2004) and/or an 'ethics of care' in various economic networks (Popke, 2006; Kneafsey et al., 2008), and doing so for quite some time now (Trentmann, 2007). In this and other work, specific attention has been paid to the mechanisms, practices, implications and limits of how the 'ethical' (Barnett et al., 2005; see also Harrison et al., 2005) or 'radical' consumer (Littler, 2009) is able to overcome the spatial 'problems' of the extended production/consumption networks of a globalized economy in order, for example, to help support the livelihoods of marginalized Caribbean banana growers or 'save' a particular part of the Amazonian rainforest to combat climate change. Thus, overall, from the 'alternative economic spaces' (Leyshon et al., 2003) and 'diverse economies' (Gibson-Graham, 2006) of small-scale, NGO-driven 'activist' businesses such as fair trade to the largest globalized corporations such as Wal-mart/Asda, the tag line of 'doing well by doing good' has the processes of SC and the figure of the sustainable consumer entrenched at its very core.

So, given the wide diversity in the origins, praxis and consequences of SC, how should we work to understand it? For us, analysing SC starts from the recognition of its *cultural* nature, function and make-up in the context of the wider environmental movement, and especially its shifts into the 'mainstream' of most industrial societies. Indeed, as just one form of 'culture', media – from TV and newspapers, to movies, to the Internet, to pop music – have worked incredibly hard to meld sustainability, lifestyles and consumption. For example, the *Ethical living* feature of *The Guardian*'s (2009) stand-alone online 'Environment' section of the newspaper is almost exclusively devoted to describing what products consumers should avoid or buy in order to consume more sustainably. And yet the specifics of what SC is and should be are decidedly fraught and uncertain but no less crucial for building more sustainable futures; thus the analytical key is understanding and exploring the cultural *politics* of SC. Here, in order to argue for the need to consider the circulating and shifting cultural politics of SC, we draw on the work of Boykoff et al. (2009: 136), who, in their specific engagement with climate change 'cultures', suggest that cultural politics are

> those politicized processes by which meaning is constructed and negotiated across space, place and at various scales. This involves not only the representations and messages that gain traction in discourses, but also those that are absent from them or silenced . . . As David Harvey (1990, p. 422) has commented, 'struggles over representation are as fundamental to the activities of place construction as bricks and mortar'. By examining these features as manifestations of ongoing and contested processes, we can consider questions regarding how power flows through the capillaries of our shared social, cultural and political body, constructing knowledge, norms, conventions and truths and untruths . . .

This resonates rather well with what some have called 'green governmentality' whereby – as in this chapter – SC produces particular truths, knowledges and subjectivities surrounding 'sustainability', 'consumption' and 'consumers', where power circulates through SC networks, working through and producing different bodies, discourses, institutions and practices in order to pursue certain sociopolitical ends. Crucially, then, a consideration of the cultural politics of SC must engage with the contemporary processes by which

> the responsibility for the environment is shifted onto the population, and citizens are called to take up the mantle of saving the environment in attractively simplistic ways. This allows for the management, self-surveillance and regulation of behaviour in such a way that lays claim to the kind of subjectivity that those who are environmentally conscious wish to have, and the governing of said subjectivity which does little to address the neoliberal order which contributes to environmental problems. In terms of becoming good environmental citizens, then, we know that there are virtuous and immoral ways to encounter nature, good and bad solutions to environmental problems and the tools for individuals to be responsible for their actions are defined already – we must only seek to apply them to our lives. (Rutherford, 2007: 299)

And lest we forget, these cultural politics and forms of governance in SC are firmly embedded in material networks; indeed, much of SC is about *altering* the very materialities of production/consumption networks – the technological as well as environmental/ ecological artefacts that construct human societies – for the 'better', again, specifically *through* consumption. Thus SC ultimately involves social and environmental governance through a cultural *material* politics of consumption; and, in particular these days, a *specific* cultural material politics that increasingly rides the tension of how individual consumption choices open up spaces for doing something at the scale of the 'everyday' versus *other* action *outside* the realm of 'shopping for change in contemporary culture' (Littler, 2009). How institutions, corporations, third-sector organizations and activist movements construct and engage with the current cultural material politics of SC forms the core focus of this chapter.

We turn now to a short historical account of the international and national (i.e. UK) policy networks and discourses surrounding SC.

Policy developments

When the first issue of this handbook was published, SC as an internationally stated policy objective was just five years old. One hundred and seventy-nine governments had signed up to the principles of *Agenda 21* (UN, 1992) at the UN Conference on Environment and Development (the Earth Summit) in 1992, officially committing to the need to make consumption more sustainable. Since that time, this political attention has been sustained in the form of a series of further international meetings and renewals of commitment. The Earth Summit was followed in 1997 by the Rio+5 conference; in 1998 by the *Human Development Report* (UNDP, 1998), which emphasized the link between SC and meeting basic human needs for all present and future generations; and then in 2002 by the 'World Summit on Sustainable Development' in Johannesburg, which affirmed international commitment to full implementation of *Agenda 21* and catalysed the International Expert Meeting on a ten-year framework of programmes for SC and production in 2003 in Marrakech. A common theme uniting these international political commitments is a focus on production-side resource efficiency in order to 'dematerialize' the economy, coupled with a programme of education and awareness-raising to encourage individuals as consumers to purchase these more sustainable products.

The continuing engagement of this international policy focus on SC is ostensibly encouraging. Yet despite naming the changing of unsustainable patterns of production and consumption as one of the top three priorities for the next two to three decades, the relevant sections of the *Johannesburg Plan of Implementation* (UN, 2002) have been criticized for paying only scant attention to SC, for having it phrased in the weakest possible language and for emphasizing energy efficiency over alternative approaches. Further, these sections of the Plan were apparently included only after controversial discussions about any reference to SC at all (Fuchs and Lorek, 2005). Whilst NGOs have been involved at the international and the national level, some argue that they have failed to bring about commitments to 'strong' interpretations of SC (i.e. interpretations that prioritize environmental and social well-being over those of economic 'health') as a result of their relative weakness as actors in global environmental governance regimes (Fuchs and Lorek, 2005).

These international policy commitments and the products of negotiations between governments around the world go on to shape domestic policy. The UK government was involved in each of the previously mentioned agreements, and since that time has created a suite of domestic policies and administrative bodies to support their delivery at a number of scales. Several new policy bodies have been created for this purpose including the Carbon Trust (2001), the Sustainable Development Commission (2002) and the Sustainable Buildings Task Group (2003). The Carbon Trust was charged with taking the lead in low-carbon technology and innovation in the UK by promoting sustainable energy technologies and practices, thus focusing on resource consumption at the aggregate level. The remit of the Sustainable Development Commission has been to act as a 'critical friend' to government, advocating sustainable development and SC across all sectors, reviewing progress and building consensus. Finally, the Sustainable Buildings Task Group brought together builders, developers, planners and environmental advisers with a focus on improving the resource and energy efficiency of buildings. For Hobson (2004), this kind of approach, which emphasizes the role of established policy networks in steering SC, is 'sustainability at arm's length' and a demonstration of overtly weak political leadership.

In 2003, the UK government launched its first SC strategy, known as *Changing Patterns*, in response to the EU's commitment at Johannesburg to develop a ten-year environmental policy framework. Yet *Changing Patterns* inherits its definition of SC and production directly from the previously developed UK Sustainable Development Strategy, *A Better Quality of Life* (UK Government, 1999). In both these policy documents, SC and production are claimed to 'exist' when economic growth has been decoupled from environmental degradation, realizable through a suite of primarily market-based measures including green taxes, innovation and green public procurement in tandem with civil-society-directed, awareness-raising information campaigns. This interpretation takes as a given that stable, continued economic growth is both necessary and compatible with 'responsible' resource use; the potential contribution of *reduced* levels of total resource consumption is quickly and thoroughly marginalized and/or dispensed with in these policy discourses. As Hobson (2002: 99) has put it, channelling the UK activist journalist George Monbiot, 'asking high-income countries what to do about overconsumption is like asking prison inmates what to do about crime'.

Furthermore, even this 'weak' interpretation of SC has not been easy to implement in the UK; implementation has been hampered by inconsistency in definitions, fluctuating political backing and poor integration of administrative mechanisms so that it fails to compete with the dominant, traditional economic concerns in UK policy-making (Russel, 2007). The mainstream approach, consisting of modest policy changes that fail to question prevailing lifestyles and consumption expectations, has been referred to as 'sustainability by stealth' (Robins, 1999). An alternative to the kind of policy-led focus on matching 'responsibilized' individuals to the production and consumption of 'green' products now in vogue in the UK, Hobson (2004) argues, is a strong political commitment to other normative and economic policy alternatives that *do not* cut out scales of action other than at that of the rational individual. The two pillars of this mainstream policy approach to SC – encouraging individuals as consumers to purchase 'sustainable' products and the emphasis on these products themselves – are the focus of the following two sections.

Information and the individualization of responsibility

The UK government has embraced public information campaigns as a strategy to generate pro-environmental behaviour change at repeated intervals since the Earth Summit in 1992. These national campaigns have included 'Helping the Earth begins at home', 'Going for Green' and most recently, 'Are you doing your bit?' Each of these campaigns called for individuals to learn about how to be responsible consumers in their everyday lives, covering a range of topics including water and energy use, or the consumption of particular products marked out as more sustainable by the presence of particular 'ecolabels'. Despite these attempts at awareness-raising, wide-scale behaviour change has been limited due to the inadequacy of such broad-brush, information-based approaches to sustainability (e.g. Collins et al., 2003; Hounsham, 2006). Indeed, as Hargreaves et al. (2008) have argued, a combination of contextualized knowledge production, a supportive social context and more rigorous practices of measurement and feedback are better able to bring about behaviour change than simple information dissemination alone.

Ecolabels have regularly featured in both international and domestic policy as important means of guiding individuals to consume more sustainable products by providing them with information about a particular good to enable them to judge its 'sustainable', 'ethical' or 'green' credentials. Technically, these labels work on the premises (1) that consumers will learn that the values embedded in a particular 'unsustainable' product conflict with their own broader environmental and social values, (2) that an ecolabelled substitute product will conflict less with or support those values, and (3) that the consumer will therefore choose the ecolabelled product (Gale, 2002; see also Barham, 2002). While increasing the consumption of such 'sustainable' products must surely contribute to the wider SC project, many commentators have taken a more critical approach to assessing the processes and promises of green labels (e.g. Guthman, 2007). Ecolabels applied to agricultural commodities have been described as representing simplified narratives of a specifically narrow ordering of ecosocial relations (Goodman and Goodman, 2001), where the checklists and codes of practices that sit behind the label potentially mystify the geographies of alternative commodity chains, 'refetishizing' consumption processes (Eden et al., 2008) and effectively suspending the need for consumers to develop other forms of environmental consciousness or critical ecological reasoning (Luke, 1997). Others have challenged the role of ecolabels in driving SC: for example, Grankvist et al. (2004) argue that ecolabels only affect the consumption decisions of those individuals with an existing interest in environmental issues, rather than with the majority of consumers.

Reifying the wider role of information – in the form of public service campaigns as well as ecolabels – in bringing about behaviour change, commonly referred to as the 'information deficit model', has been widely critiqued. At its heart, the model assumes that individuals are rational actors who make decisions solely on the basis of available information, one of the cornerstones of wider microeconomic theory. This formulation has two main difficulties: first, it ignores the often unequal structural, institutional and cultural frameworks within which we make our consumption decisions; and, second, it assumes that information is necessary but also – more importantly – sufficient to generate change. Overall, as Dolan (2002) suggests, by placing individuals and their needs and wants at the centre of policy constructions of SC, the actual praxis of consumption is decontextualized as an everyday practice to be abstracted as merely a set of microeconomic interactions devoid of their cultural, economic, and political contexts and relationalities.

Thus, merely providing individuals with information relating to SC fails to tackle the roots of society's lock-in to high-consumption lifestyles in terms of its economic, technological and cultural groundings (e.g. Michaelis, 2003). A significant body of work in environmental psychology identifies an increasing range of factors that affect whether or not we demonstrate pro-environmental behaviour; for example, personal moral and social norms, attitudes and behavioural control directly influence environmental behaviour whereas problem awareness (presumably through more and better information streams) is only indirectly implicated in developing more sustainable action (Bamberg, 2003; Bamberg and Moser, 2007). In addition, pro-environmental behaviour change is durable only if it is rooted in meaningful experience (Maiteny, 2002). A focus on generic, consumer-oriented information through impersonal media designed to engage contextualized, socially embedded consumers and issues often serves only to alienate individuals from SC. Thus Hobson (2003) argues for the need to *co-construct* SC knowledge, i.e. linking 'expert' knowledge with that of everyday consumers' experiences, which suggests that in order to be effective in generating behaviour change, a new cultural politics of SC might be needed. Here, and in parallel to these academic critiques, third-sector critics (e.g. Collins et al., 2003; Hounsham, 2006) of government-run, broad-brush, awareness-raising campaigns have drawn on conventional social marketing techniques to argue that tailored messages for different segments of the public would be more effective in getting the SC 'message' out and about.

Building on this critique of unsophisticated, blanket approaches to information dissemination, the UK Roundtable on Sustainable Consumption identified in its report, *I Will If You Will: Towards Sustainable Consumption* (SDC, 2006), that awareness-raising should involve what it terms 'community learning': informing people in groups about SC in order to cultivate new group-level social norms. A second key proposal in this document was the development of a standard social marketing approach to promoting particular behaviour-change goals, which has been taken up in the UK Department for Environment, Food and Rural Affairs' (Defra) *A Framework for Pro-Environmental Behaviours* (2008a). This framework identifies five particular behavioural goals associated with SC – personal transport, waste, energy, water and consumption of products – and then divides the public into seven segments according to their ability and willingness to act on these issues. This framework is intended to inform segment-tailored social marketing approaches to support SC, with a particular focus on reducing future contributions to climate change, and could be far-reaching given that it will inform future SC policies in the UK. Encouragingly, these newer approaches recognize that the public and their everyday practices are heterogeneous, and yet, in the end, the 'knowing expert/ ignorant public' dichotomy is still apparent. The recipients of SC information – while a bit more disaggregated – are still lumped together, and individuals are still very much held responsible for acting on this information once it is delivered to them.

Products and the production of ecological citizenship
The information circulating in SC networks encourages individuals to shift their consumption practices to include the purchase of particular kinds of 'sustainable' products often in support of the 'dematerialization' of the economy championed in policy. Individuals, through their more conscious purchases, are hereby 'responsibilized' as ecological citizens working towards a more sustainable future. A common conceptualization of ecological citizenship seeks to re-embed individuals in ethical relationships with producers of the products that they seek to consume. This approach argues for the need to socialize people as global citizens first and consumers second, constructing a particular kind of cosmopolitan or global citizenship that seeks to unveil the oppression of consumers and producers alike, tackle market myths around 'choice' and position justice at its axis (Valencia Saiz, 2005; McGregor, 2001; Luque, 2005). Echoing the discussion above, constructions of just what an ecological citizen should be are politically motivated and tend to be situated in modified 'business-as-usual' models that foreclose more 'radical' approaches to sustainability and SC in particular (Hobson, 2008).

Most often, the kinds of consumption included in ecological citizenship involve the simple shifting to the purchase of 'green' products, many of which have been produced through the deployment of environmental technologies as part of what has become known as the paradigm of 'ecological modernization' (see Mol, Chapter 4 in Part I of this volume). Ecological modernization emerged from supply-side debates and has only relatively recently been extended to the sphere of consumption by focusing on domestic routines and lifestyles across different social and environmental characteristics (Murphy, 2001; Spaargaren, 2000). The strongly productivist orientation associated with ecological modernization has been criticized for failing to challenge overconsumption and related overproduction (e.g. Carolan, 2004). Critics argue that a reliance on green products alone cannot bring about SC and that sustainability must be designed directly into systems of provision, social arrangements, sustainable home services and cultural attitudes as well as into green products (e.g. Green and Vergragt, 2002, Halme et al., 2004).

Research in the field of industrial ecology, particularly relating to lifecycle analysis, is very much linked to that on ecological modernization. Product lifecycles affect both efficiency and sufficiency (Cooper, 2005). Combining SC – in its guise as product purchasing, use and disposal – and more sustainable resource management – including resource extraction, transformation and materials management – is said to support consumers in evaluating the impacts of their purchasing decisions, help to tackle the international distanciation of production and consumption, and reduce environmental impacts across a commodity's entire lifecycle (Mont and Bleischwitz, 2007). Alternatively, applying lifecycle analysis to systems of needs *fulfilment* could provide an innovative approach to rethinking production/consumption networks, potentially enabling a move away from the sole reliance on consumerism to fulfil the needs of individuals and, indeed, societies more generally (De Leeuw, 2005).

The consumption of particular products deemed in some respect to be more sustainable has potentially interesting impacts on the formation of people's identities as 'sustainable consumers'. For example, the consumption of refillable glass milk bottles in the UK has been linked to resistance to supermarkets and disposability, as well as to the construction of individual and collective identities relating to narratives of community, sense of place, convenience and nostalgia for old England (Vaughan et al., 2007). Similarly, Hobson (2006) argues that domestic innovations such as recycling bins, low energy lightbulbs and shower timers are not only integral to what she calls the 'eco-modernization project', but these material 'moralizing machines' embody a kind of 'techno-ethics' that works to facilitate the creation of self-identifying sustainable consumers and citizens.

In addition to the purchase of such green products, consumers are encouraged to address social concerns through the consumption of particular kinds of ethical or fairly traded products in order to become even more well-rounded ecological citizens. Ethical consumption campaigns seek to motivate people as political agents by tapping into their so-called 'ordinary' and 'everyday' moralities, which are then channelled through consumption and the desire to 'perform' these (purchasing) acts as (self-)identified 'ethical' consumers (Clarke et al., 2007). Fair trade has been hailed by some as having a counter-hegemonic character that, at its more radical edges, goes beyond the current discourse of 'shopping for a better world' and into the realms of collective decision-making about consumption and about new producer/distributor relationships challenging the distribution of value along the commodity chain (Low and Davenport, 2007).

And yet, critics have charged that the fair trade approach is decidedly and narrowly market-based as it places limits on who can partake in fair trade networks – at both the consumption and production ends – in order to create value through the 'preciousness' of these quality-driven markets (Goodman, 2010; Guthman, 2007; see also Freidberg, 2003; Hughes, 2004). Moreover, as Low and Davenport (2005, 2007) argue, the current *mainstreaming* of fair trade runs the risk of reshaping the movement at the expense of its more radical and politicized edges and so far has failed to lead to the 'slop-over' of its principal tenets into conventional trade systems, as many in the fair trade movement would like to see happen. And, while ethical consumption through fair trade networks may constitute new networks of global solidarity, these depend on abstract understandings where ethical consumption remains a form of Northern benevolence, reproducing oppositions between *active* consumers and *passive* recipients and so flattening out what are already unequal power relations (cf. Barnett et al., 2005; Varul, 2008). Furthermore, a limited focus on fair trade in the context of SC may run the risk of excluding individuals' other ethical concerns, and complicating the business of ecological citizenship. Moore et al. (2006) note that supermarkets have requested a broadening of fair trade to include environmental as well as its predominantly anthropocentric concerns around the socioeconomic situation of marginalized producers in developing countries as a means of bridging this gap, with understandable resistance from the fair trade movement. Here, Hailwood (2005) argues for a combination of anthropocentric and ecocentric ideas in SC to instead develop a model of 'reasonable citizenship', which considers the ethics of our relationships with the environment and nature as well as with other people. Thus there are some calls to widen our conceptualizations of SC and sustainable consumers, since many may be simultaneously concerned with fair trade, ethical products, green products, voluntary simplicity and even ethical investing (Connolly and Shaw, 2006; McDonagh, 2006; Carter and Huby, 2005).

Downshifting, voluntary simplifiers and other challenges to consumerism
Whilst it is fair to say that most effort in delivering SC focuses on the role of products and their purchase(r)s, counter-hegemonic discourses and advocates of alternative approaches – many of which challenge consumerism more broadly – do exist. These approaches might be construed as located on a spectrum of pathways to change, moving from moderate and reformist in character at one end to more radical at the other. For example, at the moderate end there is what could be called 'alternative ownership' arrangements (e.g. car-sharing, communal washing/cooking centres and tool-sharing) that unfortunately – because of existing regulatory and normative institutional arrangements – have so far received a low profile in SC (Mont, 2004). For those at the more radical end of the spectrum, consuming particular sustainable products is simply another form of 'greenwashing' and instead, deeper changes are required through the development of alternative economic relationships and spaces (Leyshon et al., 2003), culture jamming (Klein, 2000; Littler, 2009), and even more fundamental changes to mainstream lifestyles and livelihoods (Ross, 2008).

Voluntary simplicity, or downshifting, is an example of a non-product-oriented approach to SC and, in and of itself, might be placed on a moderate-to-more-radical spectrum. Thus a range of activity is included here, from beginner voluntary simplifiers who might support some aspects of lifestyle changes based around shopping choices and limited green activities (e.g. buying fair trade products or recycling waste) to much more established voluntary simplifiers who freely choose a frugal, anti-consumption lifestyle featuring low resource use and minimal environmental impacts (McDonald et al., 2006); the contemporary phenomenon of 'freeganism', where 'freegans' consume only things that they *don't* buy, fits in this latter, more 'radical' portion of the spectrum. Voluntary simplification has always occupied a marginal position in modern societies and of necessity tends to be practised by those who have the socioeconomic capacity to 'overconsume' in the first place (Librova, 1999).

The growth of what are called new consumption communities (NCCs) is a recent focus of research into voluntary simplicity. NCCs comprise alternative communities where individuals embrace alternative consumption and production, resituating SC in a structural, embedded context to bring in elements of self-provisioning and alternative normative arrangements. These more radical voluntary simplifier groups are able to achieve partial autonomy from hegemonic market forces through forms of resistance, empowerment and reconnection to and rescaling of production networks (Bekin et al., 2006). Many of these downshifters have exhibited higher levels of happiness and enjoyment because of their lifestyles (Bekin et al., 2005), feeding into debates linking SC to increased well-being. It has been argued (ibid.) that NCCs have been able to influence other, 'non-sustainable' consumers and their relationship to consumption through educational links with local communities and volunteers.

NCCs are often involved in developing alternative economic structures, but such structures are not limited to these communities. As Curtis (2003) has highlighted, local or regional self-reliant community networks may constitute a key means of developing economic sustainability, incorporating local currencies, community corporations and regional food economies, and reducing the negative externalities of long-distance trade. Yet economic geographers such as Hudson (2005) argue that small-scale experiments to create sustainable economies such as local exchange trading schemes (LETS) are significant but ultimately occur within the existing capitalist framework, which limits sustainability unless they satisfy normal profitability criteria and fall within socially and politically acceptable limits for institutions. Similarly, Aldridge and Patterson (2002) have found that despite their potential, LETS often have a very limited economic role that is complicated by low participation and structural constraints; members typically require significant financial resources and the scheme seems to work best specifically at small scales with predominantly middle-class groups.

One interesting, emerging direction in research on alternative forms of SC is what Soper (2007, 2008) calls 'alternative hedonism'. This theory posits that consumerism ultimately creates environments that are socially and personally repressive, leading to an overall level of disenchantment in the sense that we can never satisfy our desires by simply consuming more (see also Bauman, 2007). Thomas (2008) argues that the kind of disaffection or 'ambivalent consumerism' Soper refers to is already present and being acted on in the mainstream media in the form of UK lifestyle television programmes that incorporate narratives linking downsizing, downshifting and 'the good life', where alternative hedonistic activity supports a domestic, local version of citizenship in the face of political disenchantment. Thus, by capitalizing on this disenchantment with consumerism and redirecting people's desires towards the cultural and artistic aesthetics of 'anti-consumption consumption' (Bryant and Goodman, 2004), SC could be much more effective at motivating societies beyond moral concerns alone and work towards a more holistic vision of sustainable living that *has room* for self-interest rather than centring on a kind of moral superiority.

What gets measured counts: footprinting, indicators and redefining prosperity

Measuring progress towards SC is an important means of judging the effectiveness of different approaches. In general, there are two main levels at which progress towards SC may be measured: at the individual level, through 'footprinting' and pledging; and at the national level via indicators and indices.

Footprinting and pledging are two techniques that are increasingly being encouraged by third-sector advocates as a means of measuring individual consumption against particular ideals, which of course have been constructed by particular government and advocacy groups (Hinton, 2009). Both pledging and footprinting tools are primarily administered through Internet advocacy spaces (e.g. http://www.carbonfootprint.com), where resultant scores are stored and can be used as a measure of how sustainable each individual's consumption practices are, or will be over time.

Footprinting tools tend to follow a questionnaire format, where individuals' responses to questions on aspects of their individual consumption of various resources and commodities are translated into their ecological 'footprint'. Answers to these questions are often converted into numerical values, representing either the number of global hectare equivalents this kind of consumption would require, how many planets of resources would be required if everyone were to consume in this way, or in terms of carbon equivalents in order to describe an individual's responsibility for climate change. These precise, numerical values conceal the various debates over what should and shouldn't be measured, how it should be measured and even if it is measurable. The lack of a uniform approach to footprinting (Wiedmann and Minx, 2007) inevitably leads to some degree of variability in footprint size, even when the same questions are asked and the same answers provided to different footprinting tools. Indeed, the premise of footprinting is that it is possible objectively to know and quantify what makes our consumption unsustainable, across various parameters including the amount of carbon (or CO_2) associated with certain activities, as well as water and other resource use. By including only certain activities, and within these activities including only limited aspects of their associated resource use, these tools seem inevitably to reify certain consumption actions and their particular aspects.

Where footprinting takes into account prior consumption practices, pledging focuses on future consumption and (it is hoped) emissions reductions. Pledging systems ask individuals to pledge to commit certain kinds of SC practices in the future. Conceivably there may be a degree of kudos associated with making certain pledges, or making a certain number of pledges, such that pledging may stand as a kind of conspicuous SC that may be entirely unrelated to actions that individuals actually undertake. Another potential downside of pledges is their reliance on deferred action, which suffers from the problems of hyperbolic discounting such that individuals are required to weigh up whether it is worth acting now for benefits that may or may not emerge in the future.

Moving from the individual to the national level, statistics have been collected in the

UK for several years across a range of different criteria, which collectively represent 'sustainable consumption and production indicators' (e.g. Defra, 2008b). Sustainable consumption and production (SCP) is identified here as one of four priority areas, where the relevant indicators cover mainly emissions, resource use and waste. However, ascertaining just how (un)sustainable domestic consumption and production *is* may not be straightforward, since, for example, individual commodity chains are often global in their spatial reach, blurring the geographical locations of their ecological effects (Andersson and Lindroth, 2001; see also Peters and Hertwich, 2006).

National economies are normally judged according to their levels of production in the form of GDP. Alternatives to this means of evaluating progress have long been considered a potential means to support SC, which was notably included as a recommendation in *Agenda 21* back in 1992. GDP is considered a proxy for national welfare, yet it excludes the benefits of goods and services produced and used outside the marketplace (Michaelis, 2003), and it is a rather poor measure of well-being (Jackson et al., 2004; Boulanger, 2007). Consequently, alternatives to GDP have been proposed – for instance the Indicator of Sustainable Economic Welfare, Gross National Happiness or Measure of Domestic Progress scores – in which SC could form an integral component (e.g. Michaelis, 2003; SDC, 2006). The measurement of well-being has been linked to SC, notably in the *Human Development Report* (UNDP, 1998). Instead of focusing on the microeconomics of SC products and purchases, the concept of well-being suggests the need to shift to thinking in terms of 'more units of happiness with less damage' (De Leeuw, 2005). Well-being may have more cultural salience for many, and so be more likely to elicit behavioural changes in people and communities. In a positive recognition of the importance of this concept in the context of SC, the UK government has, since 2008, measured well-being in its set of indicators for sustainable development (Defra, 2008b); yet it is doubtful how meaningful comparisons of well-being are between different people and over time, and the extent to which these can be tied directly to issues of sustainability and SC. In addition, well-being is closely tied to cultural norms and expectations, and, thus, such a measure would inevitably go to support mainstream, product-based SC and fail to disentangle SC from continued economic growth within contemporary societies. Whilst individual systems of monitoring such as the Defra suite of SCP and well-being indicators may go some way to observing whether SC is being achieved, such an approach remains at the periphery and is unlikely significantly to influence policy and practice.

The 'credit crunch': threat or opportunity?
At the time of writing, the UK economy is experiencing a recession as a result of the phenomenon colloquially termed the 'credit crunch'. Whilst initially the flow of credit was restricted in 'virtual' money markets, this eventually spilled over into real markets and has led to a restriction in the amount of credit available to both industry and consumers. In turn, this has led to growing unemployment and an increase in the cost of living, leaving increasing numbers of people with reduced disposable income, and potentially a reduction in market-based consumption.

The effects of recession on SC and its cultural politics are not immediately clear. However, past economic growth has clearly been boosted by the failure to include environmental externalities in the price of products and other consumables such as energy, and such artificially low prices have encouraged increased consumption and disposal (Schor, 2005). Furthermore, it would appear that product-based approaches to SC are not completely compatible with periods of recession since these 'sustainable' products are often more expensive. For example, the price premium associated with products such as organic and fair trade goods could make them less attractive options, with a potential negative effect on the market for these types of commodity. Yet, at the same time, restricted funds could provide greater incentives for the purchase of more durable and less disposable commodities, thus promoting more SC.

Capitalism depends upon ever-increasing production and consumption. As such, politicians are urging the public to spend more in order to help the economy to recover. Individuals as consumers are thus doubly responsibilized: they must rescue the economy, yet remain ecological citizens in the marketplace. Such an approach further marginalizes non-market forms of consumption, and reinforces the hegemonic ecological modernization perspective of product-oriented SC. Yet if consumers really do have the power to either rescue or abandon the economy through their individual consumption choices, then the recession could provide an opportunity for them to vote with their money by not responding to these calls to increase spending and instead meeting more of their needs and wants through non-marketplace consumption or other forms of well-being-oriented behaviours. Perhaps the recession affords individuals as consumers a new kind of consumer sovereignty, not just with regard to choosing between products in the market, but with regard to the opportunity to choose what sort of economic system to engage with.

What might an alternative, recession-oriented SC entail? At a minimum, there could be three key components: downshifting; a reduction in the working week; and alternative community economies. First, the recession may encourage – or even force – greater numbers of consumers to embrace voluntary simplicity and downshifting, reducing the volume of wants and needs and meeting more of the remainder outside the marketplace. Second, a reduction in market-based consumption would reduce the need to work, challenging the 'work-to-spend' lifestyle. The reduction in available jobs resulting from the recession need not necessarily result in increased unemployment, if many of the full-time jobs were offered part-time instead, or if the working week were generally reduced (e.g. Schor, 1991). Third, this increase in leisure time may support participation in alternative and local currencies, e.g. LETS and timebanking, which have historically arisen in times of recession (Seyfang, 2006).

A global economic downturn might also signal a need to further redefine SC as a concept that considers the continuing inequalities of consumption at a number of different scales – and not just for basic items like food and shelter, but *especially* for more sustainable goods. Underscoring the inequalities of consumption through the discourse of SC might work to further situate questions of justice and ethics at its core as well as shake up the contemporary consumerist product focus of SC for the better.

Concluding remarks

Whilst political, academic and practitioner interest in SC has grown over the last decade, it is still a nascent social movement. The contemporary 'post-ecologist' era and its politics of unsustainability may well necessitate a new environmental sociology that centres on the question of how advanced modern capitalist democracies try to sustain what is known to be unsustainable (Blühdorn and Welsh, 2007). It may be that the very way that we approach the issue, by creating the label of 'sustainable consumption' as a way to complement 'sustainable production', supports efforts to sustain the unsustainable by disaggregating what are two inseparable processes. Ecological modernization, information dissemination and the development of markets for SC products form the current hegemonic expressions of SC because these best fit economic understandings of individuals as rational actors and are best suited to the contemporary growth economy.

There is some support within the literature and indeed in this chapter for broadening our conceptualizations of SC. Mont and Bleischwitz (2007) argue for the integration of sustainable resource management with SC. Princen (1999) posits that SC has come to be conflated with everything from production, overall economic activity, materialism and maldistribution, to population and technology, and could be reclaimed by focusing attention on the everyday sociologies of product use and non-purchasing decisions. Similarly, Gilg et al. (2005) argue that green consumerism must be seen in the context of other aspects of sustainable living to provide a more holistic view beyond that of well-being.

Perhaps one of the most useful ways forward for the SC project could be a reinvigorated conceptualization of it as being principally about *sustainable lifestyles* and *sustainable livelihoods* rather than just about the narrow but important practices of consumption. Whichever way future work on SC goes, it will require further inter- and cross-disciplinary research and writing in order to untangle its complexities in any sort of transition to more sustainable ways of living. Yet what is even more salient at this particular historical moment is the need for SC – through both critical social science work and that of civil society – to act as a more thoroughgoing and radical challenge to everyday social ordering(s) and policy than has hitherto been the case.

Acknowledgements

We would like to thank Tom Hargreaves, Francis Fahy and the editors for their detailed comments and suggestions for improving the contents of the chapter.

References

Aldridge, T.J. and A. Patterson (2002), 'LETS get real: constraints on the development of local exchange trading schemes', *Area*, **34** (4): 370–81.

Andersson, J.O. and M. Lindroth (2001), 'Ecologically unsustainable trade', *Ecological Economics*, **37**: 113–22.

Bamberg, S. (2003), How does environmental concern influence specific environmentally related behaviours? A new answer to an old question, *Journal of Environmental Psychology*, **23**: 21–32.

Bamberg, S. and G. Moser (2007), 'Twenty years after Hines, Hungerford, and Tomera: a new meta-analysis of psycho-social determinants of pro-environmental behaviour', *Journal of Environmental Psychology*, **27**: 14–25.

Barham, E. (2002), 'Towards a theory of values-based labeling', *Agriculture and Human Values*, **19**: 349–60.

Barnett, C., P. Cloke, N. Clarke and A. Malpass (2005), 'Consuming ethics: articulating the subjects and spaces of ethical consumption', *Antipode*, **37** (1): 23–45.

Bauman, Z. (2007), *Consuming life*, Cambridge: Polity Press.

Bekin, C., M. Carrigan and I. Szmigin (2005), 'Defying marketing sovereignty: voluntary simplicity at new consumption communities', *Qualitative Market Research: An International Journal*, **8** (4): 413–29.

Bekin, C., M. Carrigan and I. Szmigin (2006), 'Empowerment, waste and new consumption communities', *International Journal of Sociology and Social Policy*, **28** (1/2): 32–47.

Blühdorn, Ingolfur and Ian Welsh (2007), 'Eco-politics beyond the paradigm of sustainability: a conceptual framework and research agenda', *Environmental Politics*, **16** (2): 185–205.

Boulanger, P.M. (2007), 'What's wrong with consumption for sustainable development: overconsumption, underconsumption, misconsumption?', in E. Zaccaï (ed.) *Sustainable Consumption, Ecology and Fair Trade*, London: Routledge, pp. 17–32.

Boykoff, M., I. Curtis and M. Goodman (2009), 'The cultural politics of climate change: interactions in the spaces of the everyday', in M. Boykoff (ed.), *The Politics of Climate Change*, London: Routledge, pp. 136–54.

Bryant, R.L. and M.K. Goodman (2004), 'Consuming narratives: the political ecology of "alternative" consumption', *Transactions of the Institute of British Geographies*, **29**: 344–66.

Carolan, M.S. (2004), 'Ecological modernization theory: what about consumption?', *Society and Natural Resources*, **17** (3): 247–60.

Carter, N. and M. Huby (2005), 'Ecological citizenship and ethical investment', *Environmental Politics*, **14** (2): 255–72.

Clarke, N., C, Barnett, P. Cloke and A. Malpass (2007), 'Globalising the consumer: doing politics in an ethical register', *Political Geography*, **26**: 231–49.

Collins, J., G. Thomas, R. Willis and J. Wilsdon (2003), *Carrots, Sticks and Sermons: Influencing Public Behaviour for Environmental Goals*, London: Demos and Green Alliance.

Connolly, J. and D. Shaw (2006), 'Identifying fair trade in consumption choice', *Journal of Strategic Marketing*, **14** (4): 353–68.

Cooper, T. (2005), 'Slower consumption: reflections on product life spans and the "throwaway society"', *Journal of Industrial Ecology*, **9** (1–2): 51–67.

Curtis, F. (2003), 'Eco-localism and sustainability', *Ecological Economics*, **46**: 83–102.

De Leeuw, B. (2005), 'The world behind the product', *Journal of Industrial Ecology*, **9** (1–2): 7–10.

Defra (2008a), *A Framework for Pro-Environmental Behaviours*, London: HMSO.

Defra (2008b), *Sustainable Development Indicators in your Pocket 2009*, London: HMSO.

Dolan, P. (2002), 'The sustainability of "sustainable consumption"', *Journal of Macromarketing*, **22**: 170–81.

Eden, S., C. Bear and G. Walker (2008), 'Mucky carrots and other proxies: problematising the knowledge-fix for sustainable and ethical consumption', *Geoforum*, **39**: 1044–57.

Freidberg, S. (2003), 'Cleaning up down South: supermarkets, ethical trade and African horticulture', *Social and Cultural Geography*, **4** (1): 27–43.

Fuchs, D. and S. Lorek (2005), 'Sustainable consumption governance: a history of promises and failures', *Journal of Consumer Policy*, **28**: 261–88.

Gale, F. (2002), 'Caveat Certificatum: the case of forest certification', in T. Princen, M. Maniates and K. Conca (eds), *Confronting Consumption*, Cambridge, MA: MIT Press, pp. 275–99.

Gibson-Graham, J.K. (2006), *A Post-capitalist Politics*, Minneapolis, MN: University of Minnesota Press.

Gilg, A., S. Barr and N. Ford (2005), 'Green consumption or sustainable lifestyles? Identifying the sustainable consumer', *Futures*, **57**: 481–504.

Goodman, D. and M. Goodman (2001), 'Sustaining foods: organic consumption and the socio-ecological imaginary', in M.J. Cohen and J. Murphy (eds), *Exploring Sustainable Consumption: Environmental Policy and the Social Sciences*, Oxford: Pergamon, pp. 97–119.

Goodman, M. (2004), 'Reading fair trade: political ecological imaginary and the moral economy of fair trade foods', *Political Geography*, **23** (7): 891–915.

Goodman, M. (2010), 'The mirror of consumption: celebritisation, developmental consumption and the shifting cultural politics of fair trade', *Geoforum*, **41**: 104–16.

Grankvist, G., U. Dahlstrand and A. Biel (2004), 'The impact of environmental labelling on consumer preference: negative vs positive labels', *Journal of Consumer Policy*, **27**: 213–30.

Green, K. and P. Vergragt (2002), 'Towards sustainable households: a methodology for developing sustainable technological and social innovations', *Futures*, **34**: 381–400.

Guthman, J. (2007), 'The Polanyian way? Voluntary food labels as neoliberal governance', *Antipode*, **39** (3): 456–78.

Hailwood, S. (2005), 'Environmental citizenship as reasonable citizenship', *Environmental Politics*, **14** (2): 195–210.

Halme, M., C. Jasch and M. Scharp (2004), 'Sustainable homeservices? Toward household services that enhance ecological, social and economic sustainability', *Ecological Economics*, **51**: 125–38.

Hargreaves, T., M. Nye and J. Burgess (2008), 'Social experiments in sustainable consumption: an evidence-based approach with potential for engaging low-income communities', *Local Environment*, **13** (8): 743–58.

Harrison, R., T. Newholm and Shaw (eds) (2005), *The Ethical Consumer*, London: Sage.

Harvey, David (1990), 'Between space and time: reflections on the geographical imagination', *Annals of the Association of American Geographers*, **80**: 418–34.

Held, V. (2006), *The Ethics of Care: Personal, Political and Global*, Oxford: Oxford University Press.

Hinton, E.D. (2009), '"Changing the world one lazy-assed mouse click at a time": Exploring the virtual spaces of virtualism in UK third-sector sustainable consumption advocacy', Environment, Politics and Development Working Paper Series, WP No. 16, Department of Geography, King's College London.

Hobson, K. (2002), 'Competing discourses of SC: does the "rationalisation of lifestyles" make sense?', *Environmental Politics*, **11** (2): 95–120.

Hobson, K. (2003), 'Thinking habits into action: the role of knowledge and process in questioning household consumption practices', *Local Environment*, **8** (1): 95–112.

Hobson, K. (2004), 'Sustainable consumption in the United Kingdom: the "responsible" consumer and government at "arm's length"', *Journal of Environment and Development*, **13** (2): 121–39.

Hobson, K. (2006), 'Bins, bulbs, and shower timers: on the "techno-ethics" of sustainable living', *Ethics, Place and Environment*, **9** (3): 317–36.

Hobson, K. (2008), 'Reasons to be cheerful: thinking sustainably in a (climate) changing world', *Geography Compass*, **2** (1): 199–214.

Hounsham, S. (2006), *Painting the Town Green: How to Persuade People to be Environmentally Friendly*, 3rd edn, London: Green-Engage Communications.

Hudson, R. (2005), 'Towards sustainable economic practices, flows and spaces: or is the necessary impossible and the impossible necessary?', *Sustainable Development*, **13**: 239–52.

Hughes, A. (2004), 'Accounting for ethical trade: global commodity networks, virtualism and the audit economy' in A. Hughes and S. Reiner (eds), *Geographies of Commodity Chains*, London: Routledge, pp. 215–32.

Hughes, A., N. Wrigley and M. Buttle (2008), 'Global production networks, ethical campaigning and the embeddedness of responsible governance', *Journal of Economic Geography*, **8**: 345–67.

Jackson, T., W. Jager and S. Stagl (2004), 'Beyond insatiability: needs theory, consumption and sustainability', Swindon, UK: ESRC Sustainable Technologies Programme Working Paper Series no. 2004/2.

Klein, N. (200), *No Logo*, London: Flamingo.

Kneafsey, M., L. Holloway, R. Cox, E. Dowler, L. Venn and H. Tuomainen (2008), *Reconnecting Consumers, Producers and Food: Exploring Alternatives*, Oxford: Berg.

Lawson, V. (2007), 'Geographies of care and responsibility', *Annals of the Association of American Geographers*, **97** (1): 1–11.

Leyshon, A., R. Lee and C. Williams (eds) (2003), *Alternative Economic Spaces*, London: Sage.

Littler, J. (2009), *Radical Consumption*, Maidenhead, UK: Open University Press.

Librova, H. (1999), 'The disparate roots of voluntary modesty', *Environmental Values*, **8**: 369–80.

Local Environment (2008), Special issue on Inequality and Sustainable Consumption, **13** (8).

Low, W. and E. Davenport (2005), 'Postcards from the edge: maintaining the "alternative" character of fair trade', *Sustainable Development*, **13**: 143–53.

Low, W. and E. Davenport (2007), 'Mainstreaming fair trade: adoption, assimilation, appropriation', *Journal of Strategic Marketing*, **14** (4): 315–27.

Luke, T.W. (1997), *Ecocritique: Contesting the Politics of Nature, Economy, and Culture*, Minneapolis, MN: University of Minnesota Press.

Luque, E. (2005), 'Researching environmental citizenship and its publics', *Environmental Politics*, **14** (2): 211–25.

Maiteny, P.T. (2002), 'Mind in the gap: summary of research exploring "inner" influences on pro-sustainability learning and behaviour', *Environmental Education Research*, **8** (3): 299–306.

McDonagh, P. (2006), 'Liberte, equalite, fraternite: reflections on the growth of fair trade and business strategy', *Journal of Strategic Marketing*, **14** (4): 295–97.

McDonald, S., C.J. Oates, C.W. Young and K. Hwang (2006), 'Toward SC: researching voluntary simplifiers', *Psychology and Marketing*, **23** (6): 515–34.

McGregor, S. (2001), 'Participatory consumerism', *Consumer Interests Annual*, **47**: 1–6.

Michaelis, L. (2003), 'The role of business in sustainable consumption', *Journal of Cleaner Production*, **11**: 915–21.

Mont, O. (2004), 'Institutionalisation of sustainable consumption patterns based on shared use', *Ecological Economics*, **50**: 135–53.

Mont, O. and R. Bleischwitz (2007), 'Sustainable consumption and resource management in the light of life cycle thinking', *European Environment*, **17**: 59–76.

Moore, G., J. Gibbon and R. Slack (2006), 'The mainstreaming of fair trade: a macromarketing perspective', *Journal of Strategic Marketing*, **14** (4): 329–52.

Murphy, J. (2001), 'From production to consumption: environmental policy in the European Union', in M.J. Cohen and J. Murphy (eds), *Exploring Sustainable Consumption: Environmental Policy and the Social Sciences*, Oxford: Pergamon, pp. 39–58.

Peters, G.P. and E.G. Hertwich (2006), 'Pollution embodied in trade: the Norwegian case', *Global Environmental Change*, **16**: 379–87.

Popke, J. (2006), 'Geography and ethics: Everyday mediations through care and consumption', *Progress in Human Geography*, **30** (4): 504–12.

Princen, T. (1999), 'Consumption and environment, some conceptual issues', *Ecological Economics*, **31**: 347–63.

Raghuram, P., C. Madge and P. Noxolo (2008), 'Rethinking responsibility and care for a postcolonial world', *Geoforum*, **40**: 5–13.

Robins, N. (1999), 'Making sustainability bite: transforming global consumption patterns', *The Journal of Sustainable Product Design*, July: 7–16.

Ross, A. (2008), 'The quandaries of consumer-based labor activism: a low wage case study', *Cultural Studies*, **22** (5): 770–87.

Russel, D. (2007), 'The United Kingdom's sustainable development strategies: leading the way or flattering to deceive?', *European Environment*, **17**: 189–200.

Rutherford, S. (2007), 'Green governmentality: insights and opportunities in the study of nature's rule', *Progress in Human Geography*, **31** (3): 291–307.

Schor, J. (1991), 'Global equity and environmental crisis: an argument for reducing working hours in the North', *World Development*, **19** (1): 73–84.

Schor, K. (2005), 'Prices and quantities: unsustainable consumption and the global economy', *Ecological Economics*, **55**: 309–20.

SDC (2006), *I Will If You Will: Towards Sustainable Consumption*, London: HMSO.

Seyfang, G. (2005), 'Shopping for sustainability: can sustainable consumption promote ecological citizenship?', *Environmental Politics*, **14** (2): 290–306.

Seyfang, G. (2006), 'Sustainable consumption, the new economics and community currencies: developing new institutions for environmental governance', *Regional Studies*, **40** (7): 781–91.

Smith, D. (2000), *Moral Geographies: Ethics in a World of Difference*, Edinburgh, UK: Edinburgh University Press.

Soper, K. (2007), 'Re-thinking the "good life": the citizenship dimension of consumer disaffection with consumerism', *Journal of Consumer Culture*, **7** (2): 205–29.

Soper, K. (2008), 'Alternative hedonism, cultural theory and the role of aesthetic revisioning', *Cultural Studies*, **22** (5): 567–87.

Spaargaren, G. (2000), 'Ecological modernization theory and domestic consumption', *Journal of Environmental Policy and Planning*, **2** (4): 323–35.

The Guardian (2009), *Ethical living*, http://www.guardian.co.uk/environment/ethical-living.

Thomas, L. (2008), 'Alternative realities: downshifting narratives in contemporary lifestyle television', *Cultural Studies*, **22** (5): 680–99.

Trentmann, F. (2007), 'Before "fair trade": empire, free trade, and the moral economies of food in the modern world', *Environment and Planning D*, Society and Space 25: 1079–102.

UK Government (1999), *Sustainable Development: A Better Quality of Life. A strategy for sustainable development for the UK*, London: TSO.

UN (1992), *Agenda 21*, http://www.un.org/esa/sustdev/documents/agenda21/english/agenda21toc.htm, last accessed 15/12/2008.

UN (2002), *Johannesburg Plan of Implementation*, http://www.un.org/esa/sustdev/documents/WSSD_POI_PD/English/POIToc.htm, last accessed 23/01/2009.

UNDP (1998), *Human Development Report*, New York and Oxford: Oxford University Press.

Valencia Saiz, A. (2005), 'Globalisation, cosmopolitianism and ecological citizenship', *Environmental Politics*, **14** (2): 163–78.

Varul, M. (2008), 'Consuming the campesino', *Cultural Studies*, **22** (5): 654–79.

Vaughan, P., M. Cook and P. Trawick (2007), 'A sociology of reuse: deconstructing the milk bottle', *Sociologia Ruralis*, **47** (2): 120–34.

Whatmore, S. (2002), *Hybrid Geographies: Natures, Cultures, Spaces*, London: Sage.

Wiedmann, T. and J. Minx (2007), '*A definition of "carbon footprint"*', Centre of Integrated Sustainability Analysis, Durham, ISA UK Research Report 07-01.

17 Globalization, convergence and the Euro-Atlantic development model
Wolfgang Sachs

Introduction

The rise of Europe to world dominance in the nineteenth century has excited the curiosity of historians for a long time. Why was Europe able to leap ahead of the rest of the world? A variety of answers has been offered by several generations of researchers. Europe was variously thought to have benefited from its rational spirit, its liberal institutions or its temperate climate.

A few years ago, however, Kenneth Pomeranz of the University of California at Los Angeles advanced an 'environmental' hypothesis (Pomeranz, 2000). Putting the question more specifically, he wondered how England had succeeded in moving ahead of China, notwithstanding the fact that China had been on a level of development comparable to England as recently as around 1750. Moreover, at the end of the eighteenth century both the Yangtze Delta and England were constrained in their economic development by the scarcity of land available to grow food, supply fuel and provide materials. Only England succeeded in overcoming this limit, however, which it achieved by tapping into two new stocks of resources. First, it gained access to biotic resources from overseas, importing tobacco, sugar, cotton and grain from colonies in North America and the Caribbean. And above all, it managed to exploit the 'subterranean forest' by learning how to utilize coal for industrial processes. Only as foreign land replaced domestic land and coal substituted for wood were the natural resource constraints left behind, enabling the British economy to 'take off'. It has been estimated that as early as 1830 virtual acres overseas and underground helped to more than double Britain's available land area (Pomeranz, 2000: 275–6), while in 1875 coal alone provided energy equal to a forest three times this area (Schandl and Krausmann, 2007: 103). In contrast, China neither developed colonies overseas nor mobilized coal reserves in distant Manchuria. Put more generally, access to biotic resources from colonies and to fossil resources from the earth's crust was essential to the rise of the Euro-Atlantic civilization. Industrial society would not exist in today's shape had not resources been mobilized from both the expanse of geographical space and the depth of geological time.

The development dilemma

With Britain's 'take-off' the landscape of inequality among nations began to change. Since the third decade of the nineteenth century the world has witnessed a growing gap in income between industrialized and non-industrialized countries. Britain, Germany and France rushed ahead, followed by Italy, the USA and Japan, leaving the non-industrialized world increasingly behind. Consequently, between 1820 and 2000 global income disparity has grown continuously, rapidly up to the Second World War and at a slower pace in the second half of the past century (Bourguignon and Morrison,

2002; Firebough, 2003; Milanovic, 2005). As a result, global inequality has continued to remain very marked, comparable only to notoriously unequal nations like Brazil or South Africa. Moreover, the conditions that had unleashed Britain's rise continued to operate throughout the twentieth century. Where previously colonies had provided access to additional land through agricultural exports, developing countries later continued to supply the industrialized world with biotic resources. For example, in 2004 Europe utilized a land area as large as one-fifth of its own agricultural area beyond its borders, predominantly in Southern countries (Steger, 2005). Where previously forest areas had been replaced by coal from the depths of the earth, it later was oil, uranium and natural gas that provided fossil energy power.

In particular, the mobilization of fossil resources from the depths of the earth triggered the transformation of agrarian societies into industrial societies, changing their socioeconomic metabolism in a profound way (Fischer-Kowalski and Haberl, 2007). While the energy system in agrarian economies is based mainly on the extraction of biomass from local ecosystems through agriculture, forestry and fisheries, the energy system in industrial economies relies to a large extent on the extraction of fossil deposits that are available independent of the make-up of local ecosystems. Three decisive advantages emerge with this transition (Altvater, 2005: 86). First, energy becomes available at much higher densities since the extraction of fossil stocks is not limited by the biological cycles of reproduction and maturation as in the agrarian economy. Second, as energy can be used from distant deposits, the limited resource assets of local ecosystems no longer act as constraints to economic expansion. And third, with respect to biomass, fossil energy carriers can be much more easily transported over long distances, making use of waterways, tankers or pipelines. All three advantages amount to a steep increase in power that marks technologies, lifestyles and beliefs in industrial societies. The shift to a fossil resource base abolished the historical limits to economic growth and triggered a surge in the use of energy and materials. Alongside successive waves of conversion technologies, such as the internal combustion engine or the electric motor, industrial societies were able to mobilize apparently infinite volumes of power for production, mobility and comfort. This achievement underpinned the superiority of industrial societies up to the end of the twentieth century. Their fossil-based 'success' provided the lead for the rest of the world; the Euro-Atlantic civilization came to set the global standard for successful development.

In hindsight, however, Europe's development path turns out to be a special case; it cannot be repeated everywhere and any time: the wealth of fossil and renewable raw materials at Europe's disposal in the nineteenth and twentieth centuries is no longer available. Although only roughly one-third of the people in the world enjoy the fruits of industrial progress, the biosphere shows signs of exhaustion. It has been calculated that the global ecological footprint currently exceeds the biocapacity of the earth annually by 20–30 per cent (Wackernagel et al., 2002; WWF, 2008: 2; see also Barcena Hinojal and Lago Aurrekoetxea on 'ecological debt', Chapter 10 in this volume). Indeed, since 1975 ecological overshoot has become a distinctive mark of human history – with still largely unforeseeable consequences. At any rate, resources, both biotic and fossil, are gradually running short on the one side, while their use is destabilizing the earth's climate on the other. As a consequence, the resources required for completing the transition from the agrarian to the industrial age for the two remaining thirds of the world population are neither easily accessible nor cheaply available. As both the looming peak oil and the onset of climate chaos indicate, the past 200 years of Euro-Alantic development are in all likelihood doomed to remain a parenthesis in world history (Wuppertal Institut, 2008).

Yet the end of the industrial era has thrown the world into a tragic dilemma. Fossil-driven development cannot simply be called off; it has already spread worldwide in both structures and minds. Obviously, urban life is underpinned everywhere by fossil-based systems of energy, transport and food production. But more importantly, fossil-driven development has colonized the minds of people across the globe, even the minds of those who live in slums, villages or forests and are excluded from enjoying the fruits of economic progress. Partly through imposition, partly through attraction, the Euro-Atlantic development model has shaped Southern desires, offering tangible examples not only of a different, but of a supposedly better, life. Countries in general do not aspire to become more 'Indian', more 'Brazilian' or for that matter more 'Islamic'; instead, assertions to the contrary notwithstanding, they long to achieve industrial modernity. More often than not the idea prevails that shopping malls and steel-mills, freeways and factory farms indicate the path to a successful society. Despite decolonization in the political sense, which has led to independent states, and despite decolonization in the economic sense, which has made some countries into economic powers, a decolonization of the imagination has not occurred. On the contrary, across the world hopes for the future are fixed on the Euro-Atlantic patterns of production and consumption. It is the tragedy of the twenty-first century that the imagination of the world is shaped by the Euro-Atlantic civilization, yet the means for everyone to live in this civilization are ever-less available.

China's emblematic case

China provides the most visible example of where the world stands in the scramble for colonies and carbon today. No doubt the rise of China is a success story in terms of conventional development. It has not only continuously achieved high growth rates, but also dramatically reduced the share of poor people earning less than one dollar a day from 33 per cent of the population in 1990 to 10 per cent in 2006 (UNESCAP, 2007: 103). Yet what is a success for China amounts to a failure for the planet. In absolute terms, China has by now become the world's largest emitter of carbon dioxide ahead of the USA, as well as the second-largest importer of oil. Even more marked than the pressure of Chinese economic growth on global resources has been the stress on local habitats: cities sick from polluted air, shrinking areas of cultivated land and dwindling water stocks are the emergency signs of a gathering environmental crisis. The annual economic costs of environmental damage as a result of economic growth were estimated in the 1990s at between 8 and 13 per cent of China's domestic product (Smil and Mao, 1998) – which would imply losses higher than the growth rate of the national economy! Furthermore, China's unsustainable development is increasingly weighing on the rest of the world. It can be compared to a vacuum cleaner sucking up resources around the globe, be it copper from Chile, soya from Brazil or oil from West Africa. It is clear that China stands out because of the size of its population, but similar tendencies are at work in Brazil, India, Malaysia, Mexico, Indonesia and other 'take-off' countries. With conventional development, the exit from poverty and powerlessness leads straight into overuse and overexploitation. A higher income beckons, but in reality these riches represent just a greater share in the environmental robber economy.

   Indeed, it is difficult to see how, for instance, the automobile society, high-rise housing, chemical agriculture or a meat-based food system could be spread across the globe. The resources required for democratizing these models of wealth globally would be too vast, too expensive and too damaging for local ecosystems and the biosphere. Since the Euro-Atlantic model of wealth has grown under historically exceptional conditions, it cannot be transferred to the world at large. In other words, the model is structurally incapable of justice. Development, therefore, is at a crossroads. Either well-being remains confined to a global minority because the prevailing styles of production and consumption cannot be generalized across the board, or sustainable models of well-being gain acceptance, opening the opportunity of sufficient prosperity for all. Since industrial affluence and global equity cannot be attained at the same time, politics in both North and South faces a crucial challenge. Countries can either opt for affluence along with oligarchy or for sufficiency with a view to equity. Production and consumption patterns will not be capable of justice unless they are resource-light and compatible with living systems. For that reason, there will be no equity without ecology in the twenty-first century (Sachs and Santarius, 2007).

Unequal appropriation of global resources
For centuries the goods of nature have been distributed around the globe through international trade. These flows generally correspond to the lines of gravity of purchasing and political power; since time immemorial control over the movement of valuable materials has been a basic factor in economic superiority. Trade has thus become the driving force of uneven appropriation. As a result, the earth's resources are used in a vastly unequal manner; at a rough estimate, 25 per cent of the world population appropriate 75 per cent of the world's resources.

   As can be expected, the gradient in appropriation between Northern and Southern countries is immediately evident (for the following, see Sachs and Santarius, 2007: 48–53). Bauxite, for example, a raw material for aluminium, is not extracted in any of the wealthy economies of the North, but predominantly in Jamaica and Brazil. Nevertheless, more than half of the world's primary aluminium is consumed in the triad of the USA, Europe and Japan, especially for vehicle production, packing, machine-building and construction. Per capita consumption in the USA is some five times higher than the world average, and 20 times higher than the average for African countries. Likewise, the triad consumes more, sometimes much more, than it possesses of metals such as iron, nickel or lead. For instance, two-thirds of nickel, an important raw material for the refinement of steel, is consumed in the triad, which has only 2 per cent of the world's reserves. A similar picture emerges in relation to fossil fuels. The industrial countries consume a good half of all oil and gas, although a somewhat smaller proportion of coal. Altogether they account for roughly 50 per cent of the world's total consumption of fossil fuels; the other half is spread among developing countries. Taking account of population, the appropriation of fossil fuels is five to six times higher in the industrial than in the developing countries, among whom, in addition, consumption varies greatly. In sum, although the main share of non-renewable resources is to be found in the countries of the South, the North consumes a disproportionately high share of them. This constellation has been at the root of numerous geopolitical conflicts that have time and again held the world in suspense for the past century or more.

However, the economic geography of the world has been shifting over the last 20 years. The old-industrial countries have lost their power to run the world economy by themselves. In a rapid, sometimes truly meteoric advance, newly industrializing countries have succeeded in acquiring a larger share of world economic activity. Notching up high and sometimes spectacular growth rates, they have reduced the distance separating them from the rich world while leaving the poorer world even further behind. They have come to occupy more favourable positions within the global division of labour in a variety of ways: whether as energy suppliers (e.g. Saudi Arabia, Venezuela or Russia), as exporters of hardware and software (e.g. Thailand, China and India) or as exporters of agricultural goods (Brazil, Argentina). China has an especially prominent position among them, being home to one-sixth of humanity and alone accounting for a big share of rising global consumption.

As about a dozen countries have forged ahead in the transition from agrarian to industrial economies, the South has started to catch up with the North in both energy consumption and CO_2 emissions. At the beginning of the 1970s the North's share was still around 60 per cent, but in recent years the South's CO_2 emissions have been increasing at the rate of 1.2 per cent annually, compared with 0.1 per cent in the industrial countries. Since economic success intensifies the claims on biotic and fossil resources, the new-industrial countries have ended up enlarging their ecological footprint to an extent that some of them have effectively joined the exclusive club of countries that live far beyond a globally sustainable level of resource use.

But the rise of economies such as China or India remains far from encompassing the entire country or the entire population. As a rule, it is concentrated in the central urban areas and more or less extensive industrial regions. Under a transnational division of labour, it is not countries or peoples but only certain places or regions that participate in global competition – and then only so long as conditions allow it (Scholz, 2002). The intended division of labour reaches out across national frontiers and binds remote areas to one another. Countless production chains cut right across the globe, as transport and communications technology make it possible to coordinate and control even far-flung networks. Against this background, the success of the newly industrialized countries may be read as an upward surge not of nations but of regional or even local spaces that present one or more favourable characteristics for global investors. Growth regions are to be regarded first and foremost as junctions of global production networks, not as trailblazers for a national economy. The fact that Shanghai and Shenzen are in China, or Mumbai and Bangalore in India, is of secondary importance: they are rather locations for cross-border processes of capital formation.

The rise of a transnational consumer class

Globalization does not encompass all areas of a country, nor all social classes. On the contrary, like cliffs in the surf, the structures of domestic inequality have defied the recurrent waves of development, growth and globalization over the last 30 years. Furthermore, the globalization period is marked by a nearly universal tendency towards an increase in domestic inequality (Cornia and Court, 2001: 8; World Bank, 2005: 44). In particular, the newly industrial countries have reached a higher national income at the price of a wider gap between rich and poor. In any case, the globalization period has produced a transnational class of winners. Looking at the world as a borderless society, it has to be registered that the upper 25 per cent of the world population own about 75 per cent of the world's income (measured in purchasing power parity) (Milanovic, 2005). Though distributed in different densities around the globe, this class is to be found in every country. In the large cities of the South even the passing observer cannot fail to be struck by their presence. Glittering office towers, shopping malls with luxury shops, screened-off districts with villas and manicured gardens, not to speak of the stream of limousines on highways or a never-ending string of brand advertisements, signal the presence of high purchasing power. As a consequence, in the newly industrial countries a consumer class of varying size is able to secure for itself a much larger share of natural resources than the majority of the population. Indeed, the uneven distribution of resource consumption between North and South globally is repeated domestically within Southern countries themselves, between the consumer class and the majority of the population.

How large is the consumer class in different countries? If one sets the boundary that separates this group from others at an annual income above $7000 (at purchasing power parity) the number of new additional consumers in emerging countries turns out to be 816 million in the year 2000 (for the following see Bentley, 2003). Above this level, people can gradually move beyond the satisfaction of basic needs and approach the kind of life-style they have learned from their models in the North. Moreover, this sum corresponds roughly to the poverty threshold in Western Europe, so that the transnational consumer class may be defined as a group possessing at least the income of the lower middle classes in Western Europe. The newly arrived consumers join the 912 million established consumers from old-industrial countries, who, however, dispose of an average income several times higher. If the net is drawn to include all the people at this level of purchasing power, the transnational consumer class amounted to a good 1.7 billion people already in the year 2000 – more than a quarter of the world's population. China and India alone account for more than 20 per cent of the global consumer class, a combined total of 362 million people, greater than in the whole of Western Europe, though with a considerably lower average income. The consumer class represents, for example, 19 per cent of the population in China, 33 per cent in Brazil and 43 per cent in Russia. If we bear in mind that the equivalent figure for Western Europe is 89 per cent, it is not hard to picture the growth potential in these countries.

Roughly speaking, the transnational consumer class resides half in the South and half in the North. It comprises social groups that, despite their different skin colour, are less and less country-specific and tend to resemble one another more and more in their behaviour and lifestyle models. In many respects, a lawyer's family in Caracas has more in common with a businessman's family in Beijing than either has with fellow country-men in the respective hinterlands. They shop in similar malls, buy the same hi-tech equip-ment, see the same films and TV series, roam around as tourists and dispose of the key instrument of assimilation: money. They are part of a transnational economic complex, which is now developing its markets on a global scale. Nokia supplies it everywhere with mobile telephones, Toyota with cars, Sony with televisions, Siemens with refrigerators, Burger King with fast-food joints, and Time-Warner with DVDs. Supply and demand reinforce each other: on the one hand, mainly transnational corporations promote inten-sive consumerism in the market; on the other hand, people with money long for a higher standard of living. This two-sided expansion means that the world economy is placing a huge extra burden on the biosphere.

In this context, three types of consumer good are mainly responsible for driving up the use of energy, materials and land area: meat consumption, electrical equipment and motor vehicles. The fattening of animals for consumption usually requires grain, and grain in turn requires farmland and water. In the decade from 1990 to 2000 alone, the quantity of livestock grain increased by 31 per cent in China, 52 per cent in Malaysia and 63 percent in Indonesia (Myers and Kent, 2003). Water for the irrigation of grain used as animal feed exhausts both surface water and groundwater: as much as 1000 tonnes is required to produce one tonne of grain, and 16 000 tonnes to produce one tonne of beef (Hoekstra, 2003). What is more, the whole range of electrical appliances – from refrigerators to air-conditioning systems, from washing machines to televisions, from microwaves to computers – increases the consumption of electricity, which is normally produced with fossil fuels. Finally there is the motor car. Whereas in 1990 the number of passenger cars in the new consumer countries stood at 62 million, by the year 2010 the figure will have soared to some 200 million, or about one-third of the world total. In sum, the consumption of resources is spreading around the globe through the lifestyles of the North, whose offshoots in the South now compete with them for environmental space.

Resource conflicts

The earth's resources do not simply fall into the arms of the transnational consumer class. Usually the provision sites are a long way from the consumption sites, with provinces or even continents in between. How does it happen that transnational consumers are able to garner the lion's share of resources? Everyone knows the name of the gravitational force which ensures that resources move from near and far to the big consumers: it is called power. By virtue of its effects, fleets of oil tankers set a safe course for the industrial countries, while tea, rice, soya and coffee find their way from poor areas of the world to supermarkets in the rich countries, and the swimming pools of the well-to-do remain supplied with water even in times of drought. So the power of the transnational economic complex operates through force fields involving innumerable decisions, in such a way that in the end a quarter of the world's population can make disproportionate use of many valuable natural resources.

Far from being just a biophysical fact, ecological limits are often the cause of social unrest. For the struggle for resources is regularly associated with conflicts of a political or ethnic nature, as injustice on this issue is often what lies behind what may be called religious or tribal feuding. Neither the crisis in the Middle East nor the civil war in Sudan can be understood without reference to the role of oil, nor the plight of refugees in Nigeria without reference to soil loss and degradation. Whether at international or sub-national level, disputes over resources contribute to social destablization whenever legitimate forms of conflict regulation are absent. It is therefore likely that, if the resource situation continues to grow tenser, conflicts will flare up in many places and make the world as a whole more inflammable.

Livelihood conflicts

Ever since the age of Pizarro, the 'New World' has been combed for valuable raw materials. But today the exploration and exploitation of new sources stretches into the remotest parts of the world's sea and land masses. Oil is extracted from deep inside the tropical forest and from deep beneath the ocean waves; timber is carried from faraway Patagonia and Siberia; and floating fish factories plough the seas from the Arctic to the Antarctic. Natural resources, however, are generally not located in a no-man's-land; they are found in places inhabited by people. As a consequence, the drive for resource exploitation often proceeds at the expense of the local population, especially in the peripheries of the South. In particular, where the frontline of resource extraction reaches for the first time, it is the lands of indigenous peoples that are caught up in the worldwide flow of resources.

For instance, since 1974, when the Texaco–Gulf consortium opened the first wells, the oil age has come to Ecuador's Amazon region, the so-called Oriente (Haller et al., 2000). Over the past 30 years, in an area covering roughly one-third of the country, oil corporations have advanced step by step, drilling holes and deploying an extensive infrastructure. The indigenous peoples in Oriente – the largest being the Quichua, Huaroni and Shuar –live mainly in subsistence societies, with their own different languages and cultural traditions. The total population of these indigenous groups is around 125 000, in an area of low population density. They depend on the natural space of the forests, riverbanks and floodplains. However, oil extraction requires blasting processes, pumping systems, pipelines and refineries. Moreover, it requires highways, landing-strips, heavy machinery and workers' camps. Clearing the forest has therefore been the first step everywhere. Furthermore, oil residue and gas were flared off, tracks and craters formed, without even sparing the holy places of the indigenous inhabitants. Especially drastic consequences have followed the pollution of the water: toxic waste and effluent have contaminated streams and rivers that local people use for drinking, cooking and washing. The disappearance of plants, fish and wildlife through deforestation and contamination has undermined the foundations of life for the indigenous groups.

As happens time and again, the use of an ecosystem as a commons that sustains local livelihoods stands opposed to its use as an economic asset that facilitates profit-making (Gadgil and Guha, 1995; Sachs, 2003). Local communities' needs for health and survival are at odds with the needs of distant consumers for energy. In other words, subsistence needs regularly compete with luxury needs. More often than not, impoverishment, social destabilization and displacement are likely outcomes. And the human dramas unfolding bear a common signature: the poor are robbed of their resources, so that the rich can live beyond their means.

But the poor come under pressure not only because they stand in the way of the extraction of natural inputs, but also because they suffer the brunt of harmful natural outputs. In particular, the bitter effects of climate change are likely primarily to hit poor countries and poor people (IPCC, 2007). As the earth's atmosphere grows warmer, nature becomes unstable. It becomes less possible to rely on rainfall, groundwater levels, temperature, wind or seasons – all factors that, since time immemorial, have made biotopes hospitable for plants, animals and human beings. Obviously, a rise in sea level will make some of the most densely populated areas of the globe impossible to live in. Less evident is the fact that changes in humidity and temperature will trigger changes in vegetation, species diversity, soil fertility and water deposits – not to speak of possible natural disasters. It is also likely that the environment will become unhealthier: more harvests will be stricken by vermin and weeds, and more people will fall ill with malaria, dengue fever or infectious diseases. Estimates have shown that, if emissions result in a moderate global temperature rise of 2 degrees, by the year 2050 some 25 million additional people will be threatened by coastal flooding, 180 to 250 million by malaria, and 200 to 300 million by water shortages (Parry et al., 2001). Far from being simply a conservation issue, climate change is pretty certain to become the invisible hand behind agricultural decline, social erosion and the displacement of people.

Geopolitical conflicts

In contrast, geopolitical conflicts are fuelled by the desire of states to gain access to essential but distant resources in competition with other states. Oil is the prominent example, but also the rivalry of countries in controlling water courses, such as the River Nile or the Euphrates–Tigris basin. Oil, at any rate, clearly exhibits the basic ingredients for an explosive resource conflict: high demand, dwindling supplies and competitors armed to the teeth (Klare, 2001). Global demand for oil rises because oil drives the consumer economy, from plastics to pesticides, from automobiles to aircraft. Moreover, the oil-based economy keeps expanding across the world, most notably in China and other Asian countries. Against the backdrop of rising demand, the looming finiteness of supplies, aggravated by the concentration of deposits in rather few and fragile countries, is about to put markets and militaries under tension. After all, the era of cheap oil is bound to draw to an end; the peak of world oil production is likely to be reached before the year 2015 (Deffeyes, 2006). Finally, competitors for the scarce supplies are superpowers who are deeply divided among themselves: China and India lead the field of Southern nations that claim their right to biospherical resources in opposition to Northern countries that have already taken more than their share (Sachs and Santarius, 2007). To be sure, the conflict does not necessarily lead to war, but even in this case, there are likely to remain sufficient victims of a rising price spiral for oil to make the world a more insecure place – the many countries that are likely to be further impoverished since they have neither oil nor money.

Dimensions of global justice

Who benefits and who loses in the process of resource extraction and consumption? This is the key question of environmental justice. What in economic language is called the 'internalization of positive effects' and, respectively, the 'externalization of negative effects' is a process that has not only a biophysical but also a social profile (Sachs, 2003). As organizations internalize benefits and externalize costs, societies are structured into winners and losers. Power relations ensure that positive effects crystallize at the top end and negative effects at the bottom. Such cost-shifting may take place in a temporal, spatial or social dimension: costs may be shifted temporally from present to future, spatially from centre to periphery, and socially from upper classes to lower classes.

Two critical dimensions can be distinguished in the distribution of benefits and costs. They point to the two most important concepts of justice: human dignity and equality. Both dimensions differ in their starting point and in their conclusions. The demand for human dignity starts from the absolute necessity of certain living standards, and insists that these must be achieved for all, whereas the demand for equality focuses on relations among people and presses for the levelling out of inequalities. In other words, the dignity concept of justice rests upon a non-comparative approach that looks at the absolute provision of certain fundamental goods and rights, while the distributive concept of justice rests upon a comparative approach that looks at the proportional distribution of various goods and rights (Krebs, 2002). Both dignity and equality go to make up the ideal of justice; therefore, any policy striving for equity will keep in mind both human rights issues and distributive issues.

Human rights
It was in December 1948, three years after the world had re-emerged from the horrors of war and the Holocaust, that the UN adopted the principles whose explosive charge is today greater than ever: 'All human beings are born free and equal in dignity and rights' (Article 1); and 'Everyone has the right to life, liberty and security of person' (Article 3). For the first time, the rights of the individual were thus solemnly rooted at an international level. Until the Second World War, international law had regarded the planet as nothing more than an arena for competing states; rights could therefore be claimed only by national states. Now, however, the human rights charter identified the people living on earth as a moral community, whose members possessed equal and inalienable rights that took precedence over the jurisdiction of national states. This may be regarded as the juridical revolution of human rights (Ignatieff, 2001: 5).

By now it is widely accepted that human rights are indivisible and interdependent (Steiner and Alston, 1996). Indeed it would be hard to understand why malnutrition or disease should impair people's capacity for action less than press censorship or religious persecution does. If someone's economic–social rights are denied, their civil–political rights are usually not worth the paper on which they are written. And, conversely, civil–political rights are often suppressed in order to avoid making any economic–social concessions to the have-nots. Livelihood rights, understood as the most elementary part of human rights, therefore define what people need for their development as living beings: healthy air and drinkable water, basic health care, suitable nourishment, clothing and housing – but also the right to social participation and freedom of action. Existential rights form the core of economic, social and cultural rights, as established in the International Pact on Economic, Social and Cultural Rights of 1996.

Very often the humiliation of poverty goes back to a denial of livelihood rights, since widespread poverty stems less from lack of money than from lack of power. In terms of resource justice, the crucial point is that natural habitats have a great value for the security of existential rights. Since savannah, forest, water or fields may, along with fishes, birds and cattle, be valuable means of providing a livelihood, the interest in subsistence coincides with the interest in environmental protection (WRI, 2008). And no one is more dependent upon intact ecosystems than the third of the world's population who rely directly on access to natural resources for their food, clothing, housing and medicine. The destruction of natural spaces therefore undermines their existential rights.

These very groups, however, are in latent or sometimes open conflict with the resource hunger of local and global upper and middle classes. For dams are built to carry water to the cities; the best land is used to grow exotic fruit for the global consumer class; mountains are broken up and rivers poisoned so that metals can be delivered to industry; and biopiracy is conducted to produce genetically engineered pharmaceuticals. It is here that the right to a livelihood overlaps with the interest in environmental protection. Since intact ecosystems reduce the vulnerability of the poor, the protection of nature is a core component of a policy that takes seriously the ending of poverty. And conversely, since effective rights provide the best guarantee that the resources of the poor will no longer be so easily diverted to the rich, the right to a livelihood is a core component of the protection of nature and species diversity. Ecology and survival rights are most closely intertwined with each other.

For this reason, conflicts over the human right to an intact environment can only grow sharper if the global class of high consumers asserts its demand for natural resources. Only if the demand for oil decreases will it no longer be worth prospecting in virgin forest; only if agriculture and industry limit their thirst for water will enough ground-water remain for village wells; and only if the excessive burning of fossil fuels is ended will insidious climate changes no longer threaten the existential rights of the poor. This means that only 'resource-light' patterns of production and consumption in the prosperous economies can create the basis for a world economy where human rights are guaranteed. Recognition of basic economic and social rights creates a duty to pursue a form of economy that does not undermine such rights.

International equity
The point of equity is not to guarantee a good life to every citizen of the world, but rather to leave everyone free to follow their own project for a good life. A theory of justice should therefore take the form of a theory of freedom, not a theory of happiness (Höffe, 1989). A cosmopolitan theory of justice will start from the fact that people and societies differ fundamentally in their ways of life and their ambitions for the future. Equality does not imply sameness. Yet everyone does have a common interest in the freedom to live in their own way and by their own lights.

Ways of handling natural resources in an interdependent world must also measure up to the criterion of freedom. They correspond to the spirit of global responsibility only if they do not seek to restrict the freedom of people and societies around the world. And the freedom of countries and societies is respected if they are not denied the natural resources necessary for their development. After the waves of industrialization that have washed over the world, every society is now dependent not only on food, plants and intact ecosystems, but also on energy, fuel, metals and minerals. If, following Amaryta Sen (1999), development is understood as a process that enlarges the real freedoms of human beings, then the freedom of societies to enjoy equal but self-chosen development cannot be achieved without a sufficiently strong resource base. However 'development' is defined, it is a codeword for the longing to draw level with the most powerful countries. In short, development stands for the overcoming of inequality among nations.

As is well known, the key move in Kant's ethics was to place universal duties rather than universal rights at the centre of attention. If all are to enjoy their space of freedom, then the freedom of some is the limit to the freedom of others. This sets a standard for every player: no one may base their conduct on principles that are not universalizable – those that cannot be adopted by everyone else. Or, to quote the first formulation of the categorical imperative in the *Groundwork of the Metaphysics of Morals*: 'I ought never to act except in such a way that I can also will that my maxim should become a universal law.' In a Kantian perspective, then, injustice may be defined in such a way that political or economic institutions are unjust if they are based upon principles that cannot be adopted by all nations. They are just if their principles can be adopted by all, because then they do not curtail anyone else's space of freedom (O'Neill, 2000).

Kant's theory applies to scarcely any other field as well as it does to that of international resource distribution. Environmental space is largely monopolized by the powerful nations, to such a degree that the weaker nations can no longer access the shares they need for autonomous and equal development. The external freedom of economically weaker societies is already severely restricted, and will be even more so in the future, in favour of opportunities made available to stronger societies. The present system of resource distribution is therefore unjust, and two additional factors reinforce this injustice: the number of citizens and the finite nature of resources. Since the weaker countries face the challenge of providing a home for a fast-growing number of people, a curtailment of their rights and freedoms is doubly onerous. Yet, more than ever before, the increasing scarcity of major resources is intensifying the injustice of uneven distribution. It is becoming a zero-sum game, in which the gains of some mean losses for others; excessive appropriation of the environment is turning into outright robbery. It is therefore the intertwining of inequality and limitation that gives global resource distribution its explosive potential. As can be gleaned from Kant's theory, a just distribution of global resources implies that each society would organize its resource consumption in accordance with rules that, in principle, could be adopted by all other societies. Overappropriation of the environment by a few strong countries at the expense of many weaker ones contradicts such rules. The cutting back of resource consumption in the rich countries therefore becomes the categorical imperative for resource justice.

Contraction and convergence

What would it imply to bring the world to a greater level of resource justice? The vision of 'contraction and convergence' (Meyer, 2000) anticipates two different development paths: one for industrial countries; one for developing countries. All nations of the world would adjust their use of resources so that in half a century from now they no longer overstretch the absorption and regeneration capacity of the biosphere. Since no nation has the right to a disproportionate share of the global environment, each one endeavours – though with individual variations – to achieve the common goal of material and energy consumption compatible with the demands of other countries, while remaining within the carrying capacity of the biosphere. In the end, there is no justification for any other distribution of globally important resources; the right of all nations to a self-defined and equal development permits it only to make claims that are socially and ecologically sustainable at a global level.

Given that the industrial countries excessively occupy the global environmental space, it follows that they are called upon to contract – that is, that they reduce their consumption of resources drastically. Resource justice in the world crucially depends on whether the industrial countries are capable of retreating from overconsumption of the global environment. The example of greenhouses gases may serve to illustrate the path of shrinking resource consumption. By the middle of the century, the overconsumers must reduce by 80 to 90 per cent the strain they put on the atmosphere by burning fossil fuels, in order to do justice to the precepts of both ecology and fairness. Clearly, the need to reduce fossil fuel consumption and carbon emissions applies to the 'global North', which includes the wealthy consumer classes of the South.

On the other hand, the contraction and convergence perspective sees developing countries as tracing an upward curve in resource consumption. First, poorer countries have an unquestionable right to attain at least a 'dignity line' of resource consumption that should apply to all citizens of the world. Without access to kerosene or biogas, without an energy and transport infrastructure, it is hard to satisfy even the basic needs of human life. Moreover, each country will try to achieve different images and forms of a prosperous society – an ambition that in turn requires access to resources such as energy, materials and land. However, this upward movement ends at an upper line of ecological sustainability for all; natural limits set the framework for justice. As it happens, a number of emerging economies are already about to hit that limit in the coming decade. The conceptual model of 'contraction and convergence' thus combines ecology and justice. It begins with the insight that environmental space is finite, and it ends with a fair sharing of the environment by the citizens of the world.

It was as early as October 1926 that Mohandas Gandhi sensed the impasse of development. In one of his columns for *Young India*, the mouthpiece of the Indian independence movement, he wrote: 'God forbid that India should ever take to industrialization after the manner of the West. The economic imperialism of a single tiny island kingdom (Britain) is today keeping the world in chains. If an entire nation of 300 million took to similar economic exploitation, it would strip the world bare like locusts.' More than 80 years later the wider implications of this statement have lost none of its relevance. Indeed, its importance has increased, since today there are no longer 300 million but 1000 million setting out to imitate the model of development that began in Britain with the Industrial Revolution. Gandhi suspected that it would not be possible to restore India's dignity, and still less China's or Indonesia's, at the economic level of Britain. The biophysical limits to the spread of the Euro-Atlantic civilization have impressively confirmed Gandhi's intuition.

References

Altvater, Elmar (2005), *Das Ende des Kapitalismus, wie wir ihn kennen*, Münster, Germany: Westfälisches Dampfboot Verlag.
Bentley, Matthew D. (2003), *Sustainable Consumption: Ethics, National Indices, and International Relations*, PhD Dissertation, American Graduate School of International Relations and Diplomacy, Paris.
Bourgignon, Francois and Christian Morrison (2002), 'Inequality among world citizens: 1820–1992', *American Economic Review*, **92** (4): 727–44.
Cornia, Giovanni Andrea and Julius Court (2001), *Inequality, Growth, and Poverty in the Era of Liberalization and Globalization*, Helsinki: UNU/WIDER Policy Brief No. 14.
Deffeyes, Kenneth (2006), *Beyond Oil: The View from Hubbert's Peak*, New York: Hill & Wang.
Firebough, Glen (2003), *The New Geography of Global Income Equality*, Cambridge, MA: Harvard University Press.
Fischer-Kowalski, Marina and Helmut Haberl (eds) (2007), *Socioecological Transitions and Global Change*, Cheltenham, UK and Northampton, MA: Edward Elgar.
Gadgil, Madhav and Ramachandra Guha (1995), Ecology and Equity. The Use and Abuse of Nature in Contemporary India, London: Routledge.
Haller, Tobias, Annja Blöchlinger, Markus John, Esther Marthaler and Sabine Ziegler (2000), *Fossile Resources, Erdölkonzerne und indigene Völker*, Gießen, Germany: Focus.
Höffe, Ottfried (1989), *Politische Gerechtigkeit*, Frankfurt, Germany: Suhrkamp.
Hoekstra, Arjen Y. (2003), 'Virtual water trade between nations: a global mechanism affecting regional water systems', *IGBP Global Change Newsletter*, **54**: 2–4.
Ignatieff, Michael (2001), *Human Rights as Politics and Idolatry*, Princeton, NJ: Princeton University Press.
Klare, Michael T. (2001), *Resource Wars. The New Landscape of Global Conflict*, New York: Henry Holt & Company.
Krebs, Angelika (2002), Arbeit und Liebe. Die philosophischen Grundlagen sozialer Gerechtigkeit, Frankfurt, Germany: Suhrkamp.
IPCC (Intergovernmental Panel on Climate Change) (2007), *Climate Change 2007: Impacts, Adaptation and Vulnerability*, Contribution of Working Group II to the Fourth Assessment Report of the IPCC, Cambridge, UK: Cambridge University Press.

Meyer, Aubrey (2000), *Contraction and Convergence. A Global Solution to Climate Change*, Totnes, UK: The Schumacher Society/Green Books.

Milanovic, Branko (2005), *Worlds Apart. Global and International Inequality 1950–2000*, Princeton, NJ: Princeton University Press.

Myers, Norman and Jennifer Kent (2003), 'New consumers: the influence of affluence on the environment', *Proceedings of the National Academy of Sciences*, **8** (100): 4963–8.

O'Neill, Onora (2000), *Bounds of Justice*, Cambridge, UK: Cambridge University Press.

Parry, Martin, Nigel Arnell, Tony McMichael, Robert Nicholls, Pim Martens, Sari Kovats, Matthew Livermore, Cynthia Rosenzweig and Ana Iglesias (2001), 'Millions at risk: defining critical climate change threats and targets', *Global Environmental Change*, **11**: 181–3.

Pomeranz, Kenneth (2000), The Great Divergence: China, Europe, and the Making of the Modern World Economy, Princeton, NJ: Princeton University Press.

Sachs, Wolfgang (2003), *Environment and Human Rights*, Wuppertal Paper No. 137, Wuppertal, Germany: Wuppertal Institute.

Sachs, Wolfgang and Tilman Santarius (2007), *Fair Future. Resource Conflicts, Security, and Global Justice*, London: Zed Books.

Schandl, Heinz and Fridolin Krausmann (2007), 'The great transformation: a socio-metabolic reading of the industrialization of the United Kingdom', in Marina Fischer-Kowalski and Helmut Haberl (eds), *Socioecological Transitions and Global Change*, Cheltenham, UK and Northampton, MA: Edward Elgar, pp. 83–115.

Sen, Amartya (1999), *Development as Freedom*, New York: Alfred A. Knopf.

Scholz, Fred (2002), 'Die Theorie der fragmentierten Entwicklung', *Geographische Rundschau*, **54** (10): 6–11.

Smil, Vaclav and Yushi Mao (1998), *The Economic Costs of China's Environmental Degradation*, Cambridge, MA: American Academy of Arts and Sciences.

Steger, Sören (2005), *Der Flächenrucksack des europäischen Außenhandels mit Agrargütern*, Wuppertal Paper No. 152, Wuppertal, Germany: Wuppertal Institute.

Steiner, Henry A. and Philip Alston (eds) (1996), *International Human Rights in Context: Law, Politics, and Morals*, Oxford: Oxford University Press.

UNESCAP (United Nations Economic and Social Commission for Asia and the Pacific) (2007), *Statistical Yearbook for Asia and the Pacific 2007*, New York: UNESCAP.

Wackernagel, Matthis, Niels B. Schulz, Diana Deumling, Alejandro Callejas Linares, Martin Jenkins, Valerie Kapos, Chad Monfreda, Jonathan Loh, Norman Myers, Richard Norgaard and Jørgen Randers (2002), 'Tracking the ecological overshoot of the human economy', *Proceedings of the National Academy of Sciences*, **99**: 9266–71.

World Bank (2005), World Development Report 2006: Equity and Development, Washington, DC: IBRD.

WRI (World Resources Institute) (2008), *World Resources Report 2008: Roots of Resilience*, Washington, DC: WRI.

WWF (World Wide Fund for Nature) (2008), *Living Planet Report 2008*, Gland, Switzerland: WWF.

Wuppertal Institut (2008), *Zukunftsfähiges Deutschland in einer globalisierten Welt*, Frankfurt, Germany: Fischer Taschenbuch Verlag.

18 Environmental hazards and human disasters
Raymond Murphy

Introduction

Risk is the concept that unites environmental research and investigations of disasters. For example, greenhouse gas emissions constitute an environmental problem causing global climate change that brings the risk of disastrous sea-level rise, extreme weather events, drought, wildfires and other difficult-to-foresee threats (Broecker, 1997; IPCC, 2001; Webster et al., 2005). This is just one of many cases where the very successes of science, technology and development create new risks of disasters in their interaction with the broader environment of nature's processes. Societies are forced to decide on a case-by-case basis how to deal with the unintended harmful side effects of developments that bring additional prosperity, comforts and leisure. Even deciding to go full speed ahead with business as usual constitutes a decision. Reflective modernity has arrived, with the significant issue being whether the reflection will be appropriate or badly chosen for society's interaction with nature's hazards.

Disasters have been referred to as 'the monitor of development . . . Whether these processes [of development] have been planned or whether they have been fortuitous, whether they have caused or exacerbated vulnerability, or whether they have reduced vulnerability, will be exposed in the manifestation of natural hazards' (Lewis, 1999: 146). Disasters have been called 'unpaid bills' and an externalized 'debt of development' (IDNDR, 1998) because costly preventive measures were not implemented. Sylves and Waugh (1996) and Quarantelli (1998) argue that the intensified activities of industrialization have exacerbated vulnerability and will increase the frequency and cost of disasters in the twenty-first century. Turner (1978: 6) concludes that 'the more extensive our use of large-scale technology becomes, the more we increase the stakes in the game which we play with nature'. Development inappropriate for nature's dynamics leads to 'disasters by design' (Mileti, 1999), 'repeat disasters' (Platt, 1999) and 'unnatural disasters' (Abramovitz, 2001). Erroneous cultural expectations of safety can result in disastrous consequences by encouraging social constructions that are incompatible with nature's constructions (Murphy, 2004). Disaster researchers (Mileti, 1999: 18; Mileti, 2002; ISDR, 2002) analyse environmental problems as catalysts of disaster, examine ways to mitigate disaster by diminishing environmental problems, and incorporate protection against natural hazards and disaster reduction as part of sustainable development. They contend that 'sustainable development is about disaster reduction' (Handmer, 2002).

All societies, including modern ones, construct expectations of safety or risk in their interaction with nature's dynamics. The question of the material reality of these prognoses is not an easy one. Will greenhouse gas emissions result in the irreversible degradation of the human-supporting environment, or will they bring the benefits of warmth to frigid areas and more oil and gas for energy-hungry societies? Disaster research attempts to learn lessons from calamities so as to prevent, mitigate, and/or adapt for the future (Murphy, 2006). Such retrospective analysis of the actualization of risk can be the basis of learning for mitigating both disasters and environmental calamities. The present chapter will expand this methodology with the goal of elaborating a categorization of different types of risk of environmental hazards.

Risk and perceptions of risk in the context of the dynamics of nature

Human beings have invented the concept of risk, but it is a *non sequitur* to conclude from this that there is no such thing as objective material risk. Sayer (1997: 482) has rigorously demonstrated the necessity that an assessment of risk avoid 'confusing its social constructs or interpretations with their material products or referents'. There is much talk about risk and safety by both experts and the public, but as Latour (2000) argued, at times things object to what people say about them. Sociologists must resist the temptation of their disciplinary specialization to reduce risk and nature to discourse and social constructions. Restricting risk to subjective perceptions jargonizes the term and contrasts with its widely understood meaning of the chance of material harm. Why add such unnecessary confusion in communicating with the wider public when an alternative that denotes constructed expectations is readily available, namely, 'perceived risk' that may or may not correspond to material risk? It is the correspondence or non-correspondence between expectations of risk and material risk that determines whether robustness or vulnerability will be constructed in the context of environmental hazards. If the threat of toxicity is denied, 'there remains only the social construction of non-toxicity. It does not, admittedly, inhibit the effect, but only its designation . . . That might be a momentary consolation, but it is no help against poisoning' (Beck, 1995b; 50–51). It is important to examine whether socially constructed risk perceptions are in step or out of sync with material dangers: 'risk perception that is at odds with the "real" risk underlies the process of risk transference which encourages development that increases long-term vulnerability' (Etkin, 1999: 69). As Beck (1992: 45) puts it: 'risks denied grow especially quickly and well'. Socially constructed conceptions of risk can correctly identify risk, but they can also be mistaken. Sayer (1997: 468) concludes that societies 'have no alternative but to attempt to assess the relative practical adequacy or objectivity of different social constructions'.

One might think that the bigger the risk, the more likely it is to be acknowledged. There are, however, theorists who have hypothesized the opposite: '*resistance* to insight into the threat grows with the size and proximity of the threat. The people most severely affected are often precisely the ones who deny the threat most vehemently' (Beck, 1995a: 3). This is because a population becomes ensnared in the material infrastructures it has constructed and upon which it is dependent; these 'underlie personal expectations and assumptions about what is normal and possible' (Nye, 1998: 7). Vested interests in normal dynamics of nature necessary for the continuation of a particular way of life can lead societies to fail to acknowledge the onset of its abnormal disturbances. However, people are also ensnared in their bodies as the ultimate material infrastructure, and this leads them to be wary of denials of risk. The relationship between perceived risk and material risk is problematic, significant and therefore vital to investigate.

Some sociologists, such as Beck (1992), and Adam (2000: 119), draw a sharp distinction between manufactured risk and risk from nature's hazards, and between a technological disaster and a natural disaster, but there is a great deal of interpenetration between the two. Technological disasters involve the inadvertent release of destructive forces of nature, or as Turner (1978) put it, nature's forces thought harnessed by technology slipped their leash. A natural disaster for its part can be unwittingly manufactured: whether a disturbance of nature becomes a disaster for human beings depends on the social construction of either vulnerable human communities or safe sustainable ones, which in turn depends on erroneous or accurate perceptions of risk or safety. Whereas nature produces disturbances, communities socially produce vulnerability in the course of everyday activities – settling a region, economic activity, population growth – as well as by failing to acknowledge and prepare for disturbances of nature. Danger results from the interaction between nature's disturbances and social constructions. A crucial issue in the social construction of vulnerability or robustness in the context of nature's forces is whether risk is accurately perceived and acknowledged.

Turner (1978: 162) studied the social, cultural and technical obstacles to accurate perception of danger during what he called the 'incubation of disaster', asking 'what stops people acquiring and using appropriate advance warning information, so that large-scale accidents and disasters are prevented?' The answer to his question consists of two distinct phenomena – lack of foresight and failure of foresight – which Turner tended to conflate. Lack of foresight occurs because of limits on the capacity of human beings at a particular time to understand and predict specific dynamics of nature. Failure of foresight happens when indications of risk are not acknowledged and unfounded claims are made about safety.

Welcoming nature's dynamics into sociology
This study of the relationship between the risk of nature's disturbances and their perception addresses a broader issue in the discipline of sociology. Latour (1996: viii) has 'sought to show researchers in the social sciences that sociology is not the science of human beings alone – that it can welcome crowds of nonhumans with open arms'. Construction by non-humans can best be understood as the processes of nature. Welcoming the study of the interaction between human beings and non-human beings into sociology involves the investigation of the articulation of human beings with the dynamics of nature, a project that is particularly important now that human beings have eliminated pristine nature, have affected our entire planet, and have unleashed new forces of autonomous nature such as climate change (Murphy, 2002).

Adam (1995: 148) cogently argues that the social sciences need to be redefined in terms of the study of 'the fundamental interpenetration of nature and culture' because industrialization has socially constructed new 'rhythms that are superimposed on those nested body and planetary times' (ibid.: 46). Some of the rhythms of nature that Adam refers to are relatively easy for human constructions to adapt to because they are regular and foreseeable. Examples are diurnal – nocturnal cycles, the seasons and the tides. But there are other long-lasting cycles of nature's disturbances that are powerful yet much more difficult to foresee (Murphy, 2001). Among the more threatening disturbances of primal nature are hurricanes, floods, tsunamis, earthquakes, volcanoes, sea-level rise and ice. The processes that have been labelled 'nature' in human discourse are far from constant. 'Nature, ecologists began to argue, is wild and unpredictable' (Worster, 1994: 420). One steady state can be tipped into a very different one, with characteristics that may not be as supportive of society.

The arrival of some disturbances of nature can be easily perceived with the senses, others require scientific knowledge and instruments, some can only be predicted stochastically over long time spans (hundred-year return periods that could arrive in a century or tomorrow), still others can only be apprehended through chaos theory, and there are those that cannot be seized at all with present scientific knowledge, instruments and data. 'Our powers of prediction, say ecologists, are far more limited than we imagined. Our understanding of what is normal in nature now seems to many to be arbitrary and partial' (Worster, 1993: 153). Foreseeability of the severity and timing of disturbances of nature are variables, as are the perception and acknowledgement by societies of whatever risk could be foreseen.

Adam's perspective carries with it a methodological principle, namely, the need to examine the interpenetration of nature and culture over time. For example, if the analysis of risk is limited to the 'point-in-time' study, as Adam (1995: 139) calls it, of perceptions, then this snapshot methodology fails to document the fallibility of perceptions of risk. Such investigations do not take into account whether or not risk is actualized into material harm. They deconstruct risk perceptions and often fail to give equal attention to deconstructing assumptions of safety, thereby neglecting its problematic status. Point-in-time investigations of risk perceptions are oblivious to unperceived risk (Murphy, 1999), unacknowledged risk, and even to unperceived safety. Socially constructed perceptions of safety or risk at one point in time can be subsequently either confirmed or refuted by nature's constructions. Expectations assuming safety or forecasts of danger can be assessed after experiencing the dynamics of nature, whether benign or destructive. The appropriateness of assumptions of safety or projections of risk can thereby be studied. This calls for a historical analysis that investigates over time the interaction of social practices with the dynamics of nature upon which those practices are superimposed.

This chapter proposes ideal types to examine the problematic relationship between risk perceptions and their referents. These ideal types assume that people do not want a disaster, but are in some cases either ignorant or reckless. When a disturbance of nature is forthcoming, it can be perceived or unperceived. If unperceived, this can be because it is (1) unforeseeable given the state of forecasting or (2) unacknowledged because of social, cultural or economic practices. Whatever the reason, this category denotes a particularly hazardous situation. Correspondence between perceptions, acknowledgement and the referent occurs when a disturbance of nature is about to strike and the risk is detected and addressed. This lays the basis for dealing with it. Correspondence also occurs when there is no disturbance of nature imminent and no perception of risk; hence perceived, acknowledged safety prevails. This 'normal' situation will not be examined here. Finally a disturbance of nature may not be looming but the population believes that it is. In this case of false risk discourse, what could be called unperceived safety, social upheaval may occur but it is the result of social dynamics rather than those of nature. There are many shades found empirically between these ideal types. The documentation that follows will be structured around them in order to examine the relationships between disturbances of nature and perceptions and acknowledgement of safety or risk. It will go beyond the study of risk as merely discourse or perceptions to investigate in addition unperceived risk, unforeseeable risk, unacknowledged risk and unperceived safety. Concrete cases will be examined that are approximations to these ideal types.

Material risk and perceptions

Unperceived risk

Long, narrow barrier islands are found all along the eastern seaboard of the USA. In 1838 investors attracted to the beautiful beaches on Galveston Barrier Island in Texas constructed a city there. By 1900 Galveston had become a prosperous shipping port of 38 000 residents rivalling nearby Houston. Twenty-six wealthy magnates lived in a five-block area of mansions. The highest point on the island was just 2.7 metres above sea level but the tides usually rose only half a metre. Tropical storms flooded the city in 1871, 1875 and 1886. In the last case there was only minor damage in Galveston but a significant number of deaths on the mainland. Subsequently a commission examined but rejected as too costly the construction of a seawall to shield Galveston from the sea.

In early September 1900, Galveston's meteorologist received telegrams of a storm building in the Atlantic and Gulf of Mexico (see Larson, 2000; Zebrowski, 1997: 157–162).[1] Flooding was noted on the low-lying parts of the island. On the morning of 8 September, people remained unalarmed and went to the beach to watch the pounding breaker waves. By early afternoon, the storm became a hurricane and no boat could resist the raging seas, so it was too late to evacuate. The sea rose 0.75 of a metre per hour and at one point surged 1.2 metres in four seconds. The whole island was inundated by 3 metres of rising water, with many waves seven metres higher. Between 6000 and 8000 of Galveston's residents drowned, a record that persists as the single-worst loss of life in an American natural disaster. About 3600 houses were destroyed, but the debris acted as a breakwater that prevented even more people from drowning. The inhabitants had not perceived the likelihood of such serious flooding. By settling this dangerous location and deciding not to spend money to make it more resistant, the community of Galveston – particularly its wealthy members – socially constructed a city that was vulnerable to the forces of nature. This resulted in the inadvertent manufacture of a natural disaster.

Tsunamis are notorious for creating unperceived risk. These waves are generated by earthquakes, volcanoes and landslides under the sea that release enormous quantities of energy into the water. In the open ocean their wavelengths are very long (hundreds of kilometres), as are their periods (20–60 minutes), and the wave height is only about a metre. As they approach shore, the shallow water shrinks their wavelength, increases their height (often to 6 to 9 metres), and concentrates their energy until they break destructively on the shore. In 1896 several Japanese fleets fishing in deep waters did not perceive a tsunami passing beneath them, but when they returned home they perceived all too well the destruction of their villages: 26 975 people dead and 9313 houses destroyed (Zebrowski, 1997: 151). When a trough of a tsunami wave arrives first, the exposed sea bottom has often been misperceived as an unscheduled very low tide. The curious attracted to see it do not perceive the danger that a 10-metre-high wave crest will hit them at formula-1 speed in 15 to 30 minutes, then drag their bodies out to sea. By 2004 tsunami monitoring had been developed, but it was judged too expensive and tsunamis too rare in the Indian Ocean for it to be installed there. When the tsunami struck on 26 December 2004, no one was evacuated and hundreds of thousands of people were killed. Perceptions determine action, and inappropriate action occurs when risk is unperceived or misperceived.

Even when some risk is foreseen, the force of the dynamics of nature may be unexpected. Disturbances of nature often demonstrate 'that safety measures are inadequate, as they did when the reinforced Nimitz Freeway in Oakland collapsed during the Loma Prieta earthquake in 1989' (Tenner, 1997: 100). Electricity grids are designed to be robust when loaded with expected amounts of ice from freezing rain. In early 1998 the El Niño effect produced warm moist air that collided with the usual cold air in Northeastern North America, resulting in intense, persistent freezing rain in wide areas of Canada and the Northeastern USA. The electricity grids collapsed because the ice loading exceeded expectations and the grids were insufficiently robust. This resulted in the most expensive disaster affecting the most people in the history of Canada, of the State of Maine, and of Northern New York State (Murphy, 2009). Perceptions of risk are social constructions that can be very different from risk itself where the processes of nature are involved. As can be inferred from the above cases, there exist different kinds of unperceived risk according to its predictability.

Unforeseeable risk

Two types of unperceived risk need to be distinguished: unforeseeable risk and unacknowledged risk. Some unperceived risks are unperceivable given the state of knowledge at the time. This was especially the case before the development of scientific knowledge of hazards and subsequent monitoring technology. Pompeii was destroyed and buried by a volcano and most of its citizens killed because, despite its advanced technology for its day, it had not developed the capacity to foresee volcanic eruptions. Unforeseeable risk still exists in modern societies. Extreme disturbances of nature have been rare in inhabited areas and long-term data upon which to construct predictions or even extrapolations do not always exist (Jones and Mulherin, 1998; Milton and Bourque, 1999). The prerequisites of accurate assessments of recurrence do not obtain in these cases. Under these conditions risk assessment is as speculative as it is scientific. 'Climatic recurrence intervals – for example, a "50-year storm" or a "200-year flood" – are simply well-informed guesses, based on brief instrumental records, of the average frequency of such events. They do not imply that storms or floods occur in fixed cycles or with regular periodicity' (Davis, 1998: 36 fn.). Davis states that the statistical abstraction of a 100-year flood has already happened twice in the twentieth century in Southern California. The Commission of Inquiry into the 1998 ice storm used the latest technical knowledge but had to admit that there is no adequate knowledge base for the prediction of intense, prolonged freezing rain and that such risk is unforeseeable (Commission scientifique, 1999).

   Litfin (1999: 89) contends that it is more important to learn how to act under uncertainty than to try to build comprehensive predictive models. But he does not specify how to act under uncertainty and how to confront the unforeseeable. Prediction is important where possible. However, the unforeseeability of some of nature's most powerful dynamics leaves no choice but to act under uncertainty. Foreseeability varies according to the particular disturbance of nature, but there is always more or less uncertainty in all disasters.

Unacknowledged risk

There are situations where nature gives prompts or hints of impending disaster, but the particular culture and social structure of the society lead to the dismissal of the warning signs. In these cases those in power often claim that the risk was unforeseeable, but it would be more accurate to conclude that foreseeable risk went unperceived by them because they did not acknowledge the indications. For example, the risk of disaster for a city constructed below sea level surrounded not only by the sea but also by a major river and a lake in a hurricane-prone region was clearly specified in advance but the levees were not reinforced and evacuation was not prepared. So Hurricane Katrina resulted in a disaster when it struck New Orleans in 2004. This failure to acknowledge risk is not unique and has occurred regularly.

The Connemaugh River in Pennsylvania, USA periodically overflowed its banks into the adjacent valley. In the distant past, lives were rarely if ever lost because of the low population density and because the flooding was gradual, giving inhabitants time to evacuate to higher ground. Then the South Fork Dam was completed in 1852: a 260-metre-wide by 24-metre-high earthen construction that held back a 5 km by 2 km lake. By 1889 Johnstown had become an industrial city of 28 000 people downstream from the dam. The hazards of a dam that was not built of masonry, not arched, and did not transmit its load to bedrock were recognized by all knowledgeable parties in 1889, and these defects in design were compounded by poor maintenance by its private owners: tycoons who had formed the South Fork Hunting and Fishing Club. Risk was not acknowledged in a way appropriate for defending against nature's dynamics. 'The failure [of the dam] was predictable, not in terms of the exact date and time, but in view of the statistical certainty that sooner or later the region was bound to be drenched by heavy rains whose runoff would exceed the capacity of the dam's spillway' (Zebrowski, 1997: 78). That happened on 31 May 1889, when the overtaxed dam exploded sending a 15-metre-high wave down the previously swollen river. In minutes, 2209 died and 967 more went missing, their bodies never to be found. The annoyance of evacuation from gradual flooding had been transformed by the dam into instant death from which no flight was possible. Thousands of homes and businesses were destroyed. The dam had increased the scale of risk. A non-disastrous heavy rain had resulted in a technological disaster because vulnerability and risk were manufactured. The disaster resulted in a liability trial, where the lawyers for the wealthy owners persuaded the court that it was an 'Act of God'. By constructing an explanation that blamed God, they held back the families of the victims more efficiently than they had held back the forces of nature and could keep their money.

In some cases physical phenomena themselves determine whether visible warning is given; for example, earthquakes give little warning whereas volcanoes often give a great deal more. Social and cultural constructions then determine what is done with the warning signs. The French colonized the island of Martinique in the West Indies. By 1902 St Pierre had become a city of 30 000, the pride of the French West Indies, and was called 'little Paris'. Birthplace of Josephine, Napoleon's empress, its economy prospered because of its deepwater harbour and numerous sugar plantations. Seven kilometres away and 1350 metres high was an ancient volcano, Mount Pelée, which had been dormant for half a century after only a minor eruption. Its mountainous crater had filled with rainwater and had become a popular lake for swimming. But in April 1901 a sister volcano – La Soufrière – on St Vincent's Island 160 km away began rumbling and its nearby inhabitants were evacuated to the other end of that island. From February 1902 St Pierre's residents could hear faint rumblings and see emissions of steam from Mont Pelée. These turned into irregular thunder and occasional ash clouds that by April were dense enough to darken the midday sun. Air began to smell of sulphur oxides, dead birds were found, and an expedition to the summit discovered that Mount Pelée had produced a new cinder cone. Horses died of asphyxiation in St Pierre, small earthquakes ruptured undersea telegraph cables, and on 30 April small streams from the mountain became raging cascades of mud, boulders and tree trunks. By 2 May, ash had accumulated to a depth of 40 cm in some parts of the city, violent ground tremors shook the city, and lightning flashed in the ash clouds. By 4 May the harbour was littered with dead birds. On 5 May a wall of the volcano collapsed, releasing a torrent of boiling water and mud that decimated the main sugar factory and interred 150 persons. To quell the panic, the governor asked a committee of experts to evaluate the need to evacuate the city. They declared that the 'relative positions of the craters and valleys opening toward the sea sanction the conclusion that St. Pierre's safety is not endangered' (quoted in Zebrowski, 1997: 198) and that the ash fall was just an inconvenience. The governor and his wife then moved from the capital Fort-de-France to St Pierre to instill confidence. The local newspaper asked in an editorial dated 7 May: 'Where could one be better off than in St. Pierre?' (ibid.: 198). Those in positions of power socially constructed a discourse to combat what they assumed was alarmism. Later that day the volcano started to roar, lightning flashed endlessly at the summit, and two vents flung glowing cinders into the sky. On the nearby island of St. Vincent, the volcano La Soufrière exploded on 7 May, killing 1350 people, a death toll kept down by the previous evacuation and the geographical accidents that no populous city lay in its path and that La Soufrière exploded in all directions, dissipating its energy rapidly. Despite all these warning signs, St. Pierre was still not evacuated. At 8:02 a.m. on 8 May an interrupted cable message dated two simultaneous blasts of Mont Pelée: one straight up, and another sideways that produced a concentrated pyroclastic flow of superheated gas and ash that charged down the mountain directly toward St Pierre at 190 km per hour. This ground-hugging cloud, whose temperature was estimated at 700–1200 °C incinerated everything in its path to the sea in only two minutes. All but one of the 30 000 people in St Pierre that fateful day were instantly cremated by the volcano, including the governor and his wife.

The socially constructed discourse of safety designed to reassure even the powerful and wealthy had been proved inappropriate by the volcano. As Beck said, the discourse did not inhibit the effect, but only its designation, which was just a momentary consolation of no help against disaster. The discourse was not alarmed enough and an appropriate response – in this case prompt evacuation – was not undertaken. Urgency was dismissed in favour of strategies to diminish fear, so the outcome was an avoidable fatal disaster. The need for urgent action and a timely response is determined by the forces of nature, not by socially constructed strategies. When communities are constructed in situations where there are potential disturbances of nature, accurate perceptions of the referent of discourse about safety or risk and of the timing of material danger are required, but these are not always socially constructed.

On 30 August 1902 Mont Pelée discharged another pyroclastic flow in a different direction, destroying several villages with 1500 more deaths. In Columbia in 1985, warnings were given to officials by scientists about probable eruptions of the Nevado del Ruiz volcano. Nothing was done, it erupted as predicted, and 22 940 people died. Because of population growth, 500 million people today reside close enough to be threatened by one of the earth's active volcanoes (see Zebrowski, 1997: 195–203).

Perceived, acknowledged risk

The inundation of Galveston provoked a dramatic transformation of perceptions of danger. Many survivors permanently left Galveston. Others decided to rebuild, but not on the island as it was. Wealth, power and knowledge provided the means for an extraordinary effort to defend inhabitants and property against extreme events of nature, and the recent experience of such an event provided the motivation. A fortune was spent to reconstruct the island. An enormous amount of fill was brought in to raise the whole city by 3.4 metres. Three thousand buildings were boosted on hydraulic jacks and stronger foundations constructed beneath them. A concrete seawall was erected: 4.9 metres wide at the base, 1.5 metres wide at the top, 5.2 metres high and 16.15 km. long, with a concave seaward face to deflect waves upward to diminish their force. This re-engineering of the barrier reef – 'one of the most amazing engineering feats of the early twentieth century' (Zebrowski, 1997: 160) – succeeded in protecting it against several hurricanes since the 1900 disaster. But the very reason for living on a barrier reef – the spectacular beach – has had to be partially sacrificed. In front of the long seawall the beach has been totally eroded and beyond the ends of the seawall the beach has been eroded 50 metres inland. Building a community in such a place exposes it to mighty forces of nature. Safety is expensive, complex, requires constant monitoring of the dynamics of nature, and is still not entirely assured. The problems are sufficiently serious that it has not been economically feasible to defend other barrier reefs against nature's forces in this way.

Tragedies such as the explosion of the South Fork Dam have led dams in the USA to be constructed with such risks in mind and operated by government or tightly regulated because unregulated private dams have proven to be so unsafe. The Red River running through Winnipeg, Canada, often caused severe flooding because the city is built on a floodplain. This was acknowledged and in the 1960s a 47-km-long channel was constructed at a cost of $60 million to divert floodwaters around the city. It has been used 17 times in 33 years and is estimated to have saved 100 times its cost in damage (*Ottawa Citizen*, 2005b). The Netherlands experienced a storm surge in 1952 that drowned 2000 Dutch residents. The population in the whole country felt threatened, so it built expensive dikes that have protected the Netherlands ever since (*Ottawa Citizen*, 2005a).

On 16 September 1929 Mont Pelée started to roar again and emitted more pyroclastic flows, but this time no one died because the population had learned from its previous errors and all the nearby residents were evacuated (Zebrowski, 1997: 201). La Soufrière started to rumble in 1975, 72000 people were evacuated for three months, and then it died down instead of exploding, and has been quiet since. Scientists forecast in 1983 that the Colo volcano in Indonesia would explode. All 7000 of the inhabitants of its tiny island were evacuated, it erupted, ravaging the island, but no one died.

At times risk has been perceived but only partly acknowledged. In 1980 the authorities at Kobe, Japan perceived the risk of earthquakes and enacted a more demanding construction code for new buildings but not old ones since retrofitting would have been extremely costly. When the earthquake hit in 1995, buildings constructed after 1980 were largely unaffected whereas 50000 older buildings were destroyed (Zebrowski, 1997: 50).

These experiences demonstrate that deaths and sometimes even property damage can be avoided if nature's dynamics are perceived accurately, acknowledged, and appropriate action taken. However, this demands complex, expensive monitoring and defences: 'in controlling the catastrophic problems we are exposing ourselves to more elusive chronic ones that are even harder to address . . . Chronic problems almost by definition demand maintenance rather than solution; while the need for vigilance and care becomes itself a chronic irritation' (Tenner, 1997: xii). Society is not always willing or able to pay the cost of protection and thus at times refuses to acknowledge the risk.

False risk discourse (unperceived safety)
Unperceived safety consists of erroneous talk about danger. Harmful consequences are produced by the prediction of peril and resulting social action rather than by the prophesied occurrence of the hazard. This is the basis of the accusation of alarmism. For example, two US scientists predicted a great earthquake off the coast of Peru to occur on 28 June 1981 that would devastate Lima (Olson, 1989). Predictions of earthquakes have been and still are probabilistic, hence unable to say whether the tremor will strike in 50 years or the next day, which would be crucial for timely defences and evacuation. The prediction of a precise date for an earthquake provoked panic in a Peruvian population already fearful because of past earthquakes. The Peruvian media highlighted the dramatic prediction by these two experts rather than the mundane scepticism of other US scientists, and a moral panic was socially constructed from nothing in nature. The uneventful passing of that day reminded all who needed a reminder of the difference between socially constructed conceptions of nature's risks and nature's risks themselves. Earthquake scientists recognized that there was a possibility these two outlier scientists were on to something new that the former still did not comprehend. So they waited until the opening shot of the putative scientific revolution (Kuhn, 1962) had misfired before unleashing the full force of their scepticism.

Shortly before the year 2000 there was much talk about risks from the millennium bug: computerized technology would run amok, fouling up banking procedures and emergency operations in hospitals and even make planes fall from the sky. Globally US$580 billion were spent to mitigate 'Y2K' problems, but now there is 'evidence that those countries and companies that did little, if anything, to avoid Y2K problems, survived largely unscathed' (Phillimore and Davison, 2002: 149). The millennium bug is a prime suspect for bogus-threat status: a social scare where material risk did not exist.

Unperceived safety at times has serendipitous consequences despite the emotional, social and economic cost. For example, the erroneous earthquake prediction resulted in measures to improve safety and earthquake preparedness for Lima (Olson, 1989). Similarly, no one complains about the enormous precautionary investment in the millennium bug scare because it brought a more sophisticated and secure information technology. Both of these proved to be no-regrets precautionary investments.

Good fortune
Accurate perceptions of risk are not the only determinants of damage and death when a disturbance of nature strikes a society. 'A direct hit on Miami could have tripled Hurricane Andrew's cost of $25 billion. If Hurricane Hugo had come ashore in Charleston, South Carolina, rather than at a nearby park, a twenty-foot wave of water would have devastated the city' (Tenner, 1997: 119). The 1998 freezing rain in Northeastern North America that crushed modern electricity grids just missed Boston (Murphy, 2009). Modern societies rely on good fortune more than they care to admit in their interaction with disturbances of nature.

In some cases cultural predispositions inadvertently mitigate or aggravate the destructive capacity of nature. In 1906, San Francisco, USA was a city of 355 000 people. In 1908, Messina, Sicily was a city of about 160 000. Both cities had experienced a series of earthquakes and both had similar scientific knowledge of them. In 1908, Messina suffered a major earthquake that killed 120 000 people. In 1906, San Francisco experienced an earthquake that released five times more seismic energy than that of Messina. The death count was 700 (Zebrowski, 1997: 53–5). The property damage was similar in the two cities. Why were the numbers of deaths so different? The answer is not to be found in planned defences. San Francisco's buildings were largely made of wood, which flexed resiliently when the quake struck. Even when buildings cracked, or subsequently caught fire, occupants had time to flee. Messina's buildings were constructed of masonry: massive stone floors and ceilings, granite walls, and brick-tile roofs. When shaken by the tremor, joists slipped from their niches, bringing down the heavy ceilings, walls and roofs to crush the occupants instantly. The disturbance of nature supplied the energy, but human constructions – buildings – actually killed people. Cultural predispositions governed the choice of building materials that unintentionally proved to be safe or deadly when shaken by tremors. The number of deaths was determined by the fit between culture and nature rather than by one or the other taken separately. Whereas San Francisco had good fortune in its disaster, Messina had bad luck. Cultural preferences can be maintained and robustness achieved reflectively by learning from experiences like these and perceiving the risk, but only if more costly defences are used, such as retrofitting with reinforced masonry.

Global risks
The year 1816 was called in New England 'the year without a summer': average temperature at least 4 °C below normal, a June snowfall in Massachusetts, frosts in June, July and August, abnormal dryness and crop failures. Europe too experienced an atypically cold summer and crop failures: there were food riots in Switzerland, France and the Netherlands, and famine made the Irish vulnerable to an epidemic of typhus. It is estimated that at least 90 000 people died in famines related to the source of the problem, and many more succumbed to associated epidemics (Zebrowski, 1997: 210). These calamities were caused a year earlier when Mt Tambora on an Indonesian island exploded, sending 180 cubic km of pulverized rock and ash into the atmosphere, reducing the height of the mountain by 1280 metres. This material was rapidly distributed by the jet streams of the stratosphere around the planet, blacking out the sun in distant lands on the other side of the earth, and much of it did not descend for a year. Mt Tambora is one of a chain of subduction volcanoes that regularly eject huge quantities of ash into the upper atmosphere. These massive forces of nature can be monitored by science and prepared for by society, but they cannot be stopped. They periodically assail society as they have always done. Only society's response can be socially constructed. For some enormous disturbances of nature, the whole planet is a hazard zone.

Modern societies may now be intensifying global disturbances of nature because of their everyday practices such as greenhouse gas emissions that increase the global risks specified at the beginning of this chapter. 'It is certainly not prudent for us humans to alter our global environment in a manner that drives it away from its current strange attractor, for we presently haven't the foggiest notion of how far we can go before the dynamics of our climate are in danger of flipping catastrophically to another strange attractor' (Zebrowski, 1997: 282). We live on nature's bubble, which we must not burst. The fact that nature produces disturbances without human activity does not diminish the risk of reckless human practices that push nature to unleash even more of them.

Is risk reduced by modern expert systems?

This study confirms a nuanced view of modern expert systems. On the one hand, those systems often yield more accurate perceptions of environmental hazards and provide important means of preparation and mitigation. As a result, fatalities originating in disturbances of nature have decreased as expert systems of defence were put in place, even though the population has grown and technologies using dangerous dynamics of nature have been deployed. Nature's disturbances provoked the most casualties where the population grew before technological protection was developed (Zebrowski, 1997: Appendix B). It is the efficacy of expert systems that results in a disaster component of environmental justice: the need to provide everyone with the modern protection from disturbances of nature that is available to some.

On the other hand, there are significant limits to the protection expert systems provide from these poorly understood, massive perturbations of nature. In 1995 Japan had one of the world's most advanced market economies and had hazard-management programmes that were the most effective in the world. Nonetheless an earthquake killed more than 6000 residents in the country's second-largest metropolitan area of Kobe–Osaka, injured more than 60 000, caused severe disruption and resulted in US$100 billion in economic losses (Mitchell, 1999: 1). Property damage from disasters is escalating worldwide (Etkin, 1999: Figure 2).

Moreover, modern expert systems have inadvertently manufactured new vulnerabilities and risks. For example, levees and dams have been constructed to control water flow, but when there is a sudden, unexpectedly large accumulation of water through rainfall, hurricanes or melting snow, these constructions have at times increased flooding. Modern societies have become dependent on centralized, tightly coupled infrastructures: nuclear reactors, distant hydroelectric megadams with long transmission lines, gas pipelines, huge oil tankers and refineries. These are technologically protected but vulnerable nonetheless when disturbances of nature exceed the upper limits of assumed risk embedded in constructed robustness, as occurred when extreme weather crushed the purportedly robust electricity grid in much of Northeastern North America (Murphy, 2009). Measures taken to control wildfires have led to an accumulation of underbrush and to the intensification of fires. The Bangladesh cyclone of 1970 killed between 225 000 and 500 000 'because engineering works designed to control high tides and salt had encouraged massive settlement on reclaimed land that appeared to be protected' (Tenner, 1997: 93). Technological measures to increase protection from the dynamics of nature have resulted in a false sense of securely controlling nature, in more imprudent social practices, and paradoxically in new vulnerabilities from those dynamics. Perceptions that risks have been reduced by expert systems have led societies to place valuable constructions in dangerous locations.

Expert systems thus cut both ways: they have improved robustness and resilience when confronted with disturbances of nature, yet have promoted risk-taking and in some cases increased vulnerability when a disturbance exceeded predictions. Scientific findings and the experience of disasters have now led such previously unperceived risks from nature's hazards to be perceived to a greater extent. But will they be acknowledged in a way that deals with them successfully? This chapter proposes a hypothesis that it hopes increases awareness and actions necessary to refute the last element of that hypothesis: with the development of science there is less unforeseeable risk and more unacknowledged risk.

Conclusions

Unlike a snapshot methodology abstracted from the context of nature's dynamics, a historical perspective inclusive of that context can study the appropriateness of perceptions of safety or risk. Expectations at one point in time concerning the future may correspond to the autonomous dynamics of nature upon which society is superimposed, or they may not. Any theory indifferent to the issue of correspondence and any methodology that brackets it out of view miss a crucial feature of societies, one that determines their fate when disturbances of nature strike. The documentation of unperceived risk and its subtypes, namely unforeseeable risk and unacknowledged risk, as well as false risk discourse (unperceived safety) in addition to accurately perceived, acknowledged safety or risk, demonstrated the problematic relationship between material danger and socially constructed understandings of safety or peril. It confirmed that the analysis of risk must not be reduced to the study of perceptions torn out of their dynamic biophysical context.

Risks that prove to be unfounded, what I have called false risk discourse and unperceived safety, have to be studied to complement and nuance the lessons learned from real material disasters. Both risk and safety are not always what they are said to be. The cases of erroneous perceptions of risk examined here showed not only that they can be an unnecessary expense, but also that precautionary protections that prove to be redundant are often less harmful (and are in some cases even beneficial) than failing to implement needed protections.

Pronouncements about safety have much to do with social regulation and are not necessarily based on accurate forecasts of the dynamics of nature. Social pressures on experts are great to produce predictions of safety that maintain prevailing social practices when confronted with the risk of nature's disturbances. Even the controllers can be taken in by their own assertions of safety and put their lives on the line to instill public confidence. Poorer people and countries suffer more from disasters because they live in the most vulnerable conditions, but wealthy people and wealthy countries have a very mixed record in defending themselves and their property against powerful disturbances of nature.

There are two general limitations on foresight. The first has to do with limitations on human understanding of the autonomous dynamics of nature. Even with the best science, perceptions of risk are fallible social constructions that can be proven erroneous by nature's dynamics. The knowledge society has to admit an abundance of ignorance concerning the dynamics of nature and hence has to recognize its fundamental lack of foresight. The second has to do with what could be correctly called a failure of foresight: social constructions that lead to a misinterpretation of prompts from nature's constructions indicating danger and hence a failure to acknowledge and act to deal effectively with risk. Failures of foresight and/or lack of foresight are prominent during the incubation of disaster.

Disasters involving disturbances of nature are not straightforwardly natural. The signs of danger may be easily visible but the risk not acknowledged and appropriate action not taken. It is then that devastation results. Or the risk may remain unperceived because the decision has been made not to pay for the necessary monitoring that is available but expensive. Or a risk may be foreseeable only probabilistically, for example, an 80 per cent chance of occurring within a 100-year return period. This general foreseeability, yet inability to predict a precise date of occurrence, may lead authorities to take the risky decision to slowly improve preparedness so as to reduce the expense at the time. Even if the risk is unforeseeable, a generous margin of safety could be built into infrastructures to take unforeseeability into account, but often it is not. These decisions about the type of society and of its infrastructure determine whether nature's disturbance will become an inconvenience or a disaster. Natural disasters are hybrids set off by nature's hazards but made destructive by vulnerability manufactured by human beings either recklessly or inadvertently.

As population grows, as previously pristine areas are colonized and reorganized by human beings, as more valuable constructions are built, and as nature's forces are recombined in new technologies, accurate forecasts are required for safety and to avoid the cost of needless defences erected because of false risk discourse (unperceived safety). Both science and experience provide rough knowledge about disturbances of nature but often not precise understanding of the elements crucial for safety: type of extreme event, severity, location, date, and duration. Modern mitigation to prepare for nature's disturbances has tended to reduce fatalities, but this difficult goal requires complex expensive measures, constant monitoring of the dynamics of nature, and is still not completely attained. When the expensive monitoring is not adequately done, risk may be unperceived or misperceived, or it may remain unacknowledged and thereby heightened. Even when perceived, acknowledged and managed as well as possible, disturbances of nature often remain disastrous in terms of property loss. Resilience after a disaster may appear preferable to mitigation because precise predictions are difficult and mitigation can be costly. But the effects of nature's disturbances studied here demonstrated that the absence of mitigation and preparedness makes disasters particularly costly and fatal. Avoidance of human disasters in modern societies requires the chronic burden of monitoring environmental hazards, acknowledging risk and supporting prevention, mitigation, adaption and preparation.

It is not enough to foresee the additional factors that constitute specific lessons learned after a disaster has occurred. Equally important is the recognition (1) that the next surprise of nature will reveal additional unexpected factors, and (2) that there is a need to build in a margin of error for them in advance by allowing for the unexpected precisely because nature's autonomous capacity to surprise society and its experts has been experienced and learned. This involves acknowledging unforeseeability and constructing a place for it in risk assessments and human constructions, rather than charging ahead at full speed as if society were confronting only the foreseeable.

All societies are heading much more blindly into the future than they care to admit, especially if they unleash new dynamics of nature such as global environmental change. Hazards of nature and human disasters have always occurred, but now human activities have created the risk of making them worse, as for example through greenhouse gas emissions. Global warming is not urgent in the sense that a volcano about to explode requires urgent evacuation. Volcanoes give visible indications of eruption even without science, whereas global climate change is creeping, with future risks contradicted by present well-being, like the coming of a tsunami. Scientific knowledge suggests that global warming is cumulative, that the longer mitigation is postponed, the more drastic mitigation must be, and that an irreversible tipping point could be reached throwing the planet into a state much less advantageous for human beings. Many of the risks are unforeseeable at present. Global warming constitutes a more complex and subtle form of urgency, which is determined by biophysical dynamics. The *sense* of urgency and resulting social actions needed to mitigate those risks are nevertheless under the control of human social constructions. Modern technological development has rendered human interactions with nature's autonomous forces much more intensive, wide-ranging and complicated than in the past, but that does not lessen the urgency of correcting human actions that unleash or aggravate nature's destructive disturbances.

Acknowledgement

I would like to thank the Social Sciences and Humanities Research Council of Canada for financial support to carry out this research.

Note

1. Zebrowski's (1997) study will be drawn on for empirical material throughout the chapter, but responsibility is mine alone for its sociological interpretation.

References

Abramovitz, J. (2001), *Unnatural Disasters*, Washington, DC: WorldWatch Paper.
Adam, B. (1995), *Timewatch*, Cambridge, UK: Polity Press.
Adam, B. (2000), 'The media timescapes of BSE news', in S. Allan, B. Adam and C. Carter (eds), *Environmental Risks and the Media*, London: Routledge, pp. 117–29.
Beck, U. (1992), *Risk Society*, London: Sage.
Beck, U. (1995a), *Ecological Enlightenment*, Atlantic Highlands, NJ: Humanities Press.
Beck, U. (1995b), *Ecological Politics in an Age of Risk*, Cambridge: Polity Press.
Broecker, W. (1997), 'Thermohaline circulation, the Achilles heel of our climate system: will man-made CO_2 upset the current balance?', *Science*, **278**: 1782–88.
Commission scientifique (1999), *Pour affronter l'imprévisible*, Québec: Publications du Québec.
Davis, M. (1998), *Ecology of Fear*, New York: Metropolitan.
Etkin, D. (1999), 'Risk transference and related trends', *Environmental Hazards*, **1**: 69–75.
Handmer, J. (2002), 'Sustainable development is about disaster reduction', *International Journal of Mass Emergencies Disasters*, **20**: 131–33.
IDNDR Technical Committee (1998), *Washington Declaration*, June, Geneva.
IPCC (Intergovernmental Panel on Climate Change) (2001), *Climate Change 2001*, Cambridge: Cambridge University Press.
ISDR (UN) (2002), *Disaster Reduction and Sustainable Development*, ISDR Background document for the World Summit on Sustainable Development, No. 5.
Jones, K. and N. Mulherin (1998), *An Evaluation of the Severity of the January 1998 Ice Storm in Northern New England*, Hannover, NH: US Army Laboratory.
Kuhn, T. (1962), *The Structure of Scientific Revolutions*, Chicago: University of Chicago Press.
Larson, I. (2000), *Isaac's Storm*, New York: Vintage.
Latour, B. (1996), *Aramis or the Love of Technology*, Cambridge, MA: Harvard University.
Latour, B. (2000), 'When things strike back', *British Journal of Sociology*, **51**: 107–23.
Lewis, J. (1999), *Development in Disaster-prone Places: Studies in Vulnerability*, London: Intermediate Technology Publications.
Litfin, K. (1999), 'Environmental remote sensing, global governance, and the territorial state', in M. Hewson and T. Sinclair (eds), *Approaches to Global Governance Theory*, Albany, NY: SUNY Press, pp. 73–96.
Mileti, D. (1999) *Disasters by Design*, Washington, DC: Joseph Henry.
Mileti, D. (2002), 'Sustainability and Hazards', *IJMED*, **20**: 135–8.

Milton, J. and A. Bourque (1999), *A Climatological Account of the January 1998 Ice Storm in Quebec*, Ottawa: Environment Canada.

Mitchell, James K. (1999), *Crucibles of Hazard*, Tokyo: United Nations University Press.

Murphy, R. (1999), 'Unperceived risk', *Advances in Human Ecology*, **8**: 99–123.

Murphy, R. (2001), 'Nature's temporalities and the manufacture of vulnerability', *Time and Society*, **10**: 329–48.

Murphy, R. (2002), 'The internalization of autonomous nature into society', *Sociological Review*, **50**: 313–33.

Murphy, R. (2004), 'Disaster or sustainability: the dance of human agents with nature's actants', *Canadian Review of Sociology and Anthropology*, **41**: 1–18.

Murphy, R. (2006), 'The challenge of disaster reduction', in Aaron M. McCright and Terry N. Clark (eds), *Community and Ecology*, JAI/Elsevier, ch. 7.

Murphy, R. (2009), *Leadership in Disaster: Learning for a Future with Global Climate Change*, Montreal: McGill-Queen's University Press.

Nye, D. (1998), *Consuming Power*, Cambridge, MA: MIT Press.

Olson, R.S. (1989), *The Politics of Earthquake Prediction*, Princeton, NJ: Princeton University Press.

Ottawa Citizen (2005a), 'Dutch seawall a model for flood protection', 2 September.

Ottawa Citizen (2005b), 'It might happen only once every 700 years, but Winnipeg will be Ready', 10 September.

Phillimore, J. and A. Davison (2002), 'A precautionary tale: Y2K and the politics of foresight', *Futures*, **34**: 147–57.

Platt, R. (1999), *Disasters and Democracy*, Washington, DC: Island Press.

Quarantelli, E.L. (1998), *What is a Disaster?*, London: Routledge.

Sayer, A. (1997), 'Essentialism, social constructionism, and beyond', *The Sociological Review*, **45** (3): 453–87.

Sylves, R. and W. Waugh (1996), *Disaster Management in the U.S. and Canada*, Springfield, IL: Charles C. Thomas.

Tenner, E. (1997), *Why Things Bite Back*, New York: Vintage.

Turner, B. (1978), *Man-Made Disasters*, London: Wykeham.

Webster, P.J., G.J. Holland, J.A. Curry and H.-R.Chang (2005), 'Changes in tropical cyclone number, duration, and intensity in a warming environment', *Science*, **309** (5742): 1844–6.

Worster, D. (1993), *The Wealth of Nature*, New York: Oxford University Press.

Worster, D. (1994), *Nature's Economy*, Cambridge: Cambridge University Press.

Zebrowski, E. Jr (1997), *Perils of a Restless Planet*, Cambridge: Cambridge University Press.

19 Structural obstacles to an effective post-2012 global climate agreement: why social structure matters and how addressing it can help break the impasse

Bradley C. Parks and J. Timmons Roberts

Introduction: shared vision?

The 'Bali Roadmap' identified a series of steps that might be taken to break the North–South impasse and solve the global climate crisis in the crucial years 2007 to 2009 to avoid a 'gap' in the functioning of the Kyoto Protocol. The Roadmap was hashed out in the presence of 10 000 representatives from developed and developing countries, intergovernmental organizations, environmental advocacy groups, research institutes and media outlets who were in Bali, Indonesia for the 13th Conference of the Parties of the UN Framework Convention on Climate Change (COP-13). The objective of the summit was to lay the groundwork for the negotiation of an ambitious 'post-2012' global climate pact in December 2009 at COP-15 in Copenhagen, Denmark.

In particular, an Ad Hoc Working Group for Long-Term Cooperative Action under the Convention (AWG-LCA) was tasked with breaking the deadlock over who should act in cleaning up the atmosphere, and how. The answer, according to the Roadmap, was that developed and developing countries would move forward with 'a shared vision for long-term cooperative action, including a long-term global goal for emissions reductions, to achieve the ultimate objective of the Convention [avoiding dangerous climate change]'. However, establishing a 'shared vision' has proven to be tremendously difficult. The USA wants binding limits on emissions by China and India. China refused, because it has not historically been a major part of the problem and because per person emissions there are a fraction of those of US citizens. The so-called 'African Group' stressed that 'a shared vision also involves sustainable development' (*Earth Negotiations Bulletin*, 2 December 2008), meaning that they continue to expect to be able to develop using cheap fossil-fuel energy. A representative of the Ghanaian government noted that '[w]e're going to have to put much more energy into bridging the growing gap between the two sides . . . It's [a] vision gap and that is not a good sign for the future' (Jaura, 2008).

The difficulty of these efforts to establish a 'shared vision' highlights the importance of better understanding competing perspectives of 'how things are' (causal beliefs and worldviews) and 'how things should be' (principled beliefs). With the first commitment period under the Kyoto Protocol set to expire in 2012 and the release of grim new scientific findings by the Intergovernmental Panel on Climate Change (IPCC) in mid-2007, there was a sense of renewed urgency at the COP-13 negotiations in Bali, Indonesia, and in the run-up to COP-14 in Poznan, Poland. There was also a broad consensus about the central task at hand: enlisting the active participation of developing countries in a post-

2012 global climate regime. Although the first round of commitments under the Kyoto Protocol was a useful political exercise, it required emissions reduction commitments from a group of wealthy countries that account for less than one-fifth of global carbon emissions and will likely have a minimal impact on atmospheric stability. In fact, during the first half of Kyoto's first commitment period, global carbon emissions rose sharply – from roughly 6 billion tonnes of carbon equivalent (GtC) per year to 7 GtC between 1996 and 2004. Climate scientists warn that to avoid 'dangerous anthropogenic interference with the climate system', atmospheric carbon dioxide (CO_2) concentrations should be capped somewhere between 450 and 550 parts per million (ppm), or at approximately 9.4 GtC per year.[1] As such, very substantial emissions reductions will be necessary in the near term to stabilize the climate.

This poses a major political dilemma. Although the current accumulated stock of CO_2 in the atmosphere is largely the responsibility of rich, industrialized countries, growth in future emissions is expected to take place primarily in the developing world. By 2030, developing-country emissions are expected to skyrocket to 60 per cent of total global emissions. It is therefore difficult to envision a scenario in which climate stabilization does not demand that 'the South . . . accept the necessity of serious, costly mitigation, and immediately embark on a low-carbon development path' (Wheeler and Ummel, 2007: 10). But the unforgiving science of future emission projections has not made the politics of negotiating a global North–South deal any less contentious. Most developing countries continue to strongly resist any binding limits on their emissions, pointing out that wealthy nations fuelled their own economic development with dirty, climate-altering energy sources and appropriated a disproportionate amount of 'atmospheric space'. As a result, they argue that the North should focus on substantially reducing its own emissions in order to free up atmospheric space for developing countries to achieve higher living standards.

As we shall describe in this chapter, North–South relations are characterized by widely divergent worldviews, perceived self-interests, principled beliefs, expectations and negotiating positions. We argue that this impasse was virtually predetermined by the profound inequality in the global system. During the COP-14 Poznan negotiations, South Korea's lead negotiator noted that 'the current culture is [one] of mistrust and finger-pointing', and called on developed and developing countries to begin implementing confidence-building measures (Eilperin, 2008: A10). South Africa's environment minister similarly argued that an effective agreement would hinge on the extent to which developed and developing countries were able to make meaningful and credible commitments. 'At what level', he asked, 'do they feel we are doing enough, and at what level do we feel they are doing enough? (ibid.)' The *Christian Science Monitor* reported that 'industrialized and developing countries bring different expectations to the talks – and the need to build trust between the two will be vital'.[2]

Poznan was a disappointment and a lost opportunity. After the negotiation of an ambitious and upbeat-sounding 'Bali Roadmap' at COP-13 in December 2007, developing-country representatives came to Poznan with concrete proposals in hand and expressed a desire to begin working towards a post-2012 global deal. However, the same issues that bedevilled previous rounds of climate negotiations – widely divergent policy positions, disagreements about the fairness principles that should guide and shape a future agreement, and deep-seated mistrust – also plagued COP-14. Delegations from the developing world expressed profound frustration and disappointment. The Director General of Brazil's Forest Service asked: 'If we can talk about decreasing [emissions] 50 percent by 2018, which is in 10 years, why can't the industrialized countries commit themselves to decreasing 80 percent by 2050, which is in 50 years?' (Eilperin, 2008: A10).[3] At the end of the COP-14 negotiations, a representative of the European think tank Third Generation Environmentalism (E3G) reported:

> if we wait until everybody looks at each other and sees what everybody exactly is going to do, we will never solve this issue . . . [W]hat is required is for [developed] countries . . . to come here and put something . . . on the table to build trust with the developing countries so that they believe that the North is actually going to act. We need developed countries to respond substantially to the proposals the G-77 and China have put on the table. We are hearing not only disappointment, . . . but anger from developing countries who have worked hard to come here to actually discuss substance, and yet . . . have not had their proposals responded to.[4]

The corrosive impact of inequality

The central argument of this chapter is that when inequality is left unchecked, it can dampen the prospects for mutually beneficial cooperation by reinforcing 'structuralist' worldviews and causal beliefs, polarizing policy preferences, making it difficult to coalesce around a socially shared understanding of what is 'fair', eroding conditions of trust, generating divergent and unstable expectations about future behaviour, and creating incentives for zero-sum and negative-sum behaviour. There are three broad types of inequality that we believe figure prominently in climate change negotiations: climate-related inequality, inequality in international environmental politics and inequality in international economic regimes. After describing these inequalities, we explain how their existence, and the industrialized world's reaction to them, has made it more difficult for rich and poor nations to forge a post-2012 global climate pact. We conclude by providing several historical examples that illustrate how countries with highly disparate worldviews, causal beliefs, principled beliefs and policy positions have resolved their differences and cooperated on issues of mutual interest.

Inequality in responsibility for climate change

A casual observer might think that the best way to resolve the issue of responsibility for climate change would be to give all human beings equal atmospheric rights and assign responsibility to individuals based on how much 'environmental space' they use. This is a basic rule of civil justice and kindergarten ethics: those who created a mess should be responsible for cleaning up their fair share. But in international politics things are not so simple.

With only 4 per cent of the world's population, the USA is responsible for over 20 per cent of all global emissions. That can be compared to 136 developing countries that together are only responsible for 24 per cent of global emissions (Roberts and Parks, 2007). Poor countries therefore remain far behind wealthy countries in terms of emissions per person. Overall, the richest 20 per cent of the world's population is responsible for over 60 per cent of its current emissions of greenhouse gasses. That figure surpasses 80 per cent if past contributions to the problem are considered, and they probably should be, since CO_2, the main contributor to the greenhouse effect, remains in the atmosphere for over one hundred years.

Yet, there are many ways to understand emissions inequality and responsibility for climate change, and each approach represents a different social understanding of fairness. Grandfathering (the basis of the Kyoto Protocol, that countries should reduce from a baseline year such as 1990) falls in line with the entitlement principle that individuals are entitled to what they have or have produced. The carbon intensity approach, which is usually associated with a measure of CO_2 emissions per unit of GDP, represents the utilitarian principle that inefficient solutions are also unjust since everyone is worse off in the absence of joint gains. Accounting for the historical responsibility of countries for the stock of greenhouse gases in the atmosphere represents the 'polluter-pays' principle. Finally, the equal emissions rights per capita approach is consistent with the egalitarian principle that every human should have equal rights to global public goods, such as atmospheric stability. These different perceptions of fairness are to a large extent shaped by the highly disparate positions that countries occupy in the global hierarchy of economic and political power. Thus we argue that inequality has a dampening effect on cooperation by polarizing policy preferences and making it difficult for countries to arrive at a socially shared understanding of what is 'fair'.

Inequality in vulnerability to climate change
Rising carbon emissions have created – and will continue to create – a warmer and wetter atmosphere, thereby increasing flooding, hurricanes, forest fires, winter storms and drought in arid and semi-arid regions. Climatologists have observed a sharp upswing in the frequency, magnitude and intensity of hydro-meteorological disasters over the past two decades – the five warmest years on historical record were 1998, 2002, 2003, 2005 and 2007 – and hydro-meteorological disasters have more than doubled since 1996 (Goddard Institute for Space Studies, 2008).

Although climate change is often characterized as 'everybody's problem' or the under-provision of a global public good, hydro-meteorological impacts are socially distributed across human populations (Kaul et al., 1999). Some countries and communities will suffer more immediately and profoundly, and they are generally not those most responsible for creating the problem. According to the latest predictions of the IPCC, rapidly expanding populations in Africa, Asia and Latin America are suffering disproportionately from more frequent and dangerous droughts, floods and storms (IPCC, 2007). The World Bank reports that '[b]etween 1990 and 1998, 94 per cent of the world's disasters and 97 per cent of all natural-disaster-related deaths occurred in developing countries' (Mathur and van Aalst, 2004: 6).

There are competing ideas about how uneven vulnerability to climate change impacts will influence the prospects for North–South cooperation. On one hand, poor countries suffering from rising sea levels, devastating droughts and storms, lower agricultural yields and increased disease burdens are unlikely to be enthusiastic about cleaning up an environmental problem that the industrialized world created in the first place. On the other hand, some rational-choice scholars have argued that self-interest may make vulnerable countries *more* likely to join global efforts to curb greenhouse gas emissions (Sprinz and Vaahtoranta, 1994).

Yet, the last 20 years of climate negotiations seem to provide more support for the former than the latter view. At the very least, it is clear that stark inequalities in vulnerability have poisoned the negotiating atmosphere and created feelings of marginalization, frustration, anger and bitterness. In some cases, there is also evidence that such feelings have led to retaliatory attitudes and negative-sum behaviour (Najam, 1995, 2004). Developing countries continually underscore their small contribution to the problem of climate change and their extreme vulnerability to its impacts in almost every round of negotiations (Müller, 2001).[5] In an April 2007 speech to the UN Security Council, the UK Foreign Secretary noted that President Museveni of Uganda characterizes climate change as 'an act of aggression by the rich against the poor' (see Green, 2008). Although some climate policy analysts dismiss this type of rhetoric as mere posturing, a recent EU report warns that '[c]limate change impacts will fuel the politics of resentment between those most responsible for climate change and those most affected by it' (European Union, 2008: 5). Fifteen years ago, Young also noted that:

> [s]ome northerners may doubt the credibility of [threats from southern nations to damage the global climate] and advocate a bargaining strategy that offers few concessions to the developing countries. But such a strategy is exceedingly risky. Many of those located in developing countries are increasingly angry and desperate . . . Faced with this prospect, northerners will ignore the demands of the South regarding climate change at their peril. (1994: 50)

Inequality in (expected) clean-up
There are also stark inequalities in who is currently doing something to reduce greenhouse gas emissions and which countries are likely to bear the greatest burden of atmospheric clean-up in the future. Although Northern governments are trying to convince the Southern governments that they need to rein in their greenhouse gas emissions, most of them are not doing so in their own countries. Under the Kyoto Protocol, 'Annex I' (developed) countries committed to a 5.2 per cent (average) reduction in greenhouse gas emissions (below 1990 levels) by 2012. However, with the exception of several European countries, greenhouse gas emissions have risen significantly throughout the industrialized world since 1990. Simply stated, the 'demandeurs' of global climate protection face a credibility problem: they need to demonstrate that they are willing to make difficult choices at home before they can enlist the support of developing countries.

Many industrialized countries have indicated that rather than making cuts at home, they would prefer to achieve their emissions reduction commitments by funding activities in developing countries. From a cost-efficiency perspective, this makes good sense: the greatest opportunities for low-cost emissions reductions exist in the developing world (Stavins and Olmstead, 2006). Stavins (2004: 8) rightly notes that 'the simple reality is that developing countries provide the greatest opportunities now for relatively low cost emissions reductions. Hence, it would be excessively and unnecessarily costly to focus emissions-reductions activities exclusively in the developed world.' But there are a multitude of moral and practical problems associated with the North simply paying the South to clean up the atmosphere on their behalf. In particular, the last 35 years of global environmental negotiations highlight the importance of addrressing the deeply held distributional concerns of developing countries, which can be a significant impediment to international environmental cooperation. Najam (2004: 128) places great emphasis on this point:

as a self-professed collective of the weak, the G-77 is inherently risk-averse and seeks to mini-
mize its losses rather than to maximize its gains; . . . [I]ts unity is based on a sense of shared
vulnerability and a shared distrust of the prevailing world order . . . [and] because of its self-
perception of weakness [it] has very low expectations.

Joanna Depledge (2002), a former UNFCCC Secretariat staff member, has similarly
reported that many non-Annex I (developing) countries fear that efforts to curb carbon
emissions in the developing world will effectively place a 'cap' on their economic
growth.

It is also important to note that even among developed countries that appear to have
reduced or stabilized their greenhouse gas emissions since 1990, there are serious questions about whether such national statistics on greenhouse gas emissions truly indicate
a shift from high-carbon to low-carbon economies and lifestyles. New research suggests
that many 'service-exporting' OECD countries, which increasingly specialize in areas
such as banking, tourism, advertising, sales, product design, procurement and distribution, are in many cases 'net importers' of carbon-intensive goods coming primarily
from developing countries. As such, they do not necessarily emit less; they may simply
displace their emissions (Machado et al., 2001; Muradian et al., 2002; Heil and Selden,
2001). This changing pattern of production and consumption has not gone unnoticed by
developing countries. In 2008, Chinese Minister of Foreign Affairs, Yang Jiechi, pointed
out that many of China's carbon emissions are the by-product of Northern demand
for manufactured goods, stating 'I hope when people use high-quality yet inexpensive
Chinese products, they will also remember that China is under increasing pressure of
transfer emission[s]' (*Economic Times*, 2008).

Inequality in international environmental regimes
International climate negotiations are also deeply embedded in the broader context of
North–South relations. In 1972, at the first international conference on the environment in Stockholm, Sweden, there was profound disagreement between developed and
developing countries on the issue of global environmental protection. 'Late developers'
feared restrictions on their economic growth, emphasized the North's profligate use of
planetary resources, and pushed for a redistributive programme that would benefit them
economically and hasten the transition towards industrialization. Developed countries
wanted Northern consumption off the negotiating table, Southern population growth
on the agenda, and non-binding language on issues of financial assistance and technology transfer (Haas et al., 1993). The South's confrontational approach intensified in the
late 1970s under the banner of the 'new international economic order' (NIEO). During
this period, developing countries put forth a 'series of proposals . . . which included
significant wealth redistribution, greater LDC participation in the world economy, and
greater Third World control over global institutions and resources' (Sebenius, 1991:
128). At the same time, late developers became strident in their criticism of Northern
environmentalism – an environmentalism that many perceived as 'pull[ing] up the
development ladder' (Najam, 1995).

In subsequent rounds of global environmental negotiations, there were calls for
increased financial compensation and more equitable representation (Sell, 1996;
DeSombre and Kaufman, 1996). Debate over the voting structure of the Global

Environmental Facility, which distributes hundreds of millions of dollars of environmental aid each year, became especially conflict-ridden. Developing countries protested 'donor dominance' and the lack of transparency in decision-making, while industrialized countries insisted that only the 'incremental costs' of global environmental projects be financed (Keohane and Levy, 1996). At the 1992 Rio Earth Summit, developed countries agreed to underwrite the participation of less-developed countries in global environmental accords. However, for a variety of reasons, wealthy nations ultimately failed to honour their policy commitments (Hicks et al., 2008).

In the mid-1990s, developing countries sought to strengthen the 'sustainable development' agenda by linking the issues of climate change, forests and biodiversity to issues of trade, investment, finance and intellectual property rights. This was flatly rejected by rich nations (Sandbrook, 1997). At the COP-6 climate negotiations, the G-77 and China also charged that many of the important decisions affecting developing countries were being made in non-transparent 'Green Room' meetings, attended only by powerful countries. This set the stage for the 2002 World Summit on Sustainable Development (WSSD), where one observer noted that 'effective governance is not possible under the prevailing conditions of deep distrust' (Najam, 2003: 370).

Inequality in international economic regimes
International climate negotiations are also inextricably linked to North–South economic relations. Stephen Krasner once said that there are 'makers, breakers, and takers' in international relations, and there is little question that developing countries are generally 'takers' in international economic regimes (Krasner, 1978). '[T]he "price" of multilateral rules', explains Shadlen, 'is that [least developed countries – LDCs] must accept rules written by – and usually for – the more developed countries' (Shadlen, 2004: 86). Gruber (2000: 8) argues that powerful states – particularly those with large markets – possess 'go-it-alone power' in that they can unilaterally eliminate the previous status quo and proceed gainfully with or without the participation of weaker parties.

Wade (2003: 622) describes a 'shrinking of development space' and argues that 'the rules being written into multilateral and bilateral agreements actively prevent developing countries from pursuing the kinds of industrial and technology policies adopted by the newly developed countries of East Asia and by the older developed countries when they were developing'. Similarly, Birdsall et al. (2005) explain how the callous – and at times opportunistic – actions of Western governments have made upward mobility in the international division of labour difficult. Other scholars of international political economy have highlighted the fact that the governance structures of international financial institutions, like the International Monetary Fund and World Bank, prevent the institutions' main clients (developing countries) from having any significant voting power (Woods, 1999; Wade, 2003).

These inequalities of opportunity have an indirect, but important, impact on how developing countries approach global environmental negotiations. Porter and Brown found that 'developing states' perceptions of the global economic structure as inequitable has long been a factor in their policy responses to global environmental issues' (1991: 124; see also Chasek et al., 2006). Similarly, Gupta (2000: 58) reported that '[Southern] negotiators tend to see issues holistically and link the issue to all other international issues. Thus linkages are made to international debt, trade and other environmental issues such as desertification'. As we have argued elsewhere (e.g. Roberts and Parks, 2007), when powerful states disregard weaker states' position in the international division of labour in areas where they possess structural power (as in international economic regimes), they run a high risk of weaker states 'reciprocating' in policy areas where they possess more bargaining leverage (as in international environmental regimes).[6]

How global inequality influences international climate negotiations
In this section, we explore some of the causal mechanisms through which inequality – in opportunity, political power and distributional outcomes – may influence global climate negotiations. We argue that global inequality makes it more difficult for rich and poor nations to identify socially shared understandings of 'fair' solutions. And even when rich and poor countries can agree on general fairness principles, the heterogeneity in preferences generated by global inequality aggravates disagreements about how to make those principles operational. Global inequality also contributes to conditions of generalized mistrust, which in turn makes developing countries less trusting of would-be cooperators and more inclined to pursue self-damaging policies.

Structuralist worldviews and causal beliefs
One of the most important causal pathways through which global inequality can impede cooperation is by promoting 'structuralist' worldviews and causal beliefs. Goldstein and Keohane (1993: 9) define worldviews as ideas that 'define the universe of possibilities for action'. For example, culture, religion, rationality, emotion, ethnicity, race, class, gender and identity all shape the way that human beings (including policy-makers) perceive the opportunities and challenges facing them. As such, having a worldview implies '[limited] choice because it logically excludes other interpretations of reality, or at least suggests that such interpretations are not worthy of sustained exploration' (ibid.: 12). By limiting one's menu of available options, worldviews and causal beliefs have an instrumental impact on how cost–benefit calculations are conducted.[7] They also influence the very way in which actors come up with their own policy agendas.

For example, depending on its position in the international system, a state may seek to maximize absolute gains, relative gains, social (fairness) preferences or emotional utility. Highly risk-averse governments may want to freeze the status quo (Shadlen, 2004; Gruber, 2000; Abbott and Snidal, 2000). Leaders who feel cheated by others may seek to punish their enemies or strengthen their relative power, regardless of the efficiency implications (Najam, 1995, 2004). Those who see themselves as marginalized by social structures may seek to overturn regimes, rather than make changes within them (Ruggie, 1983; Krasner 1985). Weak states that look down the decision tree and anticipate being exploited at the discretion of powerful states may even take self-damaging steps to promote their principled beliefs (Barrett, 2003). Whatever the particular course of action, ideas about how the world works 'put blinders on people' and '[reduce] the number of conceivable alternatives' that they choose from (Goldstein and Keohane, 1993: 12). Worldviews and causal beliefs, in this sense, influence issue definition, expectations, perceived interests, principled beliefs and ultimately the prospects for mutually beneficial cooperation.

As we have argued elsewhere, 'structuralist' ideas about the origins and persistence of global inequality form the central worldview of most developing-country leaders, including how they have viewed the issue of climate change.[8] The vast majority of goals developing-country leaders have sought since the end of the Second World War have remained elusive, and this we believe has shaped developing countries' perceptions of the world as fundamentally unequal and unjust. Twenty-five years ago, Krasner (1985) argued that ideas about 'dependency' affected how many LDC decision-makers viewed the world, their identity in relation to other states, their goals and how such goals could be most effectively realized. 'The [dependency perspective] embraced by developing countries', he argued, '[is] not merely a rationalization. It [is] the subjective complement to the objective condition of domestic and international weakness' (ibid.: 90). Najam puts it this way: 'The self-definition of the South . . . is a definition of exclusion: these countries believe that they have been bypassed and view themselves as existing on the periphery' (Najam, 2004: 226).

There are several widely held structuralist ideas related to international environmental issues, which we have argued obstruct North–South efforts to protect the climate: the idea that global environmental problems are only attributable to patterns of Northern consumption and production; the idea that a nation's ability to implement environmental reform depends upon its position in the international division of labour; and the idea that the North is using environmental issues as a ruse to thwart poor countries' economic development (Roberts and Parks, 2007). These beliefs can be seen in both the terminology and the arguments made by developing countries. Although wealthy, industrialized countries often dismiss claims of 'environmental imperialism', 'ecological debt', 'ecologically unequal exchange' and 'environmental load displacement' as empty and distracting rhetoric, the fact of the matter is that Southern governments view their interests according to their worldviews and causal beliefs, and this appears to be impeding international environmental cooperation. As we describe in greater detail below, the 'structuralist' way of making sense of the world has promoted generalized mistrust among rich and poor nations, which in turn has suppressed diffuse reciprocity, and led to divergent and unstable expectations about future behaviour. Structuralist ideas have also promoted particularistic notions of fairness, a victim mentality and, in some cases, zero-sum or negative-sum behaviour.

Principled beliefs
The second way in which we argue that global inequality influences the prospects for North–South cooperation is through its impact on 'principled beliefs'. Goldstein and Keohane (1993: 9) define principled beliefs as 'normative ideas that specify criteria for distinguishing right from wrong and just from unjust'. Such ideas can facilitate cooperation if they are widely shared by providing a so-called 'focal point' that reduces the costs of negotiating and bargaining, making agreements more palatable to domestic audiences (who frequently possess an indirect veto power over ratification and implementation), and realigning the incentives of rich and poor nations to create fewer opportunities for shirking, defection and other types of opportunistic behaviour (Roberts and Parks, 2007; Wiegandt, 2001).

First, fairness principles can reduce the costs associated with negotiating international agreements. Shared understandings of fairness provide what game theorists call 'focal points'. By isolating one point along the contract curve that every party would prefer over a non-cooperative outcome, states can stabilize expectations for future behaviour and reduce the costs of arriving at a mutually acceptable agreement (Keohane, 2001; Müller, 1999). The Montreal Protocol is a good example of an agreement that was guided by a fairness focal point. During the early negotiations, developed and developing countries staked out very different policy positions regarding what would constitute a 'fair' approach to combating ozone depletion (Sell, 1996; DeSombre and Kauffman, 1996), but all parties eventually agreed to allow the principle of 'compensatory justice' to guide the negotiations (Albin, 2001; Barrett, 2003).

Fairness principles can also influence the costs of monitoring and enforcing agreements. Due to the public-good attributes of a stable climate (i.e. non-excludability and non-rivalry) and the fact that asymmetric information reduces the 'observability' of non-compliance, states may face strong incentives to free-ride on the climate stabilization efforts of others. In a sense, it is in every state's self-interest to misrepresent their level of contribution to the collective good. Demandeurs must therefore make compliance economically rational for more reluctant participants through financial compensation schemes, issue linkage and other forms of incentive restructuring, which can weaken incentives for cheating and defection (Krasner, 1985; Abbott and Snidal, 2000; Young, 1994).[9]

Finally, norms and principles of fairness can help cement a collaborative equilibrium and reduce monitoring and enforcement costs through their impact on the domestic ratification process. Müller (1999: 10–12) lays much emphasis on this point:

> It would be foolish to assume, however, that bodies such as the US Congress or the Indian Lok Sabha could be . . . bullied into ratifying an agreement . . . [because] parties may refuse to ratify an agreement if they feel it deviates unacceptably from what they perceive to be the just solution.

Yet, norms of fairness are elastic and subject to political manipulation, and fairness focal points rarely emerge spontaneously. Therefore a truly global consensus on climate change will probably require a 'hybrid justice' solution that accommodates the different circumstances and principled beliefs of many parties (Roberts and Parks, 2007).

Generalized mistrust
Inequality also makes it harder for developing countries and developed countries to trust each other and establish mutually acceptable 'rules of the game'. Such rules are important to would-be cooperators because they reduce uncertainty, stabilize expectations, constrain opportunism and increase the credibility of state commitments.

Although few scholars have explored the causal impact of social trust in international environmental politics, there is a large literature in economics, sociology and political science on the relationship between trust and cooperation (Putnam, 1993; Keohane, 1984; 2001; Stein, 1990; and Kydd, 2000). By fostering norms of reciprocity, trust increases communication and information, reduces uncertainty and transaction costs, enhances the credibility of commitments, makes defection more costly, creates stable expectations and ultimately promotes cooperation (Durkheim, [1893] 1933; Putnam, 1993). Trust, in effect, allows would-be cooperators to bank on promises to honour policy commitments. Social inequality is strongly associated with lower levels of trust, lower levels of public-good provision (a proxy for cooperation), and higher levels of crime and other types of socially destructive behaviour (Putnam, 1993; Knack and Keefer, 1997; and Easterly, 2001).

In a domestic setting, the state has a 'monopoly of violence' and can enforce contracts and 'coerce trust' on behalf of its citizens (Putnam, 1993: 165). But states do not have the luxury of third-party enforcement in international relations; contracting takes place under conditions of anarchy (Waltz, 1979; Keohane, 1984). Countries must 'decide whom to make agreements with, and on what terms, largely on the basis of their expectations about their partners' willingness and ability to keep their commitments' (Keohane, 1984: 105). As a result, states seeking to promote international public-good provision must develop so-called 'self-enforcing' agreements (Barrett, 2003).

International relations scholarship has shed much light on how governments can convince potential partners that they will honour their commitments (Mearsheimer, 1994/95; Stein, 1990). We highlight three ways in which states may seek to enhance relations of trust: specific reciprocity, diffuse reciprocity and costly signals. Specific reciprocity refers to an 'exchange of items of equivalent value in a strictly delimited sequence' (Keohane, 1986: 4). For example, OPEC (Organization of Petroleum-Exporting Countries) and non-OPEC nations periodically agree to cut oil production at the same time in order to maximize their impact on oil prices. However, this type of strategy has significant disadvantages: unequal partners often find it difficult to reciprocate equally, contingencies may unexpectedly affect an actors' ability to reciprocate, and different interpretations and measurements can degenerate into situations of mutual recrimination. An accumulated stock of 'diffuse reciprocity' is much more valuable. Diffuse reciprocity does not require that all aspects of a contract be specified *ex ante*. Rather, it requires that states make deposits at the 'favour bank' when they can in order to build conditions of trust and stabilize expectations for future cooperative efforts (Putnam, 2000; Keohane, 1984).

When interstate relationships are characterized by mutual suspicion and deep distrust, conditions of diffuse reciprocity can be particularly difficult to build. Thus states actively seeking to foster diffuse reciprocity and build conditions of trust may need to send 'costly signals' of reassurance to would-be cooperators. Such signals 'serve to separate the trustworthy types from the untrustworthy types; trustworthy types will send them, untrustworthy types will find them too risky to send' (Kydd, 2000: 326). This has special relevance to international environmental politics: while Western countries have a long history of cooperating across a wide range of policy areas and arriving at new self-enforcing contracts, no such history exists between developed and developing countries. North–South environmental relations are characterized by high levels of mistrust and significant power asymmetries. There are many ways in which rich countries can send special signals of reassurance to developing countries – e.g. taking the lead by making deep emission cuts at home, promoting issue linkage and exercising self-restraint when the short-term return on opportunism is high. However, regardless of the tactics chosen, the overriding goal should be to clearly signal a desire to address the 'structural' obstacles facing developing countries and reverse longstanding patterns of global inequality.

Conclusion

Our research suggests that global inequality is a central, but underappreciated, impediment to North–South environmental cooperation. Therefore we argue that crafting an effective post-2012 global climate regime will require unconventional – and perhaps even heterodox – policy interventions. To date, countries have proposed different yardsticks for measuring atmospheric clean-up responsibilities based on particularistic notions of justice. But high levels of inequality make it very unlikely that a North–South consensus will spontaneously emerge on the basis of a single fairness principle. Consequently, we believe that a truly global consensus on climate change will almost certainly require a 'hybrid justice' solution that accommodates the different circumstances and principled beliefs of many parties. To break through the cycle of mistrust that plagues North–South relations, we also argue that the North needs to offer the South a new global bargain on environment and development, and signal its commitment to this new 'shared thinking' through a series of confidence-building measures. Drawing upon insights from research on US–Soviet relations in the run-up to the end of the Cold War, we argue that a series of 'costly signals' can foster mutual trust between developed and developing countries and provide a basis for long-term cooperation to stabilize the climate. These measures should offer a new vision of global environmental cooperation, provide opportunities for developing countries to transition towards less carbon-intensive development path-ways, and clearly signal a desire to address the 'structural' obstacles facing developing countries and reverse long-standing patterns of global inequality. Finally, we emphasize the central importance of exercising self-restraint when the short-term payoff on oppor-tunistic behaviour is high. When powerful states consistently treat weaker states like second-class citizens, they run the risk of weaker states 'reciprocating' in policy domains where they possess greater bargaining leverage.

Moving towards 'hybrid justice'

Earlier, we described four very different proposed yardsticks for measuring atmospheric clean-up responsibilities based on particularistic notions of justice: the grandfathering approach, which relies on entitlement principles of justice; the carbon intensity approach, which rests on utilitarian principles of justice; the historical responsibility approach, which operationalizes the 'polluter-pays' principle; and the egalitarian per capita approach. Each of these notions of justice is closely associated with where countries sit in the global hierarchy of economic and political power. It is therefore very unlikely that a North–South fairness consensus will spontaneously emerge on the basis of one of these principles. Instead, a moral compromise, or 'negotiated justice' settlement, will most likely be necessary; countries will need to be willing to reconsider and negotiate their own beliefs about what is fair.[10] As Müller (1999: 3) puts it, 'we merely need a solution which is commonly regarded as sufficiently fair to remain acceptable'.

There are already a significant number of proposals in the public domain that comport this notion of 'moral compromise'. Bartsch and Müller (2000) have proposed a 'prefer-ence score' method, which combines the grandfathering and per capita approach through a voting system. The Pew Center for Global Climate Change has developed a hybrid pro-posal that assigns responsibility based on past and present emissions, carbon intensity and countries' ability to pay (e.g. per capita GDP) and separates the world into three groups: those that 'must act now', those that 'could act now'; and those that 'should act now, but differently' (Claussen and McNeilly, 1998). The Climate Action Network International has put forward a three-track proposal, with the wealthy countries moving forward on a 'Kyoto track' of commitments to reduce absolute emissions, the poorest focused nearly entirely on adaptation, and the rapidly developing nations focused on 'decarbonization'.

Others have focused on more per capita proposals that provide for 'national circum-stances', or allowance factors, such as geography, climate, energy supply and domestic economic structure, as well as 'soft landing scenarios' (e.g. Gupta and Bhandari, 1999; Ybema et al., 2000; Torvanger and Godal 2004; Groenenberg et al., 2001).

Most recently, EcoEquity with support from the Heinrich Böll Foundation, Christian Aid and the Stockholm Environment Institute, has developed a 'Greenhouse Development Rights' framework as a point of reference to evaluate proposals for the post-2012 commitment period (Baer et al., 2008). They propose that countries below a 'global middle class' income of US\$ 9000 per capita should be assured that they will not be asked to make binding limits until they approach that level, while countries above that level should be responsible for rapid emissions reductions and payments to assist those below the line in improving their social and economic status while adjusting to a less carbon-intensive path of development. Funds raised in wealthy countries in reduc-ing emissions are also used to help poor countries adapt and develop in more climate-friendly ways. We believe that these hybrid proposals are among the most promising solutions to break the North–South stalemate.

Building trust through costly signals and creating a 'shared vision' of long-term cooperative action

At the same time, we recognize that simply asserting the importance of 'negotiated justice' settlement avoids the more central question of whether and to what extent a future agreement must favour rich or poor nations. Divergent principled beliefs are a consequence of more fundamental root causes: persistent global inequality, incongruent worldviews and causal beliefs, and an enduring trust deficit (Roberts and Parks, 2007). Therefore, along with developing a workable and fair 'hybrid justice' proposal, we believe that policy-makers must redouble their efforts to allay the fears and suspicions of developing countries, rebuild conditions of generalized trust, and work towards a new 'shared vision' of long-term cooperation across multiple issue areas.

Kydd (2000) has shown that a strategy of reassurance through costly signals can foster mutual trust between countries that do not have a long history of cooperation. He defines costly signals as 'signals designed to persuade the other side that one is trustworthy by virtue of the fact that they are so costly that one would hesitate to send them if one were untrustworthy' (ibid.: 326). Based on an analysis of US–Soviet relations in the run-up to the end of the Cold War, he notes:

> [we] can observe a series of costly signals leading to mutual trust between former adversaries. The attitudes of Western leaders, press, and publics toward the Soviet Union all underwent a substantial transformation. Soviet military and geopolitical concessions, particularly the [Intermediate-range Nuclear Forces] treaty, the withdrawal from Afghanistan, the December 1988 conventional arms initiative, and the withdrawal from Eastern Europe were decisive in changing overall Western opinion about the Soviet Union. By 1990 most observers viewed the Soviet Union as a state that had abandoned its hegemonic ambitions and could be trusted to abide by reasonably verified arms control agreements and play a constructive role in world politics. (Ibid.: 350)

Kydd's research also suggests that the more noticeable, irreversible, unconditional and costly the signal from a 'sending state', the more trust it can foster with a 'receiving state'.

We believe that the conditions of mistrust that currently plague North–South environmental relations can be understood as the product of a 'failed reassurance strategy'. In the early 1990s, the North sought to assure poorer nations that they would 'take the lead' in stabilizing the climate. But the lack of progress by the USA and other industrialized countries in meeting their own emission reduction targets provided developing nations with a ready excuse for not seriously contemplating low-carbon alternatives. As Baumert and Kete (2002: 6) put it, '[m]any developing countries believe that the industrialized countries lack credibility on the issue of international cooperation to curb greenhouse gas emissions, having done little to address a problem largely of their own making'.

However, there are some examples of (modestly) successful trust-building efforts in global environmental politics. The Multilateral Ozone Fund enshrined the 'compensatory justice' principle and gave developing countries a greater stake in the decision-making process governing the allocation of environmental aid (Woods, 1999; Hicks et al., 2008). The Montreal Protocol also gave developing countries a ten-year window to pursue 'cheap' economic development before making serious chlorofluorocarbon (CFC) reductions. Rich nations have also made some important concessions in the context of climate negotiations. For example, developing countries were invited to participate in the Kyoto Protocol's 'Compliance Committee' (despite avoiding scheduled emission reduction commitments themselves) and treated as 'equal' partners through the double-majority voting mechanism.

This idea of incremental trust-building through costly signals is not supported by some Western negotiators. In 2001, former US environmental treaty negotiator Richard Benedick described himself as being mystified as to why rich nations would ever include developing countries in the Kyoto Protocol's monitoring and compliance system. 'A major and dubious concession to the South', he noted, 'was an agreement to grant developing nations, who have no commitments, a decisive role in the protocol's compliance system, assessing and enforcing the commitments of industrialized countries' (Benedick, 2001: 73).[11] We take a very different view. We believe that textbook rational-choice models of international cooperation are simply not up to the task of explaining the low levels of diffuse reciprocity, conditions of generalized mistrust and widely divergent principled beliefs that characterize North–South environmental relations, and therefore conventional negotiating tactics need to be reconsidered. Mark Twain famously said that 'the principle of diplomacy [is to] give one and take ten', but developing a workable North–South climate pact will almost certainly require that Western negotiators transcend this principle. Human psychology research has shown that when people feel taken advantage of, marginalized, powerless, angry, envious and spiteful, they are less likely to cooperate and more likely to engage in self-damaging behaviour. We are only now beginning to come to grips with the fact that interstate relations may not be all that different. As Keohane (2001: 6) notes, '[c]ool practitioners of self-interest, known to be such, may be less able to cooperate productively than individuals who are governed by emotions that send reliable signals, such as love or reliability'.

We believe that rich countries need to build conditions of diffuse reciprocity and trust with poor countries before asking them to make costly policy commitments, and that the best way for them to do this is by launching a reassurance strategy through costly signals. Baer et al. (2008: 24) suggest that:

there is only one alternative to continued impasse: a brief but relatively formal trust-building period . . . Regarding the North, anything less than explicit and legally-binding commitments – both to ambitiously pursue domestic reductions and to greatly scale up support for mitigation and adaptation in developing countries – would be seen as a failure to seriously invest in repairing the trust deficit.

We share this view, and would add that during the early stages of a trust-building strategy it makes little sense to demand that the South adopt binding limits on their emissions. A more constructive approach would be to focus on so-called 'no-regrets' options and provide substantial financial assistance for voluntary mitigation efforts that are consistent with local development priorities. Policy 'sticks' like trade sanctions are also probably not the best way to build confidence at the early stages.[12]

Another costly signal would be the provision of adaptation assistance on a scale that is responsive to objective assessments of need.[13] Many negotiators and rational-choice scholars believe that the North should use environmental aid to either reward countries that demonstrate a credible commitment to reducing greenhouse gas emissions or provide an inducement for future cooperation. However, we would argue that this kind of textbook rational-choice institutionalism, which assumes away weak conditions of reciprocity, generalized mistrust, and divergent worldviews and causal beliefs, is misguided. Environmental aid should also be used to build trust; signal confidence, solidarity, empathy and kindness to developing countries; and offer an attractive 'new thinking' about global environmental cooperation. While critics might dismiss adaptation aid as a mere palliative, or an irrational diversion of scarce resources needed to combat climate change, we would caution against making hard-and-fast distinctions between these two types of environmental aid. While mitigation assistance might have a direct impact on climate change, it does relatively little to address global inequality's longer-term corrosive effect on North–South environmental relations. Adaptation assistance will probably foster civic and cooperative norms and thus increase the willingness of poor countries to participate in a global climate accord.

Finally, as we have argued elsewhere, sometimes trust-building is also about exercising strategic restraint (Roberts and Parks, 2007). We believe that one of the most important ways in which wealthy, industrialized countries could build trust with the global South would be to explicitly signal their concern for the 'structural obstacles' facing developing countries and aggressively support their interests and priorities across multiple international economic regimes. This type of strategy could be pursued by reining in Western agricultural subsidies, tariff escalation practices, and the ongoing 'deep integration' and anti-industrial policy crusade, which reinforce the structuralist perception that rich countries do not want poor countries to get rich the same way they did; creating a commodity support fund to insulate natural-resource-reliant countries from exogenous shocks; abandoning international economic regimes that threaten the long-term interests of developing countries; and giving developing countries a greater stake in the governance structures of international financial institutions. In the final analysis, such action could prove more important than the design features of a future climate agreement, carbon accounting schemes or environmental aid transfers. According to seasoned analyst Herman Ott and others, 'it became clear [at COP-8 in New Delhi] that developing countries would not give up their "right" for increasing emissions without serious concessions in other fields of the development agenda which satisfy the demand for global equity and poverty reduction' (Ott, 2004: 261).

To conclude, climate change is fundamentally an issue of inequality, and its resolution will probably demand an unconventional policy approach. We need a global and just transition built on diffuse reciprocity, a climate of trust, negotiated justice and a shared vision of truly long-term cooperative action.

Notes

1. The atmospheric concentration of CO_2 has already increased by almost 100 ppm – to roughly 385 ppm – over the 'pre-industrial' level (IPCC, 2007).
2. Peter N. Spotts, 'Trust tops global climate agenda', *Christian Science Monitor*, 1 December 2008.
3. We would point out that rather than 50, it is 40 years from now until 2050, but the point holds.
4. http://www.boxxet.com/Climate_change/On:UNFCCC/.
5. See Ramesh Jaura, 'Climate change: Poznan produces a "vision gap"', *IPS News*, 13 December 2008. http://ipsnews.net/print.asp?idnews=45103.
6. Baer et al. (2008: 24) point out that 'the South's distrust is rooted in the North's repeated failure to meet its UNFCCC and Kyoto commitments to provide technological and financial support for both mitigation and adaptation, and beyond these, its protracted history of bad-faith negotiations in all sorts of other multilateral regimes (the trade and intellectual property negotiations come particularly to mind)'.
7. Causal beliefs are 'beliefs about cause–effect relationships which derive authority from the shared consensus of recognized elites' (Goldstein and Keohane, 1993: 9–10).
8. Through the lens of a structuralist, the international system is characterized by a division of labour. There is a global stratification system that places nations on the top, in the middle or on the bottom, and only a few manage to move up. Nations can move up or down the hierarchy, but the structure largely remains unchanged (Roberts and Parks, 2007: 32).
9. Raúl Estrada-Oyuela, one of the leading climate negotiators at Kyoto, noted that 'equity is the fundamental condition to ensure compliance of any international agreement' (Estrada-Oyuela, 2002: 37).
10. This point is increasingly recognized by scholars and policy-makers. Blanchard et al. note that 'any future burden-sharing agreement involving developing countries will probably be based on a complex differentiation scheme combining different basic rules' (Blanchard et al., 2003: 286).
11. On the Kyoto Protocol's 'compliance committee', see Ott (2001).
12. During the COP-13 negotiations in Bali, the G-77 Chair reported that several industrialized countries had threatened trade sanctions if developing countries were unwilling to take on commitments to reduce their emissions. This seemed to engender a very negative response and reinforce the perception that the global North is more interested in limiting the South's economic development than it is in seeking to reduce its own emissions. See http://www.opendemocracy.net/global_deal/g77_threats.
13. According to the latest UNFCCC estimates, by 2030, $100 billion a year will be needed to finance mitigation activities and $28–$67 billion a year to finance adaptation activities in the developing world. Oxfam has put the cost at $50 billion a year and created an 'adaptation financing index' to provide a rough sense of who should pay how much based on the 'common but differentiated responsibilities and respective capabilities' principle. See http://www.oxfam.org/files/adapting%20to%20climate%20change.pdf.

References

Abbott, Kenneth and Duncan Snidal (2000), 'Hard and soft law in international governance', *International Organization*, **54** (3): 421–56.

Albin, Cecilia (2001), *Justice and Fairness in International Negotiation*, Cambridge, UK: Cambridge University Press.

Baer, Paul, Tom Athanasiou, Sivan Kartha and Eric Kemp-Benedict (2008), *The Greenhouse Development Rights Framework: The Right to Development in a Climate Constrained World*, Revised 2nd edn, Berlin: Heinrich Böll Foundation, Christian Aid, EcoEquity and the Stockholm Environment Institute.

Barrett, Scott (2003), *Environment and Statecraft: the Strategy of Environmental Treaty-Making*, Oxford, UK: Oxford University Press.

Bartsch, Ulrich and Benito Müller (2000), *Fossil Fuels in a Changing Climate: Impacts of the Kyoto Protocol and Developing Country Participation*, Oxford: Oxford University Press.

Baumert, Kevin A. and Nancy Kete (2002), 'An architecture for climate protection', in Kevin Baumert (ed.), *Building on the Kyoto Protocol: Options for Protecting the Climate*, Washington, DC: World Resources Institute, pp. 1–30.

Benedick, R.E. (2001), 'Striking a new deal on climate change', *Issues in Science and Technology Online*, Fall: 71–6.

Birdsall, Nancy, Dani Rodrik and Arvind Subramanian (2005), 'If rich governments really cared about development', Working Paper, Geneva: International Centre for Trade and Sustainable Development.

Blanchard, O., P. Criqui, A. Kitous and L. Viguier (2003), 'Combining efficiency with equity: a pragmatic approach', in I. Kaul, P. Conceicao, K.L. Le Goulven and R.U. Mendoza (eds), *Providing Global Public Goods: Managing Globalization*, Oxford and New York: Oxford University Press, pp. 280–303.

Chasek, Pamela, David Downie and Janet Welsh Brown (2006), *Global Environmental Politics*, 4th edition, Boulder, CO: Westview Press.

Claussen, Eileen and Lisa McNeilly (1998), *Equity and Global Climate Change: The Complex Elements of Fairness*, Arlington, VA: Pew Center on Climate Change.

Depledge, Joanna (2002) 'Continuing Kyoto: extending absolute emission caps to developing countries', in Kevin Baumert (ed.) *Building on the Kyoto Protocol: Options for Protecting the Climate*, Washington, DC: World Resources Institute, pp. 31–60.

DeSombre, Elizabeth R. and Joanne Kauffman (1996), 'The Montreal Protocol Multilateral Fund: partial success story', in Robert O. Keohane and Marc A. Levy (eds), *Institutions for Environmental Aid: Pitfalls and Promise*, Cambridge, MA: MIT Press, pp. 89–126.

Durkheim, Emile ([1893] 1933), *On the Division of Labor in Society*, trans. G. Simpson, New York: Macmillan.

Easterly, William (2001), 'The middle class consensus and economic development', *Journal of Economic Growth*, **6** (4): 317–35.

The Economic Times (2008), 'China tells developed world to go on climate change "diet",' 12 March, available at: http://www.dailytimes.com.pk/default.asp?page=2008%5C03%5C17%5Cstory_17-3-2008_pg6_19.

Eilperin, Juliet (2008), 'Developing nations plan emission cuts; shift seen as crucial to new climate pact', *Washington Post*, 12 December, p. A10.

Estrada-Oyuela, Rául A. (2002), 'Equity and climate change', in Luiz Pinguelli-Rosa and Mohan Munasinghe (eds), *Ethics, Equity and International Negotiations on Climate Change*, Cheltenham, UK and Northampton, MA: Edward Elgar Publishing, pp. 36–46.

European Union (2008), 'Climate change and international security', paper from the High Representative and the European Commission to the European Council, Brussels, 14 March.

Goddard Institute for Space Studies (2008), 'Global temperature anomalies in .01 °C', <http://data.giss.nasa.gov/gistemp/tabledata/GLB.Ts.txt>, accessed 10 July 2008.

Goldstein, Judith and Robert Keohane (eds) (1993), *Ideas and Foreign Policy: Beliefs, Institutions, and Political Change*, Ithaca, NY: Cornell University Press.

Green, Duncan (2008), *From Poverty to Power: How Active Citizens and Effective States Can Change the World*, Oxford: Oxfam International.

Groenenberg, Heleen, Dian Phylipsen and Kornelis Blok (2001), 'Differentiating commitments world wide: global differentiation of GHG emissions reductions based on the triptych approach – a preliminary assessment', *Energy Policy*, **29** (12): 1007–30.

Gruber, Lloyd (2000), *Ruling the World: Power Politics and the Rise of Supranational Institutions*, Princeton, NJ: Princeton University Press.

Gupta, Joyeeta (2000), *'On Behalf of my Delegation,. . .': A Survival Guide for Developing Country Climate Negotiators*, Washington, DC: Center for Sustainable Development in the Americas.

Gupta, Sujata and Preety M. Bhandari (1999), 'An effective allocation criterion for CO_2 emissions', *Energy Policy*, **27** (12): 727–36.

Haas, P.M., R.O. Keohane and M.A. Levy (eds) (1993), *Institutions for the Earth: Sources of Effective International Environmental Protection*, Cambridge, MA: MIT Press.

Heil, Mark T. and Thomas M. Selden (2001), 'International trade intensity and carbon emissions: a cross-country econometric analysis', *Journal of Environment and Development*, **10** (1): 35–49.

Hicks, Robert L. Bradley C. Parks, J. Timmons Roberts and Michael J. Tierney (2008), *Greening Aid? Understanding the Environmental Impact of Development Assistance*, Oxford and New York: Oxford University Press.

IPCC (2007), *Climate Change 2007: Fourth Assessment Report of the Intergovernmental Panel on Climate Change*, Cambridge: Cambridge University Press.

Jaura, Ramesh (2008), 'Climate change: Poznan produces a "vision gap"', *IPS News*, 13 December, available at: http://ipsnews.net/print.asp?idnews=45103.

Kaul, Inge, Isabelle Grunberg and Marc Stern (1999), 'Defining global public goods', in Inge Kaul, Isabelle Grunberg and Marc Stern (eds), *Global Public Goods: International Cooperation in the 21st Century*, Oxford: Oxford University Press, pp. 2–19.

Keohane, Robert (1984), *After Hegemony: Cooperation and Discord in the World Political Economy*, Princeton, NJ: Princeton University Press.

Keohane, Robert (1986), 'Reciprocity in international relations', *International Organization*, **40** (1): 1–27.

Keohane, Robert (2001), 'Governance in a partially globalized world', *American Political Science Review*, **95** (1): 1–13.

Keohane, Robert and Marc A. Levy (eds) (1996), *Institutions for Environmental Aid: Pitfalls and Promise*, Cambridge, MA: MIT Press.

Knack, Stephen and Philip Keefer (1997), 'Does social capital have an economic payoff? A cross-country investigation', *Quarterly Journal of Economics*, **112** (4): 1251–88.

Krasner, Stephen (1978), 'United States commercial and monetary policy: unraveling the paradox of external strength and internal weakness', in Peter J. Katzenstein (ed.), *Between Power and Plenty: Foreign Economic Policies of Advanced Iindustrial States*, Madison, WI: University of Wisconsin Press, pp. 51–87.

Krasner, Stephen (1985), *Structural Conflict: The Third World Against Global Liberalism*, Berkeley, CA: University of California Press.

Kydd, Andrew (2000), 'Trust, reassurance, and cooperation', *International Organization*, **54** (2): 325–57.

Machado, Giovani, Roberto Schaeffer and Ernst Worrell (2001), 'Energy and carbon embodied in the international trade of Brazil: an input–output approach', *Ecological Economics*, **39** (3): 409–24.

Mathur, Ajay, Ian Burton and Maarten van Aalst (eds) (2004), *An Adaptation Mosaic: A Sample of the Emerging World Bank Work in Climate Change Adaptation*, Washington, DC: The World Bank.

Mearsheimer, John J. (1994/95), 'The false promise of international institutions', *International Security*, **19** (3): 5–49.

Müller, Benito (1999), *Justice in Global Warming Negotiations: How to Obtain a Procedurally Fair Compromise*, Oxford: Oxford Institute for Energy Studies.

Müller, Benito (2001), 'Fair compromise in a morally complex world', paper presented at Pew Equity Conference, Washington, DC, 17–18 April.

Muradian, Roldan, Martin O'Connor and Joan Martínez-Alier (2002), 'Embodied pollution in trade: estimating the "environmental load displacement" of industrialized countries', *Ecological Economics*, **41** (1): 51–67.

Najam, Adil (1995), 'International environmental negotiations: a strategy for the South', *International Environmental Affairs*, **7** (2): 249–87.

Najam, Adil (2003), 'The case against a new international environmental organization', *Global Governance*, **9**: 367–84.

Najam, Adil (2004), 'The view from the South: developing countries in global environmental politics', in Regina Axelrod, David Downie and Norman Vig (eds), *The Global Environment: Institutions, Law, and Policy*, 2nd edn, Washington, DC: CQ Press, pp. 225–43.

Ott, Hermann E. (2001), 'The Born Agreement to the Kyoto Protocol – paving the way for ratification', *International Environmental Agreement: Politics Law and Economics*, **1** (4): 469–76.

Ott, Hermann E. (2004), 'Global climate', in *Yearbook of International Environmental Law*, **12**: 261–70.

Porter, Gareth and Janet W. Brown (1991), *Global Environmental Politics*, Boulder, CO: Westview Press.

Putnam, Robert D. (1993), *Making Democracy Work*, Princeton, NJ: Princeton University Press.

Putnam, Robert D. (2000), *Bowling Alone: The Collapse and Revival of American Community*, New York: Simon and Schuster.

Roberts, J. Timmons and Bradley C. Parks (2007), *A Climate of Injustice: Global Inequality, North–South Politics, and Climate Policy*, Cambridge, MA: MIT Press.

Ruggie, John Gerard (1983), 'Political structure and change in the international economic order: the North–South dimension', in John Gerard Ruggie (ed.), *The Antinomies of Interdependence*, New York, NY: Columbia University Press, pp. 423–87.

Sandbrook, Richard (1997), 'UNGASS has run out of steam', *International Affairs*, **73**: 641–54.

Sebenius, James K. (1991), 'Designing negotiations towards a new regime: the case of global warming', *International Security*, **15** (4): 110–48.

Sell, Susan (1996), 'North–South environmental bargaining: ozone, climate change, and biodiversity', *Global Governance*, **2** (1): 97–118.

Shadlen, Ken (2004), 'Patents and pills, power and procedure: the North–South politics of public health in the WTO', *Studies in Comparative International Development*, **39** (3): 76–108.

Sprinz, Detlef and Tapani Vaahtoranta (1994), 'The interest-based explanation of international environmental policy', *International Organization*, **48** (1): 77–105.

Stavins, Robert (2004), 'Can an effective global climate treaty be based upon sound science, rational economics, and pragmatic politics?', KSG Faculty Research Working Paper Series REP04-020, Cambridge, MA.

Stavins, Robert and Sheila M. Olmstead (2006), 'An international policy architecture for the post-Kyoto era', *American Economic Review Papers and Proceedings*, **96** (2): 35–8.

Stein, Arthur (1990), *Why Nations Cooperate: Circumstance and Choice in International Relations*, Ithaca, NY: Cornell University Press.

Torvanger, Asbjorn and Odd Godal (2004), 'An evaluation of pre-Kyoto differentiation proposals for national greenhouse gas abatement targets', *International Environmental Agreements: Politics, Law and Economics*, **4** (1): 65–91.

UNFCCC (1992), *United Nations Framework Convention on Climate Change*, New York: United Nations, <http://unfccc.int/resource/docs/convkp/conveng.pdf>, accessed 10 July 2008.

Wade, Robert (2003), 'What strategies are viable for developing countries today? The World Trade Organization and the shrinking of development space', *Review of International Political Economy*, **10** (4): 627–44.

Waltz, Kenneth (1979), *Theory of International Politics*, New York: Random House.

Wheeler, David and Kevin Ummel (2007), 'Another inconvenient truth: a carbon-intensive South faces environmental disaster no matter what the North does', Working Paper No. 134, Center for Global Development, Washington, DC.

Wiegandt, E. (2001), 'Climate Change, equity, and international negotiations', in Urs Luterbacher and Detlef Sprinz (eds), *International Relations and Global Climate Change*, Cambridge, MA: MIT Press, pp. 127–50.

Woods, Ngaire (1999), 'Good governance in international organizations', *Global Governance*, **5** (1): 36–61.

Ybema, J. Remko, J.J. Battjes, Jaap C. Jansen and Frank Ormel (2000), *Burden Differentiation: GHG Emissions, Undercurrents and Mitigation Costs*, Oslo, Norway: Center for International Climate and Environmental Research.

Young, Oran R. (1994), *International Governance: Protecting the Environment in a Stateless Society*, Ithaca, NY: Cornell University Press.

20 Environmental sociology and international forestry: historical overview and future directions

Bianca Ambrose-Oji

Introduction

Forestry is implicated in many of today's most pressing and prominent environmental issues: climate change and global warming; food, water and energy security; rapid urbanization and environmental degradation; and the environmental impacts and resilience of globalized systems of production and consumption. Trees and forests act as a global carbon sink; mediate local and regional weather systems; are a store of genetic diversity for future foods and medicines; provide traditional and novel forms of energy; impact on local hydrological systems and have the potential to alleviate flooding risk during extreme weather events; while urban forestry can improve living spaces and quality of life through greening and cooling in urban microclimates.

But how has forestry been theorized? What has sociology offered in terms of broadening our understanding of the relationship between societies and the natural resources they depend upon? This chapter will present an overview of the important trends in the history and development of international forestry, as well as tracking the parallel development of environmental sociology and the perspectives it has to offer. The chapter concludes by looking at what the discipline has to offer our understanding of the relationships between forestry and society in the future.

Catton and Dunlap (1978) were among the first sociologists to suggest that following the rise of environmental movements during the 1960s and 1970s, there should be a new period of sociological inquiry. They identified a 'new environmental paradigm' as a way to bring forward 'the study of the interaction between the environment and society': a new discipline of environmental sociology (Catton and Dunlap, 1978: 44). Notwithstanding the diverse and often conflicting approaches that have emerged since then (see both Dunlap and Vallaincourt, Chapters 1 and 3 in this volume), by 2003 Buttel was able to posit that we had moved past a period in which environmental sociologists sought to explain the nature of environmental problems, to one where they were looking to effect environmental reform through their science. For Buttel (2003) there were now four key foci within environmental sociology: social movements; state regulation; ecological modernization; and international environmental governance.

To what extent have these same concerns and the different approaches to addressing them been mirrored in forestry? What do they tell us and how far do they continue to hold currency now that we are entering the second decade of the millennium and the demands on forestry have become so diverse and substantial?

A review of the recent history of international forestry

The last two decades of the twentieth century witnessed growing global apprehension about the fate of tropical forests. Northern nations lobbied 'rainforest nations' to institute forest conservation measures, which they believed would help maintain their own access to novel genes and species, as well as retain significant tracts of forest land as a 'buffer' against global climate change. Conversely, Southern nations fought to uphold their national autonomy and defended their rights to exploit forest biodiversity as a means to achieve their own development aspirations. Although the UNCED in 1992 saw the effective formulation of the Convention on Biodiversity (CBD), agreement over tropical forests was more problematic and finally emerged only as a non-binding statement of principles. Whilst forests and forestry were expected to accommodate the often conflicting interests of global and national stakeholders, they also continued to provide livelihood resources for forest-dependent communities. Thus the demand was for foresters and conservation professionals to identify and implement methods of forest management that would protect natural forests and biodiversity while continuing to meet national and local development aims.

Action in forestry resonated with wider trends in the conservation and natural-resource-management community. Administrative decentralization and devolution of power to community level were seen as improving forest governance, with participatory or inclusive decision-making processes the key to building the local institutions necessary to effect these changes. In addition, postmodern challenges to the primacy of scientific epistemologies had begun to expose the shortcomings of technical natural-science knowledge as a means to effect conservation strategies. Rather than use prescriptions developed by forest ecologists and managers, there was a shift to using social-science-based techniques as a means to incorporate people's behaviour and societal values in the formulation of forest conservation mechanisms. Forestry had come to a crossroads. The eminent international forester Jack Westoby (1987: 302) could now declare that 'There are some people who believe that forestry is about trees. It is not. It is about people, and how trees can serve people. Forestry is *for* people.'

Added to this, social scientists and development professionals entered a period of reflexive assessment concerning the nature of 'development', how this stood alongside environmental conservation, and the increased role civil society might have in realizing sustainable development aims (Booth, 1994; Chambers, 1993; Farrington et al., 1993). New definitions of community 'organizations', 'institutions' and 'networks' began to emerge, and the meaning and potential of participation were defined (Banuri and Marglin, 1993a; Bass et al., 1995; Colchester, 1996; Fisher, 1993; Murphree, 1993; Nelson and Wright, 1995; Ostrom, 1990; Uphoff, 1992). Rural sociologists, policy-makers and development professionals began to look at participatory modes of project delivery, particularly by linking conservation to community economic development.

As a result of these changes, 'forestry', both as theoretical discipline and praxis,[1] began its own process of deconstruction and change. The social dynamic began to be more fully incorporated into a traditionally technocratic and scientific discipline. A 'paradigm shift' was hailed with the emergence of what was coined 'new forestry' (Kimmins, 1997), echoing Botkin's (1990) 'new ecology'. 'New foresters' were expected to recognize the multi-use, multi-product, ecosystem process-based management demanded by the differing cultural, social and economic values placed on forest land and resources (Ascher and Healy, 1990; McNeeley, 1994; Schreckenberg and Hadley, 1991).

Emerging frameworks of socio-environmental change in forestry
As foresters struggled to incorporate 'people' and 'society' into analytical and practical frameworks, discourse became dominated by a series of sharply polarized debates concerning the significance of the various 'social' factors that might be pivotal to the success of the 'new forestry' project. Mirroring the four foci of socio-environmental change that Buttel (2003) identified within environmental sociology, forestry discourse could be divided into four areas of interest: knowledge, power and indigenous resistance movements; community and social forestry emphasizing the structural interface between community and state regulation; the application of economic value to forests; and the integrative sustainable livelihoods framework.

Knowledge, power and indigenous resistance movements
The first area focused on the importance of culture and contextualization, arguing that: sustainable forestry was 'about issues of control, power, participation and self-determination' (Croll and Parkin, 1992: 9); power could be viewed from the perspective of the politics of knowledge (Banuri and Marglin, 1993b; Marglin and Marglin, 1990); and the incorporation of 'indigenous technical knowledge' and 'indigenous realities' was the key to success. The last claim was reinforced by evidence that tropical forests have a long history of human use, which, rather than degrading forest environments, had often added to forest biodiversity and structural complexity (Fairhead and Leach, 1995; McNeeley, 1994). These interpretations tended to view forest biodiversity as intellectual property. Arguments concentrated on developing ethnoforestry as a route to securing human rights, self determination, and equity in national and international property regimes (Amalric, 1999; Phillips et al., 1994; Posey, 1997). There were many notable examples to support these arguments.

An indigenous group in the Amazonian Sate of Acre used the Brazilian judicial courts to expel from the country for acts of biopiracy a Swiss NGO (Selva Viva) that had been cataloguing plants for international laboratories Ciba-Geigy, Hoechst, Sandoz, Lilly and Johnson & Johnson (WRM, 1997). In India, aggravated by the imposition of new rules of trade-related intellectual property rights (TRIPs), there was a series of protests between 1994 and 1996 as farmers worked against international business interests patenting natural compounds produced by the neem tree (*Azadirachta indica*). In one sense these protests were focused on property rights, but they also related to indigenous people and local communities being able to continue using the trees as they had done for generations (Dickson and Jayaraman, 1995; Kleiner, 1995; Shiva and Holla-Bhar, 1996). Under the terms of TRIPs the use of neem in traditional pesticide preparations could have put farmers in breach of international patent law.

Community and social forestry
The subdisciplines of 'community forestry' and 'social forestry' took a more structuralist approach, understanding that social organization was of prime importance, and that models of forestry built on social structure, institutions and organizations implicitly incorporated knowledge and culture (Cernea, 1985, 1990; FAO, 1995; Uphoff, 1992; Wiersum, 1984). This was expressed most clearly through debates about social organization around common property resources, relations between communities and state

forestry services, the need to work through local-level organizations such as traditional councils and user committees, and the use of 'stakeholder analysis' as the primary tool to map these varying interests (Grimble and Quan, 1994; Peluso, 1992a, 1992b). In this formulation, forest biodiversity and forest resources were understood as material property at the level of habitats and landscapes, rather than species and genes. Participation and collaborative forms of governance could be viewed as institutions supporting the transaction costs associated with tenure regimes that constrained resource degradation (Baland and Platteau, 1996; Gibson et al., 2000). From this perspective, better forest management and protection would come from the evolution of social structures that linked local and state systems of governance.

In Nepal, Yadav et al. (2003) describe how the integration of state forestry with local institutions was moving the forest sector towards more democratic and consensual models 'where local stakeholders' planning and capacity building were treated as ongoing processes' (ibid.: 48). They also note that the integration of community institutions has effects on forestry departments and their policies as they support innovations in the field and change their practice as a consequence. In Brazil, the National Institute for Colonization and Agrarian Reform (INCRA) managed national legislation during the early 1990s that allowed for the expropriation of land from large, often-absent landowners on the basis of invalid claims, or of failure to maintain land and communities as detailed in contract documents. In Rondônia, workers' collectives and cooperatives were organized to occupy such land, where they would subsequently engage in forest restoration and agroforestry work, accessing state aid for land improvement schemes such as forestry (Burford, 1993).

Forest valuation
The third approach to socio-environmental change within forestry was utilitarian and concentrated on the value (monetary and social) of forests, and developed neoclassical economic and political-economy approaches to understand the causes of deforestation. This approach assumed that forests had been undervalued by policy-makers and local communities alike, and that new forms of evaluation and natural resource accounting would provide models for management through adjustments to macroeconomic policy, the establishment of 'extractive reserves' and development based on the value of forest biodiversity (Bojo, 1993; Rudel and Roper, 1997; Ruitenbeek, 1990). This view was expressed in models that saw forestry as an important vehicle for community development through the extension of forest product commercialization initiatives, and an understanding of forest biodiversity as an economic commodity that could fuel that development (Neumann and Hirsch, 2000; Wollenberg and Ingles, 1998).

All three frameworks tended to underplay the sum of very diffuse sets of social relations – particularly the aggregate effects of actions by individuals and households on the forest ecosystem, which are not necessarily captured by understanding cultural values, institutional processes or the economic incentives for forest conservation. A very important thread running through all three models, particularly the structural and utilitarian perspectives, is the idea of forest-based livelihoods. It was this focus on livelihoods that appeared as an alternative framework to describe the mechanisms of socio-environmental change, although it was acknowledged that structure, agency, knowledge, power and value were all important.

Sustainable livelihoods

The 'sustainable livelihoods framework' (SLF) suggested that there were particular resources in the form of 'capitals' (social, human, financial, physical, natural) that could be used to realize 'environmental entitlements', and these in turn promoted particular livelihood outcomes (Bebbington, 1999; Leach et al., 1997; Scoones, 1998). So, for example, membership of a social organization might allow the realization of an entitlement through the collection or harvest of forest goods and their subsequent sale to provide income that could be used to support the family through a number of different outcomes such as improved education or better health. Importantly, however, the possibilities – the entitlements – that could be realized by individuals and households were affected by the structural policy, institutional and process contexts in which actors found themselves. Both agency and structure are implicated. Indeed the living of a life, the realization and adaptation of entitlements, could be seen as the mechanism whereby social change occurred, natural resource access and use were modified, and alternative livelihoods emerged.

The early work on forest-based livelihoods was dominated by descriptive analyses of non-timber forest product (NTFP) use and the potential value of those products measured by the cash income they could generate (Dei, 1989; Dembner, 1995; Longhurst, 1991). Many researchers found greater currency in focusing on the descriptive micro-level dynamics of livelihoods, than in being able to link with the macro-level and structural components suggested by the framework. Even though later studies using subsequent iterations of the SLF recorded more nuanced livelihood systems, it could be argued that the one structure to emerge as dominant from the livelihoods work was the market. These early works indicated an inverse relationship between household income and forest use such that the poorest groups were seen to depend most on the environment as an important mediator of livelihood vulnerability (Cavendish, 2000). In this way, forests were quickly and firmly linked to international poverty alleviation agendas through market-based mechanisms of value generation (Campbell and Luckert, 2002). The wider agendas serviced by this view developed to include the use of global transfer payments to secure biodiversity and environmental services (Putterman, 1996).

Environmental sociology and theorizing forest change

So we can see that Buttel's view of the four models of change predominant in environmental sociology certainly has currency. However, one of the questions this chapter has posed concerns how the epistemologies of environmental sociology developed during this same period and how they theorize forestry as a system at the interface of social and natural worlds. There are three major epistemological traditions that need to be explored: social constructionism; critical theory as revealed by neo-Marxian-inspired political ecology; and empiricism represented by environmental managerialism and the 'new ecology'.

Social constructionism and forestry

Social constructionists place deeply embedded practices and the language or 'discourse' around day-to-day action at the centre of any analysis of socio-environmental problems (Eder, 1996; Hajer, 1995). This approach views the way in which society acts and

interacts with the environment as conditioned by the way in which it perceives and prob-
lematizes that environment, a position summarized by the statement that 'there cannot
be a materialist analysis which is not, at the same time, a discursive analysis . . . there
is no materiality unmediated by discourse' (Escobar, 1996: 46). In other words, it is not
possible to look at material issues such as forest exploitation and degradation without
also looking at the presentation of that exploitation as 'a problem' and how that is com-
municated and linked to action through 'public transcripts' or 'narratives' (Arce et al.,
1994; Hajer, 1995; Roe, 1991; Bryant and Bailey, 1997).

These perspectives have proved useful in describing the processes driving national,
regional and global environmental trends, by identifying the 'metanarratives' and the
policy coalitions or 'discursive communities' associated with them. Useful too is the
social constructionist exposition of how the actions of people and institutions from
the global to the local level are bound together by such discursive formulations and
narratives. Hannigan (1995), Peuhkuri and Jokinen (1999) and Brown (2001) all put
forward the view that 'biodiversity' had created such a discourse, to the point where,
as an idea, a narrative, it created a 'successful career' as an environmental problem – so
much so that, until the new millennium at least, 'biodiversity' was perhaps *the* issue structuring global forest governance. Fairhead and Leach's (1998) regional study of change
to the humid forests in Africa used a social constructionist framework to demonstrate
how forest statistics were 'regarded as so authoritative . . . [they] . . . quickly become
established in the literature by default' (ibid.: 3). The statistics were used to maintain the
narrative that deforestation was occurring as populations increased and shifting cultivation cleared ever greater areas of land through 'ignorant' agricultural practice. However,
using historical analyses of the numerical and satellite data, Fairhead and Leach showed
that in many areas traditional agricultural and land management practices were actually
increasing forest cover and quality. Tiffen et al. (1994), working in the Kenyan highlands, were also able to demonstrate that contrary to the popular discourse structuring
environmental policy, an increase in population in Machakos District had halted soil
erosion and increased tree cover.

Although these ideas can inform analyses of forest management, parts of the social
constructionist repertoire have proved problematic. Any consideration of environmental issues in a developing-forest-nation context must take account of how livelihoods
are tightly bound to material conditions. It is this real-world materiality that is often
divorced from the constructionists' intellectual apparatus as they 'distance the analysis
of environmental problems from the problems themselves' (Woodgate and Redclift,
1998: 6). Woodgate and Redclift show that '[w]e are both materially and symbolically
creative and destructive; we refashion our environments physically *as well as* cognitively',
moving away from views of nature as '*either* the material conditions of our existence, *or*
as no more than a set of culturally generated symbols' to one where we can 'accept nature
as both' (ibid.: 7).

Another issue sits with the way discourse analysis often implies a lack of agency, a lack
of capability open to actors to challenge dominant 'story lines'. Even though some theorists identified the potential for 'discursive resistance' to provide campaigns and social
movements with the tools to discredit dominant narratives, it is possible to level criticism
at the constructivist approach for remaining too rigid in its interpretation of societies'
conditioning by texts and narratives.

Critical theory through political ecology

Political ecology is a broad and dynamic church (see Escobar, Chapter 6 in this volume), but taken together, its constituent views of power and resistance reinstate the agency that seems to be missing from much social constructionist analysis, recognizing the capacities of ordinary people to act and react within their politicized environments and change their own conditions and environments. Peterson (2000) took this idea one step further, by suggesting that there is a feedback loop between ecological change and human behaviour, each affecting the other over time. Casting political ecology as the study of the ever-dynamic tension between ecological and human change, Peterson also ascribed agency to ecosystems themselves, viewing them as active agents rather than just passive sets of objects transformed by human actors.

Political ecology has been used very effectively in the analysis of the social relations structuring forest management and change. Colchester's (1993) historical political analysis of the change to forest cover in Equatorial Africa illustrated how the interests of the First World coalesced with those of Third World elites to entrench the unequal power relations facilitating repression of local actors in favour of national leaders and global commercial logging interests. Brown and Ekoko (2001), working in south Cameroon, used political ecology to identify key social actors around forest exploitation and to map the relationships of power and resistance between them. Their characterizations of conflict, interactions and synergy pointed to 'spaces' for negotiation that could be used to agree new forest management prescriptions. In some of the same villages Brown and Lapuyade (2001) use political ecology to expose social cleavages along gender axes that relate to forest resource use and livelihood diversification, and show that there are different livelihood outcomes for women and men. Peluso (1996, 1992b), working in various forest nations of South-East Asia, exposed the political manipulation of forest landscapes to the exclusion and detriment of local communities which inspired civil-society responses. Finally, working in the lowland moist forests of Brazil, Shenley and Luz (1993) spent time with local communities not only documenting the political and ecological contexts, but also facilitating a process of community-based analysis of local forest value as a means of political 'empowerment' and rational decision-making in support of forest conservation and livelihood security.

Empiricism and forestry

Environmental managerialism The approach of the environmental managerialists, also described as 'environmental instrumentalists' and 'institutional' or 'technocratic eco-modernists', fills some of the gaps located within the social constructionist and political ecology approaches. Though not always thought of as environmental sociology, the main tenets of the 'school' are features that justify a place within the discipline, namely the translation of theory into practical action, and bridging positivist natural science with social science discourse.

Within ecological and environmental sciences, environmental managerialism takes a largely structuralist and positivist approach. In this formulation, community and ecosystem are not seen as different levels in a hierarchy but complementary parts of the same system, and the key focus is on adaptive management that recognizes the interplay between them. Emphasis is placed on the dynamics of species distribution and abundance, and the maintenance of ecosystem health conceived as the resilience of eco-system processes to stress within parameters suited to human occupation (Angermeier and Karr, 1994; Constanza et al., 1992; Rapport, 1995). Adaptive management is objective-driven, and the objectives may be set by local community values as much as national or global priorities. The forest management goals, and the techniques and activities used to realize them, are then treated as hypotheses that are confirmed or falsi-fied by success or failure (Walters, cited in Callicott et al., 1999).

Key proponents of this approach, Berkes and Folke (1998, p.9), state that '[t]here is no single, universally accepted way of formulating the linkage between social systems and natural systems'. They set up social 'institutions' as the cornerstone of their adaptive management approach. Local institutions are seen as the route to contextual engage-ment with nature, and thus, by implication, as an antidote to the issues of universality and prediction inherent within positivist science. However, Berkes and Folke's reliance on 'institutions' or social organizations builds a version of structuralism tending towards a view that organizational agency is technocratic and instrumental. Their vision of com-munity involvement is as a means of manipulating the coping mechanisms of local popu-lations rather than addressing the source of fundamental problems, an attitude Hajer might call 'ecologicalization of the social' (Hajer, 1995: 263).

Another limitation inherent to environmental managerialism during the 1990s was its uncritical reliance on scientific knowledge. Wallace et al. (1996) suggested that the radical changes ecosystem management ought to promote can be achieved through a fundamental change in the structures of the science it employs. They proposed that tra-ditional modes of scientific inquiry should shift from instrumental to inductive reason-ing, integrating what Dryzek (1983: 21) calls 'green reason' or 'ecological rationality'. Premised on the idea of 'civic citizen virtue' (Flyvbjerg, 1998: 229), collective altruism and the 'power of the better argument', green rationality was seen as an effective means for different social actors to resolve differences, accept different forms of scientific and expert lay knowledge, and so to build a consensus around particular courses of action. But it was precisely this that the constructionists exposed as one of the weaknesses in approaches that relied on the debate of scientific evidence in the formulation of action and policy. Indeed, the potential for discursive democracy assumes community represen-tation, democratic decision-making and exemplary critical faculties, which the political ecologists had already shown did not necessarily occur in the politicized contexts in which environmental problems were deliberated.

Accepting these limitations, the close integration of social institutions with forest man-agement and emergent ecologies is worth incorporating into sociological analyses. Also important is the ecological emphasis within environmental managerialism, which acts as a positive counterpoint to social construction in two ways: first by highlighting the importance of ecocentric values; and second by granting scientific method and knowl-edge a role in negotiating outcomes that are beneficial to both ecosystems and social systems. There was an expectation that managerialism could act as a balance to the SLF approaches that were increasingly criticized for relegating the environment to nothing more than one of a set of resource assets, and focusing more on human agency and intentions than environmental impacts. As Di Norcia (quoted in Wallace et al., 1996: 19) argued, what was required was an alternative 'ecologically sound conception of this human interest . . . that should not and can not be an anti-scientific conception'. So long as the limitations of the structuralist stance of environmental managerialism are recognized, and the scientific elements of this approach are understood as politicized, social constructs, the managerialist approach provides important tools to deal with the complexities and uncertainties inherent to biophysical systems, and interesting techniques to manage desired components of ecosystem composition, structure and function.

Sirait et al. (1994), working in the rainforests of East Kalimantan, demonstrated how local knowledge could be integrated with contemporary scientific techniques to produce viable forest management systems relevant to local social and political contexts. Looking at conservation forest management in south-west Cameroon, Abbot and Thomas (2001) demonstrate the importance of communicative rationality in changing the forest and livelihood values that are needed to support biodiversity maintenance. Warren and Pinkston (1998), working in south-eastern Nigeria, document changes to local ecologies and how the species- and process-based knowledge of indigenous communities has changed to reflect this.

New ecology   In the run-up to the new millennium, postmodern influences prompted a reappraisal of the grand theories of ecology, including the idea of 'climax communities' and habitats that endured unchanging over time. 'New' or 'non-equilibrium' ecology took the view that disturbance, change and dynamism are constant features of natural systems and are the features that drive ecological process (Attiwill, 1994; Botkin, 1990; Callicott et al., 1999; Chapman et al., 1997; Pickett et al., 1997; Sprugel, 1991). The importance of 'disturbance' began to build currency. Functionalist ecologists pushed the boundaries further, suggesting that far from being a species set apart from nature, human beings were *the* keystone species driving disturbance regimes and shaping local ecologies (Callicott et al., 1999; Peterson, 2000; Sprugel, 1991; Vandermeer and Perfecto, 1997). Consequently, conservation ecologists, forest scientists and policy-makers slowly began to accept that human decision-making and political policy choices have a direct impact on the shape of environmental and ecological conditions, and that biological conservation itself is a product of social action (Castle, 1993; Edwards and Abivardi, 1999).

These views were supported by revisiting earlier studies that noted how human agency influenced forest biodiversity. Some of the earliest West African studies suggested that African mahoganies (the *Meliaceae*) depend on human disturbance for their regeneration (Jones, 1956), while obeche (*Triplochiton scleroxylon*) was indicative of drier forest types produced after disturbance by farming (Keay, 1949 in Allison, 1962). In Latin American countries too, the reconstruction of pre-Columbian environmental histories, alongside the discovery of maize pollen and cultural artefacts in forest areas, has shown that there have been periods when forested land has been heavily influenced by human activity.

Current trends and emerging environmental sociologies

Since the turn of the millennium it has become clear that some of the more hotly debated issues of the 1990s have become twenty-first-century 'facts'. For environmental sociology three of the most important are globalization, climate change, and most recently a gathering acceptance of the distortion of 'natural time' as it fits social timescales.

Globalization is now accepted as a process and a condition of contemporary society and an important issue in environmental sociology. The impacts of the changes wrought by globalization have included a shift in the value of land and other primary resources. For example, changes to the price of cereals on world markets have produced anecdotal evidence of peasant farmers across the globe turning land over from forest fallow to more intensive wheat and maize production or opening marginal dryland forest areas for the production of bio-diesel crops such as *Jatropha curcas*. In forested nations deforestation has continued as rising prices encourage increased timber exports or, as in the case of Indonesia, Malaysia and other areas of South-East Asia, the conversion of natural forest to plantations producing important global commodities such as palm oil. It is also clear that the majority of rural populations are no longer divorced from the influences of globalized social, political and economic systems.

Climate change and global warming, so long perhaps the 'elephant in the room' as far as sociology was concerned, has also become established 'fact' (Lever-Tracy, 2008). The discussion now is about the carbon economy, of ways to mitigate and adapt to the impacts of climate change (see Redclift, Chapter 8 in this volume). For international forestry the challenge has become how to integrate forest conservation and industrial exploitation of forest resources as part of the new perspective of the global carbon system, and of moving forward on forest-based strategies that build resilient livelihoods and communities able to cope in the face of a range of future weather and climate scenarios.

Globalization studies and work on climate change have begun to add credence to the view that natural and ecological timescales have become compressed to run parallel with social timescales. Processes such as the retreat of the ice caps previously thought to take hundreds, if not thousands of years, are now shown to occur in decades, and the rapid pace of environmental change brought about by urbanization, population growth and globalized economic development have heralded in the sixth – and perhaps most rapid – period of 'mass extinction' of species. Ecologists are also revising their views of environmental change. The acceptance of non-equilibrium ecologies has moved on to the formulation of ideas about change that is brought about not by incremental steps, but by major regime shifts. These are abrupt changes where the ecology of a system switches and refigures to a different regime whose outcome is difficult to predict. Geologists, too, are gaining support for the idea of classifying a new geological epoch, the anthropocene, as a result of evidence showing that anthropogenic activity is now significant enough to influence the timescales and workings of geological as well as ecological processes (Zalasiewicz et al., 2008). Thus it may no longer be enough to claim that social processes occur through structuration and environmental changes through evolution. Society has come to a point where the seeming constant, the environment, is no longer necessarily so. Structures and processes have changed. Human agency has interrupted evolutionary processes and geological time, so that new processes of 'ecological agency' are at the point of changing social structures.

Future prospects for international forestry
There is no doubt that environmental sociology has had a significant impact on the development of the 'new forestry' project, but is it still the case that environmental sociology can provide influential analyses of current changes in forestry? The cleavages within forestry that emerged post-Rio have endured to the present, and there are clearly three major sets of claims still being made on forests by distinct communities of interest. The

developed world has continued to frame forests as a 'global commons', providing essential environmental goods and services. The developed world's early stake on accessing those commons has continued, although the focus has moved from securing rights to the more tangible products of forests, such as biodiversity, to the more intangible services proven to be important to climate change and other shared global risks. Indeed, it could be claimed that forests have been at the centre of the growth of a global risk society, while the globalization of markets and climate-change policy has certainly had an impact on the market and economic-value approaches to managing socio-environmental change.

Reports such as the 'Stern Review' into the economic impacts of climate change (Stern, 2006) had a significant impact in placing large-scale global actions to prevent deforestation high on the agenda of international environmental policy. Stern noted that whilst industrialized nations were able to include protection of carbon stocks in their Kyoto Protocol actions, most of the 18 per cent of global carbon emissions from deforestation was generated in developing nations. There have been proposals for the establishment of new global forest regimes and systems of global governance based on voluntary regulatory schemes. However, for many theorists the management of the global commons based on forests has come to be viewed as an economic problem, as much as a managerial one. A new productivism has emerged based on payment for environmental services (PES) models, which include a broad range of mechanisms designed to overcome the market failures experienced by international forestry – most particularly for biodiversity, water and carbon. This view can incorporate the claims on forests of the global North alongside the claims of less industrialized nation-states and transnational business interests among whom forests persist as natural resources to be used as a route to economic development and capital accumulation.

After the problems of developing global carbon markets based on forest conservation were exposed, 'avoided deforestation' was suggested as an alternative. Adopted at the UN Climate Convention in 2007 (see Parks and Roberts, Chapter 19 in this volume), Reducing Emissions from Deforestation and Degradation (REDD) will be the framework used in 2009 to decide how developing-country forests will be included in international climate-change mitigation regimes post-2012. Whilst discourse analysis and risk society theorists have exposed the difficulties of relying on scientific-evidence-based policy and regulatory regimes, and political ecologists have revealed the limitations of market-based regimes, REDD represents a hybrid form of forest regime that stands between the two poles. How far this approach will work to mediate forest decline or climate change has yet to be proven.

The third claim to persist comes from civil-society groups, both national and international, which have continued to push forward the rights agenda to maintain cultural integrity as well as more productive livelihoods on the basis of using a local, rather than global, forest commons. What has come through from the movement to realize participatory and collaborative forest management, and from the SLF, is a belief that entitlement, rights and social justice are the way to promote more sustainable socio-environmental forest change. This would appear to be justified by the global net transfer of tenure rights since 1985 to some 300 million hectares of forest to communities living in and around them. This has increased the share of the world's forests under community administration from 4.5 per cent in 1985 to 11.4 per cent in 2008 (Sunderlin et al., 2008). What need to be considered now are the implications of this in terms of global forest governance. The challenge for forest managers and theorists alike will be to understand the mechanisms by which communities can continue to maintain social justice within the emerging international regimes. If the focus for the next few years is to be on implementing REDD, the place of community forestry in this context will need to be established.

The language and discourse of poverty and equality, and of participation and empowerment, which were previously part of the resistance movements of civil-society groups and critical research, have been appropriated by mainstream actors in global governance systems such as the World Bank, the International Tropical Timber Organization and the organizations of the United Nations. As Foucault (1977, 1982) suggested, this 'normalization' of resistance – the requisition and integration of ideas of the resisting periphery by the powerful mainstream – has served to intensify localization politics. Resistance to the hegemony of globalized culture and the appropriation of resistance narratives has led to the redefinition of the value of culture and cultural identity attached to forests as a counter-globalization discourse. Civil-society groups are continuing to work against mainstream perceptions of forest value as purely monetary, global service values, or linked to the capital aspects of livelihoods, and there is a continuation of research documenting and explaining cultural landscapes, extended through the construction of environmental histories. In revealing ethnographic construction of landscape, and the wider social benefits of place attachment, there is an assertion of rights over local commons and contested territories (see Manuel-Navarrete and Redclift, Chapter 21 in this volume).

Concluding remarks
In summary, the themes coming through in contemporary international forestry are: the information and knowledge needs for effective management of globalized socio-environmental systems; the tension between market-based and regulatory governance of the global forest commons and global risk in an age of increasingly unpredictable ecologies; and the need to recognize and incorporate social and cultural resilience within forest tenure and management systems. After the real-world impacts that the varied scholarship of environmental sociologists has had on forestry during the last ten years, there is a clear message that environmental sociology will need to maintain its plurality of approach. It is through interdisciplinary and multiple perspectives that a fuller understanding of the complexity of future change will be revealed, and new contributions shaping appropriate actions will take place. Of the main debates in environmental sociology, risk society, political ecology and environmental managerialism as ecological modernization all offer prospects for understanding the way forests will be viewed or utilized as environments. It could be argued that to meet this challenge, the well-rehearsed arguments of these schools need to move further forward to take account of social nature and the insights of the natural sciences dealing with global change. Regardless of the switch of attention away from the rainforest campaigns of the late 1980s and 1990s, forests will remain iconic resources and landscapes in globalizing environments and the brave new world of changing global climate and ecological agency.

Note
1. Praxis is understood here as the 'real-world' practice of forestry as a technical and practical economic or development activity rather than as an academic discipline.

References

Abbot, J.I.O. and D.H.L. Thomas (2001), 'Understanding links between conservation and development in the Bamenda Highlands, Cameroon', *World Development*, **29** (7): 1115–36.

Allison, P.A. (1962), 'Historical inferences to be drawn from the effect of human settlement on the vegetation of Africa', *Journal of African History*, **III** (2): 241–9.

Amalric, F. (1999), 'Natural resources, governance and social justice', *Development*, **43**: 732–45.

Angermeier, P.L. and J.R. Karr (1994), 'Biological integrity versus biological diversity as policy directives', *Bioscience*, **44**: 690–7.

Arce, A., M. Villarreal and P. de Vries (1994), 'The social construction of rural development: discourses, practices and power', in D. Booth (ed.), *Rethinking Social Development: Theory, Research and Practice*, Harlow, UK: Longman, pp. 152–71.

Ascher, W. and R. Healy (1990), *Natural Resource Policymaking in Developing Countries: Environment, Economic Growth, and Income Distribution*, Durham, NC: Duke University Press.

Attiwill, P.M. (1994) 'The disturbance of forest ecosystems: the ecological basis for conservative management', *Forest Ecology and Management*, **63**: 247–300.

Baland, J.M. and J.P. Platteau (1996), *Halting Degradation of Natural Resources: Is There a Role for Rural Communities?*, Oxford: Clarendon Press.

Banuri, T. and F.A. Marglin (1993a), 'A systems-of-knowledge analysis of deforestation, participation and management', in T. Banuri and F.A. Marglin (eds), *Who Will Save The Forests? Knowledge, Power and Environmental Destruction*, London: UNU/WIDER Zed Books, pp. 1–23.

Banuri, T. and F.A. Marglin (1993b), *Who Will Save The Forests? Knowledge, Power and Environmental Destruction*, London: UNU/WIDER Zed Books.

Bass, S., B. Dalal-Clayton and J. Pretty (1995), *Participation in Strategies for Sustainable Development*, London: IIED.

Bebbington, A. (1999) 'Capitals and capabilities: a framework for analyzing peasant viability, rural livelihoods and poverty', *World Development*, **27** (12): 2021–44.

Berkes, F. and C. Folke (eds) (1998), *Linking Social and Ecological Systems: Management Practices and Social Mechanisms for Building Resilience*, Cambridge, UK: Cambridge University Press.

Bojo, J. (1993), 'Economic valuation of indigenous woodlands', in P.N. Bradley and K. McNamara (eds), *Living with Trees; Policies for Forestry Management in Zimbabwe*, Technical Paper 210, Washington, DC: World Bank, pp. 227–41.

Booth, D. (ed.) (1994), *Rethinking Social Development: Theory, Research and Practice*, Harlow, UK: Longman.

Botkin, D. (1990), *Discordant Harmonies: A New Ecology for the Twenty-First Century*, Oxford: Oxford University Press.

Brown, K. (2001), 'Cut and run? Evolving institutions for global forest governance', *Journal of International Development*, **13**: 893–905.

Brown, K. and F. Ekoko (2001), 'Forest encounters: synergy among agents of forest change in southern Cameroon', *Society and Natural Resources*, **14**: 269–90.

Brown, K. and S. Lapuyade (2001), 'A livelihood from the forest: Gendered visions of social, economic and environmental change in southern Cameroon', *Journal of International Development*, **13**: 1131–49.

Bryant, R. and S. Bailey (1997), *Third World Political Ecology*, London: Routledge.

Burford, N. (1993), 'A grass-roots response to landlessness in Rondônia, Brazil', Rural Development Forestry Network Paper 16 e-I, London: Overseas Development Institute.

Buttel, F.H. (2003) 'Environmental sociology and the explanation of environmental reform', *Organization & Environment*, **16** (3): 306–44.

Callicott, J.B., L.B. Crowder and K. Mumford (1999) 'Current normative concepts in conservation', *Conservation Biology*, **13** (1): 22–35.

Campbell, B. and M.K. Luckert (eds) (2002), *Uncovering the Hidden Harvest*, London: Earthscan.

Castle, E.N. (1993), 'A pluralistic, pragmatic and evolutionary approach to natural resource management', *Forest Ecology and Management*, **56**: 279–95.

Catton, W.R. Jr and R.E. Dunlap (1978), 'Environmental sociology: a new paradigm', *The American Sociologist*, **13** (4): 41–9.

Cavendish, W. (2000) 'Empirical regularities in the poverty–environment relationships of rural households: evidence from Zimbabwe', *World Development*, **28**: 1979–2003.

Cernea, M.M. (1985), *Putting People First: Sociological Variables in Rural Development*, Oxford: Oxford University Press.

Cernea, M.M. (1990), *Beyond Community Woodlots: Programmes with Participation*, London: Overseas Development Institute.

Chambers, R. (1993), *Challenging the Professionals*, London: Intermediate Technology Publications.

Chapman, C.A., L.J. Chapman, R. Wrangham R., G. Isabirye-Basuta and K. Ben-David (1997), 'Spatial and temporal variability in the structure of a tropical forest', *African Journal of Ecology*, **35**: 287–302.

Colchester, M. (1993), 'Slave and enclave: towards a political ecology of Equatorial Africa', *The Question of Indigenous Peoples in Africa*, Copenhagen: IWGIA, June.

Colchester, M. (1996), 'Beyond "participation": indigenous peoples, biological diversity conservation and protected area management', *Unasylva*, **186** (47): 33–9.

Constanza, R., B.G. Norton and B.D. Haskell (1992), *Ecosystem Health: New Goals for Environmental Management*, Washington, DC: Island Press.

Croll, E. and D. Parkin (eds) (1992), *Bush Base: Forest Farm, Culture Environment and Development*, London: Routledge.

Dei, G.J.S. (1989), 'Hunting and gathering in a Ghanian rain forest community', *Ecology of Food and Nutrition*, **22**: 225–43.

Dembner, S.A. (1995), 'Forest dependent livelihoods: links between forestry and food security', *Unasylva*, **46**: 85–90.

Dickson, D. and K.S. Jayaraman (1995), 'Aid groups back challenge to neem patents', *Nature*, 14 September, p. 95.

Dryzek, John S. (1984), 'Ecological rationality', *International Journal of Environmental Studies*, **21** (1983): 5–10.

Eder, K. (1996), *The Social Construction of Nature: A Sociology of Ecological Enlightenment*, London: Sage.

Edwards, P.J. and C. Abivardi (1999), 'The value of biodiversity: where ecology and economy blend', *Biological Conservation*, **383** (3): 83–3.

Escobar, A. (1996), 'Constructing nature: elements for a poststructural political ecology', in D. Peet and M. Watts (eds), *Liberation Ecologies: Environment, Development, Social Movements*, London: Routledge, pp. 46–68.

Fairhead, J. and M. Leach (1995), 'False forest history, complicit social analysis: rethinking some West African environmental narratives', *World Development*, **23** (6): 1023–36.

Fairhead, J. and M. Leach (1998), *Reframing Deforestation. Global Analysis and Local Realities: Studies in West Africa*, Vol. 23, London: Routledge.

FAO (1985), *Participatory Approaches to Planning for Community Forestry: Forest Trees and People Programme*, FAO Forestry Department, Rome: FAO.

Farrington, J., A. Bebbington, K. Wellard and D.J. Lewis (1993), *Reluctant Partners? Non-Governmental Organizations, the State and Sustainable Agricultural Development*, London: Routledge.

Fisher, B. (1993), 'Creating space: development agencies and local institutions in natural resource management', *Forests, Trees and People Newsletter*, **22**: 4–11.

Flyvbjerg, B. (1998) 'Habermas and Foucault: thinkers for civil society', *British Journal of Sociology*, **49** (2): 210–233.

Foucault, M. (1977), *Discipline and Punish: The Birth of the Prison*, London: Allen Lane.

Foucault, M. (1982), 'The subject and power', *Critical Inquiry*, **8**: 777–95.

Gibson, C.C., E. Ostrom and M.A. McKean (eds) (2000), *People and Forests: Communities, Institutions, and Governance*, Cambridge, MA: MIT Press.

Grimble, R. and J. Quan (1994), *Tree Resources and the Environment: Stakeholders and Tradeoffs*, Chatham, UK: Natural Resources Institute.

Hajer, M.A. (ed) (1995), *The Politics of Environmental Discourse: Ecological Modernization and the Policy Process*, Oxford: Clarendon Press.

Hannigan, J.A. (1995), *Environmental Sociology: A Social Constructionist Perspective*, London: Routledge.

Jones, E.W. (1956), 'Ecological studies on the rain forest of Southern Nigeria. IV. The plateau forest of the Okumu Forest Reserve', *Journal of Ecology*, **43**: 564–94.

Kimmins, H. (1997), *Balancing Act: Environmental Issues in Forestry*, New York: University of British Columbia Press.

Kleiner, K. (1995), 'Pesticide tree ends up in court', *New Scientist*, 16 September, p. 7.

Leach, M., R. Mearns and I. Scoones (1997), *Environmental Entitlements: A Framework for Understanding the Institutional Dynamics of Environmental Change*, Brighton, UK: Institute of Development Studies, University of Sussex.

Lever-Tracy, Constance (2008), 'Global warming and sociology', *Current Sociology*, **56** (3): 445–66.

Longhurst, R. (1991), *Dependency on Forest and Tree Foods for Food Security*, Uppsala, Sweden: Swedish University of Agricultural Sciences.

Marglin, F.E. and S. Marglin (1990), *Dominating Knowledge: Development, Culture and Resistance*, Oxford: Oxford University Press.

McNeeley, J.A. (1994), 'Lessons from the past: forests and biodiversity', *Biodiversity and Conservation*, **3**: 3–20.

Murphree, M.W. (1993), *Communities as Resource Management Institutions*, London: IIED.

Nelson, N. and S. Wright (eds) (1995), *Power and Participatory Development: Theory and Practice*, London: Intermediate Technology Publications.

Neumann, R.P. and E. Hirsch (2000), *Commercialization of Non-Timber Forest Products: Review and Analysis of Research*, Bogor, Indonesia: Centre for International Forestry Research.

Ostrom, E. (1990), *Governing the Commons: The Evolution of Institutions for Collective Action*, Cambridge: Cambridge University Press.

Peluso, N.L. (1992a) 'The rattan trade in East Kalimantan, Indonesia', *Advances in Economic Botany*, **9**: 115–127.

Peluso, N.L. (1992b), *Rich Forests, Poor People: Resource Control and Resistance in Java*, Berkeley, CA: University of California Press.

Peluso, N.L. (1996), 'Fruit trees and family trees in an anthropogenic rainforest: property rights, ethics of access, and environmental change in Indonesia', *Comparative Studies in Society and History*, **38** (3): 510–48.

Peterson, G. (2000), 'Political ecology and ecological resilience: an integration of human and ecological dynamics', *Ecological Economics*, **35** (3), 323–36.

Peuhkuri, T. and P. Jokinen (1999) 'The role of knowledge and spatial contexts in biodiversity policies: a sociological perspective', *Biodievrsity and Conservation*, **8**: 133–47.

Phillips, O., A.H. Gentry, P. Wilkin and C. Galvez-Durand (1994), 'Quantitative Ethnobotany and Amazonian conservation', *Conservation Biology*, **8** (1): 225–48.

Pickett, S.T.A., R.S. Ostfeld, M. Shachak and G.E. Likens (eds) (1997), *The Ecological Basis of Conservation: Heterogeneity, Ecosystems, and Biodiversity*, London and New York: Chapman & Hall.

Posey, D. (1997) 'National laws and international agreements affecting indigenous and local knowledge: conflict or conciliation?', http://lucy.ukc.ac.uk/Rainforest/ SML_files/Posey/posey_TOC.html, last accessed 5 May 2009.

Putterman, D.M. (1996), 'Model material transfer agreements for equitable biodiversity prospecting', *Colorado Journal of International Environmental Law and Policy*, **7** (1): 145–73.

Rapport, D.G. (1995), 'Ecosystem health: more than a metaphor?', *Environmental Values*, **4**: 287–309.

Roe, E. (1991), 'Development narratives or making the best of blueprint development', *World Development*, **19**: 287–300.

Rudel, T. and J. Roper (1997), 'The paths to rainforest destruction: crossnational patterns of tropical deforestation, 1975–1990', *World Development*, **25** (1): 53–65.

Ruitenbeek, H.J. (1990), *Economic Analysis of Tropical Forest Conservation Initiatives: Eexamples from West Africa*, Godalming, UK: World Wide Fund for Nature.

Schreckenberg, K. and M. Hadley (eds) (1991), *Economic and Ecological Sustainability of Tropical Rain Forest Management*, Paris: UNESCO.

Scoones, I. (1998) *Sustainable Rural Livelihoods: A Framework for Analysis*, Brighton, UK: Institute of Development Studies.

Shenley, P. and L. Luz (1993), *Invisible Income: The Subsistence Value of Non-timber Forest Products in Two Eastern Amazonian Caboclo Communities*, Belem, Brazil: Woods Hole Research Centre.

Shiva, Vandana and Radha Holla-Bhar (1996), 'Piracy by patent: the case of the neem tree', in J. Mander and E. Goldsmith (eds), *The Case Against the Global Economy and For a. Turn Toward the Local*, San Francisco, CA: Sierra Club Books, pp. 131–45.

Sirait, M., S. Prasodjo, N. Podger, A. Flavelle and J. Fox (1994), 'Mapping customary land in East Kalimantan, Indonesia: a tool for forest management', *Ambio*, **23** (7): 411–17.

Sprugel, D.G. (1991), 'Disturbance, equilibrium, and environmental variability: what is "natural" vegetation in a changing environment', *Biological Conservation*, **58**: 1–18.

Stern, N. (2006), *The Economics of Climate Change: The Stern Review*, London: UK Treasury.

Sunderlin, W.D., J. Hatcher and M. Liddle (2008), *From Exclusion to Ownership? Challenges and Opportunities in Advancing Forest Tenure Reform*, Washington, DC: Rights and Resources Initiative.

Tiffen, M., M. Mortimer and F. Gichuki (1994), *More People, Less Erosion: Environmental Recovery in Kenya*, Chichester, UK: John Wiley & Sons.

Uphoff, N. (1992), *Local Institutions and Participation for Sustainable Development*, London: IIED.

Vandermeer, J. and I. Perfecto (1997), 'The agroecosystem: a need for the conservation biologist's lense', *Conservation Biology*, **11**: 591–3.

Wallace, M.G., H.J. Cortuer, M.A. Moote and S. Burke (1996), 'Moving toward ecosystem management: examining a change in philosophy for resource management', *Journal of Political Ecology*, **3**: 18–32.

Warren, D.M. and J. Pinkston (1998) 'Indigenous African resource management of a tropical rainforest ecosystem: a case study of the Yoruba of Ara, Nigeria', in F. Berkes and C. Folke (eds), *Linking Social and Ecological Systems: Management Practices and Social Mechanisms for Building Resilience*, Cambridge, UK: Cambridge University Press, pp. 158–89.

Westoby, J. (1987), *The Purpose of Forests: Follies of Development*, Oxford: Basil Blackwell.

Wiersum, K.F. (1984), *Developing Strategies for Social Forestry: A Conceptual Approach*, Honolulu, HI: Environment and Policy Institute, East–West Center.

Wollenberg, E. and A. Ingles (eds) (1998), *Incomes from the Forest: Methods for the Development and Conservation of Forest Products for Local Communities*, Bogor, Indonesia: Centre for International Forestry Research.

Woodgate, G. and M. Redclift (1998), 'From a "sociology of nature" to environmental sociology: beyond social construction', *Environmental Ethics*, 7: 3–24.

WRM (World Rainforest Movement) (1997), *Bulletin N° 4*, September.

Yadav, N.P, O.P. Dev, O. Springate-Baginski and J. Soussan (2003), 'Forest management and utilization under community forestry' *Journal of Forest and Livelihood*, 3 (1): 37–50.

Zalasiewicz, J., M. Williams, A. Smith, T.L. Barry, A.L. Coe, Paul R. Bown, Patrick Brenchley, David Cantrill, Andrew Gale, Philip Gibbard, F. John Gregory, Mark W. Hounslow, Andrew C. Kerr, Paul Pearson, Robert Knox, John Powell, Colin Waters, John Marshall, Michael Oates, Peter Rawson and Philip Stone (2008), 'Are we now living in the Anthropocene?', *GSA Today*, 18 (2): 4–8.

PART III

INTERNATIONAL PERSPECTIVES ON ENVIRONMENT AND SOCIETY

Editorial commentary
Graham Woodgate

The final part of this volume reflects the first part of the book's title, providing insights into the dynamics of socio-environmental relations in Africa, Australia, China, Europe and Latin America. As well as environmental sociologists, contributors to this section include anthropologists, policy analysts and, not surprisingly, geographers.

The first contribution comes from David Manuel-Navarrete and Michael Redclift, who seek to draw sociological attention to the concept of 'place' and propose the concept of 'place confirmation' to emphasize the centrality of the notion of place as both location and the association of meanings with location. 'Like gender and nature,' they suggest, 'the meaning of place may be negotiable but its importance in the canon of concepts available to environmental sociology suggests considerable room for further development.'

Chapter 21 begins with a review of academic debate surrounding the notion of 'place', before moving to a short case study of the Caribbean Coast of Mexico. The authors' case study illustrates the dynamics of place construction and contestation, and demonstrates how economic globalization is colonizing the 'empty space' spared by the modern state and constructing new places of consumption dominated by logics of extraction and economic profit. At the same time, however, globalization also opens up new places of resistance and struggle, suggesting that the homogenizing tendencies of globalization have never completely replaced historic and alternative constructions of place: globalized spaces are being superimposed on previous meanings.

The superimposition of abstract narratives of ecological dynamics and environmental governance on local socio-environmental relations is reflected in all of the chapters that comprise the final part of this book. In Chapter 22, Bill Adams's piece on 'Society, environment and development in Africa' notes that society and environment are almost inevitably coupled in debates about rural Africa and its development, and that these debates are often conducted through a series of highly stereotyped understandings of society and nature, which provide powerful frames for theorization and analysis. Adams identifies five key environmental policy narratives that have been central to debate about society, environment and development in Africa: desertification; pastoralism and 'overgrazing'; indigenous agricultural intensification as a counter-narrative to ecological deterioration caused by overpopulation; nature as wilderness in need of preservation; and Africa as a place where ideas of 'community' have provided powerful if misleading frameworks for planning conservation and sustainable rural development.

Offering a rich variety of case-study materials, Adams demonstrates that none of these narratives has provided a satisfactory explanation of either failure or success; there is no simple blueprint for sustainable development in Africa, and no easy answers for those who would address the legacy of global 'development'. When confidence in the myth of development collapsed at the end of the twentieth century, Africa became for many 'the economic basket case of the twenty-first century'. 'Africa is no basket case', claims

Adams; 'the economic dynamism of rural Africa challenges the Western, urban, industrial notion of development'. Yet conventional colonial views of African rural people as conservative and unenterprising, whose problems could only be solved by outside expertise and technology, have persisted to the present day, entrenched within the knowledge, expertise and power of modern governments, aid donors and other external agents of change.

Adams does not doubt the importance of modern science in reducing poverty and improving the livelihoods of Africa's rural poor, and also prompts caution in respect to over-romanticizing indigenous knowledge. Nevertheless, he is adamant that local, place-based, knowledge systems are as important as Western science in providing the basis for a clear and shared understanding of what works for rural African people and why. Thus he concludes: 'What works for rural Africa is, at the end of the day, what rural Africans can make work. Without reflexivity and humility on the part of the legions of experts employed to prescribe solutions for Africa's various ills, little of value is likely to be achieved.'

In Chapter 23, attention shifts from Africa to Australia, where for many the notion of climate change has become less an artefact of arcane scientific theorizing and more a way to explain their own experience of water restrictions, severe weather events and rising food prices. As author Stewart Lockie points out, following the influential reports of economic advisers such as Nicholas Stern in the UK and Ross Garnaut in Australia, there now appears to be a clear consensus among key decision-making bodies over both the root causes of human-induced climate change and the most appropriate policy responses to it. In short, climate change is conceptualized as a market failure that is primarily to be resolved through market means. Thus the question that Lockie sets out to address is whether market instruments offer solutions to complex problems such as climate change.

While it is clearly too early to forecast exactly how effective market-based climate-change policy will be, the metanarrative of environmental governance through 'the market' already has a significant history in other arenas. Lockie's response to the question he poses is constructed through an analysis of 20 years of Australian, market-based agri-environmental policy, rolled out in initiatives such as The National Landcare Program, regional natural resource management programmes and the more recent Commonwealth Environmental Stewardship Program.

Lockie's analysis leads him to conclude that market-based instruments – no matter how well designed – do not necessarily resolve the underlying causes of so-called market failure. 'If the past two decades of experimentation in agri-environmental governance have shown anything,' suggests Lockie, 'it is that multiple programmes and grassroots political support are required if policy is in any way to match and influence the complex web of social, ecological and economic relationships that shape rural land use.' Thus the implications of Lockie's analysis for the even more complex phenomenon of climate change are clear.

The focus on governance and reform is maintained in Arthur Mol's second contribution to the handbook (Chapter 24). China, long identified as the 'sleeping dragon of the East', has awoken, and as it breathes fire into its economy the environmental impacts of its rapid industrialization are seen as cause for global environmental concern. Echoing Sachs's portrayal of the Industrial Revolution in Europe (Chapter 17), China's growing economy is scouring the globe for natural resources and mining its fossil forests to provide the energy needed to transform them into industrial products. Yet, contrary to much popular criticism, Mol claims that China's changing environmental profile is not an evolutionary treadmill of ongoing degradation. Since the mid-1990s, he notes a growing commitment to address environmental challenges in China, discernible in policies directed at promoting 'a circular economy, a resource-conserving and environment-friendly society and ecological modernization'.

Mol's objective is not primarily to evaluate whether environmental problems have been diminished or solved, but rather to understand how China is developing an environmental reform strategy and where this meets challenges and complications. By investigating developments in Chinese environmental policy, the use of market actors and mechanisms, and the role of an increasingly active civil society, the author assesses the nation's environmental reform progress over the last decade. His conclusions are mixed: the capacity of the Chinese 'environmental state' has increased significantly; major institutional innovations include new environmental laws, law enforcement, public–private partnerships and citizen participation; market signals are increasingly reflecting the full economic costs of natural resources and some of the environmental externalities of their production; and political leaders are more aware of, committed to, and accountable for, combating environmental crises. At the same time, there is more room for environmental criticism, activism and transparency while, due to continuing rapid economic expansion, the physical state of the environment has improved only marginally following these innovations in environmental governance.

The penultimate chapter of the volume (Chapter 25) retains a focus on economies in transition but switches our attention to Central and Eastern Europe (CEE). In an essay that concentrates on civic engagement in environmental governance, JoAnn Carmin considers the development of participatory institutions and the emergence of independent NGOs in the Czech Republic, Estonia, Hungary, Latvia, Lithuania, Poland, Slovakia and Slovenia.

The countries of CEE have long traditions of nature appreciation and conservation pre-dating their assimilation into the Soviet Union. Following the intense competition for industrial and military advantage that characterized the Cold War period, the significant environmental degradation that had occurred acted as a rallying point for 'oppositional activities that focused on the need to improve environmental quality and, at the same time, expressed general levels of discontent with the regimes'. When these regimes fell, it was hoped that the transitions to democracy would create space for public participation in decision-making. In particular, it was expected that the environmental policy process, from inception through to implementation, would involve the public, either through their direct participation or by means of NGOs acting on their behalf.

Carmin's essay examines progress towards participatory environmental governance in the region, examining the influence of social movements, NGOs, transitional aid agreements and, more recently, the process of accession to the European Union. In the move to align national policies with EU norms of governance, the countries of CEE have developed provisions to support participation and access to information, and to establish the right to justice in environmental matters. Nevertheless, while these formal policies represent significant advances in government transparency, accountability and access, Carmin's analysis demonstrates that the norms and routines of the Soviet era have proved resistant to change, at the same time as the realities of economic transition have caused most people to work long hours to make ends meet, leaving little time to dedicate to volunteer activities. Furthermore, NGOs seeking to promote environmental causes have encountered strong competition for funding and seen their agendas and activities channelled in directions that resemble professional organizations in Western Europe and the USA.

The impact of global norms and institutions on local livelihoods is also exemplified in the final contribution to this book. In Chapter 26, Nora Haenn examines the impact of national and international conservation initiatives on the lives of those who depend on products and services derived from ecosystems that the international conservation community and national and local politicians consider in need of protection. Drawing on her case study of the establishment of the Calakmul Biosphere Reserve in Southern Campeche, Mexico, Haenn seeks to elucidate the ways in which questions of social justice and multiculturalism play out in environmental settings earmarked for conservation initiatives. Reflecting elements of Manuel-Navarrete and Redclift's discussion of 'place' in Chapter 21 and Ambrose-Oji's piece on international forestry (Chapter 20), Haenn asserts that 'researchers interested in environmentalism, social justice and multiculturalism enter a terrain [places] where particular histories and particular social contracts matter a great deal'. Her analysis illuminates the dynamics that emerge when different place constructions overlap; in this case where a UNESCO biosphere reserve is superimposed onto frontier land occupied by *campesinos*: a place variously constructed as the right to gain justice through agrarian reform, to establish settlements and to practise slash-and-burn agriculture. For the rural inhabitants of Calakmul, the forest is a 'separate social world, one where snakes, jaguars and forest spirits threaten human existence' rather than a resource to be conserved in order to mitigate global environmental change.

Thus conservation and, we would suggest, notions of 'place' have to be negotiated. During the initial phases of reserve establishment, Haenn – while cognizant of the importance of specificity when offering prescriptions for conservation strategies – suggests that neither top-down nor bottom-up approaches are particularly successful. The former encounter resistance, while examples of broad-based local conservation initiatives are few and far between. Rather, respected local cultural brokers appear key to defining conservation in ways that make sense to a particular local audience. Yet this is no simple matter of translation, for a broker's rendition of 'conservation ideals as something more locally recognizable may result in a conservation that looks quite different from the usual protected area, but has the advantage of being practicable'.

At the same time, local brokers gain their legitimacy, at least in part, from their position and ability to act effectively within local political structures – structures that may marginalize or exclude a significant number of people. Thus, while important in the early stages of protected area establishment, local brokers may be insufficient for achieving long-term conservation: governance depends on ongoing negotiations of authority. Furthermore, if conservation is promoted without regard to local social justice – if conservation and human activities are framed as contradictory – local people are quickly alienated and, as happened at Calakmul, nature protection may have to take a back seat while local people's good faith is restored. As a suggestion for a conservation framework that might avoid such problems, Haenn proposes a 'sustaining conservation' – one that supports both the physical environment and the social relations that make conservation possible'.

In concluding, then, it seems that all routes out of our twenty-first-century socio-environmental predicament will have to be furnished with appropriate signposts. The waymarkers should all point towards a global social metabolism that is consistent with the capacity of the global ecosystem to supply resources, assimilate wastes and accommodate human living space, as well as marking our progress towards a global society in which all live in dignity, free to pursue their own happiness. Yet the legacies of Cartesian philosophy, capitalist political economy and technocratic governance mean that our various journeys into the future begin in very different places and that we shall be travelling in very different directions. For some, the itinerary will indicate economic dematerialization, a contraction of their carbon and wider ecological footprints and the ceding of geopolitical power. For others, the signposts will point towards the opening up of environmental space and improved opportunities to express their socio-ecological agency. Whatever directions our journeys take us in, as the climate warms and the pace of change quickens, the politics of moving towards a globally coherent yet locally diverse ecosociety will undoubtedly heat up!

21 The role of place in the margins of space
David Manuel-Navarrete and Michael Redclift

Introduction

In this chapter we examine the continuing importance of the concept of 'place', the revival of interest in its fortunes, and extend the analysis to what at first appear to be 'empty spaces' – areas that once appeared at the geographical 'margin', but that have assumed increased importance in the era of globalization. After reviewing the recent literature on 'place', the chapter takes as a case study the Mexican Caribbean coast, and explores the way in which a sense of place is being actively confirmed within the discourses surrounding the rapid urbanization of this coast. In the conclusion we suggest some of the ways in which the concept might be further developed, indicating several routes into 'place confirmation' as a central idea, and its conceptual potential for environmental sociology.

Before reviewing the extensive recent literature on place, it is worth reflecting on why the conceptualization of place played such a modest a role in the geographical canon until relatively recently. For such a key idea, place had not been well served by most texts before the 1990s. Subsequently it has provided a touchstone for some lively debate and has begun to attract dissenting voices – always evidence of vigour. The earlier limited attention given to place is illustrated by Cloke et al. (1991) in *Approaching Human Geography*, which has sections on Marxism, and Giddens's structuration theory, but nothing on 'place'. Similarly Holt-Jensen (1999), in a student's guide to the discipline, devotes only two pages to a discussion of place, towards the end of the book. Tim Unwin's *The Place of Geography*, published in 1992, provides an exhaustive study of the place of geography, but nothing on 'place' itself. Clearly, the publication of Yi-Fu Tuan's influential work *Space and Place: The Perspective of Experience* in 1977, which served to highlight the centrality of place, did little to energize debates before the 1990s. Yi-Fu Tuan had argued that place was a 'portion of geographical space occupied by a person or thing' and a 'centre of felt value', a repository of meaning and an object of intentionality (1977: 23). This distinction underlined earlier tensions between a largely positivist tradition of spatial science and a more hermeneutic tradition. Not until the revival of the concept of place in the last decade has the humanistic and hermeneutic tradition been more fully developed. A series of geography texts and evaluations followed, in which place was accorded parity with other geographical dimensions such as space, time and nature. As McDowell (1997: 67) wrote, 'the significance of place has been reconstituted rather than undermined' by recent discussion. The texts included Aitken and Valentine (2006), Holloway et al. (2003) and Bergman and Renwick (2008), although other ambitious texts still avoided the concept (Castree et al., 2005). The volume edited by Hubbard, Kitchin and Valentine (2004), *Key Thinkers on Space and Place*, contained many comments on key thinkers but very little illumination on 'place'. There are, however, two outstanding exceptions to the paucity of conceptual analysis of place, and they are both sufficiently important to merit close attention (Cresswell, 1996, 2004). These exceptions are Noel Castree and Doreen Massey, both of whom have made very significant contributions that have enlarged our understanding of place, and whose work is reviewed later.

In one of the classic studies of place that preceded the work of Yi-Fu Tuan, Luckermann (1964) argued that places have at least six constituent values: location; 'ensemble' (the integration of nature and culture); uniqueness; localized focusing power, emergence; and meaning (to human agents). It is striking that this analysis of place anticipates much of the regalvanized debate during the last ten years. In a prescient piece published in *Cultural Anthropology*, Gupta and Ferguson (1992) argued strongly for an analysis of place that focuses on power relations, and that links place to the contradictions arising from globalization. In essence, 'imagined communities' needed to become attached to 'imagined places'. 'The irony of these times . . . is that as actual places and localities become ever more blurred and indeterminate, ideas of culturally and ethnically distinct place become perhaps even more salient' (ibid.: 10).

Within most academic discourse, 'space' has been given much closer attention than 'place'. As McDowell suggests, this is because place is best seen as contextual: 'the significance of place depends on the issue under consideration and the sets of social relations that are relevant to the issues' (McDowell, 1997: 4). As we shall argue later, place is frequently used in a way that takes on meaning from the context in which it is employed, rather than conveying meaning itself. Modern science tended to disregard place by equating it with lack of generality (Casey, 1997). In physics, geography and social sciences the use of coordinates, maps, statistics, and other simplifying and objectifying pictures dominated the representation of places in spatial terms. The dimensions of, and actions in, space have similar meanings for everybody. Consequently, space allows scientists to adopt a role of outside observers of places, while the modern concept of 'region' is often taken as a natural unit of spatial and social organization (Curry, 2002). In social theories, space was assumed to be featureless and undifferentiated and was often used for predicting patterns of land use and economic activities without describing place in any real sense except as a product of historical accident (Johnson, 2002).

However, spatial representations of place were problematized during the second half of the twentieth century. Lefebvre (1974) and Foucault (1986) questioned the definition of absolute space in terms of Euclidean geometry, and claimed that regions are socially constructed. The human dimension of spatiality was emphasized and the notion of place acquired a renewed relevance not only among the disciplines that traditionally deal with place (e.g. geography, planning, chorography and philosophy), but also among less related disciplines (e.g. anthropology, cultural studies, ecology, psychology and phenomenology). Significant efforts for defining the concept and formulating an adequate theory of place have been developed from these disciplines. Although it is not clear whether the adoption of a unique definition would be either possible or desirable, these multiple perspectives of place agree that places are more than geographic settings with physical or spatial characteristics; they are fluid, changeable, dynamic contexts of social interaction and memory (Harrison and Dourish, 1996; Stokowski, 2002).

As we have seen, Tuan (1977) argued that experiences of places involve perception, cognition and affection. Similarly, Relph (1976) identified three components of place: physical setting, activities; and meanings. According to these authors, a place cannot simply be described as the location of one object relative to others. The concept of place has to integrate both its location and its meaning in the context of human action. As

Tuan (1977: 35) puts it: 'place is space infused with human meaning'. Working on similar lines, Agnew (1987) studied the relationship between place and human behaviour, and proposed a compositional view of places as being constituted by economic, institutional and sociocultural processes. Agnew identified three basic elements of place: location; locale; and sense of place. Location is the role a place plays in the world economy; locale, the institutional setting of a place; and sense of place, the identities forged and given meaning within places.

Among the most important recent thinking about place is that of Doreen Massey and Noel Castree. Massey (1994) suggested a more dynamic view of places as 'networks of social relations'. According to her, places are continually changing as a result of economic, institutional and cultural transformation. Places are not essences but processes, and places do not necessarily mean the same thing to everybody (Massey, 1994). In addition, for Massey, the nature of a place is a product of its linkages with other places and not just a matter of its internal features. Places appear as points of intersection, integrating the global and the local. She writes: 'displacement, most particularly through migration, depends . . . on a prior notion of cultures embedded in place' (Massey and Jess, 1995: 1). Determining place, 'drawing boundaries in space. . . is always a social act'. The authors add that the dominant notion of place, with which we are familiar, 'is one that arises as a result of the changes going on in the world around us' (ibid.: 63). For Massey, place is not a free-standing concept, but one that should be used transitively, attaching itself to another 'object' that might help illuminate it. The authors end by providing almost a 'place' advocacy, which Massey terms a 'progressive sense of place', through which geographers, and others, might take the part of communities and social classes.

Castree's contribution to the conceptualization of place is rather different. He argues that Marxist geographers were 'preoccupied with the inter-place connections more than specific place differences', in effect ignoring the saliency of place itself (Castree, 2003: 170). While broadly sympathetic to the humanistic geographers' perspective on place, which sought to 'recover people's sense of place . . . that is, how different individuals and groups . . . develop meaningful attachments to those specific areas where they live out their lives. . .' (ibid.), he invokes neurological circuit metaphors, 'switching points' and 'nodes' to suggest the degrees to which places are plugged into different sets of global relations. He argues that globalization has resulted 'in an exciting and innovative redefinition of what place means', seeing 'place differences as both cause and effect of place connections' (ibid.: 166).

Following these authors, Cresswell (2004) suggests a structural view of place that promotes a holistic and relational understanding of place instead of a compositional perspective (which just considers the socioeconomic make-up of places). According to this author, this structural view would include the following measurable components of place: economic role, institutional setting, political–cultural identity, linkages with other places; and changes over time.

Although human geographers pioneered the exploration of the concept of 'sense of place' (Relph, 1997; Hay, 1998; Cross, 2001), the configuration had several meanings. 'Sense of place' signalled: (1) a set of personal, family and community narratives that include features of a setting, (2) the attribution of non-material characteristics to a place, that is, the 'soul' of a place; its *genius loci*, (3) tacit knowledge of a place, which would include the ability to describe a plant or an outcropping of rock without being able to put a name to either, and (4) a synthetic but unsystematized body of knowledge about a place. In this last meaning, systematic knowledge of place is embedded in an unarticulated system of a higher order: *knowledge* about parts but a *sense* of the whole.

'Sense of place' has also been used in sociology. Hummon (1992: 164) suggested the following definition:

> By sense of place, I mean people's subjective perceptions of their environments and the more or less conscious feelings about those environments. Sense of place is inevitably dual in nature, involving both an interpretative perspective *on* the environment and an emotional reaction *to* the environment . . . Sense of place involves a personal orientation toward place, in which one's understanding of place and one's feelings about place become fused in the context of environmental meaning.

In anthropology, Kort (2001) argues that ethnographers and anthropologists have in the last half-century started to find place (or human spatiality) more attractive. Kort develops a theory of human place-relations in which he identifies three kinds of relations: (1) cosmic or comprehensive, (2) social, and (3) personal or intimate. But perhaps the most interesting contribution from among anthropologists is that of Arturo Escobar. Drawing on his own ethnography in coastal Pacific communities of Colombia, Escobar indicates three reasons for re-emphasizing 'place'. First, he points out that indigenous and black activists there came together in place-based struggles to defend their territory. Second, he notes that place is an important concept 'more philosophically, because place continues to be an important source of culture and identity, despite the pervasive delocalisation of social life' (Escobar, 2009: 10). More challenging is his third reason for emphasizing place:

> Third, because scholarship in the past two decades in many fields (geography, anthropology, political economy, communications etc.) has tended to de-emphasise place and to highlight, on the contrary, movement, displacement, travelling, diaspora, migration and so forth. Thus there is a need for a corrective theory that neutralises this erasure of place, the asymmetry that arises from giving far too much importance to the 'global' and far too little to 'place'. (Ibid.).

In environmental psychology, Canter (1997) developed a theory involving four interrelated facets of place: (1) functional differentiation (related to activities); (2) place objectives (related to individual, social and cultural experiences); (3) scale of interaction; and (4) aspects of design (related to physical characteristics), each with a number of subcategories. In this theory, place is considered as a holistic transactional entity and, consequently, is not reduced to isolated components. Environmental psychologists, however, often address issues of place through the concept of 'place attachment' (Altman and Low, 1992) and its two interrelated dimensions of 'place dependence' (i.e. functional attachment) (Stokols and Shumaker, 1981), and 'place identity' (i.e. emotional attachment) (Proshansky et al., 1983; Twigger-Ross and Uzzell, 1996). There is a great terminological and conceptual diversity of approaches to 'place attachment' (Giuliani and Feldman, 1993). However, Hidalgo and Hernández (2001: 274) assert that 'currently, there seems to exist a consensus in the use of the term "place attachment". In general, place attachment is defined as an affective bond or link between people and specific places.'

According to this definition, place attachment is bound up with environmental settings but not only with the physical aspects of a space. Furthermore, for some environmental psychologists, place attachment goes beyond affective bonds. Steel (2000) identified five key elements characterizing place attachment theories: (1) affective tone (either positive or negative); (2) a sense of personal involvement and interdependence linked to one's identity; (3) caring for and knowledge of a place; (4) behaviours that imply stability and continuing commitment to a place; and (5) a developmental or temporal component. Manzo (2003) identified an emergent perspective of the psychological study of people–place relationships. This perspective challenges earlier approaches that see relationships to place as individualistic, mentalist and apolitical (cf. Dixon and Durrheim, 2000). According to Manzo (2003), this new perspective reveals how people's relationships to places are complex and dynamic, include an array of places and experiences, and have a collectively shared, conscious and contested political nature. Consequently, people are seen as active shapers of places and place meanings as existing within larger sociopolitical milieux.

Another psychologist, Gustafson (2001), has articulated a tentative analytical framework for mapping and understanding the attribution of meaning to places, which is consistent with the integrative perspective. This author classified within a three-pole scheme constituted by 'self', 'others' and 'environment' the meaning of place expressed by a variety of respondents. Instead of considering the three poles as discrete categories, Gustafson (ibid.: 10) settled for a three-pole triangular model within which various meanings of place could be mapped, not only at the three poles, but also in between them. The model is complemented with four underlying dimensions of meaning: (1) 'distinction' (involving comparison with other places); (2) positive or negative 'valuation' of places; (3) continuity, and (4) change. The interplay of the last two introduces a temporal dimension in which places are regarded as processes. Places are dynamic and changing, but they also maintain an identity. The tension between these elements affords place a role both in structures and in agency.

Within the environmental literature, the concept of place, and related terms such as sense of place, bioregionalism, place attachment, environmental relationship and glocalization, are acquiring increasing relevance. Place has been proposed as a useful concept for improving ecosystem management (Mitchell et al., 1993; Williams and Stewart, 1998; Galliano and Loeffler, 1999). These proposals suggest that managers are better equipped for managing particular settings if they are aware of the divergent meanings that various stakeholders attach to these settings. Williams and Vaske (2003) operationalized this approach to management by examining the validity and generability of quantitative measures of attachment to nature-based places. According to these authors, natural places are more than containers of natural resources and staging areas for enjoyable activities. They are locations filled with history, memories, and emotional and symbolic meanings. Williams and Vaske (2003) argue that their results demonstrate how place bonds can be systematically identified and measured, and how people develop different levels and forms of attachment to different places.

Similarly, Cheng et al. (2003) report the emergence and persistence of 'place-based' collaborations for environmental management as a relatively recent phenomenon in which individuals with different perspectives work together to define and address common resource management issues bounded to a geographic place. These authors claim the existence of a politics of place in natural resource management. The politics of place emphasizes problem-solving, trust-building and on-the-ground consensual actions, rather than approving or opposing single-issue policy positions favoured by coalitions, which characterize the politics of interest. Thus the voices and values of actors are centred on places rather than on political positions. According to these authors, the existence of a politics of place could be explained by the possibility that a place (i.e. a distinct geographic area towards which all participants express value) acts as a central organizing principle for collaboration, as different actors bring their own politics of interest to bear on place.

Empty spaces at the geographical margin: the Mexican Caribbean coast

How, then, are 'places' inflected with meaning and socially constructed, while filling a specific spatial and temporal context? In the following case study we take a geographical location that has long played a role in international economic processes, but lies at the margins of spatially defined relations. Before the Spanish Conquest, the Yucatan peninsula had been densely populated with indigenous people, the Maya. However, the recent history of the Mexican Caribbean coast begins with the construction of Cancun in the 1970s. Before that, the area to the south, the coast of today's Quintana Roo (Figure 21.1), and the major focus for mass tourism in Mexico, was widely regarded as an 'empty space'. Today a myth has developed around Cancun that probably explains why so much of its history is unwritten. One of the foremost tourist guides to the area says:

> Cancun, until very recently, was an unknown area. Formerly it was a fishing town but over a period of thirty years it evolved into a place that has become famous worldwide. It is located in the south-east of Mexico with no more 'body' to it than the living spirit of the Mayas, a race that mysteriously disappeared and who were one of the great pre-Columbian cultures in Mexico. The only thing that remained was the land transformed into a paradise on earth. (Everest, 2002: 36)

This extract reveals all the major myths about the area: the coast was uninhabited when it was first 'discovered'; it embodied the spirit of the ancient Maya (who had mysteriously disappeared), while the few remaining mortals who survived the Spanish Conquest were thought to be in possession of 'paradise'. These three myths guide much of the 'Maya World' tourist discourse today, which has helped to draw millions of people into the area and provided one of the most rapid rates of urban growth in Latin America. The myths asserted that: space was devoid of culture; Indians were devoid of ancestors; and paradise was waiting to be 'discovered'. However, if we examine these claims closely, it is possible to distinguish ways in which the metaphorical grounding of tourist expansion borrows from earlier travel writing, such as the use of pioneer 'succession' as an organic process, the preference for the natural sublime over human landscapes, and the utilization of 'virgin' resources (Jones, 2003; Martins, 2000; Salvatore, 1996).

Recent research in geography, and in history, has benefited from a more reflective view of space, and an active search for its properties and significance over time (Lefebvre, 1991). Space and place are no longer 'givens' in intellectual history, the blank parchment on which human purposes are written. Some writers even argue that they should be seen as enactment or performance: constructions of the human imagination, as well as materiality. In the view of Nicholas Blomley (2004: 122), for example, 'space [is present] in both property's discursive and material enactments. Space like property, is active, not static. [And] spaces of violence must be recognised as social achievements, rather than as social

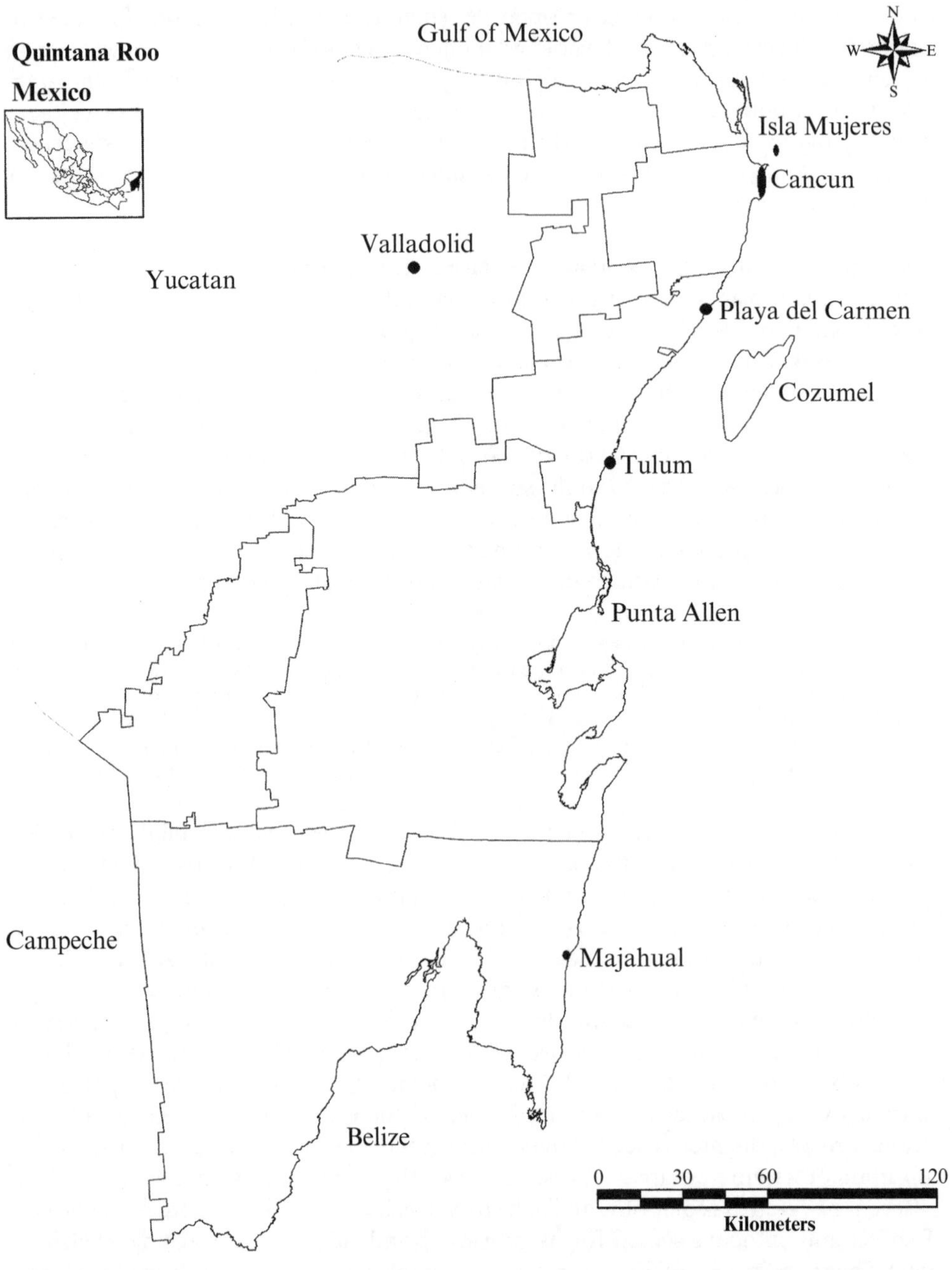

Quintana Roo

Mexico

Gulf of Mexico

Isla Mujeres

Cancun

Valladolid

Yucatan

Playa del Carmen

Cozumel

Tulum

Punta Allen

Campeche

Majahual

Belize

| 0 | 30 | 60 | 120 |

Kilometers

Source: Adapted from *Cuéntame de México*, at: http://www.cuentame.inegi.org.mx, retrieved on 28 April 2009.

Figure 21.1   Cancun and the Quintana Roo Coast, Mexico

facts.' As we have seen, this analysis of the active engagement of human populations with space has served to define much of the recent writing on place. On this reading, space and place assume a role previously denied them, and perform a transitive, active role in the making of historical events.

This 'active' conceptualization of place and space carries implications for the way in which we view resource peripheries, particularly within the context of 'globalization', a process that is increasingly seen as pre-dating modernity, rather than an outcome of it (Hayter et al., 2003: 15). Geographical places are ascribed, figuratively, temporally and spatially, in ways that serve to influence succeeding events. Their 'discovery' and 'invention' are acknowledged as part of powerful myths, which are worked and reworked by human agents, serving to create a sense of place as important as the material worlds that are described.

It is suggested that reworking place in cultural terms consists of separate but linked processes, in which location in space is associated with what Luckermann (1964) termed 'ensemble', the integration of nature and culture. These processes can sometimes be viewed sequentially, each providing a different construction of place and, in the case of the Mexican Caribbean, are characterized by distinctive generations of resource users and settlers. In charting the resource histories of places, and the histories of the visitors and tourists who have 'discovered' them, we are engaged in continually reworking a narrative. The social processes through which we come to identify place over time resemble a series of 'successions' (Cronon, 1996).

The process through which existential places are created, from within the fabric of environmental history, is seen clearly in the accounts of the Caribbean coast of Mexico: today's state of Quintana Roo. Over time we view a 'wilderness', a redoubt of pirates and looters, an 'ancient civilization' discovered by archaeologists, an abandoned space utilized by entrepreneurial hoteliers and, today, a 'tropical paradise' promising escape for international tourists.

Tropical places, abandoned spaces

The coastal resort of Playa del Carmen, today one of the most rapidly growing urban centres in Latin America, was 'discovered' in the summer of 1966, according to one account in a tourist magazine:

> Playa was discovered by a sixteen year old boy, in the summer of 1966. A momentous event, which changed forever the face of history for this small fishing village. . . In 1966 Fernando Barbachano Herrero, born of a family of pioneers, arrived there and found it inhabited by about eighty people, with a single pier made of local (Chico) zapote wood. Fernando befriended the local landowner, Roman Xian Lopez, and spent the next two years trying to talk him into relinquishing some of his land. . . (*Playa*, 1999: 4)

Two years later, in 1968, Fernando Barbachano bought 27 hectares of this land adjacent to the beach for just over US$13 000, or six cents per square metre. In 2003 it was sold for about US$400 per square metre, an increase of over 600 000 per cent. Today this piece of real estate constitutes less than 10 per cent of Playa's prime tourist development. As Playa developed, piers were built for the increasing number of tourist craft, and game-fishers, hotels and bars were constructed fronting the 'virgin' beach, and clubs were opened a short way from the shoreline. The first hotel to be constructed was Hotel Molcas, in the

1970s, next to the little ferry terminal to the Island of Cozumel. Gradually, more people were attracted to the tourist potential of Playa, and its 'history' was rediscovered when it was claimed in the local newspaper that the town had been founded by a *chicle* (the raw material for chewing gum) contractor on 14 November 1902, giving today's mega-resort a provenance that it had previously lacked. Today the town possesses shopping malls, selling designer clothes and global brands. International gourmet restaurants compete for the lucrative tourist business; 25 million tourists visited Mexico in 2007. Today, the beaches draw migrants from all over Mexico, particularly the poorer states such as Chiapas, and the town's hinterland contains squatter settlements as large as any in urban Latin America. These areas have names that sometimes suggest wider political struggles: like 'Donaldo Colosio', a 'squatter' area named after a prominent politician in the PRI (Party of the Institutional Revolution) who was murdered in Tijuana in 1994.

Tourist 'pioneers' had taken an interest in the Mexican Caribbean coast even before Fernando Barbachano stumbled upon the resort potential of Playa del Carmen. In the longer view, tourist expansion on the coast of Quintana Roo can be compared with the trade in dyewood 300 years earlier, or of mahogany and *chicle* during the last century (Redclift, 2004). All three were milestones in the development of the region, and linked it with global markets and consumers. Each possessed their own 'pioneers', like Fernando Barbachano, who 'discovered' a land of rich natural resources, apparently unworked by human hand. It is worth recalling that the account of Playa's 'discovery' in the passage above refers to a 'single pier made of local *zapote* wood. . .'. Chicozapote was the tree from which *chicle* (chewing-gum resin) was tapped. The chicle industry occupied what had become an 'abandoned space'.

After the demise of chicle production in the 1940s, the coast of Quintana Roo experienced the slow growth of specialized tourism. Between the late 1920s and 1940s several hotels were built on the Island of Cozumel, which lies off the coast opposite Playa del Carmen, the Hotels Yuri and Playa, but at this time most visitors to what are today major Mayan archaeological sites on the mainland, still slept in improvised cabins. The majority of tourists still left Cozumel by boat, landed on the mainland coast at Tankah, stayed briefly at the most important copra estate nearby, and then either cut a path through the jungle to Tulum, or took a boat along the coast.

In this, they were beating a track that had been followed by earlier pioneers, the most famous of whom were John Stephens and Frederick Catherwood, the 'giants' of Mayan archaeology in the mid-nineteenth century. Stephens and Catherwood had already explored the major Mayan sites of northern Yucatan, such as Chichen Itza and Uxmal, and arrived in Valladolid at the end of March 1841. They made enquiries about getting to the Caribbean coast, no mean feat at the time since there were no roads. 'It is almost impossible to conceive what difficulty we had in learning anything definite concerning the road we ought to take', Stephens reported to his diary (Stephens, 1988: 168). After travelling to the north coast he went on to land at Cozumel, at the only inhabited spot, the ranch of San Miguel, where they record that 'our act of taking possession was unusually exciting'. Here they stopped to feast on turtle and fresh water, strolled along the shoreline picking up shells, and went to sleep in their hammocks, 'as piratical a group as ever scuttled a ship at sea' (ibid.: 170). The Island of Cozumel had been 'discovered' several times before; once 'by accident' it is said, when Juan de Grijalva caught sight of it in March 1518, having set sail from Cuba. Unlike Grijalva, three centuries earlier, John

Stephens knew where he was in 1841 and noted for the benefit of the 'Modern Traveller' that they alone had proprietorship of 'this desolate island' (ibid.: 175).

It was another century after Stephens's visit with Catherwood that modern tourism arrived in Cozumel, with the construction of Hotel Playa and the patronage of an influential American, William Chamberlain. From about 1952 onwards Chamberlain enticed numerous foreigners to the area, and constructed the first tourist *cabañas*, which he named 'Hotel Mayalum'. This was also the first recorded attempt to link the region and its coastal tourist attractions to the cultural life of the Maya, the historical antecedents of the 'Maya World', the brand name for most of this zone today.

In Mexico, Cozumel had blazed a modest trail as a tourist destination, followed by Isla Mujeres, where relatively small hotels and guest-houses began to cluster around the small central plaza, and provided important facilities for discriminating groups of Mexicans and Americans anxious to avoid large-scale tourism. By 1975 90000 tourists were visiting Isla Mujeres annually. Behind much of this growth were powerful new political interests, later to play a part in the development of Cancun, and linked to the person of President Luis Echeverría, whose godfather was a leading businessman on the island.

During the 1960s, 14 new hotels were built in Cozumel, with a total of 400 beds; an apparently modest figure in the light of subsequent developments. But by the end of the decade, 57000 tourists had visited the island, two-thirds of them foreigners. This remarkable success prompted some of the inhabitants to examine their own histories more carefully. It was soon revealed that almost the entire population was made up of 'pioneers', or 'founders' (*forjadores*). Refugees from the Caste War had in fact repopulated the island shortly after Stephens and Catherwood's visit, contrary to the prevailing view created by global tourism that the Mexican Caribbean lacked any identity of its own. Unlike the rebel Maya who held the mainland, the 22 families of refugees who arrived in Cozumel in 1848 felt themselves to be the only surviving 'Mexicans' on the peninsula (Dachary and Arnaiz, 1998).

Cozumel had played an important advance role in tourist development because, apart from its roster of former *chicle* entrepreneurs, who were interested in putting their capital into a profitable new business, it also boasted an airport, originally built during the Second World War for US airport reconnaissance. Cozumel had traditionally been a staging post for the natural resources of the region; now it was a natural watering hole for foreign tourists, moving in the opposite direction. Unlike the case of Cancun, however, the pioneers and founders of Cozumel had been its own indigenous bourgeoisie (Antochiw and Dachary 2001; Jones and Ward, 1994).

The development of Cancun, beginning in the 1970s, made earlier tourist incursions seem very modest indeed. In the view of some observers, Cancun was chosen because the Mexican Caribbean was like a political tinderbox, liable to explode at any time. Cancun was not simply a gigantic tourist playground, in this view; it was an 'abandoned space' on the frontier, which needed to be 'settled, employed and occupied'. Even in 1970 almost half of the population of Cancun was from outside Quintana Roo; as the zone developed it pulled in people from all over southeast Mexico (Murray, 2007).

The history of Cancun, like that of Cozumel and Isla Mujeres, demonstrates that they were 'empty spaces' in the minds of planners and developers, but they were not devoid of history. The large, sophisticated resorts that have been established on the Mexican

Caribbean coast have been constructed as 'places', and are increasingly associated with accompanying myths and ascribed histories. These include connections with piracy (the all-inclusive 'Capitan Lafitte' hotel complex), with a local tourist pioneer (the Hotel Molcas in Playa, and Pablo Bush Romero, the 'founder' of Akumal) and even, most recently, with the history of *chicle*/chewing gum (in the form of a *chicle* 'village', Pueblo Chiclero, built for tourists to visit when they disembarked from their cruise liners in Majahual).

The Mexican Caribbean provides several examples of the process of 'place construction' referred to in the literature above. Following Massey (1994), we can see the area as a dense network of social relations, which at different periods of time have brought the geographical periphery close to global systems of trade and power over resources. As Massey avers, the nature of a place is a product of its linkages with other places, not just a reflection of its internal features. The ways in which places are 'plugged into' different circuits of capital also suggests something of the dynamism and innovation identified by Castree (2004). In the Mexican Caribbean, tourist economies have developed that build upon previous entrepots, notably *chicle*/chewing gum, even incorporating their historical detail, the materiality of their design, into new tourist 'products', such as '*chicle* camps' and wooden jetties. The local and 'unique' (Luckermann, 1964) are refashioned for global consumers and audiences. Place is reworked in terms of its own history.

This has also prompted different and contrasting accounts of the history of place. An example is the naming of places such as Playa del Carmen, the largest urban settlement south of Cancun. 'Playa', the resort, has a very different discursive quality from the other two alternative names that are in use. One is 'Solidaridad' (Solidarity), the official name for the municipal district of which Playa is the major part, which reflects a national history rooted in the Mexican revolutionary conflict. Similarly the Mayan term for Playa, 'X'aman H'a', carries quite different connotations of place, bound up with the importance of Playa to the symbolic world of the Mayan ancestors. 'Places' reflect and perpetuate these different parameters of culture and power, and illuminate the tension between what was 'there' or 'not there' (in Gertrude Stein's famous aphorism for her home town of Oakland, California) and what has been rediscovered subsequently.

Conclusion

The discussion of place, as we have seen, is closely linked to governing paradigms and systems of explanation. It thus possesses the potential to both signal something about location and the meaning that is attached to it. We have considered the Mexican Caribbean as a case study of the way in which place is constructed at the geographical margins of space, in economies previously dominated by extractive industries, such as hardwoods and *chicle*, places that in this case are being transformed rapidly into global tourist destinations. We have referred to this dual conceptual role as 'place confirmation', to underline the centrality of the idea of place both as location and the association of meanings with location. Like gender and nature, the meaning of place may be negotiable but its importance in the canon of concepts available to environmental sociology suggests considerable room for further development.

In the absence of systematic quantitative methods, place acquired a largely positivist mantle before the 'ideological decades' of the 1970s and 1980s, and its apologists acquired a quantitative zeal. The 'cultural turn' and postmodernism revealed a new emphasis on the human face of 'place' and its social construction, in which rather than being buried by globalization it offered a new form of conceptual revival. For both Marxists and neoliberals, place has suggested the interface of global structures and localized pockets of resistance – a regrouping of social expression in a locus of space. Its derivatives have opened up a new lexicon – emplacement, displacement, sense of place – with which to slay the dragon of global, place-less modernity, all flows and essences. One of the routes into place confirmation, then, is clearly through enlarging the way that the concept of place is employed.

A second point of entry is through recognizing the sociological processes that condition us to think about place: its naturalization. This naturalization is important not just in the more conservative, bounded sense of place as 'mosaic', the traditional way in which geographers viewed 'places', but also in the more relational way place is employed today: place and identity, place and memory, place and belonging. A sense of place clearly exists in memory (and is institutionalized in memorializing), and this sense of place appears and disappears as places are discovered, erased and rediscovered. The Mexican Caribbean coast serves as an example of this kind of process, and might lead us to ask questions about what lies behind the erasure and discovery of place. What do these processes tell us about societies and their histories? To develop conceptually, the idea of place needs to be linked to alternative visions of spatial polity in which history is an essential element, rather than a later embellishment.

One possible way of understanding the highly diverse literature on place emerging in the last two decades is to look at the politics of place from a historical and evolutionary perspective. Throughout history, place construction has played practical, sociocultural and symbolic roles. At the foundations of place construction are the processes through which individuals and groups develop survival strategies, solve common problems and make sense of their own existence. Place attachment, sense of place, affection, embeddedness, identification and other concepts are appropriate for interpreting this fundamental dimension of place. However, as human beings became more capable of controlling the environment, the construction of social and cultural meanings grew increasingly independent of physical settings. The social dimension of human experience even surpassed nature's importance in the shaping of place. For instance, the built environment served to substitute for the ecological context in some sacred places. At the same time, the colonization of vast territories by relatively small groups, in the cause of imperial expansion, brought about the possibility of transposing meanings and cultural systems from one geographical setting to another, and facilitated cultural hybridization, as happened during the Roman Empire.

With science and modernity, place construction was increasingly perceived in terms of filling 'emptiness' with 'civilization'. The concept of space (as empty place), the production of maps and the notion of private ownership of land were instrumental in the successful passage of colonialism. Concepts such as location, locale or region were linked to the modern administration of place, which achieved its ultimate expression with the hegemony of the modern nation-state. In addition, colonization opened the doors for a diverse range of new power relations that would, in turn, lead to the construction of new places (of exclusion, domination, resistance and so on). The Mexican Caribbean remained until very recently at the periphery of modernity. Its forests were constructed by Yucatecan Maya people as a place of cultural resistance, while the *chicle* and timber were exploited by the British and the *criollo* Mexicans. With the end of the Caste War, the territory of Quintana Roo was fully incorporated into the administration of the Mexican State and subjected to a number of programmes to colonize and settle the land.

In recent years, economic globalization has taken the modernization of place one step further by bypassing the constraints of national culture and state administration. Today, economic globalization is colonizing the 'empty space' spared by the modern state and constructing new places of consumption dominated by logics of extraction and economic profit. It is also creating new places of resistance and struggle, as Escobar shows in his work in Colombia (Escobar, 2009). However, this apparent homogenization has never completely replaced the historic and alternative constructions of place that are grounded in personal attachment, sense of place, cosmologies, personal intimacy and familiarity. Rather, modern and globalized spaces are being superimposed on previous meanings. Furthermore, the process of individuation that started in the early modern period and developed under liberal democracies was further deepened with postmodernity. As a consequence, the modern homogenization of place is only partial and superficial. It is a force constantly counteracted and reversed by people's impulse to find an existential meaning that the uniformity of mass consumption might never provide. It is in this context that the revival of academic interest for place construction is emerging.

The Mexican Caribbean coast shows how a place at the periphery is more vulnerable to homogenization when it is 'swallowed' by globalization and strenuously forced into space for mass-tourism consumption. Through this rapid colonization, millions of North Americans and Europeans have had the opportunity to experience a place imagined as pre-modern. Tourism in the Mexican Caribbean offers an illusion of place crafted for tourism consumption. The touristic destinations of Cancun, Playa del Carmen and Cozumel are 'engineered' places fabricated by a coalition between the Mexican State and the 'forces' of economic globalization. What it is offered to the tourist is an essentialist construction of place based on a hybrid, a concoction composed of the beach resort, colonized spaces adapted for mass consumption and reconstructions of 'others'' (Mayan or 'Mexican') assumed sense of place. The thousands of immigrants attracted to the area by economic opportunities are constructing their own places, but in Cancun, and to a lesser extent in Playa and Cozumel, these locally and spontaneously created places are hidden from the tourists' gaze. The question is then whether, in the process of engineering this illusion of place, the ecological integrity of the Mexican Caribbean is being rapidly degraded.

The analysis of place requires the acknowledgement of ambiguities that are central to thinking in contemporary environmental sociology. Places are collectively shared and contested. They do not necessarily mean the same thing to everybody. They are not 'owned' in the same way by everybody. This observation is also clearly true of the academic disciplines that have utilized place. In the world of academic discourse, place is often part of a critique, and exists on an intellectual terrain. However, in the 'lived' world of experience, place also has phenomenological import – it can be an affirmation of humanity, and in that sense critique alone does it a disservice. Acknowledging the hybridity of place provides another route into place confirmation, distancing the concept from its more descriptive history, and opening up the possibility of place as a more heuristic device, a way of understanding society rather than a point from which to view it.

References

Agnew, J.A. (1987), *Place and Politics: The Geographical Mediation of State and Society*, London: Allen & Unwin.

Aitken, S. and G. Valentine (2006), *Approaches to Human Geography*, London, Thousand Oaks, CA, and New Delhi, India: Sage.

Altman, I. and S.M. Low (eds) (1992), *Place Attachment*, New York: Plenum Press.

Antochiw, M. and A.C. Dachaty (2001), *Historia de Cozumel*, Mexico City: Consejo Nacional para la Cultura.

Bergman, E. and W. Renwick (eds) (2008), *Introduction to Geography: People, Places and Environments*, 4th edn, Upper Saddle River, NJ: Prentice-Hall.

Blomley, N. (2004) 'Law, property and the geography of violence: the frontier, the survey and the grid', *Annals of the Association of American Geographers*, **93**: 121–41.

Canter, D. (1997), 'The facets of place', in G.T. Moore and R.W. Marans (eds), *Advances in Environment, Behavior, and Design, Vol. 4: Toward the Integration of Theory, Methods, Research, and Utilization*, New York: Plenum Press, pp. 109–47.

Casey, E. (1997), *The Fate of Place: A Philosophical History*, Berkeley, CA: University of California Press.

Castree, N. (2003), 'Place: connections and boundaries in an interdependent world', in Sarah L. Holloway, Stephen P. Rice and Gill Valentine (eds), *Key Concepts in Geography*, London, Thousand Oaks, CA, and New Delhi, India: Sage, pp. 168–94.

Castree, N. (2004), 'Differential geographies: place, indigenous rights and 'local' resources', *Political Geography*, **23** (2): 133–67.

Castree, N., A. Rogers and D. Sherman (eds) (2005), *Questioning Geography: Fundamental Debates*, Oxford: Blackwell.

Cheng, A.S., L.E. Kruger and S.E. Daniels (2003) '"Place" as an integrating concept in natural resource politics: propositions for a social science research agenda', *Society and Natural Resources*, **16**: 87–104.

Cloke, P., C. Philo and D. Sandler (1991), *Approaching Human Geography: An Introduction to Contemporary Theoretical Debates*, New York: Guilford Publications.

Cresswell, T. (1996), *In Place / Out of Place*, Minneapolis, MN: University of Minnesota Press.

Cresswell, T. (2004), *Place: A Short Introduction*, London, Thousand Oaks, CA, and New Delhi, India: Sage.

Cronon, W. (ed.) (1996), *Uncommon Ground: Rethinking the Human Place in Nature*, New York: Norton.

Cross, J.E. (2001), 'What is "sense of place"?', *Archives of the Twelfth Headwaters Conference*, 2–4 November.

Curry, M.R. (2002), 'Discursive displacement and the seminal ambiguity of space and place', in L. Lievrouw and S. Livingstone (eds), *The Handbook of New Media*, London, Thousand Oaks, CA, and New Delhi, India: Sage, pp. 502–17.

Dachary, Alfredo Cesar and Stella Arnaiz Burne (1998), *El Caribe Mexicano: una frontera olvidada*, Chetumal, QR, Mexico: Universidad de Quintana Roo.

Dixon, J. and K. Durrheim (2000), 'Displacing place identity: a discursive approach to locating self and other', *British Journal of Social Psychology*, **39**: 27–44.

Escobar, A. (2009) *Territories of Difference: Place, Movement, Life, Redes*, Durham, NC: Duke University Press.

Everest (2002), *Tourist Guides to Quintana Roo, Cancun*.

Foucault, M. (1986), 'Of other spaces, heterotopias', *Diacritics*, **16**: 22–7.

Galliano, S.J. and G.M. Loeffler (1999), *Place Assessment: How People Define Ecosystems*, Gen. Tech. Rep. PNW-GTR-462. Portland, OR: US Department of Agriculture, Forest Service, Pacific Northwest Research Station.

Giuliani, M.V. and R. Feldman (1993), 'Place attachment in a developmental and cultural context', *Journal of Environmental Psychology*, **13**: 267–74.

Gupta, A. and I. Ferguson (1992), 'Beyond "culture": space, identity and the politics of difference', *Cultural Anthropology*, **7** (1): 6–23.

Gustafson, P. (2001), 'Meanings of place: everyday experience and theoretical conceptualizations', *Journal of Environmental Psychology*, **21**: 5–16.

Harrison, S. and P. Dourish (1996), 'Re-place-ing space: the roles of place and space in collaborative systems', in *Proceedings of the 1996 ACM Conference on Computer Supported Cooperative Work*, Boston, MA: ACM Press, pp. 67–76.

Hay, R. (1998), 'A rooted sense of place in cross-cultural perspective', *Canadian Geographer*, **42** (3): 245–66.

Hayter, R., T. Barnes and M. Bradshaw (2003), 'Relocating resource peripheries to the core of economic geography's theorizing, rationales and agenda', *Area*, **35**: 15–23.

Hidalgo, M.C. and B. Hernández (2001), 'Place attachment: conceptual and empirical questions', *Journal of Environmental Psychology*, **21**: 372–81.

348 *The international handbook of environmental sociology*

Holloway, L., S. Rice and G. Valentine (eds) (2003), *Key Concepts in Geography*, London, Thousand Oaks, CA, and New Delhi, India: Sage.

Holt-Jensen, A. (1999), *Geography: History and Concepts: A Student's Guide*, London: Sage.

Hubbard, P., R. Kitchin and G. Valentine (eds) (2004), *Key Thinkers on Space and Place*, London, Thousand Oaks, CA, and New Delhi, India: Sage.

Hummon, D. (1992), 'Community attachment: local sentiment and sense of place', in I. Altman and S. Low (eds), *Place Attachment*, New York: Plenum Press, pp. 253–78.

Johnson, T.G. (2002), 'Where is the place in space?', paper presented at the 2002 Southern Regional Science Association Meeting, Arlington, VA, 12 April.

Jones, G. (2003), 'Imaginative geographies of Latin America', in P. Swanson (ed.), *The Companion to Latin American Studies*, London: Edward Arnold, pp. 5–25.

Jones, G. and P.M. Ward (1994), *Methodology for Land and Housing Market Analysis*, London: UCL Press.

Kort, W.A. (2001), 'Sacred/profane and an adequate theory of human place-relations', paper presented at the 'Constructions of Ancient Space' Conference, Denver, CO, 17–20 November.

Lefebvre, H. (1974), *La Production de l'Espace*, Paris: Anthropos.

Lefebvre, H. (1991), *The Production of Space*, trans. D. Nicholson-Smith, Oxford: Basil Blackwell.

Luckermann, S. (1964), 'Geography as a formal intellectual discipline', *Canadian Geographer*, **8**: 162–72.

Martins, L. (2000), 'A naturalist's visión of the tropics: Charles Darwin and the Brazilian landscape', *Singapore Journal of Tropical Geography*, **21** (1): 19–33.

Manzo, L.C. (2003), 'Beyond house and haven: toward a revisioning of emotional relationships to places', *Journal of Environmental Psychology*, **23**: 47–61.

Massey, D. (1994), *Space, Place, and Gender*, Minneapolis, MN: University of Minnesota Press.

Massey, D. and P. Jess (1995), *A Place in the World*, Milton Keynes: The Open University.

McDowell, L. (1997), *Undoing Place*, London: Edward Arnold.

Mitchell, M.Y., J.E. Force, M.S. Carroll and W.J. McLaughlin (1993), 'Forest places of the heart: incorporating special places into public management', *Journal of Forestry*, **91**: 32–7.

Murray, G. (2007), 'Constructing paradise: the impacts of big tourism in the Mexican coastal zone', *Coastal Management*, **35**: 339–55.

Playa magazine (1999), Playa del Carmen, Mexico.

Proshansky, H.M., A.K. Fabian and R. Kaminoff (1983), 'Place-identity: physical social world socialization of the self', *Journal of Environmental Psychology*, **3**: 57–83.

Redclift, Michael (2004), *Chewing Gum: The Fortunes of Taste*, London and New York: Routledge.

Relph, E. (1976), *Place and Placelessness*, London: Pion.

Relph, E. (1997), 'Sense of place', in S. Hanson (ed.), *Ten Geographic Ideas that Changed the World*, New Brunswick, NJ: Rutgers University Press, pp. 205–26.

Salvatore, R.D. (1996), 'North American travel narratives and the ordering/othering of South America (c.1810–1860)', *Journal of Historical Sociology*, **9** (1): 85–110.

Steel, G.D. (2000), 'Polar bonds: environmental relationships in the polar region', *Environment and Behavior*, **32** (6): 796–816.

Stephens, John L. (1988), *Incidents of Travel in Yucatan*, vols 1 and 2 (originally published 1843, Harper and Bros., New York), Mexico City: Panorama Editorial.

Stokols, D. and S.A. Shumaker (1981), 'People in places: a transactional view of settings', in D. Harvey (ed.) *Cognition, Social Behavior, and the Environment*, Hillsdale, NJ: Erlbaum, pp. 441–88.

Stokowski, P.A. (2002), 'Language of place and discourses of power: Constructing new senses of place', *Journal of Leisure Research*, **34**: 368–82.

Tuan, Y. (1977), *Space and Place: The Perspective of Experience*, Minneapolis, MN: University of Minnesota Press.

Twigger-Ross, C.L. and D.L. Uzzell (1996), 'Place and identity processes', *Journal of Environmental Psychology*, **16**: 205–20.

Unwin, T. (1992), *The Place of Geography*, London: Prentice Hall.

Williams, D.R. and S.I. Stewart (1998), 'Sense of place: an elusive concept that is finding a home in ecosystem management', *Journal of Forestry*, **96**: 18–23.

Williams, D.R. and J.J. Vaske (2003), 'The measurement of place attachment: validity and generability of a psychometric approach', *Forest Science*, **49**: 830–40.

22 Society, environment and development in Africa
William M. Adams

Introduction

Sub-Saharan Africa has long been a central presence in debates about sustainability and sustainable development. Its importance derives from the views of both environmentalists and development planners. Thus, among environmentalists, it was perceived threats to Africa's megafauna that stimulated the International Union for the Conservation of Nature (IUCN) and the Food and Agriculture Organization (FAO) in 1961 to launch the 'African Special Project' to influence African leaders and promote conservation policies (Holdgate, 1999). This in turn led to IUCN work on ecology and international development (Farvar and Milton, 1973), and a 'guidebook' for development planners (McCormick, 1992: 155), *Ecological Principles for Economic Development* (Dasmann et al., 1973). These were direct forerunners of the idea of sustainable development discussed in the *World Conservation Strategy* in 1980. Africa's wildlife and its development needs still give the continent an iconic place in the worldview of conservationists, whether identifying priorities for protected areas such as biodiversity hotspots (Myers et al., 2000), or offering the challenge of finding win–win strategies to achieve conservation and poverty alleviation together.

Africa also holds a central place in debate about poverty and development. It is Africa that most challenges achievement of the 18 targets and 48 indicators of the eight Millennium Development Goals (Sachs and McArthur, 2005). Outside China, the number of people living on less than a dollar a day has increased (Chen and Ravallion, 2007). In Africa, the number of people at this level of poverty rose from 164 million to 314 million between 1981 and 2001, 46 per cent of the population (Wolfensohn and Bourguignon, 2004). Much of that poverty is rural. Even if the 2015 Goals are met in full, there will still be approximately 900 million people who are chronically poor, most of them in sub-Saharan Africa and South Asia (Chronic Poverty Research Centre, 2005). Africa is home to the largest fraction of the world's 'bottom billion' (Collier, 2007).

So society and environment are frequently – almost inevitably – coupled in debates about rural Africa and its development. These debates are often conducted through a series of highly stereotyped understandings of society and nature. The continent has, for example, repeatedly been described as in a state of crisis brought about by various systematic ills, of drought, disease and famine and war (Watts, 1989). Such stereotypes provide powerful frames for both academic and popular theorization and analysis. In 1991, Emery Roe drew attention to the way ideas about people and environment become standardized in development, through the creation of what he calls policy narratives. These are self-referencing stories that offer a definition and explanation of commonly perceived problems, and prescribe policy responses. They can be enormously powerful, structuring the way technical 'experts', government officials, donor organizations and researchers think. Once established, policy narratives are remarkably persistent: they cannot be refuted simply by showing that they are untrue in a particular instance, but only by providing a better and more convincing story (Roe, 1991, 1994; Leach and Mearns, 1996).

This chapter picks out five key environmental policy narratives that have been central to debate about society, environment and development in Africa. It discusses, first, Africa's place at the centre of global debates about desertification. Second, it discusses the related debates about pastoralism and the narrative of overgrazing. Third, it explores ideas about indigenous agricultural intensification as opposed to ecological deterioration caused by overpopulation. Fourth, it considers Africa as a continent where, despite millennia of human occupation and transformation of ecosystems, nature has been interpreted as wilderness, to be preserved against human demands. Finally, it considers Africa as a place where ideas of 'community' have provided powerful if misleading frameworks for planning conservation and sustainable rural development.

The spreading desert: desertification
The issue of desertification in the Sahel is perhaps the classic example of the power of environmental narratives (Swift, 1996, Sullivan, 2000). In 1934, the forester Edward Stebbing toured the north of Nigeria. In the dry conditions of Katsina, he concluded that open deciduous forest savanna was being degraded by human activity (shifting cultivation, burning, and livestock grazing and browsing). Famously, he reported that the areas was undergoing progressive desiccation: the very Sahara was moving southwards into farmland, a 'silent invasion of the great desert' (Stebbing, 1935: 518). Concern about the links between the management of drylands and *in situ* land degradation and soil erosion was linked to global alarm at the Dust Bowl in the American Midwest in the 1930s (Beinart and Coates, 1995). News of this environmental crisis in the USA took root in both British and French territories in Africa (Aubréville, 1949; Anderson, 1984), and the concern persisted: in 1949, Vogt concluded, 'Whether or not Africa is actually suffering a climatic change, man is most effectively helping to desiccate the continent' (1949: 248).

Stebbing described the phenomenon that subsequently became known as desertification, a term coined by Aubréville (1949). Concern about desertification was reignited during the severe drought in the African Sahel, 1972–74. Debate on the floor of the UN led to the UN Conference on Desertification (UNCOD) in Nairobi in 1977. This was organized by the UN Environment Programme (UNEP), which was then made responsible for coordinating a global Plan of Action to Combat Desertification. In UNEP, recently established following the UN Conference on the Human Environment in Stockholm in 1972, the desertification narrative had a powerful institutional champion. The problem was duly identified as a global scourge, particularly severe in dryland Africa. In 1980, UNEP estimated that about 35 per cent of the terrestrial globe was vulnerable to erosion (about 4.5 billion hectares) – land that supported about one-fifth of the world's population. Of this area, 30 per cent was severely or very severely desertified (Tolba, 1986). The extent and severity of desertification were seen to be increasing in every arid region in the developing world (Mabbutt, 1984).

The recurrence of dry years in the Sahel and Ethiopia in the 1980s confirmed ideas about human-created deserts. Thus Sinclair and Fryxell (1985) explained the crisis in the Sahel and Ethiopia not in terms of drought (a failure of rain exacerbated by warfare), but in terms of a 'settlement-overgrazing hypothesis'. They argued that until about the middle of the twentieth century the 'normal' land-use pattern in the Sahel was based on migratory grazing using seasonally available resources. They suggested that this system had been operating in a 'balanced and reasonably stable' way for many centuries, possibly since domestic cattle first appeared in the Sahel 5000 years ago. It broke down 'through well-intended but short-sighted and misinformed intervention through aid projects'. Problems began after the Second World War, exacerbated by population growth, overgrazing and agricultural practices aimed at short-term profit, not sustained yield (Sinclair and Fryxell, 1985: 992). Arguments about the possible feedback effects of bare desertified soil on climate (e.g. Charney et al., 1975) suggested that the Sahelian ecosystem was 'being pushed into a new stable state of self-perpetuating drought' (Sinclair and Fryxell, 1985: 992). It is a stark story of human being degrading the land, although in the authors' analysis the real blame is laid on the aid agencies, which fund projects that break down the older and sustainable migratory pattern. Their conclusion is that short-term food aid by itself will 'only make the situation worse', since 'simply feeding the people and leaving them on the degraded land will maintain and exacerbate the imbalance and not allow the land to recover' (ibid.).

There were contrary views. Thomas and Middleton (1994: 63) described desertification as 'a concept out of hand'. Palaeo-climatologists pointed out the extent of previous climate change over previous centuries and millennia (Grove, 1977; Roberts, 1998). The lack of an adequate definition of desertification, and of scientific measurements of ecological change, were widely discussed (Warren, 1996; Middleton and Thomas, 1997). In 1992, UNEP revised its estimate of the area desertified globally downwards to less than one-third of the area estimated at UNCOD in 1977, or in the previous 1984 survey (Thomas and Middleton, 1994; Middleton and Thomas, 1997). The new estimate suggested that just over 1 billion hectares of land suffered soil degradation, with a total of 2.5 billion hectares including vegetation change.

However, while researchers developed more subtle understandings of dryland degradation, the concept of desertification (and the argument for aid flows to some of the world's poorest countries) remained extremely attractive to policy-makers. In 1996, the 'UN Convention to Combat Desertification in Those Countries Experiencing Severe Drought and/or Desertification, especially in Africa', agreed at the Rio Conference in 1992, came into force. It defined desertification as 'land degradation in arid, semi-arid and dry sub-humid areas resulting from various factors, including climatic variations and human activities'. Desertification was an institutional fact, if a contested concept.

The narrative of desertification served the interests of specific groups of powerful policy actors: national governments in Africa, international aid bureaucracies (especially UN agencies) and scientists (Swift, 1996). In the 1970s, recently independent African governments were restructuring their bureaucracies and strengthening central control over natural resources. Drought, and the assumptions about human-induced environmental degradation linked to them, legitimated such claims and made centralized top-down environmental planning seem a logical strategy. Aid donors saw in desertification a problem that seemed to transcend politics and legitimated 'large, technology-driven international programmes' (Swift, 1996: 88).

The inexorable nibbling of goats: overgrazing
A narrative linked to that of desertification is that of overgrazing – a concept that has provided the foundation stone of policy in many African drylands. Conventional views

of rangeland management and mismanagement have been built around ideas of range conditions, class and carrying capacity. The scientific argument is that the environment is capable of supporting a certain fixed numbers (or biomass) of livestock, and that for any given ecosystem this can be calculated primarily as a function of rainfall. There is a general relationship between rainfall and the productivity of herbivores. If these regressions are taken to represent 'carrying capacity', lower stocking levels suggest that pasture is being underused, and at higher stocking levels it is being overused, with the likelihood of adverse ecological change (e.g. extinction of palatable species and eventually loss of vegetation cover) and eventually the death of excess stock.

The concepts of overgrazing and carrying capacity have led to pastoral policy to confine, control and settle nomadic pastoralists in sub-Saharan Africa (Horowitz and Little, 1987). Both colonial and independent governments have tended to distrust pastoral people who are mobile and difficult to locate, tax, educate and provide with services. Rangeland science has added to this a particular distrust of their apparently thoughtless management of seemingly fragile rangelands. Stereotyped pastoral polices (Swift, 1982) typically include (1) control of livestock numbers to match range conditions and improve stock health and weight, through destocking and especially the promotion of commercial meat sales; (2) fencing and paddocking to allow close control of grazing pressure on particular pieces of land, and provision of watering points to allow optimal livestock dispersal; (3) manipulation of range ecology through controlled burning, bush clearance and pasture reseeding; (4) disease control and stock improvement through breeding. None of these strategies fits with nomadic or semi-nomadic subsistence livestock production, so government pastoral policy has tended to emphasize sedentarization, formal (i.e. freehold or leasehold) land tenure and capitalist production.

Conventional pastoral policy has paid little attention until late in the twentieth century to the ways African pastoralists actually manage their herds and rangelands. Development emphasized the production of animals for slaughter (for meat and hides), whereas indigenous pastoral economies tend to be built on products from live animals (milk or blood). Pastoral development planning tends to focus on cattle, whereas indigenous production systems typically involve a mix of species, including browsing animals (goats or camels) that can find fodder even in the dry season (as in Turkana in northern Kenya, Coughenour et al., 1985; McCabe, 2004). Indigenous pastoral systems are well adapted to exploit the spatial and temporal variability in production, adapting herd composition and using movement to maximize survival chances. Indigenous livestock management systems offer a relatively low output compared to modern capitalist systems such as ranching. However, they are remarkably robust in terms of providing a predictable, if limited, livelihood.

Researchers have increasingly expressed reservations about the universal applicability of the concept of overgrazing (Horowitz and Little, 1987; Mace, 1991). Judgements about carrying capacity are subjective, although that subjectivity is rarely admitted (Hogg, 1983). Estimates of carrying capacity take no account of seasonal or annual variations in fodder availability in response to rainfall or fire (Homewood and Rodgers, 1987). The high spatial and temporal variability of precipitation and vegetation productivity in African drylands has increasingly been recognized.

Most estimates of carrying capacity fail to take account of the variability and resilience of savanna ecosystems (Homewood and Rodgers, 1987). They concentrate on absolute numbers of livestock and not densities, and rarely consider spatial mobility. They are therefore of little value in understanding the ecology of rangelands or the ways pastoral people manage their herds. They are a poor basis for dryland management. The attempt to identify a single 'carrying capacity' for an ecosystem is problematic: appropriate stocking densities will depend on what managers want out of the system. What suits a nomadic pastoralist may not suit a rancher; many African systems have a subsistence stocking rate higher than commercial ranchers would adopt, giving low rates of production per animal but high output per unit area (Homewood and Rodgers, 1987). Actual stocking levels can and do exceed 'carrying capacity' for decades at a time (Behnke et al., 1993).

Despite the volume of literature on overgrazing and carrying capacity, researchers now conclude that there is no one simple ecological succession towards an overgrazed state, but complex patterns of ecological change in response to exogenous conditions (especially rainfall) and stock numbers and management. Such ecological changes can take many forms, and they can proceed by diverse routes, some of which can be reversed more easily than others, and some of which are more sensitive to particular management than others. There are no 'naturally' stable points in semi-arid ecosystems that can usefully be taken to define an 'equilibrial' state.

Through the 1980s and 1990s, conventional thinking about carrying capacity and overgrazing began to be challenged by so-called new range ecology (Behnke et al., 1993). In drier rangelands, with greater rainfall variability, ecosystems exhibit non-equilibrial behaviour. Ecosystem state and productivity are largely driven by rainfall, and pastoral strategies are designed to track environmental variation (taking advantage of wet years and coping with dry ones), rather than being conservative (seeking a steady-state equilibrial output). This awareness of the non-equilibrial nature of savanna ecosystem dynamics reflects a wider understanding of the importance of non-linear processes in ecology (Scoones, 1999).

Once it is appreciated that African dryland ecosystems exhibit non-equilibrial behaviour, much of what appeared to be perversity or conservatism on the part of pastoralists is revealed to be highly adaptive (Behnke et al., 1993; Scoones, 1994; McCabe, 2004). In place of a single 'carrying capacity' for an ecosystem, represented by an equilibrium number of livestock, the balance of livestock and range resources is allowed to change over time. Drought years reduce stock condition and then (through disease, death and destitution-forced sales) stock numbers. Wet years then allow pastures to recover, allowing a lagged recovery of herd numbers as pastoralists track environmental conditions (Scoones, 1994). To cope, herd managers need extensive knowledge of environmental conditions and opportunities in different areas open to them, and resilient multi-species herds, to survive under such conditions. They also need institutions for the exchange and recovery of stock through kinship networks. Development strategies should therefore support indigenous capacity to track rainfall and maintain social and economic networks, rather than try to bring about a shift to a static, equilibrial capitalist form of production.

Alternative pastoral development strategies recognize the non-equilibrial nature of savanna ecology, that opportunistic strategies are long established and often effective, that husbandry systems may well not need drastic reform (let alone abandonment), that change can be gradual, piecemeal and fully participatory (Scoones, 1994). Strategies to help herders to balance fodder supply and stock numbers and track environmental change include a focus on enhancing feed supply (maintaining exchanges with farming communities, supplying feed), supporting mobility (supporting tenure of key dry-season grazing sites and access to trekking routes) and promoting human rights. Animal health is important to stock survival in drought, and mobile vaccination facilities can be important; while there is still a role for the stock-breeding beloved of government livestock researchers, the focus needs to be on the capacity of animals to survive disease, drought and poor dry-season grazing, in preference to milk or meat yield under favourable conditions.

It is now widely recognized that pastoralists need help to endure crises such as drought. Innovative policies include provision for purchasing stock at reasonable prices in droughts (when supply of poor animals rises and prices crash) and for helping pastoral families restock, or communal grain banks for pastoralists (thus enabling them to weather spiralling grain prices during droughts). Most important of all is the provision of security to rights in key areas of rangeland, particularly wetlands patches that support communities in surrounding drylands, and particularly in drought years (Scoones, 1991; McCabe, 2004). Finally, there is a need for more support for herders to move into and out of stock-keeping – not through mass resettlement and retraining campaigns, but by supporting a diversity of livelihood options among which people can choose. Diversity and flexibility are cornerstones of survival in both pastoral and agricultural production in drylands, and policy-makers must recognize and foster these, rather than seeking to sweep them away in the pursuit of higher productivity and a cash income (Mortimore and Adams, 1999).

Beyond Malthus: indigenous agricultural intensification
The third environment and development narrative discussed here emerged in opposition to ideas of desertification and the powerful and emotive image of environmental decline in semi-arid regions of Africa under the pressure of agricultural misuse. Empirical research in Africa in the 1990s has called into question neo-Malthusian assumptions about the inevitability of environmental degradation as population density rises, and neo-Malthusian policy narratives are increasingly under fire (Roe, 1991, 1994, Leach and Mearns, 1996; Robbins, 2004). Historically, sustainable intensive agriculture is known from a variety of contexts in Africa, for example in the irrigation systems of the Rift Valley of East Africa (Widgren and Sutton, 2004). However, generally, rural population densities in Africa are low compared to those in equivalent drylands in Asia, and historically the lack of labour for agriculture has been a critical factor in the evolution of farming systems and environmental management (Iliffe, 1995).

Comparative study of agricultural farming systems in a range of African countries shows increases in agricultural output per head, quite contrary to the customary wisdom of agrarian crisis and falling food production per capita (Wiggins, 1995). In some circumstances, rural population growth in Africa has led to agricultural intensification, not environmental degradation. Research in three regions will serve to demonstrate the challenge to the pessimistic neo-Malthusian narrative about agriculture in Africa: northern Nigeria, southern Kenya, and south-western Uganda.

In northern Nigeria, high population densities have been maintained for centuries in the close-settled zone around Kano City. This agricultural landscape is referred to in the literature as 'farmed parkland', with closely packed fields set with economic trees. By 1913, no more than one-third of the land was fallow, and by 1991, 87 per cent of it was cultivated, and rural population densities were 348 people per square kilometre (Mortimore, 1998). The farming system is complex, with several crops (particularly millet, sorghum, cowpeas and groundnuts) of a wide range of local varieties grown together in different intercropping and relay cropping mixtures (Mortimore and Adams, 1999). The key to the sustainability of cultivation without prolonged fallow periods, however, lies in the maintenance of soil fertility through the close management of nutrient cycles, use of legume crops and the integration of agriculture and livestock-keeping, particularly in the use of crop residues as fodder for small stock (sheep and goats). Some soil nutrients also arrive in the form of dust deposits. Research on farming systems further north-east in Nigeria, in areas with less rainfall than the Kano close-settled zone, suggest that similar patterns of intensification may be developing as population densities rise (Mortimore and Adams, 1999; Harris, 1999). For rural households the allocation of household labour to different tasks in cultivation, livestock keeping, off-farm activity and household work is a critical factor in their ability to achieve sustainable livelihoods (Mortimore and Adams, 1999).

In the 1990s, the possibility of a positive relationship between rural population growth and environmental sustainability started to become conventional wisdom as the results of a study of Machakos District in Kenya, published in the book *More People, Less Erosion* (Tiffen et al., 1994). Machakos in Kenya were portrayed in the 1930s as degraded wastelands, where human survival was at risk from soil erosion. When historical data from this period were used to examine changes in land use over time, they revealed a remarkable phenomenon, one of progressive improvements in soil conservation (Tiffen et al., 1994). Machakos includes some relatively high and well-watered land (2000 m above sea level, 1200 mm rainfall) and lower dry rangelands (600 m above sea level, 700 mm rainfall). Population growth rates have been high (as much as 3.7 per cent per year in the 1970s): the district's population was 240 000 in 1930 and 1.4 million in 1990.

Population growth has allowed an astonishing level of investment in land (particularly terracing) and the wholesale transformation of agriculture into highly intensive production systems (Tiffen and Mortimore, 1994; Tiffen et al., 1994). Agricultural output rose in value three times per capita and 11 times per unit of area between 1930 and 1990 as farmers invested off-farm incomes in land, intensified production, turned to cash crops such as coffee, harnessed labour to terrace hillsides, and made use of the denser networks of contacts to learn new ideas and sell their produce. The political ecology of development in Machakos is complex (Rocheleau et al., 1995). Murton (1999) notes increasing inequality and a reduction in food self-sufficiency: Machakos households with buoyant off-farm income (particularly in nearby Nairobi) can accumulate land and innovate as farmers; those dependent on agricultural labour opportunities struggle.

The third example of indigenous agricultural intensification is in Kabale District in Uganda (Lindblade et al., 1998; Carswell, 2007). Like Machakos, the area was the focus of colonial concern about overpopulation and soil erosion. However, although rural population growth and densities were high (265 per square km), research on land use change 1945–96 showed an increase in the proportion of land being fallowed, extensive terracing, and limited evidence of land degradation. Valley-bottom wetlands had been drained for grazing, and soil fertility was being maintained by using animal manure, household compost and mulching.

Wilderness Africa: conservation and society
The fourth narrative of society, environment and development addresses the relations between people and environment from the perspective that nature is something pristine, set apart from human activity. For much of the twentieth century, wildlife conservationists, film-makers, tourists and many environmentalists in the industrial North have seen Africa as a place of nature, threatened by humanity. In particular, the diversity and density of large mammals on open savannas, and the late date of their scientific discovery, led Africa to be portrayed as an 'unspoiled Eden' (Anderson and Grove, 1987: 4), or 'a lost Eden in need of protection and preservation' (Neumann, 1998: 80) and parks were planned accordingly. Ironically, as parks spread, the eviction of people to create them created true wilderness from previously inhabited lands (Neumann, 1998, 2004). Thus, when Parakuyo and Maasai pastoralists were eventually evicted from the Mkomazi Game Reserve in northern Tanzania in 1988, four decades after the reserve was first designated, the area became 'wilderness' for the first time (Brockington, 2002).

The approach taken to conservation in Africa blended experience in Europe and North America (Adams, 2003; Neumann, 2004). From Europe came the idea of exclusive royal or aristocratic hunting grounds, where the unlicensed killing of game (by rural people marked down as 'poachers') was closely policed. For the British Victorian elite, the preservation of wild 'game' for hunting was an obsession, both at home and in the Empire (MacKenzie, 1988; Adams, 2004). The British tradition of privately owned nature reserves, where non-proprietors lacked rights of access and use, was transferred to colonies, where the colonial state designated game reserves for the use of sporting gentlemen in the colonial service or on safari. This became the mainstay of British colonial conservation, a resort for gentleman hunters, whether traveller or colonial servant (MacKenzie, 1988; Adams, 2004).

From the USA came the idea of the national park, created in remote and sparsely populated areas to protect wilderness. The US national park model, epitomized by Yellowstone and Yosemite (Runte, 1987), was based on the idea of nature as something pristine and separate from lands transformed by people: nature as wilderness (Cronon, 1995). Wilderness was an important element in national identity in the USA: the extent to which the pre-Columbian American West was inhabited and transformed by human action, rather than a pristine 'wilderness', was widely recognized only in the late twentieth century (Denevan, 1992).

In colonial Africa, nature was allotted a place in the emerging map of demarcated zones for settlement, occupation and development in the form of game reserves and subsequently national parks (Adams, 2004). Government development plans expressed on the landscape of Africa the Enlightenment conceptual divide between natural and human, between empty and settled lands, between space for wild nature and for civilization (Neumann, 2004). Unlike North America, most areas of tropical forest and savanna were not emptied of people upon colonial annexation and settlement, yet for the purposes of conservation large tracts of land were routinely adjudged to be empty, or empty enough to be treated conceptually as 'wilderness' (Neumann, 1998).

In Africa, protected areas created to conserve nature were seen to be threatened by the presence of people, and their fires, hunting and livestock. As a result, rural Africans everywhere tended to be excluded, or displaced. Thus the Tanganyikan colonial govern- ment separated spaces for wildlife and for people in Liwale District in Tanzania, creating the 'wilderness' of the Selous Game Reserve by displacing some 40 000 people towards the coast, away from crop-raiding elephants and sleeping sickness, and from their homes (Neumann, 1998). Population clearance against sleeping sickness also created empty lands subsequently incorporated into protected areas, for example in the Congo, where the Parc National Albert expanded on to land cleared in 1933 as part of its drastic sleeping-sickness campaign. Population displacement from African protected areas has taken place in both the colonial period and more recently (e.g. Turton, 1987; Neumann, 1998; Ranger, 1999; Brockington, 2002).

Displacement from parks has direct effects on livelihoods (Emerton, 2001). Impacts include landlessness, joblessness, homelessness, marginalization, food insecurity, increased morbidity and mortality, loss of access to land, resources and services, now and in the future, and social disarticulation (Cernea, 1997). The value of lost agricultural production from land set aside for conservation can also be important to local and even national economies (e.g. in Kenya, Norton-Griffiths and Southey, 1995). The problem of loss of access to land of religious or cultural value is also significant (e.g. Neumann, 1998).

Conservation and community
The fifth and final society, environment and development narrative concerns the ideas that have to some extent come to replace those of wilderness preservation, the applica- tion of the concept of sustainable development in conservation programmes in Africa. Some projects that attempted to combine both conservation and development under a single project umbrella are often labelled 'integrated conservation development projects' (ICDPs; Brandon and Wells, 1992; Stocking and Perkin, 1992). Others take the form of community-based natural resource management (CBNRM).

The first generation of ICDPs enjoyed mixed success (McShane and Wells, 2004). Brandon and Wells (1992: 562) noted that the approach was 'riddled with conceptual dilemmas and design tradeoffs that can fundamentally affect project performance'. ICDPs are very little different from development projects, and conservation planners were perhaps slow to learn about the complexities of project planning, institutions and incentives, the role of participation and the issue of scale. Conservation organiza- tions have discovered that development plans are hard to transfer from paper to reality (Stocking and Perkin, 1992). ICDPs are highly complex and demand skilled staff, sub- stantial funds and a realistic (i.e. slow) timescale. Clear and precise objectives, careful evaluation of costs and benefits of project components at the level of the individual household, long-term commitment to funding and strong local participatory linkages are essential. Such projects are not cheap to implement, and do not yield results quickly. There is a risk that positive impacts of the project on the local economy will be transient and dependent on the maintenance of flows of project revenues. As in other forms of development, success depends on local perceptions, and this is vulnerable to the failure of key components.

Most CBNRM programmes involve killing or harvesting wild species: 'consumptive use'. This approach to conservation views biodiversity as an economic resource to be exploited in a sustainable way. Use may take the form of hunting by local people (e.g. for bushmeat), killing in return for a licence fee by big-game hunters, or through the collection of marketable or consumable natural products (for example no-timber forest products). The scientific task of defining a 'sustainable' level of harvesting is complex, requiring good data over long periods and regular monitoring, things often not available in most African countries. CBNRM projects also require effective institutions to enforce harvests (rules, agreement by potential hunters that these are fair and reasonable rules, and measures to deal with those who break them). There are both monetary and non-monetary reasons why people harvest illegally, whether they defy national laws or local conventions. Hunting is not always done by 'local' people, and even if it is, it is often done to supply an organized national trading network and an urban market in bushmeat (Bowen-Jones et al., 2003). It may therefore be hard for CBNRM projects to provide sufficient incentives to decouple livelihoods (e.g. of hunters and local or national traders) from unsustainable patterns of wildlife harvest. There are important wider issues relating to trade in wild species products, for example debates about the legalization of ivory trading under the Convention on International Trade in Endangered Species (CITES).

In the 1980s and 1990s, CBNRM programmes coevolved in several different southern African countries in response to a range of historical, political, social and economic experiences, conditions and challenges (Fabricius et al., 2004). In Zimbabwe, under the CAMPFIRE programme, the same benefits from wildlife use that were enjoyed by landowners on leasehold and title-hold land were extended to residents of communal lands (Duffy, 2000). In Zambia, CBNRM was a response to the challenges of engaging traditional authorities in the management of the benefits of hunting in state 'game management areas' (Wainwright and Wehrmeyer, 1998; Gibson and Marks, 1995). CBNRM programmes were based on the assumptions (1) that communities are more efficient (and cheaper managers) of natural resources than the state; (2) that community management would improve household incomes, thus helping poverty reduction and providing economic incentives for conservation; and (3) that community management reduces conflicts with wild animals, and thus the costs they impose on people, increasing tolerance of wildlife (Hutton et al., 2005).

CAMPFIRE granted *de facto* authority over wildlife resources to district authorities, such that they could profit from hunting revenues (Metcalfe, 1994). The CAMPFIRE model was seen internationally by conservation policy-makers to offer a form of conservation that is both popular and affordable (Olthof, 1994). While CAMPFIRE worked quite well in some areas (Murphree, 2001), in others, particularly those less rich in high-value trophy species such as elephant, and with rapid rates of immigration, it did not (Murombedzi, 2001). Issues of benefit distribution and governance proved problematic. Authority (and hence revenues) were devolved only to district level, not to communities themselves (Murombedzi, 2001). At best, power was decentralized from central to local government, not to community or ward level. As a result, communities lacked incentives to internalize the costs of resource management such as crop-raiding (Murphree, 1994). Decentralization *per se* is not adequate to create the conditions required for significant community control over natural resources (Ribot and Larson, 2004). Like other southern African programmes, CAMPFIRE stopped short of land tenure reform (Murombedzi, 2001). Communal tenure continues to function in ways that disadvantage its residents relative to those enjoying freehold and leasehold. CAMPFIRE was also weakened by its failure to engage with conventional rural development policy constituencies in either agriculture or land reform (Murombedzi, 2001).

Conclusions

Conventional narratives of environment and development in Africa have failed to provide a satisfactory explanation of either failure or success. There is no simple, single recipe for sustainable development in Africa, and no easy answers for those who address the legacy of global 'development', in the classic sense of progress towards universal human improvement. Confidence in the myth of development collapsed at the end of the twentieth century (Escobar, 1995), and with it Africa came for many commentators and word leaders to be labelled as the economic basket case of the twenty-first-century world.

Such views are misplaced. Africa is no basket case, and its vulnerability to external recipes for change is a cause for concern, not celebration. The economic dynamism of rural Africa challenges the Western, urban, industrial notion of 'development'. The cultural vibrancy of Africa's people amidst poverty, its continuing rurality and the number of people dependent on ecosystems challenges conventional ideas of growth before sustainability, and technology-based sustainability.

Regions such as the Sahel have shown remarkable economic resilience, with agricultural outputs keeping pace with rural population, and farmers innovating technically and sustaining livelihoods and environments in the process (Mortimore, 1998). Accounts of economic dynamism and cultural resilience at the local scale stand in marked contrast to conventional views of African rural people as conservative and unenterprising, whose problems can only be solved by outside expertise and technology. Such views were common in colonial times, but have persisted to the present day, entrenched within the knowledge, expertise and power of modern governments, aid donors and other external agents of change.

Rapid transformation in environment and production systems is still advocated by international opinion-formers as the solution for Africa: in 2008, Sir David King, former Chief Scientific Adviser to the UK government, told the British Association's Festival of Science in Liverpool that 'Africa hasn't joined Asia in the green revolution because of anti-science and anti-technology attitudes that lead to organic farming rather than GM' – non-governmental and international organizations had mistakenly supported 'traditional agricultural techniques' that would not deliver food for burgeoning African populations (http://www.the-ba.net/the-ba/News/FestivalNews/_FestivalNews2008/_King. htm, accessed 8 January 2009). King concluded: 'we have the technology to feed the population of the planet. The question is whether we have the ability to realise that we have it, and to deliver.'

Without doubt, modern science has an important role in reducing poverty and improving the livelihoods of Africa's rural poor, and King may be right inasmuch as his remarks suggest caution with respect to over-romanticizing indigenous knowledge. Yet local knowledge systems are as important as Western science in providing the basis for a clear and shared understanding of what works for rural African people and why (and what does not work, and why). In Africa, the record of outside experts and miracle technologies has been poor. University-trained experts and consultants, like their colonial predecessors, mostly fail to see order or skill in rural production systems, misunderstand the logic of practices such as mixed cropping or intercropping, seeing poor husbandry rather than carefully judged risk-avoidance. By contrast, the grand development projects in which such confidence was (and is) based have commonly been unsuccessful: over-ambitious, based on inadequate understanding of either society or environment. Thus Richards (1985) contrasts the high degree of ecological adaptation in Mende swamp rice production in Sierra Leone with the grim comedy of repeated attempts by the colonial and postcolonial developers to transform them. As long ago as 1933, Faulkner and Mackie (1993: 7) pointed out that 'the prevalent idea that the native farmer is excessively conservative is largely due to the mistakes of Europeans in the past'. This is still true. Technologies devised in the laboratory or research station rarely transfer well to the farmer's field, and scientists who prescribe development policies on the basis of their theoretical or experimental knowledge (or generalized narratives ostensibly built on someone else's science) are at best blind guides for rural Africans.

Homewood (2004) makes a series of suggestions for ways in which governments, donors and NGOs can develop more effective policies for environment, society and development. First, they must bridge the gap between an understanding based on technical and scientific analysis of natural resources and one based on political, social and cultural insights. Second, they must incorporate local perspectives on environmental processes and change. Third, they must take account of the way policy operates, and for that they need open channels for feedback from diverse groups of actors, particularly local people. As this account of policy narratives has shown, experts are resistant to data and knowledge that contradict deeply held ideas about environmental and socioeconomic processes and outcomes.

What is needed is a partnership: of modernity and tradition, of outside and local expert, or the formally educated and those with local experience. However, as Mavhunga (2007: 442) points out in the context of conservation, partnership alone is not enough: we need what he calls 'a new democracy of knowledge', a multidisciplinary collaboration rather than 'one-size-fits-all initiatives that ignore local histories and aspirations'. In making the case for a 'renaissance that tackles both poverty and environment', Mavhunga argues: 'we need first to ask ourselves: how have local villagers survived despite the odds stacked against them?' Conservationists (and I would argue, all those promoting rural change) should be

> humble enough to go in as blank slates and be more receptive to local people's views. They could find out what the villagers see as the problems and take on board how they imagine they could be solved. Thereafter, they would return and see how they could weave their own scientific ideas and money into locally generated strategies. (Ibid.)

What works for rural Africa is, at the end of the day, what rural Africans can make work. Without reflexivity and humility on the part of the legions of experts employed to prescribe solutions for Africa's various ills, little of value is likely to be achieved.

References

Adams, W.M. (2003), 'Nature and the colonial mind', in W.M. Adams and M. Mulligan (eds), *Decolonizing Nature: Strategies for Conservation in a Post-colonial Era*, London: Earthscan, pp. 16–50.
Adams, W.M. (2004), *Against Extinction: The Story of Conservation*, London: Earthscan.
Anderson, D.M. (1984) 'Depression, dust bowl, demography and drought: the colonial state and soil conservation in East Africa during the 1930s', *African Affairs*, **83**: 321–44.
Anderson, D.M. and Grove, R.H. (1987), 'The scramble for Eden: past, present and future in African

conservation', in D. Anderson and R. Grove (eds), *Conservation in Africa: People, Policies and Practice*, Cambridge: Cambridge University Press, pp. 1–12.

Aubréville, A. (1949), *Climats, Forêts et Désertification de l'Afrique Tropicale*, Paris: Société d'Éditions Géographiques, Maritimes et Coloniales.

Behnke, R.H. Jr, I. Scoones and C. Kerven (1993), *Range Ecology at Disequilibrium: New Models of Natural Variability and Pastoral Adaptation in African Savannas*, London: Overseas Development Institute.

Beinart, W. and P. Coates (1995), *Environment and History: The Taming of Nature in the USA and South Africa*, London: Routledge.

Bowen-Jones, E., D. Brown and E.J.Z. Robinson (2003), 'Economic commodity or environmental crisis? An interdisciplinary approach to analysing the bushmeat trade in central and west Africa', *Area*, **35**: 390–402.

Brandon, K.E. and M. Wells (1992), 'Planning for people and parks: design dilemmas', *World Development*, **20**: 557–70.

Brockington, D. (2002), *Fortress Conservation: The Preservation of the Mkomazi Game Reserve, Tanzania*, Oxford: James Currey.

Carswell, G. (2007), *Cultivating Success in Uganda: Kigezi Farmers and Colonial Policies*, Oxford: James Currey.

Cernea, M.M. (1997), 'The risks and reconstruction model for resettling displaced populations', *World Development*, **25**: 1569–89.

Charney, J., P.H. Stone and W.J. Quirk (1975), 'Drought in the Sahara: a biogeophysical feedback mechanism', *Science*, **187**: 434–5.

Chen, S. and M. Ravallion (2007), 'Absolute poverty measures for the developing world, 1981–2004', *Proceedings of the National Academy of Sciences*, **104**: 16757–62.

Chronic Poverty Research Centre (2005), *Chronic Poverty Report 2004–5*, University of Manchester, UK: Chronic Poverty Research Centre.

Collier, P. (2007), *The Bottom Billion: Why the Poorest Countries are Failing and What Can be Done About It*, Oxford: Oxford University Press.

Coughenour, M.B., J.E. Ellis, D.M. Swift, D.L. Coppock, K. Galvin, J.T. McCabe and T.C. Hart (1985), 'Energy extraction and use in a nomadic pastoral ecosystem', *Science* **230** (4726): 619–25.

Cronon, W. (1995) 'The trouble with wilderness, or, getting back to the wrong nature', in W. Cronon (ed.), *Uncommon Ground: Toward Reinventing Nature*, New York: W.W. Norton, pp. 69–90.

Dasmann, R.F., J.P. Milton and P.H. Freeman (1973), *Ecological Principles for Economic Development*, Chichester, UK: John Wiley & Sons.

Denevan, W.M. (1992), 'The pristine myth: the landscape of North America in 1492', *Annals of the Association of American Geographers*, **82**: 269–85.

Duffy, R. (2000), *Killing for Conservation: Wildlife Policy in Zimbabwe*, Oxford: James Curry.

Emerton, L. (2001), 'The nature of benefits and the benefits of nature: why wildlife conservation has not economically benefited communities in Africa', in D. Hulme and M. Murphree (eds), *African Wildlife and Livelihoods: the promise and performance of community conservation*, Oxford: James Currey, pp. 208–26.

Escobar, A. (1995), *Encountering Development: The Making and Unmaking of the Third World*, Princeton, NJ: Princeton University Press.

Fabricius, C., E. Koch, H. Magome and S. Turner (eds) (2004), *Rights, Resources and Rural Development: Community-based Natural Resource Management in Southern Africa*, London: Earthscan.

Farvar, M.T. and J.P. Milton (eds) (1973), *The Careless Technology: Ecology and International Development*, London: Stacey.

Faulkner, O.T. and J.R. Mackie (1933), *West African Agriculture*, Cambridge: Cambridge University Press.

Gibson, C.C. and S.A. Marks (1995), 'Transforming rural hunters into conservationists: an assessment of community-based wildlife management programs in Africa', *World Development*, **23**: 941–57.

Grove, A.T. (1977), 'Desertification', *Progress in Physical Geography*, **1**: 296–310.

Harris, F.M.A. (1999), 'Nutrient management of smallholder farmers in a short-fallow farming system in north-east Nigeria', *Geographical Journal*, **165**: 275–85.

Hogg, R. (1983), 'Irrigation agriculture and pastoral development: a lesson from Kenya', *Development and Change*, **14**: 577–91.

Holdgate, M. (1999), *The Green Web: A Union for World conservation*, London: Earthscan.

Homewood, K. (2004), 'Policy, environment and development in African rangelands', *Environmental Science and Policy*, **7**: 125–43.

Homewood, K. and W.A. Rodgers (1987), 'Pastoralism, conservation and the overgrazing controversy', in D.M. Anderson and R.H. Grove (eds), *Conservation in Africa: People, Policies and Practice*, Cambridge: Cambridge University Press, pp. 111–28.

Horowitz, M.M. and P.D. Little (1987), 'African pastoralism and poverty: some implications for drought and famine', in M. Glantz (ed.), *Drought and Hunger in Africa: Denying Famine a Future*, Cambridge: Cambridge University Press, pp. 59–82.

Hutton, J., W.M. Adams and J.C. Murombedzi (2005), 'Back to the barriers? Changing narratives in biodiversity conservation', *Forum for Development Studies*, **32**: 341–70.

Iliffe, J. (1995), *Africans: The History of a Continent*, Cambridge: Cambridge University Press.

Leach, M. and R. Mearns (eds) (1996), *The Lie of the Land: Challenging Received Wisdom on the African Environment*, London: James Currey/International African Institute.

Lindblade, K.A., G. Carswell and J.K. Tumuhairwe (1998), 'Mitigating the relationship between population growth and land degradation: land use change and farm management in southwestern Uganda', *Ambio*, **27**: 565–71.

Mabbutt, J.A. (1984), 'A new global assessment of the status and trends of desertification', *Environmental Conservation*, **11**: 103–13.

Mace, R. (1991), 'Overgrazing overstated', *Nature*, **349** (24 January): 280–81.

MacKenzie, J.M. (1988), *The Empire of Nature: Hunting, Conservation and British Imperialism*, Manchester, UK: Manchester University Press.

Mavhunga, C. (2007), 'Even the rider and a horse are a partnership: a response to Vermeulen & Sheil', *Oryx*, **41**: 441–2.

McCabe, J.T. (2004), *Cattle Bring us to our Enemies: Turkana Ecology, Politics, and Raiding in a Disequilibrium System*, Ann Arbor, MI: University of Michigan Press.

McCormick, J.S. (1992), *The Global Environmental Movement: Reclaiming Paradise*, London: Belhaven (first published 1989, Bloomington, IN: Indiana University Press).

McShane, T. and M. Wells (eds) (2004), *Getting Biodiversity Projects to Work: Towards More Effective Conservation and Development*, New York: Columbia University Press.

Metcalfe, S. (1994), 'The Zimbabwe Communal Areas Management Programme for Indigenous Resources (CAMPFIRE)', in D. Western, R.M. White and S.C. Strumm (eds), *Natural Connections: Perspectives in Community-based Conservation*, Washington, DC: Island Press, pp. 161–92.

Middleton, T. and D.S.G. Thomas (eds) (1997), *World Atlas of Desertification*, 2nd edn, Nairobi: United Nations Environment Programme.

Mortimore, M. (1998), *Roots in the African Dust: Sustaining the Drylands*, Cambridge: Cambridge University Press.

Mortimore, M. and W.M. Adams (1999), *Working the Sahel: Environment and Society in Northern Nigeria*, London: Routledge.

Murombedzi, J.S. (2001), 'Natural resource stewardship and community benefits in Zimbabwe's CAMPFIRE Programme', in D. Hulme and M. Murphree (eds), *African Wildlife and Livelihoods: The Promise and Performance of Community Conservation*, Oxford: James Currey, pp. 244–56.

Murphree, M.W. (1994), 'The role of institutions in community-based conservation', in D. Western, R.M. White and S.C. Strumm (eds), *Natural Connections: Perspectives in Community-based Conservation*, Washington, DC: Island Press, pp. 403–27.

Murphree, M. (2001), 'A case study of ecotourism development from Mahenye, Zimbabwe', in D. Hulme and M. Murphree (eds), *African Wildlife and Livelihoods: The Promise and Performance of Community Conservation*, Oxford: James Currey, pp. 177–94.

Murton, J.E. (1999), 'Population growth and poverty in Machakos District, Kenya', *Geographical Journal*, **165**: 37–46.

Myers N., R.A. Mittermeier, C.M. Mittermeier, G.A.B. da Fonseca and J. Kent (2000), 'Biodiversity hotspots for conservation priorities', *Nature*, **403**: 853–8.

Neumann, R.P. (1998), *Imposing Wilderness: Struggles over Livelihood and Nature Preservation in Africa*, Berkeley, CA: University of California Press.

Neumann, R.P. (2004), 'Nature–state–territory: towards a critical theorization of conservation enclosures', in R. Peet and M. Watts (eds), *Liberation Ecologies: Environment, Development, Social movements*, London: Routledge, pp. 195–217.

Norton-Griffiths, M. and C. Southey (1995), 'The opportunity costs of biodiversity conservation in Kenya', *Ecological Economics*, **12**: 125–39.

Olthof, W. (1994), 'Wildlife resources and local development: experiences from Zimbabwe's CAMPFIRE Programme', in J.P.M. van den Breemer, A. Drijver and L.B. Venema (eds), *Local Resource Management in Africa*, Chichester: Wiley, pp. 111–28.

Ranger, T. (1999), *Voices from the Rocks: Nature, Culture and History in the Matopos Hills of Zimbabwe*, Oxford: James Currey.

Ribot, J. and A. Larson (eds) (2004), *Decentralization of Natural Resources: Experiments in Africa, Asia and Latin America*, London: Routledge.

Richards, P. (1985), *Indigenous Agricultural Revolution: Ecology and Food Production in West Africa*, London: Longman.

Robbins, P. (2004), *Political Ecology: A Critical Introduction*, Oxford: Blackwell.

Roberts, N. (1998), *The Holocene: An Environmental History*, 2nd edn, Oxford: Blackwell.

Rocheleau, D., P.E. Steinberg and P.A. Benjamin (1995), 'Environment, development, crisis and crusade: Ukambani, Kenya, 1890–1990', *World Development*, **23**: 1037–51.

Roe, E. (1991), 'Development narratives, or making the best of blueprint development', *World Development*, **19**: 287–300.

Roe, E. (1994), *Narrative Policy Analysis: Theory and Practice*, Durham, NC: Duke University Press.

Runte A. (1987), *National Parks: The American Experience*, Lincoln, NE: University of Nebraska Press.

Sachs, J.D. and J.W. McArthur (2005), 'The Millennium Project: a plan for meeting the Millennium Development Goals', *The Lancet*, **365**: 347–53.

Scoones, I. (1994), *Living with Uncertainty: New Directions in Pastoral Development in Africa*, London: IT Publications.

Scoones, I. (1999), 'New ecology and the social sciences: what prospects for a fruitful engagement?', *Annual Review of Anthropology*, **28**: 479–507.

Sinclair, A.R. and J.M. Fryxell (1985), 'The Sahel of Africa: ecology of a disaster', *Canadian Journal of Zoology*, **63**: 987–94.

Stebbing, E.P. (1935), 'The encroaching Sahara: the threat to the West African Colonies', *Geographical Journal*, **85**: 506–24.

Stocking, M. and S. Perkin (1992), 'Conservation-with-development: an application of the concept in the Usambara Mountains, Tanzania', *Transactions of the Institute of British Geographers*, n.s. **17**, 337–49.

Sullivan, S. (2000), 'Getting the science right, or introducing science in the first place? Local "facts", global discourse – "desertification' in north-west Namibia', in P. Stott and S. Sullivan (eds), *Political Ecology: Science, Myth and Power*, London: Arnold, pp. 15–44.

Swift, J. (1982), 'The future of American hunter gatherer and postural people in Africa', *Development and Change*, **13**: 159–81.

Swift, J. (1996), 'Desertification narratives; winners and losers', in M. Leach and R. Mearns (eds), *The Lie of the Land: Challenging Received Wisdom on the African Environment*, London: James Currey/Heinemann, pp. 73–90.

Thomas, D.S.G. and T. Middleton (1994), *Desertification: Exploding the Myth*, Chichester, UK: John Wiley & Sons.

Tiffen, M. and M. Mortimore (1994), 'Malthus controverted: the role of capital and technology in growth and environmental recovery in Kenya', *World Development*, **22**: 997–1010.

Tiffen, M., M.J. Mortimore and F. Gichugi (1994), *More People, Less Erosion: Environmental Recovery in Kenya*, Chichester, UK: John Wiley & Sons.

Tolba, M.K. (1986), 'Desertification in Africa', *Land Use Policy*, **3**: 260–68.

Turton, D. (1987) 'The Mursi and National Park development in the lower Omo Valley', in D.M. Anderson and R.H. Grove (eds), *Conservation in Africa: People, Policies and Practice*, Cambridge: Cambridge University Press, pp. 169–86.

Vogt, W. (1949), *Road to Survival*, London: Victor Gollancz.

Wainwright, C. and W. Wehrmeyer (1998), 'Success in integrating conservation and development? A study from Zambia', *World Development*, **26**: 933–44.

Warren, A. (1996), 'Desertification', in W.M. Adams, A.S. Goudie and A. Orme (eds), *The Physical Geography of Africa*, Oxford: Oxford University Press, pp. 342–55.

Watts, M.J. (1989), 'The agrarian question in Africa: debating the crisis', *Progress in Human Geography*, **13**: 1–14.

Widgren, M. and J.W.G. Sutton (eds) (2004), *Islands of Intensive Agriculture in Eastern Africa*, Oxford: James Currey.

Wiggins, S. (1995), 'Change in African farming systems between the mid-1970s and the mid-1980s', *Journal of International Development*, **7**: 807–48.

Wolfensohn, J.D. and F. Bourguignon (2004), *Development and Poverty Reduction: Looking Back, Looking Ahead*, Washington, DC: World Bank.

23 Neoliberal regimes of environmental governance: climate change, biodiversity and agriculture in Australia[1]

Stewart Lockie

Introduction

In his 2008 report to the Australian government, economic adviser Ross Garnaut argued that, on the balance of probabilities, continued growth in atmospheric greenhouse gas (GHG) concentrations will heighten the risk of dangerous climate change. Echoing the 2007 report of UK economic adviser Nicholas Stern, Garnaut went on to argue that delays in action to address global climate change will impose greater costs, in the long term, than will serious and immediate measures to reduce anthropogenic GHG emissions and adapt to unavoidable climate impacts. While the Stern and Garnaut reports have attracted their critics (many of which focus on technical aspects of the analyses), there can be little doubt that they have played a major role in shifting the momentum in political debate away from so-called 'climate-change sceptics'. Further, despite considerable uncertainty over the magnitude, timing and distribution of future climate-change impacts, average temperatures in Australia have already risen 0.9 °C since 1910 while streamflows into the water supplies of Australia's major cities have fallen to between 25 and 65 per cent of their long-term average over the last decade (Garnaut, 2008). For many Australians, the notion of climate change has become less an artefact of arcane scientific theorizing and more a way to explain their own experience of water restrictions, severe weather events and rising food prices. Failure to grasp the rising public expectation of political leadership on this issue is recognized as one of the factors behind the then-incumbent Australian government's loss at the 2007 general election (Stevens, 2007).

None of this is to suggest that debates over the causes, consequences and appropriate responses to climate change have gone away. At the time of writing, there are no guarantees for a comprehensive post-Kyoto agreement on GHG emissions (see Parks and Roberts, Chapter 19 in this volume), and serious concerns regarding the potential impact of the 2008 global financial crisis on political will to commit to deep emissions reductions. Garnaut has argued that while 'climate change is a long-term structural issue', the 'Wall Street meltdown' and its 'potential impact on polluters' capacity for action' is a 'highly disruptive but "short-term" problem' (Maiden, 2008). But he has been loath to recommend that Australia commit to substantial cuts in the absence of an international agreement including all major carbon emitters (Garnaut, 2008). Other economists argue that Australia needs to push on regardless; that, advantages of an international agreement notwithstanding, a well-designed domestic climate policy would reduce uncertainty over energy infrastructure investment, lower capital costs for more carbon-efficient investments and stimulate short-term economic growth (McKibbin, 2007).

Debate over timing and magnitude aside, one of the most striking features of international and national negotiations over GHG abatement is the level of consensus among key decision-making bodies over both the root cause of human-induced climate change and the most appropriate policy responses to it. In short, climate change is conceptualized as a market failure that is primarily to be resolved through market means (Stern, 2007; Garnaut, 2008). This discourse of market failure and reform provides decision-makers with a compelling meta-narrative on environmental governance that promises flexibility, efficiency and effectiveness in the face of otherwise immensely complex problems. According to this meta-narrative, 'it is now possible to design and create markets for previously intractable policy problems' (NMBIWG, 2005: 5). Market-based instruments (MBIs) construct property rights and exchange mechanisms that allow environmental protection to occur where it can be achieved at lowest cost. Continuing the project of economic liberalization by dismantling trade barriers and removing production subsidies facilitates innovation and structural adjustment among producers as they begin to internalize the costs of environmental protection. Applied to climate change, it is postulated that these measures will allow growth in economic activity and material living standards while avoiding politically unpalatable constraints on consumption. Non-market mechanisms are not removed from the policy mix altogether (McKibbin, 2007), but are always secondary and play short-term roles in emergency management and structural adjustment (Garnaut, 2008).

So do market instruments offer elegant solutions to otherwise immensely complex problems? While it is impossible to forecast exactly how effective market-based climate-change policy will be, the meta-narrative of environmental governance through 'the market' is not unique to climate change and it is possible to examine the application of MBIs in other arenas of environmental governance with a view to engaging more productively in debates over their possibilities and limitations in relation to climate-change mitigation and adaptation. This chapter will do so in the context of agri-environmental policy measures implemented in Australia over the last two decades that have sought, in a variety of ways, to address environmental issues through economic means (Higgins and Lockie, 2002). These measures have certainly been criticized for failing to deliver sufficient environmental outcomes (Lockie, 2006) and might, on that basis, raise concerns about the adequacy of market-based approaches. However, Australian agri-environmental measures have also undergone significant adaptation over this period, and illustrate both the potential flexibility of strategies within a market paradigm and the considerable technical work that has been devoted to refining instruments of market rule. The chapter will begin by providing an overview of what will be referred to as neoliberal environmental governance and the conceptual tools that will be used to interrogate the specific case of agri-environmental governance in Australia.

Conceptualizing environmental governance through 'the market'
The term neoliberalism is used, often loosely, to denote an array of governmental ideologies and strategies based on the unitary logic of 'the market'. Market-based instruments for environmental protection do not emanate from a single uniform neoliberal manifesto or toolkit, but from a contested, spatially uneven and flexible process of experimentation in economic and social reform (see Brenner and Theodore, 2002; McCarthy and Prudham, 2004). Peck and Tickell (2002) illustrate this by contrasting two broad periods of neoliberalization in the USA and the UK. The first they characterize as 'rollback'

neoliberalization: the withdrawal of governments during the 1980s from productive activities and the dismantling of regulatory systems wherever these were seen to interfere with the efficient operation of markets (see also Larner, 2003 in relation to New Zealand). Rollback neoliberalization was evident in the sale of state enterprises, the winding back of social welfare programmes, the deregulation of financial markets, the abolition of centralized marketing authorities for agricultural commodities and so on. The second period Peck and Tickell (2002) characterize as 'rollout' neoliberalization which – in contrast to the destructive tendencies of rollback policies – saw renewed attention through the 1990s to institution-building and government intervention. These did not represent a return to the social protections of the Keynesian era, but a series of attempts to deal with the contradictions and consequences of rollback neoliberalization through the extension of market discipline to social policy. This occurred in a number of outwardly contradictory ways, including: increased reliance on technocratic and politically independent management regimes in respect of monetary policy, trade, labour market regulation and so on; the introduction of interventionist, and often punitive, social policies in relation to issues such as crime, welfare, immigration etc; and the promotion of partnerships between the public and private sectors in economic and social policy (Peck and Tickell, 2002; Larner, 2003).

At face value, dominant policy approaches to climate change represent a paradigmatic example of rollout neoliberalization – in this case through the extension of market discipline to the arena of environmental policy in response to the negative environmental externalities of economic growth and industrialization. Market-based instruments are not seen by their advocates as alternatives to state action but as the most effective and efficient ways to achieve the objectives of government (McKibbin, 2007). According to Garnaut (2008), the role of government is to fix market failures, not to pick technological or industrial winners. An effective market-based system, he argues, must be as broadly based as possible, with any exclusions driven by practical necessity and not by short-term political considerations. Policies should be avoided that seek either to impose additional regulation on specific activities or to push investment towards favoured technologies or consumption practices. Garnaut (2008) claims that such policies will not lead to any net improvement in abatement. At best, they will change the mix of mitigation activities while delivering the same emissions reduction. More likely, they will create additional transaction costs and perverse incentives that increase the total cost of GHG abatement while reducing flexibility and innovation. State interventions that stretch beyond the creation and regulation of markets, Garnaut (2008: 317) argues, 'presuppose that government officials, academics or scientists have a better understanding of consumer preferences and technological opportunities than households and businesses. This is generally unlikely and cannot ever be guaranteed.'

While economic advisers such as Stern and Garnaut recognize a role for public investment in R&D, education, transport and infrastructure, etc., such measures are complementary and limited. The primary role of government remains that of correcting market failure through the design of MBIs that place an appropriate cost on GHG emissions.

This vision of a market-based approach in which politics and politicians are removed from the day-to-day regulation of business and consumer activity resonates as much with environmentalist concerns about the need for a long-term and comprehensive approach to GHG abatement as it does with liberal ideologies of small government and individual freedom. However, the depoliticization of environmental regulation and decision-making that advocates of neoliberalization envisage is superficial and belies the extent to which market discipline – technocratically imposed and administered by centralized state and quasi-state agencies – reduces opportunity for political debate and contestation (see Peck and Tickell, 2002: 389). MBIs may, in fact, be counted among a number of techniques deployed by neoliberal regimes to extend their influence (i.e. to govern) 'at a distance' (Miller and Rose, 1990). In addition to the MBIs already discussed in this chapter, Dean (1999) identifies two interrelated categories of governmental technique associated with neoliberalization. The first are 'technologies of agency' that attempt to enable and encourage a calculative and prudent approach to self-government by members of a population. Examples include welfare-to-work programmes for the long-term unemployed (Dean, 1998), active citizenship programmes such as neighbourhood watch (O'Malley, 1992), and planning programmes designed to improve the financial and natural resource management capabilities of farmers and other producers (Lockie, 1999; Higgins, 2001). Technologies of agency may be scaled up to various aggregations of actors through partnerships between state agencies, professionals and community groups aimed at empowering targeted populations to become self-managing. The second category comprises 'technologies of performance' that provide the means through which self-government may be monitored, informed and, where necessary, held to account. Examples include audit (Power, 1994), accountancy (Miller and O'Leary, 1987) and measures of best practice (Lockie, 1998a). In combination, and despite their appearance of political neutrality, technologies of agency and performance generate novel opportunities for the imposition or expansion of centralized control by state agencies and other organizations at the same time that responsibility and accountability for tactical decision-making and outcomes (whether economic, social or environmental) are devolved to localized communities, producer/industry groups, individuals and so on (Muetzelfeldt, 1992).

It is tempting, in light of the above, to construe neoliberalization as a process that is somehow sinister or underhand. Doing so, however, potentially confuses the techniques and consequences of this process with the motivation and intent of its advocates. It is useful, therefore, to consider the analysis of neoliberalism offered by Foucault (1991) – an analysis that shifts our focus from the processes of neoliberal experimentation, and the techniques deployed through this process, to the rationalities, or ways of thinking, that underlie them. According to Foucault, rationalities of governance inform the 'conduct of conduct' by rendering potential objects of intervention knowable and actionable. Rationalities of governance define the boundaries of acceptable intervention in the affairs of others and offer strategies for that intervention. The rationality of classical liberalism, for example, constructed the individual subject as an independent actor over whom the state may legitimately exert little influence. Neoliberal rationalities, by contrast, have reconstructed the individual as a behaviourally 'manipulable being' who may be counted on to respond rationally and entrepreneurially to changing environmental variables (Lemke, 2001: 200). Through the promotion of market relations, neoliberals have thus sought to influence the environment within which people make decisions (Miller and Rose, 1990), and the ways in which they are likely to understand and respond to that environment (Burchell, 1993). Neoliberal rationality thus suggests that 'to govern better, the state must govern less' (Rose, 1999: 139); optimizing social outcomes through 'the regulated and accountable choices of autonomous agents' (Rose, 1993: 298).

While the process and techniques of neoliberalization have undergone substantial adaptation in the face of contestation and setbacks, the underlying rationality of neoliberal governance has remained the dominant ideological and political project of the post-Keynesian era (McCarthy and Prudham, 2004). Even in the face of negative environmental externalities as significant as global climate change, alternatives to the market-based approach have become almost unthinkable. Certainly, where non-market measures are implemented in other areas of environmental policy, they are, more often than not, subject to disputation over their potential to distort trade. Australian agri-environmental measures over the last two decades are of particular interest in this context. While it is impossible to extrapolate directly from experience with these measures to the likely effectiveness of market-based GHG mitigation, Australian agri-environmental measures do illustrate the ways in which experimentation in the techniques of neoliberal governance – in response to the contradictions and limitations of existing neoliberal techniques – may both extend the process of neoliberalization and generate new contradictions and limitations.

Neoliberal governance and Australian agricultural environments
Under the Australian constitution, governmental responsibility for the management of natural resources rests predominantly with state and territory governments; the role of the Commonwealth (or national government) is reserved for matters of distinctly national importance. Before the 1980s, the responses of state and territory governments to issues of agricultural land and water degradation were mostly reactive and focused on the provision, on a voluntary basis, of technical assistance and/or education to those landholders who requested it. Experimentation in various forms of integrated catchment (watershed) management was limited and what few legal provisions existed to compel landholders to improve their resource management were seldom used (see Barr and Cary, 1992). The shift to a more proactive and national approach in the late 1980s was presaged on at least three developments. First, and probably foremost, among these was the emergence, on a massive scale, of soil salinity in Victoria and Western Australia and increasingly compelling evidence of the economic and environmental cost nationwide of a range of land and water degradation issues including soil erosion, compaction and acidification, weeds, feral animals and so on (Madden et al., 2000). Second was acceptance by key figures in the Commonwealth government, including the Prime Minister, of the need for national leadership and funding to address resource degradation following a submission on this issue in 1988 by a coalition of peak farming and conservation groups: the National Farmers' Federation (NFF) and the Australian Conservation Foundation (ACF) (Toyne and Farley, 1989). Third was the consistency of measures proposed in this submission with the neoliberal rationality that was informing an ambitious and, at times, aggressive process of micro- and macroeconomic reform. Australian governments had, in fact, embarked on a programme of neoliberalization with an enthusiasm matched by few others (DAFF, 2005). On the macroeconomic front, import duties and export subsidies were removed while, on the microeconomic front, statutory marketing boards, production quotas and other means of collectivizing risk among Australian farmers were dismantled. As a consequence, Australian farmers now receive an effective rate of subsidization of only 4 per cent of gross income compared with 58 per cent in Japan, 37 per cent in Europe and 18 per cent in the USA (DAFF, 2005).

Higgins and Lockie (2002) characterize the programmes that were implemented following the Commonwealth's entry, in a major way, into agri-environmental policy as hybrid forms of neoliberal governance in which social and environmental objectives are pursued through the parallel pursuit of economic rationality. As with processes of neoliberalization more generally, the specific techniques through which neoliberal rationality has been operationalized within agri-environmental governance have adapted and changed over time in response to emergent contradictions and limitations (Lockie and Higgins, 2007). Hajkowicz (2009) thus identifies three phases of Commonwealth involvement in agri-environmental governance since the late 1980s: (1) raising awareness and changing attitudes; (2) building new institutional capacity; and (3) towards direct payments?

Phase 1: raising awareness and changing attitudes
The joint NFF/ACF proposal for a National Land Management Program argued for 'the importance of a self-help approach, which [relied] heavily upon local community groups, within a framework which recognise[d] the responsibilities of Local, State and Federal Governments' (Toyne and Farley, 1989: 6). The National Landcare Program (NLP), initiated the following year, took as its primary focus the promotion and support of community Landcare groups and limited funding was made available to groups to assist in group coordination, to establish experimental and demonstration sites, and to undertake training in property planning and other management techniques (Campbell, 1994). The main focus of financial support, therefore, was on educational, research and planning activities that were believed likely to promote change, cooperation and investment among the wider farming community. Very little was made available for direct expenditure on environmental works. Hajkowicz's (2009) characterization of this phase in Commonwealth policy as one directed towards awareness-raising and attitude change among the rural community is not inaccurate; certainly, a key goal of the NLP was to improve understanding of environmental degradation and to promote an ethic of care towards rural environments. However, community Landcare groups were not seen simply as a low-cost mechanism through which to diffuse information and promote attitude change. The networking and capacity-building activities of these groups were also seen to encourage social learning and risk-taking that capitalized on (and respected) the local knowledge of Landcare group members; encouraged landholders to coordinate their activities on a catchment or sub-catchment basis; made better use of the resources of state government agencies and the agribusiness sector; and, ultimately, reduced the personal and financial costs to landholders of redressing degradation (Lockie, 1998b; Scott, 1998).

The NLP may be described both as an early example of rollout neoliberalization and as an approach to agri-environmental governance that relied primarily on technologies of agency to promote and enable voluntary change. At the same time that institutional innovation and capacity-building were used to encourage farmers to recognize a 'duty of care' to the environment and to internalize environmental costs (Industry Commission, 1997), great care was taken not to infringe farmers' perceived property rights (Reeve, 2001), increase direct regulation, or introduce *de facto* barriers to trade. Additional programmes were introduced to address other aspects of 'market failure' by, for example, creating property rights and markets for water and by removing perverse incentives such as tax rebates for land clearing (Industry Commission, 1997). Steps were also taken to integrate the rollout features of the NLP and other natural resource management schemes with the rollback measures to which farmers were also subject at the time (see above). Most notably, the 1992 National Drought Policy (NDP) linked drought assistance to both the NLP and the Rural Adjustment Scheme (RAS) – a programme that existed principally to assist financially marginal farmers to leave the industry and free up resources for more productive investment. The NDP defined climatic variability and dryness not as 'natural disasters' but as predictable and manageable features of the Australian landscape – business risks that prudent and entrepreneurial farmers should be able to plan for and around (Higgins, 2001). It followed that the welfare measures traditionally used to support 'drought-stricken' farmers should be replaced with capacity-building programmes for those farmers who were deemed viable, or likely to achieve viability, and structural adjustment programmes for those who were not. Direct subsidies were made available for participation in property and catchment planning to farmers applying through community Landcare groups. In some respects, the NDP has been a failure. An 'exceptional circumstances' provision within the policy that enabled continued welfare support for those farmers experiencing 'rare and severe events outside normal risk management strategies' (Rural Adjustment Scheme Advisory Council, 1996: 25) became the most widely used programme within the RAS (Higgins and Lockie, 2002). However, as Higgins (2001: 312) argues, it remains the case that the linking of the NLP, NDP and RAS played a key role in redefining those circumstances where risk was deemed to be individual rather than social and, further, redefined those latter circumstances where risk was determined to be social as opportunities to encourage farmers in 'temporary difficulties' to develop their '*future capacities* for profitability'.

Phase 2: building new institutional capacity
The National Landcare Program achieved high levels of participation (over one-third of farm businesses in the broadacre[2] and dairy sectors) and was successful in promoting changes in land management among both members and non-members (ABARE, 2003). However, following over a decade of support for this programme it was found that while Landcare activities had contributed significantly to the maintenance of productivity at the field and farm levels, catchment health indicators such as water quality were continuing to decline across most of Australia (CSIRO, 2003). This review attributed the lack of cumulative regional outcomes to a combination of uneven implementation of improved management practices and the understandable (indeed, economically rational) emphasis of many groups and members on management practices that maintained or improved productivity at the farm level (see also Lockie, 1999, 2006). A more longstanding popular criticism of the NLP was that the minimal funding of on-ground works failed to recognize the difficult terms of trade faced by farmers and their limited capacity to finance such works themselves, particularly where the main benefits of environmental works were off-site, long-term, or unlikely to boost productivity (see Lockie, 2006).

In 1999, the Commonwealth released a discussion paper that signalled two key changes in its approach to natural resource management (NNRMTF, 1999; see also Dibden and Cocklin, 2005; Hajkowicz, 2009). This paper proposed that the capacity-building and awareness-raising elements of Landcare be supplemented: first, with greater use of MBIs designed to create incentives for resource protection; and second, by the devolution of significant resources to the regional level for investment in natural resource management (NRM). Further, instead of regarding these as separate measures, the discussion paper proposed that regional communities decide for themselves the appropriate mix of 'economic instruments, projects, regulations and so on' (NNRMTF, 1999: 15). Fifty-six regional NRM bodies were recognized or established with responsibility to develop regional NRM plans that identified significant natural resource issues while taking account of the environmental, social and economic aspects of these issues and ensuring that the full range of local interests, including those of non-landholders, were represented (Australian Government, 2005). Regional NRM plans were thus intended to ensure that while – through new programmes including the Natural Heritage Trust and the National Action Plan for Salinity and Water Quality – the Commonwealth was increasing direct expenditure on environmental works on private land, expenditure was targeted on works of regional priority and therefore maximum public benefit. Building the institutional capacity to do this has come, according to Hajkowicz (2009), at high cost, with expenditures through regional NRM groups between 2002–03 and 2005–06 directed in roughly equal proportions to on-ground works (including tree planting, weed control and fencing) and to capacity-building, resource assessment and planning.

The regionalization of NRM programmes relevant to agri-environmental governance appears to have deepened processes of rollout neoliberalization. While regionalization provided an avenue through which to direct higher levels of Commonwealth funding, this funding did not increase to such an extent that the need for private investment, on a much larger scale, was obviated. The institution-building activity exemplified by regional NRM groups served to reinforce the devolution of responsibility and accountability, leaving vaguely defined regional communities to resolve for themselves how to stimulate behavioural change; mobilize resources among private landholders; resolve contradictions between the public and private benefits of environmental works; monitor and report on the outcomes of government expenditure; and so on.

Phase 3: towards direct payments?
It is notable that for all the resource assessment, regional planning and institutional development that accompanied the devolution of funding to regional NRM groups, the kinds of on-ground activities that have been promoted, to date, by most of these groups have not differed substantially from those activities promoted by and through community Landcare groups. Certainly, the delivery mechanism has changed and, with it, the potential to target funding to areas identified as being of catchment-level priority and to landholders not directly involved in Landcare groups. Technologies of performance have also been introduced that, at least at the regional level, establish accountability for the monitoring and reporting of changes in resource condition. However, the use of more novel technologies of agri-environmental governance (in particular, MBIs) has been limited. This does not, it is suggested here, represent a failure on the part of regional groups. Rather, it reflects the inherent complexity involved in translating the economic theory behind MBIs into workable programmes and techniques of governance. But with government interest in new approaches to agri-environmental governance high, a National MBI Pilot Program was initiated in 2002 to encourage regional groups to test their potential to meet a variety of NRM objectives. Eleven projects were funded between 2003 and 2005 (NMBIWG, 2005). Four of these used auction systems to direct payments to those landholders prepared to provide a given environmental service at lowest cost.

In each case, the sole or primary environmental service of interest was biodiversity. Five projects used cap-and-trade and/or offset schemes to address soil salinity and water quality. Other projects examined conservation insurance and leveraged investments. The focus of nine Round 2 projects announced in late 2006 was the refinement of auction and offset instruments in order to improve cost-effectiveness, increase participation, deal better with uncertainty, ensure compliance and so on.

Official evaluations of the National MBI Pilot Program conclude that MBIs are capable of engaging landholders, encouraging voluntary change, effectively targeting public expenditure through appropriate metrics, and thereby delivering ecosystem services at significantly lower cost than grants programmes and other measures (NMBIWG, 2005). An independent study of three MBI projects undertaken by regional groups in Queensland found that low-cost, short-term and reportable outcomes certainly were possible. In particular, auction schemes were cost-effective in protecting valued ecosystems (in comparison with resuming land and establishing national parks), building understanding of the relationships between biodiversity and productivity, and promoting changes in management practice (Freckleton and Lockie, 2009). However, the extent and durability of outcomes were questionable on several fronts. First, the limited timeframe of funding support to regional groups meant that incentives were necessarily short term. Second, payments rarely covered the full cost to landholders of providing the desired ecosystem service. Third, as a consequence, MBI programmes tended to involve landholders who were likely to have provided those services without financial incentives (or, indeed, were already doing so). Fourth, despite the closed nature of the tender process, landholders were loath to underbid their neighbours and establish a genuinely competitive process. Fifth, the metrics used to measure compliance with obligations did not necessarily provide meaningful information on biodiversity or other environmental outcomes. Sixth, despite their use of a market mechanism for the allocation of resources, none of the schemes demonstrated evidence that they were likely to provide an adjustment function leading to the longer-term correction of market failure – a correction that would require the cost of protecting environmental values supporting the sustainability of agricultural production to be passed on through the value chain.

Nevertheless, the perceived success of auction schemes in delivering diffuse source environmental outcomes (NMBIWG, 2005) was behind a new Commonwealth Environmental Stewardship Program announced in 2007 (Hajkowicz, 2009). Under this programme, 'land managers will be paid to undertake agreed actions beyond their regulated responsibilities to achieve public benefit environmental outcomes' (Australian Government, 2007: 3). Hajkowicz (2009) argues that this is significant in demonstrating a growing willingness by the Australian Commonwealth to make direct payments to farmers for the provision of ecosystem services. However, it is important to note that, in doing so, the Commonwealth is not heading down a path that might be seen to compromise its commitment to neoliberalization. The environmental services that will be purchased through the 'Stewardship Program' are only those that relate to nationally endangered or vulnerable species, migratory species and wetlands, and natural values associated with world and national heritage places. In other words, not only is native biodiversity the only issue being considered for funding under this programme; the programme treats the conservation of native biodiversity as an ecosystem service in its own right. Tenders to provide this service will be evaluated according to the ability of landholders to protect native species from agriculture, not to enhance the sustainability of agriculture through the development of more biologically diverse agro-ecosystems. While this is consistent with neoliberal rationality in the sense that subsidies will not be paid for the protection of what are primarily private benefits, it remains the case that this programme is no more likely than those MBIs offered by regional groups to correct the 'market failures' that make it difficult for farmers to internalize the full environmental costs of production in the first place.

Agriculture, climate change and the market

In late 2008, the Australian government announced details of its Carbon Pollution Reduction Scheme (CPRS); a cap-and-trade MBI programme intended to commence in 2010 as the major policy response to anthropogenic climate change (Australian Government, 2008). Agriculture is not to be included in this scheme until at least 2015, and possibly not even then, with a decision on the matter deferred until 2013. This may seem surprising. It is estimated that in 2006, for example, agriculture contributed approximately 16 per cent of Australia's total GHG emissions, some 92 per cent of which came from the ruminant livestock sector (Australian Government, 2008; Garnaut, 2008). In the absence of reduced global GHG emissions, it is expected that declining rainfall in eastern and southern Australia will see significant declines in agricultural production (Hennessy et al., 2007). Further, as we have seen, governments have declared experimentation in the application of MBIs to agri-environmental management successful. So why then is agriculture to be excluded? The simple answer is that it is too complex: the technical expertise does not exist either to monitor the on-farm balance of GHG sequestration and emissions or to manage the compliance costs of including over 100000 relatively small business units in the CPRS (by comparison, only 1000 enterprises will exceed the emissions threshold set for the inclusion of non-agricultural businesses) (see Australian Government, 2008).

The Commonwealth is currently disposed to shift the obligation for GHG emissions to other points in the supply chain such as fertilizer suppliers, abattoirs and exporters, while finding other ways to encourage (or mandate) on-farm abatement that results in a similar cost of mitigation per tonne of carbon equivalent as that established through the cap-and-trade market (Australian Government, 2008). There are numerous potential problems with this proposal. First, displacing liability for GHG emissions to other points in the supply chain does not resolve the technical issues of generating a reliable estimate of the emissions on which those liabilities are based. Second, no mechanism is created in doing so for up- and downstream businesses to pass these liabilities on to farmers in a manner that is sensitive to the impact of farm management practices on emissions (thereby creating a price signal that actually addresses the source of market failure). Third, no clear purpose is served by shifting liability if alternative measures are to be set in place to mandate abatement on-farm. Fourth, basing the price of agricultural GHG mitigation on cost parity with the CPRS assumes that the most efficient and effective level of investment by farmers is the same as that determined by a market in which the only participants are 1000 of the country's largest emitters (an assumption for which there is no evidence). Fifth, no consideration is given to the potential for agricultural land managers either to sequester carbon or to capitalize on the ecosystem services that sequestered carbon may provide. Sixth, no concrete measures are proposed to assist in the process of adaptation to unavoidable climate change.

The Commonwealth may, or may not, modify its policy position on agricultural GHG emissions by 2013. The question to be addressed here is what 20 years of experimentation in neoliberal governance has revealed about the effectiveness of various agri-environmental measures and the implications of this for climate change mitigation and adaptation. To begin, neoliberal agri-environmental policy in Australia has utilized a broader conceptualization of market failure and how it might be dealt with than have most major policy documents and debates regarding climate change. In contrast, for example, with MBIs such as cap-and-trade schemes that address market failure through the creation of property rights and exchange mechanisms that, in theory, allow environmental protection to occur where it can be achieved at lowest cost, measures such as Landcare seek to address market failure by providing information and by lowering the personal and financial costs of redressing degradation (Scott, 1998). The goal remains to encourage resource users to internalize the environmental costs of production without resorting to direct subsidies or other potentially trade-distorting measures, but the perceived source of market failure (inadequate understanding of the impacts of resource use) and the means through which this is addressed (self-monitoring, social learning and collaborative activity) are not seen to lie outside existing market mechanisms. Instead, by recognizing and acting on their duty of care to the environment and other resource users, farmers secure private benefits in terms of the enhanced sustainability and productivity of the resource base. To put it more bluntly, building soil organic matter and revegetating the landscape doesn't just sequester carbon and slow soil erosion; it increases farm output over the long term and consequently the financial returns to farming through conventional commodity markets.

While a significant driver in the interest of Australian governments in MBIs has been the perceived limitations of the Landcare model, experimentation with different types of MBI suggests that these also have a relatively limited range of applicability. Auction schemes have shown most promise in relation to diffuse issues such as native biodiversity conservation, while cap-and-trade schemes appear more relevant to point-source problems where the use of scarce resources (e.g. water) or the emission of pollutants (e.g. salt) can be clearly specified, monitored and policed (NMBIWG, 2005). Treating GHGs as transferable carbon equivalents certainly suits the requirements of a cap-and-trade system. However, it also treats carbon as a pollutant, the emissions of which are not only difficult to measure from agro-ecosystems, but whose role in the provision of ecosystem services within agro-ecosystems is largely ignored. A wider range of policy options, including alternative MBIs, warrants exploration if climate-change policy is to match up with the ecological and social complexity of agriculture.

It is also important to note that the MBIs introduced in Australia over recent years have been used to supplement existing agri-environmental measures and not to replace them. The capacity and network-building focus of the first two phases of neoliberal agri-environmental policy have not only been maintained; they are playing a major role in the refinement, application and targeting of MBIs on a wider scale. In contrast, climate-change policy documents such as Garnaut (2008) argue that processes of roll-back neoliberalization have created open, flexible and prosperous market-based economies that allow scarce resources to be allocated where their economic value is highest.

The assumption appears to be that exposure to rollback neoliberalization has somehow equipped businesses to deal with cap-and-trade GHG markets and that limited capacity or institution-building activity beyond the construction of these markets is therefore necessary. This is unlikely to be the case in agriculture or other sectors dominated by small- to medium-sized enterprises.

Conclusion

Neoliberal agri-environmental measures have achieved many things. The capacity and community-building focus of the 'National Landcare Program' reconciled previously competing environmental and economic policy discourses, mobilizing significant new public and private investment in environmental management at a time of rapid rollback neoliberalization across the economy more generally. With high levels of involvement in community Landcare groups, large numbers of Australian farm businesses received training in property planning and many went on to implement improved farm management practices. The rollout, or institution-building, features of Landcare set the stage in many ways for the regionalization of NRM planning and investment and for ensuing experimentation in the use of MBIs to address NRM issues. While more debate is needed over just how successful each of these measures has been, it remains the case that Australian attempts to address agri-environmental issues through the parallel pursuit of economic rationality have had some success in focusing land managers and policy-makers on issues critical to the maintenance of biodiversity, ecological processes, agricultural sustainability and so on, at the same time that they have acted to deepen the project of neoliberalization.

What neoliberal agri-environmental measures have not achieved in Australia is improvement in resource condition at the regional or national scales. This suggests that the durability of neoliberal agri-environmental governance is in no small way related to the considerable technical work that has been devoted to developing and refining new instruments of market rule in response to emergent contradictions and limitations. While the pervasiveness of neoliberal rationality has made alternatives to governance through 'the market' difficult to think, the extension of market rule has nonetheless been marked by flexibility and innovation. The difficult questions to answer at this point are whether the recent phase of innovation in neoliberal agri-environmental policy will resolve the contradictions and limitations of earlier phases, and whether the future incorporation of agriculture within a national cap-and-trade scheme for GHG emissions will be efficient and/or effective. Experience to date does not suggest that the answer to either question will necessarily be no, but it does suggest caution. The certainty with which some economists and lead agencies have proclaimed the superiority of MBIs belies the demonstrable limitations of these as already applied within Australian agricultural environments, and the considerable difficulties facing governments as they try to determine how the proposed national Carbon Pollution Reduction Scheme can be made workable with respect to agriculture. Finding a solution to this latter dilemma requires accepting that MBIs – no matter how well designed – do not necessarily resolve the underlying causes of so-called market failure. If the past two decades of experimentation in agri-environmental governance have shown anything, it is that multiple programmes and grassroots political support are required if policy is in any way to match and influence the complex web of social, ecological and economic relationships that shape rural land use.

Notes

1. This chapter draws on research undertaken with the support of the Australian Research Council (Project No. DP0664599). The author is grateful to Dr David Carpenter, Dr Christine Dann and Rebeka Freckleton for their contributions to this project.
2. An Australian term used to refer to farms practising large-scale crop production.

References

ABARE (Australian Bureau of Agricultural and Resource Economics) (2003), *Natural Resources Management on Australian Farms*, Canberra: Australian Bureau of Agricultural and Resource Economics.

Australian Government (2005), 'About natural resource management (NRM) regions', www.nrm.gov.au/about-regions/index.html, last accessed 1 May 2009.

Australian Government (2007), *Environmental Stewardship Programme Strategic Framework 2007*, Canberra: Department of Agriculture, Fisheries and Forestry and Department of the Environment and Water Resource, Commonwealth of Australia.

Australian Government (2008), *Carbon Pollution Reduction Scheme: Australia's Low Pollution Future*, Canberra: Commonwealth of Australia.

Barr, N. and J. Cary (1992), *Greening a Brown Land: The Australian Search for Sustainable Land Use*, Melbourne: Macmillan.

Brenner, N. and N. Theodore (2002), 'Cities and the geographies of actually existing neoliberalisms', *Antipode*, **34**: 349–79.

Burchell, G. (1993), 'Liberal government and techniques of the self', *Economy and Society*, **22**: 267–82.

Campbell, A. (1994), *Landcare: Communities Shaping the Land and the Future: With Case Studies by Greg Siepen*, Sydney: Allen & Unwin.

CSIRO (Commonwealth Scientific and Industrial Research Organisation) (2003), *Assessing the Impact of Landcare Activities on Natural Resource Condition. Attachment 4. Review of the National Landcare Program*, Canberra: Department of Agriculture, Fisheries and Forestry.

DAFF (Department of Agriculture, Fisheries and Forestry) (2005), *Australian Agriculture and Food Sector Stocktake*, Canberra: Commonwealth of Australia.

Dean, M. (1998), 'Administering asceticism: reworking the ethical life of the unemployed citizen', in M. Dean and B. Hindess (eds), *Governing Australia: Studies in Contemporary Rationalities of Government*, Cambridge, UK: Cambridge University Press, pp. 87–107.

Dean, M. (1999), *Governmentality: Power and Rule in Modern Society*, London: Sage.

Dibden, J. and C. Cocklin (2005), 'Agri-environmental governance', in V. Higgins and G. Lawrence (eds), *Agricultural Governance: Globalization and the New Politics of Regulation*, London: Routledge, pp. 135–52.

Foucault, M. (1991), 'Governmentality', in G. Burchell, C. Gordon and P. Miller (eds), *The Foucault Effect: Studies in Governmentality*, London: Harvester Wheatsheaf, pp. 87–104.

Freckleton, R. and S. Lockie (2009) *Market-Based Instruments and the Conservation of Biodiversity on Private Land: An Independent Evaluation of Three Pilot Projects Undertaken by Regional Natural Resource Management Groups in Queensland, Australia*, Rockhampton, Queensland: Institute for Health and Social Science Research, CQUniversity Australia.

Garnaut, R. (2008), *The Garnaut Climate Change Review: Final Report*, Melbourne: Cambridge University Press.

Hajkowicz, S. (2009), 'The evolution of Australia's natural resource management programs: towards improved targeting and evaluation of investments', *Land Use Policy*, **26**: 471–78.

Hennessy, K., B. Fitzharris, B.C. Bates, N. Harvey, S.M. Howden, L. Hughes, J. Salinger and R. Warrick (2007), 'Australia and New Zealand', in M.L. Parry, O.F. Canziani, J.P. Palutikof, P.J. van der Linden and C.E. Hanson (eds), *Climate Change 2007: Impacts, Adaptation and Vulnerability. Contribution of Working Group II to the Fourth Assessment Report of the Intergovernmental Panel on Climate Change*, Cambridge, UK: Cambridge University Press, pp. 507–40.

Higgins, V. (2001), 'Calculating climate: "advanced liberalism" and the governing of risk in Australian drought policy', *Journal of Sociology*, **37** (3): 299–316.

Higgins, V. and S. Lockie (2002), 'Re-discovering the social: neo-liberalism and hybrid practices of governing in natural resource management', *Journal of Rural Studies*, **18**: 419–28.

Industry Commission (1997), *A Full Repairing Lease: Inquiry Into Ecologically Sustainable Land Management*, Melbourne: Industry Commission.

Larner, W. (2003), 'Guest editorial: neoliberalism?', *Environment and Planning D: Society and Space*, **21**: 509–12.

Lemke, T. (2001), 'The birth of bio-politics: Michel Foucault's lecture at the Collège de France on neo-liberal governmentality', *Economy and Society*, **30**: 190–207.

Lockie, S. (1998a), 'Environmental and social risks, and the construction of "best practice" in Australian agriculture', *Agriculture and Human Values*, **15**: 243–52.

Lockie, S. (1998b), 'Landcare in Australia: cultural transformation in the management of rural environments', *Culture and Agriculture*, **20** (1): 21–9.

Lockie, S. (1999), 'The state, rural environments, and globalisation: "action at a distance" via the Australian Landcare program', *Environment and Planning A*, **31**: 597–611.

Lockie, S. (2006), 'Networks of agri-environmental action: temporality, spatiality and identity within agricultural environments', *Sociologia Ruralis*, **46** (1): 22–39.

Lockie, S. and V. Higgins (2007) 'Roll-out neoliberalism and hybrid practices of regulation in Australian agri-environmental governance', *Journal of Rural Studies*, **23** (1): 1–11.

Madden, B., G. Hayes and K. Duggan (2000), *National Investment in Rural Landscapes: An Investment Scenario for National Farmers' Federation and Australian Conservation Foundation with the Assistance of Land and Water Resources Research and Development Corporation*, Melbourne: Australian Conservation Foundation and National Farmers' Federation.

Maiden, S. (2008), 'Garnaut argues it's time to act on climate change', www.theaustralian.news.com.au/story/0,25197,24424332-11949,00.html, 30 September.

McCarthy, J. and S. Prudham (2004), 'Neoliberal nature and the nature of neoliberalism', *Geoforum*, **35**: 275–83.

McKibbin, W. (2007), 'From national to international climate change policy', *The Australian Economic Review*, **40** (4): 410–20.

Miller, P. and T. O'Leary (1987), 'Accounting and the construction of the governable person', *Accounting, Organizations and Society*, **12**: 235–65.

Miller, P. and N. Rose (1990), 'Governing economic life', *Economy and Society*, **19** (1): 1–31.

Muetzelfeldt, M. (1992), 'Economic rationalism in its social context', in M. Muetzelfeldt (ed.), *Society, State and Politics in Australia*, Sydney: Pluto Press, pp. 187–215.

NMBIWG (National Market-Based Instrument Working Group) (2005), *National Market-Based Instruments Pilot Program: Round One. An Interim Report*, Canberra: National Action Plan for Salinity and Water Quality.

NNRMTF (National Natural Resource Management Taskforce (1999), *Managing Natural Resources in Australia for a Sustainable Future*, Canberra: Agricultural, Fisheries and Forestry, Australia.

O'Malley, P. (1992), 'Risk, power and crime prevention', *Economy and Society*, **21** (3): 252–75.

Peck, J. and A. Tickell (2002), 'Neoliberalizing space', *Antipode*, **34**: 380–404.

Power, M. (1994), *The Audit Explosion*, London: Demos.

Reeve, I. (2001), 'Property rights and natural resource management: tiptoeing round the slumbering dragon', in S. Lockie and L. Bourke (eds), *Rurality Bites: The Social and Environmental Transformation of Rural Australia*, Sydney: Pluto Press, pp. 257–69.

Rose, N. (1993), 'Government, authority and expertise in advanced liberalism', *Economy and Society*, **22** (3): 283–99.

Rose, N. (1999), *Powers of Freedom: Reframing Political Thought*. Cambridge, UK: Cambridge University Press.

Rural Adjustment Scheme Advisory Council (1996), *Annual Report 1995–96*, Canberra: Australian Government Publishing Service.

Scott, F. (1998), 'Market-based approaches for sustainability', in F. Scott, G. Kaine, R. Stringer and K. Anderson (eds), *Sustainability in a Commercial Context: Market-Based Approaches*, Canberra: Land and Water Resources Research and Development Corporation, pp. 33–59.

Stern, N. (2007), *The Economics of Climate Change: The Stern Review*, Cambridge, UK: Cambridge University Press.

Stevens, B. (2007), 'Politics, elections and climate change', *Social Alternatives*, **26** (4): 10–15.

Toyne, P. and R. Farley (1989), 'A national land management program', *Australian Journal of Soil and Water Conservation*, **2** (2): 6–9.

24 Environmental reform in modernizing China
Arthur P.J. Mol

Introduction

China's unprecedented period of high economic growth transformed the nation from a developing country in the 1980s into a new global superpower in the twenty-first century. This development process has far-reaching consequences for every facet of its society. It is not just a state-directed economy turning into a successful market economic growth model, a growing importance of the service and industrial sectors *vis-à-vis* the agricultural sector, increasing integration in the global economy, and growing inequalities among the various regions within China. The transformation taking place in China has equally far-reaching impacts on the relations between different government levels; on the multiple relations between China and the outside world; on the cultural diversification that is brought in via (new) media and international exchanges; on the openness, transparency and accountability of political processes and leaders; and on the activities and organizational structures of civil society, to name but a few. Hence China is not just a transitional economy; it is a modernizing society in full transition.

And this transitional society is faced with a rapidly changing environmental profile. Given rapidly increasing industrial production, expanding domestic consumption, exponential growth of privately owned cars and consumer mobility, rising infrastructure and construction, and growing industrial output, one should not be too surprised that China's domestic environment is rapidly deteriorating. In addition, and not unlike what most industrialized nations did before, China is increasingly scouring the region and the world for natural resources to fulfil its growth needs. Wood from South-East Asia and Latin America, minerals from Africa and Australia, oil and energy from Sudan, the Middle East and Russia, and even crops such as grain and soy from various places, are accompanied by increasing greenhouse gas emissions, and deterioration of regional water and air quality. China's ecological shadow crosses its boundaries, as much as Japan's did in the 1980s and 1990s, and those of European countries did in the colonial era.

Although some might want us to believe differently, China's changing environmental profile is not an evolutionary treadmill of ongoing environmental deterioration. Since the mid-1990s – and especially since the 10th Five Year Plan 2001–06 – a growing commitment can be identified in China to address these growing environmental challenges. A circular economy, a resource-conserving and environment-friendly society (cf. the 11th Five Year Plan; You, 2007), or ecological modernization (cf. China Centre for Modernisation Research, 2007) are some of the aspirations China has set for itself. Not that China now has a solid, undisputed, well-functioning, capable, institutionalized, well-resourced and effective system of environmental management in place. But compared to a decade ago, much has changed. In this chapter we shall assess the advances China has made in coping with its environmental crisis, domestically and overseas. The objective is not primarily to evaluate whether environmental problems have been diminished or solved (see Section 2), but rather to understand how China is developing an environmental reform strategy and where this meets challenges and complications. Hence in sections 3 to 5 we investigate respectively: developments in environmental policy; the use of market actors and mechanisms, and the role of an increasingly active – but still restricted – civil society. We conclude with a more international perspective on China's environmental reform challenges.

Assessing China's environmental profile

Assessing environmental information
Nationally, the Environmental Monitoring Centre (EMC), based in Beijing, plays an important role in environmental data collection and data processing, whereas the State Environmental Protection Agency (SEPA, in 2008 renamed the Ministry of Environmental Protection, MEP) is responsible for environmental data publication and disclosure. With around 2300 national environmental monitoring stations in more than 350 cities, China has an extensive monitoring network. The EMC is responsible for quality control and certification of the monitoring stations, and is financed from the state budget via SEPA. The EMC also partly finances local monitoring institutions (environmental protection bureaux – EPBs), but only for those tasks that are related to the national monitoring system. Wealthy local EPBs often have additional, locally funded, environmental monitoring programmes. There is very little exchange of environmental data between the EMC and SEPA on the one hand, and other ministries (such as those on water, forestry and energy) on the other.

If we disregard the national level and the more wealthy eastern provinces and cities and move instead to poorer regions and local levels, a much less favourable picture emerges of environmental monitoring and information in China:

- scarce environmental monitoring as a significant part of environmental monitoring needs to be funded by the local governments, which have limited budgets and different priorities;
- distortion in information processing;[1]
- secrecy and commoditization of environmental data for large segments of society; also, for instance, for scientific institutes;
- absence of a right-to-know code, legislation, or practice, at both the national and the local levels;
- limited publication and availability of non-secret data as a result of poor reporting at the local level, no active policy towards publication and dissemination, and limited Internet use and access.

Often only general and aggregate official data are publicly available, and then only for political decision-makers, and specific local emission data are lacking or kept secret for those directly involved in and suffering from environmental pollution. Consequently, local EPBs rely strongly on citizen complaints as monitoring data, and priorities for control and enforcement are more than incidentally set accordingly, instead of relying on 'scientific' monitoring and data collection programmes. In addition to, and partly as a consequence of, these problems, reliability and completeness of environmental data remain major problems. But there is a clear tendency to further public disclosure, and to improve and modernize environmental monitoring systems. For instance, the present 11th Five Year Plan (2006–10) has reserved RMB 60 billion (around €5.5 billion) for the entire environmental monitoring system. In 2008, China published the Environmental Information Disclosure Decree[2] and, by the end of the year, expected to have three additional satellites in the air for environmental protection and disaster control monitoring.

Within the field of environmental governance, the use of digital technologies has improved data collection and data availability. The website of SEPA/MEP, as well as many websites of provincial and local EPBs, contain numerous environmental laws and texts, large quantities of data on environmental investments and environmental quality, citizen complaints, and sometimes even data on emissions. Compared to the e-governance structures in OECD countries, however, there are very few possibilities for citizens to participate, to gain insight into the procedures of policy-making and lawmaking, or to forward ideas and comments. The e-government initiatives on the environment are also one-way, top-down initiatives, without any input from citizen discussion groups or non-governmental organizations (NGOs). Chinese government websites are superb at providing texts, regulations and laws, but generally lack possibilities for citizens to interact with the government or allow a means for citizen consultation. This means that these EPA websites can play only a minor role in issues of accountability, transparency, legitimacy and responsiveness.

Assessing environmental performance
Arguably, information distortion, the discontinuities in environmental statistics, limited data on emissions and the absence of longitudinal environmental data should make us cautious about drawing any firm conclusions on China's environmental performance. But the existing data do give us a sense of environmental performance tendencies.

All air emissions show a relative decline per unit of GDP. Concentrations of sulphur dioxide, nitrogen oxides, carbon monoxide and to some extent total particulate matter show an absolute decline in most major Chinese cities between the mid-1990s and 2000, but sometimes an increase again in the new millennium (Rock, 2002; SEPA, 2007). This is particularly the case with particulates, which continue to be one of the key worries of urban environmental authorities. Chlorofluorocarbon (CFC) production as well as consumption show continuing decreasing levels from the mid-1990s onwards, due to the closure of companies and a commitment to implement the Montreal Protocol. It is reported (but also contested) that emissions of carbon dioxide have fallen between 1996 and 2000, despite continuing economic growth (Sinton and Fridley, 2001, 2003; Chandler et al., 2002); but agreement exists on the increase of carbon dioxide emissions since then. Following strong reforestation programmes and stringent deforestation monitoring, forest coverage shows an increase in the new millennium. Most other environmental indicators show a delinking between environmental impacts and economic growth. Many absolute environmental indicators (total levels of emissions; total energy use) show less clear signs of improvements. For example, water pollution in terms of biological oxygen demand stabilized in absolute terms in the new millennium, but decreased per unit of GDP (SEPA 2007; NSB/MEP, 2009).

More indirect indicators that suggest similar relative improvements are the increase in governmental environmental investments (see Figure 24.1) and the growth in (domestic and industrial) wastewater treatment plants during the last decade. The increase of firms

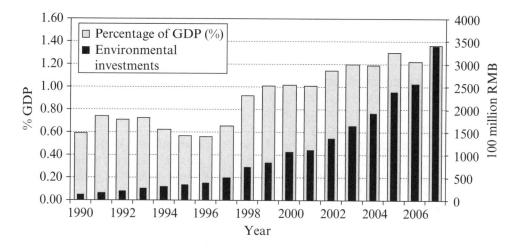

Source: *China Statistical Yearbook on Environment*, various editions.

Figure 24.1   *Chinese government environmental investments, 1990–2007: absolute (in 100 million RMB) and as percentage of GDP*

certified to ISO 14001 standards (from nine in 1996, to around 1000 in 2001, to over 30 000 by the end of 2007; http://www.iso.ch/iso/), large-scale closures of heavily polluting factories following influential environmental campaigns during the second half of the 1990s (Nygard and Guo, 2001) and also in the new millennium, and the so-called 'environmental storms' organized by SEPA/MEP during the first decade of this millennium point in a similar direction.

Obviously, these positive signs should not distract us from the fact that overall China remains heavily polluted; that emissions are more than incidentally above (and environmental quality levels below) international standards; that in 2007 less than 50 per cent of the municipal wastewater was treated before discharge (though 85 per cent of industrial wastewater, according to SEPA data); and that environmental and resource efficiencies of production and consumption processes are overall still rather low. While relative improvements can certainly be identified, absolute levels of emissions, pollution, resource extraction and environmental quality often do not yet meet standards.

How is contemporary China dealing with these current and prospective environmental threats and risks? What mechanisms, dynamics and institutional innovations can we identify in China's system of environmental governance? We shall group our analyses of innovations and transitions in China's environmental governance system into four major categories: political modernization of the 'environmental state'; the role of economic actors and market dynamics; emerging civil-society institutions; and processes of international integration.

Transitions in the 'environmental state'

The start of serious involvement by the Chinese government in environmental protection more or less coincided with the introduction of economic reforms in the late 1970s. Following the promulgation of the state Environmental Protection Law in 1979 (revised in 1989), China began systematically to establish her environmental regulatory system. In 1984, environmental protection was defined as a national basic policy and key principles for environmental protection in China were proposed. Subsequently, a national regulatory framework was formulated, composed of a series of environmental laws (on all the major environmental sectors, starting with marine protection and water in 1982 and 1984), executive regulations, standards and measures. At a national level, China now has more than 20 environmental laws adopted by the National People's Congress, over 140 executive regulations issued by the State Council, and a series of sector regulations and environmental standards set by the Ministry of Environmental Protection (MEP). More recently, several remarkable new environmental laws have been drafted and partly implemented. These include the Cleaner Production Promotion Law (cf. Mol and Liu, 2005), the Environmental Information Disclosure Decree (of 2008), and the Law on Promoting Circular Economy (of 2009).

Institutionally, the national regulatory framework is vertically implemented through a four-tier management system, i.e. national, provincial, municipal and county levels. The latter three levels are governed directly by their corresponding authorities in terms of both finance and personnel management, while the Ministry of Environmental Protection is responsible only for their substantial operation. The enactment of the various environmental laws, instruments and regulations during the last two decades was paralleled by a stepwise increase of the bureaucratic status and capacity of these environmental authorities. For instance, the National Environmental Protection Bureau was elevated to the National Environmental Protection Agency (in 1988), and in 1998 it received ministerial status as the SEPA. In 2008 it was turned into the Ministry of Environmental Protection. By 1995, the 'environmental state' had over 88 000 employees across China and by 2007 it had grown to over 170 000 (see Figure 24.2). Although the expansion of the 'environmental state' sometimes met stagnation (e.g. the relegation of EPB in many counties from second-tier to third-tier organs in 1993), over a period of 20 years the growth in quantity and quality of environmental officials is impressive (especially when compared with the shrinking of other state bureaucracies).

The state apparatus in China remains of paramount importance in environmental protection and reform. Both the nature of the contemporary Chinese social order and the character of the environment as a public good will safeguard the crucial position of the state in environmental protection and reform for some time. Environmental interests are articulated in particular by the impressive rise of environmental protection bureaux (EPBs) at various governmental levels. However, the most common complaints from Chinese and foreign environmental analysts focus precisely on this system of (local) EPBs. The local EPBs are heavily dependent on both the higher-level environmental authorities and on local governments. However, as little importance is given to environmental criteria in assessing the performance of local governments, they often display limited interest in stringent environmental reform, yet they play a key role in financing the local EPBs (see Lo and Tang, 2006). There are also poor (financial) incentives for either governments or private actors to comply with environmental laws, standards and policies. Environmental fines can be levied at a maximum of 200 000 RMB (around €18 000) at the moment, but on average they are much lower (around 10 000 RMB; cf. Table 24.1). Not surprisingly, therefore, there is a significant level of collusion between local officials and private enterprises, which 'employ' them in order to get around strict

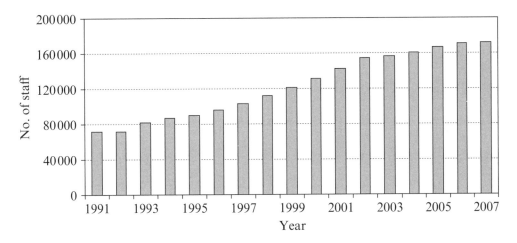

Source: China Environment Statistical Report, various editions.

Figure 24.2   Governmental staff employed for environmental protection in China, 1991–2007

Table 24.1   Environmental fines in China, 2001–06

	2001	2002	2003	2004	2005	2006
Enforcement cases	71 089	100 103	92 818	80 079	93 265	92 404
Total fines (million RMB)	240	302	329	460	641	964
Fine per case (RMB)	3377	3017	3546	5747	6868	10 427

Source: China National Environmental Enforcement Statistics, 2001–06.

environmental monitoring. Finally, local EPBs are criticized for their poor environmental capacity (in both qualitative and quantitative terms) and, more generally, for the lack (and distortion) of environmental information.

Yet the environmental state in China is clearly undergoing a political modernization process, where traditional hierarchical lines and conventional divisions of power are transformed. I shall mention four main tendencies. First, decentralization and more flexibility are paralleled by moving away from a rigid, hierarchical, command-and-control system of environmental governance. Increasingly local EPBs and local governments are given – and are taking – larger degrees of freedom in developing environmental priorities, strategies, financial models and institutional arrangements (cf. Lo and Tang, 2006). This parallels broader tendencies of decentralization in Chinese society, but it is also specifically motivated by state failures in environmental policy. The tendency is one towards greater influence and decision-making power by the local authorities and diminishing control by Beijing, both by the central state structures and by the Communist Party of China (CPC). Decentralization and greater flexibility may result in environmental policies that are better adapted to the local physical and socioeconomic situations. But in order to be effective, decentralization needs to be paralleled by accountability mechanisms and local incentives to give environment priority. There are various developments in this direction. The central state has refined its system of evaluation and accountability towards local leaders.[3] The Quantitative Examination System for Comprehensive Urban Environmental Control and the National Environmental Model City programme are key in this. Through such mechanisms, local leaders are no longer judged and rewarded only according to political and economic criteria, but also according to environmental results. Mayors are often required to sign documents guaranteeing that they meet certain environmental targets or raise their city to Environmental Model City status within a few years. In addition, citizens and civil society are given and taking more room to hold irresponsible state and company behaviour accountable, facilitated by a stronger rule of law (see below).

A larger degree of freedom for local authorities does result, for better or for worse, in a growing diversity among the Chinese provinces and towns in how they deal with local and regional environmental challenges. It also contributes to differences in success and failure, divided along lines of economic prosperity, where the richer eastern provinces and towns are systematically more concerned with, and prepared to invest in, environmental reform. But also within the eastern part of China, differences in environmental prioritization among towns can be found.

A second transition in environmental governance follows the separation of state-owned enterprises (SOEs) and the line ministries and local governments (in the case of Town and Village Enterprises) that were originally responsible for them. There is a steady process of transferring decision-making on production units from political and party influence to economic domains, where the logics of markets and profits are dominant. Although local-level governments in particular are often reluctant to give up direct relations with successful enterprises because of the linkages to financial resources, there is an unmistakable tendency for enterprises to secure growing autonomy from political agents. This development opens opportunities for more stringent environmental control and enforcement as the 'protection' of these SOEs by line ministries and bureaux at all government levels is less direct. It also sets preferential conditions for the stronger rule of – environmental – law (see below). But it does not solve one of the key problems of environmental governance: the low priority given to environmental state organizations *vis-à-vis* their economic and other counterparts. The progress in the strengthening and empowering of China's environmental authorities is ambivalent, as is common elsewhere around the world. While the national environmental authority in Beijing has strengthened its position *vis-à-vis* other ministries and agencies,[4] this is not always the case at the local level, where more than incidentally the EPBs are part of – and thus subservient to – an economic state organization.

Third, the strengthening of the rule of law can be identified as a modernization in environmental politics, closely tied to the emergence of a market economy. The system of environmental laws has led to the setting of environmental quality standards and emission discharge levels, and the establishment of a legal framework for various implementation programmes. But the environmental programmes themselves, the administrative decisions related to the implementation of standards, and the bargaining between administrations and polluters on targets have usually been more influential for environmental reform than the laws and regulations *per se*. Being in conflict with the law is usually still

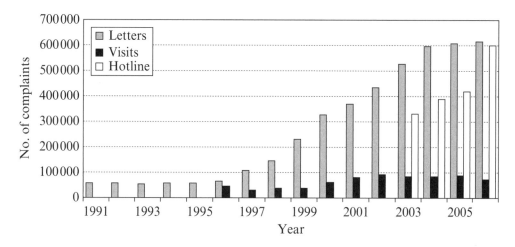

Source: *China Environment Statistical Report*, various editions.

Figure 24.3   *Environmental complaints by letters, visits and hotlines to EPBs, 1991–2006*

less problematic than being in conflict with administrations and programmes, and most of the massive clean-up programmes were not so much derived from environmental laws (although they were not in conflict with them), but rather based on administrative decisions taken at the top. The same is true for enforcement of national environmental laws at the local level. Courts have been marginally involved in enforcement and EPBs use them only as a last resort to enforce environmental laws to which polluters refuse to adhere. More recently, there are signs that the rule of law is being taken more seriously in the environmental field, also triggered by the opening up of China to the global economy and polity. This is paralleled by more formal enforcement styles of EPBs, stronger (financial) punishments of companies (see Table 24.1), and legal procedures initiated by citizens and environmental NGOs, such as the well-known Centre for Legal Assistance to Pollution Victims (CLAPV) in Beijing.

Finally, together with economic liberalization, decentralization of decision-making and experiments with local democratization, there is an increasing involvement of citizens in environmental policy-making – although still at a low level compared to Western practices. The 2003 Environmental Impact Assessment Law – and especially its 2006 public participation provisions – offers such possibilities for citizens, as the law includes stipulations on openness of information; safeguarding participants' rights; and procedures and methods for public involvement, including opinion surveys, consultations, seminars, debates and hearings. Through public hearings citizens are also involved in setting prices for water and wastewater treatment at the city level (cf. Zhong and Mol, 2008). And citizens are actively engaged in monitoring. While an environmental complaints procedure has existed for quite some time, more recently environmental authorities have stimulated (also by financial incentives) citizens to file complaints on companies and failing lower-level environmental authorities. Chinese data show sharp increases in the number of complaints sent to environmental authorities from the mid-1990s onward, to over 1 200 000 in 2006 (Figure 24.3).

Market incentives and economic actors

Traditionally, centrally planned economies did a poor job in setting the right price signals for sustainable natural resource use and minimization of environmental pollution. With a turn to a market-oriented growth model one would expect this to change. In contemporary China, environmental interests are indeed being slowly institutionalized in the economic domain of prices, markets and competition, in three ways.

First, natural resource subsidies are increasingly being abandoned so that prices for natural resources are tending to move towards cost prices. Water prices for citizens as well as industries, for instance, have increased sharply over the last decade, often at 10 per cent or more per year. The same goes for energy prices, although lower income groups are sometimes financially compensated for steep price increases (Zhong et al., 2008). Today, water and energy prices are increasingly set at cost prices, but they often do not cover costs for repair of damage and environmental externalities. Nevertheless, these increasing prices do send the right signals for water- and energy-saving measures; but also raise protests.

Second, clear attempts are being made to increase environmental fees and taxes, so that they do influence (economic) decision-making of polluters. In particular, discharge fees (on water and air), first introduced in the 1980s, have become more common, both because they are an important source of income for local EPBs and a significant trigger for the implementation of environmental measures, albeit not to the same extent everywhere. In 2007, environmental authorities received around 174 billion RMB in waste discharge fees, and this amount has been increasing over the past five years at annual rates of 20–30 per cent (NSB/MEP, 2009). Wang and Wheeler (1999) found that the fees are higher in heavily polluted and economically developed areas and that they do influence air and water emission reductions within companies. Fees are often paid only for discharging above the standard. But fees are still low, monitoring is weak, and enforcement is in the process of strengthening, so that many enterprises prefer to risk fee payment rather than installing environmental protection equipment or changing production processes. Many small and rural industries, in particular, have managed to escape payment due to lack of enforcement.

Third, market demand has started to take the environmental and health dimensions of products and production processes into account, especially in international markets that have increased so dramatically in the wake of China's accession to the WTO (see below). In China, a significant number of domestic green, organic and healthy label programmes have been established for food products[5] (but also for energy conservation, water conservation and building materials). With respect to the broad category of green food, the China Green Food Development Centre (established in 1992 under the Ministry of Agriculture) and the China Green Food Association (in 1996, also under the Ministry of Agriculture) have been active, with over 5000 certified Green Food producers, 10 million hectares (8.2 per cent of national agricultural land) and over 14000 products in 2006 (Paull, 2008). For organic food the Organic Food Certification Centre (under the Ministry of Agriculture) and the Organic Food Development Centre of China (since 1994, under SEPA/MEP) carry out inspections and certifications to national standards. Present in over one-third of the provinces in 2006, organic production comprised 600 enterprises, over 2600 products and more than 3 million hectares (Paull, 2008). Although a domestic market does exist, especially for green food products and to a lesser extent organic products, most of the organic production is destined for international, Western markets, using well-recognized labelling and certification schemes. The most important organic crops are coffee, tea, grains, nuts, dry fruits, rapeseed and sugar.

In general, however, domestic economic actors rarely articulate environmental interests. Insurance companies, banks, public utility companies, business associations, general corporations and others do not yet play any significant role in pushing for environmental reforms. Sometimes they even impede environmental improvements. For instance, local banks are not eager to lend money to polluters for environmental investments. There are three major exceptions to the absence of economic actors in the ecological modernization of the Chinese economy: large Chinese firms that operate in an international market, the environmental industry, and R&D institutions:

- Large Chinese and joint venture firms that operate for and in a global market articulate stringent environmental standards and practices, but also try to pass these new standards and practices on to their customers and state organizations, pushing the domestic playing field towards international levels. The Chinese petrochemical transnational Petrochina, for instance, is currently investing worldwide and has joint venture operations in China with several Western oil multinationals. It strongly feels the need to acquire internationally recognized environmental management knowledge, standards and emission levels, allowing it to compete in the global market. The involvement of the multinational Shell in the development of the east–west oil pipeline resulted in significant environmental and democratic improvements, also affecting its Chinese counterpart (Seymour et al., 2005).
- The expanding environmental industry presses for the greening of production and consumption processes, as it has a clear interest in growing environmental regulation and reform (Liu et al., 2005, fig. 1). Also, foreign companies and consultancies are increasingly entering the Chinese utility market (cf. Zhong et al., 2008), bringing about an upward push towards more stringent environmental standards.
- R&D institutions, from those linked to universities to those related to the line ministries and bureaux, are increasingly focusing their attention on environmental externalities, and articulate environmental interests among decision-making institutions within both the economic and the political domains. In universities a large number of environmental departments, centres and curricula were established in the late 1990s, and several environmental science and technology professional associations have been established.

Increasing room for manoeuvre: civil society

Besides an emerging NGO sector and increasing local activism and complaints, civil society's contribution to environmental reform is to be found in the rise of critical environmental coverage in the media.

Environmental protests and (GO)NGOs

China has a very recent history of environmental NGOs and other social organizations that articulate and lobby for environmental interests and ideas of civil society among political and economic decision-makers. The first national environmental NGO was only established in the mid-1990s. For a long time, government-organized NGOs

(GONGOs), such as the Beijing Environmental Protection Organisation and China Environment Fund, dominated the environmental 'civil-society' sector. They had more freedom of registration and manoeuvre than independent NGOs, because of their close links with state agencies. Through closed networks with policy-makers and their expert knowledge, these GONGOs articulate environmental interests and bring them into state and market institutions. In doing so, they play a role in bridging the gap between NGOs and civil society, on the one hand, and the state, on the other (Wu, 2002). Recently, these GONGOs have gained more organizational, financial and political independence and autonomy from the state, and are (thus) evaluated more positively by Western scholars. At the same time, independent environmental NGOs are developing rapidly, although they remain embedded in the Chinese state. Figures on the number of NGOs are unreliable, but at least several thousands of them are believed to exist.

Environmental NGOs, of which the majority are provincial or local ones, are not often very adversarial or confrontational but, rather, are expert or awareness-raising organizations, such as Global Village of Beijing. The 'political room' for a Western-style environmental movement still seems limited, but compared to a decade ago this room is expanding (and also compared to other protest issues such as Tibet, human rights, Falun Gong or Taiwan). Annually, some 50 000 environmental protests are recorded in China, showing a growing environmental consciousness of citizens, but also a growing willingness and ability of these citizens to raise their voices against one-sided modernization tendencies. Stalley and Yang (2006) show that there is little interest from potential participants (in their case, university students) in joining and supporting more institutionalized environmental NGOs, resulting in small numbers of volunteers and supporters and not very professionalized independent environmental NGOs (see also Xie, 2009). In China, the contribution of environmental NGOs in pushing for environmental reform of the Chinese economy or polity has not been very significant, but is clearly expanding. International NGOs, such as Greenpeace and World Wide Fund for Nature (WWF), have invested major efforts in further stimulating the environmental movement in China, with ambivalent successes.

Media and environment[6]

In China, the conventional media (newspapers, radio and television) have long been used primarily for propaganda and government-controlled information dissemination. In an interesting analysis, De Burgh (2003) explains the recent major changes in Chinese journalistic practices and media. After decades of state ownership and full control, parts of the media have been given economic independence, while some competition has emerged between the 2100 newspapers (but not yet on television, where China Central Television has a monopoly). These changes have created new pressures to secure a major share of newspaper funding from advertisements (up to 60 per cent in newspapers) and to pay more attention to consumer preferences. Media staff are increasingly recruited outside party control and financial incentives are used to attract good professionals. In addition, state controls have been relaxed somewhat and reporting freedom has increased, although state and party control remains tight, especially over more sensitive issues (Tibet, national security, Taiwan, Falun Gong).[7] Currently, the Chinese media clearly serve two masters, the Party and the market. They seem constantly to be testing the limits of what the Party will allow, which proves to be a moving target.

Environmental issues are increasingly considered non-sensitive issues, which have turned the reporting of environmental accidents, disasters and routine cases of pollution breaching standards into a more regular practice in China. Local newspapers in particular feel the pressure from local state authorities to refrain from reporting critically, while national bans on reporting emerge when minority issues and national (security and economic) interests are involved. Yang (2005), one of the experts on Chinese media and environment, concludes that environmental NGOs and their campaigns have been treated favourably in the Chinese newspapers from their emergence in the mid-1990s onwards. There are close ties between the Chinese conventional media (newspapers, radio, television) and environmental NGOs (Xie, 2009), and, perhaps not coincidentally, several green NGOs are led by (former) professional journalists. These close ties arise also from the fact that environmental NGOs are a source of news, and pollution victims and environmental NGOs need the media to build up pressure. While more freedom has caused greater uncertainty among journalists and media decision-makers about what is and what is not allowed, by the same token most journalists and media are decreasingly willing to accept simple top-down Party directions. Especially since the outbreak of SARS in 2001, the scope for revealing environmental information has expanded. The emerging 'investigative journalism' also focuses on scrutinizing authority, although journalists and media seldom touch upon 'Chinese leaders in action' or challenge the (local) state legitimacy, unless it is allowed from above.

The Internet has further expanded the possibilities for free media access and production, but here also the state is present. The Chinese government tries to remain in control of the Internet, for instance, via monitoring Internet use, requiring registration at local security agencies, limiting links or gateways between national and international networks, temporary bans on Internet cafés, and the placing of cameras, and requesting identification, in Internet cafés (carried out by more than 500 Internet inspectors in Beijing in 2006). The government has also closed websites, limited access to and production of news sites and weblogs, blocked access to 'undesirable' websites, intimidated actual and potential users, established restrictive policies towards Internet service providers, and jailed Internet activists. The Chinese government is even able to influence major international Internet companies such as Yahoo, Microsoft, eBay, Skype and Google, which all seem willing to accept all kinds of restrictions in order to gain access to this giant market. In China, the combination of these restrictions is often labelled 'the Great Fire Wall'. Not surprisingly, the government strongly backs international calls for further state control of the World Wide Web, for instance at the Tunis UN World Summit on the Information Society in November 2005.

At the same time, these restrictions are to a significant extent subverted and are not always very effective. Chinese environmental NGOs have been quick to use the Internet, partly because of the political restrictions in the other media in China. More than half of the environmental NGOs in China have set up websites with environmental information, bulletin boards and Internet campaigns. Some NGOs, such as the Green-web and Greener Beijing, operate only through the Web and are unregistered. They publicize environmental information, set up discussion groups, mobilise volunteers, organize activities and campaigns,[8] and catalyse offline campaigns. From a survey among urban grassroots organizations, Yang (2007) concluded that their Internet capacity is still at a low level and that especially the young organizations make active use of the Internet for publicity work, information dissemination and networking with fellow organizations, resulting in 'a "web" of civic associations in China' (ibid.: 122).

Global integration and the environment

The environmental relevance of China's global integration is first and foremost perceived in the West by the 'robbing of natural resources' from developing countries in South-East Asia, Africa and Latin America. Chinese natural resource extraction companies seem to follow the example set by Japan in the past two decades. More stringent domestic policies on deforestation following the 1998 flooding and the rise in demand for wood have forced many Chinese logging companies abroad, both in the East Asia region and beyond. And also with respect to oil and mining, Chinese companies increasingly operate globally, to direct natural resource flows to their growing economy. There is mixed evidence concerning the impact of these foreign operations. While they are reported to be among the worst environmental performers in Indonesia and Myanmar, Chinese companies seem to do better (relative to their local competitors) in Surinam and some of the African countries. But few, if any, Chinese companies abroad are among the environmental frontrunners, although they do bring home international experiences and new demands for a harmonization of standards up to international levels. In addition, Western countries express concern about the growing inflow of Chinese products, because of their substandard quality and poor environmental and labour conditions during production.

But the opening of China to the outside world also influences China's environmental governance. Global integration allows and enhances foreign – public and private – environmental development assistance coming to China. From the early 1990s onwards a steady flow of development assistance on the environment moved into China (from among others the EU member states, the USA, Japan and Korea), supporting programmes of environmental monitoring, cleaner development, wastewater treatment, international environmental policy, and the like. Parallel to that, international environmental NGOs supported the development of local NGOs. International environmental NGOs, such as Greenpeace, highlight pollution problems afflicting Chinese cities and spread green ideas such as sustainable consumption. And foreign-owned transnational and multinational corporations investing in China are contributing to developments in environmental governance by setting higher standards, technology transfer and the consequent use of environmental impact assessments. The opening up of China has also allowed Chinese firms, policy-makers and environmentalists to travel abroad, experience environmental reforms in other countries, and bring them home. Standard operating procedure in the making of new environmental laws in China is to start with a review of existing laws in other, advanced countries, and to build on these experiences.

Rapid economic growth in a more open economy has brought international pressure to adopt higher environmental standards, particularly since the entry of China into the WTO in 2001. There are a number of beneficial effects. In particular, WTO membership is directly responsible for the introduction of clearer, more even and tougher environmental standards that were essential if China was to export her goods to Western markets. As far back as 1990 the import of Chinese refrigerators to the EU was restricted due to the use of CFCs as a cooling agent, but that was still an exception. Today, these kinds of international (especially European, North American and Japanese) market trends towards greener products and production processes are felt in many more product categories, pushing for instance to higher levels of ISO certification, and growing interest for cleaner production, ecolabelling systems and circular economy initiatives. The adoption of imported cleaner technologies in the textile industry, tougher vehicle emission standards and new food and agricultural production regulations are among the direct consequence of WTO membership. Certainly, as a recent member of the WTO, China is also playing a significant role in the current Doha round of negotiations and China's position on, for instance, trade and environment will become crucial. Some observers see signs of China moving away from a defensive position of focusing on green trade barriers, towards a more offensive one, along with its active domestic policies on greening production and products.

With the perception of China as the future superpower, attention is shifting to China's outward role in global environmental politics. In recent years China has signed up to more than 50 multilateral environmental agreements. For example, it ratified the Biosafety Protocol in 2005, which was essential for the success of this treaty. China's compliance with the ozone treaty has proved critical in ensuring that it remains one of the few genuine success stories of environmental diplomacy. China was an early signer of the Kyoto Protocol in 1998, but ratified it only in 2002. As the world's largest producer of carbon emissions since 2006, the fact that China is not an Annex-I country and has thus no emissions reduction obligations, has worried many parties. It has become clear that China (and to a lesser extent India, Russia and Brazil) is turning into a key player in the new rounds of negotiations on a post-Kyoto treaty. Within China, debates on climate change are currently vibrant, preparing the country to take a role in any post-Kyoto policy. In short, future environmental diplomacy concerning almost every environmental issue will depend heavily on the role played by China. And China is increasingly becoming aware of its shifting position in global environmental politics.

While China is increasingly, and in many different ways, becoming integrated in the world, its environmental governance developments maintain a remarkably constant emphasis on national (environmental) security. Current Chinese leaders are much more open to global developments and have adopted a broader definition of China's interests and longer-term threats than did their ancestors two decades ago. However, their decisions and actions – at home and abroad – strongly reflect well-perceived domestic interests and priorities (sovereignty and security being among the most important), and there is little evidence of an acceptance of a wider global environmental responsibility as a future global hegemon – to be fair, a sentiment that is also absent from the current hegemon, the USA.

Epilogue

From a static viewpoint, China's environmental profile may look crystal clear: an undemocratic state that is ruining not only its own natural environment but increasingly also that of wider geographies. But in taking a closer look from a more longitudinal perspective, the complications of an environmental assessment of this superpower-in-the-making move to the fore. It is far from easy to draw simple, straightforward conclusions regarding current environmental developments in China. In comparing one decade ago with the current situation it seems justified to conclude that:

- the capacity of the 'environmental state' has increased significantly, on all levels;
- major institutional innovations can be identified over the last decade, for instance with respect to new laws, law enforcement, public–private partnerships and participation;
- there is more room for environmental criticism, activism and transparency;
- market signals are increasingly reflecting full costs of natural resources and some of the environmental externalities;
- the political leaders are more aware, committed and held accountable to combat environmental crises, often from a well-perceived national (environmental) security perspective;
- due to the rapid economic expansion, the physical state of the environment has only marginally improved following these environmental governance improvements.

Without doubt, developments in environmental reform in China (and India, Brazil and Russia) are of more than average importance for Planet Earth. This situation requires a continuous effort by environmental sociologists to interpret, understand and assess the social dynamics of environmental reform: to prevent simplistic conclusions; to provide balanced insights, especially where they are composed of contrasting tendencies; and to assist in designing environmental institutions that fit the new conditions of our time.

Notes

1. In an analysis of the reliability of economic data and statistics, Holz (2003) found that especially at the higher, aggregate levels of the policy-making and bureaucratic systems, there is not much chance of deliberate falsification of statistical data. But the sheer variety of data that are collected and calculated by the lower echelons and sent to the central level gives the National Bureau of Statistics a remarkable freedom in selecting which data best suit political purposes.
2. The latter is the implementation by MEP of the Regulations on Open Government Information, and took effect as of 1 May 2008.
3. The central state also remains in control through its major role in financing environmental protection projects.
4. However, at the central level, interdepartmental struggles continue to fragment environmental authority. For instance, the State Economic and Trade Commission (SETC) is the primary responsible party for the 2002 Cleaner Production Promotion Law, rather than SEPA/MEP. The former is also responsible for energy conservation policy. The Ministry of Science and Technology won the battle over the coordination of China's *Agenda 21* programme from SEPA/MEP, despite heavy influence and lobbying from UNDP.
5. Healthy food is food produced with a basic safety margin to ensure health and food safety. Green food, introduced in 1990 by the Ministry of Agriculture, refers to 'safe' food produced according to strict standards of pesticide and fertilizer use. Organic food production uses no pesticides or chemical fertilizers.
6. See also Mol (2008): 234–71.
7. Chinese news media are regulated and controlled via five mechanisms, of which the first two are the most important: government administrative system; Party committees; the legal system; social surveillance of other parties and social groups; (self-) regulations from associations in the news industries.
8. For example, Yang (2005: 63–4) reports on an online campaign in 2002 organized by Green-web, which successfully stopped the building of an entertainment complex that threatened a wetland.

References

Chandler, W., R. Schaeffer, Z. Dadi, P.R. Shukla, F. Tudela, O. Davidson and S. Alpan-Atamer (2002), *Climate Change Mitigation in Developing Countries. Brazil, China, India, Mexico, South Africa, and Turkey*, Arlington, VA: Pew Center on Global Climate Change.
China Centre for Modernisation Research (2007), *China Modernisation Report 2007: Ecological Modernisation Study* (published in Chinese), Beijing: Beijing University Press.

De Burgh, H. (2003), *The Chinese Journalist*, London: Routledge.

Holz, C.A. (2003), '"Fast, clear and accurate": How reliable are Chinese output and economic growth statistics?', *The China Quarterly*, **173**: 122–63.

Liu, Y., A. Mol and J. Chen (2005), 'Environmental industries in China: barriers and opportunities between state and market', *International Journal of Environment and Sustainable Development*, **4** (3): 269–89.

Lo, C.W.-H. and S.-Y. Tang (2006), 'Institutional reform, economic changes, and local environmental management in China: the case of Guangdong Province', *Environmental Politics*, **15** (2): 190–210.

Mol, A.P.J. (2008), *Environmental Reform in the Information Age. The Contours of Informational Governance*, Cambridge, UK and New York: Cambridge University Press.

Mol, A. and Y. Liu, (2005), 'Institutionalizing cleaner production in China: the cleaner Production Promotion Law', *International Journal of Environment and Sustainable Development*, **4** (3): 227–45.

NBS/MEP (National Bureau of Ministry of Environmental Protection) (2009), *China Environmental Statistical Yearbook 2008*, Beijing: MEP.

NBS/SEPA (2006), *China Statistical Yearbook on Environment 2005*, Beijing: SEPA.

Nygard, J. and X. Guo (2001), *Environmental Management of Chinese Township and Village Industrial Enterprises (TVIEs)*, Washington, DC and Beijing: The World Bank and SEPA.

Paull, J. (2008), 'The greening of China's food – green food, organic food, and eco-labelling', paper presented at the 'Sustainable Consumption and Alternative Agri-Food Systems Conference', Liege University, Arlon, Belgium, 27–30 May.

Rock, M.T. (2002), 'Getting into the environment game: integrating environmental and economic policy-making in China and Taiwan', *American Behavioral Scientist*, **45** (9): 1435–55.

SEPA (2007), *Report on the State of the Environment in China 2006*, Beijing: State Environmental Protection Agency.

Seymour, M., M. Beach and S. Lasiter (2005), 'The challenge of positive influence: managing sustainable development on the west–east pipeline project', *China Environment Series*, 7: 1–16.

Sinton, J. and D. Fridley (2001), 'Hot air and cold water: the unexpected fall in China's energy use', *China Environment Series*, **4**, 3–20.

Sinton, J. and D. Fridley (2003), 'Comments on recent energy statistics from China', *Sinosphere*, **6** (2): 6–11.

Stalley, P. and D. Yang (2006), 'An emerging environmental movement in China?', *The China Quarterly*, **186**: 333–56.

Wang, H. and D. Wheeler (1999), *Endogenous Enforcement and Effectiveness of China's Pollution Levy System*, Washington DC: World Bank.

Wu, F. (2002), 'New partners or old brothers? GONGOs in transitional environmental advocacy in China', *China Environmental Series*, **5**: 45–58.

Xie, L. (2009), *Environmental Activism in China*, London: Routledge.

Yang, G. (2005), 'Environmental NGOs and Institutional Dynamics in China', *The China Quarterly*, **181**: 47–66.

Yang, G. (2007), 'How do Chinese civic associations respond to the Internet? Findings from a survey', *The China Quarterly*, **189**: 122–43.

You, M. (2007), 'Annual review of Chinese environmental law developments: 2006', *Environmental Law Reporter*, **37**: 10836–40.

Zhong, L. and A.P.J. Mol (2008), 'Participatory environmental governance in China: Public hearings on urban water tariff setting', *Journal of Environmental Management*, **88** (4): 899–913.

Zhong, L., A.P.J. Mol and T. Fu (2008), 'Public–private partnerships in China's urban water sector', *Environmental Management*, **41**: 863–77.

25 Civic engagement in environmental governance in Central and Eastern Europe
JoAnn Carmin

Introduction

Throughout its history, the preservation of natural areas and monuments in countries across Central and Eastern Europe (CEE) contributed to widespread appreciation for nature and the outdoors. By the time state socialism was drawing to a close, however, many of these places had deteriorated from years of open-pit mining, toxic dumping and unbridled manufacturing. Awareness of the presence of pollution and the threats it was posing to human and ecosystem health ultimately gave rise to oppositional activities that focused on the need to improve environmental quality and, at the same time, expressed general levels of discontent with the regimes.

When state socialism collapsed under the weight of societal sentiment and stagnating economies, it was envisioned that the development of democratic systems would include changes that created opportunities for the public to participate in decision-making. Efforts were made to establish norms of participation across many domains, but the environmental arena was a priority. Given the forces that led to the transitions, this was an era characterized by optimism about the potential for remediating past damage, developing proactive laws and regulations, and building an engaged citizenry that would shape environmental policies while holding governments accountable for their actions. Consequently, it was expected that the environmental policy process, from inception through to implementation, would involve the public, either through their direct participation or by means of non-governmental organizations (NGOs) acting on their behalf.

The fall of state socialism took place at a time when existing modes of participation were being challenged and new approaches tested in Western Europe and the USA. Traditional forms of participation emphasize information dissemination and public comment on plans that are already developed. Dissatisfaction with the lack of meaningful input, and in many cases the outcomes of these approaches, was giving rise to contentious relations. Rather than continue this cycle, countries in the West were making efforts to shift the distribution of power by inviting citizens and NGOs to work collaboratively with government on all facets of environmental policy and planning (Turner and Hulme, 1997; Stoker, 1998; Kooiman, 1993). The intention was that collaboration would lead to more effective solutions while increased opportunities to participate would enhance commitment to outcomes (Durant et al., 2004; Jasanoff and Martello, 2004). When the regimes fell in CEE, it was anticipated that this latter approach, known as governance, would rapidly take root in the environmental policy arena.

The optimism that characterized the early days of the transition, and the ideals about building participatory democracies, were tempered by the realities of implementing sweeping change. Rather than quickly meet their democratic promise, government agencies found that because they were rooted in their routines and staffed by individuals who had been in their positions for many years, it was difficult to establish and implement participatory protocols. Public ideals about being involved in decision-making gave way to the realities of the economic transformations taking place as individuals found that they needed to work long hours to make ends meet and had little time to dedicate to volunteer activities. Even NGOs committed to improving environmental quality found that their efforts were hampered by the challenges of obtaining resources, coping with the pace of transition, and contending with societal attributions that lingered from the previous era about their roles, rights and responsibilities. To understand the transformations that took place and the ongoing dilemmas associated with civic engagement in environmental governance in CEE, the sections that follow examine the development of participatory institutions and the emergence of independent NGOs in the Czech Republic, Estonia, Hungary, Latvia, Lithuania, Poland, Slovakia and Slovenia.

Public participation, conservation associations and the rise of environmentalism

Environmentalism in CEE has a history that stretches back to the 1800s, when efforts were initially made to protect nature and natural resources. As was the case across the rest of Europe, some people wanted to preserve these areas for their beauty and for scientific purposes, while the aristocracy valued forests as hunting grounds and mountains as places where they could commune with nature. During the era of state socialism, many natural areas were retained, resulting in the region having some of the largest expanses of pristine wilderness and most significant levels of biodiversity in Europe (Beckmann, 2000). Although natural landscapes were preserved, the emphasis governments placed on economic production overshadowed the desire to protect environmental quality. The result was that, over time, air and water pollution began to accelerate and human health began to suffer. These trends did not go unnoticed by public officials, nor were they left unaddressed. As pollution came to be recognized as a mounting problem, policies were established that, similar to efforts in the West, set acceptable levels of toxic exposures and identified technological approaches for controlling emissions and effluents.

The involvement of scientists and experts was integral to the creation of national environmental laws and the development of local policies and plans. Members of these groups were active participants in environmental assessments during the 1970s and 1980s. These assessments typically involved reviews of proposed development with some consideration of their environmental impacts, but the main purpose was to determine whether proposals conformed to technical and financial specifications and were aligned with national-level plans (Cherp, 2001; Cherp and Lee, 1997). Although most policy decisions were made by government officials in consultation with experts, a number of provisions were in place for individuals to express their views on public matters. For instance, it was not uncommon for people to bring their concerns directly to their local officials, either by meeting with them or by writing letters. Individuals also could participate in commissions and panels, and write letters to newspapers when they wanted to comment on policy decisions and implementation (Carmin, 2003; Wolchik, 1991; Enloe, 1975).

Democratic systems grant citizens the right to form independent associations, and these often establish the building blocks for participation in public affairs. In contrast, because associations in state-socialist systems in CEE were sponsored, supported and monitored by the state and communist party, they rarely crossed into the realm of politics. Most countries sponsored trade unions, sporting leagues, women's associations and local chapters of apolitical international organizations such as the Red Cross. In the environmental arena, some national governments also sponsored nature conservation associations. Some of the larger organizations included the League for Nature Protection in Poland, Hungarian National Society of Conservationists, Czech Union for Nature Protection, Tree of Life in Slovakia, and the Latvian Society of Nature and Monument Protection. Most of these were membership organizations that had a central administration and local chapters that typically sponsored brigades engaged in activities such as tending to forests, mowing fields, leading hikes, managing wilderness trails, and maintaining the cleanliness of the country by clearing garbage from roads and streams.

Conservation associations were formed by the state to promote interest in nature and the outdoors and, at the same time, to help individuals become good socialist citizens. For instance, as brigades pursued their work, they accomplished state-approved goals that, at least on the surface, served as a means for socialization into state norms. Despite state intentions to control associational life, the interactions that many people had in the course of participating in conservation brigades led to unintended social outcomes. Some state-sponsored associations built their membership rosters by virtue of being affiliated with another group, such as when factory workers were required to become members of a trade union. While membership was sometimes a requirement, in most instances participation in conservation activities was a matter of personal choice. More often than not, individuals joined and were active members of these groups because they were attracted to the issues being addressed and wanted to spend time with like-minded colleagues. Even though the socialist state may have had other intentions, conservation and outdoor activity led to the formation of trusted relationships and supported the pursuit of personal interests (Carmin and Jehlička, 2005).

In democratic systems, associations often serve as representatives for the broader public by taking action to express generally held sentiments or ensure that marginalized views and populations have a voice in the policy process (Cohen and Arato, 1992). In contrast, associations in state-socialist systems typically engage in apolitical forms of activity and individuals interact directly with public officials when they want to voice their concerns. While this generally was the case, instances of collective opposition to government decisions that had environmental implications started to emerge across CEE in the 1980s. One of the first protests was waged in Poland in 1980, when environmental activists opposed the operation of an aluminum mill (Jancar-Webster, 1998; Hicks, 1996). Although infrequent at this time, protests with environmental themes soon followed in countries across the region. These activities were generally initiated by small groups of activists, many drawing on the networks they established by means of their affiliations with conservation associations.

By the mid-1980s, weak enforcement of policies and continued emphasis on production resulted in ongoing deterioration of environmental quality across the region (Auer, 2004; Pavlínek and Pickles, 2004; Carter and Turnock, 1996). By 1986, *glasnost* began to weaken the grip of the state. The result was that the reliance on institutional modes of participation and cautious dissent began to give way to more frequent opposition. Many of the concerns that were voiced reflected general discontent with the political systems, but because it was a relatively safe topic, numerous protests adopted environmental themes (Tickle and Welsh, 1998; Jancar-Webster, 1993; Vari and Tamas, 1993; Singleton, 1987). For instance, a catalyzing issue that gave rise to a national movement in Hungary was the proposal to build the Gabcikovo–Nagymaros Dam on the Danube River. The movement focused on the increased likelihood of flooding as well as on the cultural importance of protecting the land where the dam would be built (Carter and Turnock, 1996). Alternatively, when the nuclear accident and fire at Chernobyl occurred in 1986, it sparked environmental dissent in Poland. Environmentalists in the country used the incident, and the government's attempt to conceal what had happened, to draw attention to industrial contamination and the health impacts of pollution more broadly (Carmin and Hicks, 2002).

As the decade drew to a close, environmental activism had taken root from Slovenia to Estonia (Jancar-Webster, 1998). In response to increases in smog, toxic accidents and proposals to initiate development in natural areas, Czechoslovakia also saw rising levels of environmental activism. Residents of the North Bohemian town of Chomutov, for example, organized a public discussion about air pollution and submitted a petition asking to be informed about environmental degradation so that they could protect their health. Toxic accidents in South Bohemia and smog in Prague further raised awareness of environmental problems and, by 1989, led to additional petitions, discussions about the state of the environment, and protests in cities and towns throughout the country (Vaněk, 1996). Some of these activities were rooted in existing conservation associations, while others took place through environmental organizations that were starting to form independently and that were seeking both environmental gains and a transformation in the political regime (Baker and Jehlička, 1998; Fagin and Jehlička, 1998; Jancar-Webster, 1998).

The emergence of participatory institutions and environmental NGOs
Following the fall of the communist regimes, many aspects of environmental policy and institutional development across CEE were modeled after practices in Western-style democracies. While the pace of change varied from one country to the next, all established new environmental policies and laws, and adopted more stringent protocols with respect to implementation and monitoring compliance. Due to the role that dissidents and oppositional groups played, not only in raising the alarm about environmental degradation, but in exposing the inadequacies of the regimes, civil society was viewed as critical to building democracy, holding governments accountable and achieving environmental protection.

The creation of provisions for participation
In the early phases of transition, countries across the region made provisions for the public and civic associations to participate in environmental decision-making (REC, 1998). At that time, the emphasis was on public participation in the creation of environmental laws and regulations. However, right from the start, problems began to surface due to variable legal specificity regarding what participation should entail, including the creation of explicit procedures. As a result, participation in this domain often took place on an *ad hoc* basis. Hungary was a notable exception because NGOs had a legal right to express their views about draft legislation. However, since legal provisions were vague, other countries took a more informal approach, with officials often soliciting input from NGO representatives they knew or organizations they thought had the appropriate expertise (REC, 1998).

Relative to the formation of national legislation, Environmental Impact Assessment (EIA), Local Agenda 21 (LA21) and Local Environmental Action Plans (LEAP) had better-defined parameters for participation. In the early 1990s, the Czech Republic, Hungary, Poland, Slovakia and Slovenia started to replace existing environmental assessment procedures with EIA protocols in effect in the EU at that time (EU Directive 85/337/EEC). By the second half of the decade, Estonia, Latvia and Lithuania followed suit (Cherp, 2001). EIA involves a scientific evaluation of the impact that specified types of development projects are anticipated to have on the environment and public health. The process is initiated by the company or government agency that is proposing the particular project. Acting under this Directive, countries conduct a thorough assessment of the impacts and then make the results available to the public. The public and NGOs are given the opportunity to review documents and express their concerns in writing as well as at public hearings (Cherp, 2001; REC, 1998).

This approach to EIA draws on traditional modes of participation rooted in government-established forums, information dissemination and public comment on draft plans. In contrast, LA21 and LEAPs are more closely aligned with the vision of collaborative governance since they are characterized by the involvement of stakeholders in every aspect of the planning and decision processes (REC, 2000). LA21 is an outgrowth of the UN Conference on Environment and Development held in 1992. During the conference, nations agreed to establish action plans to achieve sustainable development. A provision of Agenda 21 is that it encourages local governments to work directly with citizens to develop a local plan, or LA21. The first LA21 initiative in CEE took place in the early 1990s, with numerous municipalities across the region subsequently engaging in this process (ICLEI, 2002).

While sustainable development was regarded as important, the newly independent countries of CEE were faced with significant environmental problems. At a meeting held in 1993 among the Ministers of the Environment from Western and Eastern Europe and representatives from the USA, it was agreed that countries in CEE could better address environmental problems if they established environmental action programs. The idea that emerged was to link national planning to local efforts and to utilize elements associated with LA21, but to focus specifically on the environment by means of a LEAP. Creating a LEAP involves forming a governance structure, eliciting a community vision, assessing environmental issues, setting priorities, establishing an action plan and creating a means for implementation to achieve the desired outcomes. Every stage of this process relies on public involvement (REC, 2000, 1998).

In addition to adopting formal policy initiatives, some environmental agencies introduced innovative approaches to engaging and promoting ongoing communication with NGOs. This was the case, for instance, with the formation of the Green Parliament in Czechoslovakia, and subsequently the Czech Republic. This forum, comprising environmental NGOs and government representatives, met regularly to discuss environmental issues. An alternative approach was adopted in Poland, where an annual national meeting of all ecology groups was held (Carmin and Hicks, 2002). Although these initiatives signaled commitment to forging ties between governments and civil-society actors, they were relatively isolated incidents. Even with many activists assuming government posts, and a desire to have open policy processes, the enthusiasm that characterized the early transition waned relatively quickly and most government agencies returned to conducting business more or less as usual. As a result, participation was often seen as a formality and NGOs were viewed as expert bodies that could support government functions.

The emergence of environmental NGOs

Across most of CEE, efforts to establish participatory forums were based on the view that non-state, non-economic actors would be integral in making environmental decisions. In other words, the expectation was that voluntary associations, unions, movements and NGOs would serve as a means through which individuals could engage holders of political authority and economic power. As a response to the history of the region, the intention was to create opportunities for these organizations to participate in decision processes so that outcomes would account for diverse perspectives and state power would be moderated and monitored.

The desire to cultivate organizations to fill these roles was reinforced by the creation of non-profit legislation enabling the formation of independent associations. In addition, many national and foreign governments, agencies and foundations dedicated resources to support the development of civil society and the creation of NGOs, including those working on environmental issues (Carmin and VanDeveer, 2004). One motivation for this support was that environmental NGOs could engage in collaborative forms of governance and, in the process, build and extend the capacity of government agencies. While some conservation organizations were the recipients of funding, most was targeted to policy-oriented NGOs since they were best able to provide support services such as drafting legislation, implementing policies and monitoring for regulatory compliance.

The transition to an open society and the presence of international funders helped build the capacities and stabilize the operations of many NGOs. However, rather than promote their independence, some organizations found that they had to conform to funder expectations and requirements. In many instances, these pressures pushed them toward adopting the norms and practices of professional organizations (Carmin and Hicks, 2002; Quigley, 2000; Jancar-Webster, 1998; Connolly et al., 1996). This trajectory helped some NGOs become more effective, but for others it meant orienting their efforts to be in line with the priorities of their funders as opposed to concerns expressed by the domestic public (Mendelson and Glenn, 2002). A critical aspect of international funding is that it rarely found its way to associations that were active under state socialism. Although these organizations had extensive networks and provided essential services, they were regarded as unwanted remnants of the former regimes and, in most cases, left to fend for themselves in the domestic arena (Carmin and Jehlička, 2005).

Through the 1990s, the region saw a rapid expansion of environmental NGOs. This growth included new national and local organizations as well as affiliations with leading transnational environmental organizations such as Greenpeace, World Wide Fund for Nature and Friends of the Earth. All of these organizations encountered administrative challenges as they navigated a dynamic sociopolitical context (DeHoog and Racanska 2003; Lagerspetz et al., 2002; Green 1999; Regulska, 1999; Jancar-Webster, 1998; Wunker, 1991). These challenges included acclimatizing to democratic norms such as responding to societal preferences and the expectations of constituents, and participating in policy-related activities (Jancar-Webster, 1998). Under state socialism, associations were often staffed at the local levels by their members, but central administration was governed by members of the *nomenklatura* (Siegel and Yancey, 1992). As a result, a further challenge for leaders taking the helms of these newly formed organizations was that they had limited administrative skills, particularly in the critical areas of fundraising and financial management (Carmin and Hicks, 2002; Jancar-Webster, 1998; Millard, 1998).

Environmental governance from transition to accession

In the period leading up to the fall of state socialism, many environmental initiatives reflected the desire for fundamental change and were rooted in open opposition and contestation. With the transition to democratic systems, the emphasis shifted to positive forms of participation, such as collaboration with authorities and engagement in public forums (Carmin and Jehlička, 2010; Jancar-Webster, 1998). Despite high hopes for inclusion, NGOs generally had difficulty becoming fully integrated into the policy process. As was the case in the past, national environmental policy-making remained concentrated in the hands of elites (Millard, 1998). Although the national policy arena remained exclusive, the local level became a site where many cooperative relationships and initiatives emerged, particularly in the period leading up to membership in the EU (Kepáková, 2004).

Redefining and implementing provisions for participation
Countries in the region applied for EU membership between 1994 and 1996. Accession negotiations were started with Czech Republic, Estonia, Hungary, Poland and Slovenia in 1998, followed by Latvia, Lithuania and Slovakia in 1999. All of these countries were granted membership in 2004. Membership in the EU required that countries adopt and implement the *acquis communautaire*. This EU body of law consists of 31 chapters, one of which focuses specifically on the environment. While countries across the region had developed new environmental institutions and policies after the fall of state socialism, the *acquis* contained over 200 environmental directives, many of which required the adoption and implementation of additional laws, regulations and standards (Carmin and VanDeveer, 2004).

In the run-up to accession, many bilateral and private funding agencies left the region. As a result, rather than being able to draw on diverse sources of funding, national governments had to rely on the EU as the primary source of support for help in meeting their accession targets. While funding enhances the capacities of state actors, it also is a means through which norms are diffused (Linden, 2002). For instance, funding during this time often focused on translating EU directives and regulations into national languages and educating and training policy-makers from CEE countries in EU requirements. The consolidation of support and focus on joining the EU meant that countries were increasingly influenced by decisions and policies originating from Brussels, including those related to participation and governance in environmental matters (Börzel, 2002; Knill and Lenschow, 2000).

A notable impact that EU membership had on institutional provisions for environmental governance is that countries in the region signed the Aarhus Convention on Access to Information, Public Participation in Decision Making and Access to Justice. The Aarhus Convention was adopted in 1998, at which time it was signed by 29 countries and the EU. It entered into force in 2001 after being ratified by 17 countries.

While the EU already had legislation in place that established standards for access to information and public participation, the Aarhus Convention expanded the definition of environmental information and granted citizens and NGOs the right to pursue legal remedies for infringements of environmental rights (Zaharchenko and Goldenman, 2004). Signatories to the Convention pledge to share documents and information about environmental quality and enforcement. This information, in turn, provides a more appropriate base for NGOs, groups and individuals to influence policy decisions (Bell et al., 2002).

Many governments have found it challenging to implement the provisions in the Aarhus Convention due to deeply entrenched views about access to information and public involvement. Under state socialism, agency representatives and experts controlled information dissemination, passing judgment on what they thought was appropriate for the public to know. While they traditionally relied on the public and associations to assist them in policy implementation, decision-making was the domain of experts. Implementing the Aarhus Convention required a shift in these traditional views and approaches (Zaharchenko and Goldenman, 2004). An example of the types of challenges administrators faced surfaced during the attempt to develop a Strategic Action Plan for the Danube Basin. Since the project emphasized access to information, efforts were made to ensure that public participants were provided with technical data and were consulted throughout the entire planning process. While the project ultimately achieved its aims, it was not easy to put into place. Ensuring access to information required not only the creation of administrative procedures for disseminating materials and tracking information requests, but also a fundamental change in the attitudes of government officials and representatives toward public rights and roles in decision processes (Bell et al., 2002).

The EIA Directive adopted by most countries in the early days of transition was amended in 1997 (Directive 97/11/EC) to include greater opportunities for notification and participation. In response to these requirements, countries enhanced their EIA provisions by requiring that developers provide notification to authorities much earlier and that authorities, in turn, inform the local municipality and residents of the proposal. In addition to being able to comment on documents and attend public hearings, the public was granted the opportunity to provide comments at the time of the initial notification about their views of the anticipated impacts and desirability of the new initiative. Further, the new provisions required that materials be made readily available, including being placed on the Internet (Cherp, 2001). The signing of the Aarhus Convention in 1998 by the European Community led to additional amendments being made to the EIA Directive in 2003 (Directive 2003/35/EC). The intention of this change was to ensure that the democratic features of Aarhus, particularly the provisions on public participation and access to justice, were aligned with the EIA process.

Although conventions have been ratified and formal provisions integrated into national policy, countries across the region continue to encounter difficulty in administering participatory processes. For example, the Water Framework Directive (WFD) specifies that the public should have access to information, be consulted, have opportunities for active participation in the planning process, and assume responsibility for outcomes (Malzbender, 2006). However, as countries worked to adopt the WFD and initiated participatory procedures, most found that they had insufficient capacity to realize their mandate. In the Czech Republic, for instance, even though river-basin authorities who were in charge of the participatory process had limited expertise in this domain, they elected to run the process themselves rather than seek out trained facilitators. As a result, they were unable to initiate information campaigns and seminars or identify key stakeholders until late in the process. In addition, since they were inexperienced, some interested groups and critical participants were excluded from the process (Slavíková and Jílková, 2008). While country variations were present in information dissemination, consultation and active involvement, region-wide assessments of WFD planning and implementation suggest that the Czech Republic is not alone in encountering difficulty in administering participatory processes (De Stefano, 2004).

Roles and activities of environmental NGOs
Two factors that had significant impacts on NGOs in the period leading up to EU accession were national government agendas and the consolidation of funding in the region. The emphasis that governments placed on harmonizing their policies with EU directives and regulations drove the environmental agenda and, in turn, shaped the priorities of many NGOs, particularly those focusing on national policy (Hicks, 2004). In addition, as funders left the region, many NGOs found that they were having difficulty obtaining resources necessary to continue their activities. Some organizations were able to retain support from their national governments, for instance through Ministries of the Environment and Ministries of Education, and remaining foreign foundations. As was the case more generally, however, the EU was one of the major sources of funding that NGOs could tap. For example, programs such as PHARE (Poland and Hungary: Assistance for Restructuring their Economics) and the 6th Environment Action Program funded NGOs in CEE candidate countries to implement environmental projects focused on education, information dissemination and environmental management initiatives. The impact of these and other programs was that rather than pursue activities of their choosing, some NGOs oriented their agendas and activities so that they could secure these resources (Hicks, 2004).

Funding was not the only international source of influence that affected environmental NGOs. Just as the diffusion of global norms can shape state agencies and initiatives, they also can influence the practices of NGOs (Frank et al., 2000). For instance, in the new climate of openness, representatives from select NGOs began to travel to international conferences and training programs, contact NGOs in other countries and make study visits to learn about their activities, and interact with international experts and staff members of foundations and aid agencies who traveled throughout the region offering advice. While these initiatives helped the participating NGOs build international ties and become integrated into transnational networks, they also had the effect of diffusing knowledge and norms about appropriate ways to manage and administer an environmental organization (Carmin and Hicks, 2002).

At the time of transition, funders focused on supporting highly visible and newly formed environmental NGOs. This preference initiated a process that contributed to the emergence of financial disparities among organizations. In the years that ensued, one of the unintended consequences of international interactions and participation in transnational networks was that they further entrenched organizational differences by giving rise to an elite class of national NGOs that was better funded, better equipped, and more professionalized than most of the smaller and less visible groups that also populated the regional landscape (REC, 2001).

Following accession, financial support from the EU continued to be extended to this group of elite NGOs with the intention of cultivating their abilities to assist the EU in formulating policies and programs, and building their capacities to help their national governments implement environmental programs (Börzel, 2006). CEE environmental NGOs have been criticized for their general inability to bring a desired degree of professionalism to their Commission-level initiatives (Hallstrom, 2004). However, it appears that they are more successful in the domestic context, as some NGOs have been effective in assisting with EU integration and advancing EU goals in their home countries. An example of how this has played out was when the Hungarian government recognized that it would be unable to mount a successful information campaign about the Natura 2000 designation process. Rather than attempt to achieve this on its own, it delegated the task to a coalition comprised of major environmental NGOs (Börzel et al., 2008).

Ongoing trends in NGO funding, international interactions and capacity-building have continued to reinforce the development of a group of NGOs that are highly professionalized. These organizations also tend to be the ones that receive the majority of their financial support from foreign foundations and EU programs, generally have the highest levels of income, and focus their efforts on national policy promotion along with related activities in the areas of education and community support. Given their funding streams, many of these NGOs focus on supporting the implementation of EU policies, Commission goals and international funder preferences rather than establishing a programmatic commitment to a particular topic that is tied to the priorities of domestic constituencies (Fagan, 2006; Carmin, 2008).

Although professional NGOs with a policy orientation tend to be the most visible actors in the CEE environmental arena, a second category of organizations comprises NGOs with an activist profile. These NGOs generally rely on a broad repertoire, but are more likely than their peers to engage in protest and other forms of direct action to advance their goals. These NGOs typically have members and, for those that derive a large portion of their income from dues and individual contributions, the lowest annual incomes. By acting on behalf of their members and supporters to sound the alarm about important environmental issues, pressuring governments, and holding public officials and corporations accountable, these organizations play a critical role in supporting democracy and advancing environmental protection (Carmin, 2008).

Associations active under state socialism had limited levels of credibility and popular support at the time the regimes fell. Over the years, however, their activities and values came to be appreciated and some that were in existence under state socialism, as well as some that have been founded based on the precedent older organizations set for directly engaging in conservation activities, have been able to endure. Therefore a third category of NGOs comprises organizations that have roots in, or have adopted the practices and values of, traditional conservation associations. These NGOs typically engage in nature protection and environmental management activities, sponsor environmental education initiatives, and disseminate information about nature and natural resources. Organizations in this category usually have modest incomes, with their national governments and dues-paying members being the major sources of their financial support. These organizations contribute to government conservation efforts through practical activities such as trail-building and forest management. At the same time, they build civil-society capacity by socializing members and volunteer participants into norms of civic engagement (Carmin, 2008).

Newer and older environmental organizations are active in the region, with some, such as those with activist and conservation orientations, more oriented toward membership than others. Although membership organizations proliferate, the tendency for individuals to join is low in comparison with both more established democracies and post-authoritarian countries. This trend cuts across most types of associations and NGOs, including those with an environmental focus (Howard, 2003). In the period following the fall of the regimes, there were two broad reasons offered for low levels of membership. One was that individuals had an aversion to membership as a consequence of state-socialist requirements to join and participate in associations. A second explanation was that the transition to a free market economy resulted in people having to focus more on their livelihoods and, therefore, having less free time to serve as volunteers or become involved in association life (Howard, 2003). In the ensuing years, membership has increased in some organizations, but many continue to struggle with recruitment and participation.

Tradition and the transformation of environmental governance
The fall of state socialism across CEE was accompanied by visions of establishing participatory democracies. The role played by civil-society actors in destabilizing the regimes, along with the emphasis placed on environmental issues in the period prior to and during the early phases of transition, created expectations about becoming environmentally proactive and promoting civic engagement in all aspects of environmental policy and planning. As is often the case when expectations encounter reality, it has been more difficult to establish participatory processes and levels of civic engagement than initially envisioned.

From transition to accession, steps have been taken to align environmental policies and practices with those of the EU. This process has included provisions to support participation, access to information, and the right to justice in environmental matters. These formal policies represent a significant advancement in government transparency, accountability and access compared to those in place under the former regime. Despite these gains, however, it is evident that norms and routines are difficult to change. To some extent, the presence of inertia reflects longstanding reliance on guidance from technical and scientific experts rather than on input from the broader public. While deeply entrenched patterns in government protocols could represent an aversion to change, in many cases they may reflect a lack of training of personnel in how to respond to the public, implement participatory processes, and work side by side with NGO representatives.

A developed civil society typically is viewed as an integral aspect of a robust democracy. It was with this goal in mind that many international funders and agencies sought to build the capacities of environmental NGOs. Whether intentional or inadvertent, many of these funders channeled the agendas and activities of NGOs in directions that resembled professional organizations in Western Europe and the USA (Mendelson and Glenn, 2002; Ottaway and Carothers, 2000; Quigley, 2000). While foreign aid has fostered the emergence of a class of professional and policy-oriented environmental NGOs, many contemporary views about associational life and appropriate approaches to civic engagement can be traced to perspectives and relationships that took root in state-socialist times (Carmin and Jehlička, 2010; Lane, 2008). In contrast to professionalized environmental organizations, many of the more traditional types of conservation organizations, as well as some activist NGOs, sponsor outdoor and nature protection activities as a means to promote social capital and advance norms of participation among their memberships (Carmin and Jehlička, 2005).

When the regimes fell, it was envisioned that the democratic transition would be swift, that foreign aid could create democratic institutions, and that a civil society based on models and principles imported from the West could be established. Many aspects of domestic and international efforts dedicated to these ends have been successful. However, over the course of time, we have discovered that the pace of democratic transition cannot be rushed, witnessed ways that the diffusion of global norms shape domestic environmental practices and seen first-hand how the persistence of social, cultural and political institutions affects environmental governance.

References

Auer, Matthew R. (2004), *Restoring Cursed Earth: Appraising Environmental Policy Reports in Eastern Europe and Russia*, Lanham, MD: Rowman & Littlefield.

Baker, Susan and Petr Jehlicka (1998), *Dilemmas of Transition: The Environment, Democracy and Economic Reform in East Central Europe*, London: Frank Cass.

Beckmann, Andreas (2000), *Caring for the Earth: A Decade of Stewardship in Central Europe*, Staré Město, Czech Republic: NP Agentura.

Bell, Ruth Greenspan, Jane Bloom Stewart, and Magda Toth Nagy (2002), 'Fostering a culture of environmental compliance through greater public involvement', *Environment*, **44** (8): 34–44.

Börzel, Tanja A. (2002), *States and Regions in the European Union; Institutional Adaptation in Germany and Spain*, Cambridge, UK: Cambridge University Press.

Börzel, Tanya A. (2006), 'Participation through law enforcement: the case of the European Union', *Comparative Political Studies*, **39** (1): 128–52.

Börzel, Tanja A., Aron Buzogany and Sonja Guttenbrunner (2008), 'New modes of governance in accession countries: the role of private actors', paper presented at the NEWGOV Cross-Cluster Workshop on Civil Society, New Modes of Governance and Enlargement, 8–10 May, Berlin, Germany.

Carmin, JoAnn (2003), 'Resources, opportunities, and local environmental action in the democratic transition and early consolidation periods in the Czech Republic', *Environmental Politics*, **12** (3): 42–64.

Carmin, JoAnn (2008), 'Investing in civil society: the diversification of environmental NGOs in Central and Eastern Europe', *Development and Transition*, **9** (1): 11-14.

Carmin, JoAnn and Barbara Hicks (2002), 'International triggering events, transnational networks, and the development of the Czech and Polish environmental movements', *Mobilization*, **7** (3): 305–24.

Carmin, JoAnn and Petr Jehlička (2005), 'By the masses or for the masses?: The transformation of voluntary action in the Czech Union for nature protection', *Voluntas*, **16** (4): 401–21.

Carmin, JoAnn and Petr Jehlička (2010), 'Navigating institutional pressure in state-socialist and democratic regimes: the case of Movement Brontosaurus', *Nonprofit and Voluntary Sector Quarterly*, **39** (1): 29–50.

Carmin, JoAnn and Stacy D. VanDeveer (2004), 'Enlarging EU environments: Central and Eastern Europe from transition to accession', *Environmental Politics*, **13** (1): 3–24.

Carter, F.W. and David Turnock (1996), *Environmental Problems in Eastern Europe*, London: Routledge.

Cherp, Aleg (2001), 'EA legislation and practice in Central and Eastern Europe and the former USSR: a comparative analysis', *Environmental Impact Assessment Review*, **21** (4): 335–61.

Cherp, Oleg and Norman Lee (1997), 'Evolution of SER and OVOS in the Soviet Union and Russia (1985–1996)', *Environmental Impact Assessment Review*, **17**: 177–204.

Cohen, Jean and Andrew Arato (1992), *Civil Society and Political Theory*, Cambridge, MA: MIT Press.

Connolly, Barbara, Tamar Gutner and Hildegard Berdarff (1996), 'Organizational inertia and environmental assistance in Eastern Europe', in Robert O. Keohane and Marc Levy (eds), *Institutions for Environmental Aid*, Cambridge, MA: MIT Press, pp. 281–323.

DeHoog, Ruth Hoogland and Luba Racanska (2003), 'The role of the nonprofit sector amid political change: contrasting approaches to Slovakian civil society', *Voluntas*, **14** (3): 263–82.

De Stefano, Lucia (2004), 'Public participation in the Water Framework Directive Common Implementation Strategy Pilot River Basin testing exercise and in the implementation of the Water Framework Directive: An environmental NGO perspective', Spain: World Wide Fund for Nature.

Durant, Robert F., Daniel J. Fiorino and Rosemary O'Leary (2004), *Environmental Governance Reconsidered: Challenges, Choices, and Opportunities*, Cambridge, MA: MIT Press.

Enloe, Cynthia H. (1975), *The Politics of Pollution in a Comparative Perspective: Ecology and Power in Four Nations*, New York: David McKay Company Inc.

Fagan, Adam (2006), 'Transnational aid for civil society development in post-socialist Europe: democratic consolidation or a new imperialism?', *Journal of Communist Studies and Transition Politics*, **22** (1): 115–34.

Fagin, Adam and Petr Jehlicka (1998), 'The Czech Republic: sustainable development – a doomed process?', in S. Baker and Petra Jehlička (eds), *Dilemmas of Transition: The Environment, Democracy and Economic Reform in East Central Europe*, London,: Frank Cass, pp. 113–28

Frank, David John, Ann Hironaka and Evan Schofer (2000), 'The nation-state and the natural environment over the twentieth century', *American Sociological Review*, **65** (1): 96–116.

Green, Andrew T. (1999), 'Nonprofits and democratic development: lessons from the Czech Republic', *Voluntas*, **10** (3): 217–35.

Hallstrom, Lars (2004), 'Eurocratising enlargement? EU elites and NGO participation in European environmental policy', *Environmental Politics*, **13** (1): 175–96.

Hicks, Barbara (1996), *Environmental Politics in Poland: A Social Movement Between Regime and Opposition*, New York: Columbia University Press.

Hicks, Barbara (2004), 'Setting agendas and shaping activism: EU influence on Central European environmental movements', *Environmental Politics*, **13** (1): 216–33.

Howard, Marc Morje (2003), *The Weakness of Civil Society in Post-Communist Europe*, Cambridge, UK: Cambridge University Press.

ICLEI (International Council for Local Environmental Initiatives) (2002), 'Second Local Agenda 21 Survey: Background Paper No. 15', Report prepared for the Second Preparatory Session of the World Summit on Sustainable Development.

Jancar-Webster, Barbara (1993), *Environmental Action in Eastern Europe: Response to Crisis*, Armonk, NY: M.E. Sharpe.

Jancar-Webster, Barbara (1998), 'Environmental movements and social change in the transition countries', *Environmental Politics*, **7** (1): 69–90.

Jasanoff, Shelia and Marybeth Long Martello (2004), *Earthly Politics: Local and Global in Environmental Governance*, Cambridge, MA: MIT Press.

Kepáková, Kateřina (2004), *The Czech Non-profit Sector before Entering the European Union: Development, Capacity, Needs and Future of Czech Environmental NGOs*, Brno, Czech Republic: Nadace Partnerství.

Knill, Christopher and Andrea Lenschow (2000), *Implementing EU Environmental Policy: New Directions and Old Problems*, Manchester, UK: Manchester University Press.

Kooiman, Jan (1993), *Modern Governance: New Government–Society Interactions*, London: Sage.

Lagerspetz, Mikko, Erle Rikmann and Rein Ruutsoo (2002), 'The structure and resources of NGOs in Estonia', *Voluntas*, **13** (1): 73–87.

Lane, David (2008), ëCivil society and the imprint of state socialismí, paper presented at the NEWGOV Cross-Cluster Workshop on Civil Society, New Modes of Governance and Enlargement, 8–10 May, Berlin, Germany.

Linden, Ronald H. (2002), *Norms and Nannies: The Impact of International Organizations on the Central and Eastern European States*, Lanham, MD: Rowman & Littlefield.

Malzbender, Daniel (2006), 'Public participation under the EU Water Framework Directive', in Anton Earle and Daniel Malzbender (eds), *Stakeholder Participation in Transboundary Water Management – Selected Case Studies*, Cape Town, South Africa: African Centre for Water Research, pp. 96–110.

Mendelson, Sarah E. and John K. Glenn (2002), *The Power and Limits of NGOs: A Critical Look at Building Democracy in Eastern Europe and Eurasia*, New York: Columbia University Press.

Millard, Frances (1998), 'Environmental policy in Poland', *Environmental Politics*, **7** (1): 146–61.

Ottaway, Marina and Thomas Carothers (2000), 'The burgeoning world of civil society aid', in M. Ottaway and T. Carothers (eds), *Funding Virtue: Civil Society Aid and Democracy Promotion*, Washington, DC: Carnegie Endowment for International Peace, pp. 3–17.

Pavlinek, Petr and John Pickles (2004), 'Environmental pasts/environmental futures in Post-socialist Europe', *Environmental Politics*, **13** (1): 237–65.

Quigley, Kevin F.F. (2000), 'Lofty goals, modest results: assisting civil society in Eastern Europe', in T. Carothers and M. Ottaway (eds), *Funding Virtue: Civil Society Aid and Democracy Promotion*, New York: Carnegie Endowment for International Peace, pp. 191–216.

Regional Environmental Center (REC) (1998), *Doors to Democracy: Current Trends and Practices in Public*

Participation in Environmental Decisionmaking in Central and Eastern Europe, Szentendre, Hungary: Regional Environmental Center.

REC (2000), *Guide to Implementing Local Environmental Action Programs in Central and Eastern Europe*, Szentendre, Hungary: Regional Environmental Center.

REC (2001), *NGO Directory: A Directory of Environmental Nongovernmental Organizations in Central and Eastern Europe*, Szentendre, Hungary: Regional Environmental Center.

Regulska, Joanna (1999), 'NGOs and their vulnerabilities during the time of transition: the case of Poland', *Voluntas*, **10** (1): 61–72.

Siegel, Daniel and Jenny Yancey (1992), *The Rebirth of Civil Society: The Development of the Nonprofit Sector in East Central Europe and the Role of Western Assistance*, New York: Rockefeller Brothers Foundation.

Singleton, Fred (1987), *Environmental Problems in the Soviet Union & Eastern Europe*, Boulder, CO: Rienner.

Slavíková, Lenka and Jiřina Jílková (2008), 'Implementing the public participation concept into water management in the Czech Republic – critical analysis', paper presented at the Annual International Conference of the Regional Studies Association, 27–29 May, Prague, Czech Republic.

Stoker, Gerry (1998), 'Governance as theory', *International Social Science Journal*, **55**: 17–28.

Tickle, Andrew and Ian Welsh (eds) (1998), *Environment and Society in Eastern Europe*, Harlow, UK: Longman.

Turner, Mark and David Hulme (1997), *Governance, Administration, and Development: Making the State Work*, West Hartford, CT: Kumarian Press.

Vaněk, Miroslav (1996), *Nedalo se tady dýchat. Ekologie v českých zemích v letech 1968 az 1989*, Prague, Czech Republic: Ústav pro soudobé dějiny AV ČR.

Vari, Anna and Pal Tamas (1993), *Environment and Democratic Transition: Policy and Politics in Central and Eastern and Europe*, Dordrecht, The Netherlands: Kluwer Academic Publishers.

Wolchik, Sharon L. (1991), *Czechoslovakia in Transition: Politics, Economics, & Society*, London: Pinter Publishers.

Wunker, Stephan M. (1991), 'The promise of non-profits in Poland and Hungary: an analysis of third sector renaissance', *Voluntas*, **2** (2): 88–107.

Zaharchenko, Tatiana R. and Gretta Goldenman (2004), 'Accountability in governance: the challenge of implementing the Aarhus Convention in Eastern Europe and Central Asia', *International Environmental Agreements: Politics, Law and Economics*, **4**: 229–51.

26 A 'sustaining conservation' for Mexico?

Nora Haenn

Introduction

If environmental protection depends on public participation and public acceptance of environmental programmes, then today's environmentalism faces two challenges. On the one hand, environmental programmes must counteract the social inequalities that disenfranchise millions of people whose actions affect local and global ecologies (Beierle and Cayford, 2002; Fischer, 2000). Environmentalism becomes a question of social justice when marginalized groups decline or are unwelcoming to protection programmes precisely because of their status. On the other hand, environmentalism must reckon with a diversity of cultural perspectives that result in radically different ways of understanding the world (Dove, 2007; Dryzek, 2005; Nazarea, 1999). From their diverse cultural standpoints, people differ over whether environmental problems exist, who is responsible for them, and what (if any) actions should be taken to ameliorate such problems. How questions of social justice and multiculturalism play out in environmental settings remains a pressing question for researchers (Brosius et al., 2005), especially those who seek a 'sustaining conservation': conservation that endures, one that supports both the physical environment and the social relations that make conservation possible. The following pages illustrate the importance of social justice and multiculturalism to lasting conservation management.

Of particular interest to the idea of a sustaining conservation are cases where a state government – a possible guarantor of social justice – acts within a culturally diverse setting. With their combination of state and private sector interests, as well as international, national and local actors, conservation sites condense class, cultural and public/private divides (West, 2006). Because they often rely on a state government for their existence, conservation sites add to concerns about social justice and multiculturalism questions of how people use ecology and environmentalism to think both with and against the state (Agrawal, 2005; Matthews, 2005; Sundberg, 2003). The presence of the state requires a shift in the way researchers connect social justice and conservation. One way of thinking of this connection is that conservation forces researchers to consider how environmentalism serves people who advocate different forms of state-related social justice (Brechin et al., 2003; Colfer, 2004).

These questions could apply to any country, but as the events below convey, their answers are highly local. Researchers interested in environmentalism, social justice and multiculturalism enter a terrain where particular histories and particular social contracts matter a great deal. Additionally, within any given country, cultural variation and the presence of inimitable personalities mean that an individual conservation–state nexus takes on its own unique form. While it is worth questioning to what extent the social justice and multicultural issues one witnesses are the result of national (or international) trends, the dynamics surrounding one protected area can appear quite distinct from those of another (Igoe, 2003).

Identities in Mexican conservation

To explore these questions, I turn to events surrounding Mexico's largest protected area for tropical ecosystems, the Calakmul Biosphere Reserve. Calakmul sits on the Yucatán peninsula, where Mexico borders Belize and Guatemala. Declared in 1989, Calakmul is part of a trend that has captured the interest of state authorities. Two-thirds of Mexico's 166 protected areas were created after 1980.[1] More dramatically, these include three-quarters of all natural resources receiving some kind of protected status in that country. The following pages describe what happened following Calakmul's declaration. Important to this story are the identities to which people in Calakmul – newly affected by a protected area – ascribe. A brief description of these identities and their associated concerns is warranted here.

Calakmul is an agricultural frontier where people categorize themselves as indigenous or non-indigenous *campesinos*, small-scale, family farmers. Crucially, they are also people who do not receive a regular salary. Their reliance on the vagaries of farming means, effectively, that they rely on state financial aid. As described below, ideals of a welfare state framed how both *campesinos* and government agents understood conservation.

Campesinos may be indigenous or not and this distinction, also, proves fundamental. Events described here took place in 1994 and 1995, soon after the world learned of the existence of the Zapatistas, the revolutionary group that continues to bring attention to the way Mexican society ignores and disrespects Native American culture. Throughout southern Mexico, the Zapatista movement has changed the way local state agents regard indigenous citizens. As we shall see, in Calakmul, Zapatismo altered conservation in profound and ambivalent ways.

In describing their identities, *campesinos* emphasize their poverty and vulnerability, but there is another aspect that distinguishes Mexican *campesinos* from those in Guatemala, Honduras, or elsewhere in Latin America. Mexican *campesinos* have a particular role to play in the nation-state, one enshrined in Mexico's constitution. Mexico's constitution is the result of a civil war, one in which *campesino* armies – led by legendaries such as Emiliano Zapata and Pancho Villa – took control of the nation's capital, its seat of power. The resulting peace had to take into account *campesino* demands for land. Although the last two decades have seen important changes to the original text, Article 27 of Mexico's constitution stipulated that the state would provide land and other support to *campesinos*.

In the mid-1990s, the weight of this promise shaped *campesino* reactions to protected areas and other state activities. For example, state policies surrounding a reserve in Chiapas were a turning point in the formation of the Zapatistas (Nigh, 2002). Readers might recall that when authorities moved to renege on Article 27's promises, the Zapatistas were spurred into action. State plans to renege on Article 27 have largely failed (Jones, 2000), partly because, as one Calakmul resident explained, 'This wasn't some agreement we negotiated, but a right we won through spilt blood.' Instead, the promise continues to link people of diverse cultural backgrounds in a single, if disputed, justice framework.

This brief background offers some key points in considering the lessons Calakmul offers for socially just environmental protection, one capable of addressing diverse cultural standpoints. As we shall see, Calakmul, like many national parks, was created from afar, with little input from the local population (Wells and Brandon, 1992), but this imposition would need to be resolved. Not only are *campesinos* and state agents accustomed to negotiation, in the mid-1990s the Zapatista uprising demonstrated the violent possibilities within *campesino* discontent.

For state agents, however, Calakmul presented a few dilemmas. One was the state's retreat from Article 27, even as *campesinos* pressed for its enforcement. A more practical issue was who might act as a negotiating counterpart. The frontier society had no natural leaders to unite dispersed settlements. State agents would resolve this problem by cultivating non-indigenous leaders, a choice that ultimately undermined the goals of those in power in the mid-1990s. Interestingly enough, these goals sought to create a *campesino* power base in which farmers – rather than state bureaucrats – would occupy key positions of regional authority. The story of conservation at Calakmul is one in which hopes for peasant empowerment were undermined by a blindness toward identity differences and where attempts at a popular environmentalism gave way to bureaucratization.

The birth of a reserve

Many people in Calakmul say they learned of the reserve only a year later, when scientists arrived to inventory the region's resources. This statement may be an exaggeration. Still, it is revealing in two ways. First, detailed scientific knowledge of the region came *after* the reserve's declaration (cf. Galindo-Leal, 1999), suggesting that something other than science motivated policy-makers at the time. Second, local people did not participate in the reserve's formation, even though, as slash-and-burn farmers, they would later be viewed as the principal threat to the reserve's existence.

Unfortunately, Calakmul is not unusual in this regard. In the early 1990s, a survey of protected areas found that they often fostered conflict, as park design held 'little or no regard for local people' (Wells and Brandon, 1992: 1). More recent surveys of protected areas similarly emphasize this social critique (Brockington et al., 2006; West et al., 2006). These critiques matter precisely because parks and reserves have proven successful in protecting forest mass (Bruner et al., 2001). They force us to ask to what extent policy success comes at the expense of creating popular, long-term support for environmentalism.

Why was Calakmul declared? Some conservationists privately assert that the declaration was connected to Mexico's sullied 1988 presidential elections. The elections, widely reported as fraudulent, brought Carlos Salinas de Gortari to power. He may have turned to environmental protection in order to curry favour with the international community. Within Calakmul, the decision had an entirely contrary effect.

The area's history of colonization helps explain local discontent. *Campesinos* complained that the reserve was an insult in an area neglected by government authorities. At the time, Calakmul was home to 15000 migrant farmers who had colonized the area beginning in the 1960s. As with agricultural frontiers in nearby Chiapas (Arizpe et al., 1996), some families arrived through state-sponsored relocation programmes. The largest portion of the population learned of land availability through word of mouth. This latter group squatted on national lands while petitioning to have their tenure legalized in the form of an *ejido* grant.

Ejidos include land given by the state to a group of farmers who manage its resources collectively. Crucially for Calakmul, *campesinos* have usufruct rights to land, but the state retains ownership. This legal technicality opens the door for state interference in *ejido* affairs. In Calakmul, it opened the way to threats of large-scale relocations following the reserve's declaration. Reserve boundaries, drawn from Mexico City without comparison with actual places on the ground, mistakenly included a number of communities. According to state environmental authorities, these people would have to move. The relocation threats applied to communities regardless of their legal status.

For *campesinos*, these threats added to a harsh life in which hunger and thirst were constant fears. Calakmul houses a seasonal tropical forest that annually undergoes marked dry periods. One out of every four years, these dry seasons result in outright drought. Because the region has no permanent streams or rivers and a low water table, wells were impracticable. Droughts brought food shortages and significantly curtailed water supplies. Until the early 1990s, these living conditions made human occupation of the region nearly impossible. A study undertaken in the late 1980s found that Calakmul *ejidos* were commonly abandoned and repopulated two and three times over the space of two decades (Boege and Murguía, 1989).

Campesinos argued that government authorities failed to ameliorate these hardships. State and county authorities, located two to four hours away by car, rarely visited the region. Calakmul had few schools or health clinics. Slighted by governing authorities, people allied themselves with the opposition PRD (Party of the Democratic Revolution). At this time Mexico's ruling PRI (Institutional Revolutionary Party) was nearing the end of its seven-decade rule over Mexico, but, in the minds of *campesinos*, it was still the country's primary power-holder. In conversation, 'PRI' and 'government' were interchangeable. Angered by neglect, *campesinos* turned their backs on the PRI. In the words of one farm leader, the PRI 'had no influence here'.

The biosphere reserve quickly became caught up in these electoral politics. In an effort to convert Calakmul's PRD supporters to PRI voters, the reserve became fused with a separate federal programme that aimed at economic development. The National Solidarity Program, known as PRONASOL (Programa Nacional de Solaridad), offered Mexican communities a new mechanism to access state development monies (Cornelius et al., 1994). Local PRONASOL committees would indicate a region's more pressing development needs. The committees might also contribute labour or matching funds to state programming. In Calakmul, PRONASOL organizers were busy building this local committee when the relocation threats and *campesino* backlash with regard to the reserve threatened their work. PRONASOL organizers, however, were able to utilize anti-PRI and anti-conservation sentiment to turn this situation around. Armed with PRONASOL development funds, they encouraged *campesinos* to demand financial aid in return for their votes and their (nominal) support for conservation.

The 1991 elections for state governor served as a platform for this votes-for-development deal, a deal that included relief from relocation. A *campesino* who served on the PRONASOL local committee – known as the Regional Council – described how conservation, development and electoral politics became intertwined:

> We wanted to form a group that could sell its product with the aid of technical advice. But then came the problem of the Reserve and that in 1990, we learned some people were inside it. When the first investigators came, birders and all those people who go into the forest, we realized there were *campesinos* inside the Reserve. SEDUE [federal environment authority under Salinas] said they had to leave, and they began to hold meetings with villages. In that time . . .

ecologist[s] . . . went to the village of Colón for a meeting, and there the people told them that if they weren't smart, they were going to be lynched. The [Regional] Council talked with the government. [We said] it wasn't right, that if the ejidal decrees were from before the Reserve's, you cannot place one decree on top of another. The Governor said, 'I promise to bring the President here, but you all are going to work out this problem with him, that you don't want to move and that you want to care for the Reserve.'

With these promises, *campesinos* voted for the PRI's gubernatorial candidate. Soon after, President Salinas de Gortari inaugurated the largesse in a personal visit to the region. In a speech to hundreds of *campesinos*, he promised programmes that would foster a 'productive ecology'. He also turned the tables on *campesino* antagonisms toward conservation. The reserve would no longer threaten *campesino* livelihoods. Instead, in the votes-for-development deal, farmers would 'care for the reserve'. In practice, this caring entailed considerable financial support for PRONASOL's Regional Council. The group became so closely tied to the reserve that the two institutions were nearly indistinguishable. In the remainder of this chapter, I indicate this close relationship by hyphenating their names: the 'Reserve-Council'. By the time of my research in 1995, the Reserve-Council's budget had reached roughly US$1 million per year (nearly US$1.5 million in today's currency), more than any other government office in the region.

A grassroots movement?

These monies supported an expansive programme of integrated conservation development. By 1995, a water management programme was damming seasonal streams and constructing ponds. An environmental educator had built an educational centre, complete with botanical garden and zoo. Organic agriculture programmes aimed at soil enrichment that would eliminate the need for field rotation. The Reserve-Council operated four nurseries that supplied hardwoods and fruit-tree saplings. In the Reserve-Council's flagship programme, *campesinos* voluntarily established protected areas on ejidal lands. As thousands of families became involved in Reserve-Council programmes, visitors to the region – especially international environmentalists – might see in all this a grassroots environmental movement (see, e.g., Kingsolver, 2003).

Reserve-Council programmes brought *campesinos* the government aid they desired, but its appeal also rested on a message of *campesino* empowerment, one that was both simple and complicated. The PRONASOL organizer who became the biosphere reserve's first director, Deocundo Acopa, crafted the message. Acopa asserted that *campesinos* 'owned' the reserve and should benefit from its presence. He billed conservation development as a redress to *campesino* poverty. At the same time, this *campesino* empowerment rested largely on Acopa's own contacts with state authorities and his ability to keep the money flowing. Acopa's populist message blended with a certain authoritarianism. Nicknamed 'the Jaguar of Calakmul', Acopa was the most powerful government agent in the region and little conservation work took place without his consent.

An example will show how this populism and authoritarianism blended in practice. In February of 1995, Reserve Director Acopa, the Regional Council and non-governmental groups met with federal environmental officers to review the conservation programmes. Acopa began by explaining the importance of having the Regional Council coordinate all non-governmental activities. He argued that independently operating NGOs could become embroiled in rivalries in which groups duplicate programmes, become territorial and operate within what he called a 'feudal' atmosphere. With Acopa's backing, *campesinos* at the Regional Council were in a position of authority over the college-educated and salaried employees of NGOs who received their funding from the World Wildlife Fund, The Nature Conservancy, and the US Agency for International Development.

After this introduction, staff employed by the Reserve-Council and NGOs presented the programmes, stressing a common focus on meeting *campesinos'* expressed development needs. Director Acopa periodically interjected the philosophy behind each programme. The water programmes aimed at stressing 'if people want water, they have to care for it'. People did not have to participate in council projects, but if they did, the projects should allow them 'to see for themselves that the forest is being destroyed'. Acopa believed that people would protect only those species they found economically valuable. He thus described the sum total of projects as supporting biodiversity by demonstrating the value of a variety of forest products (Acopa and Beoge, 1998).

At the meeting's close, a state representative described Calakmul as a national example. Calakmul's conservation community was creating 'new and rational ways to take advantage of the environment'. Most importantly, these programmes were 'based on the people, with the people, and for the people'. Donors to the programmes included the MacArthur Foundation, the World Bank, Canada's Eastern Ontario Model Forest and various Mexican federal agencies. During the 14 months I studied the Reserve-Council in action, I never saw a development programme initiated within an ejido (although Acopa instigated a few novel projects). Instead, *campesinos* acceded to the programmes offered to them.

Two points contributed to the notion that conservation development in Calakmul was popularly driven. The first was that, based on the Reserve-Council's local knowledge, programmes fitted the circumstances of particular communities. An *ejido* with a seasonal stream received a dam, while one with no running water received a rainwater catchment system. An *ejido* with an archaeological ruin received an ecotourism programme. In the context of Mexico's centralized government, this small shift could appear populist. The second point that provided a grassroots tint to conservation development was the Regional Council's democratic organization and the number of people who participated in its monthly meetings.

By 1995, more than half the villages located in Calakmul's buffer zone belonged to the Regional Council. To join, an ejido simply requested acceptance at one of the Council's monthly meetings. Because a single *ejido* could vote as many as four representatives on to the Council, meeting attendance ranged from one to three hundred people. While men voted representatives, women also voted representatives from women's groups. As such, women comprised one-third of council delegates. The Council provided the only place in Calakmul where women could hold formal power. These points made council assemblies the most representative *campesino* forum in the region. It also made the meetings a bit unwieldy. Monthly assemblies stretched to eight and ten hours. The hundreds of representatives jostled to promote their personal interests, those of their *ejidos*, and their vision of a social order in which *campesinos* would dominate.

At base, the representatives were meant to oversee a board voted from within the assembly's ranks. However, the representatives' real work went beyond this. By 1995, the Council was a quasi-governmental group with whose power everyone working in the region had to reckon. In Mexico, organizations like the Council form part of a complicated drama in which non-governmental groups strive (sometimes simultaneously) for political independence and government support for small-scale producers (Harvey 1998; Stanford 1994). Council representatives functioned mainly as a physical embodiment of this dynamic. As cantankerous hecklers, they reminded powerful outsiders of the similarly influential position held by *campesinos*. The source of this power, however, was the group's alliance with the reserve, an alliance underpinned by conservation development funds.

In this way, populism and authoritarianism, rather than standing as polar opposites, shaded into one another as a government agent mandated popular oversight of conservation and development. Meanwhile, state, federal and international authorities acknowledged and bolstered the Council's authority. In one monthly meeting, that state governor who came to office on the votes-for-development deal accompanied Canada's ambassador to Mexico to sign a bi-national pact supporting sustainable forestry in the region. At the event, a federal agent urged the representatives: 'We chose to work here because of the Reserve Director and the support of the state government. But, none of that matters without your support. If [conservation] doesn't work here, it won't work anywhere.'

As the following section describes, the ambiguous social justice on offer at the Reserve-Council paralleled the social justice setting in Calakmul *ejidos*. In fact, conservation had become caught up in *ejidal* politics, by both mimicking *ejido* land tenures and by using the *ejido* structure to implement conservation programming. Left to supervise conservation-development in their own communities, however, *ejido* members could actively resist environmentalism.

Conservation's foot soldiers

Within Calakmul *ejidos*, people struggled to put off government interference while taking advantage of conservation's development aspects. Conservation programmes touched on people's worries about their access to land. Salinas's call to 'care for the reserve' did little to calm these fears. As with their *ejidos*, *campesinos* would have some kind of responsibility toward the reserve, but ultimate authority rested with state agents. To temper state encroachment via conservation, *campesinos* invoked the spirit of Article 27 to argue that government authorities should facilitate access to farmland and agricultural inputs. They grudgingly agreed to the Biosphere Reserve, but, contrary to the Reserve-Council, saw conservation development as a kind of *quid pro quo* that compensated them for retreating from broader land claims.

Given the importance of conservation development to their livelihoods, *campesinos* had to tread carefully in their opposition to conservation. Jerónimo exemplified this selective approach. Jerónimo joined every council project on offer in his *ejido* and acted as a lead organizer for many. He spoke with me about his *ejido*'s reserve and the need to protect forests to counter global environmental change. However, when state fire-control agents pressured *campesinos* to build firebreaks around their farm fields – a hand-cut, metre-wide belt around 3–5 hectare plots – Jerónimo lost patience:

> What we are going to care for is the [Biosphere] Reserve, and we are not going to care for the forest, because the government gave it to us. If the government prohibits something on the land it gives, why give it in the first place? If we were inside the Reserve, we couldn't even cut secondary growth or collect fire wood. When people came from the Reserve, they came with other

government agents offering apiculture projects. But, they never delivered. They offered cattle so we wouldn't fell. We need pasture, tractors, water, but all we get is promises. What's the punishment for burning without a firebreak? They say there isn't one, but, believe me, they'll give you 20 years in jail.

Jerónimo might cultivate the appearance of supporting conservation to garner aid and appeal to outside interests (Tsing, 1999), but he carefully calculated what kind of conservation was worth the extra labour. His declaration notes that, in addition to threats to land and livelihood, *campesino* opposition to conservation also rested on what they saw as the unpredictability of government policies.

Juan echoed Jerónimo's position while depicting more starkly the tradeoff people expected from supporting conservation. Juan and Jerónimo were unacquainted with one another and lived at a distance of two hours driving. In contrast to Jerónimo, Juan did not participate in any Reserve-Council activities, but he still saw the need for such programmes:

Well, the government should come and explain exactly why it doesn't want [us to fell forest]. If the government gave us land, it gave us land to work. Then after giving us the land to work, it doesn't want us to fell. Then what it should do is give us other lands, give us the support to be able to live from one or two hectares, with mechanized agriculture or something else.

While Juan and Jerónimo drew on Article 27 to formulate anti-conservation positions, their relationship to Calakmul's conservation arena reflected localized *ejidal* politics. These localized politics would serve as a major source of complaint for protestors who ultimately undermined the conservation development agenda.

In both Juan's and Jerónimo's *ejidos*, Reserve-Council projects were controlled by a faction that left a significant part of each community outside the conservation agenda. Juan was not a member of his community's Reserve-Council faction, but this did not worry him. The two factions in his *ejido* had effectively divided between them all programmes entering the community, so Juan had other sources of support. Because of this division, Juan saw little need to feign support for conservation. Contrastingly, Jerónimo's statement constituted a rare utterance against conservation. Jerónimo, along with a handful of others, controlled Reserve-Council projects in his *ejido*. In addition to agricultural inputs, they benefited from the wages, foodstuffs and household supplies that programmes offered only the most active participants. Jerónimo reported that 15 per cent of his cash income derived from this sort of state aid. Other *ejido* members active in soliciting conservation development received 26–38 per cent of their cash from state programmes.

It is important to note that by dominating projects, individuals also might develop opportunities for illicit gain. Project accounting in *ejidos* was not transparent. *Ejido* members might complain of corrupt neighbours to Reserve-Council staff, but these complaints were disregarded as matters 'internal to the *ejido*' and beyond council jurisdiction. The Reserve-Council's goals of empowerment met serious obstacles in the factional politics and unaccountable leadership often typical of Mexico's *ejidos* (DeWalt and Rees, 1994; Galletti, 1998). At the same time, the Reserve-Council declined to demand transparency. Asked about *ejido* corruption, Reserve Director Acopa threw up his hands, 'What can I do if the people tolerate this?'

Acopa overlooked the way Reserve-Council programmes actually reinforced *ejidal* inequalities by employing the *ejido*'s governing structure to implement its programmes. *Ejido* offices include a president, treasurer, secretary, and a *consejo de vigilancia* or oversight council that checks on the others to see that office-holders fulfill their obligations. Reserve-Council programmes took on the exact same structure, replicated for each project an *ejido* received. Although office holders were voted in by *ejido* members, a handful of individuals dominated both *ejido* governance and the Reserve-Council programmes (Ronfeldt, 1973). The longer they were in office, the greater their chances of monopolizing contacts outside the *ejido*. Years later, a private sector conservationist commented on the tendency of NGOs to rely on particular people to access *ejido* communities: 'Is there someone else with whom you might work? You assume the person you are working with is good because you've worked with him.' The Reserve-Council's replication of *ejido* governance in its programming gave the appearance of an environmentalism rooted in local culture. In this very replication, however, *ejido* members themselves might see less an ideal of environmental protection and more power and wealth for a few.

Addressing conservation's inequalities

This power and wealth went beyond those *ejido* authorities who dominated Reserve-Council projects in their communities. At a conference with Mexican and international environmental groups, a council board member – nicknamed 'The Suitcase' by *ejido* neighbours who imagined him carrying off illicit cash – asked of the environmentalists, *'¿Qué hace esta persona en mi casa?'* 'What are these people doing in my house?' Six years after the declaration of the Calakmul Biosphere Reserve, with Reserve-Council programming at its zenith, even those at the heart of Calakmul's conservation agenda questioned the motives of state and private sector environmental staff. The notion of setting aside land that nobody would touch remained alien to *campesinos* (see below). Faced with such incomprehensibility, *campesinos* began to surmise ulterior motives (Brydon 1996). Given the overall importance of money in making conservation happen, and *campesinos*' chronic concerns for their own financial solvency, it is unsurprising that they saw conservation as a money-making enterprise.

Just how national and international environmentalists made money from conservation was unclear to people unfamiliar with the workings of a service economy. *Campesinos* imagined there must be something in the forests that environmentalists wanted to keep for themselves. For example, the Canadian aid mentioned above was interpreted as a covert land grab, as one man avowed that 'Canada owns Calakmul'. *Campesinos* guessed that international markets might have a use for forest products unknown in Mexico. A group of bat biologists was, at first, thought to be stealing the creatures, even though people could not conceive their commercial use. The biologists' tendency to work in the forests at night and their use of a black Chevrolet Suburban, the preferred vehicle of drug traffickers, provided an answer. The research was a cover for drug running. The biologists responded by painting a batman sign on their car, and soon became known as 'los Batman'.

From their vantage point, council board members had a better sense of the interests and financing associated with conservation, but they still viewed national and international agents as self-interested actors, bent on defending their class positions. As one council board member complained: 'That's why the money ecologists have for conservation doesn't arrive here. It all goes to rock concerts, exotic meals, and travel.'

These class identities went beyond whether someone listens to rock music or Mexican *norteño*. One of the most important markers of *campesino* identities was that farmers suffered as a consequence of not receiving a regular salary. *Campesinos* saw people who did receive regular salaries as wary of losing that income and willing to do whatever it took to maintain financial security. (Given the difficulty of finding employment in rural Mexico, this assessment is not far-fetched.) Salaried employees of conservation groups and government agents thus encountered a very sceptical *campesino* audience. *Campesinos* questioned whether salaried workers were willing to act hypocritically or enforce regulations known to harm farm enterprises. A few examples of corrupt environmental officers were enough to cast doubt on the whole lot. *Campesinos* were indignant but unsurprised in reporting environmental authorities that could not identify a common plant, illegally hunted wildlife or, worse, demanded bribes in exchange for not enforcing environmental laws. As conservation became caught up in class conflict, tools for resisting conservation similarly employed class statements.

At the same time, an important ethnic dimension undergirded Reserve-Council activities and *campesino* relations with environmental agents. Although indigenous people account for as much as one-half of the population in Calakmul, they had relatively little presence within the Reserve-Council. Just one of the Council's dozen or so board members was indigenous. Furthermore, none of the state or private sector environmentalists claimed an indigenous identity. This situation was both curious and untenable. Curiously, even though one rationale state agents gave for funding conservation was fear of a Zapatista-type revolt, Reserve-Council staff made no effort to reach out to indigenous people as a distinct constituency. State authorities took *campesino* militancy towards conservation as a serious threat to their ability to govern, but their response entailed pork-barrel politics aimed at non-indigenous *campesinos*. In doing so, Reserve-Council actions supported Zapatista claims that state authorities ignored indigenous people. However, the situation was untenable because, by overlooking the ethnic dynamic taking place in Calakmul, state authorities left the region vulnerable to organizers who brought a new message of indigenous empowerment.

Ethnic politics changes conservation
As the Reserve-Council grew, so did the number of its critics. As we saw, given how the projects were implemented in local *ejidos*, it was easy to object that not everyone benefited from the sustainable economy. Additionally, council board members were increasingly accused of corruption as they began to live lifestyles beyond the means of their salaries. During Easter weekend of 1995, murmured complaints were suddenly thrown into the open as a group of Zapatista sympathizers took to the streets.

The timing was strategic. Mexicans who can afford to do so go on holiday for Easter week. The roads were busy with vacationers. Bypassing Calakmul, a federal highway serves as one of two main arteries connecting the Yucatán peninsula with the rest of the country. When the protestors blocked this road, they created a problem the state would need to address.

The protestors' actions resonated with the class concerns mentioned above. They charged tolls to passing drivers, with foreign nationals and the drivers of more expensive vehicles paying a higher quota. Strikers requested the governor's personal presence to address their complaints. This was the same governor who came to power in the votes-for-development deal. To his humiliation, the strikers placed him on a stage and set before him a meal meant to represent *campesino* poverty, a plate of unsalted beans and a glass of brownish water.

The protestors did not critique the Reserve-Council alliance *per se*, nor did they advance specific ethnic claims. Instead, they focused on other development issues, namely a programme for children's scholarships (whose payments were in arrears) and the needs of individual *ejidos* for a school, electrification, or legalization of their land tenure. However, rumours circulated that the strike had been aided by PRD and Zapatista organizers. Council board members noticed, but did not elaborate on, the fact that a majority of the protestors were indigenous. The parallels between Chiapas and Calakmul were clear to all, including one protestor who, following the strike, complained about regulations that ban cutting older-growth forest:

> I don't understand them [conservationists], because if a fellow does not have land already felled, how is he going to feed his family? That's why the farmer becomes rebellious, like in Chiapas where they don't allow even a small part of the forest to be felled.

Although a few of the strike's organizers would later be jailed for their political work, in the short run the protest was effective. The governor assigned a team to meet with community leaders. Numerous problems cited by demonstrators began to receive attention. State officials began to look beyond the Reserve-Council as a means to govern Calakmul. Reserve Director Acopa received the brunt of criticism. The protest would spell the end to his tenure as director. Incredulous that Acopa had no advance warning of the Easter strike, an adviser to the state governor offered this alternative job description for a reserve director:

> Acopa should have the political structure in the palm of his hand, and he doesn't have it. If Acopa had simply organized a few plant nurseries, that would have been enough. . . . The work of a Reserve Director is political work, policy making. He shouldn't have been going about inventing things like ecotourism. His job was to influence the politics in the area without being obvious. That's what the projects were about. He had the 'façade' of being a Reserve Director.

Acopa, in contrast, reflected that the PRI's pork-barrel tactics had returned to haunt the party. People in Calakmul demanded increasingly higher prices for their allegiance.

The Easter protestors went on to form a *campesino* organization that would eclipse the Regional Council, calling their new group the 'Regional Indigenous and Popular Council'. State authorities began to shift some development funds to the group. In later years, the Indigenous and Popular Council would maintain a simultaneously present and distanced relationship to government in Calakmul. As the largest *campesino* organization in the region, state agents had to, at least, pay lip service to the group's importance. However, the group entered state terrain very carefully and only when it was assured that doing so would not undermine its long-term survival. The effect has been a preference for long-term social autonomy over short-term political influence.

Acopa himself saw the protestors as political neophytes, people who, in their focus on myriad small questions, had sacrificed a big financial prize. Acopa had been considering pressuring state authorities for the creation of a *municipio* (or county) to encompass the Biosphere Reserve and its buffer zone. As a principal political organization within Mexico, *municipios* command four to five times the budget handled by the Reserve-Council. Furthermore, these monies are relatively certain. Conservation development depended on state and NGO funding cycles lasting just one to three years. At the end of a cycle, donors could decide not to renew their support (as they ultimately did in Calakmul). By spearheading the campaign for a *municipio*, Acopa and Council board members hoped they would dominate the new institution. Indeed, many actors allied to the Reserve-Council later occupied municipal offices. Officials linked to the state governor, however, moved to assure that Acopa and his closest collaborators would have no part in Calakmul's new governing structure. Acopa left office six months after the Easter protest.

Declared in 1996, Calakmul was heralded by lawmakers as the country's first 'ecological' *municipio*, a moniker whose meaning people continue to define. With the declaration of the *municipio*, the number of state responsibilities expanded, and conservation had to compete with pressing questions of education, health care and road construction among others. Acopa's successor to the reserve directorship became the *municipio*'s first president. In this way, conservation's place in Calakmul politics became entrenched in local government, even as the thousands of families formerly active in conservation development turned to other concerns. Overall, Calakmul serves as a strong example of how conservation can extend state power and incorporate relatively underdeveloped regions into larger economic structures (Escobar, 1996).

Sustaining conservation
Today, neither reserve officers nor NGOs view the Calakmul Biosphere Reserve as under threat from *campesinos*. This turnaround, however, cannot be attributed to changed attitudes. With an end to funding cycles and the Easter protest raising doubts about its effectiveness, the conservation development programming described above ceased in the mid-1990s. Instead, agricultural expansion halted for reasons that have little to do with conservation and merit more attention than can be given here. Calakmul's agricultural frontier closed following legal changes that aimed, unsuccessfully, to privatize *ejidos* (Haenn, 2006). A new poverty relief programme now supports some 80 per cent of municipal households, providing a food security that formerly eluded *campesino* families. The declaration of the *municipio* brought significant job growth as people went to work in either the municipality itself or in the service sector that sprang up around the new institution. In the twenty-first century, numerous residents of Calakmul joined their fellow Mexicans in migrating to the USA. Precise remittance figures are unavailable. Nonetheless, one long-term actor in Calakmul's conservation scene observes of migrants, 'They're the ones with money now.'

The net effect has been decreased pressure on area forests. Deforestation takes place, but at a neglible rate (Roy Chowdhury, 2007). With little popular support for conservation, environmental policy-makers are isolated in their battle against larger threats to the Biosphere Reserve, such as highway construction and tourism development.

For conservationists working in places where protected areas are undergoing rapid ecological change, this *de facto* truce to an environmental conflict might seem satisfactory. Nonetheless, one cannot help but wonder whether an opportunity was missed, whether the Reserve-Council's original impulse to involve *campesinos* in conservation, address social inequities, and soften the cultural divide between conservation and *campesino* viewpoints wasn't important to creating support for environmental protection. Clearly, there were flaws in the implementation of these ideals. However, the approach garnered *campesino* attention toward an alien and potentially hostile programme. The possibilities Calakmul held for a broad-based conservation raises the question of how a more sustaining conservation might take shape, one that allows for lasting environmental protection because it supports both the physical environment and the social relations that make conservation possible (Haenn, 2005).

Earlier, I argued that broad-based participation in environmental programmes would be possible only if environmentalism counteracted the social inequalities that disenfranchise millions. I also noted the challenge that cultural diversity and radically different ways of understanding the world pose for such participation. Calakmul offers a few lessons for these ideas, lessons that should be considered carefully. Conservation has been criticized for its use of a one-size-fits-all methodology. Social scientists interested in conservation argue that global prescriptions for conservation strategies should operate only at the most general levels (Brechin et al., 2003). In offering lessons for conservation, researchers must acknowledge the limits to such suggestions posed by the diverse social settings in which conservation operates (Russell, 2003).

With this caveat in mind, the first lesson is that, at least in the early stages of conservation programming, both top-down and bottom-up strategies are unlikely to be successful. Conservation imposed by outside authorities is often resisted by people who view such impositions as illegitimate. Instead, top-down strategies foreground the economic and cultural differences between policy-makers and policy recipients. Regarding broad-based, bottom-up conservation initiatives, researchers are equivocal on whether such a phenomenon actually exists. Conservation employees, listing different kinds of public participation, view locally instigated programmes as very much a minority (Ericson, 2006).

Instead, in the early stages of conservation, respected, local, cultural brokers such as Reserve Director Acopa appear key to defining conservation in ways that make sense to a specific audience (cf. Shoreman, 2008). The idea of a respected local broker goes beyond the 'partner organizations' with which so many international conservation groups work, a strategy that has its own complications (Mahanty and Russell, 2002). Partner organizations often have as their primary allegiance donors (who are part of top-down structures) or conservation ideals (against which local peoples protest). Respected local brokers, in contrast, are people already established in a social realm. They are people to whom their neighbours listen. A broker's translation of conservation ideals into something more locally recognizable may result in a conservation that looks quite different from the usual protected area, but it has the advantage of being practicable.

The second lesson is that these brokers are insufficient to achieving long-term conservation. Although they can make conservation intelligible, they cannot always convince local peoples that conservation policies are legitimate. In the case of Calakmul, corruption of Reserve-Council affiliates and other state agents neatly coincided with public suspicions that conservation was about something other than ecology. Many critiques of conservation focus on this aspect of the phenomenon. Conservation policies have allowed elites to claim broad swaths of rural landscapes (Igoe, 2003). Local cultural brokers can exacerbate this tendency because they gain their power by being effective actors in existing political structures (Chapin, 2000; Lejano et al., 2007). These structures may subjugate or exclude a significant number of people, notably in the Calakmul case indigenous peoples.

Indeed, much of the debate about conservation in Calakmul centred on questions of legitimacy and social justice. Who would comprise a localized conservation community? How would such a community be organized? What rights and responsibilities would different community members hold? Neither state agents nor *campesinos* ever reached an agreement on the answers to these questions. Events at Calakmul, however, were suggestive of a diverse set of justice norms under consideration.

Campesinos' support for the votes-for-development deal and the Easter strike suggest that they sought to create a community of justice between themselves and government agents, one in which Article 27 would guide government behaviour. *Campesinos* sought a government authority that protected them from the vagaries of the marketplace, as well as the malevolent intentions of upper-class representatives. Noticeably absent from their concerns were private sector environmentalists, even though these were both present in the region and actively lobbying state authorities. Instead, *campesinos* placed a singular focus on the state, and a state that strayed too far from the ideal of protector could expect public strikes.

In this way, government–farmer relations at Calakmul support Adolfo Gilly's assertion that governance in Mexico entails ongoing negotiations of authority, built on instances of revolt (Gilly, 1998). The revolts are often settled through highly personalized negotiations such as the governor's response to the Easter protest. This personalized treatment speaks to the demand for a particular kind of justice – procedural justice (Collier 1973). In procedural justice, the outcome is determined by process rather than by regulation. The circumstances of people's individual situations take precedence over abstract bureaucratic rules or philosophical ideas of what justice should look like. This justice norm has been called 'an ethic of care' (Gilligan, 1982) by researchers who note its emphasis on obligations arising out of relationships. *Campesinos* sought a justice that took into account their personal circumstances and arose out of a personal relationship with people in authority.

Absent from this community of justice is the physical environment, an entity that many environmentalists view as deserving a place within discussions of justice. The reasons for this omission are too lengthy to explore here but rest on *campesino* ideas of forests as a separate social world, one where snakes, jaguars and forest spirits threaten human existence (see Haenn, 1999; Murphy, 1998; Schwartz, 1999). People's proper relationship to forests is based on their work. *Campesinos* go to the woods to farm, cut timber, or collect some forest product. But they cannot protect a forest both because its social difference places forests beyond the realm of human influence and because its threatening character poses doubts about whether such protection is really beneficial.

This social justice scenario is specific to Calakmul, but it points to more generalizable ideas regarding a sustaining conservation. An enduring, popularly supported conservation must view human dignity as equal to nature protection. By framing conservation and human activities as contradictory, and by acting in heavy-handed ways, environmentalists in Calakmul quickly alienated the very people whose support they needed.

For policy-makers, nature protection then took a back seat to recuperating *campesinos'* lost good faith. Forced to choose between their personal dignity and nature protection, people will probably forsake the latter. A sustaining conservation seeks to avoid this dichotomy.

An enduring, popularly supported conservation takes place within a transparent and accountable setting. The corruption that took place in Calakmul *ejidos* and at the Reserve-Council is by no means unique to Mexico. Corruption and its difficult counterpart, the appearance of corruption, undermine the notion that conservation is a scientific endeavour of value to a general public. Because notions of accountability and transparency are closely tied to cultural ideals of power and governance, a sustaining conservation would look to spell these out in locally specified ways. However, of principal concern here is that conservation financing should not exacerbate the inequalities that cause social strife.

This raises the question of the distinctive cultural orientations that cause people to view the world and value ecology in different ways. How might a sustaining conservation address multiculturalism? The lessons from Calakmul are less clear in this regard; however, findings from cognitive anthropology and research on the human brain suggest that the combination of conservation activities and the monthly council assemblies where people raised their distinct viewpoints held important possibilities for the kind of experiential learning and adjustment that underpin cross-cultural understanding (Shore, 1998).

In situations of deep ideological and practical differences, an ongoing atmosphere of experiential learning and adjustment appears key to helping people bridge their diverse cultural orientations. The idea here is that, left on their own, people tend to accept information that confirms their existing beliefs while rejecting or changing information that does not (Lewis et al., 2001). This tendency, rooted as it is in human biology, exacerbates cultural differences. By engaging and rewarding *campesinos* in conservation activities, the conservation development agenda at Calakmul created opportunities for the kind of direct experiences usually necessary for people to enact a change in thinking and see events from other perspectives.

A sustaining conservation would create spaces where this kind of learning and adjustment could take place, taking into account the variety of people involved in conservation settings (cf. Fischer, 2000). In some ways, this approach is anticipated in the notion of 'adaptive management' in conservation. The authors of adaptive management, however, conceive of learning and adjustment as ways to prove conservation success to donors, governments and local stakeholders (Salafsky et al., 2001). A sustaining conservation would use learning and adjustment to identify and work through cultural differences, keeping in mind issues of social justice.

Conclusion

Without a sustaining conservation, the programmes and policies linked to protected areas become easily turned towards other ends. In Calakmul, conservation bolstered the state by expanding state institutions into an area that had relatively little state presence. This move was controversial. Even as they were anxious for welfare aid, *campesinos* and the Reserve-Council sought to prevent *campesino* subjugation within the new state institutions.

Despite a period of broad-based participation in conservation programming, fundamental differences over whether and how to carry out conservation were never resolved. Popular support for conservation in Calakmul was never again a policy priority and has yet to be achieved. Instead, both state agents and *campesinos* have concentrated on the development portion of sustainable development. Sustainable development works as 'a metafix' (see Lele in Dobson, 1999), a set of ideas and programmes that appeals to conflicting interest groups and momentarily sweeps differences aside. Given the economic changes in Calakmul, however, the metafix is less appealing than it once was. Now that *campesinos* have economic alternatives to sustainable development, it may take a new cultural broker to invent creative ways to urge, once again, conservation on to the public conscience.

Note

1. See data available from Mexico's National Council on Protected Areas, http://www.conanp.gob.mx/q_ anp.html, last accessed 12 May 2009.

References

Acopa, Deocundo and Eckart Boege (1998), 'The Maya Forest in Campeche, Mexico: experiences in forest management at Calakmul', in Richard Primack et al. (eds), *Timber, Tourists, and Temples: Conservation and Development in the Maya Forest of Belize, Guatemala, and Mexico*, Washington, DC: Island Press, pp. 81–97.

Agrawal, Arun (2005), *Environmentality: Technologies of Government and the Making of Subjects*, Durham, NC: Duke University Press.

Arizpe, Lourdes, Fernanda Paz and Margarita Velázquez (1996), *Culture and Global Change: Social Perceptions of Deforestation in the Lacandona Rain Forest in Mexico*, Ann Arbor, MI: University of Michigan Press.

Beierle, Thomas and Jerry Cayford (2002), *Democracy in Practice: Public Participation in Environmental Decisions*, Washington, DC: Resources for the Future.

Boege, Eckart and Raul Murguía (1989), 'Diagnóstico de las Actividades Humanas que se Realizan en la Reserva de la Biosfera de Calakmul, Estado de Campeche', Merida, Yucatán: PRONATURA–Península de Yucatán.

Brechin, Steven R., Peter R. Wilshusen, Crystal L. Fortwangler and Patrick C. West (2003), *Contested Nature: Promoting International Biodiversity and Social Justice in the 21st Century*, Albany, NY: SUNY Press.

Brockington, Daniel, James Igoe and Kai Schmidt-Soltau (2006), 'Conservation, human rights, and poverty reduction', *Conservation Biology*, **20** (1): 250–52.

Brosius, J. Peter, Anna Lowenhaupt Tsing and Charles Zerner (eds) (2005), *Communities and Conservation: Histories and Politics of Community-Based Natural Resource Management*, Lanham, MD: Alta Mira Press.

Bruner, Aaron G., Raymond E. Gullison, Richard E. Rice and Gustavo A.B. da Fonseca (2001), 'Effectiveness of parks in protecting tropical biodiversity', *Science*, **291** (5501): 125–8.

Brydon, Anne (1996), 'Whale-siting: spatiality in Icelandic nationalism', in Gisli Palsson and Paul Durrenberger (eds), *Images of Contemporary Iceland*, Iowa City, IA: University of Iowa Press.

Chapin, Mac (2000), 'Defending Kuna Yala: PEMASKY, The Study Project for the Management of the Wildlands of Kuna Yala, Panama', Washington, DC: USAID, http://www.worldwildlife.org/bsp/publications/aam/panama/panama.html, last accessed 1 May 2009.

Colfer, Carol (2004), *The Equitable Forest: Diversity and Community in Sustainable Resource Management*, Washington, DC: Resources for the Future.

Collier, Jane (1973), *Law and Social Change in Zinacantan*, Stanford, CA: Stanford University Press.

Cornelius, Wayne, Ann Craig and Jonathan Fox (1994), *Transforming State–Society Relations in Mexico: The National Solidarity Strategy*, San Diego, CA: Center for US–Mexico Studies, University of California, San Diego.

DeWalt, Billie and Martha Rees (1994), *Past Lessons, Future Prospects: The End of Agrarian Reform in Mexico*, San Diego, CA: Center for US–Mexican Studies, University of California, San Diego.

Dobson, Andrew (1999), *Justice and the Environment: Conceptions of Environmental Sustainability and Theories of Distributive Justice*, Oxford: Oxford University Press.

Dove, Michael (2007), 'Globalization and the construction of Western and non-Western Knowledge', in

Paul Sillitoe (ed.), *Local Science vs Global Science: Approaches to Indigenous Knowledge in International Development*, New York: Berghahn Books, pp. 129–54.

Dryzek, John (2005), *The Politics of the Earth: Environmental Discourses*, New York: Oxford University Press.

Ericson, Jenny (2006), 'A participatory approach to conservation in the Calakmul Biosphere Reserve, Campeche, Mexico', *Landscape and Urban Planning*, **74**: 242–66.

Escobar, Arturo (1996), 'Construction nature: elements for a post-structuralist political ecology', *Futures*, **28**: 325–43.

Fischer, Frank (2000), *Citizens, Experts and the Environment: The Politics of Local Knowledge*, Durham, NC: Duke University Press.

Galindo-Leal, Carlos (1999), *La gran región de Calakmul: Prioridades biológicas de conservación y propuesta de modificación de la Reserva de la Biosfera*, México, DF: World Wildlife Fund.

Galletti, Hugo (1998), 'The Maya Forest of Quintana Roo: thirteen years of conservation and community development', in Richard Primack et al. (eds), *Timber, Tourists, and Temples: Conservation and Development in the Maya Forest of Belize, Guatemala, and Mexico*, Washington, DC: Island Press, pp. 33–46.

Gilligan, Carol (1982), *In a Different Voice*, Cambridge, MA: Harvard UniversityPress.

Gilly, Adolfo (1998), 'Chiapas and the rebellion of the enchanted world,' in Daniel Nugent (ed.), *Rural Revolt in Mexico: U.S. Intervention and the Domain of Subaltern Politics*, Durham, NC: Duke University Press, pp. 261–334.

Haenn, Nora (1999), 'The power of environmental knowledge: ethnoecology and environmental conflicts in Mexican conservation', *Human Ecology*, **27** (3): 477–90.

Haenn, Nora (2005), *Fields of Power, Forests of Discontent: Culture, Conservation and the State in Mexico*, Tucson, AZ: University of Arizona Press.

Haenn, Nora (2006), 'The changing and enduring ejido: a state and regional examination of Mexico's land tenure counter-reforms', *Land Use Policy*, **23**: 136–46.

Harvey, Neil (1998), *The Chiapas Rebellion: The Struggle for Land and Democracy*, Durham, NC: Duke University Press.

Igoe, Jim (2003), *Conservation and Globalization: A Study of National Parks and Indigenous Communities from East Africa to South Dakota*, Florence, KY: Wadsworth Publishing.

Jones, Gareth (2000), 'Between a rock and a hard place: institutional reform and the performance of land privatisation in Peri-urban Mexico', in Annelies Zoomers and Gemma van der Haar (eds), *Current Land Tenure Policy in Latin America: Regulating Land Tenure under Neo-Liberalism*, Amsterdam: Iberoamericana/Vervuert Verlag and Royal Dutch Tropical Institute, pp. 201–26.

Kingsolver, Barbara (2003), *Small Wonder: Essays*, New York: Harper Perennial.

Lejano, Raúl, Helen M. Ingram, John M. Whiteley, Daniel Torres and Sharon J. Agduma (2007), 'The importance of context: integrating resource conservation with local institutions', *Society and Natural Resources*, **20** (2): 177–85.

Lewis, Thomas, Fari Amini and Richard Lannon (2001), *A General Theory of Love*, New York: Vintage.

Mahanty, Sango and Diane Russell (2002), 'High stakes: lessons from stakeholder groups in the biodiversity conservation network', *Society and Natural Resources*, **15**: 179–88.

Matthews, Andrew (2005), 'Power/knowledge, power/ignorance: forest fires and the state in Mexico', *Human Ecology*, **33** (6): 795–820.

Murphy, Julia (1998), 'Ways of working in the forest: mediating sustainable development in Calakmul', paper delivered at the 97th Annual Meeting of the American Anthropological Association, Philadelphia, PA.

Nazarea, Virginia (ed.) (1999), *Ethnoecology: Situated knowledge/local lives*, Tucson, AZ: University of Arizona Press.

Nigh, Ronald (2002), 'Maya medicine in the biological gaze: bioprospecting research as herbal fetishism', *Current Anthropology*, **43** (3): 451–77.

Ronfeldt, David (1973), *Atencingo: The Politics of Agrarian Struggle in a Mexican Ejido*, Stanford, CA: Stanford University Press.

Roy Chowdhury, Rinku (2007), 'Household land management and biodiversity: secondary succession in a forest-agriculture mosaic in Southern Mexico', *Ecology and Society*, **12** (2): 31, available at: http://www.ecologyandsociety.org/vol12/art31/, accessed 30 August 2009.

Russell, Diane (2003), *Groundwork for Community-Based Conservation: Strategies for Social Research*, Walnut Creek, CA: Alta Mira Press.

Salafsky, Nicholas, Richard Margoluis and Kent Redford (2001), *Adaptive Management: A Tool for Conservation Practitioners*, Washington, DC: USAID Biodiversity Support Program.

Schwartz, Norman (1999), 'An anthropological view of Guatemala's Peten', in James Nations (ed.), *Thirteen Ways of Looking at a Tropical Forest*, Washington, DC: Conservation International 108, pp. 14–19.

Shore, Bradd (1998), *Culture in Mind: Cognition, Culture, and the Problem of Meaning*, Oxford: Oxford University Press.

Shoreman, Elle (2008), 'Regulation, collaboration, and conservation: ecological anthropology in the Mississpi Delta', Boston, MA: Boston University PhD dissertation.

Stanford, Lois (1994), 'Ejidal organizations and the Mexican state: confrontation and crisis in Michoacan', *Urban Anthropology*, **23**: 171–207.

Sundberg, Juanita (2003), 'Conservation and democratization: constituting citizenship in the Maya Biosphere Reserve, Guatemala', *Political Geography*, 22: 715–40.

Tsing, Anna (1999), 'Becoming a tribal elder, and other green development fantasies', in Tania Murray Li (ed.), *Transforming the Indonesian Uplands: Marginality, Power, and Production*, Amsterdam: Harwood Academic Publishers, pp. 159–202.

Wells, Michael and Katrina Brandon (1992), *People and Parks: Linking Protected Management with Local Communities*, Washington, DC: The World Bank.

West, Paige (2006), *'Conservation is Our Government Now': The Politics of Ecology in Papua New Guinea*, Durham, NC: Duke University Press.

West, Paige, James Igoe and Daniel Brockington (2006), 'Parks and people: the social impact of protected areas', *Annual Review in Anthropology*, **35**: 251–77.

Index

Titles of publications are in *italics*.